15 minutes :
Le temps maximum pour vous
apporter une solution si un petit
problème dont nous pourrions être
responsables se présentait à vous.

24H/24 :
Nous sommes là de jour comme
de nuit pour que votre
satisfaction soit complète.

Invités :
Au cas où nous ne pourrions pas
remplir ce contrat...
Vous seriez notre invité.

15 minutes :
All it takes to bring you a solution
to any little problem we may be
responsible for and you need to
cope with.

24 hours a day :
We will be there day and night
to make sure your satisfaction
is complete.

Hospitality :
If we are unable to fulfil this
contract... you will be our guest.

Managing Services

Using Technology to Create Value

The McGraw-Hill/Irwin Series, Operations and Decision Sciences

OPERATIONS MANAGEMENT

Bowerson, Closs, and Cooper,
Supply Chain Logistics Management,
First Edition

Chase, Aquilano, and Jacobs,
**Operations Management
for Competitive Advantage,**
Ninth Edition

Cohen and Apte,
Manufacturing Automation,
First Edition

Davis, Aquilano, and Chase,
**Fundamentals of Operations
Management,**
Fourth Edition

Dobler and Burt,
Purchasing and Supply Management,
Sixth Edition

Finch,
**OperationsNow.com: Processes, Value,
and Profitability,**
First Edition

Flaherty,
Global Operations Management,
First Edition

Fitzsimmons and Fitzsimmons,
**Service Management: Operations,
Strategy, and Information Technology,**
Third Edition

Gray and Larson,
**Project Management,
The Managerial Process,**
Second Edition

Harrison and Samson,
Technology Management,
First Edition

Hill,
Manufacturing Strategy: Text & Cases,
Third Edition

Hopp and Spearman,
Factory Physics,
Second Edition

Knod and Schonberger,
**Operations Management: Customer-
Focused Principles,**
Seventh Edition

Lambert and Stock,
Strategic Logistics Management,
Third Edition

Leenders and Fearon,
**Purchasing and Supply Chain
Management,**
Twelfth Edition

Melnyk and Swink,
**Value-Driven Operations Management:
An Integrated Modular Approach,**
First Edition

Moses, Seshadri, and Yakir,
**HOM Operations Management
Software,**
First Edition

Nahmias,
Production and Operations Analysis,
Fourth Edition

Nicholas,
**Competitive Manufacturing
Management,**
First Edition

Olson,
**Introduction to Information Systems
Project Management,**
First Edition

Pinedo and Chao,
Operations Scheduling,
First Edition

Sanderson and Uzumeri,
Managing Product Families,
First Edition

Schroeder,
**Operations Management:
Contemporary Concepts,**
First Edition

Simchi-Levi, Kaminsky, and Simchi-Levi,
**Designing and Managing the Supply
Chain: Concepts, Strategies, and Case
Studies,**
Second Edition

Stevenson,
Operations Management,
Seventh Edition

Vollmann, Berry, and Whybark,
**Manufacturing Planning & Control
Systems,**
Fourth Edition

Zipkin,
Foundations of Inventory Management,
First Edition

QUANTITATIVE METHODS
AND MANAGEMENT SCIENCE

Bonini, Hausman, and Bierman,
**Quantitative Analysis for Business
Decisions,**
Ninth Edition

Hillier and Hillier,
**Introduction to Management Science:
A Modeling and Case Studies
Approach with Spreadsheets,**
Second Edition

Managing Services

Using Technology to Create Value

Mark M. Davis
Bentley College

Janelle Heineke
Boston University

 Irwin

Boston   Burr Ridge, IL   Dubuque, IA   Madison, WI   New York   San Francisco   St. Louis
Bangkok   Bogotá   Caracas   Kuala Lumpur   Lisbon   London   Madrid   Mexico City
Milan   Montreal   New Delhi   Santiago   Seoul   Singapore   Sydney   Taipei   Toronto

Irwin

MANAGING SERVICES: USING TECHNOLOGY TO CREATE VALUE
Published by McGraw-Hill/Irwin, a business unit of The McGraw-Hill Companies, Inc., 1221
Avenue of the Americas, New York, NY, 10020. Copyright © 2003 by The McGraw-Hill
Companies, Inc. All rights reserved. No part of this publication may be reproduced or distributed
in any form or by any means, or stored in a database or retrieval system, without the prior written
consent of The McGraw-Hill Companies, Inc., including, but not limited to, in any network or
other electronic storage or transmission, or broadcast for distance learning.
Some ancillaries, including electronic and print components, may not be available to customers
outside the United States.

This book is printed on acid-free paper.

domestic   1 2 3 4 5 6 7 8 9 0 DOW/DOW 0 9 8 7 6 5 4 3 2
international   1 2 3 4 5 6 7 8 9 0 DOW/DOW 0 9 8 7 6 5 4 3 2

ISBN 0-07-246426-7

Publisher: *Brent Gordon*
Executive editor: *Scott Isenberg*
Senior developmental editor: *Wanda J. Zeman*
Senior marketing manager: *Zina Craft*
Producer, media technology: *Todd Labak*
Project manager: *Jim Labeots*
Production supervisor: *Gina Hangos*
Coordinator freelance design: *Artemio Ortiz, Jr.*
Photo research coordinator: *Judy Kausal*
Photo researcher: *Mary Reeg*
Supplement producer: *Joyce J. Chappetto*
Senior digital content specialist: *Brian Nacik*
Cover design: Illustration by *Dale Glasgow*
Typeface: *10/12 Times New Roman*
Compositor: *ElectraGraphics, Inc.*
Printer: *R. R. Donnelley*

Library of Congress Cataloging-in-Publication Data

Davis, Mark M., 1944–
    Managing services: using technology to create value / Mark M. Davis, Janelle Heineke.
        p. cm.
    Includes index.
    ISBN 0-07-246426-7 (alk. paper)—ISBN 0-07-119477-0 (international : alk. paper)
    1. Service industries—Technological innovations—Management. 2. Value analysis
    (Cost control) 3. Customer relations—Management I. Heineke, Janelle N. II. Title.
    HD9980.5 .D388 2003
    658—dc21   2002023965

INTERNATIONAL EDITION ISBN 0-07-119477-0

Copyright © 2003. Exclusive rights by The McGraw-Hill Companies, Inc. for manufacture and
export. This book cannot be re-exported from the country to which it is sold by McGraw-Hill.
The International Edition is not available in North America.

www.mhhe.com

To the memory of my parents, Doris and Harry Davis, in grateful appreciation for always knowing the value of education.

Mark M. Davis

To my sons, Patrick and Douglas, the lights of my life, with love.

Janelle Heineke

Education is an asset, and no one should be trod upon or hindered in such endeavors. No person can ever acquire too much learning, for it is the one thing that will always be yours, immaterial of your financial condition or physical health, immaterial of where you are or who you are.

—*Harry Davis, in a letter to his sister Nancy, dated February 22, 1945*

About the Authors

Mark M. Davis
Bentley College

Mark M. Davis is Professor of Operations Management at Bentley College in Waltham, MA. Dr. Davis earned his BS degree in Electrical Engineering from Tufts University and his MBA and DBA degrees from Boston University's School of Management. He worked as a manufacturing engineer for the General Electric Company and is a graduate of its Manufacturing Management Program. He was also a programs manager for the U.S. Army Natick Research Laboratories.

Dr. Davis's primary research interest is service operations management with a focus on customer waiting time issues. He has published articles in this area in several journals, including *The Journal of Operations Management, Decision Sciences, The Journal of Services Marketing, The Journal of Business Forecasting, OM Review, The International Journal of Production and Operations Management,* and *The International Journal of Service Industry Management.* Along with Richard Chase and Nicholas Aquilano, he has written the textbook *Fundamentals of Operations Management* (McGraw-Hill/Irwin), currently in its fourth edition.

Dr. Davis is currently Secretary of the Decision Sciences Institute and is a past president of the Northeast Decision Sciences Institute. In 2000, he was named a Fellow in the Decision Sciences Institute. In 1998, Dr. Davis received Bentley College's Scholar of the Year Award. He was appointed to the 1996 Board of Examiners for the Malcolm Baldrige National Quality Award. Dr. Davis currently serves on the editorial review board of *The International Journal of Service Industry Management.*

Janelle Heineke
Boston University

Janelle Heineke is Associate Professor of Operations Management at Boston University's School of Management. She holds a DBA degree from Boston University, an MBA degree from Babson College, an MSN degree from Boston College, and a BSN degree from Marquette University. Dr. Heineke worked in health care as both a clinician and a manager and, while practicing, held positions as a lecturer and clinical preceptor at Harvard Medical School, Boston College Graduate School of Nursing, and Northeastern University's Physician Assistant program.

Dr. Heineke's research focuses on service operations and quality management. She has published in several journals, including *The Journal of Operations Management,* the *California Management Review,* the *Quality Management Journal, The Services Industries Journal, The International Journal of Production and Operations Management, The International Journal of Service Industry Management, Health Services Research, The Journal of Medical Practice Management, Business Horizons,* and *Operations Management Review.* She is the co-author of two books, *The Physician Manager Alliance: Building the Healthy Health Care Organization* (with Stephen Davidson and Marion McCollom) and *Games and Exercises for Operations Management: Hands-on Learning Activities for Basic Concepts and Tools* (with Larry Meile) and has contributed chapters and cases to several other books. Dr. Heineke is an Associate Editor for *The Journal of Operations Management* and is a regular reviewer for several other journals.

Preface

As we enter the 21st century, we can see significant changes occurring in the ways services are being designed and delivered, and the underlying cause of many of these dramatic changes is technology. Self-service gas stations and checkout counters in supermarkets, online financial transactions including banking and stock trading, online purchases of goods formerly bought in traditional brick and mortar retail operations, e-tickets for air travel, and speed pass lanes on toll roads and turnpikes are just a few of the many examples of how technology has changed both the way in which services are being provided and the way in which customers behave.

And we have only seen the tip of the iceberg. Technology will continue to advance in the form of faster and more accurate transmission lines, more powerful computers, and larger electronic data storage equipment that is capable of storing *petabytes* of data. As technology enhances our ability to offer a broader range of always accessible and more personalized services, it also is making it possible to deliver services at lower costs. The result is both more effective and more efficient service. For all these reasons, we chose technology as the unifying framework for linking the topics that are presented in this book.

This is the first endeavor for both of us in writing a brand new, "clean slate" textbook. There is an old saying, "To really learn a subject, you should teach it." We have both taught service operations management for many years, but our efforts in writing this book have led us to offer this modification, "To really learn a subject, write a textbook about it." Before committing anything to paper, we spent many hours researching and "enthusiastically discussing" the finer points of service management that we thought we had previously understood, but that we needed to clarify and refine before we could include them in our book.

GOALS

Our primary goals in preparing this book on service management were to:

- Present the basic service concepts within a framework for managing services both effectively and efficiently.

- Integrate marketing and human resource issues throughout the text.

- Make service management concepts "come alive" by continuously reinforcing the theory and concepts with real-world examples.

- Provide students with a set of management tools to assist them to better understand the fundamental characteristics of services. These are presented primarily in the chapter supplements.

- Emphasize the internationalization of services by including examples of well-managed service organizations in different countries.

SPECIAL FEATURES OF THE BOOK

To facilitate the student's education about services, we have incorporated several pedagogical features in our book, including:

- *Chapter learning objectives:* Each chapter begins with a list of learning objectives that highlight the major topics and concepts of the chapter.

- *Opening vignettes:* Each chapter opens with a short vignette about a real company or experience that incorporates some of the material in the chapter. The purpose of the vignette is to create student interest in the chapter by demonstrating that the material presented is actually used in real-world situations.

- *The customer's perspective:* At the beginning of each chapter, concepts are introduced using easy-to-relate-to examples from everyday life. These emphasize the relevance of the concepts to the customer as well as to the service firm.

- *Managerial issues:* These provide a bridge between the examples and issues presented in the opening vignette and the customer's perspective on the theory and concepts presented in each chapter.

- *Views from the Top:* Many of the concepts presented in this book were introduced or advocated by senior executives. The Views from the Top identify senior managers, often the founder, chairman, and/or CEO of a well-known service organization that has been a strong advocate of a particular concept that is presented in the chapter.

- *Application of technology to create value:* Throughout the text are examples under the heading "Using Technology to Create Value" that illustrate how service firms are using technology to create value for both their organizations and their customers. The use of real-world examples reinforces the importance of both technology and the topics in successfully managing service operations.

- *Internet exercises:* The Internet is one of the widely available technology tools for obtaining and disseminating information. Where appropriate, an Internet exercise is provided at the end of a chapter to guide the student in obtaining the latest information on a particular topic or to reinforce the concepts presented in the chapter.

- *Examples with solutions:* Examples with solutions illustrating specific procedures and techniques follow quantitative topics. These are clearly set off from the text, and help the student to better understand the computations.

- *Key term definitions:* Key terms are in boldface when first introduced in the text and are defined at the end of each chapter with page numbers for quick reference.

- *Review and discussion questions:* These questions allow students to review the chapter concepts before attempting the problems. They provide a basis for classroom discussion.

- *Solved problems:* Representative example problems are included at the end of each of the quantitative chapters. Each includes a detailed, worked-out solution and provides another level of support for students before they try homework problems on their own.

- *Problems:* A wide range of problems follows each of the quantitative chapters.

- *Cases:* Located at the end of most chapters, short cases based on actual companies or customer experiences, allow the student to think critically about issues discussed in the chapter. These cases can also provide a basis for classroom discussions, or provide a capstone problem for the topic.

ANCILLARY MATERIALS

- *Student CD-ROM*
- *PowerPoint Presentation Slides,* which provide lecture outlines plus graphic material from the text to complement and customize lectures

ACKNOWLEDGMENTS

Although there are only two names on the cover of this book, a project of this magnitude could not be successfully completed without the assistance and cooperation of many individuals. Specifically, we would like to thank the reviewers for their evaluations and feedback on our initial manuscripts. We thank them for their suggestions and comments. The reviewers were:

Michael R. Godfrey, *University of Wisconsin—Oshkosh*

Kenneth J. Klassen, *California State University—Northridge*

Robert Klassen, *University of Western Ontario*

Robert E. Markland, *University of South Carolina*

Ann Marucheck, *University of North Carolina—Chapel Hill*

James S. Noble, *University of Missouri*

Michael J. Pesch, *St. Cloud State University*

Madeleine E. Pullman, *Colorado State University*

Richard A. Reid, *University of New Mexico*

Daniel L. Spears, *University of Hawaii*

Finally we wish to thank the staff at McGraw-Hill/Irwin for their support, encouragement, and assistance: Scott Isenberg, Executive Editor; Wanda Zeman, Senior Developmental Editor; Jim Labeots, Project Manager; and Judy Kausal, Photo Research Coordinator.

In writing this book, we have tried to practice what we preach. In applying the quality concept of continuous improvement, we have incorporated many of the suggestions made by our reviewers, and, as result, the final product represents a significant improvement over our initial manuscript.

There is an old Chinese saying that states, "May you live in interesting times." For both academics and practitioners of service management, those times are now, and we should take full advantage of the opportunity—and enjoy it while doing so!

Mark M. Davis
Janelle Heineke

Brief Contents

Contents

Managing Services

Using Technology to Create Value

CHAPTER ONE

Introduction

Learning Objectives

- Identify the major differences between services and goods.

- Introduce several broad perspectives for categorizing the different types of services that exist in an economy.

- Demonstrate how technology is changing the ways services are created and delivered.

- Present a historical perspective on services, and show how services have evolved.

OCP Delivers Orders to Paris Pharmacies in Less than Two Hours

David Young-Wolff / PhotoEdit

A customer walks into the pharmacy on *rue de Rivoli* in Paris, France, with a prescription to be filled. The pharmacist, after verifying that she does not have the medication in stock, goes to her computer where she places an order for the medication with OCP, the leading pharmaceutical distributor in Paris, along with several other items that she needs. The order is transmitted through EDI (electronic data interchange) to OCP's distribution center, which is located in St. Ouen, a Paris suburb.

Upon receipt of the electronic order, a paper requisition is generated, listing the requested items and the quantities of each. The requisition is deposited in a plastic tote bin, which has a bar code attached to the outside identifying the order. The tote bin is immediately placed on a conveyor where it wends its way through the distribution center collecting the items that were ordered. Automatic order picking equipment deposits some items in the bin without any human intervention, while other bulkier items are picked by hand. At each stop, the tote bin is weighed to ensure that the proper number of items has been put in it. Forty-five minutes after the order was received, a cover is placed on the tote box and secured with an elastic cord, and the tote box is placed in a delivery van along with other tote boxes. Less than two hours after the pharmacist placed the order, it is delivered to the pharmacy, just as the customer arrives to pick up his prescription.

Objectives of the Book

As the opening vignette illustrates, technology is changing how organizations provide service. At the same time, it is more critical today than ever for service managers to understand that the fundamentals of doing business have remained virtually unchanged. To be successful, companies still need to provide value to their customers. Those firms that do will grow and prosper; those that don't will fail and will either be absorbed by their competitors or go out of business. Ample evidence demonstrates that firms need to continually change to meet the ever increasing and changing demands of their customers. A&P supermarkets, W.T. Grant's variety stores, and the First National Bank of Boston were once leaders in their respective industries, but today either no longer exist or are mere shadows of their glory years. They ignored the fundamentals of doing business and stopped providing value to their customers. Value, as we shall learn, is defined by the customer, and in today's fast-paced ever-changing business environment, technology often plays a major role in how that value can be added.

The objectives of this book are to:

- Present the unique characteristics that services have in common, regardless of their specific industries.

- Identify the ways in which services can add value for their customers.

- Introduce the elements or basic building blocks that managers must address in designing and delivering services.

- Provide some insights into how technology is changing the ways services are being designed and delivered.

- Introduce management tools and concepts that can be applied to a wide range of services.

- Recognize the need for an organization's different functional elements, such as operations, marketing, and human resources, to interact with each other on a continuous basis.

Why the Emphasis on Services?

Services have become the focus of increasing managerial attention for several reasons. First, as we can see in Exhibit 1.1, services have experienced significant growth over the past several decades; they now represent a major portion of the economies of the world's more industrialized nations. Even in lesser developed countries, services still represent a significant portion of their economies, as shown in Exhibit 1.2.

EXHIBIT 1.1 The Growth in Services in Industrialized Countries

Source: Bureau of Labor Statistics, "Comparative Civilian Labor Force Statistics for Ten Countries (1959–2001)," Updated March 25, 2002.

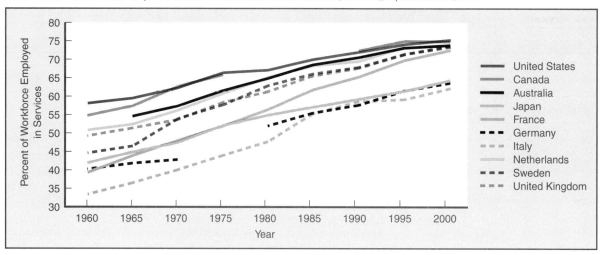

EXHIBIT 1.2

Services as a Percent of Gross Domestic Product in Lesser Developed Countries

Country	Percent of GDP
Brazil	50%
Thailand	49
Peru	45
India	45
Ghana	30

Source: *The World Fact Book 2000* (Washington, DC: Central Intelligence Agency).

Secondly, many manufacturing companies now realize they can create more value for their customers with services. These new services not only provide manufacturers with a competitive advantage but also are proving to be very profitable.

Advances in technology have also increased the emphasis on services. Many products are no longer sold as products, but instead are sold as services through the Internet. For example, you no longer need to purchase a road atlas to find a route to a particular destination. Instead, you can request the information on the Internet, from an applications service provider (ASP) that specializes in providing maps and directions. In a similar manner, many software packages are now offered on the Internet by ASPs, eliminating the need to buy and install shrink-wrapped software packages and then having to frequently upgrade them.

As Stan Davis and Chris Myers point out in their book *Blur,* technology is the underlying cause for the vast majority of changes occurring today. They identify three major elements or forces that managers need to recognize in this rapidly changing environment (which is often *blurred* because the changes are happening so quickly). These are: (*a*) speed, or quick delivery; (*b*) intangibility, or less focus on goods; and (*c*) connectivity, or electronic communications between organizations and individuals and even within organizations. Services appear to be the common factor that link all three elements, as illustrated in Exhibit 1.3. For example, the Internet now connects virtually all the distant corners of the world, allowing services in the form of e-mails and online purchases to be

EXHIBIT 1.3
**Forces Increasing
the Emphasis
on Services**

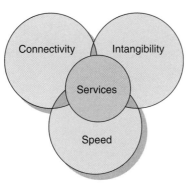

Source: Adapted from Stan Davis and Christopher
Meyer, *Blur:* Reading, MA: Addison-Wesley, 1998.

transmitted quickly and at any time. Likewise, satellite communication now permits firms such as FedEx and Wal-Mart to provide up-to-the-minute company information on an ongoing basis to their employees around the world.

Differences Between Goods and Services

The vast majority of products that we purchase consist of both a "goods component" and a "services component," as seen in Exhibit 1.4. Products that consist primarily of the goods component, such as automobiles and clothing, are considered to be goods, while products that consist primarily of services, such as a restaurant or a bank, are typically considered to be services.

Services share a common set of attributes that distinguish them from manufactured products (goods) such as automobiles, computers, clothing, or microwave ovens (which are often referred to as "things you can drop on your foot"). These characteristics of services, which, as we shall see, are interrelated, include:

• Direct customer interaction

• Intangibility

• Perishability

Direct Customer Interaction

A key factor that distinguishes manufacturing from service environments is that the customer is often present during the actual delivery of the service. Few of us have actually visited an automobile factory or a beer brewery, although many of us have purchased a car or indulged in an occasional beer. The physical presence of the customer is not required to produce the car or the beer because finished goods (FG) inventories separate the customer from the manufacturing process.

However, as seen in Exhibit 1.5, the same cannot be said for services, for which the presence and participation of the customer is required as part of the service delivery process. For example, customers must be present to have their hair done at a hair salon; to dine at a restaurant; to travel by plane, bus, or train; or to receive medical treatment at the emergency room of a hospital. In some cases, the customer is not present in the service process, but services are performed on the property of the customer. In these instances the customer's property acts as a surrogate for the customer, for the property must be present

EXHIBIT 1.4
Products Are
a "Bundle" of Goods
and Services

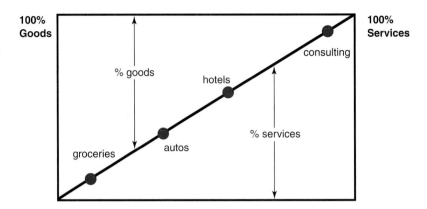

EXHIBIT 1.5
Difference
in Customer
Interaction for Goods
and Services

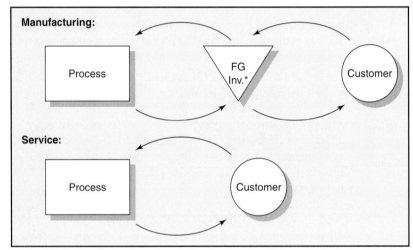

*Finished Goods Inventory.

in the performance of the service. Examples of these types of services include dry cleaning, lawn mowing, and automobile repair. Still other services are performed using information provided by the customer, for example, processing bill payments through Internet banking.

Technology is dramatically changing the way in which customers interact with many services. Bank customers now have several options for conducting their transactions, in addition to the more traditional face-to-face interaction with a bank teller. They can use an ATM or conduct online transactions through the Internet. Similarly, customers no longer have to go to a retail store location such as Barnes & Noble or Borders to purchase books. Instead they can buy their books online. For another example of how technology affects customer interaction with services, we look at EMC Corp., which manufactures data storage equipment. Advances in technology permit EMC's equipment to self-diagnose problems and even potential problems, many of which can be corrected remotely by a service technician or engineer who is located at EMC's headquarters in Hopkinton, Massachusetts. Before the introduction of this technology, the technician or engineer needed to visit the customer's facility in person to make the necessary repairs.

Intangibility

An automobile, an overcoat, or a box of cereal are tangible goods, objects that can been seen and touched and can be used or consumed now or later. Services, on the other hand, are acts that are performed for the benefit of customers, and those acts usually take place in the presence of customers (or their possessions). Services are **intangible.** We cannot actually touch a medical examination performed by a doctor, a financial transaction at a bank, the purchase of groceries at a supermarket, or a teacher's lecture in a classroom. These are services: the doctor performs a series of tests on the patient; the bank teller enters financial data into a computer for the customer; the cashier at the supermarket rings up the price of each item into a cash register; and the teacher provides knowledge and information to the students.

Perishability

Because the customer is present and participates in the delivery of a service, the capacity of the service operation is considered to be **perishable.** Service capacity that is not used immediately and remains idle cannot be saved for use in the future. For example, the empty seats on airplanes cannot be accumulated and saved for use during the peak demand periods of Thanksgiving and Christmas. Similarly, empty rooms cannot be accrued during the slow winter season at a summer resort for use during the peak periods of July and August. Customers who want to eat in a busy restaurant on a Friday or Saturday night are highly unlikely to come back on Monday morning when there is more than ample capacity to serve them. Instead, they will simply find another restaurant on Friday or Saturday night.

Types of Services

As we saw earlier in this chapter, services account for the vast majority of the economies of industrialized countries. A more detailed classification of the many different types of services is presented later in this book as an introduction to understanding service strategy. As a first step, however, Exhibit 1.6 describes services in terms of sectors, types of processes, and objects of each process.

Exhibit 1.7 provides a closer look at the two major types of service processes (transformation or transportation) and who or what is being processed (people, goods, or data), providing examples of each. The managers within each of these categories have much in common, particularly at the operational level, but at the same time, they each face their own unique set of challenges. We shall also see that technology affects each of these categories differently.

Service Sectors

As shown in Exhibit 1.6, another way to look at services is to divide them into the following three broad sectors, recognizing that there is some degree of overlap:

- Service industries
- Ancillary and support services
- Services in manufacturing

Service Industries

In looking at services by industry, we take a macro view of the categories traditionally used in determining employment by various industries within an economy. Organizations that

EXHIBIT 1.6
Categorizing Types
of Services

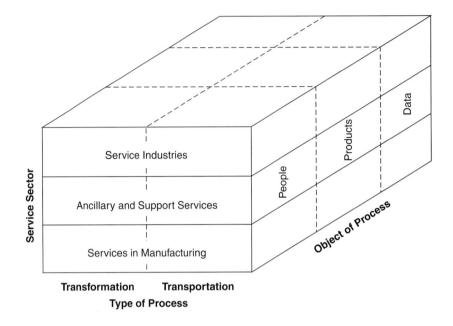

EXHIBIT 1.7
Differentiating
Services by Type
of Process and Who
or What Is Being
Processed

	Transform	**Transport**
People:	Restaurant, hospital	Airline, bus, train
Goods:	Car wash, dry cleaning	Freight line, retail sales
Data:	Payrolls, data analysis	E-mail, electronic data interchange (EDI)

fall within the service industry category focus on providing a specific type of service as their primary mission or objective. We present here some of the larger service industries that exist in every economy, recognizing that in our descriptions there is some overlap.

Health Care

Organizations in this category include primary care facilities such as hospitals (for-profit and not-for-profit), health maintenance organizations (HMOs), walk-in and specialty clinics, and health research organizations. Also included in this category are ambulance services and the professional services of doctors, nurses, and emergency medical technicians.

Hospitality

The hospitality industry covers a wide range of services from hotels and resorts to restaurants, nightclubs, and car rental agencies. Each of these can be further divided into several subcategories or market segments. Restaurants, for example, range from gourmet dining to fast food; hotels similarly range from luxury full-service hotels that are typically located in the center of major cities to budget, no-frills motels located on highways.

Financial Services

Here again there is a broad range of services, including banking, insurance, and investment brokerage services. Deregulation and advances in technology have blurred industry lines in this sector. For example, many banks now offer insurance and investment services while brokerage services such as Fidelity Investments offer check-writing services.

Professional Services

Included in this category are the services provided by doctors, lawyers, architects, accountants, teachers, and other service professionals. Often these professionals function in the role of independent contractors, each with their own client base, as in the case of medical doctors and lawyers.

Retail

Retail operations similarly cover a broad spectrum of businesses, ranging from supermarket chains such as Safeway to mom-and-pop variety stores; from large, upscale department stores like Nordstrom and Saks Fifth Avenue to small highly specialized boutiques and discount operations such as Wal-Mart and Target. Also included in this category are dry cleaning establishments, barbershops and hair salons, gas stations, and auto repair shops. These are just a few of the types of retail services available.

Transportation

This category, as suggested in Exhibit 1.6, can be subdivided into the transportation of people, the transportation of products, and the transportation of data. The transportation of people includes services that use airplanes, buses, ships, and trains. The transportation of goods is considered part of supply chain management and is addressed only tangentially here. The transportation of data is accomplished electronically through the Internet and EDI and magnetically through computer discs, as well as by fax and the traditional mail systems. It is also done orally by telephone, as when a customer speaks to a clerk at a hotel reservations call center.

Ancillary and Support Services

Ancillary and support services come under the umbrella of what we call service supply chain management (as distinguished from manufacturing supply chain management, which focuses exclusively on the delivery of products). While these services are performed within an organization, they are not the primary mission of the company. Examples of ancillary services include the cafeteria in an automobile assembly plant, the security at an office building, and the lawn care service at a university.

There has been a growing trend to outsource ancillary services instead of managing them as in-house operations, for two main reasons. First, it is usually less costly to outsource; outsourcing also allows firms to focus resources on their primary mission, thereby increasing their competitive position in the marketplace. Second, because the firm to which the service is outsourced typically specializes in that particular ancillary service, it can often provide a better level of service than if the service were provided internally.

In evaluating whether or not to outsource a service, it is important for a firm to determine if and how that service adds significant value for its customers and whether or not that service is part of the firm's competitive advantage. It would be foolhardy for a manager to relinquish control of a facet of the business that clearly differentiates it from its competitors. Some types of services within this category include:

Temporary Help

The fastest-growing segment of labor is temporary help. Increasingly, firms use temporary help as an alternative to hiring permanent full-time workers because it provides flexibility to react to marketplace changes. Service managers, in particular, need to be aware of the advantages and disadvantages of using temporary help in terms of costs, knowledge retention, and development of long-term customer relationships.

Janitorial Services

Many companies subcontract custodial care of offices and factories to outside firms that specialize in this area. ServiceMaster is one of the leading firms that provides this type of service.

Security

Guard service on either a full-time or temporary basis is also often subcontracted. This has been a strong growth industry in recent years for several reasons. More and more companies want to protect their proprietary information from getting into the hands of competitors. Another factor contributing to the growth of security services is the growth in the elderly population. Many senior citizen communities provide security to ensure the safety of members and their possessions. As this segment of the population continues to grow, so will the demand for security. The destruction of the World Trade Center towers in New York City on September 11, 2001, further fueled growth in security services.

Food Service

Many businesses, including manufacturing companies and services such as colleges and hospitals that need to provide meals to workers or "customers" (be they students or patients), often outsource these food services to firms that specialize in this area, such as ARAMARK and Sodexho.

Services in Manufacturing

At one time, manufacturing and services were viewed as two distinct segments of the economy. More recently, however, the distinction is becoming blurred, and there is more integration between the two. This merging of manufacturing and services within an organization has been driven in large part by the growing trend toward shorter product life cycles. As life cycles become shorter, the goods component of a product more quickly becomes commodity-like in nature, making it less distinguishable from its competition. Companies turn to services in many instances to obtain a competitive advantage. Examples include the support service and upgrading advertised by Gateway Computers, which makes the Gateway product bundle more attractive to many users, and the global positioning system (GPS) offered by Lincoln automobiles, which enables drivers to know where they are at any time and to obtain directions to their destinations.

Defining Value

We often hear the expression "Customers want their money's worth." Unfortunately, from a manager's point of view, satisfying customers is not that easy. Customers want more than their money's worth, and the more they receive for their money, the more value they see in the services they purchase.

In determining the **value** of a service, customers consider all the benefits derived from the service and compare it with all the costs of that service. If, in the customer's opinion, the benefits exceed the costs, then customers perceive value in the service. The more the benefits exceed the costs, the more value the service provides. In other words,

$$\text{Perceived Customer Value} = \frac{\text{Total Benefits}}{\text{Total Costs}}$$

When this ratio is greater than 1, customers perceive value; the greater the number, the more value. When this ratio is less than 1, customers feel they have overpaid for the service, that they have been "ripped off," and are highly unlikely to use that service again. Another way of looking at this is

Perceived Customer Value = Total Benefits – Total Costs

When the difference between the benefits and costs is positive, customers perceive value; when it is negative, they believe they have overpaid for the service.

Total Benefits

Total benefits consist of all the factors (which are presented in detail in Chapter 12) that affect the quality of the service being provided. Customers weight these factors differently, depending on the service. The weights for these factors will also vary from customer to customer for a given service and might even vary for the same customer at different times under different circumstances.

Total Costs

Total costs include monetary costs, but customers also can incur several other types of costs. Christopher Lovelock identifies four of these[1]:

Time

In today's fast-paced environment, time is precious. Therefore, services that require significant amounts of time can be viewed as "not being worth it" to many customers. Time can take several forms, including traveling to the service and then waiting for the service.

Physical Effort

Here the cost includes the customer's need to exert physical effort in the delivery of the service. Self-service operations are a good example of this. At a self-service gas station, customers are required to get out of their cars and pump their own gas. At a self-service supermarket, customers are required to scan their own groceries and then bag them.

Psychic Costs

These often apply to new customers, who might feel inadequate or unable to properly use a service the first time. This again would apply to some self-service operations. For some customers, purchasing goods and services the first time over the Internet may be anxiety-producing and so might be an example of psychic costs.

Sensory Costs

These costs are experienced physically by the customer, over and above the physical effort. Sensory costs pertain to the environment in which the service is being provided and can include such factors as temperature (too hot or cold), poor lighting, noise, and unpleasant smells.

For example, if we go to a restaurant for dinner on a Saturday night, the benefits of this experience include all the factors that define service quality (as presented in Chapter 12). These might include the quality of the food, its presentation and portion size, the speed of service, the atmosphere of the restaurant, the friendliness and knowledge of the staff, and the cleanliness of the restaurant. The costs, in addition to the price and tip of the

---

[1]Christopher Lovelock, *Product Plus: How Product + Service = Competitive Advantage* (New York: McGraw-Hill, 1994), pp. 60–61.

meal, also include the time it took to get to the restaurant and wait to get a table, the cost of gas for the car (or the cost of a taxi) and parking. Thus, in determining the value of going to this restaurant, we would consider all the benefits and compare them with all the costs.

How to Create or Add Value

Value can take many forms and mean different things to different customers. Value can mean something is less expensive, as when you buy books at Amazon.com. Value can mean it is more convenient, as when you order groceries online, or faster, as when you use the fast lane on the highway to pay a toll automatically. Value may take the form of information, as when Amazon.com tells you what other books have been purchased by buyers who bought the same book you did, or when Expedia.com provides a list of different airlines going to a particular city and a comparison of their airfares. Value can also take the form of more personalized service, as when you check into a hotel like the Ritz-Carlton and the staff knows you have stayed there before and have certain preferences.

The key for the service firm in creating or adding value for the customer is to provide additional benefits at an increase in cost that is perceived by the customer to be less than or equal to those benefits.

A Historical Perspective on Services

The word *service,* like the words *servant* and *servitude,* is derived from the Latin word *servus,* which means slave. Services have often been associated with menial work that is performed by low or unskilled workers. Technological advances in manufacturing during the Industrial Revolution of the 19th century decreased the labor required to produce goods and at the same time improved the standard of living. As a result, both the demand for services and the labor available to provide them increased. But it has been only within the past 50 years or so that there has been significant growth in services in industrialized countries, catalyzed in large part by advances in information technology. The current economic period is often referred to as the information or service economy, which is considered the successor to the manufacturing or industrial economy, which succeeded the agrarian economy that was dominant through the middle of the 19th century.

Services, until recently, were not considered to add value to an economy. As a result, measures of service activities were not even included in the calculation of the gross national product (GNP) of a country. Instead, services were usually lumped into a miscellaneous or *tertiary category* behind agriculture, and mining and manufacturing. In many Third World or undeveloped countries, services are still listed in the tertiary category.

Today, as we saw earlier in this chapter, services constitute a major portion of the economies in the more highly developed countries, and economic data are now available on many of the major service sectors within these economies.

In some countries, such as France, negative connotations are still associated with service, as memories linger of the oppression under the French monarchy and its need for numerous servants to support overindulgent lifestyles. As a result, many services are now fully automated, eliminating the need for service workers. For example, you can park your car in a garage in Paris and never come in contact with a parking attendant. You take a ticket as you enter, and you pay with either cash or a credit card at a machine that calculates how long you parked and the amount due. After receiving payment, the machine issues a receipt that you use to exit the garage.

The Evolution of Services in an Economy

As an economy evolves from a primarily agrarian society to an industrial society to the modern society of today, different types of services are emphasized. While nations around the world are in different stages of this transition, it appears that the role of services within these stages remains relatively consistent.

Infrastructure Services

In the early agrarian stages of an economy's development, services play a relatively minimal role. Individuals tend to be self-sufficient and have little or no discretionary income. As a consequence, there is little or no need for services. The focus at this stage is primarily on infrastructure services in the form of transportation, government agencies, and health care.

Support Services

As an economy begins to develop trade and commerce, the need for support services grows. These include banking, retail operations, hotels for business travelers, and perhaps insurance companies.

Recreational and Leisure Services

With the growth of the economy driven by industry, salaries tend to increase and so do the standard of living and the proportion of income that can be used for discretionary spending. People are very likely to spend their discretionary income eating in restaurants and taking more and better vacations or even frequent long weekend trips, thereby providing the growth for many services in the hospitality industry. Examples include restaurants, hotels, destination resorts, health clubs, and amusement parks.

Time-Saving Services

To sustain the increase in their standard of living, workers find themselves working longer hours. In many households, all adults work full time. In such an environment, time becomes more precious and people look to time-saving services as a way to cope with the time pressures and to improve their lifestyles. Examples here include mail-order businesses that save time from shopping in department stores, baby-sitting services that free both parents to work, and a wide variety of shop-at-home services that include the delivery of groceries and dry cleaning. One reason for the tremendous growth in shopping on the Internet is that it saves people time.

The Service Experience

Today, many customers are looking for something more than just good service; they are looking for a memorable experience as part of that service.[2] Customers see added value in these service experiences and are willing to pay for them. Examples of firms that provide such service experiences include Disney World, Rain Forest Café, The Discovery Zone, and Universal Studios.

Information Services

With the explosive growth of information technology and the Internet, a new type of service is emerging, which is often provided by an **infomediary.** Infomediaries act as

[2] B. Joseph Pine II and James H. Gilmore, "Welcome to the Experience Economy," *Harvard Business Review,* July–August 1998, pp. 97–105.

"brokers" between buyers and sellers, providing information to each. The services they provide occur in electronic marketplaces. Marketplaces that bring companies together are referred to as *business-to-business (B2B)*, which typically focus on a particular commodity, such as chemicals or steel. Marketplaces that bring companies and consumers together are referred to as *business to consumer (B2C)*. Examples of B2C marketplaces include shopping for an automobile and finding a bank mortgage for a house. Marketplaces that bring consumers together are referred to as *consumer to consumer (C2C)*, an example of which is eBay.

The Impact of Technology

Technology is transforming the way services are delivered today and will continue to do so for the foreseeable future. In the past, service managers typically faced a trade-off in terms of what to provide to the customer. For example, if customers wanted low cost, then it was provided with slower service or less personalized service, as shown in Exhibit 1.8A. Similarly, a trade-off existed between the degree of customization and the speed of delivery, as shown in Exhibit 1.8B.

While these trade-offs still exist, technology is allowing managers to move to a superior performance or trade-off curve, as seen in Exhibit 1.9, thereby creating or adding value for the customer in the form of faster, lower cost, and/or more personalized services.

EXHIBIT 1.8A
Traditional Trade-off between Speed of Delivery and Cost

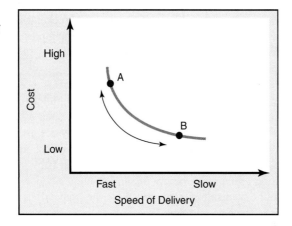

EXHIBIT 1.8B
Traditional Trade-off between Degree of Customization and Speed of Delivery

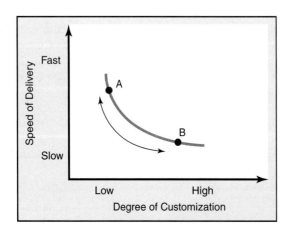

EXHIBIT 1.9
**Creating Value
by Moving to
a Superior
Performance Curve**

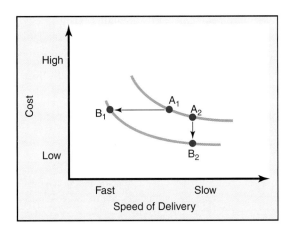

For example, in moving from A_1 to B_1, speed of delivery increases but at no additional cost. Similarly, in moving from A_2 to B_2, the speed of delivery remains the same, but the cost is significantly reduced. Both approaches increase the value of the service being provided.

Managers must also recognize that the installation of new technology must be accompanied by the proper technical support. In addition, sufficient time must be allocated in the initial start-up phase to provide proper training to both workers and, when necessary, customers. When deciding to purchase new technology, the service manager must ensure that there is compatibility between the desired technology and the overall long-term goals of the firm.

Technology will continue to advance in the form of faster and more accurate transmission lines, more powerful computers, and larger electronic data storage equipment that is capable of storing *petabytes* (a petabyte equals 2^{50} or 1,125,899,906,842,624 bytes) of data. At the same time, unit costs in all of these areas will continue to decrease. The result will be more and more innovative approaches to providing services, and this trend will continue in the coming years.

Challenges for the Service Manager

As we begin the 21st century, we can see significant changes in the design and delivery of services, and the underlying cause of these dramatic changes is technology. Self-service gas stations and checkout counters in supermarkets, online financial transactions including banking and stock trading, online purchases of goods formerly bought in traditional brick-and-mortar retail operations, e-tickets for air travel, and speed pass lanes on toll roads and turnpikes are just a few of the many examples of how technology is changing both the way in which services are provided and the way in which customers behave.

We have already seen many trends emerging in services as a result of technology, including a greater reliance on self-service, an increase in availability (24×7), a decrease in the importance of location, and a shift from traditional synchronous communication in the form of person-to-person telephone calls to IT-based asynchronous communication such as e-mail and the Internet. At the same time, there is a reverse trend toward more IT-based synchronous communication such as teleconferencing and videoconferencing.

In such turbulent times, the challenges facing service managers are many, including

- Developing new ways of adding value for customers by understanding how the Internet and other technologies affect the delivery of services.

- Managing services in an increasingly competitive global environment where customer expectations and perceptions can vary significantly from country to country.

- Working in a fast-paced and constantly changing business environment, caused in large part by the continuous introduction of state-of-the-art technologies.

- Managing a workforce where entirely new types of jobs are being created as a result of technology, and recruiting and training individuals from an increasingly diverse population.

- Providing higher levels of service to increasingly demanding customers, while maintaining or even reducing prices.

Summary

Everywhere we go we encounter services of one type or another, in the education we receive, the vacations we take, the medical exams by our doctors, the repairs to our cars, and the processing of our checks at our banks, to name a few. The growth in services, especially in the industrialized nations of the world, has reached a point where services now comprise the vast majority of their economies. Consequently, services can no longer be ignored or relegated to third-class status.

This rapid growth in services has stimulated competition. As technology continues to shrink the world, services once provided only by local or national firms are now offered by international competitors.

Advances in technology are changing the very services that can be provided—and these changes will continue into the foreseeable future.

To be successful, today's service managers need to understand, now more than ever, the basic building blocks of their businesses because these fundamentals can easily become overlooked in such a fast-paced environment. These managers also need to understand how technology can add value to their services, and how to manage the change brought on by technology. Only in this way will they be able to make intelligent, well-informed business decisions.

Key Terms

infomediary: service that provides customers with information. *(p. 13)*
intangible: services are acts or deeds that cannot be touched. *(p. 7)*
perishable: services are time sensitive and cannot be stored for future use. *(p. 7)*
value: the worth of a service as determined by what a customer is willing to pay for it. *(p. 10)*

Review and Discussion Questions

1. Identify the different types of services you come in contact with during a "normal" week.
2. What are the characteristics of the services you really like? What are the characteristics of services you dislike and as a consequence are looking to purchase elsewhere?
3. Name a product that is totally composed of service with no goods component. Name a product that is 100 percent goods with no service component.
4. Identify and compare the value created by each of the following pairs of services.
   a. Shopping at a conventional supermarket versus an online service.
   b. Eating at a fine dining restaurant versus a fast-food operation.
   c. Employing an Internet travel service versus your neighborhood travel agent.
   d. Buying stocks and bonds online versus through a traditional investment broker.
5. What does the term *service supply chain* mean?
6. Why are services more important in today's business environment?

Selected Bibliography

Brady, Diane. "Why Service Stinks." *Business Week,* October 23, 2000, pp. 118–28.

Davis, Stan, and Christopher Meyer. *Blur.* Reading, MA: Addison-Wesley, 1998.

Gale, Bradley T. *Managing Customer Value: Creating Quality and Service That Customers Can See.* New York: Free Press Division of MacMillan, Inc., 1994.

Heskett, James L. *Managing in the Service Economy.* Boston: Harvard Business School Press, 1986.

Levitt, Theodore. "Production-Line Approach to Service." *Harvard Business Review,* vol. 50, no. 5 (September–October 1972), pp. 41–52.

Levitt, Theodore. "The Industrialization of Service," *Harvard Business Review,* vol. 54, no. 5 (September–October 1976), pp. 63–74.

Lovelock, Christopher. *Product Plus: How Product + Service = Competitive Advantage.* New York: McGraw-Hill, Inc., 1994, pp. 60–61.

Pine, B. Joseph, II, and James H. Gilmore. "Welcome to the Experience Economy." *Harvard Business Review,* vol. 76, no. 4 (July–August 1998), pp. 97–105.

Vandermeer, S. *From Tin Soldiers to Russian Dolls: Creating Added Value through Services.* Oxford, England: Butterworth-Heinemann, 1993.

CHAPTER TWO

Understanding Customers and Markets

Learning Objectives

- Emphasize the importance of understanding customer needs.

- Define market segmentation.

- Present a variety of market segmentation approaches.

- Describe methods of collecting information about customers.

British Telecom's Personalized Customer Survey

Tony Freeman / PhotoEdit

British Telecommunications (BT), which was originally part of the postal system in the United Kingdom, provides services to 21 million business and residential customers, representing 90 percent of the households in that country. BT provides local and long-distance telephone communications services, Internet services, and IT solutions. Although BT had few competitors until recently, the global telecommunications industry now includes more than 100 companies. In such a highly competitive environment, BT decided to communicate more personally and regularly with its customers by conducting regular mailings to improve customer retention.

To accomplish this, BT worked with Devon Direct, a Pennsylvania-based direct marketing advertising agency, to develop a brochure with personalized savings review and order forms for each customer. "They were able to use the data in the database to make sure that every one of the million pieces mailed every week was different from every other piece. If the customers were already members of Friends and Family, the message would tell them what savings they were making. If they were not, it would encourage them to join."

Brochure copy was completely customized. "You have already saved £6 per quarter from your current Friends and Family membership. You can save £6 more if you add 8 more friends to your calling circle. Add them today, and your total annual savings will be £48!"

The customer response to the quarterly mailings was an impressive 14 to 32 percent, significantly higher than the typical response rate, which averages less than 10 percent. One mailing resulted in additional sales to one-third of the 11.5 million targeted households. The program has also resulted in higher customer retention rates.

BT credits the personalization of the brochures and the ability to address the needs of individual customers with this remarkable success, which was driven primarily by its ability to analyze its existing customer database.

Source: Arthur Middleton Hughes, "Database Marketing in Britain: A Success Story," http://www.dbmarketing.com/articles/Art164.htm, and Clive Mathieson, "BT Chief Takes the Line of Customer Satisfaction," *The* (London) *Times,* June 25, 2001.

The Customer's Perspective

Consider three busy hair salons within a block of each other in a large city. The first is brightly lit, plays new rock music at fairly high volume, offers flavored spring water to its customers, and charges $50 for a basic cut. Stylists are in their 20s, have elaborate hairstyles—many of them tinted pastel colors—and wear black leather clothes. The salon is decorated with chrome chairs and shelving and the walls are papered in a bright chartreuse foil. The second salon is quieter, playing 1970s soft rock. The walls are painted in a faux garden wall pattern, and the furnishings are beige with accents of soft jewel tones. Customers are offered lavender-scented towels and jasmine tea. Stylists, mostly in their 30s and 40s, dress primarily in stylish slacks. A basic haircut here is $40. The third salon is also brightly lit and has a street-front window that looks into a no-nonsense interior with a few wooden chairs against the wall for waiting customers. The walls are painted a pleasant blue and the floors are utilitarian vinyl tile, spotlessly clean. Stylists range in age from mid-20s to over 50. If you want a beverage, you bring it with you. A basic cut at this salon is $15.

Which of these salons would you choose? Why? How would you feel in either of the other two? It is likely that only one of these would feel comfortable to you, yet each is popular and each is profitable. These salons are different because each has focused on a particular group of customers to serve—and has carefully designed its services to meet that group's particular needs. Each salon also continuously monitors its customers to make sure that, as their needs change, so do the services and the ambience that each salon provides to continue to satisfy its particular group of customers.

Managerial Issues

The first step for managers is to define the particular market their firm is serving or wants to serve. A *market* is defined as the set of all buyers of a product, both actual buyers and potential buyers. These buyers have different wants and needs.

Once the market has been identified, managers need to learn as much about their desired customers as they can so that the services they provide can be tailored to meet the specific needs of those customers. The goal for both new and existing services is the same: to identify the major customer characteristics within that market and to design (or redesign, in the case of an existing operation) a service that best satisfies the customers' needs. Good service managers recognize that they can't serve everyone, so they focus on and learn about the customers they do want to serve and do what it takes to serve them well.

As described in Chapter 1, services are very different from tangible goods, and the meaning that services have to customers goes beyond the core service itself, so there are many ways to design and package services. The "right" way depends on what the targeted customers want and need.

Defining Services

Chapter 1 presented the fundamental characteristics that distinguish services from material goods. As we noted, services are intangible and therefore more difficult for both the service providers and the customers to measure and evaluate objectively. Services are also perishable and consequently cannot be produced in advance of demand and held in inventory. Services are produced and consumed simultaneously, meaning that either the customer or a possession of the customer is involved in the process while the service is being delivered. Services are also difficult to patent and relatively easy to copy.

To deliver services effectively, managers need to understand, beyond the fundamental characteristics of services, what they really are. James Brian Quinn, Jordan J. Baruch, and Penny Cushman Paquette define services to "include all economic activities whose output is not a physical product or construction, is generally consumed at the time it is produced, and provides added value in forms (such as convenience, amusement, timeliness, comfort, or health) that are essentially intangible concerns of its first purchaser."[1] Robert Murdick, Barry Render, and Roberta S. Russell write, "Services can be defined as economic activities that produce time, place, form, or psychological utilities."[2] More simply stated, services are deeds, processes, and performances.[3] While all of these definitions imply that services are not tangible, Chapter 1 pointed out that services are most often delivered as part of a product bundle that is composed of both goods and services. Some of these bundles are primarily services; for example, the play on Broadway that is accompanied by the playbill is primarily an entertainment service that is supported by a secondary good. Some are primarily goods with accompanying services, such as the dealer preparation service that occurs when you purchase a new car. In some bundles, it is difficult to determine which is the primary and which is the secondary element of the service. For example, is the service more important than the food in a restaurant, whether it is fast food or *haute cuisine*? Here, the tangible meal and the intangible service are intertwined.

Services consist of a number of elements or dimensions. For example, when customers enter a restaurant their experience has multiple levels. First, they experience the physical, **supporting facility** within which the service is provided. Customers also experience the **facilitating goods** that are an integral part of the dining experience, whether they are vintage wines and shrimp scampi or burgers and fries. At the same time, the customers experience the **explicit service** itself: how and by whom they are served. If they are returning customers, they expect the service to be of a particular standard and consistently per-

[1] James Brian Quinn, Jordan J. Baruch, and Penny Cushman Paquette, "Technology in Services," *Scientific American,* December 1987, p. 50.
[2] Robert Murdick, Barry Render, and Roberta S. Russell, *Service Operations Management* (Boston: Allyn and Bacon, 1990).
[3] Valarie A. Zeithaml and Mary Jo Bitner, *Services Marketing: Integrating Customer Focus across the Firm,* 2nd ed. (New York: Irwin McGraw-Hill, 2000), p. 2.

EXHIBIT 2.1
The Service Package

Supporting facility: The physical resources that must be in place before a service can be offered.
Examples: Taxi, hair salon, trading room.

Facilitating goods: Materials purchased or consumed by the customer or provided to the customer.
Examples: Food in a restaurant, X-ray film in a hospital, books in a school.

Explicit services: The essential features of a service.
Examples: The flight on an airplane, the repair of a broken arm, the cut and styled hair.

Implicit services: The ancillary features of a service.
Examples: The feeling of security after an auto tune-up, the feeling of relief after a healthy physical examination.

Source: James A. Fitzsimmons and Mona J. Fitzsimmons, *Service Management for Competitive Advantage* (New York: McGraw-Hill, 1994).

formed. Finally, customers experience **implicit services:** the friendliness and responsiveness of the staff and the characteristics of the wait for service.

These four elements—the supporting facility, facilitating goods, explicit services, and implicit services—have been called the *service package,* as shown in Exhibit 2.1. Managers of service organizations need to be very aware that each of these elements affects the impression customers have of the service—and their ultimate satisfaction with that service.

Building Customer Relationships

The fundamental characteristics of services—intangibility, simultaneity of production and consumption, customer involvement in the service system—make them easy to copy. The most significant way that service organizations can erect barriers to entry into a particular service market is by building customer loyalty, the importance of which has been recognized by a shift away from a customer acquisition/transaction focus toward a customer retention/relationship focus. (See Chapter 13 for an in-depth discussion on building customer relationships.)

Customer relationship management seeks to establish a base of customers who are committed to and profitable for the organization by targeting the customers who are likely to become long-term customers. Long-term customers are more likely to purchase additional services if they are satisfied with the current service they receive. They may also help to attract new customers through word of mouth.

When the service act consists of direct contact between a service provider and a customer and when that relationship has been established well, customers are less likely to switch to a competitor. For example, if you like your doctor, the fact that a new doctor opens an office in your town does not mean that you'll make an appointment with the new doctor for your next check-up. Similarly, if you are pleased with the work of your hair stylist, you are unlikely to switch to another stylist. Even with less personal services, such as credit card services, customers may be reluctant to switch when service has been good—or even when service is just tolerable (see Chapter 13's discussion of the zone of tolerance)—because of the trust involved with the performance of the service. On the other hand, most customers feel little guilt switching from one fast-food restaurant to another; these services are difficult to differentiate and there is little, if any, personal relationship with the service providers.

The managerial lesson is straightforward: It makes competitive sense to establish relationships with customers. It is the one reliable barrier to entry in most service markets. At the same time, service providers need to be continually on the watch for new service providers that might offer enhanced services for a similar price; customer loyalty will hold customers only when the services are of similar value.

But all services are not the same. Some firms provide services that are highly complex, some that are quite straightforward. Some services are provided to customers who are physically present when the services are provided; some are provided "behind the scenes." To build relationships with customers and to be successful, service organizations need to understand their customers and to focus every aspect of the service on meeting those customers' needs. If they don't, their competitors will!

Understanding Customers

Carefully defining services can help managers understand how the services they manage can be configured and what those services might offer customers. Managers must also understand their customers and think about how to divide the universe of possible customers into specific groups whose needs and expectations they can serve well. In other words, to know how to deliver a service, the service manager must first understand the market for the service. One challenge for every organization, therefore, is to determine which customer groups within a market it can successfully serve.

Understanding the Impact of Culture

A starting point for understanding customers is **culture.** Culture can be defined as the set of customs, beliefs, values, and practices that are shared among a group of people and transmitted to succeeding generations. Culture encompasses six universal elements, as shown in Exhibit 2.2.

Culture affects the way customers perceive services and may play a significant role in satisfaction with services. For example, in some cultures, fast service is viewed as desirable, whereas in other cultures, the same fast service would be considered rude and improper. Consequently, service managers must recognize that different cultural orientations exist and tailor the way their services are provided to incorporate sensitivity to cultural differences. This is a major challenge to managers as services expand globally.

Segmenting the Market

Some services, such as a utility or trash collection, are provided to all potential customers in essentially the same way, varying only in the amount of the service that is used. Most services, however, can be modified in various ways to make them more desirable for specific types of customers. Modifying services to meet the needs of particular groups of customers is called **target marketing,** and the groups that are targeted are called market seg-

EXHIBIT 2.2
Elements of Culture

1. *Language:* verbal and nonverbal means of communication.
2. *Values and attitudes:* what members of the culture believe is right or important or desirable.
3. *Manners and customs:* the culture's view of appropriate behavior. For example, it is considered very polite in Japan to loudly slurp one's noodles, a behavior that would be considered rude in the United States.
4. *Material culture:* the tangibles people of a culture tend to own. For example, tea is an important element of the culture in Japan and an important element of the material culture is a fine tea set to use when serving guests.
5. *Aesthetics:* ideas about beauty and good taste. For example, the traditional music of China is very different from the music of Latin America.
6. *Educational and social institutions:* where people learn and the social structures they rely upon. For example, how children are schooled and how individuals are selected for professional training.

Source: Michael R. Czinkota and Ilkka A. Ronkainen, *International Marketing* (Hinsdale, IL: The Dryden Press, 1988).

ments. **Market segmentation** divides the total market for a product or service into groups of people who are likely to be most receptive to that product or service.

How to Segment the Service Market

There are myriad ways to divide a market into segments such that each segment consists of the potential customers who are likely to have more in common with each other than with the population as a whole. To successfully target a particular segment, a service provider must be able to gain access to the segment, to measure its needs and its size, and to design a service that meets the specific requirements of that segment. We present here some of the more common ways that markets can be segmented.

Demographic Segmentation   Characteristics such as gender, age, income, and religion are likely to affect the way in which customers perceive services. A haircut may seem like a "generic" service that meets a nearly universal need, but, as we saw at the beginning of this chapter, a hair salon that offers trendy haircuts as its core service is likely to attract a different clientele than a salon that offers more traditional haircuts. The trendy salon may choose to support its core service with similarly trendy Top-40 music played in the background and a modern decor that appeals to younger customers. Another salon may target professional women, offering more traditional cuts, relaxing music, and muted colors. A salon targeting college-age men may be more utilitarian, projecting a no-nonsense image that conveys a sense of value.

Other services may not be needed or needed as often by some demographic groups as they are by others. For example, financial advising services may be targeted to the over-40 age group who are likely to have established their careers and are beginning to think ahead to their children's college needs and to their own long-term financial security; the under-25 age group who may still be getting started in their careers may not be as ready (or willing!) to think about retirement planning.

One demographic segment that has received much attention from marketers of a variety of products and services is the "Dual Income, No Kids" segment, or DINKs. DINKs tend to be very career-oriented and busy, so that time is an important factor for them. DINKs are also likely to have more disposable income than similar-aged dual-income families with children.

Exhibit 2.3 shows how household income in the United States was distributed in 2000. Note that 27 percent of households had incomes under $20,000, while only 13 percent of the households had incomes greater than $100,000.

In another demographic segmentation, Exhibit 2.4 shows the U.S. population age by gender for the year 2000. Note that as the population ages, the proportion of women begins to exceed the proportion of men.

Geographic and Geopolitical Segmentation   Whether customers live in the city or the country or in the North, Southeast, or West may affect their need for and perception of specific services. For example, customers in the southern United States are unlikely to need snow-clearing services in winter. Similarly, customers who live in rural areas may be less likely to need dog-walking services than customers in congested cities.

Psychographic Segmentation   Psychographic segmentation relates to how personality affects the needs of customers and their perception of services. Dating services for outgoing customers may be packaged as party-like get-togethers where customers mingle and meet. Similar services for more introverted customers may be packaged as "introductions" that are made after customers provide information about themselves that will enable the service to match customers with similar interests. Similarly, customers with very hectic lifestyles may make up a segment that has needs that can best be met by dry-cleaning delivery services and grocery and clothes shopping services, whereas customers with less hectic

EXHIBIT 2.3
**Distribution
of Household Income
in the U.S. in 2000**

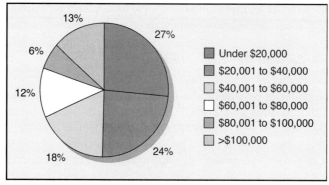

Source: U.S. Census Bureau. Last revised: December 10, 2001.

EXHIBIT 2.4
**U.S. Population
by Gender (2000)**

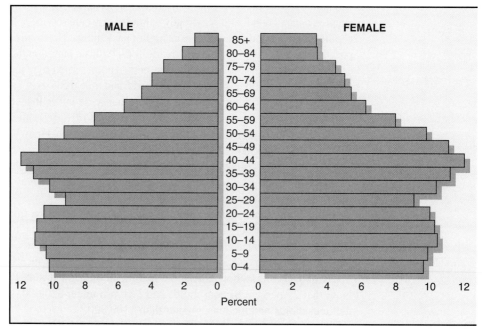

Source: U.S. Census Bureau International Database, 2000.

lifestyles may prefer to shop for themselves. Bungee jumping and skydiving opportunities can be marketed to risk-takers (or to risk-avoiders who want to be more daring!).

Lifestyle Segmentation   Markets can be segmented according to the customers' choice of hobbies, recreation, entertainment, and other leisure pursuits. For example, services might be targeted to a segment of customers who play golf. Those services might include golf lessons, vacation tours of popular golf courses, and family golf tournaments.

Life-Stage Segmentation   Life-stage segmentation divides the population into groups, such as preteens, teenagers, young parents, and empty nesters, who share similar concerns and priorities. For example, magicmaman.com, a firm located in Paris, focuses on providing information to new parents.

Product Use Segmentation   Product use segmentation focuses on the usage patterns of services to divide the market. For example, phone companies offer a wide variety of services that are based on monthly long-distance charges and/or usage by time of day.

Communication Channel Segmentation Many organizations also segment customers according to the communication channels that are used to communicate with them. Some communication channels are "real-time" or synchronous: the customer and the organization can engage in a dialogue either in person or on the telephone. Asynchronous customer interactions such as mail, FAX, e-mail, and Web communications also permit the organization to connect to the customer, but not in a way that permits back-and-forth conversation in real time.

Other Segmenting Variables The market for services can also be segmented with respect to physical size (large men, petite women); response to a trend (runners); time factors (summer vacationers); special interests (pet lovers, swing music lovers); accessibility (urban/rural; train commuters/ drivers); habits/practices (smoking, exercising); and almost any other variable that can describe a customer group.

Exhibit 2.5 summarizes the ways service markets can be segmented.

Market Segments in Relation to Industry Segments

Service industries can also be segmented. For example, the hotel industry can be divided into segments by star rating, the higher education industry can be segmented by competitiveness of admissions, and the health care industry can be segmented by the type of insurer that pays for the services provided. As an example of industry segmentation, Exhibit 2.6 shows restaurant segments sales forecasts for 2002.

One goal of segmenting the market in an industry is to match the market segments to industry segments. As demographics of the population change, for example, the growth potential for various industry segments is likely to change as well.

Risks of Market Segmentation

While market segmentation is a fundamental marketing concept, there are several criticisms of the segmentation approach. One is that segmentation describes what is happening now and tries to use that description to predict future buying behavior. Another criticism is that market segmentation assumes that the customers within each segment are alike, that is, a particular market segment is homogeneous, an assumption that the concept of market research refutes at the level of the whole market. In other words, the concept of

EXHIBIT 2.5
**Common Ways
to Segment Service
Markets**

Basis of Segmentation	Groups Customers By	Example
Demographic	Gender, age, income, religion	Male/female; preteen/30-something; upper middle class/high income; Catholic/Jewish/Muslim
Geographic/geopolitical	Geographic region or nationality	Midwesterner/New Englander; American/French
Psychographic	Personality characteristics	Extrovert/introvert; risk-taker/risk avoider
Lifestyle	Choice of hobbies, recreation, entertainment	Golfer/hiker; moviegoer/concertgoer
Life stage	Life concerns	New parents/empty nesters; undergraduate student/graduate student
Product use	Patterns of use of services	Frequent flier/infrequent flier; high/low cell phone user
Communication channel	Ways services can communicate with them	Internet/fax/phone/voicemail

EXHIBIT 2.6
Restaurant Sales
Forecasts by Segment
for 2002

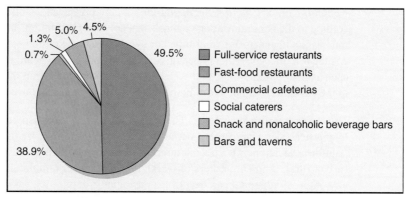

Source: http://www.restaurant.org/research/forecast_sales.cfm, April 19, 2002.

market segmentation is based on the belief that an "average" person does not exist for the whole market because individuals are different, but at the same time, segmentation promotes the idea that a few individuals can be representative of a very large segment of the market population. Lawrence Gibson, in "Is Something Rotten in Segmentation?"[4] states that the customers who are critically important for the organization to understand are the customers who are undecided about their product or service choices. Those are the customers who can still be won—or who may be lost. He also describes four common market segmentation practices that result in misleading perspectives about a market segment:

- *The random walk:* searching for patterns in data. Even randomly generated numbers will sometimes demonstrate patterns in subsets of the data, but it would be dangerous to believe that these "patterns" actually represent information that should be acted upon.

- *Guilt by association:* confusing correlation (two or more variables that are related to each other) with causality (two or more variables, one of which causes changes in the others). For example, in the 1970s, the Leboyer method of giving birth, which originated in France and involved soft lighting, relaxing music, and a warm massage and bath for the newborn, enjoyed some popularity. One study reported that the children born using this method were more creative than children born in a more traditional environment, suggesting that if parents wanted creative children they should plan a Leboyer birth. Segmenting the market this way might increase demand for a particular professional service, but increased creativity in the children birthed using the Leboyer method was probably much more likely to be attributable to creative parents, demonstrated through their desire for an alternative birthing option, rather than to the method of the birth itself.

- *Causal labeling:* assigning creative names to different segments—"trendy" or "socially responsible" or "environmentally friendly"—may focus energy on what the label conveys rather than what the data may have indicated originally. Labeling fails to acknowledge the heterogeneity within segments.

- *Analysis by index number:* using relative usage percentages to focus attention on particular segments. Understanding usage is important, but focusing on indexes can be misleading. For example, if women spent 10 percent more per month on cell phone service than men, but at the same time men made up 80 percent of the market, focusing on the higher usage per month by women might shift focus away from the larger segment of the market.

[4] Lawrence D. Gibson, "Is Something Rotten in Segmentation?" *Marketing Research* 3, no. 1 (2001).

EXHIBIT 2.7
Trade-off Between Market Size and Profit Potential

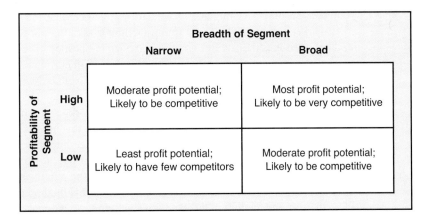

Another risk of market segmentation is related to the breadth of the target segments. Ultimately, the goal of market segmentation is to identify a profitable group of customers to serve, so two factors are important: the size of the market segment and the profitability of that segment. If the segment is small, the profit per customer must be relatively large to make serving that segment profitable. If the segment is large, the profit per customer can be lower and still result in a highly profitable business. Exhibit 2.7 illustrates this relationship. The figure also shows that when profit potential is high, competition is likely to be strong, so in every quadrant it is important to differentiate the services a firm provides from services provided by competing firms.

The final risk of market segmentation is believing that market segments are stable. Markets are very dynamic both in customer size and characteristics, so it can be dangerous for service organizations to believe that they understand their customers so well that they don't have to continue to learn about them as the world changes.

Advances in Market Segmentation

The test of the success of service market segmentation is whether the defined segments actually respond differently to different service offerings. Advances in technology make it possible to identify market segments based on multiple dimensions. For example, customers for restaurants may be targeted along the dimensions of customer interest in trendy foods, price range, and atmosphere. Looking for similarities across more than one dimension can differentiate between the customers who are looking for a fun atmosphere, trendy food, and low price and the customers who are looking for trendy food in a more elegant atmosphere, and are willing to pay higher prices.

Global market segmentation is also becoming an important challenge. Along with the other segmentation variables described above, political, legal, and business environments should be considered in global segmentation. Comparisons across countries are further complicated by differences in measures and definitions. For example, the education levels in Europe and the United States are on different scales, so "college" may not be a meaningful variable. Similarly, income levels are difficult to compare and may therefore be inappropriate as segmentation variables.

Collecting Customer Data

Managers can benefit from information about customers before the service is designed and delivered, during the provision of the service, and after the service encounter. The best data provide insights for managerial decision making.

There are a number of ways to collect data from customers. **Focus groups** are used to collect rich, detailed data from a relatively small number of customers. A typical focus group consists of 6 to 12 individuals who are selected because they are representative of the target market segment. The focus group facilitator asks the participants a series of structured but open-ended questions about the service in question. The information collected in focus groups may not necessarily be representative of all current or potential customers, but it provides insights about the service that may not be captured with other methods of data collection (see Chapter 2 Supplement for more on how to conduct focus groups).

Another way of gathering rich data about what works and what doesn't work for customers is to use the *critical incident technique.* With this approach, customers (or potential customers) are asked to relate stories about service interactions that were memorably positive or memorably negative. Analyzing such information from several customers can enable the market researcher to find patterns that may help in the service design and/or delivery. For example, one of this book's authors used this method of information gathering to find the common denominator in positive learning experiences among students. She discovered that the learning experiences that her students felt best about were those that engaged the student both actively and emotionally.

Surveys generally collect more data than focus groups, usually at least some of which is quantifiable and can be analyzed using statistical techniques that determine the probability of the information being representative of a larger population of customers. When using surveys, the surveyor must be careful about a number of factors, including what sample of the population is chosen to complete the survey and how representative that sample is of the population in terms of the demographic, geographic, psychographic, and other behavioral dimensions described earlier. The surveyor must also ascertain whether the people who responded to the survey are representative of the people to whom the survey was administered. Whether data are collected by questionnaire or by phone or face-to-face interview, the questions must be unambiguous and, at the same time, must be worded in such a way that the respondent is not led to a particular response. Good survey design is harder than it may first appear to be. For example, consider the following question: On a scale of 1 to 5, how satisfied are you with the instructor of this course? The question, if posed while the class is ongoing, may not be answered honestly if the respondent is not assured of anonymity. If posed right after an exam, the response may be biased by the exam grade. What does the scale mean? The question as worded has no "anchors" for the values in the scale. What is "great" versus "OK" versus "terrible"? The question is also ambiguous. Respondents might be thinking about any number of instructor qualities such as personality, level of organization, knowledge, lecture style, or age of materials. The answer to the question, while providing some information about the general feel that respondents have for the course, provides little information that the instructor can use to make changes in the course or in his/her teaching style—and even that insight might be confused by the fact that some respondents may think "1" is best while others think "5" is best! Another general rule for surveys is that the response rate is likely to be higher if the survey is short (see the Chapter 2 Supplement for more on survey development).

Direct observation can often provide very important insights into the customer experience during a service. Simply observing a customer's body language and facial expressions and tuning in to what a customer does and looks at can help service providers understand the customer's experience. **Mystery shoppers** can be employed to experience the service from the customer's perspective and report back to the service organization. Many service organizations, from restaurants to health care organizations, employ mystery shoppers to anonymously use the service and then record and report their experiences. The mystery shopper information is used by the organization to evaluate and improve the service provided to customers and may even be used as part of the compensation and reward program for individual managers and workers.

One often-overlooked way to learn about customer desires and needs is to ask the people who have the most contact with the customers—front-line employees. Employee feed-

View from the Top

George Gallup: Premier Pollster

When you think of surveys, chances are you think of the Gallup Poll. George Gallup was born in Iowa in 1901. In college, as the editor of the University of Iowa's *Daily Iowan,* he wanted to learn which articles people read and were interested in, a topic that later became his journalism doctoral dissertation, "An objective method for determining the reader interest in newspapers." He discovered that it was not the front-page hard news that attracted the attention of the readers, but the comics and pictures. As a journalism professor, Gallup conducted a number of reader surveys for several U.S. newspapers.

In 1932, Gallup joined the advertising agency Young and Rubicam, which was known for the quality of its research and its innovative ads. In 1935, he founded the American Institute of Public Opinion, later renamed the Gallup Organization, and applied market research techniques to gathering political opinions. Gallup's first major public opinion poll was on the 1936 presidential election. The *Literary Digest,* which had correctly predicted the previous five presidential elections, had predicted a landslide victory for Alf Landon. But George Gallup, in business for only one year, predicted that Franklin Roosevelt would carry the day.

Gallup's correct prediction established his reputation in political polling. He said, "When a president, or any other leader, pays attention to poll results, he is, in effect, paying attention to the views of the people. Any other interpretation is nonsense." He believed in market research techniques so strongly that one of his most famous quotes is, "I could prove God statistically. Take the human body alone—the chances that all the functions of an individual would just happen is a statistical monstrosity."

Some people argued that polling results influenced outcomes. Gallup's response was, "One might as well insist that a thermometer makes the weather."

But even for Gallup, understanding customers was not always easy. In 1948, his surveys had consistently shown challenger Thomas Dewey leading the election. Two weeks before the election, he stopped polling and announced that President Harry Truman would lose. Of course, Truman won—but Gallup learned from his mistakes. From that point on, he kept polling until Election Day, and the Gallup Poll has never incorrectly predicted a presidential election since.

Source: Jon Blackwell, "1935: The Poll That Took America's Pulse," *The Trentonian,* www.capitalcentury.com.
Boris Doktorov, "George Gallup: His Name Will Remain Known," http://www.marketers-hall-of-fame.com/l-george-gallup-marketing.html

back can provide valuable information about what customers say they like and also about what makes customers frustrated or angry. Similarly, having managers periodically work directly with customers brings information quickly to the decision-making levels, which keeps management focused on what customers really care about.

Some organizations meet with frequent customers who provide feedback and suggestions about the service. These *customer panels* offer a repeat-customer perspective that is particularly helpful for continuous improvement programs. In May 1997, the U.S. Internal Revenue Service established the National Partnership for Reinvention Task Force, to which it credits service enhancements such as extended phone and walk-in hours and special problem-solving days. Customer panels can also be helpful with future expectations research, providing information about what customers may want in the future as well as today.

Checkpoint evaluations are often used during the provision of a service so that the provider can determine if the service is "on track" for the customer, particularly when the service is provided over a period of time. For example, during a consulting project, consultants may ask for feedback on the customer's satisfaction at key milestones, rather than waiting for the project to be completed. Similarly, a teacher may request simple midsemester feedback that is actionable, such as: "What should I start doing, what should I stop doing, and what should I keep doing?"

Another way of learning about customer needs is to find out what went wrong with a service. When customers are dissatisfied with a service, they may not go to the trouble of providing feedback to the service organization. Actively soliciting complaints from customers, perhaps with the encouragement of a service guarantee (see Chapter 13 for more on service guarantees), helps the organization to learn why customers may be dissatisfied and may even provide information about how to improve.

EXHIBIT 2.8
Methods
of Collecting
Information
about Customers

Method	Information Collected
Focus group	Rich, detailed information from small number of customers.
Critical incident technique	Rich, detailed information about specific service elements.
Surveys	Structured information about potentially large groups of customers. If well designed, may be generalized to broader groups of customers.
Direct observation	Rich, detailed information about actual customer encounters.
Mystery shoppers	Objective information from trained third-party data collector.
Employee feedback	Rich, detailed information from employee's perspective.
Customer panels	Longitudinal information from committed customers.
Lost-customer research	Information about why customers discontinue use of service.
Data mining	Large amounts of data that can be analyzed for patterns.

When customers do not return for service, **lost-customer research** can help to identify the underlying causes. For example, a college may accept an applicant who chooses not to matriculate. Following up to determine what college the applicant did choose to attend and why can provide valuable information about the college's competitive position and student needs. Similarly, a phone service provider may contact customers who switched long-distance carriers to learn why.

Data Mining

Data mining analyzes data in large databases (which are often kept in a *data warehouse*) to find correlations or patterns that can be used to improve a service, reduce costs, and/or increase sales. Data mining enables customer-focused organizations to identify relationships among organizational variables, such as price, product positioning, or staff skills, and customer variables, such as economic and competitive factors and customer demographics, and their effect on sales, customer satisfaction, and profits.

Data mining tools extract data fields from source data, reformat them, and load them into the user's system. The data are subsequently analyzed using a statistical or other software package to classify or cluster data and to identify data patterns. The output of data mining provides information that can be used for decision making, often in the form of a graph or a table that clearly conveys information about the relationships between data variables. Companies such as Wal-Mart use data mining to analyze inventories and the rates of sales of different products in different markets. Web-based data acquisition enables organizations to collect data through their websites about customers, including other sites customers have visited, for clearer customer profiling. Exhibit 2.8 summarizes the ways services can collect information about customers.

Good market research focuses management on what matters to customers. A mix of qualitative and quantitative methods helps to ensure that the information is both rich and meaningful, and also that the conclusions can be generalized to the customer population overall. The most useful research will provide information on the customers' needs and their relative importance as well as the customers' perception of the services they receive.

The Impact of Technology

Technology has dramatically affected the ability of service firms to collect data about their customers, to analyze the data, and to use their analyses to make better managerial decisions. Data can be collected through point-of-sale scanning systems, such as those used at

Using Technology to Create Value

Fleet Bank's Expanded Customer Service

Not so long ago, commercial banks seemed to operate for the convenience of bankers rather than for the convenience of customers: They were typically open weekdays from 9:00 A.M. to 4:00 P.M. and may have had limited services available on Saturday mornings. New customers were lured with gifts for opening accounts; it seemed like no one actually ever had to *buy* a toaster or blender! Bank statements were often complicated, providing data as they came into the bank. For example, checks were listed in the order they cleared, rather than in the order they were written. Each month, customers had to painstakingly go through their statements, manually reconcile them with their own records, and hope for the best.

Now banks are actively competing on the service dimensions that are important to customers. The most common banking activities can be done 24 hours a day thanks to automatic teller machines (ATMs). Technology has made it possible for banks to readily reformat monthly statements to be much more user friendly.

Fleet Bank, for example, has its computer list checks in the order they are cleared as well as in the order they are written, and any checks that are out of order are flagged (for example, if 5426 and 5428 have cleared but 5427 is still outstanding, an asterisk appears on the statement next to 5426 to make sure the customer is aware that 5427 has not yet cleared). Advances in technology have enabled banks such as Fleet to provide even more services online for the convenience of their customers: account information, online bill paying, account transfers, and investment services. Fleet Bank provides additional options online, such as notification if an account balance dips below a customer-designated level, and e-mail communication with bank personnel. It also provides an online forum for customers to ask questions and to read the questions and responses of other customers. Fleet collects this information and uses it to more effectively focus its services to meet its customers' needs.

large retail chains. For example, the music store chain Guitar Center in 2002 had 100 stores in 29 states. Whenever a customer makes a purchase, the information is collected in the company database, enabling the store to target advertising and promotion to different segments. Customers who purchase guitars receive information about guitar and guitar-related product promotions, and customers who purchase drums receive promotional information about percussion specials. Regular customers may receive gift coupons or discounts that are unavailable to other customers.

In smaller service environments, such as the local hair salon, customer information may be collected on a personal computer, where service information, stylist preferences, payment information, and contact information can be stored.

Whether information is collected through some of the traditional market research methods described in this chapter or through point-of-sale data collection and Internet data mining, once data are collected they can be analyzed using database or spreadsheet programs, so that managers can see not only customer-specific information but also information about patterns of customer preferences and purchases. That information helps managers make better decisions about introducing new services, redesigning existing services, and adding value for their customers.

Summary

To manage successfully, service managers must understand their firms' target markets. Once the target market has been identified, managers need to learn as much about customers as they can in order to tailor their services to meet customers' needs. The service package, which includes the supporting facility, facilitating goods, explicit services, and implicit services, is designed to meet the current needs of customers and, increasingly, to build relationships with customers that will ensure their continued use of the services. Customers' needs vary widely and can be very complex, but segmenting the market to focus on particular groups of customers with common needs can help a service organization to appropriately design and continuously improve its services. But although segmentation can focus a service firm's efforts, service managers must remember that customers change, and so do their needs. Regularly collecting data about customer preferences can help service firms to maintain their focus and their competitive edge.

Key Terms

culture: the set of customs, beliefs, values, and practices that are shared among a group of people and transmitted to succeeding generations. *(p. 22)*

data mining: a process that analyzes data in large databases to find correlations or patterns that can be used to improve service provision, reduce costs, or increase sales. *(p. 30)*

explicit service: how and by whom customers are served. *(p. 20)*

facilitating goods: goods that are provided as part of a core product/service bundle. *(p. 20)*

focus group: a qualitative data collecting technique that permits collection of rich data from a small number of customers in the target market segment. *(p. 27)*

implicit services: the friendliness and responsiveness of service providers and the characteristics of the wait for service. *(p. 21)*

lost-customer research: data collection focused on customers who do not choose to purchase or repurchase a service. *(p. 30)*

market segmentation: dividing a market into groups of people who are likely to be most receptive to a product. *(p. 23)*

mystery shoppers: individuals employed by an organization to anonymously collect information on a service by experiencing the service as a customer. *(p. 28)*

supporting facility: the physical environment in which a service is provided. *(p. 20)*

target marketing: modifying services to meet the needs of particular groups of customers. *(p. 22)*

Review and Discussion Questions

1. Why is it important for a manager to consider all the elements of the service package when planning and delivering services?

2. Describe some customer needs and the value added through services for these different market segments:
   a. New parents versus empty nesters.
   b. People who trade stocks online versus through a broker.
   c. People who purchase travel tickets through a travel agency versus from an Internet site.
   d. People who dine at McDonald's, Wendy's, and Chili's

3. What risks are associated with market segmentation?

4. Describe how technology might help a supermarket manager to understand the needs of her store's customers.

5. Define customer relationship marketing and describe why it is important in the competitive service environment.

6. You are the manager of a coffee shop in a shopping mall. Describe some ways you might collect information about your customers.

7. Define data mining. What are its advantages? Disadvantages?

Internet Assignment

Go to the following sites:

Fidelity.com
Yahoo.com
Dell.com

What does each of these companies do to collect customer information from its website? How easy is it for a customer to provide information?

CASE   Charles Schwab and the Chinese Market

Charles Schwab & Co., Inc., is one of America's largest financial services firms, providing full-service investing experience to customers through the Internet and more than 350 branch offices. Schwab's commitment to its customers is evident in its mission statement: "To provide the most useful and ethical financial services in the world." Its no-pressure, no-hidden-fees advice has enabled it to grow to serving over 7.1 million accounts with $775 billion in assets.

Schwab initiated its China services when it founded its Asia-Pacific Services in 1989. By 2000, more than 250 representatives provided Mandarin, Cantonese, and Korean services via a U.S. toll-free telephone number and at 13 Asia-Pacific service offices in California, New York, Texas, and Washington. Asian investors represented Schwab's fastest-growing market. In 2000, Schwab also opened a Manhattan branch for Chinese-speaking investors and launched a Chinese-language financial information website for Chinese speakers who want to invest in the U.S. stock market. Many of these investors are wealthy immigrants to the United States from China. The site, which was developed in response to in-creasing customer demand, provides hourly market summaries, news, and analyst information.

Questions

1. What do you think are the major characteristics of the Chinese segment of the financial services market? What makes those characteristics attractive to Schwab?

2. What methods should a company such as Schwab use to collect data on customers in a new market segment such as Chinese-language investors? What special challenges would such market research impose?

3. How might a company such as Schwab collect data on its current customers?

Source: Charles Schwab press release, "Information Gap for Chinese-Speaking Investors," March 30, 2000. http://www. aboutschwab.com/sstory/missionvision.html. June 8, 2000-SINA.com. Copyright 2002 Janelle Heineke and Larry Meile.

Selected Bibliography

Czinkota, Michael R., and Ilkka A. Ronkainen. *International Marketing.* Hinsdale, IL: The Dryden Press, 1988.

Gibson, Lawrence D. "Is Something Rotten in Segmentation?" *Marketing Research* 3, no. 1 (2001).

Kumar, V., and Anish Nagpal. "Segmenting Global Markets: Look Before You Leap." *Marketing Research* 13, no. 1 (Spring 2001).

Mathieson, Clive. "BT Chief Takes the Line of Customer Satisfaction." *The* (London) *Times,* June 25, 2001.

Murdick, Robert, Barry Render, and Roberta S. Russell. *Service Operations Management.* Boston: Allyn and Bacon, 1990.

Neal, William D., and John Wurst. "Advances in Market Segmentation." *Marketing Research* 13, no. 1 (Spring 2001).

Quinn, James Brian, Jordan J. Baruch, and Penny Cushman Paquette. "Technology in Services." *Scientific American,* December 1987, p. 24.

"Treasury Names First Ever IRS Citizen Panel." *The Digital Daily,* June 23, 1998.

Zeithaml, Valarie A., and Mary Jo Bitner. *Services Marketing: Integrating Customer Focus across the Firm,* 2nd ed., New York: McGraw-Hill/Irwin, 2000.

Collecting Customer Data

Learning Objectives

- Discuss the importance of customer data in service organizations.

- Introduce several methods for collecting customer data.

- Describe how to achieve an unbiased sample.

- Define the purpose of a focus group and how to conduct one.

- Introduce various types of questionnaires and surveys, and the kinds of information they provide.

- Present how to construct a good questionnaire.

Managerial Issues

Service managers need to collect customer data regularly for many reasons. Customer data can be used as an input in the design of new services or in the redesign of existing ones. As we shall see in Chapter 13, it is also important to collect customer data in order to assess the customers' perception of the quality of services the firm is providing.

Because collecting data from customers is so important to the design and delivery of effective services, knowing how to collect good information is critical. Poorly designed data collection processes typically provide very poor data, which may result in the delivery of services that do not meet the customers' needs.

Avoiding a Biased Sample

The first step in collecting any type of customer data is to define the population group from which you want to select your sample. This is critical because some individuals and groups tend to respond from a particular point of view or with a prejudice toward one perspective or another, in other words, with a **bias.** Bias in your sample of respondents is very likely to cause bias in your results. It is nearly impossible to get a totally unbiased sample, but you need to consider potential bias and what it might mean. For example, if you survey your customers, you can discover what your customers like, but you will not find out what your ex-customers don't like or what potential customers might like. If you survey ex-customers, the results will be negatively biased, but you may find out what could have kept them from leaving. If you survey people at home during the day, you will not find out what people who work during the day may think. If you survey via the Internet, you'll learn only about Internet users, not non-Internet users.

A famous example of survey bias occurred in 1936, when the *Literary Digest* predicted that Alf Landon (the Republican) would beat Franklin D. Roosevelt (the Democrat) by a factor of 3 to 2. Roosevelt won, carrying 46 of 48 states with 62 percent of the vote! The problem occurred when the *Literary Digest* polled an unrepresentative sample of the voting population, using lists of names from car registrations and telephone books. In 1936, only the affluent could afford cars and telephones; therefore, because the affluent traditionally vote Republican, the *Literary Digest* unintentionally polled primarily Republican voters.

It is important not only to think about the bias that might result from responses from a particular set of people, but also to think about the possible bias that results from nonresponders. If, for example, you send a questionnaire to a group of people you've carefully selected to be representative of the group of people you want to understand, you need to think about whether the people who respond to the survey are similar to or dissimilar from the people who did not respond. If you sent a questionnaire to all customers of your coffee shop, half men and half women, and found, when you analyzed the completed questionnaires, that only women responded, you can probably not assume that how women responded is how men would have responded. *Nonresponse bias* can make findings of any data collection effort less usable because the responses cannot be generalized to the broader group.

Survey and focus group designers who are careful to identify possible sources of bias from their samples will be less likely to be influenced by the bias and more likely to make good decisions from the data.

However, bias is desired at times. For example, one firm wanted to find out how well its product was working in retail locations. To find this out, it conducted two separate focus groups, one for the retail store managers and the other for the workers who actually operated the equipment. The two focus groups provided different but very important information, which was used in improving the design of the product.

Focus Groups

Focus groups are in-depth interviews with a small group of people in order to learn their views about or experiences with a specific topic or product. Like group interviews, focus groups provide some insights into individuals' views, but they are particularly useful for learning about how these views are influenced by others in a group environment. Focus groups elicit information about participants' attitudes, beliefs, experiences, and reactions that would be difficult to learn from questionnaires or direct observation. They also collect information in a way that permits the researcher to learn not only *what* is important to the group, but also *why* it is important.

Focus groups are most useful during the preliminary stages of learning about customers' needs or to collect in-depth information about ongoing services. They may be used to obtain inputs from potential customers about the design of a new service or to understand what issues are important to customers before conducting a broader survey. Because focus groups are not large and are not chosen to be statistically representative, findings from focus groups cannot be generalized.

Focus Group Participants

Focus group participants should be chosen based on common characteristics that enable them to engage in a productive discussion based on personal experience about the subject of the research. Participants should not be so different that they are unable to communicate with each other, nor should they be so similar that only one point of view is expressed. Incentives such as small gifts or cash payments can be used to encourage participation.

Participants need to understand that the information they provide is not fully confidential because they share information openly within the group.

Organizing the Focus Group Session

The organization of the focus group session is critical. Typically, focus groups consist of 6 to 12 people. Most sessions last one to two hours and are held in a neutral location to avoid either positive or negative associations with a particular environment. The room should be comfortable and well-lit, and should have flip charts for taking notes so that participants can see what information is recorded. It is a good idea to offer light refreshments to help put participants at ease and to give them something to do as they enter the room for the meeting and get settled at their seats.

Focus groups are often conducted in rooms that are specifically designed for that purpose. Those rooms often have a one-way mirror so that the focus group can be unobtrusively observed from another room. The focus group room may also be designed to allow both audio and video recording of the focus group session. Focus group participants should be informed when the session is being taped or observed. It is also important not to have too many "silent observers" in a focus group because the dynamic of the participants may be affected.

The Focus Group Moderator

The moderator, or facilitator, of a focus group plays a very important role: the quality of the information collected from focus groups depends in large part on how well the moderator asks questions and keeps the discussion on target. Because so much of the valuable information from focus groups comes from the interaction between participants, the moderator has to allow participants to talk to each other, to ask questions, and to express differences of opinions. Moderators need strong interpersonal skills; they need to listen well, be nonjudgmental, and be adaptable to the different directions a focus group might take.

Exhibit 2S.1 provides some basic tips for conducting focus groups.

Types of Questionnaires and Surveys

The **questionnaire** or **survey** is a set of written or verbal questions to which the customer, called the *respondent,* provides answers. A well-designed questionnaire motivates the respondent to provide complete and accurate information.

Verbal Surveys

Verbal surveys have a number of advantages over written surveys. It may be easier for respondents to provide complete answers to open-ended questions because they don't have

EXHIBIT 2S.1
**Practical Tips
for Conducting Focus
Groups**

Before the focus group session

- Hold the session in a neutral setting.

- Limit the number of people in the group to 6–12.

- Provide comfort items such as drinks and/or light refreshments.

- Select participants who have enough in common that they can converse, but not so similar that they all think alike.

- Schedule the session at a convenient time.

- Make arrangements for parking if needed.

- Plan all questions in advance.

- Use two moderators: one to facilitate the conversation and one to take notes (unless the session is taped).

- Seat group so that everyone can see and make eye contact with everyone else (a U-shape or a circle).

- Limit sessions to two hours.

During the focus group session

- Use open-ended questions.

- Avoid leading questions.

- Minimize your involvement—act as a facilitator.

- Avoid judgmental statements—either negative or positive.

- Record comments exactly; don't paraphrase.

- Be flexible about hearing unanticipated information.

- Record information about how strongly the group feels.

- Manage the group interactions.

  - Don't let anyone control or dominate.

  - Encourage participation by all.

- Use flip charts to record opinions and comments.

After the focus group session

- Review the notes taken for clarity and understanding.

- Record observations about the group not already in your notes.

- Discuss and record any insights or ideas that the interview created while they are fresh in your mind.

to write the responses. Interviewers are able to ask respondents to clarify their responses or to answer follow-on questions that could be more difficult to build into a written survey. Experienced interviewers are also able to learn from the tone of verbal responses. When more than one interviewer is collecting data, however, it is very important to make sure that all interviewers ask questions in a consistent manner and ask clarifying or follow-on questions in the same way, or results may be biased.

Personal Interviews

Personal interviews are conducted face to face and can be conducted anywhere interviewees can be found. Doing personal interviews may make it possible to find your target segment (people who shop at your mall, for example). Personal interviewers also enable interviewers to read the nonverbal communication of interview subjects, which may provide as much information as the verbal responses! The disadvantage of personal interviews is that they can be expensive and time consuming.

Telephone Surveys

Because most homes in the United States have telephones, telephone surveys have become very popular. Dialing random numbers within an area permits wide coverage without requiring lists from which to call. However, people are getting increasingly frustrated with the large volume of telemarketing and "courtesy" calls, so finding people willing to answer the phone and be involved in an interview is becoming more difficult.

Time is an important factor to consider when conducting telephone surveys. Because the interviews are usually not scheduled in advance, interviewees may not be prepared to spend much time answering a long or in-depth survey. For the firm, of course, the longer the interviews take to conduct, the higher the cost of the survey.

Written Surveys

Mail Surveys

Mail surveys are less expensive than personal or telephone interviews, but response times are often long and response rates may be low. The best response rates are achieved from people with an interest in the subject.

Response rates to mail surveys can be improved by mailing a postcard in advance of the survey, to tell respondents when the survey will arrive. Following up with another mailing after two weeks and again in another two weeks increases response rates, too, but also increases costs. Some surveys increase response rates by sending a dollar bill or some other incentive (a gift certificate, for example), entering respondents into a drawing for a prize, or providing the results of the survey to the respondents.

E-mail Surveys

E-mail surveys are very inexpensive and can often be completed quickly, and because they are less common than mail or phone surveys, the response rate may be better because they are still somewhat novel. However, you need to obtain an appropriate list of e-mail addresses. Some people don't respond to unsolicited e-mail. It is also important to remember that e-mail users may be a biased sample of respondents.

Internet/Intranet (Web Page) Surveys

Web surveys are becoming more popular and are fast and easy for respondents to use. It is necessary to have the right software and to know how to reach the right respondents. It is also important to be aware of sample bias.

A number of companies produce software for conducting Web-based surveys. The programs enable a firm to design a survey, send it out to be completed by the target group, and collect the data into a spreadsheet or database format that permits easy analysis. The programs offer a variety of response options, from choosing a single answer (choose one) or multiple answers (choose all that apply) from a list of options; rank ordering, allocation of points, fill-in-the-blanks, fill in the numbers, and even essay questions. Exhibit 2S.2 shows

EXHIBIT 2S.2
Sample Web Survey Question

Please rate the following applications in terms of their importance to you in your decision to purchase the product:	Extremely Important	Somewhat Important	Neutral	Not Very Important	Not at All Important
Collecting information from employees	◯	◯	◯	◯	◯
Conducting market research surveys	◯	◯	◯	◯	◯
For course evaluations	◯	◯	◯	◯	◯
Customer satisfaction surveys	◯	◯	◯	◯	◯
Website feedback surveys	◯	◯	◯	◯	◯

Source: Perseus, http://www. perseusdevelopment.com/.

a sample Web survey question. The respondent would simply click on a circle to enter a response.

Many survey software packages integrate e-mail messaging, so that respondents can be invited in an e-mail message to complete the survey, then click on a URL to begin the survey process. Some software packages incorporate audio and video capability along with basic questionnaire design and data collection.

Survey and Questionnaire Design

The questionnaire should begin with an introduction or welcome message, either in a cover letter or at the beginning of the questionnaire itself. Tell your respondents who you are and why you want the information in the survey. A good introduction or welcome message encourages people to complete your questionnaire. Also mention any incentives for completing the survey. Exhibit 2S.3 outlines the basic steps involved in designing a questionnaire.

Determining What Information to Collect

To determine what information should be collected, it is often helpful to start backward from the way you intend to analyze the information. It may be useful to construct the spreadsheets or databases into which the data will be placed when collected. For example, do you want to collect data in a quantitative form so that you can calculate response averages and variances, or do you want to collect data in a qualitative form? Qualitative and open-ended questions retain the details of the responses, and therefore capture nuances that quantitative scales may not capture. There is no one "right" way to collect data, but the form in which the data are collected will determine how the data can be analyzed and reported.

EXHIBIT 2S.3
**Steps in Designing
a Questionnaire**

1. Decide what information you need to collect.

2. Decide on the basic structure of the questions.

3. Determine how the questionnaire will be administered (by phone or in-person interview, in writing, via e-mail, or in Web format).

4. Decide on the content of each question.

5. Word the questions.

6. Arrange the questions into an effective sequence.

7. Test the questionnaire and revise as needed.

Developing the Questions

The next step is to develop the questions that will collect the desired data. Several factors need to be considered to develop questions that will provide the least biased responses.

Question Structure

The structure of a question will vary, depending on the type of information desired. We present here some of the more common types of question structure.

Closed-Ended Questions   Closed-ended questions allow respondents to choose from a number of alternative answers. *Dichotomous questions* ask the respondent to choose between one of two responses, for example: yes/no; acceptable/unacceptable, true/false. *Multiple-choice questions* provide a fixed number of alternative answers from which a respondent can choose. Multiple-choice questions are appropriate when the possible replies are clear and few in number.

Closed-ended questions are easy to answer and likewise easy to analyze and compare. It is also easier to replicate research conducted with closed-ended questions (as compared to open-ended questions) because there is little ambiguity. A disadvantage of closed-ended questions is that they may influence the respondents to answer even if they have no opinion. Some respondents may also feel frustrated because the answers are constrained to a limited number of options. Watch out for overlapping categories in closed-ended questions. For example, "How old are you?: a) 15–25 b) 25–35 c) 35–45."

Open-Ended Questions   With open-ended questions, respondents have more latitude to reply in their own words, but because answers usually vary considerably among respondents, they can be difficult to analyze. In addition, respondents may be unwilling to answer certain types of open-ended questions, so this type of question may be more appropriate for verbal administration. However, open-ended questions can play an important role when new information is sought. Follow-up can be done in a later survey that uses more structured types of questions. Finally, with open-ended questions, respondents may provide different levels of detail and may not always be clear or articulate, again making the information difficult to aggregate and compare.

Projective questions, which are a subset of open-ended questions, attempt to learn about the respondent's attitudes. Questions may be posed as word associations or fill-in-the-blank sentences. Like open-ended questions, these questions may be difficult to analyze and are particularly appropriate for early, exploratory information seeking.

Scale Questions Some questions ask respondents to provide a response along some scale. We present here three types of commonly used rating scales.

Graphic scale. With a **graphic scale,** the respondent places a mark on a line. There are an infinite number of places along the line that can be marked, which frees the respondent from the limitations of an itemized scale, but the responses can be difficult for the information gatherer to interpret.

Itemized scale. An itemized scale has a limited number of responses. For example, respondents may be asked to rate their satisfaction with a service on a scale of 1 to 5, with 5 being rated the best, and 1 being rated the worst. (This is sometimes called a Likert scale.) Itemized scales collect ordinal data, which means that the relative value "distance" between the items may not be the same. For example, on that scale of 1 to 5, respondents may feel that 4 and 5 are pretty similar ("really good" and "excellent"), but that 1 is much worse than 2. Another difficulty with itemized scales is that many individual respondents may have a systematic bias; in other words, they may rate everything relatively high or low on a scale. For example, one respondent may think that to achieve a rating of 5, performance must be perfect, so that person never gives the perfect score. A second respondent may believe that 5 means excellent, but not perfect, and may be inclined to rate every question systematically higher than the first respondent.

Comparative scale. With this scale, the respondent compares the relative importance of a 0number of items to each other by allocating a given number of points among the alternatives. For example, respondents may be asked to allocate 100 points among a number of service attributes to indicate the relative importance of each attribute to them.

Exhibit 2S.4 shows examples of each of the scale question types.

A number of issues need to be considered when designing scale-type questions. For example, *Should you use an odd or an even number of steps in the response scale?* If you use an odd number, you permit the respondent to express a neutral middle response. You can force a "nonmiddle" response by using an even number of steps in the scale, but you may have some error built in because some respondents may be neutral.

How many steps should you use? Statistical reliability of the data increases sharply when the number of scale steps is at least 7, then levels off again after 11 steps. However, the more steps you have, the more difficult it is for respondents to answer.

How can you structure the answers to scale questions so that they can be compared? If you use descriptions to provide an "anchor" for one answer, then the responses may be more reliable if you have all the other answers compared to that one answer. For example, you state that "a broad menu" is worth 10 points with respect to the overall satisfaction with a fine-dining experience. You then tell the respondents that if they perceive "speedy service" to be twice as important as "a broad menu," they should assign "speedy service" 20 points.

Rank-ordering is another method for providing information about the relative importance of a small (typically under 10) number of items. With this method, respondents are asked to order the items with the first being most important and the last being least important.

Question Content

Every question in a questionnaire should have a specific purpose: to provide information about the respondent, to establish rapport with the respondent, and/or to provide the particular information that is sought in the survey.

EXHIBIT 2S.4
Examples of Scale Questions

Scale Type	Example
Graphic	*On the line below, make an "X" at the point that best depicts how important each item is to the overall dining experience in this restaurant:*
	Cleanliness of Dining Room:
	_____
	Not at all important Extremely important
	Server Friendliness:
	_____
	Not at all important Extremely important
	Menu Variety
	_____
	Not at all important Extremely important
Itemized	*For each item below, circle the number that best describes its importance to the overall dining experience at this restaurant:*
	Cleanliness of Dining Room:
	Not at all important 1 2 3 4 5 Extremely important
	Server Friendliness:
	Not at all important 1 2 3 4 5 Extremely important
	Menu Variety:
	Not at all important 1 2 3 4 5 Extremely important
Comparative	*Allocate 30 points among the following three items to indicate how important each is to your overall dining experience at this restaurant. For example, if you believe that Menu Variety is the only important item, allocate all 30 points to that category.*
	Cleanliness of Dining Room: _____
	Server Friendliness: _____
	Menu Variety: _____

Some survey questions are more sensitive than others. Sensitive questions can be posed in ways that increase the chances that the respondent will answer them—and answer them honestly. This can be accomplished in a variety of ways, including:

- Placing the more sensitive question in a series of less personal questions.
- Stating that the behavior or attitude relating to the question is not so unusual.
- Phrasing the question in terms of other people, not the respondent.
- Providing response choices that specify ranges, not exact numbers.
- Placing sensitive questions at the end of the survey.

Question Wording

Questions should be worded so that they are unambiguous and easy for the respondent to understand. Even the simplest question can be complicated by the way the respondent interprets it. Considering how a respondent might interpret a question from the "who, what, when, where, how" perspectives can be helpful. For example, asking, "Which radio station do you listen to most often?" Does "you" mean "you alone" or "you with your family?" In the morning, the respondent may consistently listen to one station, but may listen to another in the afternoon. A more clearly worded question might be, "What radio station did you personally listen to most often in the morning over the last three months?"

When asking about the frequency of use of a service, avoid ambiguous words such as *sometimes, occasionally,* or *regularly.* Instead, use more specific terms such as *once per day* and *two to three times per week.*

There are a variety of ways you can avoid ambiguity in survey questions. The language you use to construct questions should be tailored to your respondent group. Specifically, (*a*) use grammar and vocabulary that is meaningful to the respondents who are answering the questionnaire, (*b*) use jargon when it is appropriate for a particular group (for example, people employed in the same organization), (*c*) avoid language that may not be familiar to your respondents, and (*d*) avoid unnecessary abbreviations.

Questions should be worded so that respondents do not need to make assumptions about what the question is asking. For example, "What is your income?" requires the respondent to think about whether the question is asking for individual income or family income, weekly or monthly or annual income, and before- or after-tax income. A less confusing question would be, "What was your average individual monthly before-tax income last year from your salary only?" Some ways of wording questions introduce bias subtly and should be avoided. Loaded questions are questions with false presuppositions, so they cannot be directly answered without implying a falsehood. (The classic loaded question is, "Have you stopped beating your wife yet?" An answer of yes implies that you had, in fact, been beating your wife. An answer of no implies that you still are! Another presupposition is that you even have a wife.) "What should be done to improve our excellent service?" presupposes that the service is, in fact, excellent. Referring in a question to an expert's opinion may also introduce bias, as in, "Experts say that a diet high in fat is bad for your heart. Do you agree?"

Leading questions predispose respondents to answer in a particular way. Avoid leading questions that bias toward a particular answer such as, "You don't think valet parking is a good idea, do you?" More than one question embedded in a single question item can bias answers because respondents will answer one of the questions and the researcher won't know which answers relate to which questions. "Rate our food and service from 1 to 5" is asking for an answer about both food and service. Whatever the respondent answers, you will not be sure whether the first question (food), the second question (service), or both questions are being answered. Questions that include two or more questions are often referred to as *double-barreled questions.*

Some questions assume that respondents are conscious of all aspects of their behavior. For example, "Do you tip servers who smile more or less than servers who don't smile?" is a question that might be better answered by direct observation of the tipping behavior because customers may not be aware of how much, or how little, smiling actually affects their tipping practices.

Similarly, it is best to avoid questions that ask respondents to provide information they may not really have, such as, "How many times last year did you visit a fast-food restaurant?" Most respondents to that question will be guessing, rather than providing an accurate count.

For some questions, respondents may not always have an answer, so an "I don't know" option is appropriate. There are two "filter" formats, or ways of dealing with "I don't know." The first way is to simply include "I don't know" in the list of alternative answers. The other approach is to ask two questions. The first question asks, "Do you have an opinion about xyz?" If the answer is yes, the alternatives are offered; if the answer is no, the respondent goes to the next question.

Sequencing the Questions

Placing a few neutral questions at the beginning of a questionnaire can help to establish rapport with the respondent. For that reason, embarrassing or threatening questions are often placed toward the end of the questionnaire. This increases the chances that respondents will answer the difficult questions and also assures that at least the earlier questions were answered.

The sequence in which questions are presented can affect the way they are answered in two ways. First, mentioning an idea in one question may make respondents think of that idea when they are answering a later question, when they might not have thought of it otherwise. One way to correct for this effect is to distribute half of the questionnaires with one order and the other half with another order.

The order of the questions can also cause habituation, which is answering a series of questions similarly without really thinking about the question each time. Respondents may be more alert to the first questions in a series and think about them more carefully.

Other Issues Relating to Questionnaire Design

Test and Revise the Questionnaire

Questionnaires should be pretested in two stages before they are administered. In the first stage, it is helpful to administer the survey during an interview to get feedback or reactions to questions. In the second phase, it should be administered exactly the way it will be administered in practice. Patterns of missing answers or answers that don't appear to make sense may be clues that the questions are still confusing to respondents.

Questionnaire Length

In general, shorter questionnaires are better than longer ones because people are more willing to complete shorter surveys, but the ease of completion of the questionnaire may be more important than the length.

Physical Characteristics of the Questionnaire

Respondents are also affected by the way the questionnaire looks. Page layout, font type and size, question spacing, and type of paper all affect the respondent's perceptions. Some suggestions for minimizing these effects on respondents include: (a) don't change fonts often, as that can be distracting for the reader; (b) avoid having a single question span more than one page, to reduce the respondent's need to flip back and forth between pages; (c) choose fonts that are readable by respondents who have less-than-perfect visual acuity; and (d) design the survey so that there are "white spaces" on the pages; too much text can be overwhelming as well as confusing.

Errors and Variations in Questionnaire Responses

Respondents may not be able to answer all questions accurately. Two types of error are telescoping error and recall loss. **Telescoping error** results when people remember events as occurring more recently than they actually did. **Recall loss** occurs when people forget that an event occurred or how it occurs. For recent events, telescoping error dominates; for events that happened in the distant past, recall loss dominates.

Variations in responses that are not due to the characteristic being measured (for example, satisfaction with a service) may occur for several reasons, including:

- A question is ambiguous.

- Respondents have different response styles. For example, one respondent may tend to be more positive and rate everything highly, where another may tend to be more negative, and therefore rarely gives anything a top score.

- Respondents may be affected by personal factors such as fatigue and discomfort while completing the survey.

- Respondents may be affected by distractions in the environment.

- Respondents may be affected by the way in which the questionnaire is administered, such as the tone of voice or affect of the interviewer.

- The overall layout and presentation of the survey may be confusing.

Impact of Technology

Recent advances in information technology have made learning about customers and their needs easier and more convenient than ever before. The Internet has made it possible to conduct focus groups in real time online. Customers type their answers to questions and their responses to each other, and the researcher gets not only the information that would result from a traditional focus group session, but also an automatic full transcript! Some Internet companies connect into already-existing online forums to learn participants' opinions, then provide that information to their clients. While online focus groups do not capture the nonverbal reactions of participants, they are particularly appropriate for collecting information from participants who are geographically dispersed and who might not be able to participate in a traditional focus group. Online focus groups are also very useful for collecting reactions to online resources such as websites, databases, and advertising.

The Internet has also made it possible to administer surveys electronically. Some surveys are connected with particular websites and are used to gather customer reactions to a company's products or services. Other surveys are sent to respondents via e-mails that automatically link to the survey website. Respondents may simply click on closed-ended responses to questions or may fill in open-ended fields. Data are aggregated into databases for easy analysis. Some Web-based surveys even produce easy-to-design reports!

Summary

Focus groups and questionnaires are used to collect information from customers in order to make better managerial decisions. Focus groups collect rich data about the views of a small number of people and about how their opinions are affected by others. Focus group data are typically analyzed qualitatively. Questionnaires are used to collect information from larger numbers of customers and are typically analyzed using quantitative as well as qualitative techniques.

Key Terms

bias: tendency to respond with a particular point of view or prejudice. *(p. 34)*
focus group: in-depth interview with a small group of people in order to learn their views about or experiences with some topic. *(p. 35)*
graphic scale: a line on which the respondent places a mark. *(p. 41)*
projective questions: questions that attempt to learn about respondents' attitudes. *(p. 40)*
questionnaire (or survey): set of written or verbal questions to which a respondent answers. *(p. 36)*

rank-ordering: question that asks respondents to order items along some scale, such as *least important* to *most important. (p. 41)*

recall loss: when people forget that an event occurred or how it occurs. *(p. 44)*

telescoping error: the result of people remembering events as occurring more recently than they actually did. *(p. 44)*

Review and Discussion Questions

1. What is a focus group? When should it be used?
2. What is a questionnaire?
3. What are the different ways a questionnaire can be administered? What are the strengths and weaknesses of each method?
4. For each of the following surveys, identify the potential bias that might exist:
    a. A survey of computer use at home, conducted electronically.
    b. A survey to determine the incomes of typical young parents, conducted at Disney World.
    c. A survey to learn about the recreational interests of typical high school students, conducted in the advanced placement calculus class.
5. When is bias in a survey a good thing to have?
6. Identify the problem with each of these questions, state why it is a problem in a survey, and then rewrite the question to correct the problem.
    a. How would you evaluate the knowledge and friendliness of your server?
        1. Excellent
        2. Very good
        3. Good
        4. Poor
    b. What is your favorite fast-food restaurant?
        1. McDonald's
        2. Burger King
    c. How many years have you worked at X?
        1. Less than 5
        2. 5 to 10
        3. 10–15
        4. More than 15
    d. How would you evaluate your service today?
        1. Worst I've ever had
        2. Somewhere between the worst and best
        3. Best I've ever had
    e. Are you satisfied with your current dentist? (Yes or No)
    f. What percent of your income do you spend on entertainment?
    g. Wouldn't you like a free demonstration?
    h. How long did you have to wait for a CSR?

Internet Assigment

Go to the following sites:

inquisite.com
nbrii.com
customersurveystore.com

What information do these companies provide about survey design? Who are their customers? What services do they provide to their customers?

Selected Bibliography

Greenbaum, Thomas L. *Moderating Focus Groups: A Practical Guide for Group Facilitation.* Thousand Oaks, CA: Sage Publications, 2000.

http://www.statpac.com/surveys/

Kreuger, R. A. *Focus Groups: A Practical Guide for Applied Research.* London: Sage, 1988.

Morgan, D. L. *Focus Groups as Qualitative Research.* London: Sage, 1997.

Morgan, D. L., and R. A. Kreuger. "When to Use Focus Groups and Why." In *Successful Focus Groups,* ed. D. L. Morgan. London: Sage, 1993.

Stewart, D. W., and P. N. Shamdasani. *Focus Groups: Theory and Practice.* London: Sage, 1992.

CHAPTER THREE

The Role of Technology in Services

Learning Objectives

- Describe how the role of technology in services has evolved.

- Show how technology is changing the way services are designed and delivered.

- Introduce the different ways in which technology can add value to services.

- Provide a framework for defining the various types of e-services currently offered.

- Identify the issues that management must address to successfully use technology within their organizations

Technology Is Only a Tool!

Courtesy of Avis

I drove my rental car into the Avis parking lot near the Los Angeles International Airport. As I started to get out of the car and unload my bags, an attendant greeted me with a handheld computer and asked me for a copy of my rental agreement.

I said to him, "Don't bother. I need to go to the check-in desk anyway; I forgot to give Avis my frequent flier number when I rented the car last week."

"No problem," he replied, "I can handle that here too, so you don't have to go to the desk."

Impressed by his ability to handle this non-routine activity with his handheld computer, I commented, "Today's technology is truly amazing!" To which he curtly answered, "It's only a tool!"

Caught off guard by his statement, I asked him to explain what he meant. He continued, "It's only a tool. Just like a wrench is only as good as the mechanic has been trained to use it, so technology is only as good as the people who are properly trained to use it in their everyday work."

To which I could only respond, "You're 100 percent right!"

—Mark M. Davis

The Customer's Perspective

Technology in general, and information technology in particular, is dramatically affecting virtually every facet of our lives. Think about the services you have used in the last week and how they have changed in recent years. Perhaps, instead of going to the grocery store, you now order your groceries online and have them delivered to your home. Or you now do all your banking online, including transferring funds between accounts and paying your bills. You can buy books through Amazon.com and perhaps you even participate in the on-line auctions offered by eBay.

If you want to take a trip, you no longer use a travel agent, but instead purchase your airline ticket online either through the airline directly or through one of the many virtual travel agencies on the Internet that search for the lowest available airfares. You can also search the Internet for a list of good restaurants in the city you will be visiting and to find a hotel for you at the right price in the right location.

The traditional methods of delivering these services still exist, so why are we changing to these new delivery modes? We are using these new types of services because we perceive that they add value in comparison to the more traditional service delivery systems. What has enabled firms to provide these innovative approaches to service? In a word, the answer is technology.

Managerial Issues

This chapter's opening vignette captures in a nutshell the major issues confronting service managers today. (These same issues actually confront all managers in all organizations.) Information technology is changing the way services are designed, managed, and delivered. Advances in IT, especially with the explosive growth of the Internet, have enabled organizations, both for-profit and not-for-profit, to offer a myriad of new services. In so doing, technology is also making many traditional services obsolete.

However, as the Avis attendant correctly pointed out, managers must recognize that IT is only a tool, not an end in itself. Continuing the attendant's tool analogy, a multifunctional air-powered wrench that is cumbersome to hold and requires extensive training should not be used when a simple hand wrench will do the job more quickly and more easily. Similarly a 1-inch wrench should not be used when a 20-millimeter wrench is required. From an IT perspective, this means that expensive IT infrastructure should not be installed if it is not aligned with the overall goals of the firm and does not fully satisfy the needs of its customers.

Managers also need to realize that there are many times when only IT will provide the necessary infrastructure to meet their customers' needs in today's highly competitive environment. For example, if a firm's customers want to use the Internet because it is fast and efficient, then that firm needs to provide a website for its customers and have the required infrastructure in place to support it. It is equally important for managers to recognize that these new technology-driven infrastructures must be compatible with all the organization's functional elements so that information can be quickly and efficiently transmitted and shared with a minimum of errors. For example, with the proper infrastructure, a customer order that is received through a website can be sent electronically to the accounting department for credit authorization and to the operations department for fulfillment without any internal paperwork.

To properly integrate IT into their organizations, service managers need to understand both what IT can do and what IT cannot do. In addition, managers must acknowledge the need for workers at all levels to be properly trained in the use of IT, and that this training is not just a one-shot deal, but rather a continuous, ongoing process. Two key challenges to service managers today are how to properly apply IT and how to train workers to use it within the existing service environment.

The Evolving Technology-Driven Business Environment

During the second half of the 20th century, businesses evolved through four major stages of technology. Within each stage, technology affected business in a different way. These four stages are sometimes referred to as (*a*) the systems-centric (SC) stage, (*b*) the PC-centric (PC) stage, (*c*) the network-centric stage (NC), and (*d*) the information-centric (NC) stage. Exhibit 3.1 depicts these four stages in a timeline along with the estimated number of users.

Systems-centric Stage

This stage is characterized by large mainframe computers, such as the IBM-360, which were produced during the late 1960s and 1970s. These machines were capable of analyzing vast amounts of data (for that era) and producing management-related reports. The primary function of these computers was to increase the efficiency of much of the manual back-of-the-office service operations in large corporations, such as accounting and finance. Because of their size and related cost, these computers were typically centrally located in a separate department where the necessary management reports were generated.

All the work done by these computers was usually performed in batch mode, with users having to wait several hours—or even days—before their reports would be ready.

PC-centric Stage

The introduction of personal computers in the early to mid-1980s made computing power available and affordable to both individuals and small organizations. The PC decentralized computing to the individual level. Data could be analyzed in real time, eliminating the significant delays caused by waiting for the larger machines to complete their calculations in batch mode. Each PC could be configured to meet the software and usage needs of the individual. However, because most of these PCs were individual stand-alone units, it was very difficult to connect them electronically. To share information, users had to save data to discs and then use the discs to physically transfer information from one PC to another or to a mainframe computer.

Network-centric Stage

This next stage, which began in the late 1980s to early 1990s, connected the PCs within an organization into local area networks, or LANs. With LANs, PCs could communicate with

EXHIBIT 3.1
**The Four Stages
of Technology-Driven
Evolution**

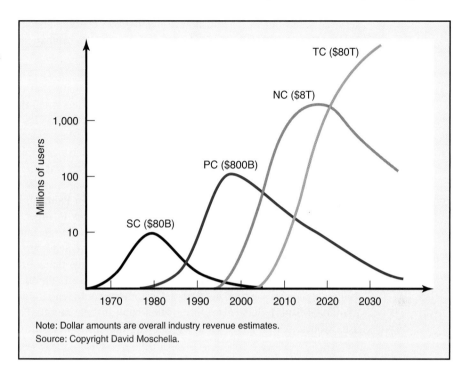

Note: Dollar amounts are overall industry revenue estimates.
Source: Copyright David Moschella.

each other electronically as well as with larger computers called *servers,* thereby reducing
the need to manually transfer data files using discs. A major challenge at this stage was the
standardization of operating systems and software packages within an organization to facilitate the transfer of the data files. Many software packages were incompatible with each
other, and even files produced by different versions of the same software could not be easily shared. For example, the software to manage the human resources department was not
compatible with the software for the operations department or the accounting department.

Information-centric Stage

The information-centric stage is defined by the introduction of the Internet coupled with
the ability to quickly transfer data inexpensively over long distances through high-speed
transmission lines and then store it inexpensively on servers. This combination of technologies has resulted in large amounts of information being available to virtually everyone
almost anywhere in the world. As a result, organizations in this stage often become bogged
down with information overload. The challenge for both management and individuals is to
decide what information is needed and how to efficiently analyze and quickly disseminate
that information throughout the organization.

Aligning Technology with the Needs of the Organization

Technology, in one form or another, has had a profound effect on how services are designed and delivered. Automated hotel checkouts through the use of in-room televisions,
automatic teller machines (ATMs) at banks, online airline reservation systems, and bar-
code readers at supermarket checkout counters provide just a few examples of how technology affects the way we design service systems, and ultimately how we deliver those

services to customers. The introduction and growing acceptance of new technologies such as the Internet and its related *e-businesses* continue to dramatically change the ways services are provided.

In the past, many service companies looked to technology primarily as a way to lower costs by increasing worker productivity, with the ultimate goal of increasing profits. But the large investments that these firms made in technology often did not yield the expected increases in productivity. The profitability of some of these firms actually declined, due in large part to the heavy debt burdens they incurred to adopt those ill-considered technologies, causing them to become less competitive in the marketplace.[1] Higher fixed costs without the expected decrease in variable costs, which was the underlying rationale for these investments, resulted in slower responses to changes in the marketplace.

Consider the following example. A bank located in Palm Springs, California, that focuses on providing a wide range of personal services to older, high-income customers would probably not gain any significant advantage by installing a large number of ATMs within its region. Most likely, the reason current customers use this bank is because they receive individual and personal attention and have the ability to interact with a real person in the form of a bank teller. The ATMs at this bank, therefore, would very likely remain idle most of the time because its customers would tend to ignore them in favor of the traditional bank tellers. Therefore, if this bank installs more ATMs that customers won't use, it increases its costs without achieving the desired benefit of savings in bank-teller labor.

The use of automated phone answering systems provides another good example of the need for alignment between technology and the goals of the firm. Such systems, while highly efficient from the company's perspective, are often frustrating and time-consuming to customers. Thus, a firm that focuses on providing very personalized service to the high end of a particular market, such as the Four Seasons hotel chain or Putnam Investor Services, might find that the installation of such an automated telephone answering system could negatively affect its business. The managers at both firms are aware of this and have all telephone calls answered by real people, rather than an automated system.

Service managers need to understand the organizational context within which the technology is to be used. Investing in technology for the wrong reasons can result in significant cost increases without the desired benefits. Service managers must also understand that investments in technology can be made for a variety of reasons other than increasing worker productivity. These include faster and more individualized services. When the customer service representatives at the Four Seasons and Putnam Investor Services answer telephone calls, they use technology to access data files on both the company and the customer, which enables them to respond to customer inquiries.

Managers must also recognize that investments in technology are often required just to maintain a firm's competitive position and that not making those investments could result in lost sales and associated lost profits. The failure of Sears to install a toll-free telephone line was a major factor in the closing of its catalog business.

Technology can affect the delivery of services in different ways. Exhibit 3.2 lists several reasons, other than increasing productivity, why a company might want to invest in technology.

Technology also needs to be properly integrated within the firm's organization to support the firm's long-term strategy. Managers must realize that some benefits of technology investments may be difficult to measure and quantify in dollars, but the effect of technol-

---

[1] Steven Roach, "Service under Siege—The Restructuring Imperative," *Harvard Business Review,* September–October 1991, pp. 82–91.

EXHIBIT 3.2
Reasons Service
Companies Invest
in Technologies

- Maintain market share.
- Avoid catastrophic losses.
- Create greater flexibility and adaptability.
- Improve responsiveness for new products.
- Improve service quality.
- Improve worker morale.
- Enhance quality of life.
- Increase predictability of operations.

Source: Adapted from J. B. Quinn and M. N. Bailey, "Information
Technology: Increasing Productivity in Services," *Academy of
Management Executive* 8, no. 3 (1994).

ogy on such relevant issues as improved worker morale and significantly shorter customer
service times may influence the long-term success of the organization.

Technology-Driven Trends in Services

Advances in technology, including improved automated equipment, voice recognition systems, high-speed data transmission lines (such as broadband), and faster and more powerful computers, have had a significant effect on services. Large amounts of data are readily accessible today and can be transmitted inexpensively over long distances. We identify several major trends in the delivery of services that are a direct result of technology. These trends are not independent; rather one trend is likely to be related to the others.

Increase in Self-Service

Many service industries have expanded self-service operations, both to control labor costs (and sometimes to permit lower prices) and to provide more rapid service to customers. Examples include self-service gas stations, ATMs, and automated toll collection on highways. Self-service is also used extensively in e-businesses, ranging from the online purchase of a sweater from Lands' End, to the purchase of airline tickets from Orbitz.com and the purchase of stocks and bonds through E*Trade. When customers enter orders from their computers, the information goes directly into the organization's databases, saving data-entry time and cost, reducing errors, and often triggering the next step in the service process.

Many supermarket chains, drugstores, and discount department store chains are currently testing self-service checkout lanes. (See "Using Technology to Create Value.") With this automated equipment, customers scan their own purchases, bag them, and pay by either cash or credit card. While customers become familiar with the technology and the process, one employee is assigned to every three or four automated lanes to assist shoppers, but in the long run, self-service checkout may produce as profound a change in the checkout process as bar-code scanning did.

One primary reason for the increase in self-service is that it reduces labor costs. With automated self-service equipment, gas station attendants are no longer needed to pump gas, bank tellers are no longer needed to make deposits and withdrawals, customer service representatives are no longer needed to answer telephone calls.

At the same time, service managers need to recognize that by going entirely to a self-service delivery system, they will exclude certain market segments. For example, some

Using Technology to Create Value

Self-Service Checkout Counters Increase Productivity and Reduce WaitingTimes at Kroger Supermarkets

Kroger, one of the nation's largest supermarket chains, is introducing self-service checkout counters. The U-Scan self-service checkout system, manufactured by Optimal Robotics, has been installed in approximately one-third of Kroger's 2,380 stores. The U-Scan system accepts all forms of payments, including cash, credit cards, and debit cards.

One of the most common complaints about shopping at supermarkets, according to Gary Rhodes of Kroger, is the time it takes to check out. No one likes waiting in long checkout lines. The self-

service units provide a checkout alternative where customers can control the length of the checkout process. As a result, the U-Scan systems have proved to be enormously popular with Kroger's customers. In addition, the U-Scan systems require significantly less labor and are therefore much more economical to operate than the traditional checkout counter with a cashier.

Source: Special thanks to Gary Rhodes of Kroger and Robin Yaffe of Optimal Robotics.

EXHIBIT 3.3
Methods of Pricing to Encourage Self-Service

Type of Service	Price Differential between Self-Service and Full-Service
Gas station	Higher price for full-service gas.
Investment firm	Higher commission for using a broker.
Airline	Special fares available only on the Internet.
Bank	Additional fee for using a teller.

customers do not want to pump their own gas; similarly, other individuals prefer to obtain advice on investing in the stock market rather than doing their own analysis. Consequently, many service firms offer self-service as one of several distribution channels. Many service firms will offer discounts when customers use self-service options or charge more when employee assistance is required. Exhibit 3.3 provides examples of how firms encourage customers to use self-service.

Decrease in the Importance of Location

Inexpensive data storage, transmission, and retrieval costs coupled with electronic access to virtually every corner of the world have decreased the importance of location for many services. Online banking services reduce the need for a customer to go to the bank. Home delivery services for groceries, dry cleaning, and so on, eliminate the need for customers to physically go to these retail locations. Similarly, any purchases made on the Internet, whether they are books from Amazon.com or airline tickets from Expedia.com, eliminate the need for the customer to visit specific retail locations that offer these services. When services can be provided remotely, the customer doesn't care where the service centers are located.

The continued development of a worldwide communication network has encouraged the crossing of national borders to locate back-office service in areas where labor is relatively inexpensive. As a result, customer call centers can be located anywhere: one U.S. airline's ticket reservation call center is located in the Caribbean, while the customer call center for a major bank whose branch offices are in the Middle Atlantic states is located in Maine. In addition to providing low-cost labor, these locations must also have in place the necessary communication infrastructure to provide the level of service required by these firms.

Shift from Time-Dependent to Non-Time-Dependent Transactions

There is a growing trend away from time-dependent service transactions toward non-time-dependent transactions. Time-dependent transactions require a service worker to be available exactly when the customer requires the service. Examples of time-dependent service transactions include table service at a restaurant, interaction with the reservations clerk at an airline call center when you reserve a flight, the check-in process at a hotel, and interaction with your stockbroker when you conduct a stock transaction. Non-time-dependent transactions do not require the presence of the service worker at the exact moment when the customer requests the service. Examples of non-time-dependent transactions include e-mail, faxes, and voice messages. Time-dependent transactions are often referred to as **synchronous transactions** or communications, while non-time-dependent transactions are referred to as **asynchronous transactions** or communications.

There are several underlying reasons for the shift toward non-time-dependent transactions. First, non-time-dependent transactions are less costly to the firm. With time-dependent transactions, service workers must always be available for the customer. To allow for the uncertainty in forecasting customer demand, as well as to keep customer waiting times reasonably short (as explained in Chapter 15), extra workers must be on duty, which is expensive. With non-time-dependent activities, the firm has some flexibility to schedule workers in a more efficient manner and also to prioritize the transactions (as explained in Chapter 10).

Asynchronous transactions are usually more efficient from the customer's perspective too. For example, rather than trying to speak to someone in person, and playing endless rounds of "phone tag," it is much more efficient to send a single e-mail message.

As the world quickly becomes a global village or single world economy that is linked electronically, a growing number of transactions do not occur during "regular business hours" (whatever that means these days!). A customer in Australia who orders something through the Internet from a small firm in England can place the order at any time, regardless of what time it is in England, and that order will be filled at the beginning of the next business day. Non-time-dependent transactions permit firms to receive transactions on a 24 × 7 basis (24 hours a day, seven days a week), and then to respond to these transactions efficiently during normal business hours.

Increase in Disintermediation

Stan Davis introduced the term **disintermediation** to mean the elimination of intermediate steps or organizations in the value chain.[2] Technology has brought buyers and sellers closer, often doing away with any intermediate organizations. For example, when travelers purchase airline tickets directly from the airlines using the Internet they eliminate the need for a travel agent. Likewise, trading stocks and bonds on the Internet eliminates the need for a stockbroker. Similarly, many manufacturers, such as Dell, now sell their products directly to consumers, eliminating the need for distributors and/or retailers.

Integrating Technology into Services

Technology needs to be properly integrated into an organization to provide it with a competitive advantage. This is achieved by enhancing the organization's effectiveness and/or efficiency, which add value for its customers. We identify three broad areas where technology can significantly contribute to the success of an organization: (*a*) strategic planning, (*b*) improved performance, and (*c*) increased efficiency.

Strategic Planning

Strategic planning is concerned with the long-range view of how an organization conducts business. Within the operations function of an organization, strategic decisions include: (*a*)

---

[2] Stan Davis, *Future Perfect* (Reading, MA: Addison-Wesley, 1987).

From the beginning, when he founded FedEx in 1971, Fred Smith has been considered a maverick and an IT visionary. He believes that the proper application of IT to be one of the critical factors in his firm's long-term success. As early as 1979, Fred recognized that information about the status of the package was as important as the package itself.

Fred traces his interest in IT to when he served as a Marine Corps captain and learned about the ARPANET, the military network, which ultimately became today's Internet. Because Fred is constantly looking to the future, FedEx is usually one of the first companies to apply new technologies to improve its operations, thereby providing it with a competitive advantage in its marketplace.

FedEx is continuously evolving its organization to better meet the needs of its customers through the introduction of state-of-the-art technologies. In 1980, for example, FedEx was already using wireless technology in the form of walkie-talkies, with couriers in constant communication with dispatchers. Around this same time, FedEx introduced COSMOS (Customers, Operations, and Service Master Online System), which was the world's first centralized global shipment tracking system. At that time, FedEx was also the first company in the ground transportation industry to use barcode labeling for packages. In 1984, FedEx introduced the first PC-based shipping system for customers who shipped as few as five packages a day (and accelerated the introduction of this program by giving the PCs to its customers). When FedEx introduced its website, www.fedex.com, in 1994, it became the first firm to allow its customers to track the status of their packages over the Internet. Two years later, using the same technology, customers could create their own shipping labels and schedule pickups for FedEx's couriers.

FedEx continues to reap the benefits of these new technologies. For example its online services now handle two-thirds of the company's 1.2 billion customer interactions a year. Without such services, it is estimated that FedEx would have to hire another 20,000 customer service employees.

The combination of Smith's vision and FedEx's success in introducing new technologies is one of the main reasons that the company continues to invest approximately 10% of its annual revenues in IT.

Sources: David Joachim, "FedEx Delivers on CEO's IT Vision," *InternetWeek,* October 25, 1999.
Sarah D. Sleeper, "FedEx Pushes the Right Buttons to Remain No. 1 in Fast Shipping," *Investor's Business Daily,* May 25, 2001.
Mark Gordon, "Next Day Change Guaranteed," *CIO, The Magazine for Information Executives,* May 15, 2001.

Where do we locate our facilities? (*b*) How big do we make them? (*c*) When do we build them? and (*d*) What processes do we adopt to produce goods or services?

Service organizations interact directly with their customers, so they must also strategically evaluate how technology will relate to customers. Service managers need to recognize that technology can significantly alter the way in which a company does business. For example, when Amazon.com started selling books over the Internet, traditional brick-and-mortar book retailers, such as Barnes & Noble and Borders, needed to strategically assess how best to respond. Should they have their own brand websites? Should the prices be different from those in the stores? Could books purchased on the Internet be returned to a retail location? Adopting the proper strategy and associated technology can result in substantial increases in revenues and market share. Failure to do so can result in losing customers to competitors.

Improved Performance

Service managers must also recognize that the decision to adopt technology is often driven by the need to improve the performance of their operations rather than to only increase productivity. (As we learned in Chapter 1, performance can be defined to include faster speed of delivery, more product variety, and improved customer responsiveness, to name a few.) Often, however, with the proper technology, both performance and productivity can be improved to create a win–win situation for the firm.

Faster Service

Technology has allowed service operations to significantly reduce and, in some cases, eliminate the need for customers to wait in line for service. In addition to providing faster service, technology can reduce labor costs by eliminating the customer/worker encounter.

For example, many hotels now offer their guests an in-room checkout option. To use it, guests simply follow the menu-driven instructions on the televisions in their rooms, leave their room keys in the room, and never go to the front desk to check out. In this case, customer waiting time is eliminated and the requirement for front-desk personnel is reduced.

As another illustration of how technology provides faster service, the deli counters in some supermarkets have computerized ordering kiosks where customers can order their favorite sliced meats and cheeses, complete their other shopping, and return to the deli to pick up their deli purchases just before going to the checkout. Deli counter workers still have to fill the orders, but customers don't have to wait.

Bar-code scanners at the checkout counters in supermarkets have significantly reduced the amount of time a customer may expect to stand in line while also reducing labor costs and errors in keying in the proper prices. Bar coding also reduces the need to frequently check inventories by providing managers with more real-time information with less effort.

Improved Knowledge about Customers

Many services maintain databases to provide managers with detailed information on their customers' purchasing characteristics and their firms' past relationships with these customers. As part of their focus on attention to personal detail, for example, the Ritz-Carlton hotel chain, through its management information system, tracks guests' preferences including the type of beds they like to sleep in (such as a queen- or king-size bed) and the types of wine they prefer. In addition, any previous incidents involving the customer, particularly complaints, are recorded in the database to assure that similar incidents do not occur again. This same database also tracks habitual complainers, who may eventually be asked to take their business elsewhere.

Marriott International is similarly collecting detailed data about its hotel guests, which allows it to target them with promotions relating to specific cities or areas of interest, such as golf or skiing, depending on each guest's individual preferences. Marriott believes such promotions based on customer-specific data will increase its annual revenues by $10 million to $20 million annually.[3]

Another method of using technology for obtaining data on individual customers is through membership cards. Many retail operations now require membership cards or provide discount incentives to encourage their use. Such cards allow the retailer to track the buying patterns of individual customers, providing in-depth information about customers that can be used for planning. For example, BJ's Wholesale Club, Costco, and Sam's Club all require their customers to purchase membership cards. Shaw's, Stop & Shop, and Price Chopper are examples of supermarket chains that have recently introduced, free of charge, a similar type of card that entitles customers to significant discounts on products. Through such membership cards, these chains can track customer purchases. In addition, Stop & Shop also prints out on the receipt the customer's annual savings from using the card, which encourages customers to keep shopping—and keep saving!

The proper use of technology enables a service company to better understand the individual purchasing patterns of and past experiences with each of its customers—information that can be used to create stronger relationships with customers and, thereby, a competitive advantage in the marketplace.

Increased Product Customization

Technology also allows service managers to provide their customers with a wider variety of options than they could offer previously. The terms *micro-niching* and *mass customization*

---

[3] Amy Borus, "A Hotel That Clicks with Guests," *Business Week Online,* September 18, 2000.

have evolved, in part, as a direct result of advances in technology that permit firms to identify and provide customized goods and services to large numbers of individual customers.

For example, Levi Strauss offers custom-fit jeans. The customer enters his or her specific measurements into the computer at the retail store and a few weeks later the jeans are delivered to the customer's home. Additional pairs can be ordered with only a telephone call, thereby eliminating the need to visit the store. L.L. Bean, the mail-order company based in Freeport, Maine, will monogram many of its products with the customer's initials. Computerized sewing machines allow operators to select the style, size, and letter(s) in a matter of seconds. A monitor screen located above the sewing machine shows the operator how the monogram will look before it is actually stitched on the article. If everything is correct, the monogram is then quickly sewn on the product with the touch of a button.

Increased Efficiency

As stated earlier, the initial thrust into technology was driven primarily by the need to reduce operating costs. This is still a major reason for purchasing new technology. Just as capital equipment is often used to reduce costs in a manufacturing company, technology can be similarly applied in a service environment. The two primary ways in which the efficiency or productivity of the operation can be increased are (*a*) economies of scale and (*b*) reduced labor costs, recognizing that there is some degree of overlap between the two.

Economies of Scale

Advances in communication technology have allowed service companies to reduce the number of locations for many types of activities. For example, reservation call centers for hotels, airlines, and car rental agencies have been consolidated to a few central locations. Economies of scale with these larger operations occur, in part, as a result of the ability to schedule a larger number of operators in one location. If the demand in a given hour (that is, the number of calls received) doubles, the number of operators necessary to provide the same level of service is less than double. Economies of scale are also reflected in the reduced per unit overhead costs, typically associated with larger facilities. An additional savings is the reduced cost associated with locating in a low-cost area. Citibank has located its credit card operations in South Dakota for this reason. Similarly, many hotel chains have their central reservation systems in Omaha, Nebraska, rather than on either the West Coast or the East Coast, where the cost of living is higher.

Reduced Labor Costs

Technology can reduce labor costs in two ways. First, it can be used as a total replacement for labor. Second, technology can provide support to existing labor, thereby increasing labor productivity.

Replacement for Labor   Technology can replace labor in several ways. For example, automatic teller machines (ATMs) in banks are a total substitute for the traditional bank teller for many routine operations, but cost only a fraction of what a teller costs. Therefore, bank customers should be encouraged to use ATMs when conducting certain types of transactions.

Organizations can also use the Internet to replace labor. The Massachusetts Registry of Motor Vehicles is now online, which allows motorists to pay speeding ticket fines and renew automobile registrations through the Internet. Increased use of the Internet in this

Using Technology to Create Value

Zara Stores Are Always Stocked with the Latest Fashions

Zara, a retail chain of high-fashion boutique clothing stores, has grown rapidly since Amancio Ortega opened his first store in Spain in 1975. Headquartered in northern Spain, Zara, with more than 400 retail stores in 25 countries, now generates sales of more than $2 billion annually, primarily in Europe, but is now beginning to penetrate the U.S. market. Its success can be attributed to several factors including competitive prices, speed of delivery, and flexibility. Merchandise is delivered to each Zara retail location twice a week. (Merchandise is airfreighted to U.S. stores.) This fast and almost continuous replenishment concept reduces the need for significant in-store inventories and the possibility of clothes going out of fashion.

A major factor in Zara's ability to react quickly to changes in customer buying is its use of information and technology. Salespeople in each retail location use handheld computers to record buyer preferences and trends. This information along with actual sales data is transmitted daily through the Internet to Zara's headquarters in Spain.

In addition, unlike its major competitors, which outsource manufacturing, Zara produces most of its merchandise in its state-of-the-art factory in Spain. Products are designed, produced, and delivered to its stores in as little as two weeks after they have appeared for the first time in a fashion show. (In contrast, competitors such as the Gap and H&M require between five weeks' and five months' lead time to fill orders from their retail operations.)

Source: William Echikson, "The Mark of Zara," *Business Week,* May 29, 2000, pp. 98–100; Jane M. Folpe, "Zara Has a Made-to-Order Plan for Success," *Fortune,* September 4, 2000, p. 80; Stryker McGuire, "Fast Fashion; How a Secretive Spanish Tycoon Has Defied the Postwar Tide of Globalization, Bringing Factory Jobs from Latin America and Asia Back to Europe," *Newsweek,* September 17, 2001, p. 36; and Richard Heller, "Galician Beauty," *Forbes,* May 28, 2001, p. 98.

manner will also reduce long lines at Registry locations and hopefully reduce annual operating expenses.[4]

A note of caution is necessary, however, when contemplating the introduction of totally automated services. First, as we have already noted, some segments of the market are not totally comfortable with automation. In addition, while automation can usually do a good job performing routine transactions, sometimes complex and highly customized transactions can be resolved only with the customer interacting directly with a knowledgeable individual.

Support for Labor   Technology in the form of automation can also be used in service operations to perform repetitive, time-consuming tasks. The use of technology in this manner not only increases worker productivity, but also reduces or eliminates errors, while at the same time assuring the delivery of a more consistent product to the customer. In some instances, technology can also increase performance in the form of faster service.

For example, in many fast-food restaurants, timed drink dispensers do not require servers to stand by the machine holding the button. Instead, a quick push of the button begins the flow of beverage permitting the server to assemble the rest of the order while the drink is being poured. Other examples of technology used in fast-food operations include a conveyor belt broiler at Burger King restaurants that assures a consistently cooked hamburger, again without the worker being continuously present during the cooking operation, and deep-fat fryers with timers that automatically lift the french fries out of the oil when they have finished cooking.

Technology in the form of computerized order-entry devices allows waitstaff to place orders in the kitchen without having to walk across the restaurant. Instead of having to make two trips to the kitchen—one to place the order and another to pick it up when it is ready—servers are now only required to make a single trip to pick up the food when it is ready.

[4] Mark Maremont, "No Waiting at This DMV," *Business Week,* August 19, 1996.

E-Services

Defining the Communication Network Environment

With the rapid growth in e-services, a new set of terms has emerged to describe the different types of networks through which information can flow. Each of these networks is defined by the type of users who have access to it. There are currently three major categories for e-services: (*a*) Internet, (*b*) intranet, and (*c*) extranet. A fourth type of network currently being used is electronic data interchange, or EDI, which is really a specialized form of extranet. Exhibit 3.4 illustrates how these various networks link an organization with its customers, suppliers, workers, and the general public.

Internet

An **Internet** network has the fewest access restrictions. Firms use the Internet primarily when dealing with the general public. For firms that sell directly to consumers, such as Amazon.com (books, etc.) and Expedia.com (discounted airline tickets, hotel rooms, etc.) the Internet is the communication network that customers use to access these firms' websites, to purchase goods and services, and to access general information about a firm. This type of website can also be used to disseminate news releases and to provide contacts within the firm, as well as directions about how to obtain additional information.

Intranet

An **intranet** is a network that operates only internally within an organization. As such, only those people who work for the organization have access to its intranet. Often the intranet is used to communicate among employees and as means for management to disseminate information quickly. For example, both Wal-Mart and FedEx have intranets that provide employees at all locations with up-to-date information on new procedures, changes in company policies, performance measurements, and recognition of outstanding employees. The FedEx intranet even includes its own television station that broadcasts company-related news 24 hours a day.

Extranet

An **extranet** is a network that allows specifically defined external sources, be they individuals or organizations, to have limited access to a firm. For example, an extranet will link

EXHIBIT 3.4

The Role of the Internet, Intranet, Extranet, and EDI in an Organization

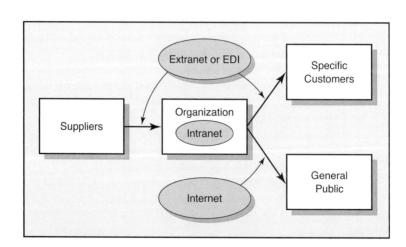

customers with an approved set of suppliers. Organizations use an extranet to share classified or highly sensitive data with their business partners. For example, through an extranet, Procter & Gamble has access to Wal-Mart's sales and inventory data. By sharing such data, these two firms both benefit through lower costs of production and distribution as well as improved levels of service to the consumer.

Electronic Data Interchange (EDI) **Electronic data interchange (EDI)** is a type of extranet that permits the electronic exchange of data between organizations in highly specified formats. Some types of transactions that can be done through EDI include (*a*) requests for quotations, (*b*) purchase orders, (*c*) acknowledgments and confirmations, (*d*) invoicing, and (*e*) payments.

While EDI is very fast and efficient, it has several shortcomings. First, companies must painstakingly link their operations to a specific EDI software and then synchronize protocols (such as which version of the software they use) with the firms with which they want to conduct business. The format for EDI is very rigid and often does not adapt well to new applications. In addition, EDI moves data in batches, so there is a time delay from when the data are sent to when the batch is received (although it is still much faster than non-electronic methods). For example, at Boston Scientific's Customer Fulfillment Center in Quincy, Massachusetts, incoming EDI orders from customers are accumulated in batches and downloaded for processing every 30 minutes.

In addition, EDI transmissions typically occur through third parties such as General Electric Information Systems that are referred to as a **value-added network (VAN).** The cost of using a VAN can be expensive, often $10,000 or more per month for medium to large companies.

Because of the many shortcomings of EDI, the extranet will most likely replace EDI eventually as a medium of communication. This is already happening with many firms that are now connected electronically with their suppliers through an extranet. These suppliers need only an extranet connection and a Web browser instead of the dedicated EDI software and connections to a VAN.

Types of E-Services

E-services have been divided into several broad categories that are defined by the types of individuals and/or organizations that provide and use these services. Three of these major categories are (*a*) business-to-consumer (B2C), (*b*) consumer-to-consumer (C2C), and (*c*) business-to-business (B2B). E-services that involve a government agency are called either government-to-business (G2B) or government-to-consumer (G2C).

Within these broad service categories, several different types of services may be provided. We present five of these. Some firms provide only one type of these services, while others may provide several. For example, an e-tailer will often also provide customer support.

E-tailers (Goods and Services)

E-tailers are firms that provide goods and services through the Internet. Pure e-tailers conduct business exclusively through the Internet, such as Amazon.com or E*Trade. These services typically have competitors in brick-and-mortar establishments. In many cases, however, e-tail operations are part of a larger organization that also has brick-and-mortar locations, such as Barnes & Noble or Wal-Mart. Some of these firms (often called *bricks and clicks,* or *clicks and mortar*), such as the Gap, also provide access to their websites at their brick-and-mortar locations, thereby making the difference between the two even fuzzier.

The major challenge for pure e-tailers that sell goods is to have the necessary infrastructure in place to efficiently and quickly deliver goods to customers. The lack of such infrastructures was evident during the 1999 holiday season when many customers who had made purchases through the Internet didn't receive their deliveries until well into January 2000. Some e-tailers, such as Amazon.com, have built their own distribution infrastructures, while others have partnered with established brick-and-mortar service operations.

E-tailers that offer services typically do not need the supply chain infrastructure required of those that provide goods. This allows faster entry into the market, significantly lower investment costs, and consequently a quicker return on investment. For example, the online travel industry is one of the first e-service industries to generate profits.

A major challenge for pure e-tailers is the lack of tangibility. With a brick-and-mortar operation, the customer has a place to go for service or to voice a complaint. There is nothing more frustrating for a customer than to wait endlessly on the phone for customer service, as happened during the 1999 holiday season.

Equally important for e-tailers is how to differentiate themselves in the marketplace. Without differentiation, these services offer only commodities and must compete solely on price. This translates into very small profit margins, which may not sustain growth.

Customer Support

This type of e-service provides customer service in a wide variety of forms. At FedEx, for example, customers can track the location of their packages through the Internet. Customer support can also take the form of chat rooms, which provide a forum for customers, or a Web page that addresses frequently asked questions (FAQs). Many firms combine their e-service customer support activities with their call center activities. With proper design, such operations can provide fast service and be highly efficient at the same time (as described in Chapter 15.)

As with e-tailers, some firms focus solely on providing customer support, to other firms, while other customer support activities can be part of a larger organization.

A major challenge for customer support services is to persuade customers, in a positive manner, to switch from requesting customer support through call centers, which are time-dependent and involve an actual person, to the Internet, which is non-time-dependent and is therefore more efficient.

Network Providers

Network providers are e-services that provide an opportunity for buyers and sellers to exchange goods and services. Electronic marketplaces are one form of network provider. These marketplaces, which are usually B2B, typically focus on a particular commodity such as chemicals, plastic, or steel. By using these marketplaces, buyers can place their order requirements on a single website and receive several quotations within hours.

Such marketplaces efficiently link buyers and sellers and provide advantages for both parties. From the buyer's perspective, less time is required to obtain quotes from many vendors, and the efficiency of the marketplace translates into significant savings. From the seller's perspective, the marketplace eliminates the need for a distributor or salesperson (an example of disintermediation), thereby reducing costs. These savings can either be passed on to the customer or go directly to the bottom line as additional profits.

Firms that conduct auctions are another example of network providers. Auctions can be between businesses and consumers (B2C), such as Priceline.com, which auctions airline tickets and hotel rooms, or between consumers (C2C), such as eBay, which will auction almost anything. Again, these firms provide networks that link a large number of buyers with a large number of sellers, thereby creating a very efficient marketplace. Intermediaries are eliminated except for the firm providing the network, which charges a percentage of an item's selling price.

Information Providers

E-service businesses that focus on providing information are referred to as **infomediaries.** Some firms focus exclusively on providing information, while others provide information as part of the value added to their core business.

These firms often provide information on several levels. For example, Hoover.com provides information on three levels. The first level, which is free, is general financial information about companies. The second level adds value by segmenting or sorting the information to fit the needs of individual users who pay a fee for this service. The third level involves custom searches that are designed specifically to meet the needs of an individual customer.

Companies that provide information as part of their total offering often also provide chat rooms where customers can discuss issues relevant to the focus of the firm. For example, Magicmaman.com, an e-service firm in Paris, provides a chat room where parents can discuss problems they are having with their young children and how some parents have dealt with them (either successfully or unsuccessfully).

Application Service Providers (ASPs)

Application service providers (ASPs) provide remote services to customers. For example, an ASP accounting firm will have on its own server the most up-to-date accounting software package that reflects the latest changes in the tax laws. Customers log into the accounting firm's website and use that accounting package to prepare their financial statements. With an accounting ASP, customers no longer need to buy a new software package every time the tax law changes.

A major challenge for ASPs is to convince customers that they are not fly-by-night operations and will be in business for the long term. Along with demonstrating the financial strength to survive in the long term, ASPs must also convince customers that they provide reliable services and that they can be trusted with sensitive customer data. Finally, customers must have confidence in the reliability of the network over which they will connect to their ASPs.

Technology-Related Issues

The integration of new technologies into an organization requires a significant amount of training and support for both workers and customers to reap the full benefits. The lack of proper training and support will, in many instances, not only fail to yield the expected improvements in performance and/or productivity, but also could prove disastrous financially as frustrated workers quit and unhappy customers take their business elsewhere.

Overcoming Barriers to Use

As new technologies become available, barriers often prevent customers from using them, and managers need to be aware of this. Such barriers can significantly hinder the organization's growth. One barrier is the "fear of the unknown," which is often associated with new technologies, the best example being purchasing of goods and services over the Internet for the first time. Because there are no tangibles associated with the firm, customers may be concerned about misuse of their credit cards and whether or not they will actually receive the goods or services purchased.

Another barrier is lack of knowledge on the part of the consumer using the service. This is especially true for self-service operations as well as for those services that use new technologies. Self-service gas stations provide a good example of this, as there are many individuals who still do not know how to operate a gas pump.

ATMs provide a good example of a service involving a new technology where the customers must both overcome their fear of the unknown as well as learn how to properly use them.

Training and Support

Significant up-front training must be built into the overall new technology process. This training is often required for both workers and customers. Failure to provide proper training will lead to inefficient operations and frustration. In addition, both workers and customers must have the necessary technical support when questions arise and/or equipment malfunctions.

Worker Training

Workers are often required to develop additional skills when a new technology is introduced. These new skills can be developed through training classes that not only describe the use of the technology but also simulate its use. This allows workers to become familiar with the new equipment and to debug the process before actually using it in the presence of a customer.

Customer Training

Customers may also be required to undergo some degree of training when the new technology interacts directly with them, as is often the case with services. Depending on the type of technology and the level of sophistication required to use it, customer training can vary from a simple pamphlet describing how to use the new equipment to attending classes that carefully document the proper use of the equipment.

Summary

Technology continues to play a significant role in the design and delivery of services. With the constant introduction of state-of-the-art technologies, this trend will most likely continue into the foreseeable future. However, service managers must realize that the adoption of technology is not a simple undertaking and must be carefully planned. In the past, many service operations looked to technology primarily to help them increase productivity. However, there are several additional reasons companies elect to incorporate new technologies into their processes, such as building stronger relationships with customers and improving their overall performance by providing better customer service.

To successfully integrate technology into an organization, service managers need to ensure that the applications of the technology are strategically aligned with the organization's goals. Failure to do so can result in significant expenditures in technology that reap no benefits and/or dissatisfied customers who take their business elsewhere.

Finally, the installation of new technology must be accompanied by the proper technical support. Sufficient time must be allocated in the initial start-up phase to provide proper training to both workers and, where necessary, to customers. When purchasing new technology, the service manager must ensure that there is compatibility between the desired technology and the overall long-term goals of the firm.

Key Terms

application service provider (ASP): firms that provide remote services to customers. *(p. 63)*
asynchronous transactions: transactions in which there is a delay in time with respect to the communication between the parties involved. *(p. 55)*
disintermediation: the elimination of intermediate steps or organizations. *(p. 55)*
electronic data interchange (EDI): the electronic exchange of data in highly specified formats that occurs between organizations. *(p. 61)*
extranet: an electronic network that allows specific external sources to have limited access to the firm. *(p. 60)*
infomediary: e-service businesses that focus primarily on providing information. *(p. 63)*
Internet: a worldwide electronic network of more than 70 million computers. *(p. 60)*
intranet: an electronic network that operates only internally within an organization. *(p. 60)*

synchronous transactions: transactions that occur in real time without any time delays, usually between individuals. *(p. 55)*

value-added network (VAN): a third-party service that is used in conjunction with EDI to provide a link between customers and suppliers. *(p. 61)*

Review and Discussion Questions

1. What are the different ways in which infomediaries add value?
2. Visit any of the following services and identify the various ways technology is changing how they are being delivered.
   a. Retail store.
   b. Restaurant.
   c. Bank office.
   d. Supermarket.
3. How can information add value to a good or a service? Provide an example.
4. Explain the differences between the Internet, an extranet, and an intranet.
5. Why are firms moving away from EDI toward extranets?
6. Identify three services you believe would be good candidates for ASPs. Why?
7. Why is it important for a firm to align its technology with its goals? Provide an example of what can happen when this alignment doesn't occur.

Internet Assignment

Visit the website of a major airline, such as American, Northwest, or Delta, and compare the different ways you can obtain information on a flight between two major cities. Then visit the website of an on-line travel agency such as Expedia.com, Orbitz.com, or Travelocity.com and do a similar comparison. What are the advantages of using an airline's website? What are the advantages of using an online travel agency's website? What are the advantages of ordering airline tickets online versus buying them through your local travel agent, who is located in a nearby shopping mall?

Selected Bibliography

Borus, Amy. "A Hotel That Clicks with Guests." *Business Week Online,* September 18, 2000.

Brin, Dinah W. "Check It Out!" *The Middlesex News,* August 11, 1996.

Davis, Stan. *Future Perfect.* Reading, MA: Addison-Wesley, 1987.

Gale, Bradley T. *Managing Customer Value.* New York: The Free Press, 1994.

Fitzsimmons, James A., and Mona J. Fitzsimmons. *Service Management for Competitive Advantage.* New York: McGraw-Hill, 1994.

Judge, Paul C. "Customer Service: EMC Corp." *Fast Company,* June, 2001, pp. 138–45.

Lovelock, Christopher. *Product Plus: How Product + Service = Competitive Advantage.* New York: McGraw-Hill, 1994, pp. 60–61.

Maremont, Mark. "No Waiting at This DMV." *Business Week,* August 19, 1996.

Ostrofsky, Ken. "Mrs. Fields' Cookies." *Harvard Business School Case,* no. 9-189-056, 1989.

Quinn, J. B. "Technology in Services: Past Myths and Future Challenges." In *Technology in Services: Policies for Growth, Trade and Employment.* Washington, DC: National Academy Press, 1988.

Quinn, J. B., and M. N. Bailey. "Information Technology: Increasing Productivity in Services." *Academy of Management Executive* 8, no. 3 (1994).

Richman, Tom. "Mrs. Fields' Secret Ingredient." *Inc.,* October 1987.

Roach, S. S. "Services under Siege—The Restructuring Imperative," *Harvard Business Review,* September–October 1991.

Scott, Karyl. "EMC Shores Up Its Offense." *InformationWeek,* October 2, 2000, pp. 72–82.

Zellner, Wendy. "Where the Net Delivers: Travel." *Business Week,* June 11, 2001, pp. 142–44.

CHAPTER FOUR

The Integration of Manufacturing and Service

Learning Objectives

- Demonstrate the importance of aligning the goods and services components of the product bundle.

- Present several frameworks that provide insights for integrating manufacturing and services.

- Introduce alternative approaches for using services to create value for manufacturing firms.

- Illustrate how services can add value to goods.

GE's Diagnostic Medical Systems Self-Diagnose Potential Failures Before They Occur

Stephen McBrady / PhotoEdit

A call comes into the customer service center at General Electric's Medical Systems–Europe (GEMSE), which is located in Buc, France, a suburb of Paris. However, this call is not from a customer, but instead is from one of GEMSE's own medical systems, an MRI (magnetic resonance imaging) system, which assists doctors in the diagnosis of patient illnesses. The MRI, using a system referred to as *telemaintenance,* is informing the call center through built-in self-diagnostic equipment that it has identified a potential defect in a component, and that this component should be replaced before it actually fails. A technician is dispatched to the site of the MRI with the replacement part, and the first time the customer is even aware that there is a potential problem is when the technician shows up at the door. The part is replaced and, with virtually no downtime, the MRI continues to provide images to doctors to assist them in their diagnoses.

MRI systems are very sophisticated medical imaging equipment that help hospitals perform a wide variety of diagnostic procedures critical for their patients. The downtime of such equipment disrupts the hospital organization by requiring patients to be rescheduled and/or seeking alternative methods for diagnosing patients in emergencies, both of which result in unnecessary additional costs. From a medical and cost perspective, it is therefore very important to maximize equipment uptime. This service that GEMSE provides to its customers adds significant value to its medical systems, thereby providing GEMSE with an advantage over competitors that also make high-quality diagnostic medical systems.

The Customer's Perspective

What do you look for when you go shopping for a computer? On what criteria do you base your decision? Do you think about the product's reliability and durability? Probably not, as you assume the top brands all make very reliable and durable products. Do you look at price? Definitely, especially when comparing the actual physical products. However, if the quality of the top-name computers is comparable and they are evenly priced, how do you decide which one to buy?

If you look at the advertisements for Gateway's personal computers or General Electric's kitchen appliances, the focus is not on the quality of the products themselves, but rather on the services that are provided as part of the overall package when you buy these products. Why? Because, as noted above, you consider the high quality of these products to be a given, as is the quality of their competitors' products (Dell, IBM, and Apple for Gateway; Amana and Maytag for GE). In such highly competitive markets, the goods themselves are often viewed as commodities. As a result, the difference in the prices of these commodity-like products is usually minimal.

With such a wide variety of high-quality, comparably priced products to choose from, you look to other criteria for deciding which one to buy. For many customers, the primary decision criterion is often the additional service that distinguishes one product from others.

Managerial Issues

Through a combination of factors that include the Internet, the lowering of international trade barriers, and a trend toward lower transportation costs, customers now have a much wider variety of high-quality products to choose from. This trend toward a single global economy has created a hypercompetitive environment, shifting the power from the producers to the buyers. Customers no longer are forced to buy only from local or regional manufacturers; instead they can buy products from virtually every corner of the world. This significant increase in competition has forced firms to look for new ways to differentiate themselves in the marketplace.

One strategy that many companies have adopted for addressing this growing competition is to constantly introduce new products. In 1995, for example, 70 percent of the sales at Hewlett-Packard's Medical Products Group in Andover, Massachusetts, were from products that were less than two years old.[1] This constant introduction of new products has resulted in shorter product life cycles. As a consequence, many products now reach their maturity or *commodity stage* much sooner than they did in the past. When purchasing commodities, customers tend to buy primarily on price, because products of competing firms have similar primary operating characteristics and features. In such an environment, profit margins shrink significantly.

As we learned in Chapter 1, the vast majority of products that we purchase today are actually a **bundle of benefits** consisting of both a goods component and a services component (see Exhibit 1.4). Products that consist primarily of the goods component, such as automobiles and clothing, are usually referred to as goods, while products that consist primarily of services, such as a dinner at a restaurant or a financial transaction at a bank, are typically referred to as services.

To maintain high profit margins, as well as to separate their firms from the competition, managers, particularly those in manufacturing, now look more and more to the service component of the bundle. Providing high-quality goods is no longer the sole criterion for purchasing. Rather, a high-quality good is now viewed, in Terry Hill's terms, as an **order qualifier,**[2] or the minimum criterion for a product to even be considered. The **order winners,** or the criteria by which the customer ultimately decides to buy, are often the services that are included as part of the product bundle.

In other words, because of today's intense competition, the quality and performance characteristics of a physical product are taken as given. This does not mean that customers are willing to accept poor-performing products. In fact, just the opposite is true. Customers demand high-performance, state-of-the-art products that are of high quality as the minimum criterion for purchase. Managers must therefore develop new ways to differentiate their products in the marketplace, and that often means providing services as part of the overall product offering.

The Increasing Role of Service in Manufacturing

The growing battle for customers can be attributed, in large part, to the significant increase in international competition over the past several decades. For example, in the late 1960s, only 7 percent of all U.S. companies were exposed to international competition, but by the late 1980s, this figure had grown to more than 70 percent.[3] The formation of economic trading blocs, such as the European Union (EU) and the North American Free Trade Agreement (NAFTA), has further accelerated the growth in international competition.

In this highly competitive business environment, manufacturing firms need to find new and innovative ways to stay ahead of the competition. To maintain and even increase profit margins, many manufacturing firms now focus on services to obtain a competitive advantage in the marketplace. This increasing emphasis on services can be attributed, in some degree, to the advances in information technology, especially the explosive development and growth of the Internet.

As seen in Exhibit 4.1, the trend toward greater emphasis on services applies to both goods and services. For example, Internet-based retailers (or *e-tailers*) add more value than their traditional brick-and-mortar counterparts, by delivering products to your house,

---

[1] Mark M. Davis, Nicholas J. Aquilano, and Richard B. Chase, *Fundamentals of Operations Management,* 3rd ed. (Burr Ridge, IL: Irwin/McGraw-Hill, 1999).

[2] Terry Hill, *Manufacturing Strategy: Text and Cases,* 3rd ed. (Burr Ridge, IL: Irwin/McGraw-Hill, 2000), pp. 49–85.

[3] S. C. Gwynne, "The Long Haul," *Time,* September 25, 1992, pp. 34–38.

EXHIBIT 4.1
Increased Emphasis on Services

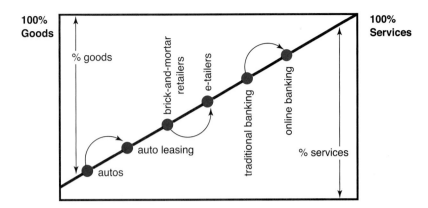

thereby eliminating the need for you to go to the retail store. Similarly, the value added by online banking through the Internet eliminates the need to visit your bank's branch office for many types of transactions.

The value added by services can be seen in virtually every industry, from warranties on automobiles and appliances to customer support in personal computers and software. In fact, in some cases, service is even replacing the need to purchase the product. Examples here include equipment leasing, software licensing, automobile leasing, and video rentals.

Added services create a win–win situation. From the customer's perspective, the service adds value, thereby creating a competitive advantage for the firm. In addition, the profit margin for the service component is very often significantly greater than that for the goods component.

Defining Levels of Added Service: Little "s" and Big "S"

There are several ways to integrate service with a manufactured product. As a starting point for understanding how services can be successfully integrated, we first distinguish between two major levels of providing services: what we define as little "s," or operational applications of services, and big "S," or strategic approaches to services. Both are important to an organization, although the focus of this chapter is on big "S" services, because that is where leading-edge firms are currently focusing their efforts and where the managerial challenges currently exist.

Little "s" or Operational Services

Little "s" or operations-related services are provided primarily within the operations function of an organization. These types of services are usually applied to existing products to make them more attractive to customers. As a result, they don't usually require the major resource commitments that are associated with long-range strategies that typically require cross-functional coordination within an organization.

We present here two broad categories of little "s" services: (*a*) availability and (*b*) customization. Time and location can be viewed as two components of availability, and customization is an extension of the concept of process flexibility that is externally oriented toward the customer rather than internally focused on the production process.

Availability

Speed of delivery is an important factor in buying a product. When it comes to delivery, the faster the better. But short delivery times are not the only way in which firms can enhance their value to customers. Companies that can serve their customers when they want to be served also have a competitive advantage in the marketplace. That is why more and more firms are offering $24 \times 7 \times 52$ service (that is, they are open 24 hours a day, seven days a week, 52 weeks a year). For example, Fidelity Brokerage Services provides such service to its customers through a combination of automated Internet services and telephone access to brokers and advisers. ATMs are another good example. In addition to being available 24 hours a day, ATMs are conveniently located in shopping malls, airports, and supermarkets, thereby further increasing their availability to customers.

Customization

Customization means modifying the standard product offering to meet the needs of each individual customer. To accomplish this, the manufacturing process must be sufficiently flexible to accommodate a wide variety of individual customer specifications. In addition, customized products, by their very nature, are made to order rather than made to stock, as is the case with standard products. Dell Computers provides an excellent example of a firm that provides customized products (and with short delivery times too!).

Big "S" or Strategic Services

Strategic services are defined as those services that require coordination across organizational boundaries. These boundaries can exist between functions within a strategic business unit (SBU), between SBUs, or even between independent organizations. As an example of coordination between functions within an organization, consider product redesign, where the service becomes an embedded feature of the product. These embedded services typically require coordination among the engineering, manufacturing, and customer support functions, as is the case with Honeywell's Airplane Information Management System, which integrates the aircraft's operating systems with microprocessors and software or GE's telemaintenance system described in the opening vignette. Other examples of strategic services that cross functional and even organizational boundaries include Boeing Capital's financing the purchase of Boeing aircraft and Coca-Cola's decision to move downstream toward the customer by taking over the distribution function. These types of integrated services are viewed as being strategic because they have significant long-term implications, and consequently require a major organizational commitment.

To understand how service can be successfully integrated with manufacturing, we present here three established frameworks: (*a*) the service factory, (*b*) the customer's activity cycle, and (*c*) downstream services. We also introduce some new approaches that provide additional insights into how this integration can be successfully accomplished.

The Service Factory

Dick Chase and David Garvin were two of the first scholars to recognize that manufacturing firms can use service to obtain a competitive advantage in the marketplace. They identified several roles that a manufacturing firm could play by having a **service factory** that would provide services to enhance the products being sold. Those roles are (*a*) consultant, (*b*) showroom, and (*c*) dispatcher.[4]

[4] Richard B. Chase and David Garvin, "The Service Factory," *Harvard Business Review* 67, no. 4 (July–August 1989), pp. 61–69.

Consultant

In the role of consultant, a manufacturing firm can utilize the expertise of its factory workers to address customer-related issues, especially with respect to problem solving. Allowing factory personnel to work directly with customers provides an opportunity for them to become part of the customer's design team, enabling the manufacturer to better understand how the customer's end product is used and to suggest alternative, and often more economical, solutions.

Some firms even have toll-free phone numbers that go directly to the factory floor. With a minimum of training in telephone etiquette, factory workers are able to answer many of the customers' questions and, in the process, suggest new ways for using their products, or even suggest new products that better address the needs of their customers. This concept can be expanded to include B2B situations where factory workers visit customers' operations to better understand how their products are used, allowing the workers to offer more insightful suggestions for improvement.

Showroom

As a showroom, the factory floor can be used to demonstrate to customers the technical expertise and the quality of the processes that are used to manufacture goods or components. However, three things are necessary for the factory to operate successfully as a showroom. First, marketing and manufacturing personnel need to work closely together to understand customers' expectations and then to fulfill these expectations. Second, factory workers and their supervisors must be trained to communicate with customers and even to make formal presentations to them. Finally, the layout of the factory floor must permit stopping points for visitors and perhaps even audiovisual aids to emphasize those aspects of the production process that provide the greatest value added for customers. For example, as part of the tours conducted at Peugeot's automotive assembly plant in Poissy, France, visitors wear headphones so they can clearly hear the tour guide over the noise on the factory floor. Hewlett-Packard's facility near Stuttgart, Germany, has wide-screen televisions located throughout the factory to describe the different operations.

Dispatcher

In the role of dispatcher, the factory can provide the link to after-sales service support. This is especially important for new products where unforeseen problems often occur. A firm's ability to quickly repair or replace defective equipment can be a competitive advantage. In addition, information collected in the field can be fed directly back into the product design and manufacturing processes to reduce future problems.

To successfully adopt the role of dispatcher, however, requires a significant amount of flexibility from the manufacturing processes. Customer demands must be anticipated and planned for so that they can be responded to quickly and without any major disruption in production.

The Customer's Activity Cycle

A second framework that provides insight into how services can provide manufacturers with a competitive advantage is the **customer's activity cycle (CAC).** Sandra Vandermerwe introduced the concept of the customer's activity cycle (CAC), which is presented in Exhibit 4.2.[5] According to her, the larger the portion of the CAC that a firm participates

[5] Sandra Vandermerwe, *From Tin Soldiers to Russian Dolls: Creating Added Value through Services* (Oxford, England: Butterworth-Heinemann, 1993).

EXHIBIT 4.2
Customer's Activity Cycle

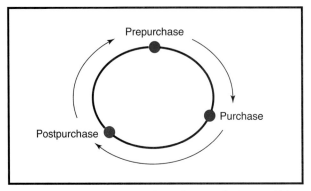

Source: Sandra Vandermerwe, *From Tin Soldiers to Russian Dolls: Creating Added Value through Services* (Oxford, England: Butterworth-Heinemann), 1993.

in by providing related services, the greater the competitive advantage that firm has in the marketplace. As part of the overall CAC concept, Vandermerwe suggests that firms shift their emphasis from selling only goods to their customers to providing their customers with solutions to their problems, that is, to offer services.

Activities within the Customer's Activity Cycle

The three major components of the CAC are the: (*a*) prepurchase activities, (*b*) purchase activities, and (*c*) postpurchase activities.

Prepurchase Activities

At this stage of the CAC, the customer is primarily concerned about "what to do." However, for many purchases today this question is too complex or strategic in nature to be answered by one individual or buyer within the customer's organization. As a result, prepurchase activities often involve individuals from several functional areas such as engineering and manufacturing, as well as individuals from the suppliers' organizations. For example, at the individual purchase level, customers wishing to buy a computer may not know how much speed or memory they need to conduct the tasks that they are likely to perform. During the prepurchase stage, the firm should listen to their customers' descriptions of how they think they will use the computer and how much they can afford to spend and help them to match those needs with a computer that will be both appropriate for their work and within their budgets. Similarly, corporate customers may know that they need certain components for their products, but may not be as knowledgeable as the supplier about how to best design those components for both effective performance and efficient use of the purchasing budget. Their suppliers also need to listen to the customer's needs and to work with individuals within the customer's organization in choosing among alternatives, or designing a new solution.

Purchase Activities

The purchase activities center around the actual sale of the product. Here the firm's activities focus on executing the decision that resulted from the prepurchase activities. These include processing the purchase order, arranging financing (if necessary), and actually delivering the product to the customer.

EXHIBIT 4.3
Examples
of Activities within
the Customer's
Activity Cycle

		Hendricks Voeders	SKF
Prepurchase:		Managing breeding environment	Advice on bearing management
		Arranging financing	Inventory management
		Advising on stock	Warehousing
Purchase:		Delivering feed	Delivering bearings
		Managing nutrient intake	Training
		Managing health conditions	Mounting bearings
Postpurchase:		Delivery to slaughterhouse	Repair and replacement
		Delivery to processors	Maintenance and support
		Distribution to retailers	Environmental management

Postpurchase Activities

Postpurchase activities focus on "keeping things going." These include the maintenance and repair of products that are under warranty or have extended service contracts. Emphasis here is on ensuring that the customer's investment in the product is very successful. These activities also include looking to the future, to the next CAC. For example, the Foxboro Company has a customer friend program where each customer is assigned to an individual in manufacturing who continues to stay in contact with the customer on a regular basis after the product has been purchased.

Applying the Customer's Activity Cycle

Two examples of firms that have successfully applied the CAC framework are Hendrix Voeders, a Dutch producer of animal feed, and SKF, a Swedish ball-bearing manufacturer.

Today, Hendrix Voeders is no longer in the business of providing only livestock feed to pig farmers in Holland (that is, goods); it also provides a wide range of services to these farmers, including consulting on pig breeding, nutrition management, delivery to the slaughterhouse, and distribution of pork products to retail outlets. Similarly, SKF in Sweden no longer produces only ball bearings for its aftermarket or replacement business. It also now provides advice to its customers on spare parts management, training, and installation, and it suggests good preventive maintenance practices that will extend the life of the bearings.[6]

Some of the activities that these two firms perform during each of the three stages of the CAC are presented in Exhibit 4.3. These two companies exemplify the trend among today's world-class businesses of turning to services to obtain a competitive advantage in the marketplace. Where once manufacturing was considered to be totally separate from services, now both are considered to be essential, and they must be properly integrated and aligned for a firm to succeed.

Downstream Services

More recently, Richard Wise and Peter Baumgartner have developed a framework that encourages manufacturing firms to look downstream from the production process to identify services that can be integrated with their physical products. Their rationale for this approach is that the market for product-related services is significantly larger than it is for the

[6] Ibid.

products themselves. For example, in both the automobile and personal computer markets, the sales of product-related services are five times greater than the sales of the actual products. In addition, as cited earlier, the profit margins for these services are significantly larger than they are for the products alone.[7]

Wise and Baumgartner have identified four types of services that manufacturers can provide downstream: (*a*) embedded services, (*b*) comprehensive services, (*c*) integrated solutions, and (*d*) distribution control.

Embedded Services

Embedded services consist of specific functions that are part of the product itself. For example, Honeywell, as mentioned earlier, has developed an Airplane Information Management System (AIMS) that provides a series of self-diagnostic tests on an airplane's equipment. Previously these tests were performed manually by airline mechanics. Embedding the diagnostic service in the product enables problems to be identified early and corrected before passengers and equipment are endangered.

Comprehensive Services

With comprehensive services, the manufactured product is usually "married" to additional services, which makes the purchase of the product easier for the customer. For example, the purchase of a locomotive from GE Transportation Systems is facilitated when GE Capital is willing to provide the financing. For similar reasons, Boeing Capital finances the purchase of Boeing Aircraft. For individuals, GMAC Financial Services and Ford Credit provide similar financial services to facilitate the purchase of their automobiles.

Integrated Solutions

Integrated solutions focus on combining products and services into a seamless offering that addresses a specific customer requirement. For example, Nokia, the Finnish manufacturer of cell phones, has used this approach with telephone carriers, going beyond simply selling cell phones to addressing all the equipment and service needs of the cellular carriers. So in addition to providing carriers with a wide variety of products that include handsets, transmission equipment, and switches, Nokia also assists carriers in planning and managing their networks to meet local zoning requirements for transmission tower construction and provides maintenance and technical support. Carriers can purchase totally compatible products and services from a single source, saving them the time it would require to coordinate among a variety of suppliers—and thereby saving them considerable money!

Distribution Control

With distribution control, the manufacturing firm moves downstream in the value chain to assume responsibility for product distribution that was previously performed by an independent firm. For example, Coca-Cola has been taking over the bottling and distribution of Coke products, activities that were previously performed by independent bottlers.

Additional Approaches to Integrating Service and Manufacturing

The three previous frameworks for integrating services into manufacturing firms all focus on specific areas. Chase and Garvin focused on the use of the manufacturing facility as a means

---

[7] Richard Wise and Peter Baumgartner, "Go Downstream: The New Profit Imperative in Manufacturing," *Harvard Business Review* 77, no. 5 (September–October 1999), pp. 133–41).

of providing service. Vandermerwe focused almost exclusively on the customer activities that occur before, during, and after the purchase of the product. Wise and Baumgartner preferred to look only downstream from the production process for ways to introduce service.

Four additional and different approaches to integrating services with manufacturing are presented here. Some of these strategies have been directly adopted from service firms. As noted among the previous frameworks, some overlap also exists. These four approaches are:

- Demonstration of knowledge and expertise.

- Improved product performance.

- Customer training.

- Expanded product capabilities.

Demonstration of Knowledge and Expertise

As Chase and Garvin pointed out in their service factory, firms can achieve a competitive advantage by demonstrating their technical knowledge and expertise in the production process. By showing customers the steps involved in the production process and how quality is ensured at each of these steps, customers obtain a level of comfort, especially when the specific details of the inner workings of the product itself are difficult to comprehend, as is often the case with sophisticated high-technology products.

In addition, when customers tour the manufacturing facility, they can be introduced to new products and options for existing ones. EMC Corp. in Hopkinton, Massachusetts, a leading manufacturer of electronic storage equipment, understands the benefits of providing plant tours to potential as well as existing customers. The company conducts more than 1,000 tours a year at its manufacturing facilities in Massachusetts. Visitors are impressed by the extensive product testing at each stage of the process, ensuring that a highly reliable product is shipped to customers. Employees are also readily available throughout the plant to answer questions. The plant tours have proved to be very successful, with a majority of the potential customers buying EMC products, often more than they had initially planned.

For similar reasons, the Foxboro Company also encourages both current and potential customers alike to visit its manufacturing facilities in Foxboro, Massachusetts. Visitors to the manufacturing facility are immediately greeted by a display showing the many awards that Foxboro has won over the years, including the Shingo Prize, the Massachusetts' Quality Award and *Industry Week*'s Plant of the Year Award. During tours of the manufacturing processes, employees often take time from their work to talk to visitors about specific projects they have worked on to improve the quality of the product and/or to make the processes more efficient. These employee presentations again reinforce knowledge and skill about the processes and products.

The benefits of demonstrating knowledge and expertise are not limited to high-technology products. Green Giant of Minneapolis, Minnesota, which produces a wide variety of high-quality canned and frozen food products, had difficulty penetrating the Japanese markets. Only after Green Giant invited Japanese food distributors to visit its production facilities in Minnesota, where the company demonstrated the quality of both its processes and the resulting products, was it able to successfully conduct business in Japan.[8]

Improved Product Performance

Through technology, firms can now provide improved product performance either by anticipating and correcting potential problems before they occur or by reducing response time. This service characteristic is especially important to firms buying products requiring significant capital investments, which translates into costly downtime. It is also important where product reliability is critical, as with financial institutions and state lotteries. These types of services can also be viewed as imbedded services.

For example, both GE Medical Systems–Europe (as noted in the opening vignette) and EMC Corp. have built into their products self-diagnosing software that constantly monitors the product's performance. When a specific performance characteristic falls outside acceptable limits, the product software can do one of two things. First, it can self-correct the problem, if that is possible. Second, it can automatically call the manufacturer's service support center where an engineer can either correct the problem remotely, or if a part needs to be replaced, dispatch a technician with the replacement part, which is then installed before the breakdown occurs. Under this scenario, the first time that a customer is even aware of a potential problem is when the technician shows up at the facility to replace the questionable part.

However, as GE is learning, a major challenge with this approach is visibility. When the equipment self-corrects, or technicians correct the problem remotely, the customer never knows that the service has been provided, and may ultimately question the need for it.

Customer Training

Some manufacturers have recognized the benefits of providing extensive customer training in the use of their products. Training quickly familiarizes their customers with how the products are used. Training can be viewed as a competitive advantage in that it acts as a barrier to entry for similar products that are offered by competitors. For example, why would a firm invest time and money to train workers in how to use another product if they are satisfied with the product they are currently using and have already been trained on? FedEx provides a good example of a service firm that does an outstanding job of this. Even if a customer ships only a few packages a day, FedEx will provide that customer with a dedicated computer that is directly linked to the FedEx system and will teach the customer

[8] Jane Ameson, "When in Rome," *Northwestern Airlines World Traveler,* March 1993.

how to use it. This is a major reason competitors have trouble convincing FedEx's customers to switch.

Le Grand, which is located in Limoges, France, produces electrical components such as outlets, switches, and junction boxes, all of which are considered to be commodity-type products. To gain a competitive advantage, Le Grand constructed a large training facility in Limoges where architects and electrical contractors are invited to view its wide variety of products and also to learn how to install them in various settings. To accomplish this, the training facility has been designed with different rooms to demonstrate how the equipment should be installed. These rooms include a kitchen, bathroom, and bedroom, as well as a hospital room.

The Foxboro Company also uses training to differentiate itself from its competition. Before the equipment is delivered, customers are invited to Foxboro's manufacturing facility where their equipment is set up so they can learn how to use it under the guidance of Foxboro instructors. Foxboro attributes its very high percentage of repeat business, in part, to its training programs.

Expanded Product Capabilities

Some manufacturers look to provide services in the form of additional product capabilities that go beyond the primary function of the product itself. In services, for example, many airlines offer to connect you directly with hotels and car rental firms when you make a flight reservation. The concierge service at an upscale hotel is another illustration of expanded service. In both of these cases, the services that are provided go beyond the core product or service that the firm provides.

Mercedes-Benz is a good example of a manufacturer that is providing services that go well beyond the core driving performance characteristics of the automobile. With its S class cars, customers now have the option of purchasing the following services:

- If your car breaks down, the push of a button sends a signal to the nearest garage with your exact location, as determined by a satellite from a signal in your car using the global positioning system (GPS).

- If you are involved in an accident, the push of another button uses the GPS to notify an emergency vehicle of your location. The same signal is automatically sent if the automobile's air bag system is activated.

- If you are traveling and want to stop to eat, the push of a third button will identify restaurants in the vicinity of your car, and if you want, it will also make a reservation for you!

The Impact of Technology

Technology has played an important role in the shift in emphasis from goods to services and the strategic advantage that manufacturing firms can now achieve by providing services. As stated earlier, the Internet is significantly affecting both the book and music industries, offering services that replace goods. Internet websites now allow firms to offer $24 \times 7 \times 52$ service while at the same time being cost effective. Telecommunication technology and satellite communications have significantly reduced the cost of transmitting information and have also increased the speed and the amount of data that can be sent between individuals and organizations, regardless of their locations. In essence, technology, in many of these cases, has been both the catalyst and the means by which firms are now looking to use service as a competitive advantage.

Summary

As goods more quickly become commodities in today's business environment, manufacturers need to seek out new ways to differentiate their products from those of their competition. One way that they can achieve an advantage in the marketplace is by offering services as part of the total product's bundle of benefits. These services can be divided into two categories: (a) little "s" services, which relate to those services primarily within the operations function, and (b) big "S" services or strategic services that require a much broader and longer-term perspective.

With big "S" services, manufacturers can strategically incorporate services into their product offering. If these services are properly designed and aligned with the overall goals of the firm and its products, manufacturers can realize not only a competitive advantage, but also new business opportunities and markets that often have significantly larger profit margins than those associated with the manufactured products themselves.

Key Terms

bundle of benefits: the overall product offering that includes goods and services. *(p. 68)*
customer's activity cycle: all of a customer's activities related to the purchase of a product. *(p. 71)*
order qualifier: minimum characteristics of a firm or its products to be considered as a source of purchase. *(p. 68)*
order winner: characteristics of a firm or its products that distinguish it from its competition so that it is selected as the source of the purchase. *(p. 68)*
service factory: a manufacturing facility that can also provide services to a firm's customers. *(p. 70)*

Review and Discussion Questions

1. For each of the following products, identify at least one service that could be provided that would make the product more attractive to customers:

    man's suit   videocassette recorder
    used car   cell phone
    medical prescription office supplies

2. Why are customers more likely to buy products with services, even if they are more expensive than just the physical products themselves?
3. What issues must manufacturers address when looking to integrate services into their products?
4. Compare the customer's activity cycle framework for integrating services with that of downstream services. How do they differ?
5. Why are services gaining increased recognition in manufacturing companies?

Internet Assignment

Go to the home page of one of the following companies. Describe the products they make and the various services they offer. How do these services provide these firms with a competitive advantage?

    John Deere Company (www.deere.com)
    Pitney Bowes Company (www.pitneybowes.com)
    Xerox Data Systems (www.xerox.com)

CASE Women's Clothing Manufacturer Faces Price Pressures from Customers Even as the Cost of Raw Materials Increases

Tuncalilar Tekstil, Ltd. (TTL) is a manufacturer of women's clothing and apparel with its headquarters in Istanbul, Turkey. Founded by Sezer Mavituncalilar in 1978 with three sewing machines, TTL now has 450 production employees in two manufacturing locations. In addition, it has a 30-person sales force to promote its products.

As a contract manufacturer, TTL produces primarily private label clothing for major retail chains that are located in western Europe and the United Kingdom, such as Marks & Spencer, H&M, Campione, and Country One. Its major competitors are located in Greece, Portugal, and Spain, including Inditex, a publicly traded company in Spain, which markets under the Zara and Mango labels.

In the 1990s, TTL tried to introduce two new product lines, Vento and Kromozome, which were its own labels, in the hopes of increasing profit margins. It also tried to penetrate the U.S. market, but found it was not profitable due to the very small profit margins.

Its current business strategy is to deliver sample orders to its customers within two weeks, and to deliver production orders within 40 days, with the goal of continuously providing its customers with the latest in women's fashions.

The raw materials (that is, the fabrics) interestingly enough are mostly purchased from Italy and Spain because many of the designs specify technically advanced fabrics that are synthetic mixtures. However, basic cloths like cotton and linen are supplied from Turkey, Egypt, and Russia. Accessories, such as buttons, zippers, and threads are mostly purchased from Turkish suppliers.

Currently, TTL is being squeezed by its customers to reduce its prices. At the same time, it is facing an increasing trend in the price of the raw materials that are used in the clothing it produces.

Questions

1. What types of services could TTL offer its customers to provide it with a competitive advantage over its competitors?

2. How would these services add value for both TTL's customers and the end consumers who are buying these products?

Selected Bibliography

Ameson, Jane. "When in Rome." *Northwestern Airlines World Traveler,* March 1993.

Chase Richard B., and David A. Garvin. "The Service Factory." *Harvard Business Review* 67, no. 4 (July–August, 1989), pp. 61–69.

Davis, Mark M., Nicholas J. Aquilano, and Richard B. Chase. *Fundamentals of Operations Management.* Burr Ridge, IL: Irwin/McGraw-Hill, 1999, pp. 20–41.

Davis, Stanley M. *Future Perfect.* Reading, MA: Addison-Wesley, 1987.

Davis, Stanley M., and Chris Meyer. *Blur.* Reading, MA: Perseus Books, 1998.

Gwynne, S. C. "The Long Haul." *Time,* September 25, 1992, pp. 34–38.

Hill, Terry. *Manufacturing Strategy: Text and Cases,* 3rd ed. Burr Ridge, IL: Irwin/McGraw-Hill, 2000, pp. 49–85.

Holmes, Stanley, Carol Matlack, Michael Arndt, and Wendy Zellner. "Boeing Attempts a U-Turn at High Speed." *Business Week,* April 16, 2001, pp. 126–28.

Vandermerwe, Sandra. *From Tin Soldiers to Russian Dolls: Creating Added Value through Services.* Oxford, England: Butterworth-Heinemann, 1993.

Wise, Richard, and Peter Baumgartner. "Go Downstream: The New Profit Imperative in Manufacturing." *Harvard Business Review* 77, no. 5 (September–October 1999), pp. 133–41.

CHAPTER FIVE

Defining Service Strategies

Learning Objectives

- Explain how competition among service firms differs from competition among manufacturing companies.

- Describe why barriers to entry are low in service environments.

- Introduce several strategy models that enable service managers to formulate clear, focused strategies.

- Explain how the degree of customer contact affects decisions about a firm's workforce configuration.

- Describe how the complexity of the service and the degree of service customization interact to affect workforce decisions.

Starbucks' Internet Strategy: Focus on Coffee

Michael Newman / PhotoEdit

Starbucks understands its Internet strategy. Darren Huston, senior vice president for new ventures, states simply, "Our job is to sell more coffee."

Starbucks opened its first store in Seattle's Pike Place Market in 1971, but it wasn't until 1984 that Howard Schultz, then director of retailing and marketing, struck with the popularity of coffee bars in Milan, Italy, convinced Starbucks founders to establish a coffee bar in downtown Seattle. Within five years, there were 55 Starbucks locations and the company introduced a mail-order catalog that enabled the company to sell coffee throughout the United States.

A decade later, in 1998 and 1999, Starbucks embraced the Internet as a strategic opportunity but experienced problems getting it right—costly problems. Forays into the online communication (customers chat in cafés, right?), furniture retailing, and home delivery services didn't fare well. Today, Starbucks is aligning its Internet strategy with its core strategy: achieving customer loyalty to its coffee products.

Starbucks' website now sells only products that are directly related to the products sold in its stores: coffee beans, cups, and coffee brewers. Although its customers are young and often tech-savvy (Starbucks estimates that 90 percent of its customers are Internet users), Starbucks learned that its Internet presence needed to complement and support its core brick-and-mortar business. In keeping with that approach, Starbucks has begun to provide high-speed wireless Internet connections in its cafés. But Starbucks doesn't want to turn its stores into just cybercafés; it prefers to maintain its comfortable image and sense of community while offering wireless Internet connections for customers who want to sip and work.

At the same time, its online store, Starbucks Direct, brings in about $20 million per year, which represents 1 to 2 percent of total company revenues. Customers who shop online can see a broader array of products such as espresso machines that are expensive and can't be stocked in every model and color at each café location.

Today Starbucks Internet strategy is to focus on its core business—coffee. Huston says, "I'll be happiest if people start telling us, 'I used to come in just for my morning coffee. Now that you've got Internet connectivity, I'm coming back for coffee and a snack in the afternoon as well.'"

Sources: George Anders, "Starbucks Brews a New Strategy," *FastCompany,* August 2001, p. 144, and www.starbucks.com.

The Customer's Perspective

You've decided that your modem is too slow; it's time to bite the bullet and order a cable Internet connection. You ask around and discover that, although several cable Internet providers serve your area, the technical connection service provided by Company X is most reliable. So you call.

First you get an automated voice message that asks you to identify whether you are calling to inquire about a sale or for service. You push the appropriate key on the phone pad. And then you wait. For about eight minutes. About every 30 seconds during that eight minutes you hear an automated voice say, "Your order is important to us. Please stay on the line. Your call will be answered by the next available operator." After about two more minutes of waiting you question whether, in fact, your call really *is* important to them. But you stick it out because you want the cable connection.

When your call is finally really answered, the operator, without any greeting, asks for your area code and phone number. You try to inform him that you are calling only for information at this point, but he curtly replies that first he needs your area code and phone number. When he is ready to speak with you, he asks whether you want the basic or deluxe service. You're not sure, so you ask for more information. His speech is so unclear that you have to ask him to repeat himself several times. At last you feel you've gotten enough information to sign up for the deluxe service. The operator asks where you live and you reply. He then says, "Oh, deluxe service is unavailable in your area." You seethe, but state that you'll purchase the basic service for the price he just quoted. He replies, "Actually, that price isn't available in your area. It will be an additional $10 a month." Frustrated, but still wanting the service, you agree. You're delighted when he informs you that a technician will be there the next afternoon, Saturday, between 1:00 and 3:00 P.M. The technician will format your computer, add a card, and install any wiring you need. At least, you sigh, the installation sounds organized.

The next morning at 9:30 your doorbell rings; it's the Internet cable technician. You welcome him in, a bit frazzled by the unexpected early arrival, and say, "I'm sorry that I don't have my office ready for you to go to work; I wasn't expecting you until after 1:00." He shrugs his shoulders in reply and follows you to your office. A quick glance around the room shows him that you have no TV—and therefore no cable—in your office. You agree; the cable is connected to the TV in the family room downstairs. With an irritated look, he says, "I'll have to run some cable then." You think, Yeah—so? but say nothing.

The technician runs the cable into your office, then says, "Hey. You don't have an Ethernet card in your computer." You reply, "That's right. Your office told me you'd install one." He answers, "You'll have to pay an additional $50." You reply, "Your office told me the card was part of the installation price." He replies, "They did?" and installs the card without further comments.

Twenty minutes later, he explains the equipment to you and tells you that he will call the company and have them do the hardware and software configuration as soon as possible—certainly within the hour. He tells you to watch for four little lights on the box he's left on your desk to be on at the same time to indicate that service is ready. You agree, sigh deeply, and see him out.

Three hours later, your Internet connection is still not working. You call the company. After waiting about four minutes (and hearing the same recorded message every 30 seconds!), you finally get an operator, who says, "He never called us. Can you give me your phone number . . ." She assures you that the two other computers in your home can be connected to the cable with no additional charge; all you have to do is buy some cable at a computer store and set up a LAN. One of your buddies knows how to do that, so you agree and hang up as soon as you can.

Later that day, you discover that the LAN doesn't work. You call again (another wait and another series of recorded messages) and speak to a different operator. He tells you that the last operator was mistaken. A LAN is the right approach, but a special configuration needs to be done. He'll take care of it right away. In fact, he does, and the connection is working before you hang up.

As you set the receiver in the cradle, you mutter to yourself, "What in the *world* are they thinking? They may have the best technical product, but their service is awful—from sales to installation to problem solving. Don't they understand that some other company will jump in and serve customers better, and in the process take away the whole market? How can they possibly be so shortsighted?"

The cable company has a good product, but no service strategy. However, there are many companies that have good products. Without a plan for how those products will be sold, customers served, and problems solved, the long-term success of any company is in serious question.

Managerial Issues

All services are not the same. Some service firms provide services that are highly complex, some that are quite straightforward. Some services are provided to customers who are physically present at the time the services are provided, some are provided "behind the scenes." To manage a service operation so that customer needs are consistently met (effectiveness) and in a way that makes best use of the resources available (efficiency), a service manager needs to understand how to think about service strategically, that is, how to understand the nature of the service itself, rather than the specifics of a particular service within a particular industry.

Starbucks is a clear example of strategic focus. The company started as a coffee company, then built a brand and reputation around coffee as an experience beyond the beverage itself. As Starbucks grew, it tried to move beyond coffee into competitive environments where it had few advantages. But these unsuccessful forays refocused Starbucks on coffee and the company is now expanding in a way that is much more likely to be successful, because its new offerings are linked to what it does best: coffee.

What distinguishes Starbucks coffee from that at Dunkin' Donuts or the local convenience store? What makes FedEx different from the U.S. Postal Service or UPS? What is so special about Dell Computers that they have captured such a large share of the PC market? Why have Amazon.com and eBay been such successes as pure Internet companies?

These companies are successful because their customers perceive that they add more value in the products and services they sell than their competitors do. Customers are willing to pay for that added value. Each company has developed a strategy that distinguishes it from its competitors.

A strategy defines the road map for everyone in the organization to follow. That road map shows not only the destination but also the directions that need to be followed to reach that destination. In other words, managers try to develop strategies that differentiate their firms from their competitors, so that customers will perceive added value in the services and be willing to pay for that value. Equally important, the strategy should address the organizational decisions that will allow the firm to move ahead of its competition.

The Generic Strategy Model

To be successful, an organization needs a strategy, which is simply a carefully developed long-range plan for achieving specific desired results. A good strategy defines how an organization will compete in the marketplace. It incorporates how the organization will obtain funding (debt, equity, external sources, internal sources), with whom the organization will compete, and who its customers will be. Strategy also determines along which dimensions the organization will compete. The "classic" competitive dimensions are cost (low price), quality (high quality), flexibility (ability to respond to changes in demand volume and product mix), and delivery (speed of service). During the last decade or so, service has been added to these **competitive priorities** (see Chapter 4 for how service is used as a competitive advantage in manufacturing).

At one time, managers believed that organizations needed to excel at only one of these competitive priorities. However, due to both increased competition and advances in technology, customers expect excellence along several dimensions—and many firms have risen to the challenge and now provide just that.

To excel at any of the competitive priorities, a firm must determine its *critical success factors:* the activities, conditions, or other deliverables that are necessary for the firm to achieve its business goals—in other words, the things the organization must get right. For example, if the goal of a bank is to achieve a certain percentage of Internet-based transactions, a critical success factor will be a user-friendly website that encourages customers to bank online rather than at an ATM or at a teller window.

Once the critical success factors have been identified, the firm must develop a set of distinctive competencies. A *distinctive competency* is an exceptional capability that creates a preference for a firm and its products or services in the marketplace, enabling it to achieve a leadership position over time. From a strategic perspective, particularly in services, which are relatively easy to copy, it is critical for firms to develop some capabilities into distinctive competencies that are difficult for other firms to replicate. The terms *distinctive competency* and *core competency* are often used interchangeably. If there is a difference between the two, it is probably a perspective difference. Distinctive competencies are perceived by the customer and hence relate directly to the firm's success in the marketplace. For example, the ability to offer stylish haircuts at a low price may be the distinctive competency perceived by the customer. Core competencies may not be perceived directly by the customer, but they relate to what the customer perceives as distinctive competencies. For example, the distinctive competency of stylish haircuts at a low price may be related to the hair salon chain's ability to attract and retain talented well-trained young stylists.

In large organizations, strategy can be viewed from a number of levels. **Corporate strategy** determines how the organization will be financed, its financial performance expectations, and who its competitors are. Each **strategic business unit (SBU)** within a corporation has a separate mission and objectives that are planned independently of other company businesses. Each SBU strategy is based on who their customers are. Corporate and business unit strategies determine the organization's competitive priorities. The competitive priorities, in turn, determine what decisions are made within each business function within the strategic business unit. Because marketing and operations functions are so closely linked in service organizations, the decisions relating to those functional strategies are emphasized here.

Strategic Marketing Decisions

The functional strategic decisions in marketing are called the **marketing mix.** The marketing mix has traditionally been summarized as incorporating the four Ps: (*a*) product, (*b*) price, (*c*) place, and (*d*) promotion. The marketing mix for services has been expanded to include three more elements: (*e*) people, (*f*) physical evidence, and (*g*) process.[1]

The Traditional Marketing Mix

Product   Product refers to benefits that will be provided to the customer through the good or service. Product decisions relate to the ways the firm differentiates its product from those of competitors, including how the product will be branded, trademarked, packaged, and warranted; what features will be included in the product design; and what models and sizes will be included in the product line.

Price   These decisions relate to how the product or service will be positioned in relation to competitors' prices. From the point of view of the customer, price is related to value; from the point of view of the firm, price is related to profit. Pricing decisions include whether the firm will price the service at a premium or for customers on a budget; what discounts will be offered for volume purchases; and how to price for retailers, wholesalers, and agents.

Place   Place decisions relate to where the goods or services will be delivered. Some place decisions include whether the goods or services will be sold directly to customers, through telemarketing, or via the Internet and what geographic area will be served.

Promotion   Promotion decisions relate to how the product or service will be advertised and what means will be used to stimulate sales.

[1] Bernard H. Booms and Mary Jo Bitner. "Marketing Strategies and Organizational Structures for Service Firms," in *Marketing of Services,* ed. J. H. Donnelly and W. R. George (Chicago: American Marketing Association, 1981), pp. 47–51.

The Expanded Marketing Mix for Services

People These decisions relate to both the people who are employees and those who are customers. Employee decisions include how workers will be recruited, trained, evaluated, and rewarded. Customer decisions relate to how customers will be treated by the service firm to influence their own service experience and the experiences of other customers.

Physical Evidence These decisions relate to how the service facility and service providers look: the ambience of the facility, the dress of employees, and the physical appearance of other service tangibles such as menus in a restaurant, signs in a deli, and performance reports for financial institutions.

Process Process decisions relate to how activities are performed in the service firm, the steps in the service process, and how customers will be involved in the service delivery.

Strategic Operations Decisions

Robert Hayes and Steven Wheelwright classified the strategic operations decisions into two categories: **structural decisions,** which relate to physical facility issues, and **infrastructural decisions,** which relate to less tangible issues.[1a]

Structural Decisions

Structural decisions include (*a*) location, (*b*) capacity, (*c*) vertical integration, and (*d*) process technology.

Location For services that deal directly with the customer (which we will learn later in the chapter are defined as high-contact services), the location decision is driven by where the customers are. For example, economies of scale may be realized by having all Dunkin' Donuts production done in a single huge facility—say in Ottumwa, Iowa, near the geographic center of the United States—and it might be most convenient for the company to have all customers come to that single location to purchase Dunkin' Donuts products. But most of its customers in the United States (or even in Iowa, for that matter!) aren't willing to travel to Ottumwa on their way to work in the morning just to grab a quick cup of coffee and a donut! On the other hand, low-contact services, such as a credit card call center, which don't require the physical presence of the customer, may be able to locate in a part of the country, or even the world, where labor and other operating costs are lower. Telecommunication technology enables that service location decision.

Capacity Physical capacity decisions are critically important. Too much capacity is costly, because it represents unnecessary fixed costs, and may reduce profits to the point of bankruptcy. Conversely, too little capacity may lead to poor service that frustrates customers and reduces their loyalty, leading to opportunity cost of lost sales when customers take their business elsewhere.

Vertical Integration Vertical integration relates to how much of the supply chain is controlled by the organization. Backward integration involves purchasing or controlling suppliers; forward integration involves purchasing or controlling customers. For example, a coffeehouse chain might purchase coffee bean growers (backward integration) or an airline might purchase a company that provides tours in the cities to which the airline flies (forward integration). Technology has enabled organizations to work together as closely as if they were vertically integrated without actual change of ownership. This virtual vertical

---

[1a] Robert H. Hayes and Steven C. Wheelwright, "Restoring Our Competitive Edge: Competing through Manufacturing" (New York: John Wiley), 1984.

integration makes it possible for organizations to share information and engage in joint planning that produces an advantage for all parties involved.

Process Technology   The most basic definition of technology is how work is done. The choice of the technology that will be used to provide service is very important for most service organizations. For example, some colleges and universities may decide to employ face-to-face teaching technologies in a classroom while others may choose to develop Internet distance-learning technologies. Similarly, some restaurants choose to provide table service, while others provide only counter service, and still others have customers serve themselves.

Infrastructural Decisions

Until recently, infrastructural decisions were thought to be more quickly changed than structural decisions, although anyone who has ever had managerial responsibility knows that these decisions cannot be "turned on a dime." The infrastructural decisions relate to (*a*) workforce, (*b*) quality management, (*c*) policies and procedures, and (*d*) organizational structure.

Workforce   Service managers need to establish the skills requirements for their workers and to determine how they will be scheduled, trained, and evaluated. For example, a walk-in medical clinic may choose to staff its workforce with nurse practitioners who can assess and treat a wide variety of problems, but whose salaries are likely to be lower than those of physicians. Some restaurants may choose to employ professional waiters and others may choose high school or college students as their major server pool.

Quality Management   Service managers also need to decide how quality will be defined, measured, and monitored within their organizations. Quality decisions are critically important for every firm, but particularly for service organizations, because of the intangibility of services and their simultaneity of production and consumption. (See Chapters 12 and 12S for a complete discussion of quality management topics.)

Policies and Procedures   Managers also need to define how the work will be performed and how decisions will be made. These policies and procedures can make a tremendous difference in the consistency of the service and the way customers perceive the service. For example, one reason for McDonald's success is the consistency of its products and services around the world, which can be attributed in large part to the very clear procedures that have been developed for how hamburgers and fries should be prepared and served to customers. McDonald's customers expect that wherever they go, McDonald's food will taste essentially the same, and it probably would not if the established procedures were not consistently followed in every store.

Organizational Structure   The hierarchical structure of an organization defines who reports to whom, which in turn determines how the work gets done. For example, hospitals may be organized according to traditional departments, such as medicine, surgery, nursing, and pharmacy, or they may be organized around specific types of services, such as women's health care and cardiac care. Hospitals that are organized around these specific types of services, often called service lines, may have nurses and pharmacists reporting to physicians, whereas in a more traditional organization, nurses would report to a head nurse who would, in turn, report to a supervisor, who, in turn, would report to the director of nursing. Similarly, in a functional organization, pharmacists would report to the pharmacy shift supervisor, each of whom would report to the chief of pharmacy. The way people interact in organizations that are structured in one way is likely to be very different from the way they interact in the other.

As stated previously, the marketing and operations functional decisions are highly interrelated. When the operations and marketing decisions are aligned, the strategy has a good chance of success. When the decisions are not aligned, intraorganizational conflicts arise—and customers can usually feel the disconnect, too.

The strategic decisions made within the various functions determine how and which processes are established, as well as how performance is measured. Optimally, throughout the strategy development process, information is continuously fed back through the system so that customers' needs are identified and addressed and performance goals are achieved. The service delivery process, then, is continuously driven by strategy, which is continuously being monitored by established performance measures. Exhibit 5.1 illustrates the generic strategy model.

EXHIBIT 5.1
Generic Strategy Model

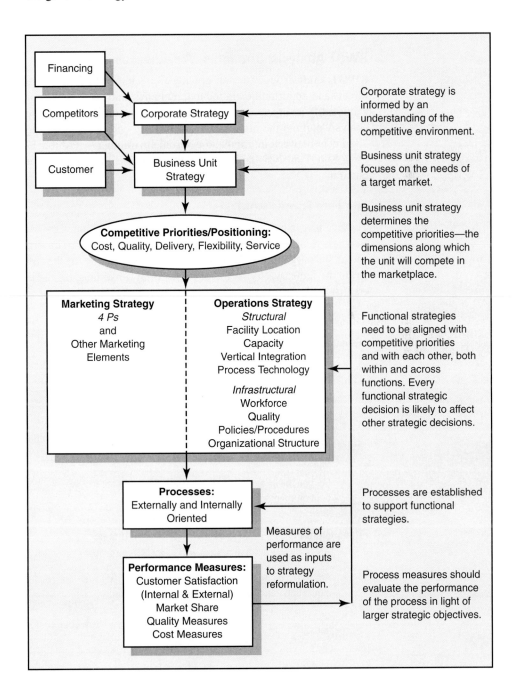

Financing

Competitors → Corporate Strategy

Customer → Business Unit Strategy

Competitive Priorities/Positioning:
Cost, Quality, Delivery, Flexibility, Service

Marketing Strategy
4 Ps
and
Other Marketing
Elements

Operations Strategy
Structural
Facility Location
Capacity
Vertical Integration
Process Technology

Infrastructural
Workforce
Quality
Policies/Procedures
Organizational Structure

Processes:
Externally and Internally
Oriented

Performance Measures:
Customer Satisfaction
(Internal & External)
Market Share
Quality Measures
Cost Measures

Corporate strategy is informed by an understanding of the competitive environment.

Business unit strategy focuses on the needs of a target market.

Business unit strategy determines the competitive priorities—the dimensions along which the unit will compete in the marketplace.

Functional strategies need to be aligned with competitive priorities and with each other, both within and across functions. Every functional strategic decision is likely to affect other strategic decisions.

Processes are established to support functional strategies.

Measures of performance are used as inputs to strategy reformulation.

Process measures should evaluate the performance of the process in light of larger strategic objectives.

It is critically important to remember that strategy is what an organization actually does, not what it says it does. The strategy formulation process is a dynamic, ongoing process that incorporates changes in the environment and information about performance.

Specific Strategy Models

SWOT analysis and five forces analysis are specific strategy models that were developed as tools for strategy formulation and evaluation. Each model provides a specific structure for the strategic analysis process so that important elements are addressed. While each of the models is equally applicable to both manufacturing and services, the emphasis here will be on service organizations.

SWOT Analysis: Strengths, Weaknesses, Opportunities, and Threats

SWOT analysis identifies an organization's internal strengths and weaknesses as well as threats and opportunities in the external environment. A well-thought-out SWOT analysis can identify an organization's distinctive competencies and critical success factors. SWOT analysis permits the organization to identify and develop strategies that ensure the best alignment between internal and external environments. Exhibit 5.2 shows a typical layout for a SWOT analysis and some of the questions that might be asked in each of the four quadrants.

The Five Forces Analysis

The **five forces model** shown in Exhibit 5.3 was developed by Michael Porter of Harvard Business School. It provides a structure for the analysis of an organization's environment and an industry's attractiveness. The five forces include (*a*) the risk of new competitors entering the industry, (*b*) the threat of potential substitutes, (*c*) the bargaining power of buyers, (*d*) the bargaining power of suppliers, and (*e*) the degree of rivalry between the exist-

EXHIBIT 5.2
SWOT Analysis

Strengths

- At what does your organization excel?

- How strong is your organization in the market?

- Do you have a clear direction?

- What differentiates you from competitors?

- Do you have a skilled workforce? Exceptional product? Strong customer base?

Weaknesses

- Will your workforce be inadequately skilled?

- Does your organization have sufficient resources?

- What does your organization do poorly?

- Is your organization adequately financed?

Opportunities

- What are the current market trends?

- Are there niches in the market your organization can fill?

- Does technology offer new service options?

Threats

- What are your competitors doing?

- Are your products aging?

- What policies/laws affect your options?

- Are your customers' needs changing?

EXHIBIT 5.3
The Five Forces Model

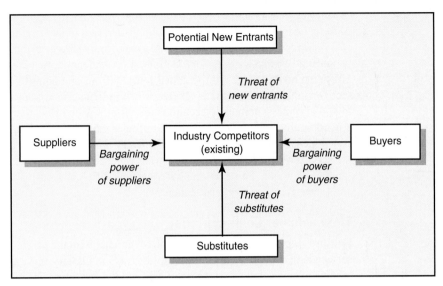

ing competitors.[2] Like SWOT analysis, five forces analysis structures the factors that affect the potential success of an organization in the marketplace so that a meaningful—and it is hoped successful—strategy can be defined.

Economies of Scale

One strategic challenge of managing in a service environment is the competition that typically exists and that is becoming even more intense as the Internet becomes more widely accepted by consumers. Services are relatively easy to copy and many do not require large capital investments, so barriers to entry are low. One strategic approach that manufacturing firms have adopted to create barriers to entry in their markets is to quickly gain market share to take advantage of economies of scale. For many services, however, there are very limited opportunities to achieve similar scale economies. With brick-and-mortar services whose customers are a part of the service delivery process, like McDonald's, Jiffy Lube, and H&R Block, a large number of similar service outlets that are relatively small in size are required so that they are close to the markets they serve. This precludes any savings from economies of scale that are associated with large physical facilities, but may provide opportunities for gaining competitive advantage through the infrastructural decisions.

However, advances in technology are enabling economies of scale for some service operations. Telecommunications call centers and e-service businesses are examples of services that can take advantage of such scale economies.

Service Classification Models

Chapter 2 introduced the four elements of the service package: the *supporting facility, facilitating goods, explicit services,* and *implicit services.* Managers of service organizations need to be very aware that each of these elements affects the impression customers have of

---

[2] Michael E. Porter, *Competitive Advantage: Creating and Sustaining Superior Performance* (New York: The Free Press, 1985).

the service and ultimately their satisfaction with that service. Understanding the concept of the service package is therefore an important step to understanding services in general.

When facilitating goods are of little or no importance to the service, the service has been called a *pure service.* For example, a taxi ride, although it involves a supporting facility (the taxi), consists of the actual journey from one point to another (the explicit service) and the attitude of the taxi driver (the implicit service), but involves no real supporting good (unless, perhaps, a receipt is requested). A taxi ride, therefore, can be considered a nearly pure service. Other examples of nearly pure services might be a symphony concert, a dental checkup, or a package delivery. Pure services are actually the exception in the service sector, however. Most of what we consider to be services usually include some facilitating goods. This section addresses how different types of services can be classified and managed for strategic advantage.

The Customer Contact Model

Because customers often come into direct contact with the service provider at the time the service is performed, one of the simplest ways to classify services is according to the relationship between the service employee and the customer. Dick Chase's customer contact model describes services as either (*a*) pure services, (*b*) mixed services, or (*c*) quasimanufacturing services.[3]

Types of Services

Pure Services   In the customer contact model, pure services are those in which the major service production occurs in the presence of the customer (this is a slightly looser definition of *pure* than the one used above, with the emphasis on the degree of customer contact rather than the lack of supporting goods). Examples of pure services in the customer contact model are an examination by a physician, a stay at a hotel, or participation in a degree program at a university: all have a high degree of direct contact between customers and service providers.

Mixed Services   These involve elements of close customer contact and elements of back-office work. Postal services would be an example of a mixed service. Although there is some customer contact with either the postal workers at the counter in the post office or with the mail carrier, there is also significant back-office work that is done in the form of sorting and transportation.

Quasimanufacturing Services   Virtually no face-to-face contact occurs between the customer and the service provider in quasimanufacturing services. Here, the "interaction" involves a customer's possession and the service. The processing of checks in the back office of a bank, government administration offices such as the noncontact arm of the Internal Revenue Service, and the automated mail sorting processes at a central branch of the post office are examples of quasimanufacturing services, all of which are performed for the customer on the customer's possessions (a check, a tax document, a letter to Uncle Mitch).

It is important to emphasize here that the examples of each of these types of services is at the *service* level—not at the organization level. An organization may deliver a variety of services that have different degrees of customer contact. For example, in health care, an examination by a physician, during which a blood test is drawn, is a high-contact service, but the processing of the blood sample in the lab is a quasimanufacturing service, as is the processing of the bill for the examination.

---

[3] Richard B. Chase, "The Customer Contact Approach to Services: Theoretical Bases and Practical Extensions," *Operations Research* 29, no. 4 (1981).

Degree of Proximity to the Customer

Customer contact can further be characterized by the degree of proximity between the service provider and the customer. Face-to-face contact between the customer and the provider is *direct customer contact*. Most high-contact services we encounter day to day are direct contact services, such as schools, restaurants, and barbershops. When services are provided by telephone, the degree of contact may be high (say, a suicide hot line or a computer support line), but it is *indirect customer contact*. Services that can be provided indirectly are more likely to be able to take advantage of location and scale economies.

No-contact services are performed without any personal contact. These services correlate highly with those that are called, in the customer contact model, quasimanufacturing services, such as back-office check processing or mail sorting. Mail is often the medium for communication between customers and service providers in no-contact services.

Some services are difficult to characterize using these models. Automatic teller machines (ATMs) and Internet services clearly involve no face-to-face or even indirect contact, but there is connection between the service and the customer.

Services Performed on People versus Services Performed on Things

Considering not only the degree of contact but also whether the service is directed at people or things is another way to characterize services.[4] Some low-contact services require high skill levels, such as accounting services or legal services, while others, such as housekeeping or janitorial services, may require considerably less skill.

Two important dimensions of the service interaction that are affected by the degree of customer contact are the skills required of the service worker and service efficiency.

How the Degree of Customer Contact Affects Worker Skills and Service Efficiency

Understanding the degree of customer contact helps to determine how a service should be managed. The skills required of the service worker are clearly affected by the degree of customer contact. Workers in high customer contact services not only must master the technical skills associated with the specific service being delivered, but also must possess interpersonal skills to properly interact with customers. For example, a secretary in a physician's office not only must be competent at data entry, filing, scheduling, and other clerical tasks, but also must be able to interact appropriately with patients—from pleasantly dealing with the details of appointments to supporting and comforting patients who are upset. Similarly, physicians must not only master the technical skills of diagnosis and treatment but also learn an appropriate "bedside manner." As another example, professors must not only know their fields, but also have the skill to bring their material to life in the classroom and to relate to students one on one.

In contrast, workers in service environments with virtually no contact with customers need not possess the same degree of people skills that customer contact workers require (although people skills may be important for contact with coworkers within the organization). Indirect-contact services, such as phone-based services, may require more people skills than no-contact services, but perhaps fewer people skills than face-to-face services. In high-contact systems, the emphasis is on effectiveness: meeting the customer's needs. Efficient use of resources is still important, but it takes a back seat to effectiveness. (See Chapter 11 for more on efficiency and effectiveness measures.)

In manufacturing, customers are separated from the production of goods; the technical core of the operation is buffered from the customer. In high-contact services, however, the

---

[4] Christopher H. Lovelock, "Classifying Services to Gain Strategic Marketing Insights," *Journal of Marketing* 47 (Summer 1983), pp. 9–20.

customer is directly involved. This high degree of customer contact introduces an element of uncertainty into the service environment that can negatively affect efficiency. For example, interaction with customers in a bank may slow the speed of processing a transaction, perhaps because customers are slow to find the materials required to complete their transactions (like their checkbooks and bank cards) or because they need to ask the teller questions. Likewise, a physician may have difficulty keeping on schedule, even when appointments are appropriately booked, because patients have concerns or problems that were not anticipated when the schedule was made.

Dick Chase has also suggested that the proportion of time the customer is in contact with the service in relation to the total service delivery time for that customer is the key factor in determining efficiency.[5] This model would predict, for example, that a bank's back-office check-clearing operation is likely to be more efficient than the teller operation. The bank's customers at the tellers' counter all vary in the way they interact with the teller. The uncertainty introduced by these differences makes the teller operation inherently less efficient than the check-clearing operation.

Although high customer contact may reduce the service system's efficiency, high customer contact also provides the opportunity to involve the customer in the process—and thereby to reduce the uncertainty involved with providing complex services.

Complex Services and Customized Services

Chase's customer contact model has been countered by others who argue that the amount of time required to provide the service is less important than the degree of complexity of the service for strategically managing a service operation.

The degree of service complexity and customization also affects the nature of the service interaction and the decision about who should provide those services.[6] Professional services, such as medical care, engineering, consulting, and legal advice, are examples of services that provide complex and customized services. All of these services require a workforce that has the ability to exercise judgment in the provision of the service. Professional workers tend to be highly educated and trained to manage the ambiguity associated with the problems their customers may bring to them. However, while professional workers may require little or no additional training on the technical aspects of their work, they are likely to need—and appreciate—orientation to the goals of the organization, because there often may appear to be a conflict between the goals of the individual professional and his or her customer and the goals of the organization. For example, physicians may need to understand that their HMO employer controls costs by limiting the vendors from which drugs can be ordered, and therefore limiting the number of name-brand drugs. If the physicians are not given the proper orientation to this policy, the organization may be stymied in its attempt to control costs and the physicians may be frustrated in their efforts to provide the care they want to provide to their patients.

In professional services it is likely that the worker knows considerably more about the technical nature of the service than the manager, and consequently these service professionals may balk at "being managed." Managing this type of service therefore primarily involves providing the professionals with the information and the support that they need to be effective and efficient. This is not to say that professionals do not need to be "managed," but it does imply a very different style of management. Managers need to establish standards and goals jointly with professionals, so that both managerial and professional objectives can be met. Managers also need to regularly provide information about perfor-

---

[5] Chase, "The Customer Contact Approach to Services."
[6] Lovelock, "Classifying Services to Gain Strategic Marketing Insights."

mance outcomes, so that the professionals can modify their actions to better meet their service standard objectives.

Services that are less complex and less customized require less judgment on the part of the service worker. A fast-food restaurant, for example, provides meals that are less customized than a full-service restaurant and the degree of complexity and judgment involved in taking and filling the order is quite low. Service workers in such an environment can be trained more quickly because of the narrow scope of the service interaction, as there are few menu items and little flexibility in the way those items are prepared. For example, customers at a fast-food restaurant cannot specify that they want an "extra chocolaty" milkshake. In contrast, customers at a fine restaurant may be impressed—or even overwhelmed—by the amount of information that the servers provide about special menu items, ingredients, the steps in the preparation of meals, and the degree to which their meals can be customized. To capture these differences between services, Roger Schmenner classified services in his service process matrix (see Exhibit 5.4) as either *service factories, service shops, mass services,* or *professional services* based on two dimensions: the degree of labor intensity and the degree of interaction and customization.

Service factories provide services to large numbers of customers. They tend to be capital-intensive and the level of interaction with and customization of service for customers is fairly low. In contrast, *mass services* are provided in high-labor-intensity environments but have relatively low levels of service customization. *Service shops* also tend to be capital-intensive but provide customized services, while *professional services* are very labor-intensive as well as highly interactive and customized. As noted above, service classifications are most useful when classifying specific processes rather than whole organizations. Within schools, for example, there are examples of both labor-intensive and customized processes in the form of directed or independent studies conducted by agreement between individual instructors and students. Within hospitals, there are low-customization processes, such as accounts payable and receivable processes, and in hotels, the services provided to VIPs are likely to be highly customized. Each of these service types has particular challenges for managers, as shown in Exhibit 5.5.

Services with high levels of labor intensity require control of processes related to workforce, while those with high levels of interaction and customization require cost and quality controls. Services with low levels of customization require differentiation from other services and attention to the customers' perception of the environment and, at the same

EXHIBIT 5.4
The Service Process Matrix

		Degree of Interaction and Customization	
		Low	High
Degree of Labor Intensity — Low		**Service Factory** Airlines Trucking Hotels Resorts/recreation	**Service Shop** Hospital Auto repair Other repair services
Degree of Labor Intensity — High		**Mass Service** Retailing Wholesaling Schools Retail banking	**Professional Service** Physicians Lawyers Accountants Architects

Source: Roger W. Schmenner, "How Can Service Businesses Survive and Prosper?" *Sloan Management Review* 27, no. 3 (Spring 1986), p. 25.

EXHIBIT 5.5   Service Challenges

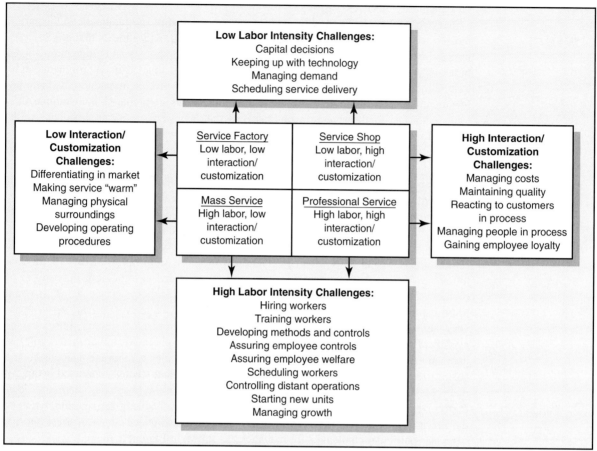

Source: Roger W. Schmenner, "How Can Service Businesses Survive and Prosper?" *Sloan Management Review* 27, no. 3 (Spring 1986), p. 27.

time, standardization of processes to assure consistency of service. On the other hand, services with low labor intensity (in other words, services with high capital intensity) require constant attention to changes in technology and processes that permit efficient use of capital resources.

Lovelock points out that services can be high in complexity and low in customization, as seen in Exhibit 5.6, citing classroom lectures as an example, or high in customization and low in complexity, citing hotel services and telephone services (you can call anywhere by simply dialing a series of numbers) as examples.[7] As these examples illustrate, complexity is probably the dimension that determines the nature of the workforce, but the degree of customization of the service probably determines how much orientation the workforce will need to reach the organization's goals.

Services with Wide Fluctuations in Demand

One of the greatest challenges associated with managing service operations is dealing effectively with wide fluctuations in demand. Goods-producing organizations have the edge here; they can produce goods in slow periods to meet demand in peak periods, although even goods producers have to worry about product obsolescence and spoilage. Because of

[7] Lovelock, "Classifying Services to Gain Strategic Marketing Insights."

EXHIBIT 5.6
**Customization
and Judgment
in Services**

<table>
<tr><td colspan="3" align="center">Degree of Customization</td></tr>
<tr><td></td><td align="center">High</td><td align="center">Low</td></tr>
<tr>
<td rowspan="2" align="center">Degree of Service Worker Judgment
in Meeting Customer Needs</td>
<td>**High**
Professional services
Surgery
Taxi service
Beautician
Plumber
Education (tutorials)
Upscale restaurant</td>
<td>Education (large classes)
Preventive health programs
College food service</td>
</tr>
<tr>
<td>**Low**
Telephone service
Hotel service
Retail banking
Family restaurant</td>
<td>Public transportation
Routine appliance repair
Movie theater
Spectator sports
Fast-food restaurant</td>
</tr>
</table>

Source: Christopher H. Lovelock, "Classifying Services to Gain Strategic Marketing Insights," *Journal of Marketing* 47 (Summer 1983), pp. 9–20.

the intangibility of services and the simultaneity of service delivery and consumption by the consumer, service managers have no choice but to try to match their firm's ability to provide services when customers require them. For example, delivering flowers on a special occasion such as Valentine's Day needs to be done on Valentine's Day; no other day will do! In 1996, the three Greenworks florist shops in Washington, D.C., expected to sell more than 30,000 roses on Valentine's Day. To meet that demand, the manager added 12 phone lines to his usual 10 and hired 20 couriers to back up his regular fleet of six trucks.[8] This example illustrates a seasonal or onetime peak demand situation. Similar challenges occur on much smaller scales, however. Demand for services may fluctuate considerably by season of the year, day of the week, time of the day, and even from minute to minute. If the perceived value of the service is high, customers may be willing to wait to be served, but there is always the risk that they will choose not to wait for the service—or even to seek the service from another provider (see Chapter 15 for more on waiting lines).

When demand fluctuates widely, the service manager needs to be very attuned to the workforce issues, particularly the number of workers that need to be scheduled, the stress on workers in busy times, and the boredom that can accompany slow periods. Quality control is important here because of the way the pace of the work may vary when demand is high versus when it is low. Strategies for matching supply and demand include increasing capacity when it is needed, serving customers more quickly (without sacrificing quality), and shifting demand to periods when more capacity is available. (The issue of matching supply and demand in services is addressed in more detail in Chapter 14.)

The Impact of Technology

Technology has significantly changed the way service managers develop strategies. The Internet has not only increased competition in an already crowded and highly competitive environment, but also forced managers to react much more quickly to changes in the marketplace. Where once managers had the luxury of months and even years to develop their strategies, they now have, in many instances, only weeks—or maybe months, if they are lucky.

[8] Rochelle Sharpe, "Hearts of Gold," *Wall Street Journal,* February 15, 1996.

In 1984, at the age of 19, Michael Dell founded Dell Computer Corporation, the first computer company to sell customized systems directly to customers. In 2002, net revenues for the company were $31 billion.

On November 1, 1999, in his address to the Detroit Economic Club, Michael Dell spoke about "Building a Competitive Advantage in an Internet Economy."

At Dell, we have integrated virtually our entire business with the Internet. We currently take about 40 percent of our orders online through dell.com, which saves money for both our customers and Dell. It increases customer satisfaction and customer loyalty by reducing support costs. And many routine service kinds of inquiries that would normally occur over the phone can now happen on the Internet. For instance, order status calls, which can cost up to $13 a call, can be handled over the Internet for essentially no cost at all. And of course, turning our inventory faster allows us to save cost, and it gives our suppliers a direct view into our demand trend so that they can tune their output to meet our exact requirements.

Companies need to consider the implications of leveraging the Internet for their business. Simply establishing a website—putting a Web front-end on top of your company—is not going to create the efficiencies you need. You must rethink how you're going to use information more efficiently, and drive inefficiencies out of the system.

In the traditional physical world, the field of consideration was limited to a geographic area that you could travel in. But now, of course, all that's changed. The field of consideration is the world. We have pricing transparency. We don't buy things only from companies that are physically close to us. And those companies that are physically close to us, with expensive assets like real estate and inventory and buildings, are carrying a lot of additional cost, which may or may not be necessary.

I'm not suggesting that all physical businesses are doomed for disaster. But consider the example of two extremes. One extreme is a café where you go for some social interaction and a cup of coffee. You're not going to replace this kind of experience online. The other extreme is purchasing something at a drugstore. How many of you like to go to the drugstore to stand in line while people are buying embarrassing things? This is not a highly differentiated, experiential sort of thing. My point is that every physical experience now has to be held to a higher standard. If you're in a physical business, you've got to deliver something that is more valuable than can be delivered online.

In this speech, it is clear that Internet technology has dramatically affected Michael Dell's strategy for Dell Computer. It is also clear that the Internet, alone, is not the strategy. Rather, it enables companies that are forward-thinking to develop new ways to serve customers and to achieve competitive advantage.

Strategy is critical to virtual service businesses such as Amazon.com or E*Trade, because they lack the physical structures of brick-and-mortar operations, which lend credibility and the ability to come into direct contact with customers. Unless they can develop a successful strategy, they will be forced to compete only on price, which results in insufficient profit margins to sustain long-term growth.

Likewise, strategy is critical for brick-and-mortar services that are trying to expand their services through the Internet. As Starbucks learned in the opening vignette, an Internet strategy must properly support the existing physical operations.

The Internet is only one example of how technology is forcing service managers to rethink their strategies. As mobile devices increase in popularity and other new technologies are developed and become affordable, these too will need to be considered in the strategic development process.

Summary

When they develop a strategy, a service firm's managers establish its long-term direction by defining the markets it will serve and how it will serve the customers within those markets. A firm's strategy also establishes the framework for the different functional decisions, which need to be in alignment with the overall strategy. Operations strategy includes both structural and infrastructural decisions. Marketing strategy includes decisions regarding pricing, placement, and the type of delivery process. Human resource strategy decisions include the skill levels of the workers hired and the type of training they require. Information systems strategy decisions include what information will be available to suppliers and customers and how that information will be accessed.

Several classification models have been developed to provide managers with some insights for developing a service strategy. These models focus internally on the factors such as the type and degree of customer contact, the degree of customization of the service, and the skill requirements of the workers.

In addition, frameworks have been developed to assist managers with strategy development. These frameworks look externally at the factors that can affect the business, including suppliers, customers, and the competition.

Key Terms

competitive priorities: the dimensions along which a firm chooses to compete: cost, quality, flexibility, delivery, and service. *(p. 83)*

corporate strategy: the level of strategy that focuses on financing and the competition. *(p. 84)*

five forces model: a strategy model for understanding an organization's competitors, suppliers, customers, potential new market entrants, and potential substitute products or services. *(p. 88)*

infrastructural decisions: operations strategic decisions that relate to workforce configuration, quality management, policies and procedures, and organizational structure. *(p. 85)*

marketing mix: the set of marketing strategic decisions that include product, price, place, and promotion. *(p. 84)*

strategic business unit (SBU): a unit of a company that has a separate mission and objectives that are planned independently of other company business. *(p. 84)*

structural decisions: operations strategy decisions that relate to location, physical capacity, process technology, and vertical integration. *(p. 85)*

SWOT analysis: a strategy formulation/evaluation model that structures information about an organization's strengths, weaknesses, opportunities, and threats. *(p. 88)*

Review and Discussion Questions

1. What is strategy?
2. Describe how the elements of the generic strategy model may interrelate for a service organization you know well, such as McDonald's.
3. Describe the elements of SWOT analysis.
4. Describe the elements of the five forces model.
5. If you were the manager of a bank, describe how the customer contact model could help you to develop an e-banking option for your customers.
6. How does management of services provided for people differ from management of services performed on things? How might the operations strategic decisions differ for a carryout pizza shop and an upscale pizza dine-in restaurant?
7. How do complexity and customization affect service strategy? What are the challenges associated with high and low levels of complexity and customization?
8. How does technology affect service strategy?

Internet Assignment

Go to the following URLs for the Ritz Carlton Hotels and Resorts and the University of Phoenix.

http://www.ritzcarlton.com/html_corp/home/index.asp
http://www.phoenix.edu/index_flat.html

What do their sites tell you about their strategy?

CASE   HollyRock

In the fall of 2001, Hannah Simmons had just started a new venture in her hometown of Hollistown: a restaurant, called HollyRock, that would cater to teenagers. Hollistown was a comfortable middle-class bedroom community that offered little for teenagers to do after school, having few stores and no place for its 1,000 high school students to hang out. The nearest movie theater was 20 minutes away and the nearest fast-food restaurant was 10 minutes by car. Hollistown's zoning laws were very strict in an attempt to maintain its quiet and peaceful atmosphere. Chain businesses were generally unsuccessful in obtaining licenses to operate; Hollistown preferred to support local, small businesses. Hannah's idea had been to provide a welcoming atmosphere for the town's young people after school, on evenings, and during weekends.

Hannah found a location that she thought would be perfect. The building was an old house with a large front porch that had been converted to retail space some time before and that had been recently vacated. It was on the town's main street across from a pizza/Italian food restaurant and a few small shops and about a 15-minute walk from the high school. The building offered ample parking in front and in back. Next door was a vacant lot, on the other side of which was Hollistown's only other restaurant, Robb's, which was open for breakfast and lunch Monday through Saturday, on Friday evenings for dinner, and on Sunday morning for breakfast.

HollyRock had seating for 75, and Hannah found that the average table turnaround was one hour. Restaurant hours were Monday through Thursday from 3 to 9 P.M. and on Friday and Saturday from 3 to 10 P.M. Menu items were geared to the tastes of young people: burgers, pizza, ice cream, and shakes. Customers placed their orders at the counter and were given a number when the order was ready, so there was no need for waiters. HollyRock employed one person to bus and clean tables, one person to work the counter, and one person to cook.

HollyRock was decorated in an appealing casual style. There were booths along one side of the restaurant and pic-

nic tables in the center, which customers often moved around to accommodate larger groups. The walls were covered with posters of rock bands, a large blackboard for customers to write messages to each other, and a jukebox in one corner with a small area for dancing. On Friday and Saturday nights, local bands and singing groups could sign up to perform for their friends.

HollyRock was an immediate success. Young people were excited about having a welcoming place to go and parents were supportive of the concept of a safe, local "hangout." One of Hannah's concerns was that HollyRock might be too successful. On Friday and Saturday nights, there was more demand than could be accommodated. On the other hand, although Hannah thought the restaurant's hours were appropriate for her target market, she wanted to be able to maximize the restaurant's profitability by considering other markets for daytime hours.

Questions

1. Who are HollyRock's customers?

2. Who are likely to be HollyRock's competitors?

3. Consider the structural (location, capacity, technology) and infrastructural (workforce, quality management, organization design, policies and procedures) decisions Hannah made. Do the decisions support each other? Are the decisions aligned to support her overall strategy for HollyRock?

4. Hannah is considering opening weekdays at 8 A.M. and offering gourmet coffee, baked goods, and quiche for stay-at-home mothers and nutritious sandwiches and finger foods for small children. She thinks this will enhance revenues. What issues should she consider?

Copyright 2002 Janelle Heineke and Larry Meile.

Selected Bibliography

Anders, George. "Starbucks Brews a New Strategy." *FastCompany* 49 (August 2001), p. 144.

Chase, Richard B. "The Customer Contact Approach to Services: Theoretical Bases and Practical Extensions." *Operations Research* 29, no. 4 (1981).

Fitzsimmons, James A., and Mona J. Fitzsimmons. *Service Management for Competitive Advantage.* New York: McGraw-Hill, 1994.

Joachim, David. "FedEx Delivers on CEO's IT Vision." *Internet Week.com,* October 25, 1999.

Lovelock, Christopher H. "Classifying Services to Gain Strategic Marketing Insights." *Journal of Marketing* 47 (Summer 1983), pp. 9–20.

Porter, Michael E. *Competitive Advantage: Creating and Sustaining Superior Performance.* New York: The Free Press, 1985.

Project Management

Learning Objectives

- Explain the difference between service projects and repetitive service processes.

- Identify the challenges associated with managing projects.

- Describe the activities involved in planning projects.

- Introduce tools that are used to schedule projects.

- Present the tools used to monitor project progress.

The e.Schwab Project: Online Service at Charles Schwab

© Jean Miele / CORBIS

The Charles Schwab Corporation, which was founded in 1974 as one of the country's first discount brokerages, provides a broad array of financial services to individual investors, independent investment managers, retirement plans, and institutions through a network of nearly 400 branches, offices, telephone service centers, automated phone services, and the Internet.

In 1995, Schwab had no Internet presence. By 1998, Schwab had 2.2 million online accounts and traded $4 billion of securities each week on its website—more than half its total trading volume. But Schwab's Internet success did not just happen. Co-CEOs Charles Schwab and David Pottruck believed that while lowering prices to compete on the Web could cost them millions in revenues, Internet service was the key to future success.

In 1995, Chief Information Officer Dawn Lepore got a message from a member of her staff who wanted her to see some software that would link Schwab's different computer systems. The technical challenge could be solved a number of ways, but the engineers chose a simple Web-based system that enabled a Schwab server to take a Web order, execute it, and send a confirmation back to the customer's PC. While this sounds straightforward today, it was groundbreaking at the time, since most existing Web trading systems required that each order first be printed and then reentered manually into another system.

Lepore and Schwab immediately recognized the implications of the proposal. Within weeks, a Web trading project team was formed. The team grew to 30 people and evolved into an electronic brokerage unit called e.Schwab, which reported directly to Pottruck.

At the same time, brokerages such as E*Trade and Ameritrade were working on their Web trading products, so competition was fierce and pressure was high. In 1996, e.Schwab went live. To open an account, investors sent a check (or wire transfer), but after that first transaction they could trade any security by logging on to e.Schwab's website where for a flat fee of $39 (later reduced to $29.95) they could trade up to 1,000 shares, rather than the usual sliding scale of higher commissions for larger trades.

The announcement of e.Schwab was made at the annual shareholders' meeting, but without any further publicity, the new service was an immediate success, reaching 25,000 Web accounts in the first two weeks—the goal for the entire first year. By the end of 1997, Schwab's online accounts had grown to 1.2 million and online assets to $81 billion.

Sources: Erick Schonfield, "Schwab Puts It All Online," *Fortune,* December 7, 1998, pp. 84–99, and http://www.aboutschwab.com/.

The Customer's Perspective

Your family has decided that it's finally time to move away from the vintage 1950s look of your kitchen and expand it to include a great room with a view of your backyard. The first step was interviewing general contractors and obtaining proposals and estimates for the work—and right from the beginning what seemed like a simple, straightforward renovation became complicated and stressful. You interviewed three contractors. The first estimated that the renovation would take three months and cost $112,000, the second estimated four months and $65,000 and the third estimated two months and $73,000. After some discussion, it became clear that only the third contractor had included an allowance for new appliances, despite your careful explanation that "everything would need to be new."

After considerable discussion and refinement of the plans, you decided on the third contractor, primarily because the two-month completion estimate meant your family would be disrupted as little as possible. The first day went well. The contractor came and removed all your appliances and began to remove the cabinets. In less than three days, the room had been emptied and the general contractor pulled down the exterior wall and arranged a temporary plastic enclosure to keep out the elements. The builders arrived promptly the next morning and began work on framing the new addition. The first four days went smoothly, then, without explanation, the crew disappeared for nearly a week.

Your family's frantic calls to the general contractor made no difference; the builder was nowhere to be found.

When they finally returned, there followed what seemed like an endless series of "We can't do our work until the plumbers (or electricians or tile installers or cabinetmakers or inspectors) do theirs." It seemed as though every step depended on every other step being done first—and no one seemed to be directing the process.

Nearly five months later, the kitchen was completed. The new kitchen is both beautiful and functional, and the final cost was precisely what was estimated, but the family has all agreed that before you undertake another major renovation, you'll move!

Coping with the uncertainty of major project work is a challenge for all customers. Time and cost are always important factors, whether you're an individual planning your wedding or a manager representing a large corporate customer contracting for a major advertising campaign.

Managerial Issues

Most managers in service organizations deal both with ongoing processes and with special, one-of-a-kind endeavors that arise out of a particular need or problem. The skills and tools required to manage one-of-a-kind endeavors, or projects, are somewhat different from the skills and tools required to manage ongoing processes, and they challenge managers along many dimensions, ranging from team-building skills to technical scheduling and monitoring techniques.

Because projects tend to be large in scope and complex, and are usually very important to the organizations involved, managing them well is also very important. At the same time and for the same reasons, it is important not to try to manage too many of the small details centrally. The effective project manager walks a fine line between being in control and being overcontrolling!

Effective project managers work closely with customers both internal and external to define the scope of the project and to clarify the time and budget goals, then monitor the project's progress closely to ensure that those goals are met.

Defining and Selecting Projects

Launching an advertising campaign for a new video game, developing a new financial services instrument, and planning a wedding all share something in common: They are distinctive types of processes called projects. A **project** is a set of related and interdependent activities that are directed toward the creation of some major identifiable product or service that is usually one of a kind. Because they are often large and are either not repeated or repeated very infrequently, projects are particularly challenging to manage. Projects are also likely to be complex in scope, often requiring the involvement of several functional areas within a single organization or even across several organizations. They may span weeks, months, or years, so effective management usually means continuously monitoring, updating, and replanning throughout the project timeline. But because projects produce a particular product or service, they have definable start and end points as well as specific events or tasks to be completed at certain points in time—called *milestones*—along the way.

Definition of Project Management

Project management is defined as the planning, scheduling, and controlling of project tasks to meet project objectives, including accomplishing the project's goal within an established schedule using the appropriate level of resources. When projects are large, long, and complex, the stakes for the organization may be very high and the projects usually involve a great deal of coordination and cooperation between different departments, functions, and organizations. Large, complex projects also generally incorporate a great deal of uncertainty. When projects are smaller, the timeline may be shorter, the stakes may be lower, the degree of complexity may be less, but the fundamental principles of project management still apply.

There are some distinct differences between managing repetitive processes and managing projects. One difference relates to organizational structure: Repetitive processes are likely to be managed within the formal organization structure, while the people working together on a project are often brought together specifically to accomplish the project and may stop working together when the project is completed. Because project teams are so often newly formed groups, it can take time, the conscious effort of those involved, and a major focus on communication to be effective. Team functioning is further complicated by the fact that the people working on the project team often continue to be active in other groups.

Another difference between ongoing process management and project management relates to the tasks themselves. Since projects are by definition not repetitive, flexibility is an important aspect of successful project management. Unique tasks cannot normally be totally understood until they are well under way so project plans continue to evolve over the life of the project. Effective management usually requires continuously monitoring, updating, and replanning throughout the project timeline.

Many management positions encompass characteristics of both project and repetitive process management. Consider, for example, developing a new service such as e.Schwab did in the opening vignette. The development and introduction of a specific new service is a onetime undertaking, or project, that would almost certainly involve a specially formed project team that would face the challenges of team development while also working toward completion of the project tasks. Once the service is introduced, however, the delivery, monitoring, and continuous improvement of the service would normally be the responsibilities of the appropriate functional organizations and would be guided by the organization's standard operating procedures (which might be modified, of course, to address new needs introduced by the new product).

Selecting a Project

Most organizations have many projects ongoing at the same time, and there are usually many more proposals for projects than the organization has the resources to undertake. As a result, managers should have a method for clearly evaluating the projects to decide which to take on and which to pass on. It is important for organizations to have an evaluation process in place to minimize the confusion and negative effect on morale that can occur when the project selection process is ambiguous or unduly complicated. Project selection models should be capable of capturing the dimensions that are important to the decision, sophisticated enough to differentiate between projects, flexible enough to provide reliable results within a range of business conditions, and reasonably easy for managers to use and understand.

We present here several models for evaluating potential projects and the strengths and weaknesses of each.

Cost/Benefit Analysis

Cost/benefit analysis is a traditional financial approach to choosing from among a number of potential projects. This approach attempts to quantify the costs and the revenues or profits. A number of measures can be used to calculate the cost/benefit of projects, including net present value (NPR), payback period, internal rate of return (IRR), and return on investment (ROI). While these measures are well understood, they may be difficult to apply to many projects. The qualitative or strategic benefits of a project may not be easily quantified, and failure to account for some of the less quantifiable factors may result in choosing projects that are, in the long term, not the best for the firm.

Scoring or Ranking Models

Scoring or ranking models for project selection were developed to address the shortcomings of cost/benefit analysis. These models use a limited set of both qualitative and quantitative criteria that are considered to be particularly important to the firm. Typically the criteria are given weights to indicate their relative importance and a single score is computed for each project. One disadvantage of this approach is that assigning weights is often highly subjective and therefore can be difficult. Another is that these models focus on one project at a time, reducing each to a single number, and then comparing them. There is no attempt to consider the impact of undertaking a number of projects at the same time.

The criteria used in scoring or ranking models should be aligned with the organization's overall success factors. These might include important cost/benefit measures described earlier, such as payback period or return on investment, as well as nonfinancial measures such as market share and/or product/service mix. For example, if a service firm's mission is to be the technology leader in its industry, ensuring that some proportion of the services being offered, say, 20 percent, incorporate the newest technologies might be an important factor in the project selection decision.

The selection criteria and their weights can be compared using a project screening matrix, which is similar to the factor rating system described in Chapter 8 (which is used for evaluating potential new service site locations). Exhibit 6.1 shows an example of a project screening matrix that incorporates some factors that might be used to evaluate projects in a technology-leader service.

According to this project matrix, Project 3 scores highest at 56 points, followed by Project 4, which scores 47 points. Project 3, therefore, would have the highest priority and Project 4 would be next.

Management Science Models

These models attempt to create an optimized portfolio of projects using an objective function such as minimizing costs or maximizing revenues or profit. Management science models consider resource constraints across a number of projects and can model both qualitative and quantitative factors. A disadvantage of management science models is that they can be difficult to formulate and interpret.

EXHIBIT 6.1 Project Screening Matrix

Criterion	Criterion Weight	Project 1	Project 2	Project 3	Project 4	Project 5
Strategic fit	2	2	3	5	5	1
Leverages core competencies	2	5	2	3	2	4
Technology advance	3	2	2	5	4	1
Improves customer retention	2	5	3	4	2	2
Internal leadership availability	1	2	5	5	2	3
25% contribution	3	1	2	4	5	2
Total		**35**	**33**	**56**	**47**	**26**

The Portfolio Management Approach

The portfolio management approach to project selection is based on the concept of diversification. With this method the organization chooses projects based on the level of risk for the portfolio of projects as a whole. This approach attempts to select projects based not only on the merits of each individual project but also on how the projects interact with each other.

Another factor that is always important is the political factor. If the CEO wants to design a new service, it is likely that his or her project will have a high priority. Idealistically, one could argue that politics should not enter into the decision, but realistically it should be recognized that all important organizational decisions have political implications that need to be considered. Having a structure in place to evaluate and prioritize project proposals helps to reduce the effect of politics on project choice decisions.

Whatever model is used in the project selection process, managers should also remember that the models do not *make* the decisions; they only provide a structure for making them. Models do just that: They *model* reality and therefore capture only part of the story.

The Project Life Cycle

Projects can generally be divided into six key phases: (*a*) defining the project's goals, (*b*) developing the detailed project plan, (*c*) scheduling the project, (*d*) launching and implementing the project plan, (*e*) monitoring and controlling the project, and (*f*) closing out and evaluating the project. These six phases together define the *project life cycle*. Envisioning the project life cycle in its entirety enables the project manager to see the "big picture," which is particularly important because most organizations have many projects under way concurrently. Each phase of the project life cycle is critical to a project's success.

Defining the Project's Goals

Whether a project is large or small, it is always important to begin on the right foot. Once the decision has been made to initiate a project, a steering committee is usually formed to define the project more clearly and in more detail. The steering committee typically consists of a group of senior people in the organization, often including the person who will take on the role of project manager. The steering committee is responsible for the work in the earliest phase of the project life cycle, in particular defining the scope of the project. Carefully defining the project helps ensure that all stakeholders in the project agree on exactly what the project is so everyone will be working toward a common set of objectives. There should be agreement on (*a*) what is to be accomplished, (*b*) what is outside the boundaries of the project, (*c*) when the project should be completed, (*d*) what resources are to be used, and (*e*) what measures of success are to be used.

Because a project begins with a challenge or opportunity, preliminary investigation may be needed before the stakeholders agree on what the actual challenge/opportunity is. Different stakeholders, including customers, may have different objectives for the project, and compromises may be necessary. Understanding what the end results will look like will still be preliminary at this point and may be limited to interim results, such as a statement of requirements. The scope of the project is likely to change as it proceeds, but a clear understanding of the scope at the beginning of the project is critical to determine who should lead the project and who the project team members should be.

This is the time for conflict resolution. Many projects are initiated before a common goal is established with the hope that the goal will become clear as the project progresses. This approach is dangerous. Clear agreement on the nature of the project and the project's goals helps to focus the decision-making process as alternative approaches for addressing the problem or opportunity are considered. Some issues to resolve at this stage are: Will members of the project team already have the skills needed to accomplish the project or should training, hiring, contracting for consultants, or forming partnerships with other organizations be used to bridge the gaps? Will the same team stay with the project throughout the project life cycle? Will they use leading-edge tools and techniques, or ones with which they are experienced or that have been previously used within the organization? Other project approaches might include prototyping, pilots, and incremental rollout or phase-in methods. The risks and advantages associated with each option should be carefully considered before selecting the specific approach.

The Project Manager

Once the project's scope and objectives have been initially defined and mapped out, the project manager will usually assume responsibility for the project. All managers are responsible for understanding how to use the resources available most efficiently and effectively to accomplish a specific objective. To be successful, managers must be able to: (*a*) plan work, (*b*) motivate workers, and (*c*) measure and control performance. Project managers face additional challenges because they manage a finite amount of work and because they often are required to work outside the formal organizational structure. The project manager is responsible for completing the project on time, on budget, and within specifications. Given the characteristics of projects, it should not be surprising that very important skills for project managers include leading, communicating, negotiating, and problem solving, all of which are key team skills. Specific project management tools have also been developed to help managers focus on the big picture while at the same time allowing them to track the specific details through the different phases of a project. The people and leadership skills required of the project manager represent the "art" of project management, while the technical skills represent the "science." Too much emphasis on either the art or the science can result in poor results, missed deadlines, and increased costs. Successful project managers find the proper balance between the two.

The Project Team

After the goals have been defined and a project approach selected, the appropriate team of people can be assembled to form the project organization, which is a temporary organization structure created to incorporate the skills and expertise that are required for completing the project. Teams may include people from functional areas such as marketing, operations, and information systems, as well as from support functions such as risk management, auditing, and legal departments. Consequently, project managers often need to cross traditional functional lines to complete a project. The roles, reporting relationships, and responsibilities of the project leader and of each member of the project team must be carefully defined to minimize role confusion and lack of ownership for project activities. Good project managers create a collaborative culture that relies on strong teaming skills as well as technical expertise. Without the authority of a traditional manager and the formal system of rewards and punishments, project managers must earn their authority by building trust, respect, and credibility among project members.

Firms can create a number of different organizational structures for managing projects: (*a*) project teams within the functional organization, (*b*) dedicated project teams, and (*c*) matrixed organizations. Each of these structures has particular advantages and disadvantages.

Project Teams within the Functional Organization   Projects managed within the existing organizational structure are typically overseen by someone in a top management position. There is no formal project team; rather, each function within the organization completes activities for which it is usually responsible. For example, if a hospital's management decided to expand its women's health services to include an outpatient service, the marketing department would do the advertising and promotion, the nursing department would hire and train nursing and support staff, and the chief of obstetrics and gynecology would hire and orient the physician staff. All of these activities might be overseen by the hospital's vice president of operations, and coordination among departments would happen through the usual communication channels.

The advantages of this project structure are that the usual operations of the organization as a whole are disrupted only minimally, and there is no confusion about roles and reporting relationships. Another advantage is that the expertise of everyone in a functional area can be drawn upon to complete the project. A disadvantage of functional project organizations, however, is that the organization may find it difficult to maintain its focus on the project while the functional areas continue to perform their normal work. People assigned to the project may not be as motivated as they might be if their time was dedicated to project work. In addition, unless the communication and cooperation between functional areas are already very strong, there is some risk that a project's success may be compromised because the people involved in the project focus primarily on their functional responsibilities.

Dedicated Project Teams　　In this project organization, team members are recruited by the project manager and operate as a separate organizational unit for the duration of the project. An advantage of this model is that project team members are no longer responsible for working in other processes, so the ongoing processes are not disrupted directly by project work. Team members focus on the project and work together across functions, so they are more likely to understand how the functional elements of the project relate to each other. In other words, the level of functional integration in well-managed dedicated project teams is likely to be high. Projects are also likely to be completed more quickly when dedicated project teams are used because of the higher levels of focus, commitment, and integration.

A disadvantage of the dedicated project team organization is that the functional expertise of the project team is limited to the individuals who are on the team. Another disadvantage is that when the project is completed, project team members need to be reassigned, either to another project or back to their original functional departments. The risk for team members is that the organization may not have another project for them to work on or the jobs they left to join the project may no longer be available.

Matrixed Project Organizations　　Many organizations use matrixed approaches to project organization. A common approach is to have project team members continue to work in their usual functional jobs and also become part of a project team led by a project manager. These teams, like the dedicated project teams, are typically composed of members from different organizational functions. Project team members may continue to report to their functional managers or they may report to both the project manager and their functional managers. One advantage of this approach over the functional organization is that the project manager is more clearly responsible for integrating across functions. Another advantage is that, because team members continue to work within their functional roles, they are more readily able to draw upon the expertise of others within the function. The main disadvantage of the matrixed organizational form is that there is likely to be some level of tension between project managers and functional managers related to how resources should be used and how decisions are made. There is also a risk that project team members will be overloaded with work on both their projects and their "day jobs."

Critical Project Success Factors

The factors that contribute to a project's success can be grouped into four categories:

Task-related variables. These are direct measures of task performance, such as the ability to produce quality results on time and within budget, innovative performance, and the flexibility to change.

People-related variables. These affect the inner workings of the team and include good communications, high involvement, the capacity to resolve conflict, mutual trust, and commitment to the project's objectives.

Leadership variables. These include the ability to organize and direct tasks, facilitate group decision making, motivate, assist in conflict and problem resolution, and foster a work environment that satisfies the professional and personal needs of individual team members.

Organizational variables. These consist of the overall organizational climate, command-control-authority structure, policies, procedures, regulations, regional cultures, values, and economic conditions.[1]

Once the project team has been formed, the goals of the project should be reviewed and re-stated as clearly and concisely as possible. Revisiting the goal definition step at this point ensures that the goals are achievable, that the timelines are feasible, and that the required resources and expertise are understood. Most people experienced in project management will agree that the beginning of a project is the most important part of the project's life cycle.

Developing the Detailed Project Plan

The next phase of project management is project planning, which focuses on developing the road maps that will be followed during project implementation. The first step in project planning is developing the work breakdown structure.

Work Breakdown Structure (WBS)

A **work breakdown structure (WBS)** takes a complicated task, subdivides it into smaller tasks, and then subdivides each of these smaller tasks into still smaller tasks until responsibility for completing each task can be assigned to a specific person or entity. These smaller tasks are used for estimating the amount of work required, determining the time duration, estimating costs, and assessing risk. The smaller tasks are also used for scheduling. Groups of subtasks that can be assigned to a single organizational unit are often called *work packages.*

The WBS is often depicted graphically, as shown in Exhibit 6.2, which resembles an organizational chart. It can also be listed in table or outline form, as presented in Exhibit 6.3.

When a project is fairly large and complex, it may be too difficult to complete the WBS all at once. When this occurs, it is often necessary to do the WBS in steps, perhaps defining activities only until the next major milestone.

The work breakdown structure has many uses in planning a project. The first is to help identify tasks that might otherwise have been missed. The second is to identify all the tasks that will be individually planned. To accomplish this, each task or activity in the WBS must

---

[1] Hans J. Thamhain, "Managing Technologically Innovative Team Efforts toward New Product Success," *Journal of Production Innovation Management* 7, no. 1 (March 1990), and Hans J. Thamhain, "Effective Leadership Style for Managing Project Teams," in *Handbook of Program and Project Management,* ed. P. C. Dinsmore (New York: AMACOM, 1992).

EXHIBIT 6.2
Work Breakdown Structure (Graphical Form)

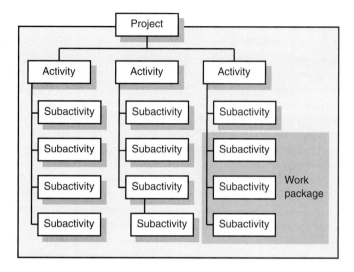

EXHIBIT 6.3
Work Breakdown Structure (Table or Outline Form)

```
Project
   Activity
      Subactivity Level 1
         Subactivity Level 2
         Subactivity Level 2
      Subactivity Level 1
   Activity
      Subactivity Level 1
         Subactivity Level 2
         Subactivity Level 2
```

be defined. This includes identifying all the inputs and outputs for the activity and describing what must be done to transform the inputs into the outputs. For each task, it is wise to consider risks and potential pitfalls so that plans can be developed that do not take unnecessary risks. In addition, planning for each activity includes identifying what skills will be required for the activity and determining if anyone on the team possesses those skills. Sometimes the skills among the team members are inadequate, and as a result, new activities must be added for training or for adding other individuals to the team.

Task Responsibility Defining who has preliminary responsibility for the task is also part of the WBS. Teams often develop responsibility matrices during this phase of the project so that they can map team member skills and backgrounds to tasks and distribute responsibilities for the project fairly. Exhibit 6.4 illustrates an example of a responsibility matrix for a college commencement planning project.

Another important element of the WBS is the estimation of the time duration for each activity. Prior experience, databases, experts, and/or common logic can be used to estimate these duration times. In addition, a consistent unit of time (hours, half days, days, or weeks) should be selected and used throughout the project.

Cost Estimates Estimating the cost of each activity is also part of the WBS. Costs are usually categorized as either direct or indirect. Direct costs are costs that can clearly be charged to a particular work package and typically include labor and materials and equipment

EXHIBIT 6.4
Responsibility Matrix

Activity	Person Responsible
Develop script	Maxine
Plan menu	Barb, Julie
Recruit volunteers	Julie
Produce graduation list	Barb, Stephanie
Produce program	Barb, Stephanie, Pam
Communicate with dean's office	Maxine
Work with Building and Grounds Department	Maxine
Conduct transcript audits	Stephanie, advisors
Choose faculty award winner	Don
Coordinate walk-through	Maxine
Check diplomas	Stephanie, advisors
Practice hooding	Don
Coordinate check-in	Barb
Conduct post review	Maxine

purchases and/or rental. The level of direct costs can be heavily influenced by the people responsible for each work package. Indirect or project overhead costs, on the other hand, are costs that are not directly related to a specific activity or work package, but are, instead, associated with the project as a whole. Overhead costs may include the salary of the project manager, the cost of equipment used for a set of activities (copying, etc.), consulting fees, and general project training expenses. Indirect costs, such as general and administrative (G&A) expenses, are allocated to projects much as they are allocated to departments within large organizations. Examples of G&A costs that can be allocated to a project include the organization's overall facility-related costs (a share of the rent and/or maintenance for the space the project team uses) and centralized support function costs such as those associated with payroll, accounts payable, personnel, and utilities.

Sometimes allocated costs can be specifically related to some projects rather than others. For example, the costs associated with a three-year research grant for a university may include space and equipment usage, but if no additional hiring is done, an allocation of personnel costs may "overtax" that project. So even allocated costs can sometimes be allocated more on an activity basis rather than a less project-specific allocation basis.

It is rare that a project has more resources than it needs. Once costs are estimated, the project team can then explore creative, less-expensive ways to accomplish a given task.

Uncertainty in Project Estimates   For project management to be truly effective, estimates of time and resource requirements need to be as accurate as possible. Although projects, by definition, are unique and contain a high degree of uncertainty, the project manager can apply the following six fundamental principles to ensure the estimates are as good as they can be.[2]

1. *Estimates should be made by the persons most familiar with the task.* The people "on the line" are most likely to base their estimates on past experience with similar activities and are less likely to be biased. Having the people responsible for completing the activity do the estimating also increases their buy-in to the timeline.

2. *Estimates should be based on normal conditions, efficient methods, and a normal level of resources.* Time estimates for each task should be based on the typical workday (for

---

[2] Clifford F. Gray and Erik W. Larson, *Project Management: The Managerial Process* (New York: Irwin/McGraw-Hill, 2000).

example, eight hours) and should be made considering only the project in question and should not include other demands that might be placed on an individual or a department. Although the problem of many projects converging and creating stress in a single work unit is real, it should not be built into the initial estimates of time, but rather it should be managed through the scheduling process. Similarly, costs should be realistically estimated. If, for example, software programming costs are expected to rise dramatically because of market conditions, those increases need to be reflected in the real cost of programming resources.

3. *Time estimates should all be expressed in the same units.* The project team should consistently use the same unit of time throughout the project. Workweeks, calendar weeks, workdays, or hours, can all be appropriate units of time. For example, the time units for a large building restoration project may appropriately be workweeks (since most of the work will be conducted on workdays, Monday through Friday), while the time units for a very time-sensitive project such as a fire evacuation at a hospital or school would most likely be measured in minutes.

4. *Estimates should treat each activity as independent of every other activity.* Independence of estimates tends to result in more realistic estimates than those that combine a number of activities and estimate the total time required.

5. *Time and cost estimates should not include allowances for contingencies.* Each estimate should be based on normal operating conditions. The project manager should consider potential unusual circumstances in their entirety for the overall project and should plan a separate budget accordingly. Individual activities may come in over or under budget for time and/or cost, but the overall time and costs for the entire project are likely to be estimated more accurately if contingencies are not built into individual activities.

6. *The project management culture should allow errors in estimation to occur.* Punishment for over- or underestimates is likely to result in either overly tight or overly cushioned estimates in the future. If the estimators trust that management will understand that even the most thoughtful estimates will not always be correct, there is a better chance that future estimates will be as realistic as they can be.

Projects, because they are inherently "new," are inherently risky. Risk can be assessed through the work breakdown structure. The types of risks can be identified for each activity, and the likelihood of each risk can be assessed. For example, for a project with a long duration, there is a risk that costs will change, but it is unlikely that the costs for all the activities will change in the same way. Labor costs, in a low-unemployment economy, may rise significantly while material costs may be fairly stable. But even labor costs may not change much if the contract specifies the labor rate. The risk associated with a project is usually related to time (the longer the project, the higher the risk), degree of technological change (more change leads to more risk), and size (the more activities and interactions between activities, the greater the risk that problems will occur).

Precedence Relationships   Once the project activities have been defined, the persons responsible for the activities have been identified, and the costs have been estimated, the team needs to determine the order in which the tasks will be performed. For each project activity, the team must identify which other activities are immediate *predecessors* (that is, the activities that come immediately before and upon which the task in question is dependent) and which other activities are immediate *successors* (that is, the activities that come immediately after and are dependent upon the activity).

One critical caution for project managers in these early phases of a project is not to define tasks in too great detail, for several reasons. First, at the start of any large project, it is virtually impossible to accurately estimate all the times and costs. Second, trying to manage time in small increments is micromanaging, and no one likes to be micromanaged! A project manager cannot compensate for unclear goals with a long, detailed laundry list of activities. The project plan should not be a "to do" list of all the tasks that need to be completed; rather it should serve as a map that leads toward the project goal. A good project plan is one that is used as a tool for planning and tracking project milestones.[3]

Scheduling the Project

After the work breakdown structure has been developed and the project activities defined, the project team can proceed to the next phase of the project: scheduling the project.

The Project Network

Once all the project activities have been arranged in sequential order, a network diagram can be constructed. A **network diagram** is a graphical presentation of the relationships between the activities that makes it possible to identify the longest path of activities through the project. This longest path is called the **critical path** because it defines the shortest time in which the project can be completed for a given configuration of estimated activity times. (A more detailed explanation of this is presented in the supplement to this chapter.) Knowing which activities are on a project's critical path is very important to the project manager; only by reducing the times for the activities on the critical path will the overall project duration time be reduced. The critical path in a project, therefore, is similar to the bottleneck in a repetitive process in that both are process constraints.

Consider the WBS for a project to renovate the dining room in a restaurant, shown below in table form. The restaurant manager will hire contractors to do the renovation and has identified the activities in the project and the time requirement for each, as shown in Exhibit 6.5.

As we can see, activity A has no immediate predecessor activities. The remaining activities in the table follow at least one other activity; for example, activity B must follow activity A and activity G must follow both activity B and activity E. The network diagram for this project is shown in Exhibit 6.6.

The project network also identifies where there is **slack time** in the project network. Slack time is the "wiggle room" in a project, defined as the amount of time an activity can be delayed without affecting either the completion of the project overall *(total slack time)* or the earliest start time of any other activity in the network *(free slack time)*. Understanding where there is slack time in a project is extremely important for project managers.

Consider a single-project example in which a project manager has two weeks of slack time between two activities, X and Y, each of which has been predicted to require three

EXHIBIT 6.5
Precedence Table

Activity	Activity Description	Time (days)	Immediate Predecessor
A	Remove furniture and draperies	1	none
B	Launder draperies	1	A
C	Sand walls and woodwork	3	A
D	Paint walls and woodwork	4	C
E	Install carpet	2	D
F	Rehang draperies	1	D
G	Rearrange furniture	1	B, E

[3] The Hamilton Group, 4PM website, URL: http://www.4pm.com/.

EXHIBIT 6.6
Network Diagram for Restaurant Renovation

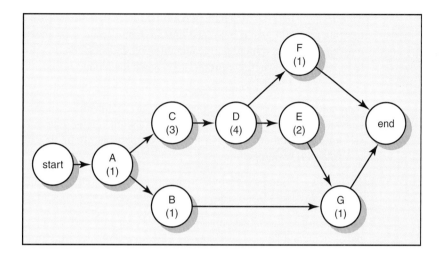

weeks to complete. Activity X is an immediate predecessor activity for activity Y, which means that activity X must be completed in order to start work on activity Y. If activity X uses up both weeks of slack and takes five weeks to complete, activity Y must be completed in its predicted three weeks. If activity Y, because of bad time estimates or some unexpected difficulties, also exceeds its expected three weeks, it will affect the start of a new activity—or may even shift the critical path.

Consider also an example in an organization that is managing several projects at once. If the managers know where there is slack along a noncritical path, they can schedule the workforce more effectively, perhaps permitting workers who don't need to start an activity for project A immediately to work on a more time-sensitive activity for project B. Or managers may decide to get work done on the activity for project A early, knowing that project C is coming along and that the workers on the project A activity will be needed for critical project C activities as soon as the project A activity is completed. Mismanaging slack time across projects could cause shifts in both project critical paths, possibly extending the completion dates of one or both of the projects.

Launching and Implementing the Project Plan

Once the project schedule has been developed and approved, the actual project work can begin. Most of the resources assigned to the project are usually consumed in this phase. The work that is undertaken when the project is launched can be divided into two broad categories: teamwork and task work.

Teamwork

As the actual project work is initiated, the project team tends to evolve through a series of five developmental stages:[4]

Forming During this stage, team members become acquainted with each other and with the scope of the project. Team members start to establish ground rules for both their roles within the project team and their interpersonal relationships. This stage is completed when the members begin to view themselves as a team.

[4] B. W. Tuchman and M. C. Jensen, "Stages of Small Group Development Revisited," *Group and Organizational Studies* 2 (1977), pp. 419–27.

Storming   This stage is characterized by internal conflict. Team members recognize that they are part of a group but resist the constraints placed on their individuality. There also may be in conflict about team leadership and decision-making processes. The team moves to the next stage when the project manager's leadership is accepted by the members.

Norming   During this third stage, strong relationships among team members begin to form and the team becomes cohesive. Team members become more aware of shared responsibilities and a sense of camaraderie also develops. The norming stage is completed when team members establish and agree upon the common expectations about how the team should work together.

Performing   Here, the team structure is primarily functional and accepted by team members. Energy has shifted from understanding each other to achieveing the project goals.

Adjourning   During this phase, the team prepares to disband, because the project goals have been completed. The reactions of team members at this stage can vary from a strong sense of accomplishment and looking forward to the next project to one of depression over the loss of the team's camaraderie and friendship.

This five-stage model is important for project managers to understand because it demonstrates that attention must first be paid to team development for the team to be effective in accomplishing the project's task goals. Some project managers find that sharing this model with the team helps to facilitate movement through each of the stages.[5]

Task Work

Because a project is a unique undertaking and a new activity for the team, uncertainty is to be expected. Individual assignments that result from the detailed work plan will need to be developed, and sometimes these new plans will lead to changes in other parts of the plan.

In addition to filling in the previously undefined portions of the work plan, the project team should constantly be attuned to potential problems in the plan. When such problems do arise, the original work plan may no longer be appropriate. Consequently, the team must remain flexible to look for innovative alternative ways to accomplish the project objectives.

With either uncertainty or problems in the work plan, project managers should expect that the members of the project team will continuously seek ways to improve the project outcome as they learn more about the project. However, if these improvements mean the project will cost more than the organization is willing to pay, or that a critical deadline will not be met, they should probably not be made.

During the implementation phase, it is crucial for the project team to record its activities and accomplishments. This information is important for communicating the status of the project to both the other team members and the project stakeholders. While schedules and budgets are important, it is at least as important to know that the quality of the output being produced meets the expectations for the project.

Changes are inevitable and so are the pressures they place on the team to meet project objectives. Keeping the team motivated and resolving team conflicts are critical challenges for the project manager during the implementation phase.

Monitoring and Controlling the Project

Once the project has been planned and scheduled and the actual work has begun, project control becomes critically important. Attention must be paid to whether the tasks have been started and completed on schedule, whether the costs have changed, and whether new risks

[5] Gray and Larsen, *Project Management.*

or uncertainties have developed since the project planning phase. Determining what data to collect, how often to collect the data, and how to assess the difference between what was expected to occur in terms of time and costs and what has actually occurred are key decisions.

Since most projects are large and complex, real-time adjustments to the project plan must be made. It is important to keep an eye on the project's critical path because changes in time and uncertainty may shift the critical path, which should also shift the management challenge to a different set of activities.

Monitoring Time

A tool commonly used for monitoring a project's timeline is the Gantt chart, which is presented in Exhibit 6.7. A **Gantt chart** depicts on a timeline the time required to complete activities. Gantt charts can also be constructed so that precedence relationships, critical paths, and slack times are clearly depicted.

The advantage of Gantt charts over network diagrams is that the timeline for the project is clearly shown. The disadvantage is that the critical path and interdependencies of very complicated projects are less clearly depicted.

Monitoring Costs

Network diagrams and Gantt charts focus the manager's attention on time as a critical resource. Another critical resource is money. Several graphical depictions of cost relationships are commonly used in project management. Project cost breakdown graphs (see Exhibit 6.8) show the relationship between labor, material, and overhead costs. It can also be helpful to show the relationship between dollar costs and labor hours (see Exhibit 6.9) and the difference between projected and actual costs (see Exhibit 6.10).

Projects usually involve trade-offs between time and costs. In our restaurant renovation example, the project could probably be completed faster if the restaurant manager was willing to pay more to have the workers work overtime.

Costs for project activities are generally considered in terms of normal costs and crash costs. *Normal costs* are the costs associated with completing the activity within the normal time under normal conditions. But for many projects it may be necessary to complete some activities in less than normal time. Completing an activity faster generally means that it will cost more. **Crash costs (or expedited costs)** are the costs associated with completing the activity in shorter-than-normal time, or **crash time (or expedited time).** Crash costs are

EXHIBIT 6.7
Gantt Chart

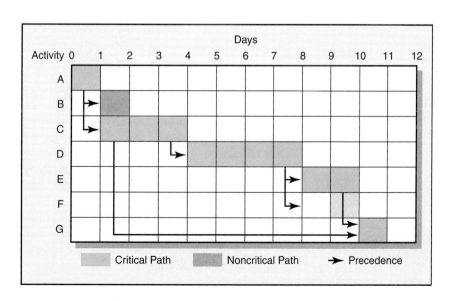

EXHIBIT 6.8
Project Cost Breakdown

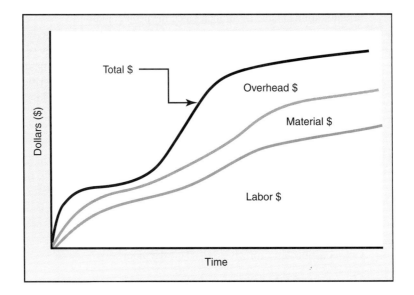

EXHIBIT 6.9
Divisional Breakdown of Costs and Labor Hours

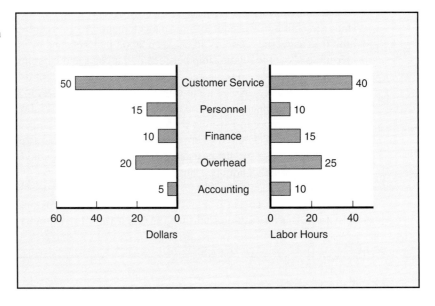

higher than normal costs because they include, for example, overtime premiums for labor and the additional expenses of the coordination involved in the expediting.

For each activity in a project, the normal costs and crash costs can be computed, along with the time reduction expected from crashing the activities. The project manager can then decide on how much time to take to complete each activity based on the trade-off between time and money for the project. For example, suppose the restaurant renovation project is scheduled for completion in late November. The manager might be willing to pay more to have the project completed before Thanksgiving, when the restaurant usually experiences high demand. An analysis of the activities in the project will determine how much it will cost to complete the project early. If the cost of early completion is less than or equal to what the firm is willing to pay, "crashing" the appropriate activities makes sense. However, if the cost of early completion is greater than the firm is willing to pay, crashing is not a rational alternative.

EXHIBIT 6.10
**Actual versus
Projected Costs Graph**

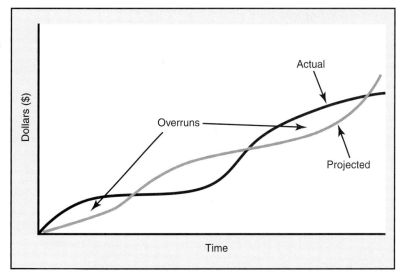

Not all activities can be effectively crashed. Some do not respond to additional labor (such as writing a chapter in a textbook), some are limited by physical processes (it takes a certain amount of time for paint to dry), and some do not respond well to additional pressure (people don't think faster if the stress increases!).

The Critical Chain

As noted previously in this chapter, most organizations have several projects ongoing at any time and it is likely that the same resources within the organization will be required for more than one project at the same time, creating a chain of projects across the organization. Eli Goldratt refers to this concept as the *critical chain*.[6] If the activities along the critical path in project B cannot be completed because resources are being used for completing activities in project A, project A and project B are part of the same critical chain of activities that are linked by the need for common resources. Furthermore, project B will not be able to be completed in the time expected because an activity on its critical path has been delayed.

The critical chain phenomenon is likely to affect how people in organizations estimate activity times for projects. The people doing project work in an organization understand that they may be expected to complete activities of more than one project at a time; therefore, they are likely to overestimate the time it requires to complete an activity just in case the requirements of more than one project become active at the same time. These estimates are longer than the actual time for an activity, hence total project duration is likely to be overestimated.

Then, you might ask, why do so many projects run late? There are several possible explanations. First, as Parkinson's Law states, work fills the time available. Within many organizations, completing an activity early may increase the expectation that all activities will be completed ahead of schedule. Completing an activity early will not always enable the next activity to begin early because of other demands on the resources for that activity.

The critical chain concept reinforces the importance of good time estimates and also emphasizes the importance of maintaining a "big picture" view from the top: Someone should be watching how resource demands across many projects affect each individual project and the organization as a whole.

[6] Elihahu M. Goldratt, *Critical Chain* (Croton-on-Hudson, NY: North River Press, 1998).

Closing and Evaluating the Project

Eventually, every project comes to an end. When a project is completed, it is important for the project members to "debrief" to assess what worked well and what didn't. Although a true project is not repeated often, the process of managing a project is repeated and much of what is learned about the management of one project can be directly applied to the management of other projects. Unfortunately, many organizations skip this important step, for myriad reasons:

- "It's time to move on." In today's fast-paced world there is always another project on the horizon. It is easy to believe that reviewing a completed project is wasting precious time that could be spent on the new project.

- "We know we made mistakes—there's no point in dwelling on them." Like individuals, most organizations don't like to think about their mistakes; it is easier and more pleasant to think about successes. However, the only way to avoid similar mistakes in the future is to thoroughly understand the mistakes of the past.

- "The team has changed." Since projects, especially large projects, usually have long time horizons, often the people involved at the end are not the same ones who started the project. Debriefing about early steps in the process may be less complete than if the original team was in place, but the team at the end of a project can still identify elements that could have been managed differently.

- "It's costly to have meetings about something that's already done." Costs are associated with debriefing, but rather than costs associated with a project that is past, these costs are really associated with preventing problems in the future, and while they are real costs (primarily the time of the individuals involved) these costs are likely to be much lower than the costs associated with addressing the same problems in the next project.

Project Life Cycle Compression

As time becomes an increasingly important factor for business competitiveness, there is growing emphasis on applying project management techniques to compress the project life cycle. Sometimes activities that are normally performed in sequence, for example, design and implementation, can be performed in parallel. Compression of a project schedule by overlapping phases or activities that were originally planned be to done sequentially is called **fast-tracking.** Fast-tracking differs from crashing in that the tasks are overlapped without incurring additional project costs.

A firm's ability to introduce new services into the marketplace faster than its competitors can determine whether it will win or lose the battle for new customers, which ultimately affects the bottom line. Although newer technologies have certainly played a role in developing our expectations about both how long projects should take and how much they should cost, they have also improved the ability to complete many tasks more quickly, which only raises the expectation for accelerating projects even more!

Relating Projects to Repetitive Processes

As stated earlier, projects are a special type of process that are one of a kind and often large and complex. Many processes, however, share the characteristics of both projects and repetitive processes. For example, an advertising firm rolls out new advertising campaigns for clients on a regular basis. Each campaign is different, but all the campaigns share certain common characteristics that make those "repeated projects" more like processes. The astute manager recognizes that the efficiency orientation of repetitive process management can be applied to projects. For example, when the advertising campaign is over, a thoughtful after-action review can pinpoint what aspects of the project were particularly successful and what aspects were particularly challenging—or just didn't work. Sharing these insights with members of the next advertising campaign team may help them to learn from both the successes and the problems of the prior project.

The Impact of Technology

Technology has significantly improved the tools that are available to a project manager. Many project management software packages produce the kinds of reports and graphs described in this chapter in seconds, rather than in hours of painstaking manual work. The Project Management Center, a central source for project management information on the Internet, provides a directory of project management software (http://www.infogoal.com/pmc/pmcswr.htm), listing more than 50 Windows-based packages, nearly 80 Web-based programs, and nearly 30 programs that run on other platforms! There is a project management software package for nearly every type of project, from the most straightforward to the most complex. Nearly every day, enhancements are made to these tools to make them more user-friendly and more informative about all the variables that project managers want to track.

Project management software can be divided into two major categories: (*a*) desktop products, such as Microsoft Project and Primavera Project, and (*b*) Web-enabled products, such as that provided by PlanView.

One key factor to consider when purchasing a project management software package is price. Dick Billows of the Hampton Group in Denver, Colorado, has divided today's project management software into three price categories.[7] In the low end of the market at less than $100 are products such as TurboProject, Milestone Simplicity, and Project Vision. With these products, project managers can automate the network drawing process, prepare occasional status reports, and produce some simple Gantt and network diagrams.

Larger, cross-functional projects place additional requirements on both the project manager and software. Products that fall in this intermediate price level can simulate the project and have the ability to reschedule activities to optimize results, based on the latest developments. With these larger projects, budgets are an important consideration, and project management needs to include estimates of the projects' labor requirements. Software in this category has the ability to schedule and track labor hours and costs. The cost of software in this category can range from $300 to $500, with Microsoft Project and Primavera products being the market leaders.

The high end of the software market ranges from $400 to $20,000 and differs considerably in terms of what is provided. These software packages are typically for project managers who are managing more than one project simultaneously. Products available in this category include Microsoft Project 2000 (with Project Central), Primavera Project Planner, Open Plan, Cobra, and Enterprise PM.

The combination of improved software and advances in telecommunications allows larger projects to be better managed across greater distances. The same tools permit team members to work effectively together although members may be physically located all over the world.

---

[7] Richard Billows, "A Buyer's Guide to Selecting Project Management Software," The Hampton Group, 2001 (www.4pm.com/articles/selpmsw.html).

Technology has also enhanced an organization's ability to collect good data on past projects, thereby improving time and cost estimates. And communication technology, from Web connections to teleconferencing, now supports virtual project teams on the "soft side" of project management: team dynamics and interpersonal connection.

Summary

Projects are a special type of process that are one of a kind and are often large and complex, spanning both internal and external organizational boundaries. Since projects are by definition not repetitive, flexibility is an important aspect of successful project management. The unique tasks associated with projects cannot normally be totally understood until the projects are well under way so project plans continue to evolve over the life of the project. Effective project management usually requires continuously monitoring, updating, and replanning throughout the project timeline.

Effective project management also involves managing people from a variety of disciplines and helping the project team to cope with the stress associated with project uncertainty. A variety of tools can be used to more effectively monitor and control both project time and resources.

Key Terms

crash costs (or expedited costs): the costs associated with completing the activity in shorter-than-normal time. *(p. 115)*

crash time (or expedited time): the project duration time after expediting. *(p. 115)*

critical path: The longest path through a project network, representing the shortest duration of the project as a whole, analogous to the bottleneck in a sequential process. *(p. 112)*

fast-tracking: the compression and/or overlapping of activities to reduce the overall duration of the project. *(p. 118)*

Gantt chart: A diagram that depicts the activities in a project and clearly shows the time required to complete each activity. *(p. 115)*

network diagram: A diagram that graphically demonstrates the relationship between the activities and makes it possible to identify the longest path of activities through the project. *(p. 112)*

project: A set of related and interdependent activities that are directed toward the production of some major identifiable product or service—usually one of a kind. *(p. 102)*

slack time: the time an activity can be delayed without affecting either the completion of the project overall (total slack) or the earliest start time of any other activity in the network (free slack). *(p. 112)*

work breakdown structure (WBS): subdivides a complicated task into smaller tasks, and then subdivides each of these smaller tasks into still smaller tasks until the tasks are small enough to be easily understood. *(p. 108)*

Review and Discussion Questions

1. Describe the difference between projects and repetitive processes.
2. You are planning a graduation party. Using the work breakdown structure, identify the components of this project.
3. How does the role of a project manager differ from that of a traditional functional manager?
4. Why are projects difficult to schedule?
5. Define critical path.
6. "Project control should always focus on the critical path." Comment.
7. Describe some of the graphical tools that can be used to monitor and control projects.
8. You are responsible for selecting a project audit leader. What characteristics would you look for? Why?
9. Project managers have sometimes been compared to orchestra conductors. What characteristics do these two roles have in common?

Internet Assignment

Connect to your favorite Internet search engine and do a search on "service projects" or "projects and services." Visit at least four sites to identify at least five projects about which you can find the following information:

1. The nature of the project: What is the key goal?
2. The people involved in the project: Who are they? Is this a business or a public service project?
3. How large is the project? Is it expected to take weeks? Months? Years?
4. How is the project funded? Are workers paid or do they volunteer?

Selected Bibliography

Goldratt, Elihahu M. *Critical Chain.* Croton-on-Hudson, NY: North River Press, 1998.

Gray, Clifford, and Erik Larsen. *Project Management.* New York: Irwin/McGraw-Hill, 2000.

The Hamilton Group, 4PM website, URL: http://www.4pm.com/.

Schonfield, Erick. "Schwab Puts It All Online." *Fortune,* December 7, 1998, pp. 84–99.

Thamhain, Hans J. "Effective Leadership Style for Managing Project Teams." In *Handbook of Program and Project Management,* ed. P. C. Dinsmore (New York: AMACOM, 1992).

Thamhain, Hans J. "Managing Technologically Innovative Team Efforts toward New Product Success." *Journal of Production Innovation Management* 7, no. 1 (March 1990).

Tuchman, B. W., and M. C. Jensen. "Stages of Small Group Development Revisited." *Group and Organizational Studies* 2 (1977), pp. 419–27.

Project Scheduling, Cost, and Risks

Learning Objectives

- Introduce tools that enable managers to monitor and control project duration and costs.

- Demonstrate how to determine a project's duration.

- Illustrate how to identify which resources have priority in a project.

- Show how to shorten a project's duration by crashing activities.

- Demonstrate how to calculate and interpret the costs associated with crashing project activities.

Managerial Issues

Project managers strive to complete every project with the desired end result on time and within budget. In other words, project managers are concerned about quality, schedule, and costs.

As described in Chapter 6, managers use a variety of tools to monitor and control both the costs of projects and the time it takes to complete them. Among the most useful of these tools is the network diagram, which illustrates the relationship between tasks. It also identifies the critical path, which is the sequence of activities that takes the longest time to complete and which therefore determines the shortest time in which the project can be completed. But before managers can schedule projects, they need to determine the order in which activities must be performed.

Identifying Precedence Relationships

The project-related work described in Chapter 6—defining the project's goals and developing the detailed project plan—is the critical front end to successful project scheduling. Included in that work is the development of the work breakdown structure (WBS), which identifies what activities are involved in the project and estimates how long it will take to complete each activity.

To construct a network diagram, the project team first needs to determine the sequence of activities in the WBS—in other words, which activities must be preceded by other activities. These dependency relationships between tasks are called *precedence relationships*.

EXHIBIT 6S.1
Restaurant Renovation Precedence Table

Activity	Activity Description	Time (days)	Immediate Predecessor
A	Remove furniture and draperies	1	none
B	Launder draperies	1	A
C	Sand walls and woodwork	3	A
D	Paint walls and woodwork	4	C
E	Install carpet	2	D
F	Rehang draperies	1	D
G	Rearrange furniture	1	B, E

Typically, the activities identified in the WBS are arranged in a table that shows those relationships. The table of precedence relationships for the restaurant renovation project presented in Chapter 6 is shown in Exhibit 6S.1.

Activity A has no immediate predecessor activities. The remaining activities in the table follow at least one other activity: activity B must follow activity A; activity G must follow both activity B and activity E. Once the precedence relationships are understood, the project network diagram can be created.

Types of Network Diagrams

Historically, there were two basic methods for producing network diagrams. The **critical path method (CPM)** used *activity-on-the-node* diagrams, with circles representing each activity in the project and arrows indicating the relationships between the activities. CPM diagrams were usually constructed using the most-likely or best estimates for activity completion times. The **program evaluation and review technique (PERT)** used *activity-on-the-arc* diagrams depicting activities as arrows and using circles to show the start and end point of each activity, called an *event*. PERT diagrams allowed for the use of three time estimates for each activity: optimistic, most-likely, and pessimistic estimates. Optimistic times are the shortest times; they are based on the assumption that everything goes smoothly within each activity. Pessimistic times are the longest times; they consider some of the more likely problems that could, but will not necessarily, occur. (Note: Pessimistic times are based on likely problems, not unlikely problems such as tidal waves in New England.) Most-likely times are the best estimate of how long project activities will take if normal conditions apply.

The distinctions between CPM and PERT diagrams have blurred over time because CPM users can (and often do) use three time estimates, and PERT users can (and do) place activities on nodes rather than arcs. Since the proliferation of PC-based project management software, virtually all network diagrams are developed using activity-on-the-node notation. Exhibit 6S.2 graphically illustrates the differences between CPM and PERT diagrams.

Activity-on-the-arc diagrams are generally more difficult to construct because they sometimes require the use of "dummy" activities in order to show precedence relationships between activities that share an end event and to preserve precedence relationships.

Before we demonstrate how network diagrams are constructed, it is important to note that managers of projects with more than just a few activities would never construct network diagrams manually; they would use project management software. Many project management software packages are available with features that vary from package to package. All project management software packages produce network diagrams, provide information about slack time, produce timelines and calendars, and track costs. All the software algorithms use the techniques described here to identify the critical path and to calculate slack time. Having a basic understanding of how these tools work enables the project manager to more appropriately manage projects using the output provided.

EXHIBIT 6S.2
Comparison between CPM and PERT Network Diagrams

CPM (Activity-on-the-Node) Network Diagram

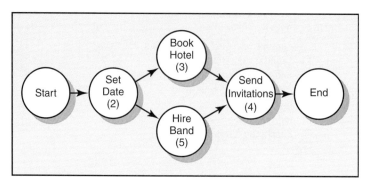

PERT (Activity-on-the-Arc) Network Diagram

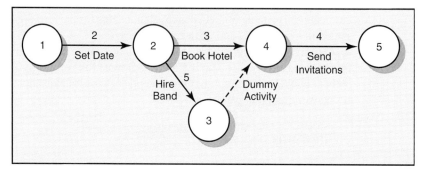

Constructing a Network Diagram with Single Completion Time Estimates

The first step to constructing a project network diagram is to draw the network of activities. The network begins with a circle, or *node*, labeled "Start." A node is drawn to depict each activity and an arrow is drawn between each activity and its immediate predecessors and successors. Activities with no immediate successors are connected to a node labeled "End." Each activity node is labeled with the activity name and the time required to complete the activity.

The network diagram or CPM chart for the restaurant renovation project activities listed in the precedence table above is shown below.

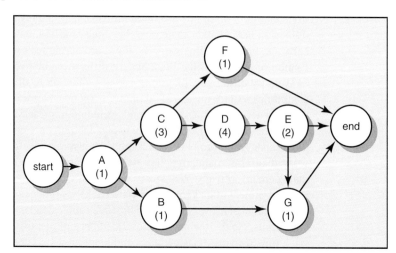

Calculating Earliest Start and Earliest Finish Times: The Forward Pass

The next step is to determine the earliest possible start time and the earliest possible finish time for each activity in the project network. The procedure for identifying the *earliest start* and *earliest finish* times is called the **forward pass** because it moves forward through the network from the "start" node toward the "end" node. The earliest start time for the "start" node is zero. Because the "start" activity does not require time to complete, the earliest finish for that node is also zero. For each activity, the earliest finish time is that activity's earliest start time plus that activity's completion time.

Proceeding forward through the network, the earliest finish time for each predecessor node becomes the earliest start time for its successor nodes.

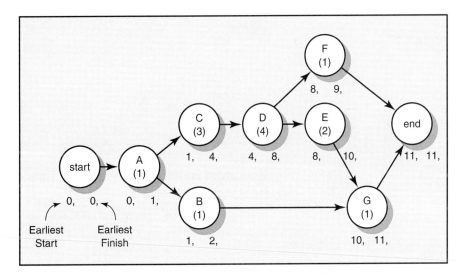

When an activity has more than one predecessor activity (in other words, when more than one arrow points to an activity node), the *latest* early finish time among its predecessor activities determines the earliest start time for that activity (see activity G in the figure below). This is because the successor activity cannot begin until all the immediate predecessor activities have been completed.

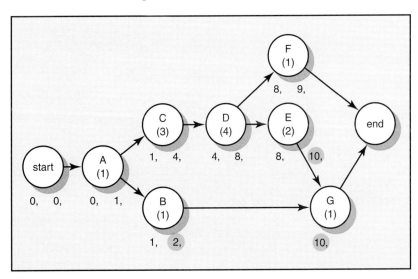

When the "end" node is reached, the forward pass is completed and the earliest finish time for each activity has been determined. The completion time for the "end" node is called the *project completion time* or *project duration time.*

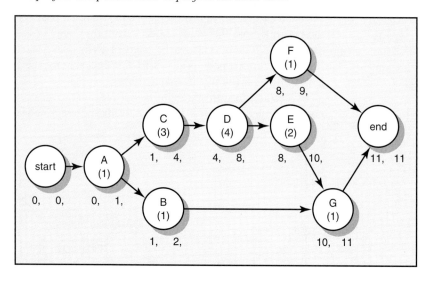

Calculating the Latest Finish and Latest Start Times: The Backward Pass

The next step in identifying a project's critical path is to go through the project network again, this time working *backward* through the network from the "end" node to determine the *latest finish* and *latest start* times for each activity. This process is called the **backward pass.**

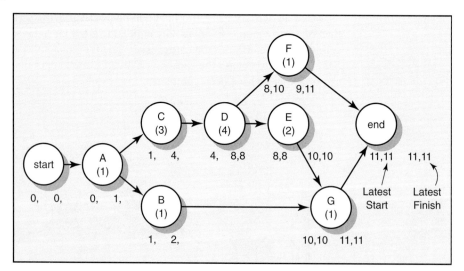

Unless the project's customer specifies a later completion time, the earliest finish time is also used at the "end" node as the latest finish time. To do the backward pass, the latest start of each successor activity is used as the latest finish for its predecessors, subtracting the activity time at each node. For the restaurant renovation example, the forward pass determined that the project could be completed in 11 days because it was the earliest finish time for the project. We start the backward pass using 11 days as the latest finish time. Proceeding backward to activity F, the latest finish time for the project (11 days – 0 days at the end node) is the latest finish time for activity F. At activity F, we subtract its completion time (1 day) from its latest finish time (11 days) to get its latest start time of 10 days. As with the forward pass, this procedure is followed through the network along each path until a node with more than one successor (or a node with more than one arrow leading to it when working *backward*) is reached.

A node with more than one successor node uses the earliest of the latest start times of its successors as its latest finish time because the predecessor activity must be completed before the latest start among all its successor activities. In the restaurant renovation example, activity D has two successor activities, F and E. The latest start time for activity F is 10 and the latest start time for activity E is day 8. Because activity E's latest start is eight, activity D's latest finish can be no later than day 8.

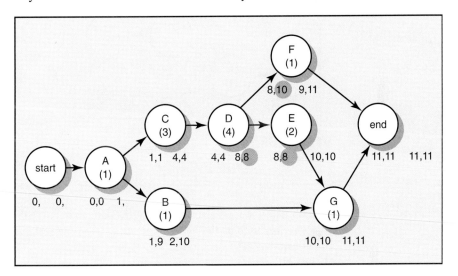

When the "start" node is reached, the backward pass is completed and the latest finish and latest start times for each activity have been determined.

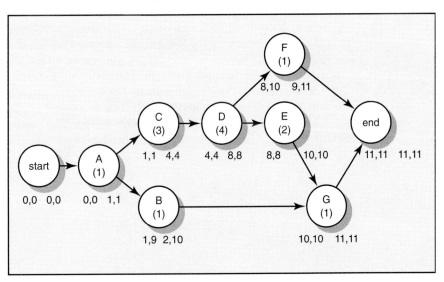

Computing Slack Times and Identifying the Critical Path

After completion of the forward and backward passes through the network, the *difference between the earliest start and latest start* and the *difference between the earliest finish and the latest finish* is computed for each activity. (These differences should be the same for a given activity; a check on your computations!) These differences are called **total slack time,** which is the maximum amount of time an activity may be delayed beyond its early start without delaying the overall project completion time.

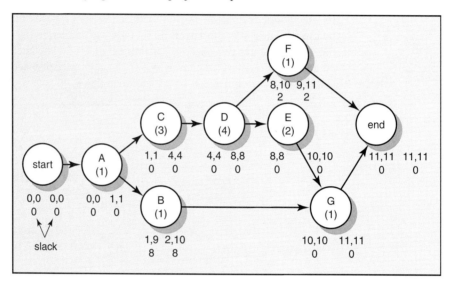

The path with the least slack is the critical path. Whenever the earliest finish time for the project is also used as the latest finish time, as in the restaurant renovation example, the critical path has zero slack time.

The critical path is the longest path through a project network, so you may have been wondering why you couldn't simply identify the critical path by identifying that longest path. In this simple example, finding that path is not difficult because there are only three paths through the network: A-B-G, A-C-D-E-G, and A-C-D-F. In large networks, however, even enumerating all the possible paths through a network can be extremely difficult, even without determining the length of each path. Project scheduling software identifies the critical path by performing the forward and backward passes, thereby identifying the slack at each node and, in turn, identifying the path with the least slack (which, if the default of earliest finish = late finish is used, will be zero) as the critical path.

In the restaurant renovation network below, the critical path, A-C-D-E-G, is the longest path through the network and has zero slack at each activity node. It is, therefore, the critical path for this project. Reducing the time required to complete activities not on the critical path will have no effect on overall project completion time.

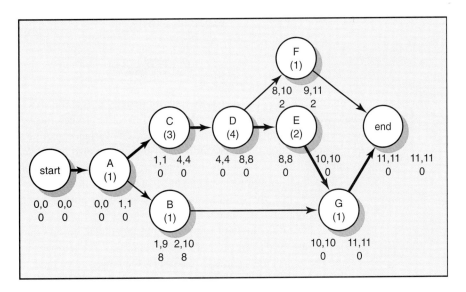

Total slack time was defined above as the maximum amount of time an activity may be delayed beyond its early start without delaying the overall project completion time. Another type of slack time is **free slack time.** Free slack time is defined as the amount of time an activity can be delayed without delaying the early start of any other activity. In the restaurant renovation example, activity B has total slack time of eight days; it can be delayed eight days without affecting the overall project duration. Activity B also has free slack time of eight days; it can be delayed eight days without affecting its successor activity's earliest start. An activity that has total slack time may or may not have free slack time, but free slack time can never exceed total slack time for an activity. For example, activity F has total slack time of two days but no free slack time.

Probabilistic Activity Estimates

As noted previously, activity times are often uncertain in large projects, so it may be useful to estimate activity completion times using optimistic, best-estimate, and pessimistic times. These times are estimated based on the judgment of people who understand the activities. The optimistic time is the least amount of time in which the activity can be completed if all goes smoothly. The most-likely or best-estimate time is the time the experts think it *should* take. The pessimistic time takes into consideration reasonable delays in the activity. Revisiting our original project chart for renovating the restaurant, we might modify the time estimates as shown in Exhibit 6S.3.

For a rough estimate of the expected activity time, these times are weighted based on the beta probability distribution. The **beta distribution** is a flexible distribution that can take on a variety of forms that typically characterize project management activities. It has finite end points that limit the possible activity times to the area between o and p and, in the simplified version, permits a straightforward computation of the activity mean and standard deviation. The optimistic and pessimistic times are given a weight of 1 and the most likely or "best estimate" is given a weight of 4, indicating that the "best estimate" is four times more likely to occur than either the optimistic or pessimistic times. The expected time for each activity, then, would be calculated as the sum of the weighted times, divided by the total weight (6). For activity C, the calculation would be:

$$\text{Expected Activity Time} = \frac{o + 4m + p}{6}$$

$$\frac{(1)2 + (4)3 + (1)7}{6} = 3.5 \text{ days}$$

In this case, the expected activity time for activity C is somewhat higher than the "best estimate." To determine the expected time for the entire project, the expected times for activities on the critical path would be added together. The variance and the standard deviation for the project completion time probability distribution can also be calculated, permitting the project manager to understand the likelihood of completing the project within a given time.

The beta distribution should be used as a first estimate for the weights. As the manager gains experience, the weights should be empirically adjusted until the resulting estimates most closely match the actual times.

Using three different time estimates for calculating a project's duration can be confusing for the people involved in the project, and with confusion often comes distrust and obstruction. The role of the project manager is to make sure the project team understands the tools adequately so that they are helpful to the team, rather than a source of annoyance or misunderstanding.

Assumptions of Critical Path Network Management of Projects

Several assumptions need to be made when applying network analysis to projects, but these are not always valid in actual projects.

1. *Assumption:* Project activities can be defined with clear beginning and end points.
   Reality: Real projects, with all their complexity, change over time, so a network diagram developed at the beginning of a project is very likely to change as the project progresses toward completion. To manage large projects, it is usually necessary to frequently update the project network as better information becomes available.

2. *Assumption:* Project activity precedence relationships can be clearly specified.
   Reality: Precedence relationships are not always clear before the work actually begins. In some projects, the sequencing of later activities depends on the outcomes of earlier activities. Again, this generally means that project networks must be updated as the project moves forward.

3. *Assumption:* Project control should focus on the critical path.
   Reality: The critical path often shifts as a project proceeds and estimated activity times change. An experienced project manager recognizes the need to pay attention to all the paths in a network with an understanding of the relative slack time on each path. Contributing to the difficulty of managing the critical path is what Eli Goldratt calls the **critical chain.** As

EXHIBIT 6S.3
Restaurant Renovation Precedence Table with Probabilistic Activity Times

Activity	Activity Description	Time Estimates (days)			Immediate Predecessor
		Optimistic (o)	Most Likely (m)	Pessimistic (p)	
A	Remove furniture and draperies	1	1	2	none
B	Launder draperies	1	1	2	A
C	Sand walls and woodwork	2	3	7	A
D	Paint walls and woodwork	2	4	6	C
E	Install carpet	1	2	3	D
F	Rehang draperies	1	1	1	D
G	Rearrange furniture	1	1	1	B, E

discussed in Chapter 6, Goldratt notes that most organizations that do project work have workers engaged in more than one project at a time—and they are likely to be working with people in other organizations who are also working on more than one project at a time. Since these projects intersect, a chain of activities is affected not only by uncertainty in the activities themselves and by the activities in their own project network, but also potentially by the uncertainties in the activities in those other projects with which they intersect—another argument for the wise project manager to keep an eye on all the paths in the network!

Another problem that sometimes arises is the attempt to beat the network by getting on or off the critical path. Many contracts provide incentives for finishing a project early. Contractors on the critical path generally have more leverage for obtaining funds since they have a major influence on project duration.

Project network techniques have proved themselves for more than three decades and promise to be of continued value in the future.

Time–Cost Trade-offs

There is usually a relationship between how long it takes and how much it costs to complete an activity. Some costs are associated with completing a project more quickly, but other costs are incurred when a project's duration is longer than originally planned.

The costs associated with shortening a project's duration are called crash costs. Crash costs include worker-related costs, such as overtime pay, hiring additional workers, transferring workers from other jobs, as well other resource-related costs, such as buying or leasing additional equipment or drawing on other support facilities. Crash costs can also include the costs to expedite the delivery of material and project-related documents (for example, using FedEx instead of regular mail).

When a project takes longer than anticipated to complete, costs such as overhead and project-related space costs, such as rent, continue and therefore add to the overall cost of the project. Projects that are completed after the deadline may also incur penalty costs, and the firm may incur opportunity costs if other work cannot be started until the current project is completed.

Chapter 6 defined crash costs (or expedited costs) as the costs associated with completing an activity in less than normal time. Consider the consulting project example presented in Exhibit 6S.4. The total cost for completing the project in normal time is $57,000. Each activity can be crashed and the cost of shortening each activity by one week is shown.

EXHIBIT 6S.4 **Consulting Project Precedence and Cost Table**

Activity	Immediate Predecessor	Activity Description	Normal Time (weeks)	Normal Activity Cost	Minimum Time to Complete (weeks)	Total Cost if Crashed to Minimum Time	Cost to Reduce Time by One Week
A	none	Prepare proposal	3	$5,000	2	$10,000	$5,000
B	A	Discuss proposal with client	2	$3,000	1	$4,000	$1,000
C	B	Collect data	4	$22,000	2	$34,000	$6,000
D	C	Analyze data	3	$9,000	1	$12,000	$3,000
E	D	Write report	3	$8,000	2	$10,000	$2,000
F	D	Present findings to client	2	$10,000	1	$14,000	$4,000
		Totals:		$57,000		$87,000	

The network diagram for the consulting project is:

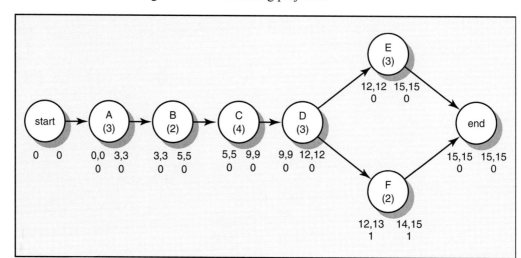

The critical path for the project is A-B-C-D-E. The time–cost trade-offs can be shown by calculating the total project costs as it is reduced in length by one day at a time. To reduce the project duration by one day, select the activity along the current critical path that has the lowest crash cost per day, as shown in Exhibit 6S.5

EXHIBIT 6S.5 **Reducing Consulting Project Completion Time One Week at a Time**

Current Critical Path(s)	Remaining Number of Weeks Activity May Be Shortened			Cost Per Week to Expedite Each Activity			Least Cost Activity to Expedite	Total Cost of All Activities in Network	Project Completion Time
A-B-C-D-E								$57,000	15
A-B-C-D-E	A-1, B-1, C-2, D-2, E-1, F-1			A-5, B-1, C-6, D-3, E-2, F-4			B	$58,000	14
A-B-C-D-E	A-1,	C-2, D-2, E-1, F-1		A-5,	C-6, D-3, E-2, F-4		E	$60,000	13
A-B-C-D-E, A-B-C-D-F	A-1,	C-2, D-2,	F-1	A-5,	C-6, D-3,	F-4	D	$63,000	12
A-B-C-D-E, A-B-C-D-F	A-1,	C-2, D-1,	F-1	A-5,	C-6, D-3,	F-4	D	$66,000	11
A-B-C-D-E, A-B-C-D-F	A-1,	C-2,	F-1	A-5,	C-6,	F-4	A*	$71,000	10
A-B-C-D-E, A-B-C-D-F		C-2,	F-1		C-6,	F-4	C*	$77,000	9
A-B-C-D-E, A-B-C-D-F		C-1,	F-1		C-6,	F-4	C*	$83,000	8
A-B-C-D-E, A-B-C-D-F			F-1*						

* Crashing F will not shorten total project duration.

EXHIBIT 6S.6
Total Consulting Project Cost with Penalties

Project Completion Time (weeks)	Normal Plus Crash Costs	Penalty Costs at $4,000/Week over 8 Weeks	Total Project Cost
15	$57,000	$28,000	$92,000
14	$58,000	$24,000	$88,000
13	$60,000	$20,000	$85,000
12	$63,000	$16,000	$83,000
11	$66,000	$12,000	$81,000
10	$71,000	$8,000	$81,000
9	$77,000	$4,000	$82,000
8	$83,000	$0	$83,000

Note that although activity F is less expensive to crash than activity A or C, crashing activity F would not shorten the overall project duration. The shortest possible project duration is eight weeks at a total cost of $83,000.

What if the consulting firm in this example had agreed to pay penalty costs of $4,000 per day if the project was not completed by week 8? The total cost table, including penalty costs, is shown in Exhibit 6S.6.

Exhibit 6S.6 demonstrates that when penalty costs are considered, the total cost of the project is minimized at either 10 or 11 weeks total completion time. But the project manager must consider other factors when deciding which project completion time is most appropriate. For example, it may make sense to have the total cost of the project be $2,000 more than the minimum possible cost in order to satisfy the customer. Completing the project earlier also reduces the opportunity costs that might be incurred if another project cannot be started during the time between the minimum time and the 10th or 11th week. On the other hand, the project manager may need the resources that could be deployed to expedite this consulting project on a different project, so he or she might choose to pay the penalty costs rather than risk having the other project delayed by pulling resources away from it. Strategic issues as well as immediate cost issues should always be considered when project time–cost decisions are made.

Note that the total project cost at 8 weeks in Exhibit 6S.6 is $83,000, not the $87,000 shown in Exhibit 6S.4 that represents the cost of crashing all activities to their minimum time. Crashing an activity only shortens project duration when that activity is on the critical path, so it is necessary to work through the iterative process shown in Exhibit 6S.5.

Evaluating and Managing Risk in Projects

In Chapter 6 we defined a project as a set of related and interdependent activities that are directed toward the creation of some major identifiable product or service that is usually one of a kind. They are often large and are either not repeated or repeated very infrequently. These characteristics make projects inherently risky.

Risks are more likely to occur at the beginning of a project, when uncertainty is highest. When risks do occur early in a project, it is often possible to develop alternatives that keep costs in line. When risks occur later in a project, they are likely to be more costly to address and there are likely to be fewer alternatives available because the project has already progressed along a certain path. For example, a project for developing a new website can change the tone of its message to customers with little expense before the site is

EXHIBIT 6S.7
Probability and Cost of Risk as Project Progresses

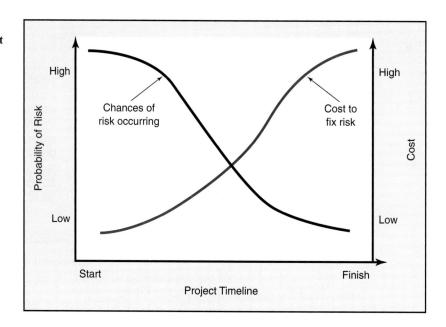

mapped out and before text has been written. After the site is mapped and the pages of the site are populated with data, changing the overall tone of the website is much more costly. Exhibit 6S.7 illustrates the relationship between the probability of risk occurring, the cost associated with risk, and the timeline of the project.

Types of Project Risks

The risks associated with projects can be classified into four major categories: (*a*) organizational risks, (*b*) financial risks, (*c*) technical risks, and (*d*) scheduling risks.

Organizational Risks

Organizational risks are risks associated with the relationships that are affected by a project. Some affected relationships are inside the firm. When a project organization is formed, the relationships among people in the organization are affected by new organizational structures. There may be risks to individual project team members. For example, if the project is not successful, project team members may lose their status in the organization or may find that the jobs they held before they were assigned to the project are no longer available to them. Projects can also affect relationships between firms because many projects cross organizational boundaries. If a project does not meet its cost or completion time objectives, relationships between the firm and its suppliers and/or customers may be strained, which can have significant long-term implications beyond the project.

Another risk for both individuals and for the firm is related to developing new capabilities. One objective for a project manager may be to provide opportunities for project team members to learn new skills. If, however, the team members do not develop the skill set required by the project, the project objectives may not be met and the team members again risk their status within the organization.

One major organizational risk for most firms that do project work is the opportunity cost associated with having employees focus their efforts on their assigned project activities in addition to their regular job responsibilities. In other words, focusing primarily on a project, no matter how important, may make it difficult or impossible for employees to perform as well in their "day jobs." The nonproject work of the organization and the well-being of the overloaded employee may be jeopardized by the project.

Financial Risks

Financial risks are directly related to project costs. Because project activities are difficult to understand fully before the onset of most projects, costs may be considerably higher than projected. If the project runs late or does not meet its objectives, there may be significant financial penalties. Opportunity costs are also associated with taking on one project versus another or with undertaking a project that distracts workers from their other responsibilities.

Technical Risks

Many projects are subject to significant technical risks. Again, because projects are unique undertakings, it may be difficult to completely understand the technical requirements of a project until the project is well under way. A very clever television commercial demonstrated this risk by showing a top manager standing in the midst of his staff and holding a consultant's strategy report. The manager tells his staff how excited he is about moving forward with a key strategic initiative and then says, "I have just one question for you: Can we do this with our current technology?" After a short dramatic pause and some furtive glances between the staff members, one staff member speaks up and says, "No. We can't. No way." The manager is last shown looking stunned and disheartened. This manager was lucky; he found out about the technical risks before the project began. Sometimes the technical problems are not encountered until later. If the problems are significant, the project's costs may soar or the project may not be completed.

Another technical risk is associated with the technical skill set of the project team members. Not only does the technical ability to complete a project need to exist, but it also needs to exist within or be available to the project team. Whenever a project requires state-of-the-art technology, the technical risks are likely to be considerable. Every new technology has the potential to fail.

Scheduling Risks

Another category of risk associated with projects is scheduling risk. The uncertainty related to individual activities makes their duration difficult to estimate accurately. Because activities in a project are related to other activities in the project network, uncertainty in any one activity can affect other tasks as well as the project overall. The larger the project, the more likely it is that the inherent uncertainty related to the activities will be significant.

These four types of risks are related to each other. For example, when activity uncertainty leads to scheduling risk, there are likely to be associated financial costs. Scheduling and organizational risks are related when tensions arise over competing project resources. Exhibit 6S.8 illustrates the relationships among the four categories of risk.

Managing Risks

A major goal of any project manager is to identify the likely risks, to understand their implications, and to formulate plans for dealing with risks if and when they arise. The first step is to try to identify potential risks before they actually become problems. If the right people have been assembled to work on the project, they will probably be able to anticipate some problems that are likely to occur—or that are perhaps not likely to occur, but if they do occur will become major roadblocks. Once potential risks have been identified, it is important to analyze the information available and evaluate the probability of each risk, its significance to the project overall, and its possible costs. The project team can then use the risk information to identify steps that can be taken to reduce the impact of each risk. As the project progresses, careful monitoring of project status will identify early indicators

EXHIBIT 6S.8
The Relationship between Types of Project Risks

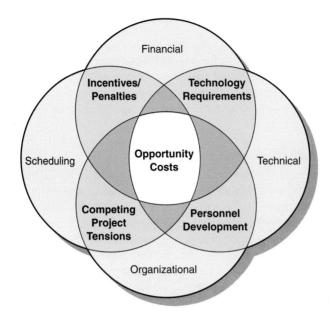

of risk and enable the team to carry out the actions it had planned or, in the case of unanticipated problems, develop action plans to deal with the problems without delay. Clear communication among the project team members throughout the project is essential for identifying risks and actual problems and activating the risk contingency plans.

Impact of Technology

As presented in Chapter 6, technology has dramatically enhanced the ability of project managers to monitor the details of project scheduling and costs with state-of-the-art software. After information about project activities, their durations, their costs, and the resources required to complete them are entered, project management software produces network diagrams, Gantt charts, task resource usage charts, resource requirements charts, costs charts, and calendars. The charts can show milestones and compare budgets for activities against actual costs. Project management software can also help project managers to evaluate the risks associated with project activities and to plan for various contingencies. Complicated, time-consuming analyses are now available almost instantaneously, at the click of a mouse.

All these tools enable project managers to frequently assess project status and regularly evaluate project performance. Because project managers have more complete information more readily available, they can make better decisions about managing project resources and meeting project goals.

Summary

A variety of project management tools enable managers to monitor and control a project's duration and costs. Network diagrams show the relationship between tasks and the earliest and latest times that each activity can begin and end to keep the project on schedule. Network diagrams also identify the critical path, which is the longest path through a project network, and which therefore determines the project's duration. Once the activities on the critical path are identified, the manager can also identify which activities are not critical to the project's duration and can manage resources assigned to those noncritical path activities more effectively. For organizations that undertake several projects at the same time, the concept of the critical chain, which identifies the resource links between seemingly unrelated projects in project-oriented organizations, can help managers to deploy resources more effectively.

There are specific relationships between time and costs in projects. The trade-offs between time and costs are seen when project completion time is reduced by crashing certain activities.

There are several categories of risks associated with projects, and managers can take specific actions to reduce these risks.

Key Terms

backward pass: identification of the latest finish time and latest start time for each activity in a project network. *(p. 126)*

beta distribution: a flexible statistical distribution which provides a starting point for developing project activity duration estimates. *(p. 129)*

critical path method (CPM): network diagramming technique that uses activity-on-the-node diagrams, with circles representing each activity in the project and arrows indicating the relationship between the activities. *(p. 123)*

critical chain: the set of interconnected projects that may cause activities within a single project network that do not appear to be on the critical path to affect project duration. *(p. 130)*

forward pass: identification of the earliest start time and earliest finish time for each activity in a project network. *(p. 125)*

free slack time: the amount of time an activity can be delayed without delaying the early start of any other activity in the project network. *(p. 129)*

program evaluation and review technique (PERT): network diagramming technique that uses activity-on-the-arc diagrams, depicting activities as arrows and using circles to show the start and end point of each activity, called an event. *(p. 123)*

total slack time: the maximum amount of time an activity may be delayed beyond its early start without delaying project completion time. *(p. 128)*

Review and Discussion Questions

1. Describe the process used to identify the critical path in a project network.

2. Describe the difference between optimistic, pessimistic, and most-likely or best time estimates. Discuss why all three estimates are used in probabilistic activity time estimation.

3. You have been asked to lead the planning for the 50th anniversary of your company next year. Who would you want to have on your project team? What information would you need from management to create appropriate boundaries for the project? What project tools could you use to monitor the project as it progresses?

Internet Assignment

Using your favorite search engine, search the Internet using the keywords *project management software* and *project management tools*. Visit at least four sites and compare some of the tools and services that are available to help project managers be successful. Try to find at least one site that offers a demonstration version of the company's project management software. Identify which tools are included in the package and compare them to some of the tools described in this chapter supplement.

Solved Problem

Larry manages a landscaping service and has accepted the following project.

	Activity	Time (days)	Immediate Predecessor
A	Determine landscape design.	5	none
B	Prepare soil.	3	none
C	Grade property.	2	A, B
D	Lay out planting beds.	4	C
E	Plant trees.	2	D
F	Plant shrubs.	5	D
G	Plant flowers.	3	F
H	Plant grass.	2	D
I	Mulch beds.	2	F
J	Place birdbath.	1	G

a. Draw the project network.

b. Find the critical path.

Solution: *a.* The project network looks like this:

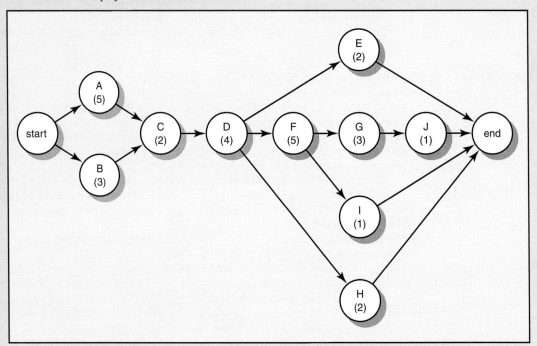

b. To find the critical path, we need to identify the earliest start and finish times, the latest start and finish times, and the slack for each activity. The critical path is the path with the least slack.

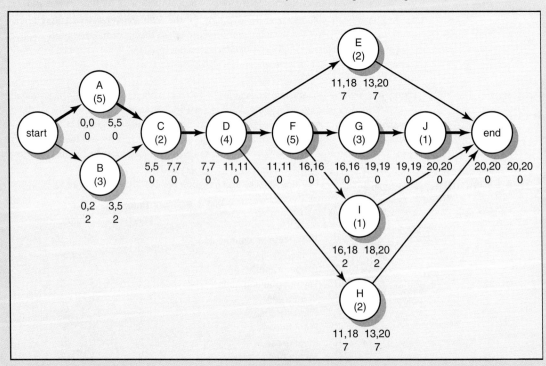

Problems

1. A project has the following list of activities and completion times.

Activity	Immediate Predecessors	Time to Complete (days)
A	–	2
B	A	2
C	A	4
D	B	3
E	C	7
F	C, D	6
G	E, F	2

Construct a network diagram for the project. Do the forward and backward pass and identify slack time for each activity. What is the critical path? What is the expected project completion time?

2. The project team for the project described in question 1 has reassessed its time estimates and provided optimistic, most-likely, and pessimistic time estimates.

Activity	Immediate Predecessors	Time to Complete (days)		
		Optimistic	Most Likely	Pessimistic
A	—	1	2	4
B	A	1	2	3
C	A	2	4	6
D	B	1	3	4
E	C	3	7	12
F	C, D	4	6	9
G	E, F	1	2	4

Construct the project network diagram using these probabilistic activity times. How did slack times change for each activity? Has the critical path changed? What is the expected project completion time?

3. The activities and precedence relationships for tasks in a service project have been identified as follows:

Activity	Immediate Predecessors	Time to Complete (weeks)
A	—	4
B	A	2
C	B	3
D	A, C	4
E	A, C	2
F	D	5

a. Construct a network diagram for the project.
b. Do the forward and backward pass and identify the slack time for each activity.
c. What is the critical path?
d. What is the expected project completion time?

4. The normal and crash costs for the activities in question 3 are shown in the following table:

Activity	Immediate Predecessor	Normal Time (weeks)	Normal Cost	Minimum Time to Complete Activity	Cost to Reduce Activity Duration by One Week
A	—	4	$5,000	3	$2,000
B	A	2	$3,000	1	$3,000
C	B	3	$12,000	2	$1,000
D	A, C	4	$17,000	3	$4,000
E	A, C	2	$3,000	1	$5,000
F	D	5	$8,000	3	$4,000

There is a penalty cost of $4,000 per week for each week the project is delayed beyond 10 weeks.
 a. Construct a table that shows the total project costs for the project.
 b. If you were the project manager, which completion time would you target? Explain.

5. The following represents a plan for a project:

Job No.	Predecessor Job(s)	o	m	p
1	—	2	3	4
2	1	1	2	3
3	1	4	5	12
4	1	3	4	11
5	2	1	3	5
6	3	1	2	3
7	4	1	8	9
8	5, 6	2	4	6
9	8	2	4	12
10	7	3	4	5
11	9, 10	5	7	8

 a. Construct the appropriate network diagram.
 b. Identify the critical path.
 c. What is the expected completion time for the project?
 d. What is the probability that the project will be completed in 30 days or less?

6. The following is a network with the activity times shown above the nodes in days:

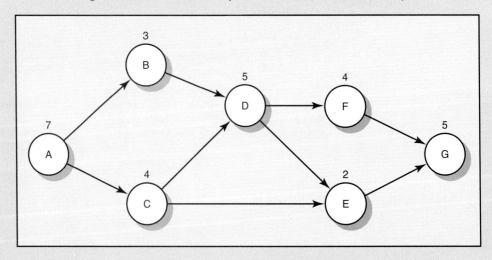

a. Find the critical path.

b. The following table shows the normal times and the crash times, along with the associated costs for each of the activities.

Activity	Normal Time	Crash Time	Normal Cost	Crash Cost
A	7	6	$7,000	$ 8,000
B	3	2	5,000	7,000
C	4	3	9,000	10,200
D	5	4	3,000	4,500
E	2	1	2,000	3,000
F	4	2	4,000	7,000
G	5	4	5,000	8,000

If the project is to be shortened by four days, show which activities in order of reduction would be shortened and the resulting total project costs.

7. The home office billing department of a chain of department stores prepares monthly inventory reports for use by the stores' purchasing agents. Given the following information, use the critical path method to determine:

a. How long will the total process take?

b. Which jobs can be delayed without delaying the early start of any subsequent activity.

Job and Description	Immediate Predecessors	Time (hours)
a	Start	—	0
b	Get computer printouts of customer purchases	a	10
c	Get stock records for the month	a	20
d	Reconcile purchase printouts and stock records	b, c	30
e	Total stock records by department	b, c	20
f	Determine reorder quantities for coming period	e	40
g	Prepare stock reports for purchasing agents	d, f	20
h	Finish	g	0

8. For the network and the data shown:

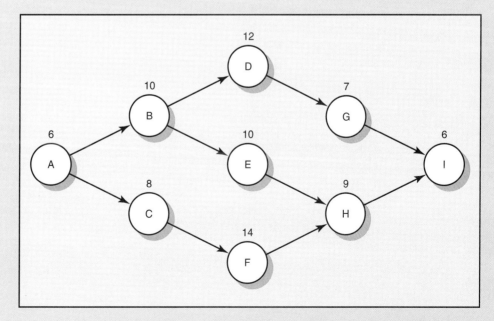

a. Determine the critical path and the early completion time for the project.

Activity	Normal Time (weeks)	Normal Cost	Crash Time (weeks)	Crash Cost
A	6	$ 6,000	4	$12,000
B	10	10,000	9	11,000
C	8	8,000	7	10,000
D	12	12,000	10	14,000
E	10	10,000	7	12,000
F	14	14,000	12	19,000
G	7	7,000	5	10,000
H	9	9,000	6	15,000
I	6	6,000	5	8,000

b. Reduce the project completion time by four weeks and identify the critical path. (An activity cannot be shortened to less than its crash time.)

9. The following CPM network has estimates of the *normal time* listed for the activities:

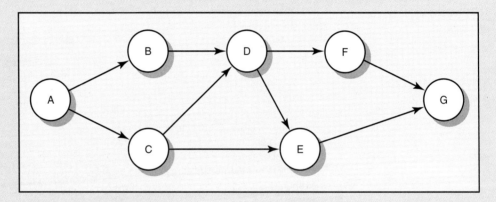

Activity	Time (weeks)
A	7
B	2
C	4
D	5
E	2
F	4
G	5

a. Identify the critical path.
b. What is the length of time to complete the project?
c. Which activities have slack time and how much?

10. The following is a table of normal and crash times and costs. Which activities would you shorten to cut two weeks from the schedule? What would be the incremental cost? Does the critical path change?

Activity	Normal Time	Crash Time	Normal Cost	Crash Cost	Possible Number of Weeks Decrease	Cost/Week to Expedite
A	7	6	$7,000	$ 8,000		
B	2	1	5,000	7,000		
C	4	3	9,000	10,200		
D	5	4	3,000	4,500		
E	2	1	2,000	3,000		
F	4	2	4,000	7,000		
G	5	4	5,000	8,000		

Selected Bibliography

Goldratt, Elihahu M. *Critical Chain.* Croton-on-Hudson, NY: North River Press, 1998.

Gray, Clifford, and Erik Larsen. *Project Management.* New York: Irwin/McGraw-Hill, 2000.

Tuchman, B. W., and M. C. Jensen. "Stages of Small Group Development Revisited." *Group and Organizational Studies* 2 (1977), pp. 419–27.

CHAPTER SEVEN

Designing Service Processes

Learning Objectives

- Present the challenges associated with designing new services.

- Describe the different degrees of innovation and how they affect service design.

- Introduce process flow diagramming and service blueprinting.

- Identify the factors that should be considered when designing services.

Service Design at Disney Theme Parks

© Robert Holmes / CORBIS

Disney theme parks are a wonderful example of services that have been very thoughtfully designed. Every detail of the experience has been carefully planned from the customers' point of view. From the moment the family car pulls into the parking lot until it pulls out at the end of a day of fantasy, the visitors' experiences are mapped out and each element of the service is aligned with the overall experience.

Disney planners know that vacationers want everything to be fun and nothing to be a hassle, so smiling employees are always in sight, ready to help if you need anything. All the facilities are spotlessly clean, and there is enough variety in attractions, food, and price levels to suit everyone's tastes. To keep you coming back, Disney regularly expands its offerings—12 new rides, facilities, or experiences were added at DisneyWorld in the past two years and 22 in the past five! At the same time, Disney continues to improve all the elements of its services and to delight customers of all ages.

Disney's management understands that processes matter to customers. Some of those processes take place behind the scenes: food preparation, costume design, employee training, layout, and scheduling shows. Other processes take place within the view of the customer: characters' interactions with customers, parades, meal service, and entertainment shows. Careful attention to every step in every process—whether visible to the customer or not—lays a strong foundation for successful service delivery.

Source: http://disneyworld.disney.go.com.

The Customer's Perspective

Two days after his 16th birthday, Doug went with his mother to the Massachusetts Registry of Motor Vehicles to apply for his driving learner's permit. The parking lot was full when they arrived, but a spot soon opened up and the two of them entered the building and immediately encountered a sign with an arrow pointing left that said, "Take a Number and Check in at Desk." There were two people in line ahead of Doug, one young man about his age and another man speaking with the woman behind the counter. While they waited, Doug and his mother looked around the room and saw no lines at any of the counters, although several people were waiting on benches.

After waiting about three minutes, Doug reached the counter and the woman asked, "What can we do for you today?" Doug replied that he needed a learner's permit—also known as a Class D license—and she handed him a form and said, "Down at the end."

Doug took the form and walked to the other end of the building. He found a pen, completed the form, and waited for just a moment before his number was called. A personable young woman named Judy greeted him, took his $15, and pointed him toward a room around a corner where he would take the written test. The "written" test was actually a multiple-choice test administered one question at a time on a computer terminal. Doug's mother waited for him for just over five minutes, watching more customers enter the building and move through the process.

When Doug emerged, he returned to Judy's counter, where he waited about 30 seconds for the customer she was serving to complete his transaction. Judy administered Doug's eye test, which he passed when he wore his glasses, then took his picture, a two-step process that involved first taking the picture, then having Doug view it on a screen and decide whether to have another taken. Doug preferred to try another shot and approved the second one immediately. Two more minutes and he was out the door—his coveted learner's permit in hand!

Doug thought the service was just fine, but his mother, who had experienced a very different process the last time her license was renewed, was amazed! She remembered always taking a book to the registry because the lines were so long. Signs were so unclear that it was not uncommon to wait in one long line only to find that you had been waiting in the wrong one, and that you had to start all over again in another. You didn't expect any smiles from the employees—and *forget* having a choice about your picture! The design of the new registry process seemed to her to be an unqualified success!

Think about the services you've encountered in the last week or so. How many services were there? Which of those services delighted you? Which were disappointing? Which of those services left you feeling either angry or frustrated? Which services were just there—not memorable one way or the other? Do you ever catch yourself thinking, "If I were in charge here, I'd sure do this differently"?

Managerial Issues

Service design issues encompass everything from developing something new for an undefined group of customers to enhancing current services by changing service features. Whether the service design issues are large or small, a service operation should be designed to meet the specific needs of its customers. The proper approach to service design should consider what the service should entail, where customers should be served, when they should be served, who should serve them, and how they should be served. Incorporating these customer-related issues into the service system design process assures that the service elements are compatible and focused on satisfying the customer.

Service Design Challenges

Because services are intangible they can be difficult to describe, and that difficulty creates a challenge for service designers. Lynn Shostack identifies four risks inherent to describing services in words:[1]

- *Oversimplification.* Shostack writes, "To say that 'portfolio management' means 'buying and selling stocks' is like describing the space shuttle as 'something that flies.' "

- *Incompleteness.* Customers are able to describe only the parts of the services with which they are familiar and with which they have direct contact.

- *Subjectivity.* People are biased by their own experiences with services.

- *Biased interpretation.* In describing services to others, people add another bias in the way they use words, which are open to the interpretation of the listener. For example, what one person may mean by "polite and responsive" may be very different from what other people think when they hear those words.

The service design process, like any process, can be improved by using a structured approach that systematically collects information from customers and service providers to objectively design a service that meets customer needs, rather than a service that seems like a good one to the manager! Chapter 2 Supplement describes in detail ways that information about customers can be collected and analyzed.

Meeting the Needs of the Customer

The first step toward successful service design is identifying and understanding the specific needs of the customer, which is the focus of Chapter 2. Through thoughtful market research, the target market can be identified and its needs understood. The next step is to determine what customers really expect from a particular type of service. Even within a given industry, customer expectations will vary significantly with the type of service and the particular need. For example, consumers of health care services expect 24-hour availability for emergency care but will usually not have the same expectation for the availability of routine medical examinations.

The challenge of learning about customer needs is magnified for new services. Whether customers can, in fact, correctly identify what they want in a new service is much debated. Customers may not be able to articulate a new service concept, but they can describe their basic needs and expectations from a service delivery system. For example, services such

[1] G. Lynn Shostack, "Designing Services That Deliver," *Harvard Business Review,* January–February 1984, pp. 133–39.

as Chuck E. Cheese restaurants are the answer to customers who are interested in a place where parents can take small children to have a fun meal away from home. They offer safe games and activities with small prizes for "winners" (all children win something) and animatronic music and entertainment. Kids are permitted—and are encouraged—to run around the facility and have fun while their parents enjoy an afternoon or evening away from home. The prizes and animatronics might not have been identified by prospective customers as part of a desired service, but the notion that kids like to move around and play games, that they like to win and be rewarded, and that they are attracted to animals, music, and movement would certainly be recognized by most parents! This chain's service concept clearly incorporates both an understanding of the needs of the customers and the creativity of the service designer.

Similarly, the Borders bookstore chain has responded creatively to meeting its customers' needs. Some book purchasers know exactly what they're looking for and want to immediately locate their choice and pay for it quickly. Others, however, wish to wander, browse, and relax in a bookstore. Borders has successfully addressed the needs of both of these groups of customers into its service design. A carefully organized and well-labeled floor plan, a computer-search help desk, and an efficient checkout system are available for customers who want efficiency and speed of service, and an airy, open layout with chairs and benches scattered throughout the store satisfies the needs of the browsers. Borders has accommodated the needs of browsers even a step further by offering upscale refreshments, which include gourmet coffees and teas, freshly baked cookies and brownies, bottled spring waters and juices, and even full lunch menus. Again, there is clear evidence of the direct link to customers' identified preferences—and the creative addition that differentiates Borders from other bookstores.

Designing the Customer Service Encounter

Service encounters can be structured in a number of different ways. The *service-system design matrix* in Exhibit 7.1 identifies six common alternatives.

The top of the matrix shows the degree of customer/server contact: the *buffered core,* which is physically separated from the customer; the *permeable system,* which the customer can penetrate via phone or face-to-face contact; and the *reactive system,* which is both penetrable and reactive to the customer's requirements.

Production efficiency decreases as the customer contact time increases, enabling the customer to influence the system. To offset this, however, the face-to-face contact provides greater opportunity to sell additional products. Conversely, low contact, such as mail, allows the system to work more efficiently because the customer is unable to significantly affect (or disrupt) the system. However, there is relatively little, if any, sales opportunity for additional product sales at this end of the spectrum.

There can be some shifting in the positioning of each entry. Consider the "face-to-face tight specs" entry in Exhibit 7.1. This refers to situations where there is little variation in the service process—neither customer nor server has much discretion in creating the service. Fast-food restaurants and Disneyland come to mind. "Face-to-face loose specs" refers to situations where the service process is generally understood, but there are options in the way it will be performed or the physical goods that are a part of it. A full-service restaurant or a car sales agency are examples. "Face-to-face total customization" refers to service encounters whose specifications must be developed through some interaction between the customer and server. Legal and medical services are of this type, and the degree to which the resources of the system are used for the service determines whether the system is reactive or merely permeable. Examples would be the mobilization of an advertising firm's resources in preparation for an office visit by a major client, or an operating team scrambling to prepare for emergency surgery.

EXHIBIT 7.1 Service-System Design Matrix

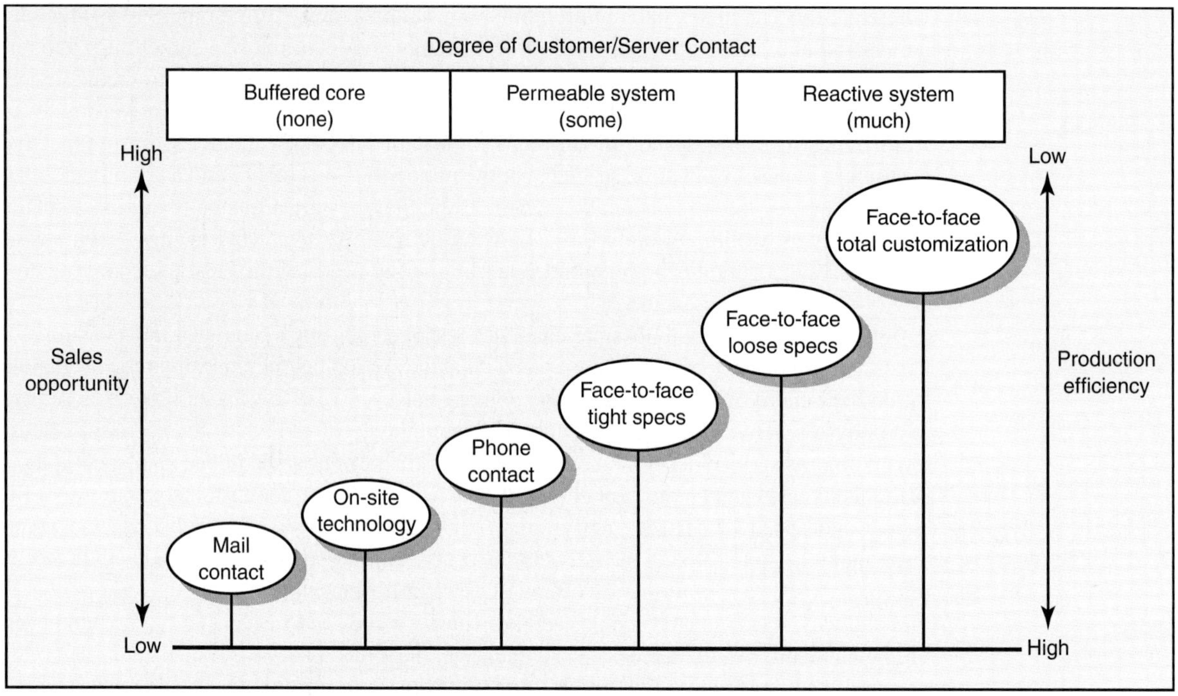

Source: Mark M. Davis, Nicholas J. Aquilano, and Richard B. Chase, *Fundamentals of Operations Management,* 3rd ed. (New York: Irwin/McGraw-Hill, 1999), p. 54.

Strategic Uses of the Matrix

The service-system design matrix has both operational and strategic uses. Its operational uses are reflected in its identification of worker requirements, focus of operations, and innovations previously discussed. Some of its strategic uses are

1. *Enabling systematic integration of operations and marketing strategy.* Trade-offs become more clear-cut, and, more important, at least some of the major design variables become evident. For example, the matrix indicates that a service process would probably not increase sales if it invested in high-skilled workers who would operate using tight specs.

2. *Clarifying exactly which combination of service delivery the firm is actually providing.* As the company incorporates the delivery options listed on the diagonal, it diversifies its production process.

3. *Permitting comparison with the way other firms deliver specific services.* This helps to pinpoint a firm's competitive position.

4. *Indicating the need for evolutionary or life cycle changes as the firm grows.* The evolution of service delivery can move in either direction along the diagonal as a function of the trade-off between efficiency and the potential to generate additional sales.

5. *Providing flexibility.* The matrix can be used to understand individual service products or the aggregated service offerings of the firm as a whole.

Designing the Service Process

Designing the service process involves defining three key elements:

• Service concept, which focuses on satisfying customer needs.

- Service content, which defines what is included in the service itself.

- Service style, which describes how the service will be delivered.

Service Concept

Service design begins with the **service concept.** The service concept is a detailed description of the customers' requirements and how they are to be satisfied. The "what" focuses on understanding the needs of the target customers, and the "how" involves understanding the organization's competitive priorities as well as the specifics that go along with the service. The service concept encompasses four areas:[2]

- The service operation—the manner in which the service is delivered.

- The service experience—the customer's direct experience of the service.

- The service outcome—the benefits and results for the customer receiving the service.

- The service value—the benefit that customers perceive to be the result of the service in comparison to the cost of that service.

In defining the service concept, the manager must also be attuned to the skills, qualifications, and interests of the workforce. For example, nurse practitioners can perform physical examinations and treat medical problems that in the past could be done only by a physician. Using nurse practitioners to deliver care achieves two workforce goals: providing good care for patients and freeing physicians to concentrate on the more complicated cases that may be more interesting to them and that use their skill set more efficiently. Using nurse practitioners to provide care formerly provided only by physicians may also reduce the total cost of providing care.

Service Content

The "what" of service design relates to the actual **service content** and includes: (*a*) the steps that are followed to serve customers, (*b*) the points in the process at which workers might need to make decisions, and (*c*) the points in the process at which customers might need to wait. These steps can be shown effectively as a **process flow diagram,** which is sometimes referred to as a **service blueprint.**

Service Process Flows

A process flow diagram is a very effective tool for depicting the steps in a process. Process activities are depicted as rectangles, the movements from one step in the process to another are shown as arrows, waits are drawn as inverted triangles, and decision points are drawn as diamonds. Process flow diagrams can be drawn from the perspective of either the customer or the worker and can be used to show the movement between service areas or departments. Exhibit 7.2 illustrates the process flow diagram for restaurant service from the perspective of the customer, and Exhibit 7.3 illustrates the process flow diagram from the perspective of the staff.

Service Blueprints

When used specifically for designing service operations, process flow diagrams are often referred to as service blueprints.[3] As planning tools for service design, service blueprints help to identify the points in the service process where special attention must be paid: where

[2] R. Johnston and G. Clark. *Service Operations Management* (Harlow, England: Prentice Hall, 2001), and G. Clark, R. Johnston, and M. Shulver. "Exploiting the Service Concept for Service Design and Development," in *New Service Design,* ed. J. Fitzsimmons and M. Fitzsimmons (Thousand Oaks, CA: Sage Publications, 2000), pp. 71–91.
[3] G. L. Shostack, "Designing Services That Deliver." *Harvard Business Review,* January–February 1984, pp. 133–39.

EXHIBIT 7.2
Process Flow
Diagram:
Customer's
Perspective

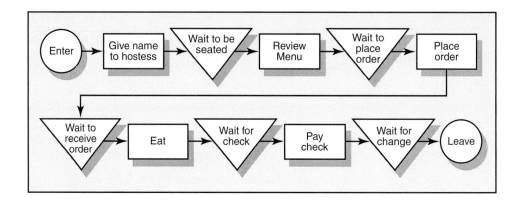

customers may be confused, where employees must make decisions (and might therefore be prone to errors), where waits are likely to occur in the flow of customers or in the flow of work, and where additional intervention (such as attention from a manager) might be required. Service blueprints are often drawn to indicate where the part of the operation that is visible to the customer (that is, the front office or front-of-the-house operations) is separated from the part of the operation that is visible only to the workers (that is, the back office or back-of-the-house operations). Customers are most concerned with the parts of the operation with which they come into direct contact. "Contact" need not imply that the customer must be physically present at the service site. Customers interact with service systems in many ways: personal face-to-face contact, voice contact, e-mail, and some services have no contact with service workers (such as automatic teller services). Regardless of the type of service, customers expect prompt attention (efficiency), appropriate action (effectiveness), and courteous service from front-of-the-house operations.

Valerie Zeithaml and Mary Jo Bitner describe four specific components of service blueprints that differentiate "blueprints" from process flow diagrams: (*a*) customer actions, (*b*) onstage contact employee actions, (*c*) backstage contact employee actions, and (*d*) support processes. These components are separated in the blueprint by three lines: the *line of interaction,* the *line of visibility*, and the *line of internal interaction.*[4]

The physical elements of the service are listed at the top of the service blueprint. In a hotel, for example, physical elements include the lobby, room keys, and elevators to the floors on which guest rooms are located. Exhibit 7.4 shows the components of a service blueprint.

Customer actions are the steps in the process performed by the customer. **Onstage-contact employee actions** are the steps performed by the service provider in the presence of the customer. For example, the waiter at a restaurant takes an order at a customer's table. **Backstage-contact employee actions** are the activities undertaken by the service provider behind the scenes, outside the customers' view. The backstage activities of that same waiter may include communicating with the chef about the order, plating the salad course, and printing a check. **Support processes** are any actions taken by other members of the service team that support the activities of the service providers. In the restaurant, a number of kitchen staff may be involved with preparing a meal in the kitchen. Other employees may order ingredients and clean up.

The process flow diagrams in Exhibits 7.2 and 7.3 have been combined and redrawn in Exhibit 7.5 as a service blueprint.

By comparing the service blueprint to the process flow diagram, you can see that each approach to depicting the service shows some detail that the other does not. The process

[4] Valerie A. Zeithaml and Mary Jo Bitner. *Services Marketing: Integrating Customer Focus across the Firm,* 2nd ed. (New York: Irwin/McGraw-Hill, 2000), pp. 206–7.

EXHIBIT 7.3 Process Flow Diagram: Staff Perspective

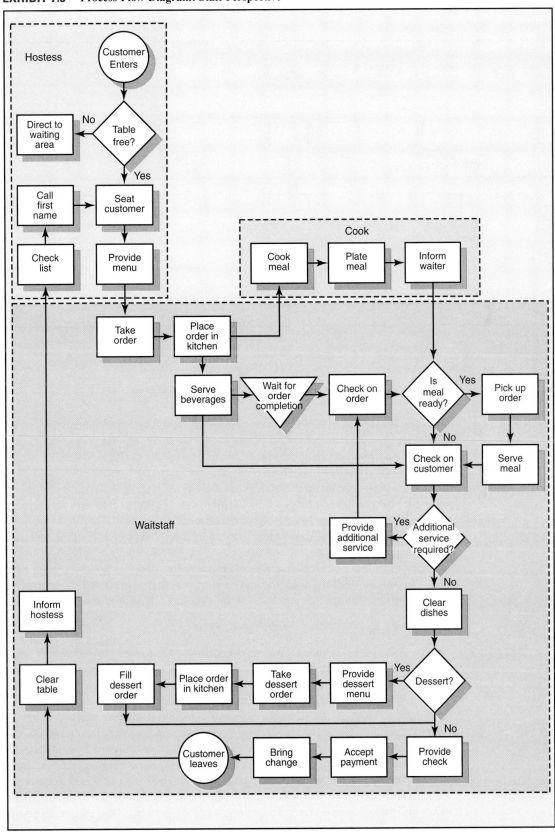

EXHIBIT 7.4 **Service Blueprint Components**

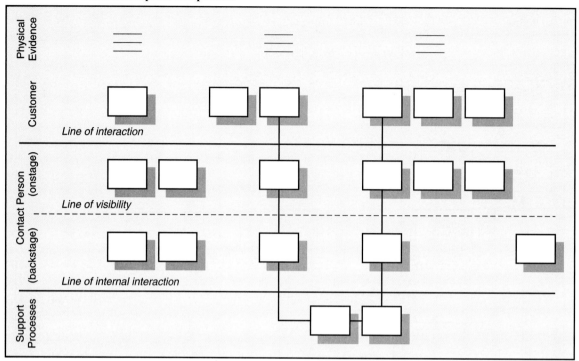

flow diagram approach shows decision points and waits, which traditionally are not shown on the service blueprint. Decision points are particularly important to understand thoroughly when a process is being designed because it is at the decision points that judgments take place and errors are likely to occur.

The service blueprint, on the other hand, shows the interaction between different players in the newly designed process, which demonstrates how important it is for everyone involved in the new service to understand the process, the handoffs, and how they interrelate. The line of visibility makes clear to everyone involved in providing the service what the customer should and should not see.

A "hybrid" of the service blueprint and process flow diagram is shown in Exhibit 7.6. This diagram shows all the decisions and connections that the process flow diagram shows at the same time that it illustrates the concepts traditionally shown in a service blueprint.

Service Style

Service style is the "how" of the service delivery. Customers may expect or desire a particular mood or ambience to be associated with a service. The atmosphere of a direct-contact service involves all of the senses: sight, hearing, smell, and even tactile sensations. For example, the ambience of a *haute cuisine* restaurant might entice the customer by using pleasant decor and candlelight, soft background music, the aromas of good food, and the comfort of cushioned armchairs. Patients in a hospital are accustomed to a different set of sensory inputs, but a successful hospital service design might incorporate some of the elements of a fine hotel or restaurant to create the perception of high value-added service. For example, the Massachusetts General Hospital and the Brigham and Women's Hospital, both located in Boston, have added gourmet room service menus with amenities such as linen-covered carts and fresh flowers to promote their maternity and postoperative services. These same hospitals have remodeled their maternity rooms

EXHIBIT 7.5 Service Blueprint of Restaurant Service

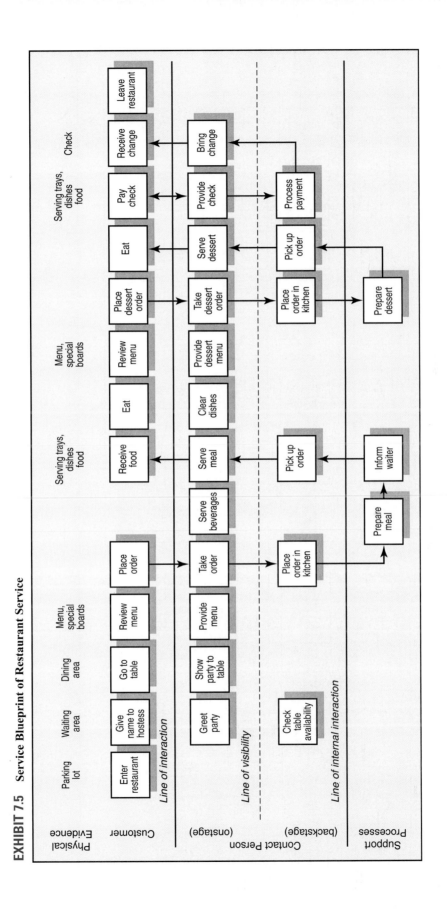

153

EXHIBIT 7.6 Hybrid Process Flow/Service Blueprint Diagram

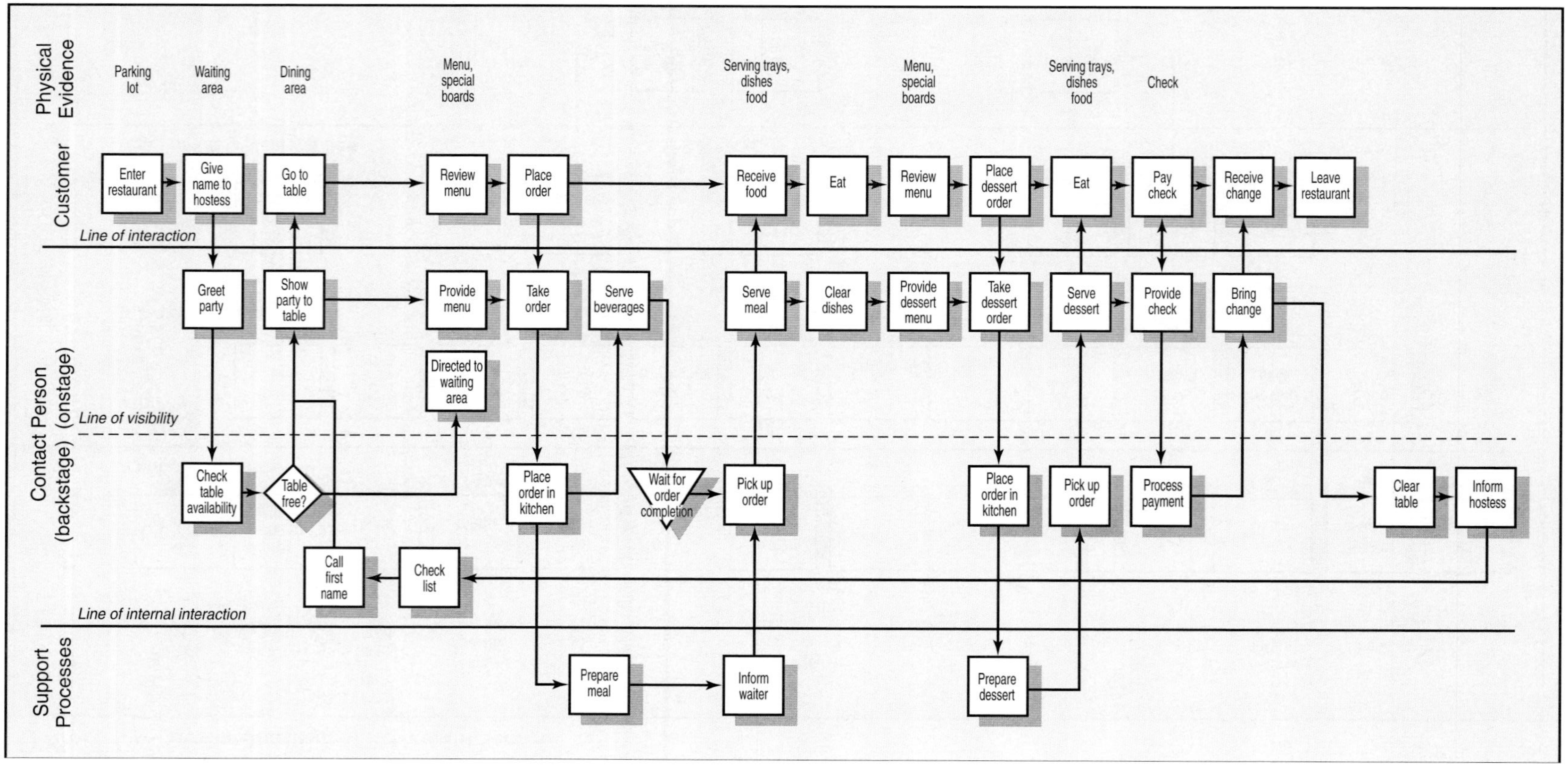

154

to be more like hotel rooms, complete with armoires that hide color television sets and that also offer handheld showers and wall-mounted hair dryers in the private bathrooms.

While customers expect a certain style and atmosphere in the front-of-the-house service operation, the back-of-the-house operations are invisible to customers. Therefore, while the front of the house should focus on improving customer service, the back-of-the-house design should focus on increasing efficiency.

Operations Decisions in the Design Process

Chapter 5 introduced the strategic implications of operations decisions, which were classified as either structural or infrastructural. Those strategic decisions need to be closely aligned in order to design a service that is perceived by the customer to be coherent. The strategic operations decisions are used in this chapter as the conceptual framework for making systematic service design decisions.

Structural Decisions

The structural decisions relating to the physical elements of service design are (*a*) location, (*b*) capacity, (*c*) technology, and (*d*) vertical integration.

Location

Manufacturing firms select locations for factories for a variety of reasons, including proximity to raw materials, energy sources, labor, and the desired transportation infrastructure. Although these factors may also be important for services, the primary criterion for choosing a location for personal-contact services is proximity to the customer. Service design must consider how the location of the service can best meet the customers' needs. Fast-food restaurants, for example, are often located near highway exits, within business districts, and, increasingly, even within schools, which are all very convenient locations that are likely to be near to the demand for fast, inexpensive, "eat-as-you-go" food. Upscale fine-dining restaurants, on the other hand, are more likely to be located within cities or towns, possibly near other "evening out" services such as the theater or the symphony or in particularly attractive getaway spots.

Services that do not require direct customer contact, such as call centers, can use the criteria used by manufacturers: low cost of real estate and proximity to appropriate labor. (A more detailed discussion of service location issues is presented in Chapter 8.)

Locating Direct-Contact Services

For many personal-contact services, customers are served at the service organization's facility. For example, one gets a haircut at a barbershop, groceries at the supermarket, a physical examination at the doctor's office, and a meal at a restaurant. The design of personal-contact services that are provided at the service's site should consider several location dimensions. Is the location convenient to the target market? If the target customers are likely to use public transportation, is there convenient access by bus or subway? If the customers are likely to drive, is the location easy to find? Is there ample parking? Is the area safe, well lit, clean, and attractive?

An alternative to having customers come to the service site is taking the service to the customer. Many personal services are now also offered at the customer's home or business. Home health care is the fastest-growing segment of the health care industry. Personal trainers can supervise your workout in your home. Groceries and even meals from restaurants can be ordered by phone and delivered to your door. Personal computers can be repaired on site at your office. Bringing the service to the customer can provide an important competitive advantage to the firm, differentiating the service and adding value in a society where an individual's time is becoming increasingly important.

Probably no one is more renowned for his attention to service design detail than Walt Disney. Disneyland and DisneyWorld theme parks consider every aspect of the customer's experience in their designs. For example, before the opening of Disneyland's Pirates of the Caribbean ride, Walt toured the ride and had a vague sense that something was not quite right. He led a team of employees through the attraction and asked again and again whether it felt authentic. All agreed that the costumes, the buildings modeled after those in New Orleans' French Quarter, the voices and sounds, the smells of Cajun food and gunpowder, and even the temperature and humidity evoked the Caribbean.

But Walt was not satisfied. One young housekeeping crewman finally spoke up and said that he had grown up in the South, and on summer nights he'd expect to see lightning bugs. Walt grinned, gave him a bonus, and shipped in live lightning bugs until his design crew could simulate them.

Walt knew the secret of successful design: "You don't build it for yourself. You know what people want and you build it for them." Walt would stoop down to look at buildings from a child's perspective. He waited until he saw paths across lawns where customers took shortcuts, then built sidewalks before fencing in grassy areas. He refused to sell chewing gum in his parks, because he didn't want customers to be frustrated with gum on their shoes.

Walt Disney died more than 30 years ago, but his uncompromising attention to detail lives on in his theme parks. Perhaps the most meaningful demonstration of Disneyland staff's ongoing commitment to detail is in Walt's small apartment on the second floor of the Main Street Firehouse: As a tribute to Walt, a light is always kept burning in the window.

Source: Jack Canfield, Mark Victor Hansen, Maida Rogerson, Martin Rutte, and Tim Clauss, *Chicken Soup for the Soul at Work: 101 Stories of Courage, Compassion & Creativity in the Workplace* (Deerfield Beach, FL: Health Communications, Inc., 1996); and Roger B. Jones, Jr., "Sharing Walt's Dream," http://www.kazrak.com/disney/Dream.html, 1995.

Locating Remote-Contact Services Remote-contact services, such as phone, mail-order, and Web-based operations, can locate their operations to take advantage of economies such as lower wage rates, less-expensive real estate costs, and lower overall expenses. Customers have ready and inexpensive access to these operations by toll-free phone numbers and mail and can share in the benefits of lower costs because these services can be provided at lower prices. Moving work to a central location can also reduce the size requirements of a retail outlet or free additional space for front-of-the-house operations, with the goal of increasing revenues.

Like phone and mail-order operations, the infrastructure that supports Internet services can be located anywhere. Many service systems locate their Internet operations near their other operations to achieve scale economies and to promote communication among the different channels.

Layout

Layout is another important element of service design. Issues to consider are the costs of the space itself, the efficiency of the service staff, and the comfort and convenience of customers. Back-of-the-house layouts typically focus on efficiency, while front-of-the-house layouts typically focus on effectively meeting customer needs. Chapter 8 describes several types of service system layouts, including process layouts, which organize materials and equipment according to the process performed, such as the different departments in a hospital; product layout, which organizes the steps in a service process in the order they are provided, such as the layout of the self-service stations at a cafeteria-style restaurant; and fixed position layout, such as an operating room or the special services desk at a bank, where all new account transactions occur. Chapter 8 also describes the importance of ambience; the functionality of the space; and the signs, symbols, and artifacts that provide cues to the customers about the nature of the service.

Capacity

The size of the service facility is an important design consideration. When capacity is inadequate, customers may be uncomfortable or may choose not to purchase the service, which argues for excess capacity. But when there is too much capacity, operating costs may be too high to permit delivering the service at a price customers are willing to pay. Chapter 14 provides a detailed examination of service system capacity issues.

Technology

At its simplest level, technology is the way work is done. One can write a check with a checkbook and a pen or "write" a check with a computer and an electronic link to a bank. The technology an organization chooses to use may determine its ability to deliver new service products and to compete in new markets. A classic example is the comparison between McDonald's and Burger King. McDonald's configured its restaurants with grills that are multipurpose pieces of equipment, while Burger King chose to cook hamburgers using a specialized broiling process, which many customers argued produced a tastier hamburger. When the demand for breakfast fast-food service became evident, however, McDonald's had an advantage: Eggs can be cooked on a grill, but not on a broiler. Burger King had to add new equipment to its kitchens to produce simple breakfast foods, and by the time this was accomplished, McDonald's had captured much of the breakfast market. The decision between adopting multipurpose equipment and specialized equipment continues to be important in services. Typically, larger volumes make specialized (and often faster) equipment cost-effective, but the flexibility afforded by more labor-intensive multipurpose equipment can also be a competitive advantage in a fast-paced society where customers' needs change quickly.

Today, technology decisions often focus on whether to provide services through the Internet rather than through the more traditional face-to-face or telephone interfaces. Which interface is the right choice depends on the market being served and their needs—not only for the core service, but also for the broader experience. For example, during the holiday season, a Boston-area mall ran radio ads that asked, "Do you *really* want to do your holiday shopping on the Internet? Come to the North Shore Mall, where you can see and hear and smell and taste before you buy! You'll be served by real people who care about you and about making your holiday a happy one!"

Vertical Integration

Traditionally, vertical integration refers to owning either suppliers or customers in the supply chain. The notion of *virtual vertical integration* is now often used to describe firms that work very closely with their suppliers and customers to achieve many of the advantages of vertical integration without actual ownership of the up- or downstream operations. Decisions related to either ownership of the supply chain or linkages to other organizations in the supply chain clearly need to be considered in service design. For example, building in the linkages to acute care hospitals is important for skilled nursing facilities or rehab hospitals. The handoffs between these organizations should be seamless to ensure that patients receive appropriate care. Similarly, elementary schools, junior high schools, and high schools in a town need to coordinate their services to make sure that students' needs are met.

Infrastructural Decisions

Workforce Configuration

The people who provide services to the customer are also an important part of the service design. While this might seem like a straightforward decision in many services, in others it is critical to the customer and can provide a considerable competitive advantage.

Service organizations should consider several important factors when deciding how to configure the workforce. As in any hiring decision, service organizations need to think about the nature of the work that must be performed and the qualifications required of the workers. Does the job require a particular type of skill or training? How much experience should the worker have? Along with task-related capabilities, workers who will come into direct contact with customers must also have people skills that might not be as critical for workers in the back-of-the-house operations. For example, a back-of-the-house worker in a fast-food restaurant whose job is to cook need not have the well-developed people skills that make a counter server more successful: an easy smile, a pleasant demeanor, the ability to defuse the emotion of an angry or irritable customer.

Another important factor to consider when making workforce decisions is cost. There are times when a firm should hire the worker with the most training and experience and be willing to incur the higher costs associated with that worker. At other times, however, a more cost-efficient alternative will not only be adequate, but also may even be service enhancing, thereby creating a win–win situation. For example, hospitals learned in the 1970s and 1980s that many expectant parents wanted birth experiences other than the controlled, problem-focused experiences they could expect with high-risk-oriented medical care. When midwives were introduced as alternative care providers in some hospitals, large patient followings were built up. Because women generally make the health care decisions for their families, the loyalty to a hospital that developed when a midwife delivered a healthy baby and the parents had a positive experience was demonstrated through return visits to that hospital for other types of health care services. Nurse practitioners and physician assistants were also found to be highly regarded by their patients, providing high-quality services and enhancing the experience for their patients. While midwives, nurse practitioners, and physician assistants increased customer satisfaction, they also decreased costs for the organizations that employed them, since they were paid significantly less than the physicians who would have provided similar care.

Many service systems can be designed with the goal of minimizing customer contact with service workers. This requires attention to the basic technology of the service: how the work is organized and accomplished and what kinds of workers and equipment are needed. Self-service operations such as supermarkets have made it possible to have customers select their own items and bring them to a cashier for payment. Many supermarkets and discount department stores are now introducing self-checkout lanes as well. Gas stations offer self-service pumps, customers are handed empty beverage glasses that they fill themselves at Burger King, and customers deposit and withdraw funds themselves at ATMs. Generally the types of services where customers can self-serve are not highly complex and do not require the customer to have specialized knowledge about the service. Even in very complex services such as health care delivery, however, the customer can be asked to take on some tasks that had been previously performed by the service provider. For example, it is common for a patient to be asked to complete a medical history form when visiting a physician or dentist for the first time. In the past, this information was obtained by the service provider during a face-to-face interview with the patient, requiring more time of the service provider. Shifting that task to the customer frees the service provider to perform the tasks that cannot be performed by the customer and may actually improve the quality of the information obtained if the form to be completed is detailed and well constructed.

Quality

The design of a service system must address two important aspects of service quality: performance quality and conformance quality. (See Chapter 12 for a more detailed discussion of these dimensions of quality.) Performance quality relates to the primary operating characteristics of the service. For example, the design of a restaurant must consider whether the service will provide a gourmet dining experience or a fast-food experience or something in between. Many other design decisions will depend on the performance quality decision, including workforce decisions and policies and procedures.

The other important aspect of service quality is conformance quality. Whether the restaurant is gourmet or fast food, the service should control the process variables that are seen as important to customers so that the quality of the service is perceived as excellent by the market being served. For example, in a fast-food restaurant, customers are likely to be concerned about the freshness of the food, whether the hot foods are hot and the cold foods are cold, whether the restaurant is clean and attractive, whether servers are prompt and polite, and whether customers have convenient access to the restaurant (which may mean parking or may mean a drive-up window). For each of these variables a standard can be established and conformance can be monitored over time. At what temperature should hot foods be maintained? For how long? At what point should unsold food be discarded? Designing quality into the service system is critical to the success of the service firm.

Policies and Procedures

Policies and procedures for doing work contribute to building a strong service system design and can support the decisions made about workforce and quality. For example, in a health care environment, hiring nurse practitioners rather than physicians to provide primary health care requires that there be clear guidelines about when nurse practitioners should refer patients to physicians for care. Similarly, if health care aides are used in a hospital environment to provide basic care for patients, there need to be clear guidelines about when these aides should summon a nurse. Failing to establish policies and procedures that support the service design can mean failing to properly provide the service.

Hours of Operation An important policy decision relates to when the customer wants to be served. Banks used to be the classic examples of services that were not attuned to the needs of their customers; 10:00 A.M. to 3:30 P.M. Monday through Friday became known as "banker's hours"—pleasant for the workers but very inconvenient for most of their customers. In recent years, banks have expanded their branch hours to be more accessible to customers and have offered automated teller machine (ATM) services to make most common transactions possible 24 hours a day, 7 days a week, 52 weeks a year. Some McDonald's now offer 24-hour drive-through service and some pharmacies are open 24 hours a day. Similarly, "doc-in-a-box" services opened to offer walk-in primary and urgent care to patients who were tired of having to take time off from work for a routine visit or treatment of a minor illness by their physicians. Many retail stores are now open earlier and stay open later, service stations have expanded their hours, universities offer evening and weekend classes, all to better meet the needs of the customers in their specific target markets. While it is easy for competitors to follow an expanded-hour strategy, customer loyalty may be won by the first to enter the market by offering increased customer convenience.

Organizational Structure

Understanding reporting relationships within a service organization is critical for service design. Building in appropriate coaching and mentoring enables the firm to consistently serve customers well. Similarly, service managers need to understand the flow of the service design to know at which points service workers may encounter challenges and when they need to be ready to intervene to either help the frontline service provider or interact with the customer.

Service as a Performance

Stephen Tax and Ian Stuart describe services as performances and suggest that service managers "look to the theater" to learn how to deliver services well.[5] From studying the production of a play, they discovered four key elements of service design:

1. *Integrating design processes.* Performances have three components: business functions, technical functions, and artistic functions. Tax and Stuart see the script as the service concept, providing the cast and crew with a shared understanding of what needs to be done. The stage manager is the service manager, who hires, trains, and motivates the team.

2. *Ready, aim, fire.* Theatrical productions open on time and ready for peak performance, unlike many service systems that open late, with details not thought out, and with a need for tweaking—a "ready, fire, aim" approach. The constant experimentation that accompanies the preopening period provides an opportunity for everyone to be involved and creative. Managers of all services should involve the service team in focusing on the details that make the difference to the customer.

3. *Efficient design.* Because rehearsals don't generate revenues, theaters are as efficient as they can be. Communication is key here; daily rehearsals, weekly production meetings, and dress rehearsals all prepare everyone for the performance and create an opportunity to voice concerns about decisions made along the way. Again, the message for all services is clear: Communication about customer requirements; practicing how to manage customer interactions, particularly the challenging ones; and identifying potential problems before they occur result in smooth service delivery and fewer customer complaints.

4. *Do it right at first.* Experimenting during the design phase makes it possible to deliver a superior "performance" when the service opens.

Even services that do not involve direct customer contact can benefit from these service-as-performance design elements. Functional integration, focus on the needs of the customer, communication among the members of the service team, and identifying and eliminating problems in the design phase all result in services that are more likely to be both efficient and effective.

The Impact of Technology

Technology has made every aspect of service design more effective and efficient. Managers can use computer software to make better decisions about service system capacity by simulating different service configurations and how well they meet varying levels of customer demand. For example, these programs can demonstrate when and where waiting lines will form and how long customers may have to wait when different numbers of servers are scheduled. Other computer programs enable service managers to experiment with different facility layouts. They can then visualize how customers would move through the facility and determine if any physical bottlenecks occur. A number of layouts can be tried electronically before any physical structures are built.

Policies and procedures can be readily accessed online by employees and maintained and updated by managers, enabling everyone in the service system to be "on the same

---

[5] Stephen S. Tax and Ian Stuart. "Designing Service Performances," *Marketing Management* 10, no. 2 (July/August 2001), pp. 8–9.

page" regarding how to serve customers. Process flow diagrams and service blueprints can be produced and modified with ease, enabling everyone in the service system to see exactly what the service process is intended to be.

The Internet has made it possible to design many services that complement already existing services. Online banking, online retail purchasing, and even online local weather reports enhance services offered by existing service firms. New software technologies have transformed Web page development from a complicated process that could be done by only a highly skilled programmer to a point-and-click process that enables anyone to develop attractive and fully functional websites. And completely new services such as e-mail have become so much a part of our lives that it is hard to remember what it was like without them!

Summary

The basic elements of service design focus on the needs and desires of the customer, service content and style, service system location, hours of operation, workforce configuration, management of quality, and policies and procedures. All of these are integral components in designing a successful service operation. Strong service system design spans the boundary between marketing and operations, differentiating the service in the marketplace and promoting efficiency and effectiveness, which in turn enhance the service firm's competitive advantage.

Service process flow diagrams and service blueprints detail every step in the service delivery process, enabling managers to identify the points in the service process where special attention must be paid. In order for a service to be perceived as coherent by customers, managers need to closely align decisions made about physical elements (location, capacity, technology, and vertical integration) as well as infrastructural elements (workforce configuration, quality management, policies and procedures and organizational structure). Technology has had a major impact on service design, enhancing both effectiveness and efficiency by making information readily available to managers and workers and by enabling new service delivery options.

Key Terms

customer actions: the steps in the process performed by the customer. *(p. 150)*
backstage-contact employee actions: steps performed by the service provider behind the scenes. *(p. 150)*
onstage-contact employee actions: steps performed by the service provider in the presence of the customer. *(p. 150)*
process flow diagram: an illustration of the steps, flows, and decision points in a process. *(p. 149)*
service blueprint: specialized process flow diagrams that depict the different elements of the service design. *(p. 149)*
service concept: a detailed description of what customer needs are to be satisfied and how they are to be satisfied. *(p. 149)*
service content: the *what* of the service. *(p. 149)*
service style: the *how* of the service. *(p. 152)*
support processes: actions taken by members of the service team who do not have direct contact with the customer but whose activities support the activities of the contact service providers. *(p. 150)*

Review and Discussion Questions

1. What are the risks associated with designing new services?
2. What is meant by the service concept?
3. You are planning to open an Internet café in your hometown. You plan to serve nonalcoholic beverages and a variety of pastries, cold made-to-order sandwiches, bagged chips, and fresh fruit.
   a. Develop a service design using the operations decisions framework described in this chapter.
   b. Draw a service blueprint for a typical customer interaction.

Internet Assignment

Go to Amazon.com. Compare the book shopping experience online with the shopping experience at your favorite bookstore. What elements do the two service designs share? What elements are different?

CASE   White International Airport

On December 20, 2001, Peter Dixon, facility manager at White International Airport (WIA), walked slowly through the terminal and thought how much had changed in just a few months. What had been a calm, relaxing environment for travelers had become crowded and tension-filled. While he applauded the new safety standards, he regretted the loss of the homey atmosphere and wondered what could be done to restore at least some of the original "feel" at WIA.

WIA began operations in 1931 as Wellgrove State Airport and was renamed in 1940 to honor local military hero and U.S. Senator Charles White. In the early 1990s, the State Port Authority assumed financial and operational responsibility for the airport and began an aggressive renovation and expansion campaign. When the attractive 15-gate terminal opened in 1997, passenger traffic nearly doubled, due in large part to White's proximity to two large New England cities whose airports were congested and, to many travelers, overwhelming. At White, the pace was slower and passengers enjoyed browsing through inviting shops and dining in restaurants and coffee shops along the corridors just inside the security checkpoints. White was small, with only 15 gates in a single terminal, and flights were scheduled evenly throughout the day to avoid large crowds. Therefore, family, friends, and colleagues were able to pass through the security checkpoints and be there at the gate to greet arrivals or to wave good-bye as travelers boarded their flights.

Everything changed, however, on September 11, 2001. The terrorist hijacking and the crashing of two large passenger planes into the World Trade Center towers in New York City led to much more stringent airport security regulations. Airports no longer permitted people without tickets to pass beyond the security checkpoints. Peter was confident that security staff members at White were following the new procedures to the letter, but he was concerned about the how the policy and procedural changes affected WIA's "feel."

As he strolled through the terminal, Peter was struck by the length of the lines both at the airline ticket counters and at the security checkpoints leading to the gates. White was laid out with baggage claim on the ground floor and ticket counters and gates on the second floor. Signs encouraged everyone but passengers to wait in the baggage claim area; combat-fatigue-clad soldiers carrying automatic weapons stood at the escalators, discouraging anyone who might have thought about trying to find their families or friends nearer the gates.

Today, on the baggage claim level, large numbers of people sauntered about as they waited. At each end of the large open area, there was a soda machine and a snack machine. The entire area offered only about 20 seats. Several people sat in groups on the carpeted floor or perched on the edge of the baggage conveyors, apparently ready to jump up if the conveyors began to move. As the escalator brought Peter to the second floor, he saw ticketed passengers waiting wearily in a line that surely required at least a 40-minute wait. The only place for passengers to get a cup of coffee or snack before their flights was in the gate area, on the other side of the security checkpoints.

Peter knew that the current layout of the terminal would not satisfy either passengers or their families and friends if the more stringent safety regulations continued, and he had no reason to believe that the safety standards would be relaxed enough to permit nonpassengers to enter the gate area. He wanted WIA to provide the most relaxing environment it could for travelers who would only be more anxious about flying than they might have been before 9/11.

Questions

1. Who are White International Airport's customers?

2. What do WIA's customers want?

3. Identify the front-of-the-house and back-of-the-house processes that are important for an airport.

4. What processes are needed to meet customer needs and at the same time to support new safety standards?

5. Draw blueprints for a traveler both arriving at and departing from WIA. Draw a process blueprint for someone meeting or dropping off a traveler.

Copyright, 2002 Janelle Heineke and Larry Meile.

Selected Bibliography

Canfield, Jack, Mark Victor Hansen, Maida Rogerson, Martin Rutte, and Tim Clauss. *Chicken Soup for the Soul at Work: 101 Stories of Courage, Compassion & Creativity in the Workplace.* Deerfield Beach, FL: Health Communications, Inc., 1996.

Chase, Richard B. "The Customer Contact Approach to Services: Theoretical Bases and Practical Extensions," *Operations Research* 29, no. 4 (1981).

Jones, Roger B., Jr. "Sharing Walt's Dream." http://www.kazrak.com/disney/Dream.html, 1995.

Shostack, G. L. "Designing Services That Deliver." *Harvard Business Review,* January–February 1984, pp. 133–39.

Shostack, G. L. "Understanding Services through Blueprinting." In *Advances in Services Marketing and Management,* ed. Teresa A. Swartz, David E. Bowen, and Stephen W. Brown. Greenwich, CT: JAI Press, 1992, pp. 75–90.

Tax, Stephen S., and Ian Stuart. "Designing Service Performances," *Marketing Management* 10, no. 2 (July/August 2001), pp. 8–9.

Zeithaml, Valarie A., and Mary Jo Bitner. *Services Marketing: Integrating Customer Focus across the Firm,* 2nd ed. New York: Irwin/McGraw-Hill, 2000.

CHAPTER EIGHT

Facility Location and Design

Learning Objectives

- Define the different types of service facilities and their site location requirements.

- Identify the different factors, both qualitative and quantitative, that should be considered when evaluating potential site locations.

- Present methods and criteria for evaluating potential brick-and-mortar retail locations.

- Introduce the concept of geographic information systems (GIS) and discuss its impact on the site location process.

- Identify alternative approaches for designing facility layouts.

Bruegger's Bagel Bakeries and Au Bon Pain Restaurants Use Commissaries to Support Retail Operations

Courtesy Au Bon Pain

The success of most brick-and-mortar retail operations, especially restaurants and other food service outlets, has often been attributed to their locations. Major food service chains now view site location as a two-stage process: the first involves locating the actual retail operations, and the second focuses on locating a central commissary where the initial food preparation takes place.

Bruegger's Bagels, for example, mixes the dough and forms the bagels in its regional commissaries and then ships them fresh to retail outlets where they are boiled and baked in front of customers. In contrast, Au Bon

Pain, a cafe and bakery chain that offers a variety of French breads, croissants, muffins, and other pastries, uses a single central facility in Missouri to support its approximately 250 Au Bon Pain and Saint Louis Bread locations throughout the United States. The ingredients are mixed and formed at the central location and then frozen, to be baked later at the retail operations.

The site selection criteria are significantly different for each of the two stages of the site location process. For the retail site the criteria are determined by customer demographics such as average household income, average family size, population density, and automobile and/or pedestrian traffic counts; at the central production facility, the criteria are determined by labor costs, building costs, and distribution costs.

The Customer's Perspective

Why is location important to you when you just want to grab a quick bite to eat at McDonald's or Taco Bell? Or when you need to choose a restaurant during your lunch hour? What about the location of a Dunkin' Donuts or Starbucks if you want a cup of coffee or café latte? How does the importance of the location of these food outlets compare with the importance of the location of the haute cuisine restaurant where you have a reservation on Saturday night for that special occasion? *Why* are they different?

How important is the location of the supermarket where you shop, your bank branch, or the dry cleaners where you take your clothes? Why is location so important for these types of services?

Why do you choose a particular hotel in San Francisco or Rome when you go there on vacation? What is the primary reason for selecting a hotel or motel if you are driving across country?

In contrast to the above services, how important to you is the location of the Delta Air Lines call center when you telephone to make an airplane reservation? Or where your bank's website is maintained when you want to conduct an online transaction? Does it matter to you where the Bruegger's regional commissary or where Au Bon Pain's central production facility are located?

For traditional brick-and-mortar service operations, location is very important for a variety of reasons. The layout and design of the facility is also important. Compare the ambience of a gourmet French restaurant with that of Burger King. Why are they different? What are the different messages each is trying to deliver? There are many factors to consider in designing a layout for a service facility. These include not only operational issues such as speed and efficiency but also financial issues such as potential revenues and marketing issues such as decor and ambience.

Managerial Issues

Technology has significantly reduced or eliminated the need for customers to directly interact with many service delivery processes. This is due in large part to the growth of the Internet. For example, online grocery shopping services such as Peapod.com have freed customers from going to the supermarket. Similarly, hotel and airline reservations can be made and tickets can be purchased through the Internet. As a result, services that no longer require the physical presence of the customer don't have to be located close to their customers. However, at the other end of the spectrum, many services still require direct interaction with the customer. Examples here include restaurants, hotels, and hair salons. For each of these businesses, the selection of a location that is convenient for customers still remains a key success factor, as clearly expressed by the often quoted saying, "The three most important factors for a successful restaurant are location, location, and location."

For those services where technology has eliminated or significantly reduced the need for direct customer contact, the choice of location is still an important decision. The site selection process for many of these service operations often resembles the process for locating a manufacturing facility, with one important difference: the cost of distribution for these service facilities typically remains constant, regardless of where they are located.

In addition to selecting the proper location, the customer's participation in the service process requires that customer-related factors be included in the design and layout of the service facility. The design of the facility thus needs to address a wide variety of often conflicting goals, ranging from maximizing the efficiency of the operation, to maximizing sales, to providing the proper ambience for the customer. These goals all need to be aligned with the overall strategy of the firm and the service experience that management wishes to convey to the customer.

Finally, management must recognize the growing role of IT in analyzing and selecting locations and in designing facilities. The use of IT not only significantly improves the site selection process, but also speeds it up. IT has also changed the way service facilities are designed.

Types of Facilities

Where to locate a service facility depends on the type of service that is being provided and how it will be delivered to the customer. We identify the following three major types of service facilities, based on the degree and type of contact each has with the customer:

- Facilities with direct interface with the customer.

- Facilities with indirect customer contact.

- Facilities with no customer contact.

Facilities with Direct Interface with the Customer

Businesses that provide for the actual presence of the customer as part of the service process are often referred to as **brick-and-mortar operations** because of their physical structures. Examples of these types of services include restaurants such as McDonald's and Outback Steakhouses, hotels and motels like the Ritz-Carlton and Fairfield Inn, branch offices of banks, hospitals, and traditional retail operations such as supermarkets like Safeway, large department stores like Nordstrom, and clothing boutiques like The Limited. A critical factor in the success of these firms is the volume of sales that a given location can generate. Consequently, many multilocation services have developed sophisticated forecasting models for predicting the sales that potential new locations can generate. (The supplement to this chapter introduces forecasting models that are used to evaluate potential new locations based on predicted sales.)

Facilities with Indirect Customer Contact

Services, such as telephone call centers and virtual firms, which only link to the customer through a website, do not require the customer's physical presence in order to deliver the service. Examples of the wide variety of services that have call centers include hotels, airlines, and car rental agencies (for reservations); brokerage and financial services (for trading transactions); and mail-order businesses such as L.L. Bean and Lands' End (for customer orders). Call centers can also provide customer service support for both services and manufacturing companies. These same services may be offered on a website as an alternative channel of communication with the customer. For these types of facilities, location near the customer is not an issue. Consequently, the site selection process in these cases is very similar to that of back-of-the-house service operations, as discussed in the following section. In fact, both the call centers and website staff are frequently located in the same facility to take advantage of economies of scale.

Facilities with No Customer Contact

Services that have no direct interaction with the customer are often referred to as **back-of-the-house operations.** Because the customer is absent from the process, these services tend to resemble a manufacturing operation in many respects. Services with these characteristics can be further divided into two broad categories: (*a*) the processing (sometimes) and distribution of physical goods (as illustrated by a central commissary for a restaurant chain) and (*b*) the processing and distribution of information (as illustrated by a credit card billing operation). As in selecting a manufacturing site, the location of a physical distribution center needs to consider not only the facility's operating costs but also the distribution or delivery costs, with the goal of minimizing the combined costs of both. Wal-Mart's regional distribution centers provide a good example of this type of facility.

In addition to distributing products, some of these back-of-the-house facilities also include manufacturing processes and are therefore often called *quasi-manufacturing operations.* A central commissary for Bruegger's Bagels, as stated earlier, where the dough is mixed and the bagels are formed, is a good example of a quasi-manufacturing operation.

However, for back-of-the-house services that are exclusively involved in processing information, there are only the facility operating costs to minimize, as the differences in delivery costs between alternative locations are usually nonexistent or negligible. For example, the cost of long-distance telephone services is the same throughout the United States, as is the cost of mail delivery. Thus, the site selection criteria for a check processing operation of a bank or a customer billing operation for a retail chain or credit card company will focus primarily on minimizing operating expenses.

Factors to Consider in Evaluating Potential Sites

To properly analyze the advantages and disadvantages of potential sites, managers need to consider both qualitative and quantitative factors. These factors will vary in type and relative importance, depending on the kind of service facility being evaluated.

Qualitative Factors

The qualitative factors used in the evaluation of a site will vary significantly, depending on the type of service to be provided. Some of the more common factors include: (*a*) local infrastructure, (*b*) availability and skills of workers, (*c*) local work environment, and (*d*) quality of life.

Local Infrastructure

The local infrastructure includes such factors as availability of high-speed telecommunication lines, access to major highways and airports, and availability of support services. This last factor is especially important when evaluating international locations. For example, when McDonald's opened its first restaurant in Moscow, it also had to build a central commissary to provide rolls, hamburger patties, and other prepared products that are typically provided by the existing network of suppliers in the United States.

Availability and Skills of Workers

A key factor in selecting a site is the size of the available workforce. Equally important is the level of education of those workers. The increasing complexity of many services requires that today's workforce be highly educated. This is particularly true for IT-intensive, back-of-the-house operations.

Local Work Environment

The attitude of local governments toward business is very important in choosing a site. Are local government leaders supportive of the business being located in their community? Are there restrictive labor laws? Are there strong labor unions in the area? All these issues need to be considered.

Quality of Life

To provide incentives for existing employees to move and also to attract new employees, a location must offer a high quality of life. Included here are the quality of the local school systems, neighborhood safety, restaurants, availability of cultural activities such as theaters and museums, as well as other forms of entertainment such as sporting events and recreational activities, like boating, camping, and skiing.

Quantitative Factors

Some operations-related quantitative factors that should be included in selecting a service site are (*a*) labor costs, (*b*) taxes and tax incentives, and (*c*) utility costs. For services with direct customer contact, additional marketing factors also need to be considered. These include (*d*) population size, (*e*) population demographics, and (*f*) automobile and/or pedestrian counts.

Labor Costs

Labor costs can vary dramatically, even within a country. For example, one major reason Citibank's credit card operations are located in Sioux Falls, South Dakota, or that the reservation call centers for many hotel chains are located in Nebraska is that the labor costs in these areas are very low. Labor costs are low because housing and other costs are also low. For services that are very labor intense, this is an important issue.

Taxes and Tax Incentives

Taxes also vary significantly from region to region. Some states within the United States have neither personal income taxes nor sales taxes (New Hampshire, for example), while others have both. Real estate taxes and business income taxes can also vary significantly from area to area. To encourage businesses to locate in their areas, local governments often provide tax incentives in the form of reduced real estate taxes and/or income taxes for a fixed time period (for example, 5 or 10 years) or subsidies for worker training programs. Such tax incentives have contributed to Ireland's ability to attract foreign businesses in recent years.

Utility Costs

Utility costs again can vary between regions. Historically, for example, water and electricity costs have been less expensive in the western part of the United States than along the eastern seaboard.

Population

The number of people residing and/or working within a given radius of a potential location can significantly affect the sales for services that require direct interaction with the customer. The distance of the population from the location should be measured in time, in additional to the more traditional measure of miles. In Wyoming, for example, traveling 20 miles may take 20 minutes, while traveling 20 miles in metropolitan Boston or Los Angeles may take an hour or more. Thus, a service firm might also consider the population that lives and/or works within a 20-minute driving time.

Population Demographics

Population demographics can include such factors as (*a*) household income, (*b*) household size, (*c*) age, and (*d*) level of education. The importance of these factors will vary significantly, depending on the type of service. For example, a fast-food operation such as McDonald's is concerned with the number of children living near a location in contrast to a copying center like Kinko's, which looks at the number of offices within a given area.

Automobile and/or Pedestrian Counts

These two measures are often used to predict how much demand there might be for a service. Which measure to use depends on the location. For a location in a downtown area or a mall, pedestrian counts are critical. For a location on a major highway or interstate, automobile or total traffic count is more appropriate. In both cases, to be reliable, data need to be collected several times during the day and over different days of the week.

Exhibit 8.1 shows some criteria used to identify potential locations for a back-of-the-house operation.

Methods for Evaluating Potential Locations

Both qualitative and quantitative methods are available for evaluating and comparing potential site locations. These include the factor-rating system and the center of gravity method. In addition, there are forecasting models that use regression analysis to predict sales for **front-of-the-house operations.** (See the supplement to this chapter.) Often, a

EXHIBIT 8.1
**Typical Criteria
for Locating a Back-
of-the-House Service
Operation**

- Population characteristics (size, education, diversity, etc.).
- Workforce characteristics (size, type, education, employed, etc.).
- Availability of alternative workforces (military spouses, students).
- Distance to commercial airports.
- Distance to population centers.
- Distance to telecommunication infrastructure.
- Distance to higher education facilities.
- Quality-of-life characteristics.
  - Quality of living index.
  - Cost of living index.
  - Cultural amenities.
  - Crime statistics.
  - Quality of education.
- Distance to highways/interstates.

Source: Provided courtesy of Fluor Global Location Strategies.

combination of these methods is used so that management can evaluate sites from several perspectives.

Factor-Rating Systems

Factor-rating systems are probably among the most widely used location selection techniques because they can combine very diverse issues into an easy-to-understand format. (The methodology presented here is the same as that for the project management screening matrix in Chapter 6.) At the same time, it is important to recognize that although the end result from this type of analysis is a number, factor-rating systems are used to evaluate both qualitative and quantitative factors.

Another reason the factor-rating system approach is popular is that it is relatively simple to use, requiring only six steps:

1. Identify the specific criteria or factors to be considered in selecting a site (for example, those shown in Exhibit 8.1).

2. Assign a weight to each factor indicating its importance relative to all the other factors being considered.

3. Select a common scale for rating each factor (for example 1–100).

4. Rate each potential location on each of the factors.

5. Multiply each factor's score by the weight assigned to that factor.

6. Sum the weighted scores for all the factors and select that location with the highest total score.

Example

To illustrate the factor-rating system, consider the Low-Credit Card Interest Bank, which is looking to locate its credit card operations. Two potential sites have been identified. Management has decided to use some of the criteria shown in Exhibit 8.1 and has assigned weights to each based on their relative importance. The two locations are rated on each of these factors and a total score for each location is calculated.

Solution

Factor	Weight	Rating Site A	Rating Site B	Score Site A	Score Site B
Size and education of workforce within 15 miles	20	60	75	1,200	1,500
Availability of part-time workers (students)	10	45	20	450	200
Distance to telecommunication infrastructure	25	80	90	2,000	2,250
Distance to higher education facilities	5	50	35	250	175
Cost of living index	15	85	80	1,275	1,200
Cultural amenities	10	65	40	650	400
Crime statistics	15	95	90	1,425	1,350
Totals	100			7,250	7,075

Using this evaluation method, site A should be selected because it has the higher of the two scores.

Although the weights for the factors in this example totaled 100, this is not a requirement. What is important is that the weights assigned to each factor reflect their relative importance in selecting a site. Equally important, the scale for rating each factor, as stated earlier, should be the same. The actual total score value is not as critical as its value compared to those for the other sites under consideration. In the example above, site A's total score is higher, but only 2.5 percent higher, which might suggest that there is little difference between the two locations based on the criteria employed.

Center of Gravity Method

The **center of gravity method** is a quantitative technique that can be used to determine the optimal location for a facility that prepares and/or delivers physical goods to other service facilities. For these services, the goal is to minimize the combined operating and distribution costs that are associated with the facility.

The center of gravity method can also be used to select locations for traditional brick-and-mortar retail operations such as supermarkets, department stores, and wholesale discount operations like Sam's Club and Costco. For these services, the location decision usually depends on the population density and the average sales per customer for the different areas to be served.

Consider a distribution center location decision. The first step in applying the center of gravity method is to identify each of the existing retail operations to be supported on an X and Y coordinate grid map, which establishes the relative distances between the retail locations. (Distance is used as a proxy for the distribution cost of one unit of product.) Exhibit 8.2 illustrates such a grid map.

The center of gravity, which is the optimal location for the distribution facility, is found by calculating the X and Y coordinates that minimize the distribution costs among the retail facilities it will support. To determine this location on the grid map, the following formulas are used:

$$C_x = \frac{\Sigma\, d_{ix}\, V_i}{\Sigma\, V_i} \qquad\qquad (8.1)$$

$$C_y = \frac{\Sigma\, d_{iy}\, V_i}{\Sigma\, V_i} \qquad\qquad (8.2)$$

EXHIBIT 8.2
Grid Map of Ye Olde Bake Shoppe's Retail Locations

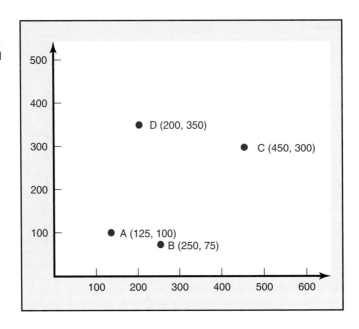

where:

C_x = X coordinate of the center of gravity for the distribution facility.

C_y = Y coordinate of the center of gravity for the distribution facility.

d_{ix} = X coordinate of the ith retail location.

d_{iy} = Y coordinate of the ith retail location.

V_i = Volume of goods transported to the ith retail location.

Example

Ye Olde Bake Shoppe Company has four retail locations within the metropolitan area of a major city. These locations are shown on the grid map in Exhibit 8.2. Currently each retail outlet makes all its own breads and pastries from scratch (that is, the breads and pastries are prepared on site from basic ingredients such as flour, sugar, shortening, etc.). Management, to both reduce costs and ensure consistent quality of the firm's products among all locations, has decided to build a central commissary where the dough will be mixed and the products formed and frozen. The products will then be distributed to the four retail stores for baking. The issue facing management is where to locate the commissary.

The estimated amounts of product sold weekly (in pounds) in each store along with its respective grid coordinates are provided in the table below:

Store Location	X Coordinate	Y Coordinate	Pounds of Product Sold
A	125	100	1,250
B	250	75	3,000
C	450	300	2,750
D	200	350	1,500

Solution

To determine the center of gravity, which will be the theoretical optimal location for the commissary, we set up the following spreadsheet for applying formulas 8.1 and 8.2:

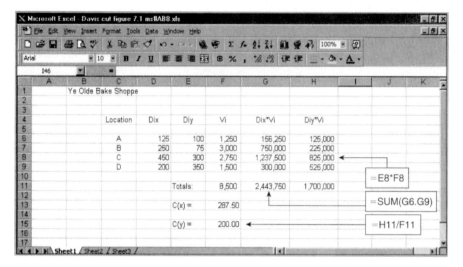

The X and Y grid coordinates for the center of gravity, which serve as a starting point for locating the new commissary, are calculated as

$$C_x = 2,443,750/8,500 = 287.5$$
$$C_y = 1,700,000/8,500 = 200.0$$

Another Approach for Locating Facilities

While the center of gravity method provides a theoretical optimal solution for minimizing distribution costs, the resulting location is very often not feasible for a variety of reasons. For example, the site selected might be in a residential neighborhood, may not have access to major highways, or may already be occupied by another business. Nevertheless, the center of gravity method does provide a starting point for searching for a location.

A more realistic approach to selecting a location is to identify several sites within the desired area that not only meet the requirements of the firm but also are available. Each site can then be evaluated using the same criteria as in the center of gravity approach, that is, to minimize the total costs of distribution. However, unlike the center of gravity method, where the solution can draw from an infinite number of possibilities, the solution with this approach is limited to the sites selected for evaluation.

Example

We again use Ye Olde Bake Shoppe chain of retail stores to illustrate this approach and to provide a basis of comparison between the methods. Management has identified two potential sites on which to locate the commissary. Because the two sites are within the same general area, production costs are estimated to be the same at both locations. Management's goal in selecting a site, therefore, is to minimize distribution costs. The following information is provided on each site:

Store Location	Pounds of Product Sold	Distance to Site 1 (miles)	Distance to Site 2 (miles)
A	1,250	19.5	23.0
B	3,000	17.5	12.5
C	2,750	20.6	18.0
D	1,500	11.2	25.0

Solution

Using logic similar to that of the center of gravity method, we set up the following table to calculate the total distribution costs associated with each site. (For consistency with the center of gravity method, we define distribution costs here as total pound-miles.)

Because site 1 has the lower distribution costs, it should be selected for the new commissary.

Geographic Information Systems (GIS)

Advances in information technology, such as faster computers, more flexible databases, and improved geographic mapping software, have resulted in the rapid growth of **geographic information systems (GIS).** The Environmental Systems Research Institute (ESRI), a leading GIS software producer located in Redlands, California, offers the following definition of GIS: "A GIS is an organized collection of computer hardware, software, geographic data, and personnel designed to efficiently capture, store, update, manipulate, analyze, and display all forms of geographically referenced material."[1]

Functionally, GIS is a spatial database that combines geographic information such as the location of roads, waterways, and specific building structures (for example, office buildings and apartment complexes) with the geographic distribution of regional demographic data such as populations, household incomes, and age. These data are combined or overlaid on a map of the geographic region being analyzed, providing management with a pictorial representation of the different factors that affect the service location decision. The benefit of graphically displaying such data is best expressed in the old adage, "A picture is worth a thousand words." GIS is not meant to substitute for the traditional feasibility studies that are typically done in evaluating new sites, but rather to provide management with additional inputs and perspectives.

[1] Thomas G. Exter. "The Next Step Is Called GIS," *American Demographics* 14, no. 5 (May 1992).

Using GIS, companies can conduct location analysis more quickly and with greater confidence than was previously possible. Because GIS provides a graphical display of large amounts of data, it offers the service manager a bird's-eye view of the region of interest.

Service Facility Design Layouts

Many issues must be considered when designing a layout for a service facility. Managerial decisions made at this time usually have long-term consequences, not only in terms of costs, but also in terms of the ability of the firm to properly serve its customers.

The overall goal in designing a layout for a service facility, from an operations perspective, is to minimize travel time for workers and often also for customers. From a marketing perspective, however, the goal is usually to maximize revenues. Frequently these two goals conflict with each other. It is management's task to identify the trade-offs that exist in designing the layout, considering both perspectives. For example, the prescription center in a pharmacy is usually located at the rear, requiring customers to walk through the store. This encourages impulse purchases of nonprescription items. Borrowing from manufacturing, we identify three basic types of service facility layouts: (*a*) process layout, (*b*) product layout, and (*c*) fixed-position layout.

Process Layout

In a **process layout** (often referred to as a *job-shop layout*), similar pieces of equipment or processes are grouped together in a common area. The support services for an emergency room in a hospital provide a good example of a process layout, with radiology, blood analysis, and the pharmacy each being located in a specific area of the hospital. Patients requiring any of these services must go to the locations where they are being provided. The kitchen of a large restaurant is likely to be designed with a process layout. All the desserts and breads are prepared in the bake shop; fruits and vegetables are peeled, sliced, and diced in the prep area; and raw meats and seafood are prepared for cooking in the butcher shop. Even the cooking line in a restaurant is often subdivided by the type of process, with all of the deep fat frying occurring in one area, broiling and roasting in another, and sautéing in a third.

Product Layout

In a **product layout** (also known as a *flow-shop layout*), equipment and/or processes are arranged according to the progressive steps in which the service is being provided. A good example of this type of layout is a cafeteria line, where all the stations (for example, salads, hot and cold entrees, desserts, and beverages) are arranged in a specific order, and customers visit each station as they move through the line.

Fixed-Position Layout

In a **fixed-position layout,** the service occurs in a given location and all the processes, equipment, and products are brought to the customer at that location. Examples of fixed-position layouts in services include: (*a*) automobile repair shops (where all the processes such as brake repair, oil change, etc., typically take place in the same location); (*b*) operating rooms in a hospital (where the patient remains in a given location on the operating table); and (*c*) tables at a restaurant, where all the courses in a meal are brought to the customer (and in some cases even prepared at the table in front of the customer).

Additional Considerations in Designing Facilities

Other factors also should be considered when designing service facilities. First, the cost per square foot for retail locations is usually very expensive (in comparison to the cost of manufacturing facilities). Because the cost of retail space is so high, brick-and-mortar services try to design their facilities to maximize the sales generated per square foot or square meter. To accomplish this, operations such as restaurants minimize the area that is devoted to back-of-the-house operations, like the kitchen, and maximize the area that generates revenue, like the dining room and lounge. This can be accomplished, as discussed earlier in this chapter, through the use of a central commissary where food can be prepared in a relatively low-cost area. Another approach is that taken by Benihana, a chain of Japanese steak houses. At Benihana's the strategy is to move the kitchen to the front of the house so the customers can observe the food preparation as entertainment.

Another factor that also needs to be considered is the customer's presence in the transformation process. For services where the customer is physically present, the decor package of the service operation plays an important role in determining the customer's overall satisfaction with the service encounter.

Mary Jo Bitner introduced the expression **servicescape** to describe the physical surroundings in which the service occurs.[2] The servicescape of a facility comprises three major elements: (*a*) ambient conditions, (*b*) spatial layout and functionality, and (*c*) signs, symbols, and artifacts.

Ambient Conditions

These refer to the background characteristics of the facility, including noise level, lighting, and temperature. (It is often said that the prices in restaurants are inversely related to the amount of lighting in the dining room—the darker the restaurant, the more expensive the food.) Hanging lights over tables, as seen in some of the better restaurants, suggest privacy; recessed lighting in ceilings, on the other hand, as seen in many fast-food operations, sends different signals to the customer.

Spatial Layout and Functionality

Unlike manufacturing firms where the goal in designing a layout is to minimize the cost of moving material between areas, one goal of a service operation is to minimize the travel time of employees and, in some instances, customers. At the same time, the service firm tries to maximize revenues per customer by providing them with as many opportunities as possible to spend their money. For example, the long lines to get into the shows at the casinos in Las Vegas and Atlantic City wend their way through the slot machine areas so the customers have an opportunity to play the slots while they are waiting.

[2] Mary Jo Bitner. "Servicescapes: The Impact of Physical Surroundings on Customers and Employees," *Journal of Marketing* 52 (April 1992), pp. 57–71.

Other examples of retail layouts where management attempts to maximize revenues are Ikea, a chain of Swedish furniture stores, and Stew Leonard's Dairy Store in Norwalk, Connecticut. Both of these facilities are designed so that the customer, once entering the store, must go through much of the facility to exit, as though they are in a maze with a single path through it.

Signs, Symbols, and Artifacts

These refer to those aspects of the service operation that have social significance. For example, the design of banks often includes columns and stone to give the feeling of security. The offices of large law firms and consulting practices are often done in dark woods and thick carpets to connote success and traditional values. Waiters in tuxedos and waiters in white shirts with white paper hats and aprons each give different signals to customers' expectations about what they might expect from the service.

The Impact of Technology

Information technology has had a significant impact on the site selection process for services as well as in the design layout of these facilities. Geographic information systems play an increasing role in evaluating alternative sites. GIS significantly enhances the site selection process by presenting management with a wide variety of data in easily understandable graphical form.

The increase in the use of the Internet has decreased the need for customers to actually be present in many service delivery systems, making site selection less dependent on the location of the firm's customers. At the same time, the Internet has shifted customer demand from being synchronous (or time dependent) to being asynchronous (or time independent), thereby allowing firms to more efficiently manage their facilities.

Technology has also played a significant role in the design layout of service facilities. A concept known as **push technology**, where information is pushed electronically to designated individuals or work areas, eliminates the need to consider the flow of paperwork in designing back-of-the-house services. For example, at Putnam Investor Services' operation in Franklin, Massachusetts, all incoming mail is scanned into its computer system using electronic imaging. Then, depending on the type of work the documents require, the scanned files are "pushed" electronically to the responsible work areas for the appropriate actions. In such IT-enriched environments, there is little or no need to consider the flow of work between work areas when designing the layout.

The use of IT-driven reservation systems for specific customer groups such as Hertz's Gold Club for its frequent rental car customers has resulted in Hertz's pickup areas being redesigned to provide faster service as well as increased efficiency with more emphasis on self-service. With a reservation, Gold Club members are taken directly to their cars, eliminating the need to check in. In supermarkets and other retail stores, using UPC bar codes on products results in more accurate inventory management and lower inventories, requiring smaller back-of-the-house storage areas.

Other IT-related technologies are having a profound effect on layout designs. Consider touch-screen shopping kiosks, electronic shelf labels and signs, handheld shopping assistants, self-scanning checkout systems, and virtual reality displays.[3] Each of these technologies changes the way customers and employees move through the stores, which has resulted in more efficient and effective layout designs.

[3] Regina F. Maruca, Raymond Burke, Sir Richard Greenbury, and Robert A. Smith. "Retailing: Confronting the Challenges That Face Brick-and-Mortar Stores," *Harvard Business Review,* July–August 1999, pp. 3–12.

1 Line Long

The Internet is segmenting customers into two broad categories. The first consists of those customers who are focused primarily on the efficiency of the transaction with the service firm, both in terms of cost and time, and who therefore prefer to use the Web. The second group is made up of customers who are focused on the total experience of the interaction with the service firm, which includes the encounter with service workers and the overall layout and ambience of the service facility. This second group prefers to visit the actual service facility. Segmenting customers along these two dimensions is a trend that is likely to continue and will therefore strongly influence the design of service facilities to further enhance the customer's overall experience.

Summary

The site selection process is critical for services, especially for those that interact directly with the customer. The evaluation of a potential site needs to include both qualitative information, which can be presented and compared with the factor-rating system, and quantitative data that is typically included in a detailed financial analysis. Quantitative approaches, like the center of gravity method, also exist for evaluating potential locations.

The design layout of the physical facilities is also important. Again, when the customer participates in the process, consideration must be given not only to the efficiency of the operation, but also to the desired customer experience, which may include maximizing sales.

Key Terms

back-of-the-house operation: a service facility, or that part of the service process, that does not come in contact with the customer. *(p. 167)*

brick-and-mortar operation: a front-of-the-house service that requires a physical structure to interact directly with the customer. *(p. 166)*

center of gravity method: a quantitative approach for determining the optimal location for a facility based upon minimizing total distribution costs. *(p. 171)*

factor-rating systems: a qualitative approach for evaluating alternative site locations. *(p. 170)*

fixed-position layout: a facility where the service is provided to the customer at one specific location. *(p. 176)*

front-of-the-house operation: a service facility, or that part of the service process, that interacts directly with the customer. *(p. 169)*

geographic information system (GIS): a computer tool that is used to assess the feasibility of alternative locations for service operations. *(p. 174)*

process layout: a facility layout where similar services or processes are performed in a common designated area, independent of a specific sequence. *(p. 175)*

product layout: a facility layout where the services are performed in a designated sequence according to the progressive steps required to provide that service. *(p. 175)*

push technology: the automatic transfer of electronic documents to specific work areas or stations. *(p. 177)*

servicescape: a term used to describe the various aspects of the physical surroundings in a service operation that can affect a customer's perception of the service received. *(p. 176)*

Review and Discussion Questions

1. Identify some of the site selection criteria that should be considered by a high-end, full-service hotel chain such as the Hilton, Hyatt, or Marriott. (By full-service we mean that the hotel has a restaurant, cocktail lounge, meeting rooms, and catering facilities to accommodate large functions like conferences and weddings.)

2. Identify some of the site selection factors that should be considered for a budget motel that primarily provides only rooms, such as Motel 6, Days Inn, and EconoLodge.

3. What factors should be considered when evaluating potential sites for a distribution center or quasi-manufacturing operation that directly supports retail operations?

4. Visit a major hotel in your area and describe the layout of its front-of-the-house operations.

5. Describe the front-of-the-house layout of a bank's branch office.

6. What are the major differences between selecting a location for a retail clothing store and an airline reservation call center? What are the major causes for these differences?

7. How might you design the layout for a walk-in clinic?

8. Visit two different supermarkets. What similarities do their layouts share? What differences did you notice?

Internet Assignment

Visit the website of an ASP (applications service provider) that will give you detailed maps that include the distance and time between any two locations. What is the estimated time it takes to go from your home to your school and how many miles is it? Use the same ASP to determine how far it is from your school to the nearest McDonald's or Burger King.

Solved Problems

1. Luxury Hotels, Inc., is looking to relocate its reservations call center and has identified the following factors and respective weights for evaluating each potential site:

Factor	Weight
Available workforce	30
Level of skills	15
Telecommunication infrastructure	45
Cost of labor	50
Access to major highways	25
Total	165

A site location consultant has identified the following three sites and has rated each of these locations on the above factors as follows:

Factor	Ratings Site A	Ratings Site B	Ratings Site C
Available workforce	65	80	90
Level of skills	50	45	75
Telecommunication infrastructure	90	70	40
Cost of labor	75	90	85
Access to major highways	80	85	55

a. Which site would you recommend for locating the call center?

b. How much does the rating for the labor cost factor have to increase for site A so that the scores for sites A and B are the same?

c. How much does the weight for the infrastructure factor have to increase before site A becomes the preferred location for the call center?

Solution

    a. We set up the following spreadsheet to calculate the scores for each location:

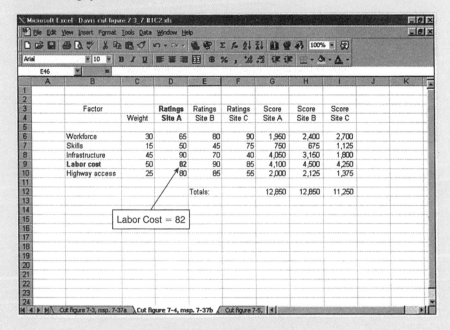

On the basis of this analysis, we recommend that the new call center be located at site B, which has the highest score of 12,850.

    b. To determine the rating for the labor cost factor at site A that makes the scores for sites A and B identical, we again use a spreadsheet and increase the labor cost rating for site A until the scores for the two sites are the same. The desired labor cost rating for site A is 82 as illustrated in the following spreadsheet:

c. As shown in the spreadsheet below, the weight for the infrastructure has to be increased to 63 before site A becomes the preferred location.

	Factor	Weight	Ratings Site A	Ratings Site B	Ratings Site C	Score Site A	Score Site B	Score Site C
Workforce		30	65	80	90	1,950	2,400	2,700
Skills		15	50	45	75	750	675	1,125
Infrastructure		**63**	90	70	40	5,670	4,410	2,520
Labor cost		50	75	90	85	3,750	4,500	4,250
Highway access		25	80	85	55	2,000	2,125	1,375
				Totals:		14,120	14,110	11,970

Infrastructure = 63

2. Personal Nursing Services (PNS) provides individualized nursing care to patients in three hospitals in the metropolitan area of a major city. For a variety of reasons, the number of patients to be cared for at each hospital often changes at the last minute. As a result, the nurses working for PNS report each morning to PNS's headquarters for their daily assignments. PNS then provides vans to take the nurses to their assigned hospitals. The vans also pick them up at the end of the day and return the nurses to the headquarters so that they can file their reports before going home. Consequently, the vans make two round trips a day to each hospital. The location of each hospital is shown on the grid map below.

PNS has experienced rapid growth in the demand for its services and is looking to move into larger facilities.

a. Using the center of gravity method, determine the ideal location for its new headquarters.

b. PNS has submitted a proposal to a fourth hospital, which is located at coordinates X = 20, Y = 5. If it is awarded the contract for this hospital, where should its headquarters building now be located?

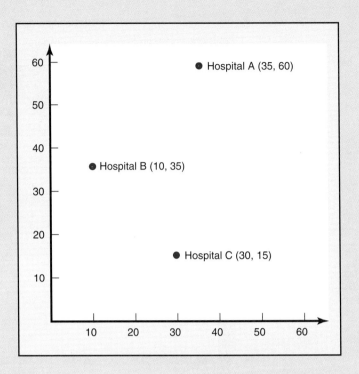

Solution

From looking at the grid map, we calculate the coordinates of each of the three hospitals now being served as follows:

Hospital	X Coordinate	Y Coordinate
A	35	60
B	10	35
C	30	15

a. Using a spreadsheet and based on the three hospitals that are currently under contract, we calculate the coordinates for the new headquarters as follows:

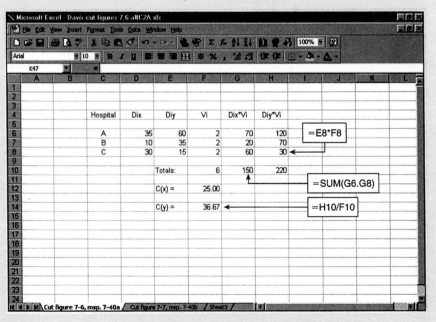

Thus, the new headquarters' location should be at coordinates X = 25.0, Y = 36.7.

b. To add the fourth hospital, we simply update the spreadsheet with the fourth hospital's coordinates and recalculate the X and Y coordinates for the new headquarters location.

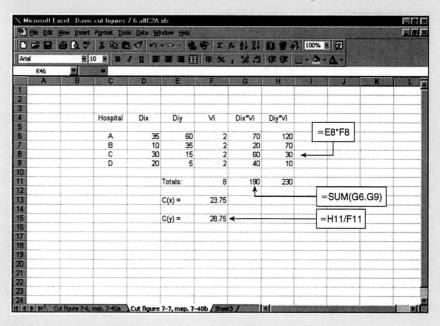

Thus, if PNS is awarded the contract for the fourth hospital, then the ideal location for the its new headquarters would be at coordinates X = 23.8 and Y = 28.8

Problems

1. The Speedy Ambulance Service is searching for a location that will serve both as its headquarters and as a garage for its ambulances. You have been asked to chair the site selection search team. The team has identified the following factors to consider in choosing a location and has assigned the following weights to these factors:

Factor	Weight
Proximity to hospitals	25
Population over age 65	30
Access to major highways	15
Number of nursing homes	20
Local tax incentives	10
Total	100

The search team has found three sites and has assigned the following factor ratings to each of them:

Factor	Ratings Site A	Ratings Site B	Ratings Site C
Proximity to hospitals	30	45	75
Population over age 65	60	55	35
Access to major highways	80	90	65
Number of nursing homes	45	60	55
Local tax incentives	85	70	80

a. Which site would you recommend to the search committee?

b. What is the impact on the site selection if the weight of the "access to highways" factor is reduced to 5 and the weight of the "local tax incentives" factor is increased to 20?

2. Edtoys.com is a virtual company that offers a wide variety of educational children's toys through its website. When an order is received, it is immediately sent electronically to the manufacturer

for direct shipment to the customer. With this type of structure, Edtoys.com does not have to maintain inventories or become involved in delivery. Management focuses primarily on making its website as customer friendly as possible and expanding its product offerings.

Edtoys.com has seen tremendous growth in the past several years and needs to find a new and larger location for its offices. On the basis of conversations with several members of Edtoys.com's top management team, a consulting firm has identified the following factors that should be considered in choosing a new site for its offices and has assigned the following weights to each of these factors:

Factor	Weight
Proximity to business schools	20
Access to highways	20
Telecommunications infrastructure	40
Quality of life	30
Proximity to major airport	25
Total	135

The consulting firm has identified two possible locations and has assigned each of them the following factor ratings:

Factor	Ratings Site A	Ratings Site B
Proximity to business schools	70	55
Access to highways	40	75
Telecommunications infrastructure	75	90
Quality of life	60	85
Proximity to major airport	80	50

Which site should the consulting firm recommend to Edtoys.com?

3. Patorano's Pizza, a chain of Italian pizza restaurants, wants to expand its operations into Asia, specifically in the People's Republic of China (PRC). Unfortunately, due to a lack of food purveyors and suppliers, management must build its own distribution center and commissary where many of the foods used in the restaurant will be either partially or fully prepared. (For example, the dough for the pizza will be mixed and portioned at the commissary.) The first stage of its business plan has identified specific locations for the first three restaurants to be opened. The X and Y coordinates and estimated annual sales for each of these three locations are presented below:

Location	X Coordinate	Y Coordinate	Forecasted Sales (in yuan)
A	20	45	2,500,000
B	35	15	4,000,000
C	5	50	1,800,000

  a. Draw a grid map and locate each of the planned restaurants on it.
  b. Assuming that the volume of products to be shipped is directly proportional to sales, calculate the coordinates for the central commissary that will minimize distribution costs. Plot these coordinates on the grid map.
  c. The second phase of the business plan calls for two more locations at the following grid locations and with estimated sales shown below:

Location	X Coordinate	Y Coordinate	Forecasted Sales (in yuan)
D	45	10	3,200,000
E	30	30	1,400,000

What is the impact of these additional restaurants on the location of the central commissary?

4. Jane's Office Supplies is a small retail chain that sells high-priced designer office supplies to senior executives. It has recently opened three locations in the metropolitan Washington, D.C., area which are currently being supplied from the corporate warehouse in Dallas, Texas. The X and Y coordinates for these locations are provided in the table below along with the annual sales that each location generates. To reduce shipping costs, management has decided to open a distribution center in the Washington area.

Store Location	X Coordinate	Y Coordinate	Annual Sales
Downtown Washington	60	53	$745,000
Suburban Maryland	13	78	483,000
Suburban Virginia	21	42	612,000

a. Draw a grid map and locate each of the three stores on it.

b. Assuming that the volume of products to be shipped is directly proportional to sales in each store, calculate the coordinates for the distribution center that will minimize distribution costs. Plot these coordinates on the grid map.

5. Having determined the optimal location for its distribution facility, Jane Davajian, the president of Jane's Office Supplies, found two sites that were available. The distance each site is from each of the three retail locations is as follows:

Retail Location	Distance from Site A (miles)	Distance from Site B (miles)
Downtown Washington	17	14
Suburban Maryland	10	12
Suburban Virginia	25	18

Which location should Jane choose to minimize her distribution costs?

6. Gourmet Specialty Foods, an upscale grocery chain that caters to high-income families, wants to build a new supermarket that will serve three affluent communities. A market research study revealed that the average weekly food purchases per family are the same for each of these three communities.

Community	Number of Families	X Coordinate	Y Coordinate
Smithtown	12,800	93	81
Jonesville	17,300	27	116
Moore City	9,500	75	34

Determine the optimal grid location for the supermarket.

7. A real estate consulting firm has found two locations that will meet Gourmet Specialty's requirements. The distance each of the locations is from the three communities is as follows:

Community	Site A (miles)	Site B (miles)
Smithtown	7.5	9.7
Jonesville	4.6	3.1
Moore City	8.0	6.2

On which site should Gourmet Specialty build its new supermarket?

CASE   Bruegger's Bagel Bakery

Founded in 1983 in Burlington, Vermont, Bruegger's Bagel Bakery is a retail bagel concept that has grown to more than 300 neighborhood bagel bakeries throughout the United States. These stores are located in major downtown areas, suburban strip shopping centers, and easy to drive to, quick-service locations. In addition to bagels, the bakeries also offer a wide variety of cream cheeses, soups, coffees, and deli-style sandwiches, which customers can enjoy either on the premises or take out.

Every Bruegger's bakery bakes its own bagels throughout the day, providing customers with fresh hot bagels. However, to ensure that only the highest-quality bagels are served and that there is consistency in both the quality and size of the bagels among its many retail locations, Bruegger's initially prepares the raw bagels at central commissaries. These commissaries are responsible for mixing the dough, forming the bagels, and proofing them (that is, allowing them to rise properly under a controlled temperature and humidity environment). The raw bagels are then distributed to individual locations where they are first boiled in water and then baked. Currently, Bruegger's has more than 30 retail locations in the greater Boston area, most of them being located in downtown Boston, and in the suburbs north and west of Boston. There are also four stores that are located south of Boston. The addresses for each of these bakeries and the average number of dozens of bagels that each receive daily are shown below:

Address	City/Town	Average Number of Dozens of Bagels Delivered per Day
45 Morrissey Blvd.	Dorchester, MA	180
356 Granite Ave.	East Milton, MA	135
2100 Washington St.	Hanover, MA	165
211 Lincoln St.	Hingham, MA	120

Currently these four locations are provided with bagels from a central commissary that is located in Woburn, Massachusetts, northwest of Boston. Because this commissary is reaching its maximum capacity, management has decided to locate a new commissary south of Boston to provide bagels for these four locations. (It is expected that there will be additional future locations south of Boston that will also be served by this commissary.)

Nord Brue, founder and current CEO at Bruegger's, working with a real estate consultant in Massachusetts, has identified the following two potential locations for this commissary:

Address	City/Town
50 Derby St.	Hingham, MA
100 Independence Ave.	Quincy, MA

Issues to Be Addressed

a. Find an ASP on the Internet that provides detailed maps that include directions with distances and times between locations. Determine the travel times and distances between the two potential commissary sites and each of the four retail locations.

b. One alternative is for Nord to subcontract out the delivery of the bagels to a local food delivery service that has quoted a delivery charge of five cents per dozen bagels per mile. With this cost as a criterion, which site should Nord select for the commissary?

c. Another option is to use a company truck, which is available, for the deliveries. With this alternative, Nord estimates that the driver will have to make one delivery per day to each of the four locations, and that the driver and truck will cost $30 per hour, including the driver's benefits. Under this scenario, which commissary site should Nord select?

d. Which of these two alternative methods of delivery (that is, outsourcing or keeping it in-house) do you recommend and why?

e. What additional factors should Nord consider in selecting a new commissary site south of Boston?

Selected Bibliography

Bitner, Mary Jo. "Servicescapes: The Impact of Physical Surroundings on Customers and Employees." *The Journal of Marketing,* April 1992, pp. 57–71.

Exter, Thomas G. "The Next Step Is Called GIS." *American Demographics* 14, no. 5 (May 1992).

Garrison, Sue. "After Push Came to Shove." *Business Geographics,* February 2000, p. 11.

Joerger, Albert, Stephen D. DeGloria, and Malcolm A. Noden. "Applying Geographic Information Systems: Siting of Coastal Hotels in Costa Rica." *Cornell Hotel and Restaurant Administration Quarterly* 40, no. 4 (August 1999), pp. 48–59.

Lovelock, Christopher. "Strategies for Managing Capacity-Constrained Services." *Managing Services: Marketing, Operations Management and Human Resources,* 2nd ed. Englewood Cliffs, NJ: Prentice Hall, 1992.

Lovelock, Christopher, and Lauren Wright. *Principles of Service Marketing and Management.* Upper Saddle River, NJ: Prentice Hall, 1999.

Maruca, Regina F., Raymond Burke, Sir Richard Greenbury, and Robert A. Smith. "Retailing: Confronting the Challenges That Face Brick-and-Mortar Stores." *Harvard Business Review,* July–August 1999, pp. 3–12

Moutinho, Luiz, Bruce Curry, and Fiona Davies. "Comparative Computer Approaches to Multi-Outlet Retail Site Location Decisions." *The Service Industries Journal* 13, no. 4 (October 1993), pp. 201–20.

Reid, Hal. "Retailers Seek the Unique." *Business Geographics* 5, no. 2 (February 1997), pp. 32–35.

Strazewski, Len. "Silicon Valley Holds Fertile Kids' Market." *Franchise Times,* February 1997.

Tayman, Jeff, and Louis Pol. "Retail Site Selection and Geographic Information Systems." *Journal of Applied Business Research* 11, no. 2, pp. 46–54.

Forecasting

Learning Objectives

- Present the fundamental concepts of forecasting and its importance to a service organization.

- Introduce some common forecasting methods and show how they can improve the operational performance of services.

- Recognize that errors exist in all forecasts and demonstrate how to measure and assess these errors.

- Discuss how information technology has affected forecasting models while also increasing their use.

Outstanding Customer Service at FedEx Starts with Forecasting

FedEx is the world's largest express transportation company. To support its global transportation network, FedEx has established 51 customer service call centers throughout the world. The 16 call centers located in the United States handle about 500,000 calls a day. The service level goal for all call centers is to answer 90 percent of all calls within 20 seconds or less. Three major networks are supported by these call centers: domestic, international, and freight.

For each network, FedEx has developed four types of forecasts, based on forecasting horizons. The strategic or long-range plan, which is revised and updated once a year, forecasts the number of incoming calls per week, the average handling time per call, staffing requirements, and the number of technology-handled calls. The business plan addresses the same items in the strategic plan but is revised on an as-needed basis, as decided by upper management. The tactical forecast provides a daily forecast of incoming calls and is done once a month. The operational forecast, which is done weekly, forecasts the number of incoming calls and average handling time in half-hour increments for each day of the week.

Because of the large number of calls handled daily at Federal Express, even a small increase in forecasting accuracy of 1 to 2 percent can translate into an annual savings in labor costs of more than $1 million.

Source: Weidong Xu, "Long Range Planning for Call Centers at FedEx," *Journal of Business Forecasting,* Winter 1999–2000, pp. 6–11; and conversations with Weidong Xu, forecasting specialist at FedEx.

Managerial Issues

Services, because they are perishable and interact directly with the customer, must be able to satisfy customer demand as it occurs. In other words, customers cannot typically be "inventoried" to some future time or to another location when or where sufficient capacity is available. For example, a busy restaurant on a Saturday night will not be able to persuade those customers that it cannot serve to come back the following Sunday morning. Similarly, a hotel that is full on a given night will most likely not be able to persuade those guests it cannot accommodate to either make a room reservation for another night or to stay at another hotel within the same chain that is 50 miles away.

As a result, services must have adequate capacity to meet peak periods of customer demand. However, capacity costs money, and unused capacity is a waste of money, ultimately driving up the cost of providing the service.

Service managers therefore use various forecasting techniques to predict customer demand. As illustrated in the opening vignette about FedEx, forecasting for service operations can be divided into three major categories: (*a*) long range, (*b*) intermediate range, and (*c*) and short range.

Long-range forecasting might focus on estimating the annual sales for a potential location for a restaurant chain to determine that location's feasibility and the appropriate size for the restaurant. The more accurately the forecast can predict sales for a location, the higher the probability that the location will be successful. An airline uses long-range forecasting to determine the number of airplanes it needs to buy, when it should buy them, and where they will be used. Long-range forecasting can also be used to determine capacity requirements at a customer service call center, to determine the number of incoming telephone lines or workstations that are needed, as illustrated at FedEx in the opening vignette.

Intermediate-range forecasting is used to manage existing capacity through a technique known as yield management (presented in detail in Chapter 14). Airline managers need to forecast passenger demand for each flight by market segment to determine how many seats to allocate to each of these segments. Similarly, a hotel needs to forecast guest demand by market segment for each night to determine when it should offer discounted room rates. Call centers use intermediate-range forecasting to determine how many people to hire to meet seasonal demand fluctuations.

Short-range forecasting in services typically focuses on estimating customer demand for each day of the week in small time periods such as an hour or half-hour. The forecasted demand for each period is then used as an input for determining the number of workers required in each period to satisfactorily meet that demand. (Worker scheduling is presented in detail in Chapter 11.) The ability to accurately forecast customer demand in short time increments translates into efficient scheduling of workers while still providing a given (or even improved) level of service. For example, McDonald's and Burger King have high levels of customer demand during lunch and dinner, and consequently they need to schedule more

EXHIBIT 8S.1
**Comparing
the Incremental
Costs and Benefits
of Forecasting**

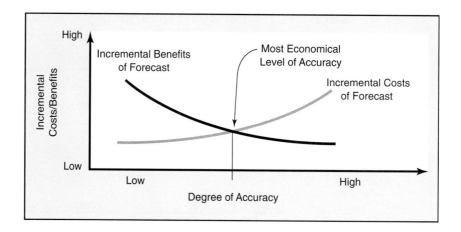

workers for these busy periods than they do during slower times. Similarly call centers like FedEx's have seasonal demand fluctuations as well as peaks and valleys in their daily demand patterns and need to forecast demand as a first step in determining worker schedules.

As with FedEx, managers of leading-edge service companies now recognize the importance of forecasting at all levels of the organization. At the highest levels, it is the basis for corporate, long-range, strategic planning. In the functional areas of finance and accounting, forecasts provide the basis for budgetary planning and cost control. The operations management function uses forecasts in the intermediate term to make periodic decisions that involve capacity planning. More recently, a growing number of service operations, such as FedEx, are using forecasting techniques to predict customer demand so they can better serve their customers while at the same time control their labor costs.

However, while forecasting can provide service managers with information that will allow them to run their operations more effectively and efficiently, these managers must also recognize that these forecasts are not perfect. Inaccuracies in forecasting occur because many factors in the business environment cannot be predicted or controlled with certainty. Rather than search for the perfect forecast, it is far more important for managers to establish the practice of continually reviewing their forecasts and to learn to live with their inaccuracies. This is not to say that we should not try to improve the forecasting model or methodology, but that we should try to find and use the best forecasting method available, *within reason.* In this respect, as shown in Exhibit 8S.1, the cost of obtaining small improvements in forecasting accuracy is very high after *reasonable* forecasts have been developed.

The goal of this supplement is to present an introduction to several different forecasting techniques and models (both qualitative and quantitative) commonly used in services, recognizing that additional and more sophisticated forecasting techniques and models are available for people seeking more in-depth knowledge in this area. We address primarily time series techniques and causal relationships, including a discussion of the sources of errors and their measurement.

Types of Forecasting

Forecasting techniques can be classified into three broad categories—*qualitative, time series analysis,* and *causal relationship forecasting.*

Qualitative techniques are subjective or judgmental and are based on estimates and opinions. Such techniques are used primarily when there are limited or no data available, which is often the case with start-up businesses. **Time series analysis** is based on the idea that data describing past demand can be used to predict future demand. In other words, the time-related trends that generated demand in the past will continue to generate demand in the future. **Causal relationship forecasting,** on the other hand, assumes that demand is related to some underlying factor or factors in the environment, and that cause-and-effect relationships are at work.

Time series analysis is typically used in short-range situations, like forecasting daily and hourly worker requirements for the next week. Causal relationship forecasting is usually used for longer-term issues, such as selecting a site for a retail operation. Exhibit 8S.2 briefly describes some different varieties of the three basic types of forecasting models. In this chapter we discuss the time series analysis methods and the first of the causal relationship forecasting techniques.

Exhibit 8S.3 shows a comparison of the strengths and weaknesses of these different forecasting methods. The moving average and exponential smoothing methods tend to be

EXHIBIT 8S.2
Forecasting Techniques and Common Models

I.	**Qualitative**	*Subjective, judgmental. Based on intuition, estimates, and opinions.*
	Delphi method	An interactive consensus-building process involving a group of experts who respond to a questionnaire. A moderator compiles results and formulates a new questionnaire, which is again submitted to the same group of experts.
	Market research	Collects customer data in a variety of ways (surveys, interviews, etc.) to test hypotheses about the market. This information is typically used for long-range forecasts including changing consumer preferences.
	Historical analogy	Relates what is being forecast to a similar service. Important in planning new services where a forecast may be derived by using the history of a similar existing service.
II.	**Time Series Analysis**	*Based upon the idea that the history of occurrences over time can be used to predict the future.*
	Simple moving average	The data points from several time periods are averaged by dividing the sum of the point values by the number of data points. Each, therefore, has equal influence. These data points may be weighted equally or unequally, based on experience.
	Exponential smoothing	Recent data points are weighted more, with weighting declining exponentially as data become older.
	Regression analysis	Fits a straight line to past data generally relating the data values to time. Most common fitting technique is least squares.
	Trend projections	Fits a mathematical trend line to the data points and projects it into the future.
III.	**Causal**	*Tries to understand the system underlying and surrounding the item being forecast. For example, sales may be affected by advertising, quality, and competitors.*
	Regression analysis	Similar to least squares method in time series but may contain multiple variables. Basis is that the forecasted variable is caused by the occurrence of other events or factors.
	Input/output models	Focuses on sales of each industry to other firms and governments. Indicates the changes in sales that a producer industry might expect because of purchasing changes by another industry.
	Leading indicators	Statistics that move in the same direction as the series being forecast but move before the series, such as an increase in the price of gasoline indicating a future drop in the sale of large cars.

EXHIBIT 8S.3
Comparison
of Forecasting
Techniques

Technique	Time Horizon	Model Complexity	Data Requirements
I. Qualitative			
Delphi method	Long	High	High
II. Time Series			
Moving average	Short	Very low	Low
Exponential smoothing	Short	Low	Very low
Linear regression	Long	Medium high	High
III. Causal			
Regression analysis	Long	Fairly high	High

the best and easiest techniques to use for short-term forecasting with little data required. The long-term models are more complex and require much more data. In general, the short-term models compensate for random variation and adjust for short-term changes. Medium-term forecasts are useful for seasonal effects, and long-term models identify general trends and are especially useful in identifying major turning points. Which forecasting model or models a firm should adopt depends on several factors, including: (*a*) forecasting time horizon, (*b*) data availability, (*c*) accuracy required, (*d*) size of the forecasting budget, and (*e*) availability of qualified personnel.

Components of Demand

In most cases, the demand for services can be broken into five components: (*a*) average demand for the period, (*b*) trends, (*c*) seasonal influence, (*d*) cyclical elements, and (*e*) random variation. Exhibit 8S.4 illustrates a plot of demand over a four-year period, showing the trend, cyclical, and seasonal components, and randomness (or error) around the smoothed demand curve.

Cyclical factors are more difficult to identify since either the time span or the cause of the cycle may not be known. For example, cyclical influence on demand may come from such occurrences as political elections, war, economic conditions, or sociological pressures.

Random variations are caused by chance. Statistically, when all the known causes for demand (average, trend, seasonal, and cyclical) are subtracted from the total demand, what remains is the unexplained portion of demand. If one is unable to identify the cause of this remainder, it is assumed to be purely random chance. This unexplained portion is often referred to as the *noise* or error in the forecast.

In addition to these five components there is often autocorrelation, which denotes the persistence of occurrence. More specifically, the demand expected at any point is highly correlated with its own past values. For example, if demand has been high during December for the past 10 years, then one would expect high demand during December for the coming year. When demand is random, the demand from one time period to another may vary widely. Where high autocorrelation exists, the demand is not expected to change very much from one time period to the next.

Trend lines are the usual starting point in developing a forecast. These trend lines are then adjusted for seasonal effects, cyclical, and any other expected events that may influence the final forecast. Exhibit 8S.5 shows four of the most common types of trends. A linear trend reflects a straight continuous relationship. An S-curve is typical of a service's growth and maturity cycle. The critical points on the S-curve are where the trend makes a

EXHIBIT 8S.4
Historical Monthly Customer Demand Consisting of a Growth Trend, Cyclical Factor, and Seasonal Demand

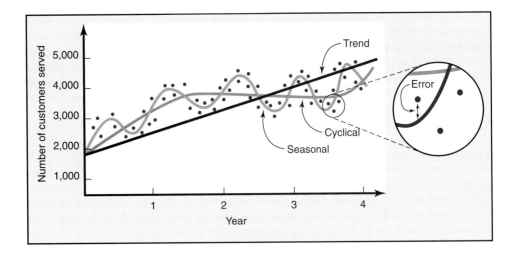

EXHIBIT 8S.5
Common Types of Trends

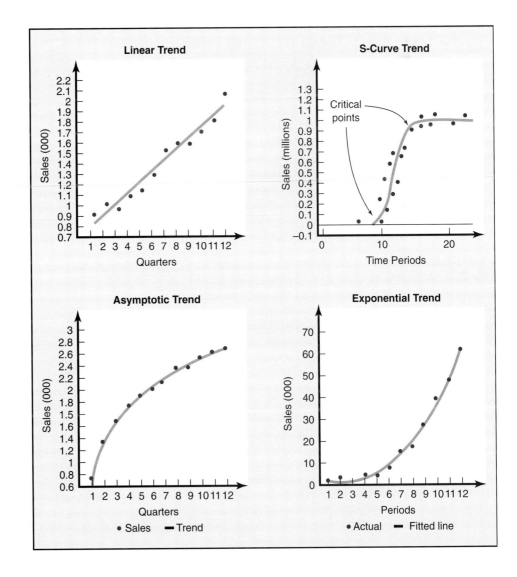

transition from slow growth to fast growth and from fast to slow. An asymptotic trend starts with the highest demand growth at the beginning, then tapers off. Such a pattern could occur when a firm enters an existing market with the objective of saturating and capturing a large share of the market. An exponential curve is common in new services with explosive growth as is often experienced with new e-business services. The exponential trend suggests that sales will continue to increase rapidly for some period—an assumption that may be questionable for longer time periods.

Time Series Analysis

Time series forecasting models attempt to predict the future based on historical data. For example, the number of customers served in a restaurant at lunchtime on Mondays for each of the past six weeks can be used to forecast the number of customers that will eat lunch there on the seventh Monday.

We present here three types of time series forecasting models: (*a*) simple moving average, (*b*) weighted moving average, and (*c*) exponential smoothing. To determine the most appropriate model, the data should first be plotted on a graph. If the data points appear to be relatively level, a moving average or exponential smoothing model would be appropriate; if the data points show an underlying trend, then exponential smoothing with trend adjustment would be appropriate. In addition, the errors associated with each model should be calculated and compared.

Simple Moving Average

If the demand for a service is neither growing nor declining rapidly, and does not have any seasonal characteristics, a **simple moving average** can be very useful in identifying a trend within the data fluctuations. For example, if we want to forecast the number of calls to be received in a call center in June with a five-month moving average, we can take the average of the sales in January, February, March, April, and May. When June passes, the forecast for July would be the average of February, March, April, May, and June. The formula for a simple moving average forecast is:

$$F_t = \frac{A_{t-1} + A_{t-2} \cdots + A_{t-n}}{n} \qquad \textbf{(8S.1)}$$

where

F_t = Forecasted sales in period t

A_{t-1} = Actual sales in period $t - 1$

n = Number of periods in the average

Suppose we want to forecast weekly demand using both a three-week and a nine-week moving average, as shown in Exhibits 8S.6 and 8S.7. These forecasts are computed as follows:

To illustrate, the three-week forecasting for week 4 is:

$$\frac{800 + 1{,}400 + 1{,}000}{3} = 1{,}067$$

and the nine-week forecast for week 10 is:

$$\frac{800 + 1{,}400 + 1{,}000 + \ldots + 1{,}300}{9} = 1{,}367$$

EXHIBIT 8S.6
Forecast Demand Based on a Three- and a Nine-Week Simple Moving Average

Week	Demand	Forecast (3-Week)	Forecast (9-Week)	Week	Demand	Forecast (3-Week)	Forecast (9-Week)
1	800			16	1,700	2,200	1,811
2	1,400			17	1,800	2,000	1,800
3	1,000			18	2,200	1,833	1,811
4	1,500	1,067		19	1,900	1,900	1,911
5	1,500	1,300		20	2,400	1,967	1,933
6	1,300	1,333		21	2,400	2,167	2,011
7	1,800	1,433		22	2,600	2,233	2,111
8	1,700	1,533		23	2,000	2,467	2,144
9	1,300	1,600		24	2,500	2,333	2,111
10	1,700	1,600	1,367	25	2,600	2,367	2,167
11	1,700	1,567	1,467	26	2,200	2,367	2,267
12	1,500	1,567	1,500	27	2,200	2,433	2,311
13	2,300	1,633	1,556	28	2,500	2,333	2,311
14	2,300	1,833	1,644	29	2,400	2,300	2,378
15	2,000	2,033	1,733	30	2,100	2,367	2,378

=Average(C5:C7) =Average(C5:C13)

EXHIBIT 8S.7
Moving Average Forecast of Three- and Nine-Week Periods versus Actual Demand

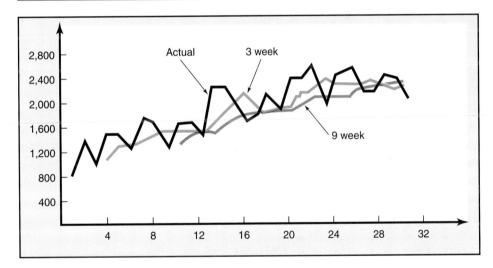

As noted in the accompanying "Creating Value through Technology," it is important to select the proper number of periods to include in the moving average. To determine the right number of time periods to use, management must consider several conflicting effects. As noted in Exhibit 8S.7, the larger the number of periods included in the average, the greater the random elements are "smoothed," which may be desirable in some cases. However, if a trend exists in the data—either increasing or decreasing—the resulting moving average has the adverse effect of constantly lagging this trend. Therefore, while a smaller number of periods in the moving average produces more oscillation, the resulting forecast will more closely follow the existing trend. Conversely, the inclusion of more periods in the moving average will give a smoother forecast, but at the same time it will lag the trend by a greater amount.

Exhibit 8S.7 graphs the data shown in Exhibit 8S.6, illustrating how the number of periods that are included in the moving average can affect the forecast. Note that the growth trend appears to level off at about the 23rd week. The three-week moving average responds

At Taco Bell, a large fast-food chain specializing in Mexican food, labor is a major cost component, averaging 30 percent of sales. Scheduling the proper number of workers for a given time period is therefore critical in the highly competitive fast-food industry. Too many workers results in excessive costs and reduced profits. Too few workers, on the other hand, results in lost sales and/or poor service. With the demand being highly variable throughout the day (52 percent of daily sales occur between 11:00 A.M. and 2:00 P.M.), Taco Bell needs to accurately forecast sales to schedule the proper number of workers.

After evaluating several forecasting techniques, Taco Bell adopted a six-week moving average. The number of customer transactions is recorded in 15-minute time intervals for each day of the week. For example, the forecasted number of customers to be served next Friday between 10:30 A.M. and 10:45 A.M. is the six-week average of the number of customers served in that same time period for the previous six Fridays.

This forecasting model is a major element in Taco Bell's labor-management system, which is estimated to have saved Taco Bell $16.4 million in labor costs in 1996 (in comparison to the previously existing management system).

Source: Jackie Hueter and William Swart, "An Integrated Labor-Management System for Taco Bell, *Interfaces* 28, no. 1 (January–February 1998), pp. 75–91.

better in following this change than the nine-week, although overall, the nine-week average is smoother.

The main disadvantage in calculating a moving average is that all the individual elements used in the average must be carried as data since a new forecast period involves adding the newest data and dropping the oldest data.

Weighted Moving Average

Whereas the simple moving average gives equal weight to each component of the moving-average database, a **weighted moving average** allows each element to be weighted by a factor, where the sum of all the weighting factors equals one. The formula for a weighted moving average forecast is:

$$F_t = w_{t-1}A_{t-1} + w_{t-2}A_{t-2} \cdots w_{t-n}A_{t-n} \tag{8S.2}$$

where

$$F_t = \text{Forecasted sales in period } t$$

$$A_{t-1} = \text{Actual sales in period } t - 1$$

$$w_{t-1} = \text{Weight assigned to period } t - 1$$

$$n = \text{Number of periods in the moving average}$$

An additional constraint when using the weighted moving average forecast is:

$$\sum_{i=1}^{n} W_{t-i} = 1$$

For example, a department store may find that in a four-month period the best forecast is derived by using 40 percent of the actual sales (in units) for the most recent month, 30 percent of two months ago, 20 percent of three months ago, and 10 percent of four months ago. The actual unit sales were as follows,

Month 1	Month 2	Month 3	Month 4	Month 5
100	90	105	95	?

The forecast for month 5 would therefore be:

$$F_5 = 0.40(95) + 0.30(105) + 0.20(90) + 0.10(100)$$
$$= 38.0 + 31.5 + 18.0 + 10.0$$
$$= 97.5 \text{ units.}$$

Suppose sales for month 5 actually turned out to be 110; then the forecast for month 6 would be:

$$F_6 = 0.40(110) + 0.30(95) + 0.20(105) + 0.10(90)$$
$$= 44.0 + 28.5 + 21.0 + 9.0$$
$$= 102.5 \text{ units.}$$

The weighted moving average has a definite advantage over the simple moving average because it can vary the effects between older data and more recent data. If there is a disadvantage to the weighted moving average, it is that someone must determine the weights to be used.

Exponential Smoothing

In the two previous forecasting methods, a major issue is the need to continually carry a large amount of historical data. Nevertheless, in many applications (perhaps even in most), the most recent data points are more indicative of the future than those in the distant past. If this premise is valid—that the importance of data diminishes as the past becomes more distant—then **exponential smoothing** may be the most logical and easiest method to use.

This is called "exponential smoothing" because each increment in the past is decreased by $(1 - \alpha)$, as shown below:

	Weighting at $\alpha = 0.3$
Most recent weighting $= \alpha(1 - \alpha)^0$	0.3000
Data 1 time period older $= \alpha(1 - \alpha)^1$	0.2100
Data 2 time periods older $= \alpha(1 - \alpha)^2$	0.1470
Data 3 time periods older $= \alpha(1 - \alpha)^3$	0.1029

Therefore, the exponents 0, 1, 2, 3 . . . give this method its name.

Exponential smoothing is the most commonly used of all forecasting techniques. It is an integral part of virtually all computerized forecasting programs and is widely used for ordering inventory in retail firms, wholesale companies, and other service operations.

Exponential smoothing accomplishes virtually everything that can be done with moving average forecasts, but requires significantly less data. The **exponential smoothing constant alpha** (α) is a value between 0 and 1. If the actual demand tends to be relatively stable over time, we would choose a relatively small value for α to decrease the effects of short-term or random fluctuations, which is similar to having a moving average that involves a large number of periods. If the actual demand tends to fluctuate rapidly, we would choose a relatively large value for α to keep up with these changes. This is similar to using a moving average with a small number of periods.

The major reasons that exponential smoothing techniques have become so well accepted are:

1. Exponential smoothing models are surprisingly accurate.

2. Formulating an exponential smoothing model is relatively easy.

3. The user can readily understand how the model works.

4. Very little computation is required to use the model.

5. Computer storage requirements are small because of the limited use of historical data.

In the exponential smoothing method, only three pieces of data are needed to forecast the future: the most recent forecast, the actual demand that occurred for that forecast period, and a smoothing constant alpha (α). As described above, this smoothing constant determines the level of smoothing and the speed of reaction to differences between forecasts and actual occurrences. The value for the constant is arbitrary and is determined both by the nature of the item being forecasted and the manager's sense of what constitutes a good response rate. However, error-measuring techniques, such as MAD (discussed later) can be used to evaluate different values for α until that value is found which minimizes the historical error. For example, if a service exhibits relatively stable demand, the reaction rate to differences between actual and forecast demand would tend to be small, perhaps just a few percentage points. (For example, the number of automobiles arriving at a gas station on Thursdays between 8:00 A.M. and 11:00 A.M.) However, if the service were experiencing growth, it would be desirable to have a higher reaction rate, to give greater importance to recent growth experience. The more rapid the growth, the higher the reaction rate should be. Sometimes users of the simple moving average switch to exponential smoothing but like to keep the forecasts about the same as the simple moving average. In this case, α is approximated by $2 \div (n + 1)$ where n was the number of time periods that were used in the moving average.

The equation for an exponential smoothing forecast is:

$$F_t = (1 - \alpha)F_{t-1} + \alpha A_{t-1}$$

or rewritten as

$$F_t = F_{t-1} + \alpha(A_{t-1} - F_{t-1}) \tag{8S.3}$$

where

F_t = Exponentially smoothed forecast for period t

F_{t-1} = Exponentially smoothed forecast made for the prior period

A_{t-1} = Actual demand in the prior period

α = Desired response rate, or smoothing constant

This equation states that the new forecast is equal to the old forecast plus a portion of the error (the difference between the previous forecast and what actually occurred).[1]

When exponential smoothing is introduced, the initial forecast or starting point may be obtained by using a simple estimate or an average of preceding periods. If no historical forecast data are available, then the forecast for the previous period (that is, last month) is set equal to the demand for that period.

Example

To demonstrate how the exponential smoothing method works, assume that the number of calls into a call center on Mondays between 10:00 A.M. and 11:00 A.M. is relatively stable and a smoothing constant (α) of 0.05 is considered appropriate. If the exponential smooth-

---

[1] Some writers prefer to call F_t a smoothed average.

ing method were used as a continuing policy, a forecast would have been made for last month. Assume that last month's forecast (F_{t-1}) was 1,050 calls, and 1,000 were actually received (A_{t-1}), rather than 1,050.

Solution

The forecast for this month would then be calculated as follows:

$$F_t = F_{t-1} + \alpha(A_{t-1} - F_{t-1})$$
$$= 1,050 + 0.05(1,000 - 1,050)$$
$$= 1,050 + 0.05(-50)$$
$$= 1,047.5 \text{ calls}$$

Because the smoothing coefficient is relatively small, the reaction of the new forecast to an error of 50 calls is to decrease the next month's forecast by only 2.5 calls.

Example

In another example, suppose Kevin Alexander owns a small restaurant that is open seven days a week. Until just recently he forecasted the daily number of customers using his "gut feel." However, he wants to open another restaurant and recognizes the need to adopt a more formal method of forecasting that can be used in both locations. He decides to compare a three-week moving average, and exponential smoothing with $\alpha = .7$ and $\alpha = .3$. The actual sales for the past three weeks are shown below, along with his forecast for last week.

Week	Customers per Day						
	Sun	Mon	Tue	Wed	Thu	Fri	Sat
Actual:							
3 weeks ago	138	183	182	188	207	277	388
2 weeks ago	143	194	191	200	213	292	401
Last week	157	196	204	193	226	313	408
Forecast:							
Last week	155	191	192	198	204	286	396

a. Forecast sales for each day of the next week using:

- A three-week moving average

- Exponential smoothing with $\alpha = .7$

- Exponential smoothing with $\alpha = .3$

b. The actual sales for the next week are as follows:

Week	Customers per Day						
	Sun	Mon	Tue	Wed	Thu	Fri	Sat
Actual:	160	204	197	210	215	300	421

Evaluate each of the three forecasting techniques based on the one week's data. Which technique would you recommend to Kevin?

Solution

a. The forecasts for each of the three methods are presented below.

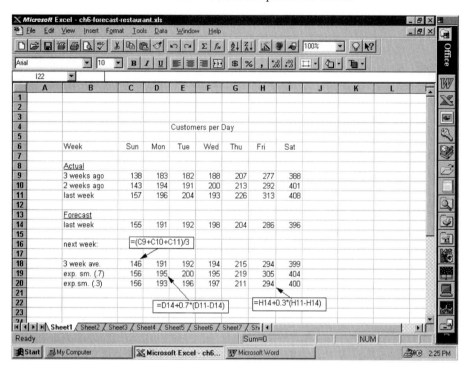

b. Using the average mean absolute deviation (MAD) as a criterion for measuring error, a comparison of the three forecasting methods is presented below:

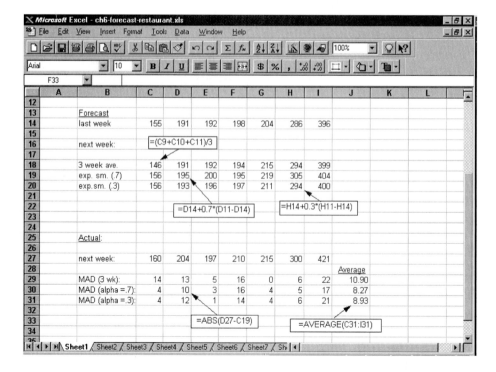

On the basis of this analysis, Kevin should use the exponential smoothing method with $\alpha = .7$, as that method has the lowest average MAD of 8.27. (MAD, which is a measure of how much the forecasted demand differs from the actual demand, is presented later.)

As discussed above, exponential smoothing has the shortcoming of lagging changes in demand. Exhibit 8S.8 shows actual data plotted as a smooth curve to show the lagging effects of the exponential forecasts. As noted, the forecast lags the actual demand during increasing or decreasing periods of demand. Also note that the higher the value of alpha, the more closely the forecast follows the actual. To more closely track actual demand, a trend factor may be added. In addition, the value of alpha can be adjusted to improve the accuracy of the forecasting. This is termed *adaptive forecasting.* Both trend effects and adaptive forecasting are briefly explained in the following sections.

Trend Effects in Exponential Smoothing

As stated earlier, an upward or downward trend in data collected over a sequence of time periods causes the exponential forecast to always lag behind (that is, to be above or below) the actual occurrence. Exponentially smoothed forecasts can be corrected somewhat by including a trend adjustment. To correct for the trend, we now need two smoothing constants. In addition to the smoothing constant α, the trend equation also requires a **trend smoothing constant delta** (δ). Like alpha, delta is limited to values between 0 and 1. The delta reduces the impact of the error that occurs between the actual and the forecast. If both alpha and delta are not included, the trend would overreact to errors.

To initiate the trend equation, the trend value must be entered manually. This first trend value can be an educated guess or computed from past data.

The equation to compute the forecast including trend (FIT) is:

$$FIT_t = F_t + T_t \qquad\qquad (8S.4)$$

where

$$F_t = FIT_{t-1} + \alpha(A_{t-1} - FIT_{t-1}) \qquad\qquad (8S.5)$$

EXHIBIT 8S.8
Exponential Forecasts versus Actual Number of Calls Received over Time Showing the Forecast Lag

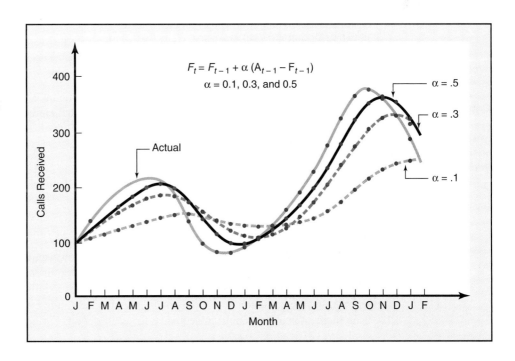

$$T_t = T_{t-1} + \alpha\delta(A_{t-1} - \text{FIT}_{t-1}) \tag{8S.6}$$

Assume an initial starting point for F_t of 100 calls, a trend of 10 calls, an alpha of .20, and a delta of .30. If the actual demand turned out to be 115 rather than the forecast 100, calculate the forecast for the next period.

Adding the starting forecast and the trend, we have:

$$\text{FIT}_{t-1} = F_{t-1} + T_{t-1} = 100 + 10 = 110$$

The actual A_{t-1} is given as 115. Therefore,

$$F_t = \text{FIT}_{t-1} + \alpha(\text{A}_{t-1} - \text{FIT}_{t-1})$$
$$= 110 + .2(115 - 110) = 111.0$$

$$T_t = T_{t-1} + \alpha\delta(A_{t-1} - \text{FIT}_{t-1})$$
$$= 10 + (.2)(.3)(115 - 110) = 10.3$$

$$\text{FIT}_t = F_t + T_t = 111.0 + 10.3 = 121.3$$

If, instead of 121.3, the actual turned out to be 120, the sequence would be repeated and the forecast for the next period would be:

$$F_{t+1} = 121.3 + .2(120 - 121.3) = 121.04$$

$$T_{t+1} = 10.3 + (.2)(.3)(120 - 121.3) = 10.22$$

$$\text{FIT}_{t+1} = 121.04 + 10.22 = 131.26$$

Determining Alpha (α) with Adaptive Forecasting

A key factor to accurate forecasting with exponential smoothing is the selection of the proper value of alpha (α). As stated previously, the value of alpha can vary between 0 and 1. If the actual demand appears to be relatively stable over time, then we would select a relatively small value for alpha, that is, a value closer to zero. On the other hand, if the actual demand tends to fluctuate rapidly, as in the case of a new service that is experiencing tremendous growth, then we would select a value of alpha that is nearer one.

Regardless of the initial value selected, α will have to be adjusted periodically to ensure that it is providing accurate forecasts. This is often referred to as *adaptive forecasting*. There are two approaches for adjusting the value of alpha. One uses various values of alpha and the other uses a tracking signal (which is discussed later).

1. *Two or more predetermined values of alpha.* The amount of error between the forecast and the actual demand is measured. Depending on the degree of error, different values of alpha are used. For example, if the error is large, alpha is 0.8; if the error is small, alpha is 0.2.

2. *Computed values of alpha.* A tracking signal computes whether the forecast is keeping pace with genuine upward or downward changes in demand (as opposed to random changes). The tracking signal is defined here as the exponentially smoothed actual error divided by the exponentially smoothed absolute error. Alpha is set equal to this tracking signal and therefore changes from period to period within the possible range of 0 to 1.

In logic, computing alpha seems simple. In practice, however, it is quite prone to error. There are three exponential equations—one for the single exponentially smoothed forecast as shown in the previous section, one to compute an exponentially smoothed actual error, and the third to compute the exponentially smoothed absolute error. Thus, the user must keep three equations running in sequence for each period. Further, assumptions must be

EXHIBIT 8S.9A
Additive Seasonal Factor
EXHIBIT 8S.9B
Multiplicative Seasonal Factor

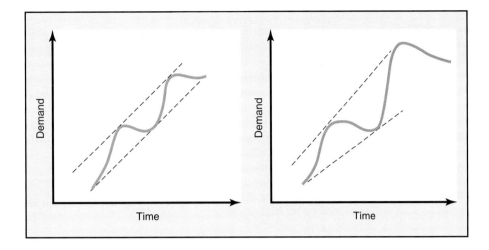

made during the initial time periods until the technique has had a chance to start computing values. For example, alpha must be given a value for the first two periods until actual data are available. Also, the user must select a second smoothing constant, in addition to alpha, which is used in the actual and absolute error equations. Clearly, those who use adaptive forecasting on a regular basis rely on technology for the calculations.

Seasonality Effects

Many services, such as airlines, hotels, restaurants, and even hospitals, encounter seasonal demand fluctuations in addition to the trend effect. For these types of services, a seasonality effect should also be included in the forecasting model. When both trend and seasonal effects are used in the forecast model, the question is how are the two related. We present two types of relationships pertaining to seasonal variation: (*a*) additive and (*b*) multiplicative.

With additive seasonal variation, we assume that the seasonal factor remains constant relative to the trend line or average. In this case, as shown in Exhibit 8S.9A, the forecast would simply be the sum of the trend value and the seasonal adjustment factor or

$$\text{Forecast} = \text{Trend} + \text{Seasonal factor}.$$

With multiplicative seasonal variation, the seasonal factor is multiplied by the trend value, as shown in Exhibit 8S.9B, or

$$\text{Forecast} = \text{Trend} \times \text{Seasonal factor}.$$

The following example illustrates forecasting with trend and an additive seasonal factor.

Example

A customer service call center for a financial services firm has received the following average daily number of calls per quarter over the past three years:

Forecasting Model Saves L.L. Bean $300,000 Annually in Labor Costs

L. L. Bean, the mail-order company located in Freeport, Maine, depends on customer telephone orders for 72 percent of its business. Scheduling telephone operators at its call centers is therefore a critical element in its success. Having too few operators results in long customer waiting times and the real possibility of losing customers to competitors. On the other hand, having too many telephone operators results in unnecessary labor costs, which negatively affects profits. The key to scheduling the proper number of operators to be on duty at any given time depends on the ability to accurately forecast the number and type of customer

calls that will occur in that time period. Using a time series forecasting model developed by professors at the University of Southern Maine, L.L. Bean has been able to save approximately $300,000 annually in labor costs by scheduling its operators more efficiently. This has been done without incurring any decrease in service quality!

Source: Bruce H. Andrews and Shawn M. Cunningham, "L.L. Bean Improves Call Center Forecasting," *Interfaces* 25, no. 6 (November–December 1995), pp. 1–13.

Year	Quarter	Average Number of Calls per Day
1	1	345
	2	315
	3	270
	4	300
2	5	365
	6	330
	7	285
	8	315
3	9	380
	10	340
	11	305
	12	320

Forecast the average number of daily calls for each quarter in year 4 using an additive seasonal factor.

Solution

1. Using times series regression analysis, calculate the trend line for the historical data. The resulting regression equation is:

    Average daily number of calls = 315 + 1.15(Quarter)

2. Set up an Excel spreadsheet, as shown here to calculate the differences between the forecast for each quarter that is calculated from the regression equation and the actual number of calls that occurred.

3. Calculate the average differences for each of the four quarters over the three years, as shown in the spreadsheet.

4. Using the regression equation, forecast the average number of daily calls for each quarter in year 4.

5. Adjust the quarterly forecasts obtained in step 4 by the average quarterly difference for each of the four quarters, respectively. As shown in the accompanying spreadsheet, the forecast of the average number of daily calls for each quarter in year four are:

Year	Quarter	Trend Forecast		Seasonal Factor		Adjusted Forecast
4	13	330.0	+	42.6	=	372.6
	14	331.1	+	6.4	=	337.5
	15	332.3	+	−36.4	=	295.9
	16	333.4	+	−12.5	=	320.9

Forecast with Trend and Additive Seasonal Factor

Year	Quarter	Actual Ave. No. of Daily Calls	Trend Forecast Ave. No. of Daily Calls	Difference	Trend Plus Seasonal Forecast	Note 1	Note 2
1	1	345	316.2	28.9	358.8	28.9	13.8
2		315	317.3	-2.3	323.7	2.3	8.7
3		270	318.5	-48.5	282.1	48.5	12.1
4		300	319.6	-19.6	307.1	19.6	7.1
2	5	365	320.8	44.3	363.4	44.3	1.6
6		330	321.9	8.1	328.3	8.1	1.7
7		285	323.1	-38.1	286.7	38.1	1.7
8		315	324.2	-9.2	311.7	9.2	3.3
3	9	380	325.4	54.7	368.0	54.7	12.1
10		340	326.5	13.5	332.9	13.5	7.1
11		305	327.7	-22.7	291.3	22.7	13.8
12		320	328.8	-8.8	316.3	8.8	3.7

=315+1.15*B18

=315+1.15*B18−12.5

Average Difference: 24.9 7.2

Average Seasonal Factors:

Q1	42.6
Q2	6.4
Q3	-36.4
Q4	-12.5

Note 1: Absolute Difference without Seasonal Factor
Note 2: Absolute Difference with Seasonal Factor

Forecast:	13	372.6
	14	337.5
	15	295.9
	16	320.9

=(E10+E14+E18)/3

=315+1.15*B33−12.5

Summary Output

Regression Statistics

Multiple R	0.131112488
R Square	0.017190484
Adjusted R Square	-0.081090467
Standard Error	32.99184048
Observations	12

ANOVA

	df	SS
Regression	1	190.3846154
Residual	10	10884.61538
Total	11	11075

	Coefficients	Standard Error
Intercept	315	20.30507418
X Variable 1	1.153846154	2.7589163

X coefficient   Constant

Forecasting Errors in Time Series Analysis

When we use the word *error,* we are referring to the difference between the forecast value and what actually occurred. Demand is generated through the interaction of a number of factors that are either too complex to describe accurately in a model or are not readily identifiable. Therefore, all forecasts contain some degree of error. In discussing forecast errors, it is important to distinguish between *sources of error* and the *measurement of error.*

Sources of Error

Errors can come from a variety of sources. One common source that many forecasters are unaware of is caused by the projection of past trends into the future. For example, when we talk about statistical errors in regression analysis, we are referring to the deviations of observations from our regression line. It is common to attach a confidence band to the regression line to reduce the unexplained error. However, when we subsequently use this regression line as a forecasting device by projecting it into the future, the error may not be correctly defined by the projected confidence band. This is because the confidence interval is based on past data; consequently it may or may not be totally valid for projected data points. In fact, experience has shown that the actual errors tend to be greater than those predicted from forecasting models.

Errors can be classified as either bias or random. *Bias errors* occur when a consistent mistake is made, that is, the forecast is always too high or always too low. Sources of bias include: (*a*) failing to include the right variables, (*b*) using the wrong relationships among variables, (*c*) employing the wrong trend line, (*d*) mistakenly shifting the seasonal demand from where it normally occurs, and (*e*) the existence of some undetected secular trend. *Random errors* can be defined simply as those errors that cannot be explained by the forecast model being used. These random errors are often referred to as "noise" in the model.

Measurement of Error

Several of the common terms used to describe the degree of error associated with forecasting are *standard error, mean squared error* (or *variance*), and *mean absolute deviation.* In addition, *tracking signals* may be used to indicate the existence of any positive or negative bias in the forecast.

Standard error is discussed in the section on linear regression. Since the standard error is the square root of a function, it is often more convenient to use the function itself. This is called the *mean square error,* or variance.

The **mean absolute deviation (MAD)** was at one time very popular but subsequently was ignored in favor of the standard deviation and standard error measures. In recent years, however, MAD has made a comeback because of its simplicity and usefulness in calculating tracking signals. MAD is the average error in the forecasts, using absolute values, which measures the dispersion (or variation) of observed values around some expected value.

MAD is computed using the differences between the actual demand and the forecast demand without regard to whether it is negative or positive. It is therefore equal to the sum of the absolute deviations divided by the number of data points, or, stated in equation form:

$$\text{MAD} = \frac{\sum_{t=1}^{n} |A_t - F_t|}{n}$$

(8S.7)

where

t = Period number

A_t = Actual number of customers for period t

F_t = Forecasted number of customers for period t

n = Total number of periods

$||$ = A symbol used to indicate the absolute value of a number and thus disregarding positive and negative signs

When the errors that occur in the forecast are normally distributed (which is assumed to be the usual case), the mean absolute deviation relates to the standard deviation as

$$1 \text{ standard diviation} = \sqrt{\frac{\pi}{2}} \times \text{MAD, or approximately } 1.25 \text{ MAD.}$$

Conversely,

$$1 \text{ MAD} \approx 0.8 \text{ standard deviation}$$

The standard deviation is the larger measure. If the MAD for a set of points at a hotel reservations call center, for example, was found to be 60 calls, then the standard deviation would be 75 calls. And, in the usual statistical manner, if control limits were set at ±3 standard deviations (or ± 3.75 MADs), then 99.7 percent of the points would fall within these limits. (See Exhibit 8S.10.)

A **tracking signal** is a measurement that indicates whether the forecast average is keeping pace with any genuine upward or downward changes in demand. As used in forecasting, the tracking signal is the *number* of mean absolute deviations that the forecast value is above or below the actual occurrence. Exhibit 8S.10 shows a normal distribution with a mean of zero and a MAD equal to one. Thus, if we compute a tracking signal and find it equal to –2, we can conclude that the forecast model is providing forecasts that are quite a bit above the mean of the actual occurrences.

A tracking signal can be calculated using the arithmetic sum of forecast deviations divided by the mean absolute deviation, or

EXHIBIT 8S.10

A Normal Distribution with a Mean = 0 and a MAD = 1

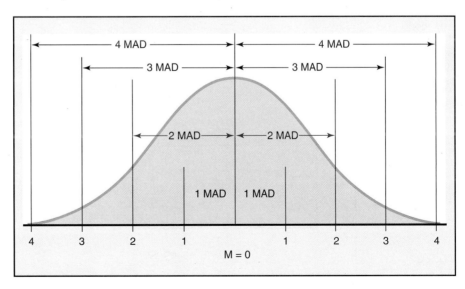

$$TS = \frac{RSFE}{MAD} \qquad \text{(8S.8)}$$

where

$RSFE$ = Running sum of forecast errors

MAD = Mean absolute deviation

Exhibit 8S.11 illustrates the procedure for computing MAD and the tracking signal for a six-month period where the forecast had been set at a constant 1,000 and the actual demands that occurred are as shown. In this example, the forecast, on the average, was off by 66.7 calls and the tracking signal was equal to 3.31 mean absolute deviations.

We can obtain a better interpretation of the MAD and tracking signal by plotting the points on a graph. While not completely legitimate from a sample size standpoint, we plotted each month in Exhibit 8S.12 to show the drifting of the tracking signal. Note that it drifted from −1.00 MAD to +3.31 MADs. This occurred because the actual demand was greater than the forecast in four of the six periods. If the actual demand doesn't fall below the forecast to offset the continual positive RSFE, the tracking signal would continue

EXHIBIT 8S.11
Computing the Mean Absolute Deviation (MAD), the Running Sum of Forecast Errors (RSFE), and the Tracking Signal from Forecast and Actual Data

Month	Forecasted Number of Calls	Actual Number of Calls	Deviation	(RSFE)	Abs Dev	Sum of Abs Dev	MAD*	$TS = \frac{RSFE}{MAD}$
1	1,000	950	−50	−50	50	50	50.0	−1.00
2	1,000	1,070	+70	+20	70	120	60.0	.33
3	1,000	1,100	+100	+120	100	220	73.3	1.64
4	1,000	960	−40	+80	40	260	65.0	1.23
5	1,000	1,090	+90	+170	90	350	70.0	2.43
6	1,000	1,050	+50	+220	50	400	66.7	3.31

*Mean absolute deviation (MAD). For Month 6, MAD = 400 ÷ 6 = 66.7 calls.

†Tracking signal = $\frac{RSFE}{MAD}$. For Month 6. TS = $\frac{RSFE}{MAD}$ $\frac{220}{66.7}$ = 3.3 MADs.

EXHIBIT 8S.12
A Plot of the Tracking Signals Calculated in Exhibit 8S.11

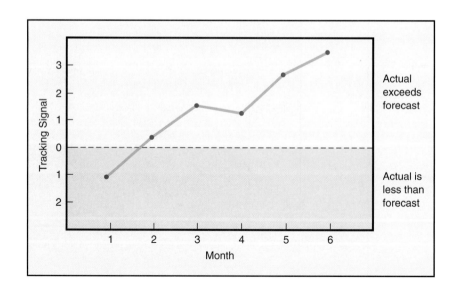

EXHIBIT 8S.13
The Percentages
of Points Included
within the Control
Limits for a Range
of 0 to 4 MADs

Control Limits		Percentage of Points Lying within Control Limits
Number of MADs	Related Number of Standard Deviations	
=1	0.798	57.048
=2	1.596	88.946
=3	2.394	98.334
=4	3.192	99.856

to rise and we would conclude that the assumption that demand is 1,000 calls is a bad forecast. When the tracking signal exceeds a preestablished limit (for example, ±2.0 or ±3.0), the manager should consider changing the forecast model or the value of α.

Acceptable limits for the tracking signal depend on the number of calls being forecast (high-volume or high-revenue items should be monitored frequently) and the amount of personnel time available (narrower acceptable limits cause more forecasts to be out of limits and therefore require more time to investigate). Exhibit 8S.13 shows the area within the control limits for a range of zero to four MADs.

In an ideal forecasting model, the sum of the actual forecast errors would be zero; that is, the errors that result in overestimates should offset the errors that are underestimates. The tracking signal would then also be zero, indicating an unbiased model that neither leads nor lags the actual demands.

Often, MAD is used to forecast errors. It might then be desirable to make the MAD more sensitive to recent data. A useful technique to do this is to compute an exponentially smoothed MAD (often identified as MAD_t) to forecast the next period's error range. The procedure is similar to exponential smoothing, which was presented earlier. The value of the MAD_t forecast is to provide a range of errors; in the case of call centers, this is useful in establishing service levels with respect to how fast the calls are answered. MAD_t is defined as:

$$MAD_t = \alpha|A_{t-1} - F_{t-1}| + (1 - \alpha)MAD_{t-1} \tag{8S.9}$$

where

MAD_t = Forecast MAD for the *t*th period

α = Smoothing constant (normally in the range of 0.05 to 0.20)

A_{t-1} = Actual demand in the period $t - 1$

F_{t-1} = Forecast demand for period $t - 1$

There are occasions when it is more desirable to assess the accuracy of the forecast model in relative terms rather than in absolute terms, as presented above. When this occurs, we use the **mean absolute percentage error (MAPE)** to determine the forecasting errors as a percentage of the actual. The MAPE is calculated using the following formula:

$$MAPE = \frac{\sum_{t=1}^{n} \frac{|Y_t - \hat{Y}_t|}{Y_t}}{n} \times 100 \tag{8S.10}$$

where

Y_t = Actual demand

Y_t = Forecasted demand

n = Number of periods in the forecast

For example, using the data presented in Exhibit 8S.11, we calculate the MAPE as follows:

Period	Forecasted No. of Calls	Actual No. of Calls	Deviation $(Y_t - Y_t)$	Absolute Deviation $Y_t - Y_t$
1	1,000	950	−50	50
2	1,000	1,070	+70	70
3	1,000	1,100	+100	100
4	1,000	960	−40	40
5	1,000	1,090	+90	90
6	1,000	1,050	+50	50

$$\text{MAPE} = \frac{\sum_{t=1}^{n} \frac{|Y_t - \hat{Y}_t|}{Y_t}}{n} \times 100$$

$$\text{MAPE} = \frac{50/950 + 70/1,070 + 100/1,100 + 40/960 + 90/1,090 + 50/1,050}{6} \times 100$$

$$\text{MAPE} = \frac{.053 + .065 + .091 + .042 + .082 + .048}{6} \times 100$$

$$\text{MAPE} = \frac{.381}{6} \times 100 = 6.4\%$$

Linear Regression Analysis

Linear regression analysis is used to define a relationship between two or more correlated variables. This relationship is usually developed from observed data where one or more parameters (the independent variable) is used to predict another (the dependent variable). Linear regression refers to a special class of regression where the relationship between the variables is assumed to be represented by a straight line. The equation for *simple linear regression* includes only one independent variable and takes the form:

$$Y = a + bX \tag{8S.11}$$

where

Y = Dependent variable we are solving for

a = Y intercept

b = Slope

X = Independent variable (in time series analysis, X represents units of time)

This forecasting method is useful for long-term forecasting of major occurrences and aggregate planning. For example, linear regression would be very useful to forecast sales at a potential new location for a restaurant or retail store.

The major restriction in using linear regression analysis is that, as the name implies, past data and future projections are assumed to fall around a straight line. While this does limit its application, sometimes, if we use a shorter time period, linear regression analysis can still be used.

Linear regression is used for both time series forecasting and for causal relationship forecasting. When the dependent variable (which is usually represented on the vertical axis of a graph) changes as a result of time (which is plotted on the horizontal axis), it is referred to as time series analysis. If the dependent variable changes due to a change in the independent variable, then it is referred to as causal relationship forecasting (such as the sales at a supermarket is related to the number of people who live within a five-mile radius).

The following example illustrates time series analysis using the least squares method for obtaining the linear regression equation that forecasts sales for future quarters.

A new e-business specializing in educational toys for children has received the following orders per month for the previous year:

Month	Sales	Month	Sales
1	600	7	2,600
2	1,550	8	2,900
3	1,500	9	3,800
4	1,500	10	4,500
5	2,400	11	4,000
6	3,100	12	4,900

The firm wants to forecast the number of orders for the next four months, that is, months 13, 14, 15, and 16. The least squares equation for linear regression is:

$$\hat{y} = a + bX$$

where

$\hat{y}$ = Dependent variable computed by the equation (sales in this example)

y = Dependent variable data point (see below)

a = Y intercept

b = Slope of the line

X = Independent variable (time period in this example)

The least squares method is used to determine the line that *minimizes the sum of the squares of the vertical distances* between each data point (y) and its corresponding point on the line (y). If a straight line is drawn through the general area of the points, the difference between the point and the line is ($y - \hat{y}$). Exhibit 8S.14 shows these differences. The sum of the squares of the differences between the plotted data points and their corresponding points on the line is:

$$(y_1 - \hat{y}_1)^2 + (y_2 - \hat{y}_2)^2 + \cdots + (y_{12} - \hat{y}_{12})^2$$

The best line to use is the one that minimizes this total.

EXHIBIT 8S.14   Least Squares Regression Line

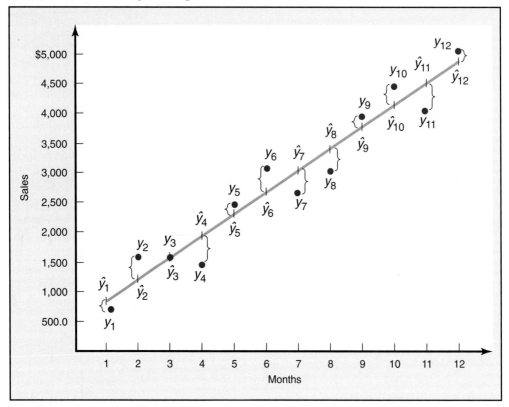

In the least squares method, the equations for solving for a and b are obtained using calculus and are:

$$a = \bar{Y} - b\bar{X}$$

$$b = \frac{\sum XY - n\bar{X}\bar{Y}}{\sum X^2 - n\bar{X}^2}$$

where

   $a = Y$ intercept

   $b =$ Slope of the line

   $\bar{Y} =$ Arithmetic mean of all Ys

   $\bar{X} =$ Arithmetic mean of all Xs

   $X = X$ value at each data point

   $Y = Y$ value at each data point

   $n =$ Number of data points

   $\hat{y}_i =$ Value of the dependent variable computed with the regression equation

Exhibit 8S.15A shows the computations that are required for the 12 data points. From these calculations we determine that the final equation for Y has an intercept (a) of 441.6 and a slope (b) of 359.6. The slope can be interpreted to mean that for every unit change in X, Y changes by 359.6.

EXHIBIT 8S.15A
Least Squares
Regression Analysis

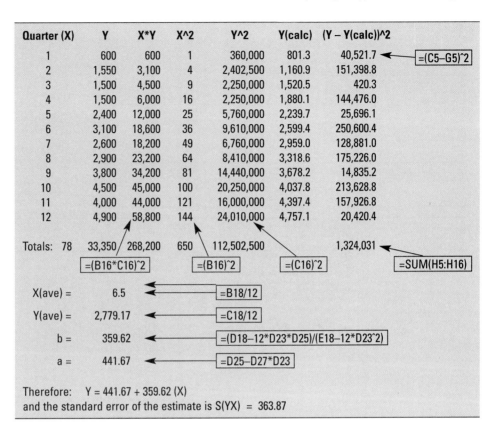

Quarter (X)	Y	X*Y	X^2	Y^2	Y(calc)	(Y – Y(calc))^2	
1	600	600	1	360,000	801.3	40,521.7	◀ =(C5–G5)^2
2	1,550	3,100	4	2,402,500	1,160.9	151,398.8	
3	1,500	4,500	9	2,250,000	1,520.5	420.3	
4	1,500	6,000	16	2,250,000	1,880.1	144,476.0	
5	2,400	12,000	25	5,760,000	2,239.7	25,696.1	
6	3,100	18,600	36	9,610,000	2,599.4	250,600.4	
7	2,600	18,200	49	6,760,000	2,959.0	128,881.0	
8	2,900	23,200	64	8,410,000	3,318.6	175,226.0	
9	3,800	34,200	81	14,440,000	3,678.2	14,835.2	
10	4,500	45,000	100	20,250,000	4,037.8	213,628.8	
11	4,000	44,000	121	16,000,000	4,397.4	157,926.8	
12	4,900	58,800	144	24,010,000	4,757.1	20,420.4	

Totals: 78   33,350   268,200   650   112,502,500   1,324,031

=(B16*C16)^2   =(B16)^2   =(C16)^2   =SUM(H5:H16)

X(ave) =   6.5   ◀ =B18/12

Y(ave) = 2,779.17 ◀ =C18/12

b =   359.62 ◀ =(D18–12*D23*D25)/(E18–12*D23^2)

a =   441.67 ◀ =D25–D27*D23

Therefore: Y = 441.67 + 359.62 (X)
and the standard error of the estimate is S(YX) = 363.87

Using this linear regression equation, the forecasts for months 13 through 16 would therefore be:

$$Y_{13} = 441.6 + 359.6(13) = 5,116.4$$

$$Y_{14} = 441.6 + 359.6(14) = 5,476.0$$

$$Y_{15} = 441.6 + 359.6(15) = 5,835.6$$

$$Y_{16} = 441.6 + 359.6(16) = 6,195.2$$

To calculate the regression line with the Excel regression function, use the following commands: tools → data analysis → regression.

In the table provided, input the Y-range, which in this case is C5:C16, and the X-Range, which is B5:B16. Then under "Output options" select "New worksheet." The spreadsheet in Exhibit 8.15B provides the same information as calculated in Exhibit 8.15A along with additional information on the regression line.

A measure of how well the data fit the regression line can be determined by calculating the **standard error of the estimate** (S_{yx}). The standard error of the estimate is similar in many ways to the standard deviation (σ). Just as the standard deviation is a measure of how widely the data points are dispersed around the arithmetic mean, so does the standard error of the estimate reflect how widely the errors are dispersed around the regression line. If the error points are assumed to be normally distributed around the regression line, then, as with the standard deviation, we can conclude, for example, that 68.26 percent of the data points around the regression line fall within one standard error of the estimate.

EXHIBIT 8S.15B   **Least Squares Regression Analysis**

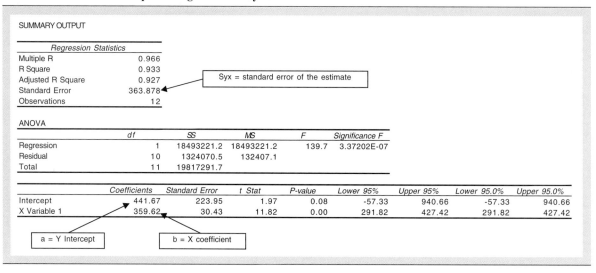

SUMMARY OUTPUT

Regression Statistics	
Multiple R	0.966
R Square	0.933
Adjusted R Square	0.927
Standard Error	363.878
Observations	12

Syx = standard error of the estimate

ANOVA

	df	SS	MS	F	Significance F
Regression	1	18493221.2	18493221.2	139.7	3.37202E-07
Residual	10	1324070.5	132407.1		
Total	11	19817291.7			

	Coefficients	Standard Error	t Stat	P-value	Lower 95%	Upper 95%	Lower 95.0%	Upper 95.0%
Intercept	441.67	223.95	1.97	0.08	-57.33	940.66	-57.33	940.66
X Variable 1	359.62	30.43	11.82	0.00	291.82	427.42	291.82	427.42

a = Y Intercept

b = X coefficient

The formula for the standard error of the estimate, or how well the line fits the data, is[2]

$$S_{YX} = \sqrt{\dfrac{\sum\limits_{i=1}^{n}(y_i - \hat{y}_i)^2}{n-2}}$$
(8S.12)

The standard error of the estimate in the previous example is computed from the second and last ($\hat{y}$) columns of Exhibit 8S.15:

$$S_{YX} = \sqrt{\dfrac{(600 - 801.3)^2 + (1,550 - 1,160.9)^2 + \cdots + (4,900 - 4,757.1)^2}{10}}$$

$$S_{YX} = 363.9$$

Causal Relationship Forecasting

Any independent variable, to be of value from a forecasting perspective, must be a leading indicator. For example, if the weather service or the *Farmer's Almanac* predicts that next winter is going to have an abnormally large number of snowstorms, people would probably go out and buy snow shovels and snow blowers in the fall. Thus, the weather prediction or the *Farmer's Almanac* is said to be a leading indicator of the sale of snow shovels and snow blowers. These relationships between variables are causal relationships—the occurrence of one event causes or influences the occurrence of the other. Running out of gas while driving down a highway, however, does not provide useful data to forecast that the car will stop. The car will stop, of course, but we would like to know enough in advance in order to do something about it. A "low gas level" warning light, for example, is a good leading indicator that forecasts that the car will stop shortly.

[2]An equation for the standard error that is often easier to compute is

$$S_{XY} = \sqrt{\dfrac{\sum Y_i^2 - a \sum Y_i - b \sum Y_i X_i}{n-2}}$$

EXHIBIT 8S.16
Causal Relationship:
Sales to Housing
Starts

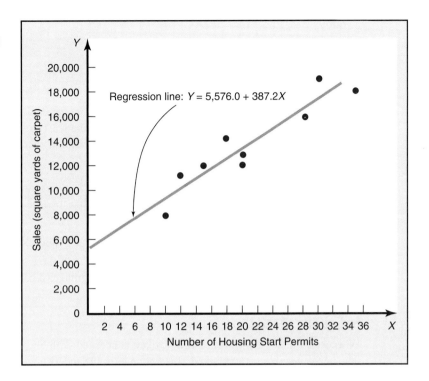

The first step in causal relationship forecasting is to identify those occurrences that are really the causes of the change. Often leading indicators are not causal relationships but in some indirect way may suggest that some other things might happen. Noncausal relationships are simply coincidences. For example, one study some years ago showed that the amount of alcohol sold in Sweden was directly proportional to teachers' salaries. Presumably this was a noncausal relationship.

The following problem illustrates one example of how a forecast is developed using a causal relationship.

Example

The Carpet City Store has kept records of its sales (in square yards) each year, along with the number of permits that were issued for new houses in its area. Carpet City's operations manager believes forecasting carpet sales is possible if the number of new housing permits is known for that year.

Year	Number of Housing Permits	Sales (in sq. yds.)
1993	18	14,000
1994	15	12,000
1995	12	11,000
1996	10	8,000
1997	20	12,000
1998	28	16,000
1999	35	18,000
2000	30	19,000
2001	20	13,000

Solution

First, the data are plotted on Exhibit 8S.16, with

X = Number of housing permits

Y = Sales of carpeting in square yards

Since the points appear to be in a straight line, the manager decides to use the linear relationship $Y = a + bX$. We solve this problem by using the least squares method. Solving for a and b, using the equations presented earlier in this chapter, we obtain the following forecasting equation:

$$Y = 5,576.0 + 387.2X$$

Now, suppose that 25 new housing permits are granted in 2002. The 2002 sales forecast would therefore be:

$$Y = 5,576.0 + 387.2(25) = 15,256.0 \text{ square yards}$$

In this problem, the lag between filing the permit with the appropriate agency and the new homeowner coming to Carpet City to buy carpet makes a causal relationship feasible for forecasting.

Reliability of the Data

With causal relationship forecasting, we are concerned with how much of a change in the dependent variable is "explained" by a change in the independent variable. This is measured by the variance. The greater the proportion of the variance that can be explained by the independent variable, the stronger the relationship. The **coefficient of determination** (r^2) measures the proportion of the variability in the dependent variable that can be explained by changes in the independent variable and is calculated as follows:

$$r^2 = \frac{\Sigma (y_i - \bar{Y})^2 - \Sigma (y_i - \hat{y}_i)^2}{\Sigma (y_i - \bar{Y})^2} \tag{8S.13}$$

where

y_i = Actual value of Y that has been observed for a given value of X

$\bar{Y}$ = Arithmetic mean for all values of y

$\hat{y}_i$ = Value of Y corresponding to a given value of X that has been calculated from the regression equation

The relationship between these variables is shown in Exhibit 8S.17. In equation (8S.13), the first term in the numerator and the term in the denominator are the same ($\Sigma (y_i - \bar{Y})^2$). This term represents the total variation of the Y variable around the arithmetic mean $\bar{Y}$. The second term in the numerator represents the error or that variation in the Y variable that cannot be explained by the regression equation. Thus, the numerator represents that amount of variation that can be explained by the regression equation, and the denominator represents the total variation. As stated above, the coefficient of determination therefore measures the proportion of variation in Y that can be explained by changes in X.

Another measure for evaluating the reliability of a regression forecast is the **mean squared error (MSE)**. Using the same notation as above, the MSE is calculated as follows:

$$\text{MSE} = \frac{\Sigma (y_i - \hat{y}_i)^2}{n - 2} \tag{8S.14}$$

where n = the number of observations.

EXHIBIT 8S.17
The Relationship between $\bar{Y}, y_i,$ and $\hat{y}_i$ in Determining r^2

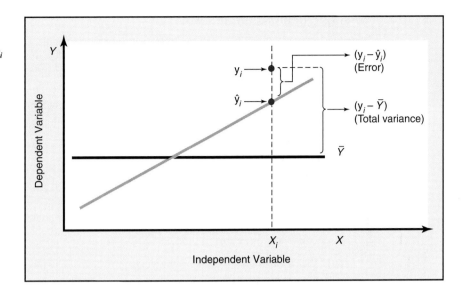

The following example will demonstrate the use of both of these terms.

Example

Using the data from the Carpet City Store example presented above, we can compute the coefficient of determination (r^2) and the MSE as follows:

Year	Actual Sales (Sq. Yds)	Predicted Sales (Sq. Yds)	Total Variance	Error Variance
1993	14,000	12,546	111,111	2,114,116
1994	12,000	11,384	2,777,778	379,456
1995	11,000	10,222	7,111,111	605,284
1996	8,000	9,448	32,111,111	2,096,704
1997	12,000	13,320	2,777,778	1,742,400
1998	16,000	16,418	5,444,444	174,724
1999	18,000	19,128	18,777,778	1,272,384
2000	19,000	17,192	28,444,444	3,268,864
2001	13,000	13,320	444,444	102,400
		Totals:	98,000,000	11,756,332

$$r^2 = \frac{98,000,000 - 11,756,332}{98,000,000} = .88$$

or 88 percent of the change in carpet sales from year to year can be attributed to a change in the number of housing permits issued.

Similarly, we compute the mean squared error:

$$\text{MSE} = \frac{11,756,332}{9-2} = 1,679,476$$

The operations manager can use these values for r^2 and MSE to evaluate other forecasting techniques with the technique that is currently being used.

Multiple Regression Analysis

Another forecasting technique is multiple regression analysis, in which more than one independent variable is considered, together with the effects on sales of each of the items of interest. For example, the gross annual sales for a retail operation such as a home furnishings store can be affected by several factors. These factors can include the number of marriages, housing starts, disposable income, and trends, as they relate to the geographical location of the store. The effects of these different factors can be expressed in a multiple regression equation as

$$S = b + b_m(M) + b_h(H) + b_i(I) + b_t(T)$$

where

S = Gross sales for year

b = Base sales, a starting point from which other factors have influence

M = Marriages during the year

H = Housing starts during the year

I = Annual disposable personal income

T = Time trend (first year = 1, second = 2, third = 3, and so forth)

and b_m, b_h, b_i, and b_t represent the influence on expected sales of the number of marriages, housing starts, income, and trend, respectively.

Forecasting by multiple regression is very appropriate when a number of factors might influence a variable of interest—in this case, sales. The primary difficulty in applying multiple regression analysis is in the data gathering and the mathematical computations. Fortunately, standard software programs for multiple regression analysis are now available.

The Impact of Technology

Increased sophistication in forecasting software programs, coupled with faster computers, has allowed service managers to develop more accurate forecasts that can be performed more frequently. This improvement in forecasting accuracy allows the service manager to improve operational efficiency as well as customer service. Point-of-sale (POS) equipment can now readily provide the service manager with historical sales data in as small as 15-minute time increments. The availability of this data permits accurate forecasting of future sales for corresponding time periods, thereby permitting the manager to schedule workers more efficiently.

Advances in software development have also facilitated their use. Users of these programs are no longer required to have advanced degrees in mathematical modeling. In fact, anyone with a working knowledge of an electronic spreadsheet can create a forecast on a PC.

Many of the commercial forecasting software programs now available exist as library routines within a mainframe computer system, while some may be incorporated or "bundled" as part of a larger program. Still other programs can be purchased separately from software companies specializing in this area. Many of these programs are also available for PCs.

Forecasting is also an integral part of *yield management* (also known as revenue management), which is discussed in greater detail in Chapter 14. The role of forecasting here is to project customer demand for various prices charged for a service. This information allows the service manager to establish a selling price that will maximize capacity utilization and therefore also maximize revenues.

A wealth of information concerning forecasting is also available on the Internet. This includes reviews of different forecasting programs.

Summary

Forecasting is fundamental to any planning effort. In the short run, a forecast is needed to predict customer demand patterns so that a firm can determine the number of workers required to provide a given level of service. In the long run, forecasting is required for strategic changes, such as developing new markets and locations, developing new services, and expanding or creating new facilities.

For long-term forecasts that lead to heavy financial commitments, great care should be taken to derive the forecast. Several approaches should be used. Causal methods such as regression analysis or multiple regression analysis are beneficial, as they provide an initial basis for decision making. Economic factors, product trends, growth factors, and competition, as well as a myriad of other possible variables, need to be considered and the forecast adjusted to reflect the influence of each.

Short- and intermediate-term forecasts, such as those required for labor scheduling, may be done with simpler models, such as exponential smoothing with perhaps an adaptive feature or a seasonal index. The forecasting routine should therefore be simple and should also detect and respond rapidly to identifiable short-term changes in demand while at the same time ignoring the occasional spurious demands. Exponential smoothing, when monitored by management to adjust the value of alpha, is also an effective technique.

A Chinese fortune cookie once stated that "Forecasting is difficult, especially about the future." A perfect forecast is like a hole-in-one in golf: great to get but we should be satisfied just to land on the green. The ideal philosophy for managers is to create the best forecast possible, and then have sufficient flexibility in the system to adjust for the inevitable forecasting errors. As stated earlier, managers must recognize the trade-offs that exist in developing forecasting models: the greater the accuracy required, the more expensive the model. At some point, the cost of improved accuracy cannot be economically justified.

Key Formulae

Simple moving average forecast

$$F_t = \frac{A_{t-1} + A_{t-2} \cdots + A_{t-n}}{n} \tag{8S.1}$$

Weighted moving average forecast

$$F_t = w_{t-1} A_{t-1} + w_{t-2} A_{t-2} \cdots w_{t-n} A_{t-n} \tag{8S.2}$$

and

$$\sum_{i=1}^{n} w_{t-i} = 1$$

Exponential smoothing

$$F_t = F_{t-1} + \alpha (A_{t-1} - F_{t-1}) \tag{8S.3}$$

Exponential smoothing with trend effects

$$\text{FIT}_t = F_t + T_t \tag{8S.4}$$

$$F_t = \text{FIT}_{t-1} + \alpha (A_{t-1} - \text{FIT}_{t-1}) \tag{8S.5}$$

$$T_t = T_{t-1} + \alpha\delta (A_{t-1} - \text{FIT}_{t-1}) \tag{8S.6}$$

Mean absolute deviation (MAD)

$$\text{MAD} = \frac{\sum_{t=1}^{n} |A_t - F_t|}{n} \tag{8S.7}$$

Tracking signal

$$TS = \frac{RSFE}{MAD}$$ (8S.8)

Exponentially smoothed MAD

$$MAD_t = \alpha \left| A_{t-1} - F_{t-1} \right| + (1 - \alpha)MAD_{t-1}$$ (8S.9)

Mean absolute percentage error (MAPE)

$$MAPE = \frac{\sum\limits_{t=1}^{n} \frac{\left| Y_t - \hat{Y}_t \right|}{Y_t} \times 100}{n}$$ (8S.10)

Linear regression

$$Y = a + bX$$ (8S.11)

Standard effor of the estimate

$$S_{YX} = \sqrt{\frac{\sum\limits_{i=1}^{n} (y_i - \hat{y}_i)^2}{n-2}}$$ (8S.12)

Coefficient of determination

$$r^2 = \frac{\sum (y_i - \bar{Y})^2 - \sum (y_i - \hat{y}_i)^2}{\sum (y_i - \bar{Y})^2}$$ (8S.13)

Mean squared error

$$MSE = \frac{\sum (y_i - \hat{y}_i)^2}{n-2}$$ (8S.14)

Key Terms

causal relationship forecasting: relating demand to an underlying factor other than time. *(p. 191)*
coefficient of determination (r^2): proportion of variability in demand that can be attributed to an independent variable. *(p. 216)*
exponential smoothing: time series forecasting technique that does not require large amounts of historical data. *(p. 197)*
exponential smoothing constant alpha (α): value between 0 and 1 that is used in exponential smoothing to minimize the error between historical demand and respective forecasts. *(p. 197)*
linear regression analysis: type of forecasting technique which assumes that the relationship between the dependent and independent variables is a straight line. *(p. 210)*
mean absolute percentage error (MAPE): the average absolute difference between the actual and forecasted demands expressed as a percentage of the actual demand. *(p. 209)*
mean absolute deviation (MAD): average forecasting error based upon the absolute difference between the actual and forecasted demand. *(p. 206)*
mean squared error (MSE): measure of variability in the data about a regression line. *(p. 216)*

qualitative techniques: nonquantitative forecasting techniques based upon expert opinions and intuition. Typically used when there are no data available. *(p. 190)*

simple moving average: average over a given number of time periods that is updated by replacing the data in the oldest period with that in the most recent period. *(p. 194)*

standard error of the estimate: measure of dispersion of the data about a regression line. *(p. 213)*

time series analysis: analyzing data by time periods (for example, hours, days, weeks) to determine if trends or patterns occur. *(p. 190)*

tracking signal: measure of error to determine if the forecast is staying within specified limits of the actual demand. *(p. 207)*

trend smoothing constant delta (δ): value between 0 and 1 that is used in exponential smoothing when there is a trend. *(p. 201)*

weighted moving average: simple moving average where weights are assigned to each time period in the average. The sum of all of the weights must equal one. *(p. 196)*

Review and Discussion Questions

1. Why is forecasting especially important for a service firm, as compared to a manufacturing company?

2. As the real estate development manager for an upscale hotel chain, you have been asked to develop a forecasting model for predicting sales at potential new locations. Which forecasting technique(s) would you use and why?

3. You are developing a forecasting model to predict the hourly customer demand at a fast-food outlet located in a major metropolitan area. What are some factors that might influence hourly customer demand at this location?

4. In terms of forecasting errors, why would a manager want to use the least squares method when conducting simple regression analysis?

5. In comparing simple moving average, weighted moving average, exponential smoothing, and simple linear regression analysis, which forecasting technique would you consider to be the most accurate? Why?

6. What is the main disadvantage of using regression analysis to predict hourly sales in a bank or a department store?

7. What is the main purpose of using a tracking signal?

8. Discuss the main differences between the mean absolute deviation (MAD) and the standard error of the estimate.

9. Examine Exhibit 8S.3 and suggest which forecasting technique you might use for: (*a*) locating a high-priced clothing boutique; (*b*) estimating the number of calls for roadside assistance; (*c*) locating a health service clinic; (*d*) determining customer orders at a mail-order toy company.

10. In terms of the errors, why would the service manager wish to use the least squares method when doing simple linear regression?

11. What is the main disadvantage of daily forecasting using regression analysis?

12. Discuss the basic differences between the mean absolute deviation (MAD) and the standard error of the estimate.

Internet Assignment

The Wharton School at the University of Pennsylvania has a website devoted to forecasting at www.marketing.wharton.upenn.edu/forecast/welcome.html. Visit this website and select a firm that provides business forecasting software. Visit that firm's website and:

Solved Problems

a. Describe the company.

b. Select one of its forecasting software products and describe it in detail, including costs.

c. Identify specific applications for which this program would be most suitable.

1. Sunrise Baking Company markets doughnuts through a chain of food stores and has been experiencing over- and underproduction because of forecasting errors. The following data are its daily demands in dozens of doughnuts for the past four weeks. The bakery is closed Saturday, so Friday's production must satisfy demand for both Saturday and Sunday.

	4 Weeks Ago	3 Weeks Ago	2 Weeks Ago	Last Week
Monday }	2,200	2,400	2,300	2,400
Tuesday }	2,000	2,100	2,200	2,200
Wednesday	2,300	2,400	2,300	2,500
Thursday	1,800	1,900	1,800	2,000
Friday	1,900	1,800	2,100	2,000
Saturday Sunday	2,800	2,700	3,000	2,900

Make a forecast for this week on the following basis:

a. Daily, using a simple four-week moving average.
b. Daily, using a weighted average of 0.40 for last week, 0.30 for two weeks ago, 0.20 for three weeks ago, and 0.10 for four weeks ago.
c. Sunrise is also planning its purchases of ingredients for bread production. If bread demand had been forecast for last week at 22,000 loaves and only 21,000 loaves were actually demanded, what would Sunrise's forecast be for this week using exponential smoothing with $\alpha = 0.10$?
d. Supposing, with the forecast made in (c), this week's demand actually turns out to be 22,500. What would the new forecast be for the next week?

Solution

a. Simple moving average, 4 weeks.

Monday $\qquad \dfrac{2,400 + 2,300 + 2,400 + 2,200}{4} = \dfrac{9,300}{4} = 2,325$ doz.

Tuesday $\qquad\qquad\qquad\qquad\qquad\quad = \dfrac{8,500}{4} = 2,125$ doz.

Wednesday $\qquad\qquad\qquad\qquad\qquad = \dfrac{9,500}{4} = 2,375$ doz.

Thursday $\qquad\qquad\qquad\qquad\qquad\ = \dfrac{7,500}{4} = 1,875$ doz.

Friday $\qquad\qquad\qquad\qquad\qquad\quad = \dfrac{7,800}{4} = 1,950$ doz.

Saturday and Sunday $\qquad\qquad\quad = \dfrac{11,400}{4} = 2,850$ doz.

b. Weighted average with weights of .40, .30, .20, and .10.

	(.10)		(.20)		(.30)		(.40)		
Monday	220	+	480	+	690	+	960	=	2,350
Tuesday	200	+	420	+	660	+	880	=	2,160
Wednesday	230	+	480	+	690	+	1,000	=	2,400
Thursday	180	+	380	+	540	+	800	=	1,900
Friday	190	+	360	+	630	+	800	=	1,980
Saturday and Sunday	280	+	540	+	900	+	1,160	=	2,880
	1,300	+	2,660	+	4,110	+	5,600	=	13,670

c. $\begin{aligned} F_t &= F_{t-1} + \alpha(A_{t-1} - F_{t-1}) \\ &= 22,000 + 0.10(21,000 - 22,000) \\ &= 22,000 - 100 \\ &= 21,900 \text{ loaves} \end{aligned}$

d. F_{t+1} = $21{,}900 + \alpha(22{,}500 - 21{,}900)$
   = $21{,}900 + .10(600)$
   = $21{,}900$ loaves

2. A specific forecasting model was used to forecast patient visits to an emergency room. The forecasts and the corresponding actual number of visits that subsequently occurred are shown below.

Month	Actual	Forecast
October	700	660
November	760	840
December	780	750
January	790	835
February	850	910
March	950	890

Use the MAD, tracking signal, and MAPE to evaluate the forecasting model.

Solution

Evaluate the forecasting model using MAD and tracking signal.

Month	Actual Demand	Forecast Demand	Actual Deviation	Cumulative Deviation (RSFE)	Absolute Deviation
October	700	660	40	40	40
November	760	840	−80	−40	80
December	780	750	30	−10	30
January	790	835	−45	−55	45
February	850	910	−60	−115	60
March	950	890	60	−55	60

Total dev. = 315

$$\text{MAD} = \frac{315}{6} = 52.5$$

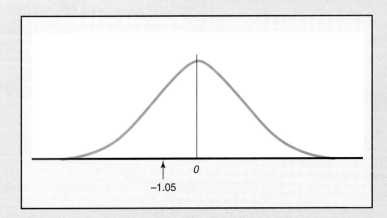

$$\text{Tracking signal} = \frac{-55}{52.5} = -1.05$$

$$\text{MAPE} = \frac{40/700 + 80/760 + 30/780 + 45/790 + 60/850 + 60/950 \times 100}{6}$$

$$\text{MAPE} = \frac{.059 + .105 + .038 + .057 + .070 + .063}{6} \times 100$$

$$\text{MAPE} = .392/6 \times 100 = 6.5\%$$

Forecast model is well within the distribution.

Problems

1. A year ago, Deborah Young-Kroeger started a home delivery service for the elderly. Customers place their orders with a local supermarket, drugstore, or other retail establishment that has agreed to participate in this service. Each retail operation then fills its order and Deborah's firm picks up and delivers the merchandise. In addition to a fixed fee she receives per order from her customers, Deborah also receives a small percentage or commission from the retailers. Because she has been able to promise deliveries within three hours, her company has experienced significant growth, as shown in the table below:

Month	Number of Orders Delivered
January	420
February	430
March	400
April	440
May	500
June	470
July	530
August	490
September	540
October	570
November	630
December	600

Because she leases her delivery vans on an annual basis, she wants an estimate of the number of deliveries for each month in the coming year. Using least squares regression analysis, forecast the number of deliveries for each of the next 12 months.

2. From past history, the number of customers who have eaten lunch at Jane Forte's restaurant for the past six Fridays is:

Date	Number of Customers
Six Mondays ago	120
Five Mondays ago	110
Four Mondays ago	150
Three Mondays ago	120
Two Mondays ago	160
Last Monday	150

a. With the following weights, use a weighted moving average to forecast the number of customers for next Monday's lunch.

Date	Weight
Three Mondays ago	.20
Two Mondays ago	.45
Last Monday	.35

    b. Using a simple three-period moving average, find the forecast for next Monday's lunch.

    c. Using single exponential smoothing with $\alpha = 0.2$ and a forecast for last Monday's lunch of 130 customers, calculate the forecast for next Monday's lunch. Make whatever assumptions you wish. List these assumptions.

    d. Using simple linear regression, calculate the regression equation for the data presented above.

    e. Using the regression equation in part *d,* calculate the forecast for next Monday's lunch.

3. Accel Automotive specializes in the major repairs and maintenance of foreign automobiles. The following data represent the number of cars that were actually repaired each month for the previous six months and a starting forecast for January.

Month	Actual	Forecast
January	100	80
February	94	
March	106	
April	80	
May	68	
June	94	

    a. Calculate the forecast for each of the remaining months using simple exponential smoothing with $\alpha = 0.2$.

    b. Calculate the MAD for these forecasts.

4. The number of patients visiting a walk-in health clinic over the past two years has been aggregated into two-month periods as presented below:

Period	Number of Visits	Period	Number of Visits
Jan.–Feb.	1,090	Jan.–Feb.	1,150
March–April	1,040	March–April	1,120
May–June	1,500	May–June	1,590
July–Aug.	1,700	July–Aug.	1,820
Sept.–Oct.	1,200	Sept.–Oct.	1,260
Nov.–Dec.	1,000	Nov.–Dec.	1,060

    a. Plot the data on a graph.

    b. Fit a simple linear regression model to the data.

    c. Using the results from part *b,* forecast the number of patients for each of the six bimonthly periods for the next year.

5. Peter Arnold, as manager of a hotel reservations call center, has been collecting data on the number of calls received per hour for each day of the week to forecast future calls. Using these historical data, and comparing them with the forecasted number of calls, Peter has calculated the tracking signals for three different time periods as follows:

Time Period	Mondays 10:00–11:00 A.M.	Fridays 7:00–8:00 P.M.	Sundays 3:00–4:00 P.M.
Week 1	−2.70	1.54	0.10
Week 2	−2.32	−0.64	0.43
Week 3	−1.70	2.05	1.08
Week 4	−1.10	2.58	1.74
Week 5	−0.87	−0.95	1.94
Week 6	−0.05	−1.23	2.24
Week 7	0.10	0.75	2.96
Week 8	0.40	−1.59	3.02
Week 9	1.50	0.47	3.54
Week 10	2.20	2.74	3.75

Discuss the tracking signals for each time period and what the implications are.

6. To determine the future capacity requirements for your call center, prepare a forecast using simple linear regression for each quarter of the coming year from the past two years' historical data.

Quarter	Number of Calls Received
1	16,000
2	19,500
3	15,000
4	14,000
5	21,500
6	24,000
7	20,500
8	19,000

7. Terry Tierney has created a website that offers discounted travel packages for senior citizens and has collected the following data on the number of travel packages she has sold per month over the past nine months:

Month	Actual
January	1,110
February	1,300
March	1,500
April	1,700
May	1,600
June	1,800
July	1,400
August	1,300
September	1,400

She wants to test two different forecasting methods to determine which was better over this nine-month period.

a. Forecast the number of travel packages sold monthly from April through September using a three-month simple moving average.

b. Use simple exponential smoothing to estimate April through September. (Use $\alpha = 0.3$ and assume that the forecast for March was 1,300.)

c. Use MAD to determine which forecasting method produced the better forecast over the six-month period.

8. Test the validity of your forecasting model. The following are the forecasts for a model you have been using along with the actual demands that occurred:

Week	Forecast	Actual
1	800	900
2	850	1,000
3	950	1,050
4	950	900
5	1,000	900
6	975	1,100

   Use the method stated in the text to compute the MAD and the tracking signal and draw a conclusion as to whether the forecasting model you have been using is giving reasonable results. Justify your conclusion.

9. A forecasting method you have been using to predict the number of daily calls into a call center is shown in the following table along with the actual demand that occurred.

Forecast	Actual
1,500	1,550
1,400	1,500
1,700	1,600
1,750	1,650
1,800	1,700

   a. Compute the tracking signal using the mean absolute deviation (MAD) and running sum of forecast errors (RSFE).
   b. Do you believe the forecasting method is giving good predictions?

10. After using your forecasting model for six months, you decide to test it using MAD and a tracking signal. Following are the forecasted and actual number of patient visits to a walk-in clinic for the six-month period:

Period	Forecast	Actual
May	450	500
June	500	550
July	550	400
August	600	500
September	650	675
October	700	600

   a. Calculate the tracking signal.
   b. Decide whether your forecasting routine is acceptable.

11. Consolidated Edison Company of New York, Inc., sells electricity, gas, and steam to New York City and Westchester County. Sales revenues for the years 1989 to 1999 are shown below. Forecast the revenues for 2000 through 2003. Use your own judgment, intuition, or common sense concerning which model or method to use, as well as the period of data to include. Obtain the actual revenues for three years and evaluate your forecasting model.

Year	Revenue ($ millions)
1989	5,550
1990	5,739
1991	5,873
1992	5,933
1993	6,020
1994	6,260
1995	6,537
1996	6,960
1997	7,121
1998	7,093
1999	7,491

12. Dana and Kerry own a chain of aerobic and fitness centers for women. They recently hired a consultant to help identify which factors significantly affect the volume of sales at a location. Based on the consultant's analysis, the three most significant factors were: (1) average age of adult females within a three-mile radius, (2) number of adult females living or working within a three-mile radius, and (3) average household income within a three-mile radius. Using multiple regression analysis, the consultant developed the following equation to forecast sales for a new location:

Sales = 410, 411 − 4,417 (average age) + 4.62 (number of females) + 1.55 (average income)

Dana and Kerry are currently evaluating four potential sites. The data for each of these sites are as follows:

Site	Average Age	Number of Females	Average Income
A	47 yrs	14,000	$77,000
B	22	21,000	49,000
C	32	9,000	54,000
D	37	16,000	83,000

Calculate the forecasted sales for each site. Which one should Dana and Kerry select for their next location if their goal is to maximize their sales?

13. Josh Francis has been recently named director of franchising for a chain of gourmet coffee shops. The company has divided the United States into different territories, with a franchise manager assigned to each territory. The sales and populations for the current territories that the firm now does business in are as follows:

Territory	Population (millions)	Sales (thousands)
A	2.53	410
B	1,76	240
C	6.81	595
D	4.22	325
E	12.77	990
F	5.09	665
G	10.82	840
H	16.84	1,450
I	7.65	825
J	11.34	935
K	6.18	830

a. Using an electronic spreadsheet, calculate the least squares regression line that fits the above data.
b. What is the regression equation? What is the coefficient of determination?
c. Josh's company is planning to expand into two additional territories in the coming year. The populations of these two territories are 7.43 million and 3.87 million. What are the estimated sales that Josh can expect from these two territories?

14. David has recently graduated from a business school and has taken a position as the assistant manager at a small hotel with 35 rooms. One of his first assignments is to develop a model to forecast the number of room-nights that are expected to be sold in each month in 2003. (A room-night is the sale of one room for one night.) He has collected the following historical data on how many room-nights have been sold for each month in each of the past three years.

Month	Room-Nights Sold		
	2000	2001	2002
January	307	275	316
February	257	209	251
March	290	304	338
April	323	312	370
May	425	469	472
June	589	548	593
July	791	734	777
August	643	658	702
September	454	420	513
October	725	690	766
November	547	493	639
December	605	584	668

a. Using exponential smoothing with an electronic spreadsheet, develop a forecast for the number of room-nights to be sold in each month of 2003. Since this is the first time you are doing this forecast, use $\alpha = 0.3$ and $\alpha = 0.7$ and develop two forecasts. (Assume that the forecast for each month in 2000 is equal to the actual demand.)
b. Which α would you recommend using and why?

15. A customer service call center for a major appliance manufacturer has collected the following data for the last four Mondays on incoming calls:

Time	Four Mondays Ago	Three Mondays Ago	Two Mondays Ago	Last Monday
6:00–8:00 A.M.	35	42	39	33
8:00–10:00 A.M.	66	71	78	80
10:00–noon	90	105	112	98
noon–2:00 P.M.	99	123	114	107
2:00–4:00 P.M.	87	101	96	94
4:00–6:00 P.M.	55	43	51	38
6:00–8:00 P.M.	25	31	34	30

a. Use exponential smoothing with $\alpha = .3$ and $\alpha = .7$ to forecast the number of calls for next Monday.

b. Using MAD as a criterion, which of the two values of α do you recommend?

16. Chez George is a haute cuisine restaurant that is open only for dinner. To determine the proper number of servers to schedule for each day, Aspen Wang, the dining room manager, needs to forecast the number of meals that will be served. To do this, she has collected the following data:

Day of the Week	Four Weeks Ago	Three Weeks Ago	Two Weeks Ago	Last Week
Sunday	56	44	63	65
Monday	87	72	79	81
Tuesday	90	93	88	95
Wednesday	101	92	107	102
Thursday	120	114	106	118
Friday	125	131	143	157
Saturday	166	152	178	179

a. Using exponential smoothing and $\alpha = .5$, forecast the number of meals for each day next week.

b. Calculate the MAD for each day.

Selected Bibliography

Andrews, Bruce H., and Shawn M. Cunningham. "L.L. Bean Improves Call Center Forecasting." *Interfaces* 25, no. 6 (November–December 1995), pp. 1–13.

Carlberg, Ralph. "BioComp Systems on Demand Forecasting." Biocomp Systems, Inc., Redmond, WA, 1996.

Davis, Mark M., and Paul D. Berger. "Sales Forecasting in a Retail Service Environment." *The Journal of Business Forecasting,* Winter 1989, pp. 8–17.

DeLurgio, Stephen A. *Forecasting Principals and Applications.* New York: Irwin/McGraw-Hill, 1998.

Diebold, Francis X. *Elements of Forecasting.* Cincinnati, OH: Southwestern College Publishing, 1998.

Hample, Scott. "R U Ready for AI?" *Marketing Tools,* May 1, 1996, p. 60.

Hanke, John E., and Arthur G. Reitsch. *Business Forecasting.* 4th ed. Boston: Allyn and Bacon, 1992.

Hueter, Jackie, and William Swart. "An Integrated Labor-Management System for Taco Bell." *Interfaces* 28, no.1, January–February 1998, pp. 75–91.

Jain, Chaman L. "Explosion in the Forecasting Function in Corporate America." *The Journal of Business Forecasting,* Summer 1999, pp. 2, 28.

Makridakis, Spyros, Steven C. Wheelwright, and Rob J. Hyndruan. *Forecasting: Methods and Applications.* 3rd ed. New York: John Wiley & Sons, 1998.

Moore, Karl, Robert Burbach, and Roger Heeler. "Using Neural Networks to Analyze Qualitative Data." *Marketing Research* 7 (January 1, 1995), p. 34.

Newbold, Paul, and Theodore Bos. *Introductory Business Forecasting.* Cincinnati, OH: South-Western Publishing Co., 1990.

Wilson, J. Holton, and Barry Keating. *Business Forecasting.* New York: Irwin/McGraw-Hill, 1998.

Xu, Weidong. "Long Range Planning for Call Centers at FedEx." *The Journal of Business Forecasting,* Winter 1999–2000.

CHAPTER NINE

Managing the Workforce

Learning Objectives

- Introduce the concept of the service profit chain.

- Identify some of the emerging trends that are changing the ways people work.

- Describe the role of the manager as team leader and coach, and the skills required to be effective.

- Define the concept of employee empowerment and show how it affects management and the organization.

- Distinguish between traditional work groups, self-managed teams, and cross-functional teams.

- Present the ways technology affects jobs and the workplace.

- Introduce both behavioral and physical factors that should be considered when designing jobs.

At Southwest Airlines, the Customer Isn't Always Right—the Employee Is!

AP / Wide World Photo / Southwest Airlines

It may be hard to believe, but some people actually have fun at work. They hug and kiss each other as if they are part of one big happy family; in this case, that "family" happens to be a corporation named Southwest Airlines (SWA). At the same time, they are a group of hardworking, dedicated professionals who are committed to providing excellent service to customers, which is clearly stated in SWA's mission statement: "The Mission of Southwest Airlines is dedication to the highest quality of customer service delivered with a sense of warmth, friendliness, individual pride and company spirit."

At the same time, the customer is not always right at SWA, but the employee is! Customers who treat employees rudely or don't like the service that SWA provides may be asked to take their business elsewhere.

SWA's employees are clearly its biggest asset, and its investment in them over the years has paid off many times over. In the highly competitive airline industry:

- SWA is the only U.S. airline to have made a profit every year since 1973, and its profit margins are the highest in the industry.
- SWA consistently offers the lowest fares in the markets that it serves.
- SWA has the most productive workforce with the lowest cost per passenger mile.
- SWA has the lowest employee turnover rate.
- SWA has the best performance record, based upon baggage handling, on-time arrivals, and customer complaints statistics, winning the Department of Transportation's annual triple crown five times (1992, 1993, 1994, 1995, and 1996).

Sources: Kevin Frieberg and Jackie Frieberg, *Nuts!* (Austin, TX: Bard Press, 1996), and http://www.southwest.com.

The Customer's Perspective

Have you ever asked a waiter in a restaurant or a teller in a bank a question for which they didn't have an answer, and they didn't even try to get you one? Have you ever asked someone in a hotel or a retail store to do something for you and they simply replied, "That's not my job!" Have you noticed a constant changeover in employees in many services? Sometimes it seems that you actually know more about the business than they do. Have you ever been served by rude employees or by employees who don't seem to care about their jobs or the place where they work?

Every one of us has experienced one or more of these situations, probably on more than one occasion. All these types of encounters between employees and customers reflect poor workforce management practices resulting in high employee turnover and unmotivated employees. These encounters also suggest that the employees lack the necessary training to do their jobs properly.

On the other hand, you may have been pleasantly surprised when an employee went out of his or her way for you, or when you were warmly greeted by a worker, or an employee seemed genuinely interested in helping you. These types of encounters between customers and employees usually indicate that these organizations understand the value of their employees and have made a major commitment to meet their needs, as well as to educate them and have the proper incentives in place so that they will provide excellent service to customers.

Managerial Issues

As we have seen earlier in the book, services compete in the marketplace in many ways as they constantly look for new opportunities to distinguish themselves from their competition. However, as we have also seen, many of these advantages often are short lived because they are easily duplicated by the competition.

One area that appears to provide firms with a sustainable long-term competitive advantage is their ability to attract, motivate, and retain highly skilled workers. Firms that are able to accomplish this successfully on a consistent long-term basis, such as General Electric under Jack Welch, Southwest Airlines under Herb Kelleher, and FedEx under Fred Smith, have also achieved enviable long-term financial success, and that is no coincidence. The management team in each of these firms knows the value and contribution of their workers and continuously invests in training, motivating, and retaining them.

Moreover, the growing use of intranets, which include Enterprise Resource Planning (ERP) systems, opens up new approaches for integrating organizations that had never before been contemplated. These new technologies provide greater employee flexibility by allowing them to work from remote locations, including their homes. As a consequence, managers, in many instances, must now oversee the work of employees with whom they rarely meet face to face.

The Service Profit Chain

Jim Heskett, Earl Sasser, and Len Schlesinger introduced the concept of the service profit chain, the basic elements of which are presented in Exhibit 9.1.

The first element in the service profit chain is the employee. Management's goal should be to develop a corporate culture that promotes worker loyalty and worker satisfaction. In such an environment, not only are workers very productive, but the quality of their output is also very high. This leads to higher customer perception of value in the service, which is the second element in the service profit chain. Customers who perceive high value in a service are willing to pay more for it, which leads to greater profitability for the firm, the third element in the service profit chain. The firm then reinvests a portion of the profits back into the firm in the form of training and incentives that continue to develop worker skills and promote worker satisfaction and loyalty. FedEx has adopted a similar approach, which is shown in Exhibit 9.2.

In essence, FedEx believes that if you treat your workers properly, they will provide customers with a high level of service, which will then generate significant profits for the firm. FedEx reinvests a significant portion of those profits back into training and rewarding its people, which supports the continuation of the cycle.

EXHIBIT 9.1
**Elements of the
Service Profit Chain**

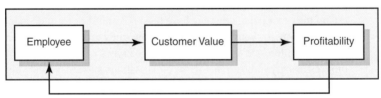

Source: Adapted from James L. Heskett, W. Earl Sasser, Jr., and Leonard A. Schlesinger, *The Service Profit Chain* (New York: Free Press, 1997), p. 12.

EXHIBIT 9.2
**FedEx's
People–Service–Profit
Concept**

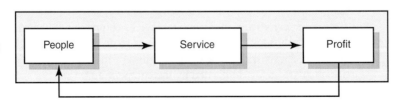

Emerging Trends in the Workplace

The workplace is changing. Some of these changes are externally driven, such as the changing demographics of the workforce and the impact of technology, and some are internal changes organizations are making to become both more efficient and more effective.

Workforce Diversity

Today's workforce is more diverse than ever before. In the United States, for example, the two-income family is almost a necessity; as a result, more women than ever before are in the workforce. Liberal U.S. immigration policies have also contributed to this increase in workplace diversity. In the European Union, workers are no longer restricted to working only in their country of origin, but can now seek employment in any one of the EU's member nations.

Flexible Work Hours

Many companies offer employees flexible work schedules, which can be seen as a benefit for both workers and the organization. For example, in the United States, in a firm with flexible work hours, an employee can report to work any time between 7:00 and 9:00 A.M. and leave after working eight hours. However, in some companies in Germany, flexible work hours mean that an employee can work up to 70 hours a week (without being paid overtime, and provided the work is there) during parts of the year and take extended time off at other times. These employees work as many hours as they would in a traditional work year, but have far more flexibility in their personal lives, so both the organization and the individual win!

Part-Time Work and Job Sharing

Part-time work in services is related both to the needs of the workforce and the service organization. People choose to work part time for a number of reasons: some work primarily for extra spending money, some work during the hours that their children are in school but plan their workdays so that they can be available for their children both before and after school, some have health problems or other reasons they must limit their work hours. From the organizational perspective, many services experience wide variations in demand throughout the day or seasonally. For example, coffee shops and donut shops may have very high demand early in the morning, but lower demand throughout the rest of the day. Restaurants have highest demand during mealtimes, and retail stores experience demand peaks when most people are free to shop—evenings and weekends. Services near ski and beach resorts experience highly seasonal demand. One advantage of employing part-time workers is that payroll taxes and benefits are usually significantly less than they are for full-time workers. However, many firms that rely heavily on a part-time workforce may provide full benefits for these employees to attract and retain them. FedEx, for example, provides full medical and insurance benefits to part-time workers who may work only 20 hours a week.

With job sharing, two or more individuals work together to perform the duties of a full-time position. They will often share the same office, which is less expensive for the firm than providing each with his or her own office. Job sharing may be particularly attractive to employees who have small children or elderly parents who need care.

Temporary Labor

Hiring and firing workers is expensive. In some countries, such as Germany and France, laws and social conventions make it almost impossible to fire an employee (although this is changing). As a result, more companies in these countries are choosing to hire temporary workers. In addition to enabling the firm to quickly adjust its workforce to meet changing demand for its services, a temporary workforce also allows the firm to retain its full-time workers on a more permanent basis. For example, a firm may hire enough full-time workers to handle the stable portion of demand over time; it then hires temporary workers when demand increases due to seasonal or other short-term variation. The full-time employees work year-round, while the temporary workers work only during the busy season.

Increasing Emphasis on Teamwork

Nowhere is the need for effective management and the focus on employee empowerment more obvious than in the increasing use of teamwork by organizations. Although some organizations have successfully used team models for organizing work for more than 20 years, the surge in the number of American organizations now using teams has been relatively recent. There are many reasons for the growing popularity of teams, including that teams typically outperform individuals when doing tasks that require judgment, experience, and multiple skills. Companies using self-managed teams have found that they increase productivity, quality, customer satisfaction, and flexibility; allow for the streamlining of functions; and produce higher worker commitment.[1]

To better understand the power of teams, it is important to highlight some differences between teams and traditional work groups. In traditional work groups, the emphasis is on sharing information and making decisions that help group members perform their functions more effectively. Work groups do not need to work collectively on tasks that require a group effort, and their members are individually accountable for their performance. Work teams, in contrast, emphasize collective performance. Work team members are both individually and mutually responsible for their contributions and performance. Work teams are characterized by a high degree of synergy. This synergy combines and improves the knowledge and skills of individual members to create products and/or decisions that are of higher quality than those made by individuals alone. Katzenbach and Smith define the difference between a team and a group of people with a common assignment as "a small number of people with complementary skills who are committed to a common purpose, performance goals, and approach for which they hold themselves mutually accountable." They go on to say that truly high-performance teams have the added ingredient of "members who are also deeply committed to another's personal growth and success."[2]

As more organizations embrace the use of work teams, the variety of team structures and projects on which teams work continues to increase. Two types of work teams that are prevalent in today's organizations are self-managed work teams and cross-functional teams.

Self-Managed Work Teams

Unlike traditional work groups, **self-managed work teams** tend to operate very autonomously. They have responsibility for not only solving problems, but also for implementing solutions and measuring outcomes. Typically composed of 10 to 15 employees, these teams take on many of the activities and responsibilities that were formerly the duties of their supervisors. Members of a self-managed team are likely to have collective con-

---

[1] J. D. Orsburn, L. Moran, E. Musselwhite, and J. H. Zenger, *Self-Directed Work Teams: The New American Challenge* (Burr Ridge, IL: Business One Irwin, 1990).
[2] Jon R. Katzenbach and Douglas K. Smith, *The Wisdom of Teams: Creating the High Performance Organization* (Boston: Harvard Business School Press, 1993), pp. 45, 92.

trol over (*a*) work assignments for team members, (*b*) the pace at which work gets done, (*c*) assessing the quality of team and individual output, and (*d*) who joins the team.

There are, however, some unique problems with self-managed work teams, especially in service operations. For example, a guest at the front desk of a Ritz-Carlton Hotel became very upset when she was told there was no manager for the front desk. To address that problem, each team member becomes "manager for a day" on a rotating basis.

Effective self-managed teams have produced some important benefits for organizations and their employees. The greater autonomy and responsibility given to employees in self-managed teams tend to increase worker motivation and job satisfaction. Employees are empowered and can see how their efforts contribute to organizational success. This motivation and satisfaction also positively affects productivity and the organization's bottom line. For example, an employee on a self-managed team at ACES, an independent electric power producer, noticed that fans similar to those used in his plant were being sold at a local discount store for one-third the cost of those bought by ACES from the original manufacturer. He took the initiative to buy the discount store's entire inventory of fans. Because of his participation in a self-managed team, he knew the cost of the ACES fans, understood the purposes for which the fans were used and how often they would need to be replaced, and felt authorized by the company to implement a solution that would save money.

The successful implementation of self-managed teams, however, is not easy. It takes considerable time, effort, and organizational commitment. Team members not only must have technical expertise but also must develop skills in problem solving, decision making, interpersonal communication, and team management. The organization must be willing to create innovative reward and incentive systems that reflect both individual and team performance. Managers must learn to become facilitators and coaches of empowered, self-managed teams rather than directors and bosses of individual contributors.

Cross-Functional Work Teams

Cross-functional work teams come together to tackle large, complex projects or solve organizational problems that cut across traditional functional lines and require the input and expertise from several areas within an organization. The members of a cross-functional team may come from the same organizational level but represent different departments and areas of expertise.

As in the case of self-managed work teams, the successful implementation of cross-functional teams requires organizational commitment. The members of a cross-functional team must learn to appreciate and understand the perspectives of representatives from other parts of the organization. They must also learn to communicate their expertise and opinions in ways that representatives from other functional areas can understand. Developing an effective cross-functional team can take considerable time and effort. The organizations that have done so, however, believe that the effort pays off.

Employee Turnover

Firms that treat their workers well have very low employee turnover compared to the average turnover in their industries. Ritz-Carlton hotels, for example, have an employee turnover rate of less than 20 percent in an industry that averages more than 100 percent annually! Similarly, Southwest Airlines' employee turnover rate of 4.5 percent is one of the lowest in the airline industry. Although all the material presented in this chapter relates to employee turnover, we focus here on those topics that are directly related to the cost of turnover.

Employee Turnover Costs

The cost of employee turnover has several components, some of which are readily quantifiable while others are less easily measured. Every time an employee leaves, these costs are incurred.

Loss of Knowledge

When employees leave a firm, they take with them knowledge that they gained over time. This can include knowledge of internal systems and processes, as well as knowledge of customers. Also included here is the knowledge of the organization's culture and relationships with other employees, which facilitates completing work in an efficient and effective manner.

Loss of Output

When an employee leaves and the position is not filled immediately, the firm loses that worker's output while the position remains vacant. In a strong economy with low unemployment, as occurred in the United States during the late 1990s, this lag time can be considerable. For example, if a firm averages $300,000 in sales per employee, then a sales position that remains unfilled for three months costs the firm $75,000 in revenues.

Hiring Costs

The cost of hiring new employees includes advertising costs, as well as interview and testing time. Recruitment costs also include travel expenses related to hiring. In addition to the direct costs of actually attracting, screening, and hiring employees, new employees may be significantly less productive during their first few months on the job. A new employee must learn the organization's systems and procedures. For example, employees, on average, are only 75 percent productive during their initial six months of employment. In a retail environment, for example, if the average revenue per employee is $293,000 per year (revenue per employee being a surrogate for productivity), then revenue for six months would be 50 percent of that or $146,500. The cost associated with an employee's lower productivity in the first six months is 25 percent of that, or $36,625.[3]

Termination Costs

In addition to the costs associated with employees leaving an organization, such as conducting exit interviews and changing employee personnel records and payroll status, firms often must pay unemployment insurance. Firms with high employee turnover tend to have higher unemployment insurance rates, particularly when workers are laid off due to a lack of work. Termination costs can also include severance pay and extended health benefits.

The Hiring Process

The first step in reducing employee turnover is to have an effective hiring process that screens out individuals who do not have the characteristics and skills that are necessary for them to succeed. Companies that invest in good recruiting can readily identify individuals who are not compatible with the firm's culture and goals before they are hired, rather than discovering the incompatibility later. For example, as stated above, in the hotel industry, which is notorious for having average employee turnover rates of more than 100 percent annually, both the Ritz-Carlton and the Four Seasons hotel chains have turnover rates that are less than 20 percent. A major contributor to this low rate is the extensive screening that

---

[3] J. Fitz-Enz, "It's Costly to Lose Good Employees," *Workforce,* August 1997, p. 50.

potential employees must undergo before they are hired. This process includes in-depth interviews with several managers as well as personality and skills tests to ensure not only that they have the technical skills required, but also that they will fit in well with these organizations' cultures.

The New Managerial Role

Managers in today's organizations face a rapidly changing and often unpredictable environment. Large-scale corporate restructuring, layoffs (or "downsizing"), and mergers and acquisitions mean that today's managers must identify new and innovative ways to produce more with fewer workers and fewer organizational layers. Attempts to create more profitable "lean and mean" organizations have resulted in an unexpected by-product: a sharp decline in perceptions of loyalty between the employee and the organization. In 1993, for example, 77 percent of workers surveyed said that companies were less loyal to employees than five years before. In addition, 60 percent of these workers judged that employees were less loyal to the organization.[4] Today's managers are challenged to motivate employees who may feel less commitment to their organizations than was previously the norm.

One way to foster employee commitment is to encourage workers to be involved in decisions and responsible for their work. This requires managers to view workers from a new perspective, as partners in the decision-making process rather than subordinates. No longer are employees expected "to leave their brains at the door" when they come to work each day. In addition, fax machines, e-mail, and videoconferencing have influenced the speed with which information is available and the way in which employees work together. Wal-Mart, for example, holds weekly employee meetings via satellite communication, ensuring that everyone in the company receives the same information at the same time.

The growing diversity in the workforce, if properly managed, can improve creativity and decision making as well as make the organization more responsive to a wider variety of customers. But failure to effectively manage a diverse workforce can lead to high turnover of valuable employees, unproductive conflicts, communication breakdowns, and expensive legal actions. For example, Southern California Edison agreed to pay $11.25 million to as many as 2,500 employees who were victims of job discrimination since 1989, and employees of Texaco filed a $520 million class-action discrimination lawsuit against the company in 1996.[5]

Expanded Managerial Skill Set

All these changes, along with other issues like the increasing pressures generated by worldwide competition and/or the need to respond to new environmental regulations, mean that managers must now have a wider range of skills than ever before and be adept at playing a variety of organizational roles. In a study of 402 highly effective managers, Kim Whetten and David Cameron identified 10 skills that were most frequently cited as being critical to managerial effectiveness.[6] They are:

1. Communicating verbally (including listening).

2. Managing time and stress.

3. Managing individual decisions.

4. Recognizing, defining, and solving problems.

[4] B. B. Moskal, "Company Loyalty Dies, a Victim of Neglect," *Industry Week,* March 1, 1993.
[5] *USA Today,* November 15, 1996; *Boston Globe,* November 17, 1996.
[6] Kim Whetten and David Cameron, *Developing Management Skills* (New York: Harper Collins, 1995).

5. Motivating and influencing others.

6. Delegating.

7. Setting goals and articulating a vision.

8. Possessing self-awareness.

9. Team building.

10. Managing conflict.

At first, some of the skills may appear to be contradictory. Effective managers must have skills that foster employee participation and group work as well as skills in individual decision making and leadership. They must be visionary and, at the same time, manage day-to-day decision making. Robert Hoojberg and Robert Quinn use the term *behavioral complexity* to highlight the need for today's managers to use a variety of different, even conflicting, competencies and behaviors in an integrated way. A manager's ability to play multiple and competing roles has been related to a number of positive outcomes. These include better firm performance, higher overall managerial effectiveness as assessed by subordinates, better managerial performance, charisma, and the likelihood of making process improvements in the organization. Robert Quinn et al. depict the behavioral complexity required of managers in a model that includes eight managerial leadership roles and the core competencies required for each role. These are shown in Exhibit 9.3.

A review of these eight roles and related core competencies highlights the need for managers to work through and with other people. This, however, has a different meaning for managers today than it did in the past. The traditional managerial role was based on the following set of assumptions: (*a*) a good manager always has more technical expertise than any subordinate; (*b*) a good manager can solve all the problems; (*c*) a good manager has the primary (or only) responsibility for how the department works; (*d*) a good manager knows at all times exactly what is going on in the department.

In contrast, today's effective manager is rarely someone who: (*a*) knows it all, (*b*) does it all alone, or (*c*) regularly instructs others in exactly what to do. Instead, a manager delegates, negotiates, communicates, develops, and is often a coach and teacher. In the emerging models of effective management, a key managerial skill is no longer "bossing" others around. "Bossing" may get the work done in the short term, but does little to develop a workforce that has either the creativity or the initiative to respond quickly to changing customer requirements, a new technology or competitor, or an unexpected obstacle. Increasingly, today's managers focus on developing employees who can manage and lead themselves to achieving the organization's goals both individually and by working in teams.

Charles Manz and Henry Sims describe managers who can lead others to lead themselves as "superleaders." A key to their managerial success is their ability to empower employees, helping them become "self-leaders." Empowered employees are highly motivated and committed to taking joint responsibility for the overall excellence of the organization. They find personal meaning in their work, know that they have the competence to perform their job well, believe that they have control over how to do their work, and understand that they have an impact on the outcomes that make a difference to the organization.[7]

To foster employee empowerment, managers, on a continuous basis, must share with frontline employees four organizational ingredients:

1. Information about the organization's performance.

2. Rewards based on the organization's performance.

---

[7] Charles C. Manz and Henry P. Sims, Jr., *Business Without Bosses* (New York: John Wiley and Sons, 1995).

EXHIBIT 9.3
Eight Different
Managerial Roles
and Their Required
Core Competencies

Type of Role	Core Competencies Required
Mentor	1. Understanding self and others. 2. Communicating effectively. 3. Developing subordinates.
Facilitator	1. Building teams. 2. Using participative decision making. 3. Managing conflict.
Monitor	1. Monitoring individual performance. 2. Managing collective performance. 3. Managing organizational performance.
Coordinator	1. Managing projects. 2. Designing work. 3. Managing across functions.
Director	1. Visioning, planning, and goal setting. 2. Designing and organizing. 3. Delegating effectively.
Producer	1. Working productively. 2. Fostering a productive work environment. 3. Managing time and stress.
Broker	1. Building and maintaining a power base. 2. Negotiating agreement and commitment. 3. Presenting ideas.
Innovator	1. Living with change. 2. Thinking creatively. 3. Creating change.

Source: R. E. Quinn, S. R. Faerman, M. P. Thompson, and M. R. McGrath, *Becoming a Master Manager: A Competency Framework* (New York: John Wiley and Sons, 1996), p. 23.

3. Knowledge that enables employees to understand and contribute to organizational performance.

4. Power to make decisions that influence organizational direction and performance.[8]

These four ingredients of empowerment relate directly to what research and common sense tell us about what motivates individuals to achieve peak performance. Individuals perform better when they understand the impact of their personal contribution on the success of the overall effort. They are more motivated when they can see the direct linkages between their contributions, the success of the overall effort, and the rewards they receive. They are also motivated to perform better if they know they have the requisite knowledge and skills to do the job well. And finally, individuals perform best when they have the autonomy and discretion to exercise their own best judgment about how to do the job.

The new managerial role of integrating seemingly contradictory competencies and creating empowered employees is not an easy one. It requires a manager to have not only technical and organizational skills, but also excellent people skills. To succeed in today's work environment, a manager must understand what it takes to effectively manage the organization's human resources.

[8] David E. Bowen and Edward E. Lawler, "The Empowerment of Service Workers: What, Why, How and When," *Sloan Management Review,* Spring 1991, pp. 31–39.

The Manager as Role Model, Coach, and Mentor

In the old management model, managers tell workers what to do, monitor their work, and evaluate their performance. The newer model views managers as resources who help workers to understand their jobs, who coach workers and provide opportunities for their growth and development, and who act as role models for workers.

Role Modeling

Probably the most effective way for the service manager to train workers is to act as a role model. "Do what I say, not what I do" gives the wrong message to the workforce. When service managers serve customers or answer phones, they demonstrate their own commitment to customer service and they model the behaviors they want their workforce to exhibit. For example, when a secretary in a medical office is clearly having a difficult time with a patient on the phone, the office manager could volunteer to take over and show how to diffuse the patient's emotion and offer the appropriate options for care. We've spoken with service workers who remember previous managers fondly, saying, "Whenever I have a difficult time with a customer, I think to myself, 'What would Mary Jane say?' and I can generally figure it out." There is a very powerful message here: No amount of objective, in-depth training substitutes for watching someone with particular skills and capabilities in action.

Acting as a role model, particularly for difficult situations, also sends another message to the service worker. By taking the time to demonstrate appropriate behavior, the manager is treating the worker with respect and acknowledging his or her needs. This is exactly what the service manager wants the workforce to be able to do with customers. As noted above, many organizations have come to recognize that satisfied workers are more able to satisfy customers. The role of the service manager in those environments shifts from watching the workers to ensure they do what is expected, to supporting workers in their efforts to satisfy customers.

Coaching

A coach engages in a number of activities intended to help employees perform more efficiently and effectively in their current jobs and develop the capability to advance within the organization. Coaches provide instructions on how a job should be done and correct mistakes when they occur. But coaches also expect their employees to develop additional skills and capabilities. They work with employees to design individualized development plans and periodically review those plans to assure that the development goals are being met. Coaches think about how workers may rotate through different jobs to acquire new knowledge and skills and provide time for workers not only to perform their current jobs but also to acquire new capabilities.

Effective managers think about coaching both from the employee's perspective and from the organization's perspective. They are always on the watch for people who show the potential to grow into more challenging roles and who may be promoted when higher-level jobs open up.[9]

Mentoring

The term *mentor* has its roots in Homer's *The Odyssey:* Mentor was given charge of Telemachus, the son of Odysseus, when Odysseus went off to war. Mentor helped Telemachus with every aspect of his life, acting as teacher, counselor, athletic coach, and

[9] Accel-team.com, http://www/accel-team.com/human_resources/coaching.html.

adviser. Modern mentors are people, usually of higher rank and seniority in an organization, who help junior people develop their technical and managerial skills and also develop as people. They help their protégées to maneuver through the organization's culture and politics. Mentors also encourage their protégées to take risks and to rise to greater challenges within the organization.

Performance Monitoring

Capable service managers know they need to monitor specific indicators over time to make sure they are on target with both efficiency and effectiveness. The data collected will vary from service operation to service operation but will generally fall into two categories, both of which pertain to worker capabilities: technical aspects and interpersonal customer satisfaction aspects. For example, in a fast-food restaurant, the technical aspects of the service would relate to the food preparation and to the service tasks. Food data might include how long made-to-inventory items have been in bins, how often the griddle is cleaned, how fresh raw materials are, and the temperatures of the food after cooking. Service task data might include how long it requires, on average, to take an order, to fill an order, and to make the correct change. Objective data on customer service that would also be considered part of the technical aspect of the service might be whether servers remember to greet customers and to offer items such as desserts or fries. Customer service data might include customer satisfaction with waits, with food variety, and with the attitude of the server.

In a hospital, technical aspects of care that need careful monitoring might include incidence of hospital-based infection, incidence of medication errors, death rates, and average lengths of stay. Customer satisfaction data might include information about general satisfaction with the service.

It is also important for the service manager to monitor and provide feedback to workers on their individual performance—again, both in terms of technical performance and interpersonal interactions.

Structuring Incentives and Sanctions

Another important workforce management role for the service manager is the structuring of incentives and sanctions. Managers can say that the organization is focused on customer satisfaction, but if the incentives pull workers in another way it should not be surprising if customer satisfaction is not achieved. For example, in a department store, if the workers are evaluated only on whether the register sales balances with the cash at the end of the shift, there is no reason to believe that workers will be intrinsically motivated to interact pleasantly with customers—or even to pay any attention to them at all! If, on the other hand, it is determined that clean, tidy dressing rooms (with clothing from previous customers removed) relates to customer satisfaction with the shopping experience, workers can be informed of the importance of this customer satisfaction element and the manager can monitor dressing room status to make sure this task is consistently performed. Similarly, if clerks are made aware that their employment is contingent upon paying attention to the customers (and not each other) during the purchase transaction, they are more likely to pay attention to the customer.

Incentives are very important. It is also important, however, to have ways to sanction employees who are not performing appropriately. It is the role of the service manager to train, support, encourage, and be a role model, but if, in the end, the worker's performance does not improve, it is also the role of the service manager to remove the worker from the customer service environment. The customer–service provider interaction is too important to the organization to permit repeated bad service to continue.

Job Design

The proper design of jobs is central to an organization's ability to effectively manage its human resources, especially from an operations perspective. Without a proper job design to support new styles of management, empowered employees, and teamwork, these innovative approaches to transform the workplace and increase organizational competitiveness are likely to fail.

In this section, we explore several job design issues and present some guidelines for carrying out the job-design function. We begin by noting some trends in job design, some of which were mentioned earlier:

1. *Quality as part of the worker's job.* Now often referred to as "quality at the source," improved quality is linked with the concept of **worker empowerment.** Empowerment, used in this context, refers to workers being given the authority to give a customer an on-the-spot refund if service is not satisfactory, or doing whatever else is necessary "to make things right."

2. *Cross-training workers to perform multiskilled jobs.* This is more often seen in the factory than in the office despite pressures on the clerical workforce. Indeed, bank check processing centers and the majority of high-volume clerical jobs are far more factory-like than those in many factories.

3. *Employee involvement and team approaches to designing and organizing work.* This is a central feature in total quality management (TQM) and continuous improvement efforts. Virtually all TQM programs are team based.

4. *"Informating"* ordinary workers through telecommunications network and computers, thereby expanding the nature of their work and their ability to do it. In this context, informating is more than just automating work, it is revising the fundamental structure of work. Northeast Utilities' computer system, for example, can pinpoint a problem in a service area before the customer service representative (CSR) answers the phone. The CSR uses the computer to troubleshoot serious problems, to weigh probabilities that other customers in the area have been affected, and to dispatch repair crews before other calls are even received.

5. *Anytime, anyplace production.* The ability to do work away from the office, again due primarily to advances in information technology, is a growing trend throughout the world.

6. *Automation of heavy manual work.* Examples abound in services (one-person trash pickup trucks). These changes are driven by safety regulations as well as economics and personnel reasons.

7. *Most important of all, organizational commitment to providing meaningful and rewarding jobs for all employees.*

Job design may be defined as the specification of the work activities for an individual or group within an organizational setting. Its objective is to develop work assignments that meet the requirements of the organization and the technology, and that satisfy the personal and individual requirements of the jobholder. The term *job* (in the context of nonsupervisory work) and the activities involved in it are defined as follows:

1. *Micromotion:* the smallest work activity involving such elementary movements as reaching, grasping, positioning, or releasing an object.

2. *Element:* Two or more micromotions, usually thought of as a more or less complete entity, such as picking up, transporting, and positioning an item.

3. *Task:* Two or more elements that make up a complete activity, such as wiring a circuit board, sweeping a floor, or cutting a tree.

4. *Job:* A set of all the tasks that must be performed by a given worker. A job may consist of several tasks, such as typing, filing, and taking dictation (as in secretarial work), or it may consist of a single task, such as attaching a wheel to a car (as in automobile assembly).

Job design is a complex function because of the variety of factors that enter into arriving at the ultimate job structure. Decisions must be made about who is to perform the job, where it is to be performed, and how. And, as we can see in Exhibit 9.4, each of these factors may have additional considerations.

Behavioral Considerations in Job Design

Degree of Labor Specialization

Specialization of labor is a two-edged sword in job design. On the one hand, specialization has made possible high-speed, low-cost production, and has greatly enhanced our standard of living. On the other hand, extreme specialization, such as that encountered on traditional assembly lines in mass-production industries, often has serious adverse effects on workers, which in turn are often passed on in the form of low-quality or defective work. In essence, the problem is to determine how much specialization is enough: At what point do the disadvantages outweigh the advantages? (See Exhibit 9.5.)

EXHIBIT 9.4   **Factors in Job Design**

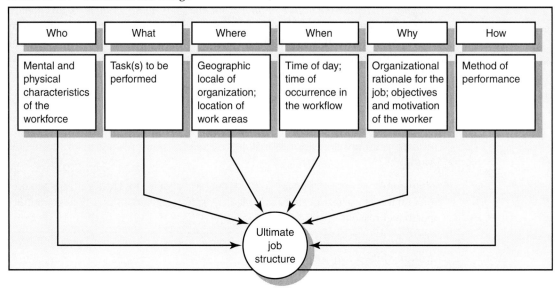

EXHIBIT 9.5
**Advantages
and Disadvantages
of Specialization
of Labor**

Advantages of Specialization

To Management

1. Rapid training of the workforce
2. Ease in recruiting new workers
3. High output due to simple and repetitive work
4. Low wages due to ease of substitutability of labor
5. Close control over workflow and work-loads

To Labor

1. Little or no education required to obtain work
2. Ease in learning job

Disadvantages of Specialization

To Management

1. Difficulty in controlling quality since no one person has responsibility for entire process.
2. "Hidden" costs of worker dissatisfaction, arising from
   a. Turnover
   b. Absenteeism
   c. Tardiness
   d. Grievances
   e. Intentional disruption of process
3. Reduced likelihood of obtaining improvement in the process because of worker's limited perspective
4. Increased labor–management friction
5. Increased potential for unionization

To Labor

1. Boredom stemming from repetitive nature of work
2. Little gratification from work itself because of the small contribution to each item
3. Little or no control over the work pace, leading to frustration and fatigue (in assembly-line situations)
4. Little opportunity to progress to a better job because significant learning is rarely possible on fractionated work
5. Little opportunity to show initiative through developing better methods or tools
6. Local muscular fatigue caused by use of the same muscles in performing the task
7. Little opportunity for communication with co-workers because of layout of the work area

Recent research suggests that the disadvantages may outweigh the advantages. However, simply stating that specialization should be avoided is risky. People differ in what they want from their work and what they are willing to put into it. Some workers prefer not to make decisions about their work, some like to daydream on the job, and others are simply not capable of performing complex work. Still, there is a good deal of worker frustration with the way many jobs are structured, leading organizations to try different approaches to job design. Two popular contemporary approaches are job enrichment and sociotechnical systems. The philosophical objective underlying these approaches is to improve the quality of work life of the employee, and so they are often applied as central features of what is termed a quality of work life (QWL) program.

Job Enlargement and Job Enrichment

Job enlargement generally entails making adjustments to a specialized job to make it more interesting to the jobholder. A job is said to be *enlarged horizontally* if the worker performs a greater number or variety of tasks, and it is said to be *enlarged vertically* if the worker is involved in planning, organizing, and inspecting his or her own work. Horizontal job enlargement is intended to counteract oversimplification and to permit the worker to perform a "whole unit of work." Vertical enlargement attempts to broaden the workers' influence in the transformation process by giving them more control over their own activities. Today, the common practice is to apply both horizontal and vertical enlargement to a given job and refer to the total approach as **job enrichment.**

Physical Considerations in Job Design

One way of viewing the general nature of the physical requirements inherent in work is through the work task continuum shown in Exhibit 9.6. In this typology, *manual tasks* put stress on large muscle groups in the body and lead to general fatigue. *Motor tasks* are controlled by the central nervous system, and their measure of effectiveness is the speed and precision of movements. While these tasks lead to fatigue, the effect is localized in the smaller muscle groups, such as the fingers, hands, and arms and, hence, cannot be adequately measured by indexes of *general* fatigue. *Mental tasks* involve rapid decision

EXHIBIT 9.6
Work Task:
Continuum (Human
Work)

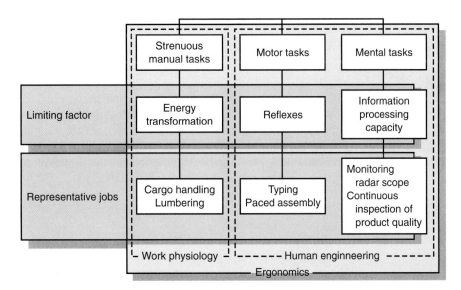

making based on certain types of stimuli, such as blips on a radar screen or defects in a product. Here the measure of effectiveness is generally some combination of response time and the number and types of errors.

As noted in Exhibit 9.6, motor tasks and mental tasks fall under the heading *human engineering,* while the study of the physical aspects of work in general is called *ergonomics* (from the Greek noun for "work" and the Greek verb for "to manage").

The Impact of Technology

Technology has affected the workplace in many ways, from how recruiting is done to the kinds of jobs that are available and how work is done.

Recruitment

It used to be difficult for people to find out about job openings beyond the area in which they lived, and, likewise, it used to be difficult for organizations to recruit beyond their local areas. The Internet has removed many of these geographic barriers. Websites such as Monster.com, HotJobs.com, and JobFind.com provide electronic marketplaces that bring individuals and organizations together from every corner of the world. Not only do these sites provide companies with the ability to reach a larger audience of potential employees, but they also make it possible for people to find job opportunities in places and in organizations that were previously unknown to them.

Telecommuting

The decrease in communications costs and the increase in the speed of transmission allows many businesses to employ workers that live in geographically remote locations. There were approximately 2 million telecommuters in the United States in 1990, and this number is expected to increase to 50 million by 2030.[10] Organizations that employ telecommuters have lower facilities and overhead costs because they don't have to provide office space (and the associated utilities and maintenance) for every worker.

Training and Development

Continued advances in state-of-the-art technology are requiring firms to spend more on employee training and development. Training is no longer considered to be a one-shot deal but is now understood to be something that must be updated on a regular basis. In 1997, U.S. businesses budgeted more than $59.8 billion to provide formal training and development courses to more than 49.6 million employees, or more than $1,200 per employee.[11]

The use of technology in the workplace has increasingly divided the workforce into two categories: those whose jobs require ever-increasing skills and knowledge to operate the technology-oriented equipment and those whose jobs are becoming more menial as a result of this technology. Unless workers receive additional training in managing, operating, and maintaining this high-technology equipment, they will have to settle for work that has lower skill requirements with correspondingly lower pay.

[10] Jack M. Nilles, *Managing Telework: Strategies for Managing the Virtual Workforce* (John Wiley and Sons, New York, 1998.)
[11] P. J. Guglielmino and R. G. Murdick, "Self-Directed Learning: The Quiet Revolution in Corporate Training and Development," *NSAM Advance Management Journal* 62, no. 3 (Summer 1997), p. 10.

Summary

Today's service managers face increased pressure to improve organizational performance. This has come about for several reasons, including the growth in competition and the need to excel simultaneously in a wide variety of areas. To produce more output with a smaller workforce, managers are now turning to their employees for ideas on how to improve worker productivity and performance. Much of the improvements in this area are the result of work teams. However, changes in management style are required for the successful implementation of these teams.

How we manage our workforce and how we specifically design jobs are both critical elements in the success of a company. Many management gurus suggest that a firm's employees are the only sustainable competitive advantage.

In the end, it takes people to run a business. Regardless of a company's strategy or degree of automation, a business cannot function without highly motivated workers who have been properly trained in the technical aspects of their jobs. This is especially true for services, where labor is often a major cost component and employees frequently interact directly with customers.

Good managers know the long-term value of employee incentives and training, because they know that customer loyalty is directly related to employee loyalty, and that both contribute significantly to the long-term profitability of the firm. In essence, how managers treat their employees is the same way their workers will treat customers.

Key Terms

cross-functional work teams: teams within an organization that have representatives from different areas of the firm. *(p. 237)*

job design: tasks and sequences that have to be accomplished and are within an individual's job assignment. *(p. 245)*

job enlargement: redesigning a job, usually by increasing the number of tasks, to make it more interesting. Also referred to as horizontal enlargement. *(p. 247)*

job enrichment: broadens the workers' knowledge of a job to better understand their contribution and make broader-based suggestions for improvement. Also referred to as vertical enlargement. *(p. 247)*

self-managed work teams: autonomous teams responsible for identifying problems, implementing solutions, and measuring outcomes. *(p. 236)*

specialization of labor: dividing tasks into small increments of work, resulting in efficient operations due to highly repetitive tasks. *(p. 245)*

worker empowerment: providing employees with authority to make decisions pertaining to the organization. *(p. 244)*

Review and Discussion Questions

1. Think of three examples of ways in which an organization has changed to become more competitive. What impact do you think these changes have on the employees of the organization?

2. Which of the eight managerial roles do you practice in your role as a student, in activities in which you participate, in your job? Which of Cameron and Whetten's 10 skills do you use in these roles?

3. What problems might arise from empowering employees? What are some of the hurdles that managers must overcome in empowering employees? What could the organization do to address these issues?

4. Would you prefer to work in a traditional work group or in a self-managed work team? Why?

5. This chapter mentioned some benefits of and the difficulties in implementing cross-functional and self-managed work teams. What other difficulties can you predict? What other benefits do you see?

6. Is there any inconsistency when a company requires precise time standards and, at the time, encourages job enlargement?

7. How is technology affecting the workplace in service organizations?

CASE   AT&T Credit Corp.

Millions of clerical employees toil in the back offices of financial companies, processing applications, claims, and customer accounts on what amounts to electronic assembly lines. The jobs are dull and repetitive and efficiency gains minuscule—when they come at all.

That was the case with AT&T Credit Corp. (ATTCC) when it opened shop in 1985 as a newly created subsidiary of American Telephone & Telegraph Corp. Based in Morristown, New Jersey, ATTCC provides financing for customers who lease equipment from AT&T and other companies. A bank initially retained by ATTCC to process lease applications couldn't keep up with the volume of new business.

ATTCC President Thomas C. Wajnert saw that the fault lay in the bank's method of dividing labor into narrow tasks and organizing work by function. One department handled applications and checked the customer's credit standing, a second drew up contracts, and a third collected payments. So no one person or group had responsibility for providing full service to a customer. "The employees had no sense of how their jobs contributed to the final solution for the customer," Wajnert says.

Unexpected Bonus

Wajnert decided to hire his own employees and give them "ownership and accountability." His first concern was to increase efficiency, not to provide more rewarding jobs. But in the end, he did both.

In 1986, ATTCC set up 11 teams of 10 to 15 newly hired workers in a high-volume division serving small businesses. The three major lease-processing functions were combined in each team. No longer were calls from customers shunted from department to department. The company also divided its national staff of field agents into seven regions and assigned two or three teams to handle business from each region. That way, the same teams always worked with the same sales staff, establishing a personal relationship with them and their customers. Above all, team members took responsibility for solving customers' problems. ATTCC's new slogan: "Whoever gets the call owns the problem."

The teams largely manage themselves. Members make most decisions on how to deal with customers, schedule their own time off, reassign work when people are absent, and interview prospective new employees. The only supervisors are seven regional managers who advise the team members, rather than give orders. The result: The teams process up to 800 lease applications a day versus 400 under the old system. Instead of taking several days to give a final yes or no, the teams do it in 24 to 48 hours. As a result, ATTCC is growing at a 40 percent to 50 percent compound annual rate, Wajnert says.

Extra Cash

The teams also have economic incentives for providing good service. A bonus plan tied to each team's costs and profits can produce extra cash. The employees, most of whom are young college graduates, can add $1,500 a year to average salaries of $28,000, and pay rises as employees learn new skills. "It's a phenomenal learning opportunity," says 24-year-old team member Michael LoCastro.

But LoCastro and others complain that promotions are rare because there are few managerial positions. And everyone comes under intense pressure from co-workers to produce more. The annual turnover rate is high: Some 20 percent of ATTCC employees either quit or transfer to other parts of AT&T. Still, the team experiment has been so successful that ATTCC is involving employees in planning to extend the concept throughout the company. "They will probably come up with as good an organizational design as management could," Wajnert says, "and it will work a lot better because the employees will take ownership for it."

Questions

1. Besides few opportunities for promotion and intense peer pressure, what other factors might contribute to the high employee turnover rate?

2. What would you do to reduce the employee turnover rate at ATTCC?

Source: John Hoerr, "The Payoff from Teamwork," *Business Week*, July 10, 1989, p. 59, by special permission © 1989 by The McGraw-Hill Companies.

Selected Bibliography

Bowen, David E., and Edward E. Lawler. "The Empowerment of Service Workers: What, Why, How and When." *Sloan Management Review,* Spring 1991, pp. 31–39.

Cusumano, Michael. *Japan's Software Factories: A Challenge to U.S. Management.* New York: Oxford University Press, 1991.

Fitz-Enz, J. "It's Costly to Lose Good Employees." *Workforce,* August 1997, p. 50.

Frieberg, Kevin, and Jackie Frieberg. *Nuts!* Austin, TX: Bard Press, 1996.

Gittel, Jody Hoffer. "Investing in Relationships." *Harvard Business Review,* June 2001.

Guglielmino, P. J., and R. G. Murdick. "Self-Directed Learning: The Quiet Revolution in Corporate Training and Development." *NSAM Advance Management Journal* 62, no. 3 (Summer 1997), p. 10.

Heskett, James L., W. Earl Sasser, and Leonard A. Schlesinger. *The Service Profit Chain.* New York: Free Press, 1997.

Hoerr, John. "The Payoff from Teamwork." *Business Week,* July 10, 1989, p. 59.

Hoojberg, Robert, and Robert Quinn. "Behavioral Complexity and the Development of Effective Managers." In *Strategic Leadership: A Multiorganizational-Level Perspective,* ed. R. Phillips and J. Hunt. Westport, CT: Quorum Publishing, 1992.

Katzenbach, Jon R., and Douglas K. Smith. *The Wisdom of Teams: Creating the High Performance Organization.* Boston: Harvard Business School Press, 1993.

Konz, Stephan. *Work Design: Industrial Ergonomics.* 2nd ed. New York: John Wiley & Sons, 1983.

Lipin, Steven. "A New Vision." *The Wall Street Journal,* June 25, 1993.

Manz, Charles C., and Henry P. Sims, Jr. *Business Without Bosses.* New York: John Wiley and Sons, 1995.

Moskal, B. B. "Company Loyalty Dies, A Victim of Neglect." *Industry Week,* March 1, 1993.

Nilles, Jack M. *Managing Telework: Strategies for Managing the Virtual Workforce.* New York: John Wiley and Sons, 1998.

Orsburn J. D., L. Moran, E. Musselwhite, and J. H. Zenger. *Self-Directed Work Teams: The New American Challenge.* Burr Ridge, IL: Business One Irwin, 1990.

Quinn, R. E., S. R. Faerman, M. P. Thompson, and M. R. McGrath. *Becoming a Master Manager: A Competency Framework.* New York: John Wiley and Sons, 1996, p. 23.

Sasser, W. Earl, and William E. Fullmer. "Creating Personalized Service Delivery Systems." *In Service Management Effectiveness,* ed. D. Bowen, R. Chase, and T. Cummings. San Francisco: Jossey-Bass, 1990, pp. 213–33.

Wetten, Kim, and David Camerson. *Developing Management Skills.* New York: Harper Collins, 1995.

Yang, D. J. "When the Going Gets Tough, Boeing Gets Touchy-Feely." *Business Week,* January 17, 1994, pp. 65–68.

CHAPTER TEN

Scheduling

Learning Objectives

- Introduce the different scheduling issues that exist in a service environment.

- Recognize the difference between scheduling work in back-of-the-house operations and scheduling workers in front-of-the-house operations.

- Identify the different priority rules that can be used to schedule work.

- Present a framework for scheduling workers in a service organization.

- Illustrate how technology can facilitate the scheduling of workers.

Scheduling Priorities at Tax Time

© Richard Pasley

"Every year it's the same thing. We have our corporate clients who need their tax returns completed by March 15 and our individual clients who need their personal income tax returns done by April 15, but it seems that whatever plan we have in place to schedule the work, these three months of February, March, and April are still crazy."

Ron Rice, managing partner of Weiner and Rice, a medium-sized CPA firm in Chestnut Hill, Massachusetts, was holding his annual meeting in January with his staff of accountants to address the workload for the upcoming tax season. "What it boils down to," Ron continued, "is that we try and cram a year's worth of work into two and a half months, and that's not realistic, regardless of how many hours a week each of us works. In addition, no matter how hard we try, we always end up with complaints from our clients that we take too long to get their tax returns done."

"The issue is establishing priorities for doing the returns," chimed in Bob Mazairz, a senior accountant who had been with the firm for about five years. "We need to decide which returns we work on first, which get second priority but still get completed by the March or April deadline, and which returns we put on extension and, therefore, don't need to file until August 15."

"It's not as simple as that," Ron replied. "We tell our clients that if they don't get us the information to do their personal tax returns before March 23, they may have to go on extension. However, for those we put on extension, we still need to estimate their taxes. Even then, there may be interest and penalties to pay. On the other hand, we could also get complaints from those customers that have refunds coming if we put them on extension."

"And what do we do when we get a corporate return at the last minute and have several individual clients who have given us their tax information in early March?" asked Bob. "Do we delay the individual tax returns to work on the corporate return?"

"Good point," said Ron. "All I know is that I am tired of facing this same fiasco every year. There has to be a better way of scheduling these returns than the one we're using. Anyone have any ideas on this?"

Source: Special thanks to Ron Rice and Bob Mazairz, Weiner and Rice, CPA, Chestnut Hill, Massachusetts.

The Customer's Perspective

How often have you been at a bank, a fast-food restaurant, or an airline ticket counter and noticed that there were more teller booths, cash registers, or check-in counters than there were workers on duty? And because of the lack of workers, you had to wait in line before being served? Have you ever noticed the express checkout line with no customers and lines at every other register in a supermarket? Or a cash-only line at a discount department store? Or the first-class check-in at an airline counter?

In each of these situations, why aren't there enough workers on duty when there are service stations available? Why do businesses have these different types of lines with different priorities?

At the bank or McDonald's, it is an issue of scheduling the proper number of workers throughout the day. With specialized queues, such as the express checkout in the supermarket or the first-class check-in at the airline ticket counter, there is the additional issue of determining which customers receive priority.

All these issues pertain to the scheduling of workers and the priority rules that managers use to decide which customers will be served next and which customers will wait.

Managerial Issues

Scheduling services can be divided into two broad categories: (*a*) the scheduling of work in back-of-the-house operations, and (*b*) the scheduling of workers in front-of-the-house operations. With back-of-the-house operations, managers typically focus on the scheduling of work to be done, as determined by priority rules. An example of a back-of-the-house operation would be the order-fulfillment process of a mail-order catalog company such as L. L. Bean or Lands' End, or an e-tailer such as Amazon.com or E-toys. With these service firms, individual orders that are received by mail, telephone, and the Internet are usually accumulated over a given time period and then scheduled for *picking* in batches (or "waves," as they are sometimes called) to maximize worker efficiency. Other examples of back-of-the-house services include the processing of insurance claims and the approval of home mortgage applications. As the buffer time between workers and customers decreases, management's emphasis begins to shift from prioritizing work to scheduling workers. For example, e-mail inquiries usually permit a short time period before the customer becomes impatient (as measured in hours), providing some flexibility to efficiently schedule workers. But maximizing the efficiency of the operation cannot be achieved at the expense of response times that are unacceptable to the customer.

The scheduling of front-of-the-house workers is complicated by the fact that they must interact directly with customers, and as a result, the response times are usually measured in seconds and minutes, rather than hours or days. The direct interaction with the service delivery process can often cause customers to wait before receiving the desired service. Basically, waiting lines occur when there is insufficient service capacity (be it in the form of workers or service stations, or both) to meet customer demand.

The determination of the proper number of front-of-the-house workers to schedule at any particular time is critical to the success of every service operation. On the one hand, scheduling too few workers results in unnecessarily long customer waiting times. On the other hand, scheduling too many workers translates into overstaffing, resulting in unnecessarily high labor costs. The service manager, consequently, needs to schedule workers in a way that effectively satisfies customer demand and at the same time minimizes labor costs.

The cost of labor in most services is a major cost component, often running 35 percent of sales and higher. For some services, virtually all the direct cost is labor. Examples of these types of services include consulting, legal work, home care nursing, and hair salons. Thus, a small but necessary increase in labor can have a very significant impact on a firm's profits.

The managerial issues related to scheduling, therefore, focus on several major issues. For back-of-the-house operations, these are (*a*) determining the total number of workers required to complete the existing and/or forecasted workload within a given time period, and (*b*) establishing priority rules by which this work is to be completed. For front-of-the-house operations, managers need to be concerned with (*a*) determining the proper level of service to provide customers, (*b*) scheduling workers throughout the workday to properly satisfy the varying customer demand, and (*c*) managing customer waiting times when they do occur to minimize dissatisfaction.

Scheduling Work in Back-of-the-House Operations

Priority Rules

The process of determining what assignment or task to do first is known as sequencing or priority sequencing. **Priority rules** are the criteria by which work is sequenced. These rules can be very simple, requiring that the work be scheduled according to a single piece of data, such as the processing time, due date, or order of arrival. Other rules, though equally simple, may require several pieces of information to formulate a criterion for scheduling work, such as the *least slack rule* and the *critical ratio rule* (both of which are defined shortly). Still others, such as Johnson's rule (also discussed later), apply to the scheduling of assignments based on the sequence of those assignments and require a computational procedure to specify the order of sequencing the tasks. Ten of the more common priority rules for sequencing tasks are:

1. *FCFS—first come, first served.* Orders or customers are assigned in the same sequence in which they arrive. This is the normal, most accepted priority rule for front-of-the-house operations, because the customer perceives it as being the fairest.

2. *SPT—shortest processing time.* Address that assignment or customer with the shortest completion time first, next-shortest second, and so on. (This is also known as SOT—shortest operating time.)

3. *Due date—earliest due date first.* Complete that order or assignment with the earliest due date first.

4. *Start date—due date minus normal lead time.* Complete the order or assignment with the earliest start date first.

5. *STR—slack time remaining.* This is calculated as the difference between time remaining before the due date minus the processing time remaining. Orders with the shortest STR are run first.

6. *STR/OP—Slack time remaining per task or operation.* Orders or assignments with the shortest STR/OP are run first, calculated as follows:

$$STR/OP = \frac{\text{Time remaining before due date} - \text{Remaining processing time}}{\text{Number of remaining tasks}}$$

7. *CR—critical ratio.* This is calculated as the difference between the due date and the current date divided by the work time remaining. Orders or assignments with the smallest CR are run first.

8. *QR—queue ratio.* This is calculated as the slack time remaining in the schedule divided by the planned remaining queue time. Orders or assignments with the smallest QR are run first.

9. *LCFS—last come, first served.* This rule occurs frequently by default. As orders or assignments arrive they are placed on the top of the stack and the worker usually picks up the order on top to complete first.

10. *Random order-whim.* The managers or the operators usually select whichever order or assignment they feel like running.[1]

Schedule Evaluation Criteria

The following standard measures of schedule performance are used to evaluate priority rules:

• Meeting due dates of customers' orders and/or downstream tasks and assignments.

• Minimizing order completion time, which is the time from when an order is received to when it is completed and ready for the customer. (Terminology for this time is not standardized. Some companies call this order cycle time, some use throughput time, and others may have their own internal nomenclature.)

• Minimizing work in process.

• Minimizing workers' idle time.

[1] This list is modified from Donald W. Fogarty, John H Blackstone, Jr., and Thomas R. Hoffman, *Production and Inventory Management* (Cincinnati: South-West Publishing, 1991), pp. 452–53.

Scheduling *n* Orders or Tasks with One Worker and/or Machine

To illustrate the impact of different scheduling criteria, let us compare some of these 10 priority rules in a static scheduling situation involving two orders or tasks that are to be completed by one worker on one machine. (In scheduling terminology, this class of problems is referred to as an "*n* job—one-machine problem," or simply *n*/1.) The theoretical difficulty of this type of problem increases as more machines are considered; therefore, the only restriction on *n* is that it be a specified, finite integer.

Consider the following example: Marc Ginsburg is the supervisor of Legal Copy-Express, which provides copying services for law firms in Philadelphia. Five customers have submitted their orders at the beginning of the week. Specific scheduling data on each of these orders are as follows:

Order (in order of arrival)	Processing Time (days)	Due Date (days hence)
A	3	5
B	4	6
C	2	7
D	6	9
E	1	2

All orders require the use of the only color copy machine that Legal Copy-Express has. Marc must therefore decide on the processing sequence for the five orders. The evaluation criterion is to minimize the mean order cycle time. Suppose Marc decides to use the FCFS rule in an attempt to make Legal Copy-Express appear fair to its customers. The FCFS rule results in the following order completion times:

FCFS Schedule

Order	Processing Time (days)	Due Date (days)	Start	Cycle Time (days) Processing Time			Finish
A	3	5	0	+	3	=	3
B	4	6	3	+	4	=	7
C	2	7	7	+	2	=	9
D	6	9	9	+	6	=	15
E	1	2	15	+	1	=	16

Total order completion time = 3 + 7 + 9 + 15 + 16 = 50 days

Mean order completion time = 50/5 = 10.0 days

Comparing the due date of each order with its order completion time, we observe that only order A will be on time. Orders B, C, D, and E will be late by 1, 2, 6, and 14 days, respectively. On the average, an order will be late by (0 + 1 + 2 + 6 + 14)/5 = 4.6 days.

Let's now consider the SPT rule. Here Marc gives the highest priority to the order that has the shortest processing time. The resulting order completion times are:

SPT Schedule

Order	Processing Time (days)	Due Date (days)	Start	Order Completion Time (days) Processing Time			Finish
E	1	2	0	+	1	=	1
C	2	7	1	+	2	=	3
A	3	5	3	+	3	=	6
B	4	6	6	+	4	=	10
D	6	9	10	+	6	=	16

$$\text{Total order completion time} = 1 + 3 + 6 + 10 + 16 = 36 \text{ days}$$

$$\text{Mean order completion time} = 36/5 = 7.2 \text{ days}$$

The SPT rule results in lower average order completion time. In addition, orders E and C will be ready before the due date, and order A is late by only one day. On the average, an order will be late by $(0 + 0 + 1 + 4 + 7)/5 = 2.4$ days.

If Marc decides to use the DDate rule, the resulting schedule is:

DDate Schedule

Order	Processing Time (days)	Due Date (days)	Order Completion Time (days)			
			Start	Processing Time		Finish
E	1	2	0	+	1	=	1
A	3	5	1	+	3	=	4
B	4	6	4	+	4	=	8
C	2	7	8	+	2	=	10
D	6	9	10	+	6	=	16

$$\text{Total order completion time} = 1 + 4 + 8 + 10 + 16 = 39 \text{ days}$$

$$\text{Mean order completion time} = 39/5 = 7.8 \text{ days}$$

In this case orders B, C, and D will be late. On the average, an order will be late by $(0 + 0 + 2 + 3 + 7)/5 = 2.4$ days.

In a similar manner, the order completion times of the LCFS, random, and STR rules are as follows:

LCFS Schedule

Order	Processing Time (days)	Due Date (days)	Order Completion Time (days)			
			Start	Processing Time		Finish
E	1	2	0	+	1	=	1
D	6	9	1	+	6	=	7
C	2	7	7	+	2	=	9
B	3	6	9	+	4	=	13
A	4	5	13	+	3	=	16

$$\text{Total order completion time} = 13 \text{ days}$$

$$\text{Mean order completion time} = 9.2 \text{ days}$$

$$\text{Average lateness} = 4.0 \text{ days}$$

Random Schedule

Order	Processing Time (days)	Due Date (days)	Order Completion Time (days)			
			Start	Processing Time		Finish
D	6	9	0	+	6	=	6
C	2	7	6	+	2	=	8
A	3	5	8	+	3	=	11
E	1	2	11	+	1	=	14
B	4	6	14	+	4	=	16

$$\text{Total order completion time} = 55 \text{ days}$$

$$\text{Mean order completion time} = 11.0 \text{ days}$$

$$\text{Average lateness} = 5.8 \text{ days}$$

STR Schedule

Order	Processing Time (days)	Due Date (days)	Order Completion Time (days)				
			Start		Processing Time		Finish
E	1	2	0	+	1	=	1
A	3	5	1	+	3	=	4
B	4	6	4	+	4	=	8
D	6	9	8	+	6	=	14
C	2	7	14	+	2	=	16

Total order completion time = 43 days

Mean order completion time = 8.6 days

Average lateness = 3.2 days

A comparison of the results of these different priority rules is summarized below:

Scheduling Rule	Total Completion Time (days)	Average Order Completion Time (days)	Average Lateness (days)
FCFS	50	10.0	4.6
SPT	36	7.2	2.4
DDate	39	7.8	2.4
LCFS	46	9.2	4.0
Random	55	11.0	5.8
STR	43	8.6	3.2

For this example, the SPT rule is better than the rest of the scheduling rules, but is this always the case? The answer is yes. It can be shown mathematically that the SPT rule yields an optimum solution for the $n/1$ case with respect to the SPT rule and for other evaluation criteria such as mean waiting time and mean completion time. In fact, this simple rule is so powerful it has been termed "the most important concept in the entire subject of sequencing."[2] However, the SPT rule ignores the due dates of orders. As a consequence, jobs with longer processing times can often be late.

Scheduling *n* Orders with Two Workers and/or Two Machines

The next step up in scheduling complexity is referred to as the $n/2$ case, where two orders or assignments must be processed by two workers and/or machines in a common sequence. As in the $n/1$ case, there is an approach that leads to an optimal solution according to certain criteria. Also, as in the $n/1$ case, we assume it is a static scheduling situation. The objective of this approach, termed Johnson's rule or method (after its developer), is to minimize the overall order completion time, from the beginning of the first order until the completion of the last. Johnson's rule consists of the following steps:

1. List the completion time for each task for both workers or machines.

2. Select the order with the shortest completion time.

3. If the shortest time is for the first worker or machine, do that order first; if the shortest time is for the second worker or machine, do that order last.

4. Repeat steps 2 and 3 for each remaining order until the schedule is complete.

---

[2] R. W. Conway, William L. Maxwell, and Louis W. Miller, *Theory of Scheduling* (Reading, MA: Addison-Wesley Publishing, 1967).

Example

We can illustrate the application of Johnson's rule by scheduling four jobs through two workers:

Step 1: List operation times for each order.

Job	Completion Time with Worker 1	Completion Time with Worker 2
A	3	2
B	6	8
C	5	6
D	7	4

Steps 2 and 3: Select shortest completion time and assign. Order A is the shortest with worker 2 and is assigned first and performed last. (Order A is now no longer available to be scheduled.)

Step 4: Repeat steps 2 and 3 until all orders are scheduled. Select the shortest completion time among the remaining orders. Order D is the second-shortest with worker 2, thus it is performed second to last (remember job A is last). Now orders A and D are no longer available for scheduling. Order C is performed first. Now, only order B is left with the shortest completion time with worker 1. Thus, according to step 3, it is performed first among the remaining jobs, or second overall (order C was already scheduled first).

In summary, the solution sequence is C – B – D – A, and the overall completion time is 25 days, which is a minimum. Also minimized are total idle time and mean idle time. The final schedule appears in Exhibit 10.1

These steps result in scheduling the orders having the shortest task time in the beginning and ending of the schedule. As a result, the amount of concurrent operating time for the two workers is maximized, thus minimizing the total completion time required to complete the orders.

Scheduling Front-of-the-House Workers

A Framework for Scheduling Front-of-the-House Workers

Worker schedules are usually developed on a weekly basis for several reasons. First, state and federal laws in the United States, for example, specify the maximum number of hours and/or days that an employee can work in a given day or week, after which overtime premiums must be paid. Second, the distinction between full-time and part-time workers is often made on the basis of the number of hours worked in a calendar week. In addition,

EXHIBIT 10.1
Optimal Schedule of Orders Using Johnson's Rule

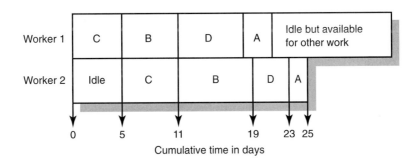

full-time versus part-time status often determines the benefits paid by an employer and may be related to union contracts that specify the minimum number of hours that workers in each category may work. Finally, many workers, especially hourly workers, are paid on a weekly basis that is often mandated by local or state law.

The procedure for developing worker schedules for front-of-the-house operations can be divided into the following four major elements, as illustrated in Exhibit 10.2: (*a*) forecasting customer demand, (*b*) converting customer demand into worker requirements, (*c*) converting worker requirements into daily work schedules, and (*d*) converting daily work schedules into weekly work schedules.

Forecasting Demand

Since the delivery of most services occurs in the presence of the customer, the customer's arrival rate is directly related to the demand level for the service operation. For example, customers must be present at a restaurant to be served; the patient must be present in the hospital to be treated. In addition to the customer's presence at the point of service, the potential for high variability in the pattern of customer demand makes it extremely important for service managers to efficiently schedule workers. The first step, therefore, in developing a schedule that will permit the service operation to meet customer demand is to accurately forecast that demand.

Several patterns of demand need to be considered: (*a*) variation in demand within days (or even hours), (*b*) variation across days of the week, (*c*) variations within a month, and (*d*) seasonal variations. Because demand is often highly variable throughout a day, forecasting within-day variation is usually done in either hour or half-hour increments. Today, with the use of computers and more sophisticated point-of-sale (POS) equipment, the ability to record customer demand in even smaller time increments is possible (for example, 15-minute intervals). However, while technology can provide customer demand in relatively small time increments, this does not affect the scheduling of workers, because people do not work in such small time increments. It is also important to remember that the smaller the forecast time period, the more likely it is that the forecast will be inaccurate, simply because of variation in customer arrivals.

To develop a forecast, we need to collect historical data about customer demand. The actual number of customers expecting service in a given time interval (that is, half-hour or hour) is the preferred data. Fortunately, a wide range of POS equipment is available that can capture this type of data and, in many cases, even download it onto a computer for subsequent analysis.

Converting Customer Demand into Worker Requirements

A necessary element in the conversion of customer demand into front-of-the-house worker requirements is the establishment of a customer-service level. For example, many restaurants offer express lunches within a specified time period. Another example of a specified

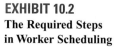

EXHIBIT 10.2
**The Required Steps
in Worker Scheduling**

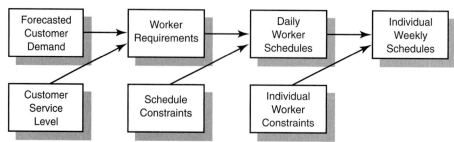

EXHIBIT 10.3
An Example
of Labor
Requirements
for a Fast-Food
Operation

Volume Guidelines (Sales($)/Hour)		Total Number of Workers	Grill	Windows	Drive-Through	Bin	Fry	Floaters*
$140	(Minimum)	4	1	1	1	0	0	1
150		5	1	1	1	0	0	2
180		6	2	1	1	0	0	2
210		7	2	2	1	0	0	2
240		8	2	2	2	1	0	1
275		9	2	2	2	1	0	2
310		10	3	3	2	1	0	1
345		11	3	3	2	1	1	1
385		14	3	3	3	1	1	1
425		13	4	3	3	1	1	1
475		14	4	3	3	1	1	2
525		15	4	4	3	1	1	2
585		16	5	4	3	1	1	2
645	(Full Staff)	17	5	4	3	1	1	2

*Floaters help out; they patrol the lot, lobby, and restrooms; restock; and cover on breaks.

Source: Adapted from "McDonald's," Harvard Business School case no. 681-044, 1980.

level of service is at Putnam Investments in Andover, Massachusetts, where Liam McMakin states that Putnam's established service level at its call centers is that "93 percent of all calls should be answered in 20 seconds or less."[3]

Knowing the average number of customers who require service in a given time period and the average length of time it takes to provide service to each customer, a manager can determine how many workers to schedule for that time period to provide the desired level of service. Queuing theory, which is presented later in Chapter 15S, is a mathematical approach for establishing the relationship among the three following variables: (*a*) customer demand (for example, customers per hour); (*b*) available capacity, expressed in the number of workers on duty and the average time to service a customer; and (*c*) average customer waiting time.

To facilitate this process of converting customer demand into the required number of workers, a service organization will often develop a labor requirements table. This table tells the manager how many workers are needed for different levels of demand. For some companies, these tables also indicate where the workers should be assigned. To determine how many workers to schedule and where they should be assigned, the service manager has only to look up in the table the forecasted demand for a given time period. A labor requirements table for a fast-food restaurant is shown in Exhibit 10.3, where, for example, eight workers in total are required when the forecasted hourly demand is $240 in sales.

Converting Worker Requirements into Daily Work Schedules

The next step in the scheduling process is the conversion of worker requirements for each time interval into a daily work or shift schedule. The basic goal is to schedule a sufficient number of workers in a given time period to meet the expected demand at the target service level. However, additional factors usually need to be included, such as (*a*) the minimum length of a shift that might be prescribed either by law or by a union contract (for example, when workers are called in by UPS, they are guaranteed by their union contract a minimum of three hours work), (*b*) the maximum shift length permitted by state or local

---

[3] Conversation with Liam McMakin, vice president, Putnam Investment Services, on February 15, 2002.

labor laws, and (*c*) the company's policies about rest and meal breaks. These factors can significantly affect how efficiently the organization can meet the target service level. These shift constraints often result in a worker schedule where the total number of labor hours needed to meet the minimum shift requirement(s) is greater than the actual number of labor hours required to satisfy customer demand.

To develop these schedules, many organizations use part-time rather than full-time workers to effectively meet customer service goals while simultaneously controlling costs. Since part-time workers are typically paid less and may also be entitled to fewer (or even no) fringe benefits, the average hourly cost of the part-time worker is lower than that of the full-time worker. Part-time workers can be used to meet demand at peak periods (such as meal times in restaurants) or during periods when full-time workers would prefer not to work (such as weekends in hospitals).

Converting Daily Work Schedules into Weekly Work Schedules

The conversion of daily work schedules into weekly work schedules is more complicated than simply repeating the daily schedule procedure. In developing weekly schedules, managers need to consider workers' days off for illness, holidays, and vacations. They also need to factor in the additional cost of paying workers to work on holidays if services are offered on those days. Workforce scheduling in a hospital, for example, can be particularly challenging on major holidays. In addition, these weekly schedules need to be assigned to specific individuals. Therefore, managers need to include here individual worker constraints such as days off, hours available for work, and so forth.

Scheduling Consecutive Days Off

A practical problem encountered in many service organizations is setting schedules so that employees can have two consecutive days off, even though the operation is open seven days a week. The U.S. Fair Labor Standards Act requires, as mentioned previously, that overtime be paid for any hours worked (by hourly workers) in excess of 8 hours per day or 40 hours per week, and most people probably prefer two consecutive days off per week. The following heuristic procedure was modified from that developed by James Browne and Rajen Tibrewala to deal with this problem.[4]

[4] James J. Brown and Rajen K. Tibrewala, "Manpower Scheduling," *Industrial Engineering* 7, no. 8 (August 1975), pp. 22–23.

Example

Objective: Find the schedule that minimizes the number of five-day workers with two consecutive days off, subject to the demands of the daily staffing schedule and assuming that the workers have no preference for which days they get off.

Solution

Procedure: Starting with the total number of workers required for each day of the week, create a schedule by adding one worker at a time. The procedure for doing this is as follows:

Step 1: Circle the lowest consecutive pair of days of worker requirements. The lowest pair is the one where the highest number in the pair is equal to or lower than the highest number in any other pair. This ensures that the days with the highest requirements are covered by staff. (Monday and Sunday may be chosen even though they are at opposite ends of the array of days.) In case of ties, choose the days-off pair with the lowest requirement on an adjacent day. This day may be before or after the pair. If a tie still remains, choose the first of the available tied pairs. (Do not bother using further tiebreaking rules, such as second-lowest adjacent days.)

Step 2: Subtract 1 from each of the remaining five days (i.e., the days not circled). This indicates that one less worker is required on these days, since the first worker has just been assigned to them.

Step 3: The two steps are repeated for the second worker, the third worker, and so forth, until no more workers are required to satisfy the schedule.

Example

	Monday	Tuesday	Wednesday	Thursday	Friday	Saturday	Sunday
Worker Requirement:	4	3	4	2	3	1	2
Worker 1	4	3	4	2	3	1	2
Worker 2	3	2	3	1	2	1	2
Worker 3	2	1	2	0	2	1	1
Worker 4	1	0	1	0	1	1	1
Worker 5	0	0	1	0	0	0	0

Solution

The solution consists of five workers covering 19 worker days, although slightly different assignments may be equally satisfactory.

Worker	Days Off
1	Saturday, Sunday
2	Friday, Saturday
3	Saturday, Sunday
4	Tuesday, Wednesday
5	Works only Wednesday

Additional Scheduling Issues in Services

This chapter has focused primarily on the scheduling of work in terms of presenting the different priority rules that can be applied and the scheduling of workers to meet customer demand. However, additional scheduling issues exist in services that are beyond the scope of this book. These include (*a*) the scheduling of equipment, such as airplanes and buses; (*b*) the sequential scheduling of deliveries to customers (such as that done by FedEx and UPS) in order to minimize travel time; and (*c*) resource allocation issues in terms of whether people and/or equipment should be dedicated to a narrow set of tasks (and therefore highly

Using Technology to Create Value

How Worker Scheduling Is Automated at Kronos

Kronos, Inc., located in Waltham, Massachusetts, provides a fully automated workforce management system that consists of the following three major modules: Business Forecaster, Workforce Planner, and Smart Scheduler.

The Business Forecaster module uses historical data from POS systems, traffic counters, and other sources to develop a forecast of future sales. The system is sufficiently flexible to allow the service manager to determine which variables to forecast and the amount of historical data to use. The system can provide projections on a daily basis, as well as in hour, half-hour, and 15-minute intervals.

Combining the sales projections from the Business Forecaster module with previously determined staffing guidelines and con-

straints, the Workforce Planner module develops worker staffing requirements that will meet the forecasted demand efficiently by minimizing labor costs and effectively by meeting established levels of customer service. These staffing requirements can be provided in the same time intervals as the forecast.

Kronos considers the Smart Scheduler to be the heart or "engine" that drives its overall system. The staffing requirements generated by the Workforce Planner module combined with general work rules and specific constraints for individual employees are the inputs to this module. The output of the Smart Scheduler is a detailed work schedule for the next forecast period, matching specific employees with specific shift assignments.

---

efficient) or more flexible to perform a wide variety of tasks (and therefore highly effective at the cost of efficiency).

The Impact of Technology

Information technology has had a significant impact on the ability of the manager to schedule workers. Early computer programs for scheduling workers were often cumbersome to use and also very limited in their applications. However, the advent of faster and more powerful computers coupled with newer software programs has resulted in worker scheduling programs that are both significantly more user-friendly and, at the same time, more flexible in their applications.

The use of these automated scheduling programs has several advantages. First, it significantly reduces the amount of time a manager has to devote to developing a weekly work schedule. When worker scheduling was done manually, it was not uncommon for a manager in a complex service environment to devote one entire eight-hour day each week to developing a schedule for the following week. With an automated scheduling system, managers are no longer required to commit such a large amount of time to scheduling, so they have more time to devote to actually managing the operation.

In addition, scheduling software typically contains highly sophisticated mathematical formulas designed to minimize labor hours, subject to the constraints and conditions identified earlier in this chapter (such as the minimum number of hours per shift). Worker productivity is therefore also increased. Thus, by using an automated scheduling system, a more efficient worker schedule can be generated in only a fraction of the time previously required with a manual procedure.

Many of the automated systems available today are fully integrated systems that consist of several modules. Kronos, Inc., in Waltham, Massachusetts, one of the leading producers of automated workforce scheduling systems, offers a fully integrated service worker scheduling system, as described in the accompanying "Using Technology to Create Value."

The continued development of more sophisticated worker scheduling software has allowed service managers to increase the efficiency of their operations while at the same time maintaining, or even improving, the level of service provided. As a result of using these software programs, some firms have been able to move to a higher performance

EXHIBIT 10.4
**The Impact
of Technology
on Worker Efficiency
and Service**

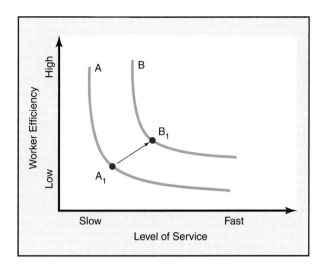

curve, as shown in Exhibit 10.4, where the move from A to B results in both increased efficiency and faster service.

Summary

Worker scheduling is especially important in service operations where labor is often a significant cost component. Here, too much labor negatively influences profits, but insufficient labor has a negative impact on customer service and, hence, adversely affects future sales. Worker scheduling can be divided into two broad categories: (*a*) the scheduling of back-of-the-house work, and (*b*) the scheduling of front-of-the-house workers. Back-of-the-house work is typically separated from the customer and can therefore be scheduled much like a job shop in a manufacturing environment. Front-of-the-house worker scheduling, because of the direct interaction with the customer, must take a different approach that recognizes the trade-off between the level of service provided and the overall efficiency of the staff.

Information technology, in the form of software programs for scheduling workers in a service environment, has had a significant impact on the worker scheduling function in service operations. First, these programs have reduced the amount of time managers must devote to this often tedious task. In addition, they provide very efficient worker schedules, which allow the service manager to reduce labor costs while often providing a higher level of service in comparison to that previously obtained from manual labor scheduling techniques.

Key Terms

priority rules: the criteria by which work is scheduled. *(p. 254)*

Review and Discussion Questions

1. Identify some practical deterrents to using only the SPT rule in a service.
2. What priority rule do you use in scheduling your study time for midterm examinations? If you have five exams to study for, how many alternative schedules exist?
3. Why is it more difficult to schedule front-of-the-house workers than it is back-of-the-house workers?
4. In the United States, certain assumptions are made about the customer-service priority rules used in banks, restaurants, and retail stores. What rules might be used in other countries? To what factors might you attribute the differences, if any?
5. In what way is the scheduling of work in the home office of a bank different from that of a branch office?

6. Assume you are the desk clerk at an upscale hotel and that you handle all room registrations. You are dealing with your customers on a first-come, first-served basis when a professional football team arrives. Team members are playing a team from your city and will be staying at your hotel. How will you handle their registrations?

7. In many services, the percentage of work done by automated processes is increasing. For example, in a copy center, copy machines now collate and staple automatically. In hospitals, more and more diagnoses are made by machines with remote sensors. Discuss how the capacity of machines to "do more" affects the overall operation from a worker scheduling perspective.

8. What is the impact of self-service on worker scheduling?

Solved Problem

1. Joe's Auto Seat Cover and Paint Shop is bidding on a contract to do all the custom work for Smiling Ed's used car dealership. One of the main requirements in obtaining this contract is rapid delivery time, since Ed, for reasons we shall not go into here, wants the cars facelifted and back on his lot in a hurry. Ed has said that if Joe can refit and repaint five cars that Ed has just received (from an unnamed source) in 24 hours or less, the contract will be his. The following times (in hours) are required in the refitting shop and the paint shop for each of the five cars. Assuming that cars go through the refitting operations before they are repainted, can Joe meet the time requirements and get the contract?

Car	Refitting Time (hours)	Repairing Time (hours)
A	6	3
B	0	4
C	5	2
D	8	6
E	2	1

Solution

This problem can be viewed as a two-machine flow shop and can be easily solved using "Johnson's rule."

	Original Data		Johnson's Rule	
Car	Refitting Time (hours)	Repainting Time (hours)	Order of Selection	Position in Sequence
A	6	3	4th	3rd
B	0	4	1st	1st
C	5	2	3rd	4th
D	8	6	5th	2nd
E	2	1	2nd	5th

Graph of Johnson solution (not to scale):

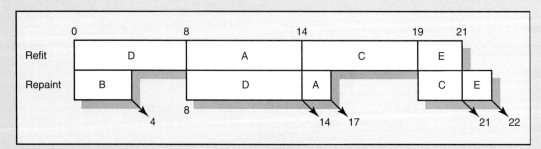

The total time for the five cars is 22 hours.

Problems

1. Joe has three cars that must be overhauled by his ace mechanic, Jim. Given the following data about the cars, use the STR/OP priority rule (least slack remaining per operation) to determine Jim's scheduling priority for each.

Car	Customer Pickup Time (hours hence)	Remaining Overhaul Time (hours)	Remaining Operations
A	10	4	Painting
B	17	5	Wheel alignment, painting
C	15	1	Chrome plating, painting, seat repair

2. There are seven customer orders that each require two tasks: A and B. All seven orders must go first through A and then B.
   a. Determine the optimal sequence in which the orders should be scheduled using these times:

Customer Order	Task A Time	Task B Time
1	9	6
2	8	5
3	7	7
4	6	3
5	1	2
6	2	6
7	4	7

   b. Draw a graph similar to the solved problem showing the sequence of orders.
   c. What is the total completion time for all seven orders?

3. The following list of applications in a bank's mortgage application department includes estimates of their required times:

Application	Required Time (days)	Days to Delivery Promise	Slack
A	8	12	4
B	3	9	6
C	7	8	1
D	1	11	10
E	10	−10	−
F	6	10	4
G	5	−8	−
H	4	6	2

   a. Use the shortest operation time rule (SOT) to schedule these applications. What is the schedule? What is the mean service completion time?
   b. The boss doesn't like the schedule in *a.* Applications E and G must be done first, for obvious reasons (they are already late). Reschedule and do the best you can while scheduling applications E and G first and second, respectively. What is the new schedule? What is the new mean service completion time?

4. Orders A, B, C, D, and E must go through processes I and II in that sequence (i.e., process 1 first, then process II). Use Johnson's rule to determine the optimal sequence to schedule the orders to minimize the total required time.

Order	Required Processing Time on A	Required Processing Time on B
A	4	5
B	16	14
C	8	7
D	12	11
E	3	9

5. Joe was able to land a job scheduling cars in a brand-new custom refinishing auto service shop. This system is capable of handling 10 cars per day. The sequence now is customizing first, followed by repainting.

Car	Customizing Time	Painting (hours)	Car	Customizing Time	Painting (hours)
1	3.0	1.2	6	2.1	0.8
2	2.0	0.9	7	3.2	1.4
3	2.5	1.3	8	0.6	1.8
4	0.7	0.5	9	1.1	1.5
5	1.6	1.7	10	1.8	0.7

In what sequence should Joe schedule the cars to minimize the total required time?

6. The MedSports Clinic provides specialized medical care for sports-related injuries. A patient's visit to MedSports usually involves two separate stages. First, the patient meets with the doctor to explain the nature of his or her injury and, if necessary, to have a physical examination by the doctor. Following the visit with the doctor, a set of X rays is taken of the injured part of the patient's body. The amount of time spent at each stage of the patient's visit can vary significantly, depending on the type of injury and whether or not this is the patient's first visit to the clinic. As MedSports has just recently opened, currently only one doctor is available at any one time, and only one X-ray technician and machine. On a given day, six patients have made appointments. It is estimated that each patient requires the following time (in minutes) for each of the two stages:

Patient	Time (minutes)	
	Examination	X Ray
A	30	15
B	45	50
C	75	35
D	20	40
E	90	25
F	60	70

   a. Using Johnson's Rule, determine the optimal order for scheduling these patients throughout the day.
   b. If the clinic opens at 9:00 A.M. with the first patient, what times should each of the patients be told to come into the clinic?

7. A fast-food restaurant has forecasted hourly sales (in dollars) for next Monday to be the following:

Hour:	11:00	12:00	1:00	2:00	3:00	4:00	5:00	6:00	7:00	8:00	9:00	10:00
Sales:	$250	$625	$500	$375	$150	$100	$175	$400	$475	$300	$275	$125

Using the staffing table shown in Exhibit 10.3, determine the number of workers required for each hour of the day. (Note: The times stated above represent the beginning of each hour in which the sales are forecasted.)

Selected Bibliography

Baker, K. R. "The Effects of Input Control in a Simple Scheduling Model." *Journal of Operations Management* 4, no. 2 (February 1984), pp. 99–112.

Conway, Richard W., William L. Maxwell, and Louis W. Miller. *Theory of Scheduling.* Reading, MA: Addison-Wesley Publishing, 1967.

Dilworth, James B. *Operations Management: Design, Planning and Control for Manufacturing and Services.* New York: McGraw-Hill, 1992.

Fogarty, Donald W., John H. Blackstone, Jr., and Thomas R. Hoffman. *Production and Inventory Management.* Cincinnati: South-Western Publishing, 1991.

Gershkoff, I. "Optimizing Flight Crew Schedules." *Interfaces* 19, no. 4 (July–August 1989), pp. 29–43.

Johnson, S. M. "Optimal Two Stage and Three Stage Production Schedules with Setup Times Included." *Naval Logistics Quarterly* 1, no. 1 (March 1954), pp. 61–68.

Moody, P. E. *Strategic Manufacturing: Dynamic New Directions for the 1990s.* Burr Ridge, IL: Richard D. Irwin, 1990.

Richter, H. "Thirty Years of Airline Operations Research." *Interfaces* 19, no. 4 (July–August 1989), pp. 3–9.

Sipper, Daniel, and Robert L. Buflin, Jr. *Production: Planning, Control, and Integration.* New York: McGraw-Hill, 1998, p. 531.

Vollmann, Thomas E., William L. Berry, and D. Clay Whybark. *Manufacturing Planning and Control,* 4th ed. Burr Ridge, IL: Irwin, 1997.

CHAPTER ELEVEN

Measuring Process Performance

Learning Objectives

- Introduce process analysis as a tool for understanding service delivery processes.

- Demonstrate how to use process flow diagrams to analyze processes.

- Define efficiency and effectiveness in service organizations.

- Identify several measures of process performance.

Measuring Performance at Nordstrom

Amy Etra / PhotoEdit

In the *Nordstrom 2000 Annual Report,* company President Blake Nordstrom wrote, "We have narrowed our focus to include the following priorities:

- Achieving a balanced mix of merchandise, appropriately tailored by market, to better serve our broad base of customers.
- Utilizing information technology as a selling tool—in the form of a perpetual inventory system—to help us offer not only the right merchandise, but the right amount of merchandise, in every store.
- Identifying efficiencies in back-of-the-house areas of our business to both control costs and offer greater support to the selling floor.
- Managing our growth—maintaining focus on our existing business while capitalizing on favorable expansion opportunities."

These priorities emphasize the department store chain's legendary focus on customer service and at the same time they demonstrate Nordstrom's recognition of the need to use resources wisely as an important part of the firm's overall growth and profitability. Blake Nordstrom continues in the report,

> Some of these initiatives will have an impact on our business this year; some will produce benefits realized over time. The bottom line: even in the face of a changing economy, we are confident that by concentrating on doing what's right for our customers, we will also do what's right for our shareholders. We have many reasons to be optimistic—over 45,000 to be exact. After all, our people continue to be our greatest asset. They are the ones who maintain and build upon our reputation. They understand it is their business, their customer, their legacy.

Source: Nordstrom Annual Report, 2000.

The Customer's Perspective

Think about your favorite fast-food restaurant at lunchtime. How many servers are usually at the counter when you enter? How many are busy serving customers? How many seem to be "just waiting" for the next customer to arrive? When servers are busy, what happens to how long you wait for service? When servers are idle, you can be served immediately, but what are the implications of idle staff for the cost of your hamburger, burrito, or pizza? What are your expectations as a customer? Do you think they are the same as or different from the expectations of the manager of the restaurant? In other words, how would you, as a customer, measure performance? And how might that be different if you were the manager?

Now think about an emergency room at a hospital. What do you as a customer expect in terms of service? Chances are you expect to be seen and treated immediately—with no wait at all—if you or a friend or family member has a serious illness or injury. On the other hand, you expect to wait if you have a less urgent problem. As you wait to have a minor injury stitched, you may think about the high costs of health care and how they are reflected in a high-tech environment like an emergency room. As you wait, you have a chance to look around. If you have to wait, how often do you see a doctor or nurse idle?

In a fast-food restaurant, all customers want essentially the same thing: a meal. Idle workers mean that customers can be served more quickly when they arrive—and that's important when it's *fast* food. In an emergency room, all customers don't need the same thing; some illnesses or injuries are much more severe and therefore more sensitive to waits than others. What are the implications of these characteristics for the managers of these services?

How the performance of service organizations is measured is important to both customers and managers. Both groups are concerned with how well the service is provided and, in one way or another, about how much those services cost.

Managerial Issues

There has been considerable controversy about productivity performance in the U.S. service sector during the past two decades. One perspective denies there is a productivity problem and suggests that current measurement techniques don't reflect all the improvements that have occurred. Another perspective argues that productivity in services will improve only when there is increased competition, particularly from foreign countries. A third view blames low service productivity on poor management, particularly the management of information technology.

Another view, however, is that services have started to focus less on productivity and more on building long-term relationships with customers that ensure long-term revenue streams. That view is supported by many case studies that demonstrate how firms have achieved success by focusing on customer-retention activities. Service performance is not only about productivity, but must also consider other important measures to properly assess the overall performance of the firm.

Still another view is that productivity in services has actually decreased because of the shift toward self-service. In other words, any increases in worker productivity actually reflect that the customers do much more of the service work than they did in the past.

There are two major categories of performance measures for every organization: measures of **efficiency,** or how well resources are used, and measures of **effectiveness,** or how well process objectives are being met. Another way of thinking about efficiency is "doing things right," while effectiveness focuses on "doing the right things." Examples of measures of efficiency include how often equipment is being used and how busy and productive workers are. Measures of effectiveness include customer and employee satisfaction levels and financial profitability and return measures.

Managers know they need to use resources wisely. It is easy to put together a service process that always meets the goal of serving every customer as if there were infinite resources available, but that is unrealistic. Similarly, it is easy to use resources very efficiently if you are not concerned about customers and their individual needs, about fluctuations in demand for your services, or about making sure the quality of the service is always what it should be. But service managers *do* have to worry about both of these issues. Consequently, the balance between efficiency and effectiveness involves some tension and trade-offs. Good managers know that the right balance is when resources are used as efficiently as they can be used, given the effectiveness goals that need to be met.

Analyzing Service Processes

A process is any conversion activity that transforms inputs into outputs. *Process analysis* involves understanding *what* the process does, *how* and *why* it does it, and how it might be improved. Much like the diagnostic work of a physician, which involves technical analysis, observation, and judgment, process analysis assesses the work or conversion activity performed by some working unit. All processes convert inputs into outputs, through some conversion or transformation process, as shown in Exhibit 11.1.

The Process Flow Diagram

The four components always specified in every process analysis are tasks (or operations), flows, storages (or queues), and decision points. Drawing a diagram or flowchart of the process is a useful first step to analyzing any process. In a typical **process flow diagram,** tasks are depicted as circles or rectangles, flows as arrows, storages (in the form of customer waits) as inverted triangles, and decision points as diamonds.

Consider a routine cleaning and checkup at a dentist's office. The office has four workers: a receptionist who performs the first task of registering patients; a hygienist who does the second task, which is routine teeth cleaning; a dentist who does the third task of examining the patient's teeth; and an appointment secretary who performs the final task of scheduling the patient's next appointment(s). Exhibit 11.2 shows the process flow diagram for this simple process. The number associated with each task is the amount of time in minutes required to perform that task. For example, it takes the receptionist four minutes, on average, to register a patient.

EXHIBIT 11.1
Converting Inputs to Outputs

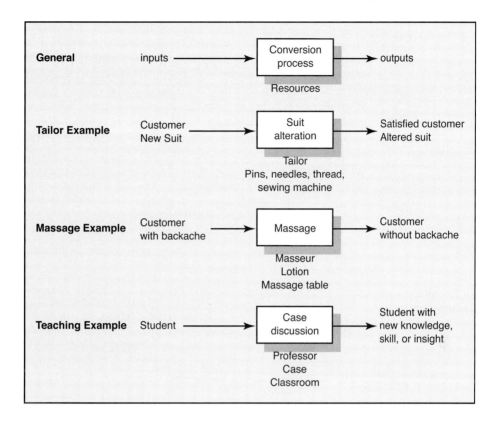

EXHIBIT 11.2
Simple Process Flow Diagram for Routine Dental Checkup

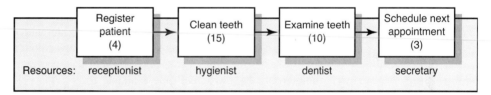

Constructing a process flow diagram is something of an art. A given process may have more than one "correct" process flow diagram. The degree of detail incorporated in the diagram, sometimes referred to as **granularity,** depends on why it is being drawn. For an overall picture of a complex process, a fairly simple diagram might be drawn, whereas if the diagram is being constructed to analyze and improve a particular series of process steps, each step might be broken into very minute detail.

The focus of process analysis is the operating unit, which in this case is the dentist's office. In some analyses, this focus might be a department of a service organization, the overall work of the service organization, or even an entire service supply chain. Work orders (scheduled routine appointments in our example) are one input to the operating unit. Other inputs are purchased material (paper "bibs," cleaning paste, dental floss), equipment (dental instruments, X-ray machine), and worker knowledge. The inputs are transformed into outputs by the tasks performed.

Capacity, as discussed in Chapter 14, is defined as the ability of the process to do work per unit of time and can be expressed in either units of output per unit of time (such as pages per minute or tons per day) or simply in units of time (such as available hours per day), depending on which provides the most useful information for the manager. Typically, capacity for standardized outputs is expressed in units per time period and capacity for more variable outputs is expressed in available hours per time period. For example, the capacity of a tollbooth on a turnpike is measured in vehicles per hour and the capacity of a bank teller is measured in customers per hour. However, the capacity of a surgeon or a college professor may be measured in hours per week because of the wide variety of tasks that each performs. Within an operating unit, service tasks are performed by people or pieces of equipment, called a *work center*. The rate at which a work center produces units of output is called its *task time*. To express capacity in units of time at a particular work center, the following formula is used:

$$\frac{\text{Time available}}{\text{Task time}} = \text{Capacity}$$

Exhibit 11.3 shows the capacities for the four workers in the dentist office example.

EXHIBIT 11.3
**Work Center
Capacities, Dentist
Office**

Receptionist:	(60 minutes/hour) ÷ (5 minutes/patient) = 12 patients/hour
Hygienist:	(60 minutes/hour) ÷ (15 minutes/patient) = 4 patients/hour
Dentist:	(60 minutes/hour) ÷ (10 minutes/patient) = 6 patients/hour
Appointment secretary:	(60 minutes/hour) ÷ (3 minutes/patient) = 20 patients/hour

As Exhibit 11.3 shows, the capacity of each worker (or work center) is different from the capacities of other workers (or work centers). If only patients having routine examinations are seen in the office, the hygienist's task, teeth cleaning, would limit how many patients could be seen in a day by the office overall, because the hygienist's task has the longest task time. The longest task time in a sequential process determines the maximum output the process can produce because it is the limiting step in the process. Stated another way, the hygienist's task in this example is the **bottleneck** of the process.

If each worker in the office works an eight-hour day, taking a half hour for lunch and two 15-minute breaks, the actual time available for serving patients is seven hours per worker per day. How many patients can the office see during those seven hours?

Since the hygienist is the bottleneck, the capacity for the overall process would seem to be:

$$\frac{(7 \text{ hours/day} \times 60 \text{ minutes/hour})}{(15 \text{ minutes/patient})} = 28 \text{ patients per day}$$

However, this would be true only if the hygienist started four minutes after the receptionist. If they started at the same time, the time the hygienist would be in the office would be the same, but he or she could not see the first patient immediately because that patient would need to be checked in first. Exhibit 11.4 illustrates how patients might flow through the dentist's office.

Notice that the dentist cannot start seeing the second patient immediately after finishing with the first patient because the second patient does not finish with the hygienist until five minutes later. When a worker is not busy, that time is referred to as **idle time.** Notice, too, that the receptionist could start to see the second patient immediately after seeing the first patient, but it would be irrational to schedule patients that way because they would have to wait until the hygienist could see them. When customers (or units of production) are not able to move forward in a process because the next stage is already busy, that is called a *wait*. To prevent a wait for the hygienist, it would make sense for this dentist's office to schedule patient appointments every 15 minutes.

EXHIBIT 11.4
Possible Patient Flow
through Office

	Receptionist		Hygienist		Dentist		Appointment Secretary	
Patient	**Start**	**End**	**Start**	**End**	**Start**	**End**	**Start**	**End**
1	9:00	9:05	9:05	9:20	9:20	9:30	9:30	9:33
2	9:05	9:10	9:20	9:35	9:35	9:45	9:45	9:48
3	9:10	9:15	9:35	9:50	9:50	10:00	10:00	10:03
4	.	.	.	.	.	.	.	.
5	.	.	.	.	.	.	.	.

The process flow diagram for the dentist's office can be drawn to incorporate more detail. Exhibit 11.5 expands the process flow diagram presented in Exhibit 11.2 to incorporate specific waits and decision points.

The total time required for a unit of output, in our example, a dental patient, to pass through an operating unit—including waiting time between operations—is called **elapsed time.** (Note: The terminology used to describe the sum of the waiting times and service process times is not standardized in practice. Some organizations call this "throughput time," others use "cycle time" or "total time" in the system.) With no waiting time, the elapsed time for a single patient to move through the entire routine examination process is 33 minutes (Greet + Clean + Examine + Schedule = 5 + 15 + 10 + 3). However, patients do not all arrive exactly on time and there is variation in the time a routine examination takes (the times we were using were *average* times, and averages do not occur, they are calculated). The elapsed time for individual patients can vary widely because of variation in task times and in waiting times.

After the process flow diagram has been constructed and the fundamental characteristics of the process understood, the process can then be evaluated for efficiency and effectiveness.

Measures of Efficiency

There are two basic ways to capture efficiency: efficiency in the process, or how much of the available time a resource is used, and efficiency in the outcome, or the amount of work that is done by each resource. Capacity utilization is a measure of process efficiency; worker productivity is a measure of output productivity.

Capacity Utilization

Capacity utilization is a measure of how much of the available capacity is being used; it relates the capacity required by the demand for the work center to the capacity available (or supply) at the work center. Capacity utilization is expressed as a percentage and is calculated by dividing the capacity required by the capacity available:

$$\text{Capacity utilization} = \frac{\text{Capacity required}}{\text{Capacity available}}$$

For example, if three patients are seen in one hour, the capacity utilization for each worker in the dentist's office for that one hour would be calculated as shown in Exhibit 11.6.

If the workers in the office did nothing else in that hour except see the three routine patients, then the receptionist was busy 25 percent and idle 75 percent of the hour, the hygienist was busy 75 percent and idle 25 percent of the hour, the dentist was busy 50 percent and idle 50 percent of the hour, and the appointment secretary was busy 15 percent and idle 85 percent of the hour. Capacity utilization is, then, a measure of how efficiently those labor resources were used.

EXHIBIT 11.5   Expanded Process Flow Diagram of Routine Dental Exam

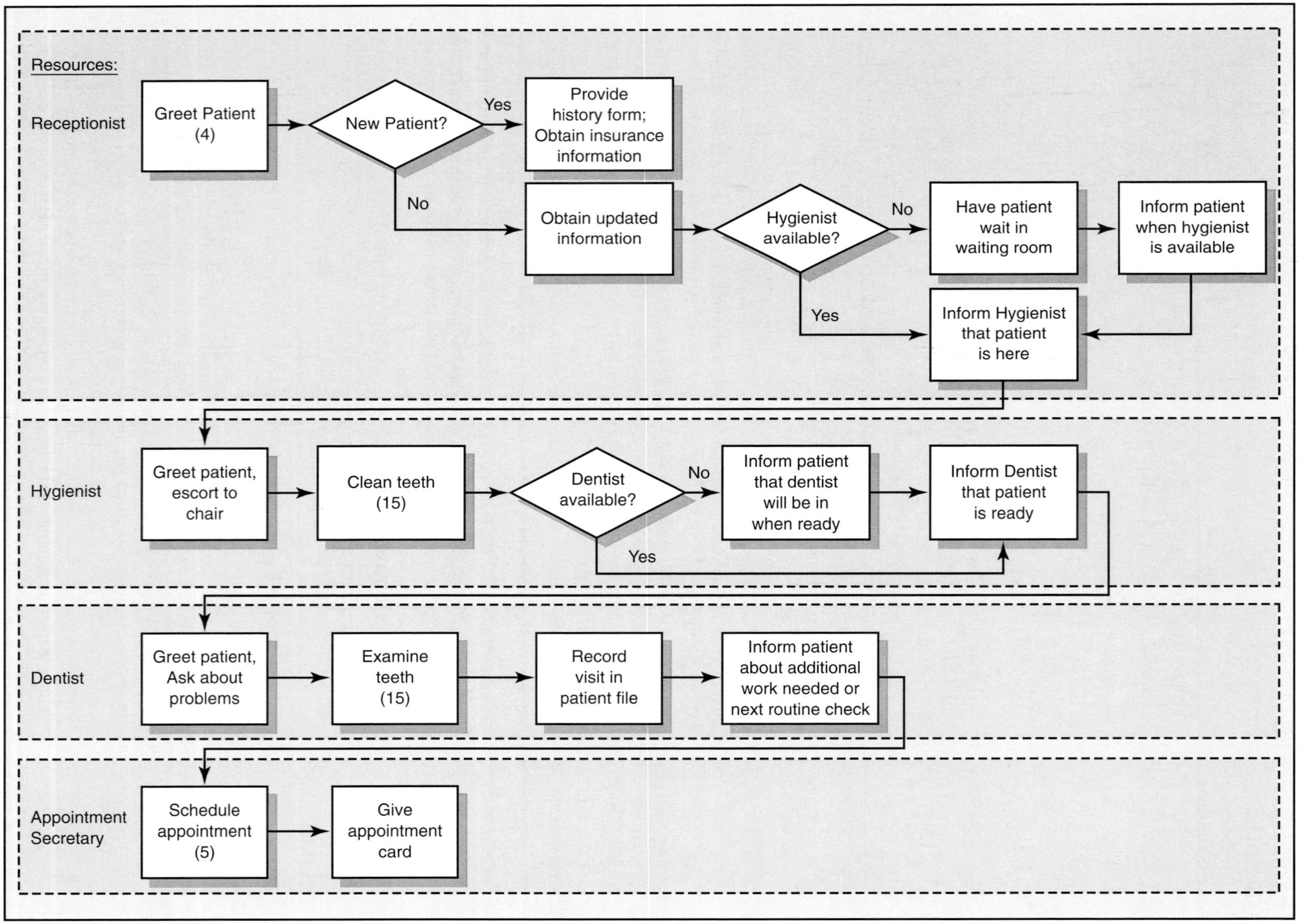

EXHIBIT 11.6
Work Center Capacity Utilizations for a Dentist Office

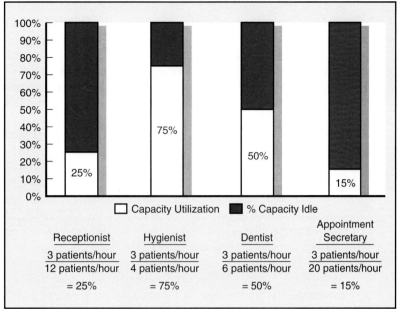

Of course, it is likely that each of the workers in a dentist's office would have tasks to perform in addition to those related to routine examinations. All of the time that the worker is busy as a percentage of the time the worker is available to work would represent that worker's capacity utilization.

Because

$$\text{Capacity utilization} = \frac{\text{Capacity required}}{\text{Capacity available}}$$

and

$$\text{Capacity available} = \frac{\text{Time available}}{\text{Task time}}$$

it is clear that there are three ways that capacity utilization can be changed: (*a*) change the capacity required (demand), (*b*) change the time available, or (*c*) change the task time.

What is the right capacity utilization for a work center? It depends. When capacity utilization is 100 percent, a work unit's productive resources are fully employed. Efficiency is high, but other measures of the work unit's performance, such as speed of delivery and quality, may be low. A fast-food restaurant operating at 95 percent capacity utilization might be very efficient, but it would not remain profitable for very long because customers would have to wait in long lines for service and it would not be very fast (see Chapter 15 for more about managing waiting times). Customers' expectations for cost, quality, speed, and reliability of delivery determine the appropriate capacity utilization for a work unit. There is no universal "right" capacity utilization for all processes. For each service, the proper balance between the efficient use of resources and meeting other performance goals must be assessed.

What can be done to lower a work center's capacity utilization if it is too high? Remember that capacity utilization is a way of expressing the relationship between the capacity available and the demand for it. To decrease capacity utilization, either capacity needs to be increased or demand must be decreased. One way to increase capacity is to add productive resources: hiring another hygienist at the dentist's office, for example. Another way to increase capacity is to use existing productive resources more effectively (for example, decrease the longest task time of the process). Thoughtful managers and workers continuously look for opportunities to improve service process efficiency.

For any given process, serving fewer customers is easier than serving more customers, but serving fewer customers is also likely to result in less revenue and lower profits. Therefore, decreasing demand is not usually a goal for service processes. In services, shifting demand from one time period to another to level the demand is often a goal because matching capacity with demand is easier to do when the demand is relatively stable (see Chapter 14 for a discussion of yield management in services). There are also some services for which the goal actually *is* to reduce demand. For example, fire departments go to great lengths to educate the public so that the demand for fighting fires decreases.

Capacity utilization can be too high in some services, but it is also possible for capacity utilization to be too low. When capacity utilization is low, costs are high because resources are not being used: Either employees are not working or equipment is not being used (they are idle). Capacity utilization can be increased by decreasing capacity or increasing demand. Decreasing capacity is usually achieved by reducing productive resources, rather than by purposely using productive resources less efficiently. Layoffs, or "downsizing," occur when organizations have more resources than they need to meet demand and costs are too high for the organization to remain profitable.

Productivity

Another measure of efficiency is productivity, or how much work is done per time period by a worker. Like capacity utilization, productivity relates the demand for a service to the capacity of a service—because how much a worker *can* do is likely to be affected by how much a worker *must* do. For example, the productivity of a loan officer might be measured in customer loan applications processed per day. If the process is analyzed and improved so that the loan officers have all the training and information they need to answer customer questions quickly and to provide information accurately, and if the process technology is up to date, the loan officers may each be able to evaluate 10 loan applications a day; however, if demand is lower than 10 applications a day, the output of the loan officers will be lower and the loan officer will appear to be less productive.

Which measure of productivity should be used depends on the service being evaluated. For example, in retail services, sales per square foot of selling space is an important measure because retail space is expensive. In an electrical utility company, kilowatt-hours per gallon of oil used might be the important productivity measure.

Cost

Cost is an important measure of the efficiency of any operation. Costs that should be considered include the cost of materials used to provide the service; the cost of labor, which includes both the costs of delivering the service and the costs associated with supervising workers; and overhead costs, which include the costs of running the organization as a whole, such as the costs of space, equipment, utilities, and centralized processes (for example, payroll, accounts payable and receivable, the personnel department, etc.). Labor and material costs are determined in large part by the overall design of the process and by how much waste and rework occur.

Measures of Effectiveness

Customers generally don't care how efficient service organizations are or what the organization's costs are; they want service that meets their needs for the price they are willing to pay.

Each year, states must process huge numbers of income tax documents: California receives more than 13.5 million, New York nearly 10 million, and Texas, even though it has no state tax, processes 13 million! To deal with these staggering numbers, the larger states have begun to use imaging technology to automate tax processing.

The State of New York began to use imaging in 1998 as part of its ongoing contract with Fleet Bank. Using the new technology, New York was able to meet its goal of mailing refunds within 45 days, rather than the typical 90-day turnaround. In addition to faster turnaround, imaging systems have enabled managers to shift workers to meet variations in demand. For example, when phone demand is high, managers can use the work-flow software that is part of the imaging system to shift workers from processing returns to customer service.

Fleet Bank also used labor more efficiently than the state could have. New York expected to save $7 million to $10 million each year through labor cost reductions alone. Fleet Bank used high-speed scanners, work-flow software, bar coding, and a high-capacity network to manage the volume. Returns generated by professional tax preparers, about 55 percent of the state's total, were simpler to process, but the remaining 45 percent took more processing time because most were handwritten.

Many other states have also turned to imaging systems to process annual tax returns. As the technology becomes cheaper and more reliable, efficiency and productivity have increased and the states can use their tax dollars for something other than processing tax returns!

Source: Tod Newcombe, "How Big States Use Tax Imaging," *Government Technology,* January 1998; and Tod Newcombe, "Documenting the Tax Byte," *Government Technology,* January 2002.

Price, one might argue, reflects costs, and in a perfect world, that would be true. But the relationship between price and cost is more complicated than that. Customers are willing to pay for value, and if the value offered to customers by a service is greater than the organization's cost of delivering that service, the organization can earn profits. If the organization is not efficient (that is, it does not use its resources well) or does not satisfy the customers' needs, the organization may not be able to sell the service for more than it costs to deliver it.

Measures that relate to customer satisfaction and market performance are measures of effectiveness.

Customer Satisfaction

The most obvious indicator of effectiveness is customer satisfaction. Customer satisfaction can be measured directly through interviews and questionnaires, but it can also be measured indirectly in a variety of ways, such as customer retention and loss, number of new customers, sales volume and market share, and customer complaints.

Customer Retention/Loss

Customers who are pleased with services will generally become repeat customers. It is less costly for a service organization to keep current customers than to attract new ones (see discussion on zero defections in Chapter 13), and repeat customers represent a continued revenue stream. Of course, some services do not wish to have prior customers return—emergency room services do not want to see customers returning, funeral homes don't ever expect to have the same customer return—but both of these services rely on "household" customers and positive word-of-mouth advertising. Because new customers are also important, measuring the inverse of customer retention, customer loss or defection (how many customers do not return), may be more informative.

New Customers

No matter how loyal current customers are, all organizations need to attract new customers to be viable in the long run: customers relocate, they experience changes in their economic status, and eventually they die. The percentage of new customers that the organization at-tracts is an important measure for most services. Some customers may be encouraged by current customers to try a service. The number of *word of mouth referrals* can be a mea-sure of the satisfaction of current customers.

Sales Volume and Market Share

Sales volume is certainly a measure of service effectiveness. Increasing sales volume usu-ally means that more customers are purchasing the service and/or customers are purchas-ing more, on average; conversely, decreasing sales volume means that fewer customers are purchasing the service or customers are purchasing less, on average. Market share is the percentage of total industry sales that are attributed to a particular service organization and is a more macro-level measure of customer satisfaction. Growth in sales in a stable market coincides with growth in market share and both mean that customers prefer the growing service over other competing services. Sales in an expanding market, however, can grow when market share is declining, so it is important to consider both to learn how customers evaluate a service in light of other competing services.

Complaints

An obvious indicator of the level of customer satisfaction is the number of complaints a service receives. Complaints are not just an indicator, they also provide an opportunity to learn about what customers want from a service.

Many customers choose not to complain when they are dissatisfied with a service, how-ever; it's too much hassle for many customers, who, instead, simply choose a competing service next time. In contrast to the *talkers,* who are customers who do complain, these customers are sometimes referred to as *walkers.* It is important for service organizations to develop processes for collecting customer complaints and to aggregate and analyze the information, seeking patterns that might provide insights into how to better serve their customers.

Technical Quality

Technical quality relates to the core element of a service, as opposed to functional quality, which relates to the customers' perception of the quality of the service. Technical quality may not be something that customers can accurately assess because they do not have the technical knowledge to do so. Customers may not have the ability to immediately evaluate whether their cars have been correctly repaired, their cavities properly filled, their stock portfolios managed well, or their illnesses accurately diagnosed. Because customers are not able to evaluate technical quality, measures of technical quality, which vary from ser-vice to service, must be monitored and evaluated by the professionals who provide the ser-vice (see Chapter 12 for a more detailed discussion of technical quality).

Customer Cancellation and No-Show Rates

In many service organizations, the rate of customers who cancel or do not show up for their scheduled appointments is an important measure of effectiveness. There are always legiti-mate reasons for both cancellations and no-shows, but when either rate is very high, it may indicate there is a problem, either with the process itself or with customer satisfaction with the process. For example, the no-show rate in pediatric offices in an inner city may be much higher than in a wealthy suburb because inner-city families may have less structured lives, more language difficulties, or less understanding of the need to keep routine appointments. Any of these reasons for no-shows may be an indication that the process needs to incor-porate more patient education or an appointment reminder system.

No-show rates may also mean that customers do not value the service. Whenever no-show rates increase, managers should investigate to determine whether the process needs to be modified or whether customer dissatisfaction might be a cause.

Employee Satisfaction

Blake Nordstrom, quoted in the opening vignette, believes that satisfied employees lead to satisfied customers. Employee *turnover,* the percentage of employees who leave per period, and **absenteeism,** the percentage of employees who call in sick or fail to report to work, are good indicators of the service organization's overall health.

Employee turnover is not always a bad thing. Some service systems employ a workforce strategy that expects turnover. For example, McDonald's employs many young people working part time during high school and college, and Starbucks employs many college students as baristas. These organizations do not expect workers to stay for years (although some do move up through the ranks to become managers). Turnover should be evaluated in light of the workforce strategy and not in a vacuum.

Employee satisfaction can be measured directly, too, through interviews, focus groups, and surveys. Employees will not be frank with the information they provide, however, if they believe there is a risk that managers will retaliate against them if they do not report satisfaction on all dimensions. In some organizations, honest information about employee satisfaction may need to be solicited anonymously. In healthy organizations, there is regular dialogue between supervisors and subordinates at all levels, and job satisfaction can be a matter of open discussion and continuous improvement.

Flexibility/Bandwidth

Service organizations vary in their ability to be flexible to changes in customer demand and changes in service content. The ability of a service to tolerate wide variation in demand content or volume is called **bandwidth.** Some services have a greater ability to handle variations in service content. For example, in health care, a physician has greater service content bandwidth than a nurse practitioner because a nurse practitioner's scope of practice is narrower. A branch bank has more service mix bandwidth than an ATM, because an ATM offers a limited menu of services (deposits, withdrawals, payments, and account transfers) and a branch bank offers all the services available at an ATM as well as new account services, investment services, and so on. Bandwidth also relates to tolerance to volume surges. McDonald's, for example, can handle two busloads of tourists that arrive unexpectedly, but a haute cuisine restaurant would not be able to manage such a surge. McDonald's can be said to have a wider-volume bandwidth or higher-volume flexibility than an upscale restaurant.

Measures of Both Efficiency and Effectiveness

Some performance measures span both efficiency and effectiveness because they reflect not only the use of resources but also how well the process meets customer expectations. Yield, dependable delivery, waiting time, and certain financial measures are included among these measures.

Yield

Yield is defined as:

$$\text{Yield (\%)} = \frac{\text{Good Outputs}}{\text{Total Outputs Produced}}$$

Yield is a very applicable measure in manufacturing environments. It is easy to see that for any production process, if materials and components are available to make a given number of units of a product, the number of good units that are actually produced can be expressed as a percent of the total number of units produced. For example, if you are making widgets and you have enough materials to make 1,000 widgets but 50 of them do not pass the quality inspection, your yield is 950/1,000, or 95 percent. Yield is also an applicable measure in many services. For example, in a telemarketing process, yield would be the percentage of calls that result in a sale:

$$\text{Yield (\%)} = \frac{\text{Number of sales}}{\text{Number of calls}}$$

Similarly, in a university, if 5,000 students are accepted into a program and 3,000 choose to attend, the yield on offers of matriculation is 60 percent (3,000/5,000). Yield for a retail website might be:

$$\text{Yield} = \frac{\text{Number of sales}}{\text{Number of people who visit the website}}$$

Yield is not a good measure for all service processes, however. It is difficult, for example, to see how yield might apply to a dry-cleaning service, a computer repair service, a physician's office, or a beauty salon.

Dependable Delivery/Waiting Time

Dependable delivery, or delivering a service in the promised time, is important to customers, not only for actual delivery services such as UPS or FedEx, but also for travel services such as airlines, buses, and trains as well as for any service that schedules appointments or reservations (hair salons, physician's offices, accounting services, and restaurants, to name a few) or that competes on speed of service (fast-food restaurants, walk-in copy services, convenience stores, oil-change services). The ability to meet delivery promises is determined to a great extent by how the process is designed, but it is also determined by how well the process is understood and managed, and therefore how work is scheduled and expedited. If the manager of a process does not have a solid understanding of processing and wait times for a given service, it can be very difficult to accurately establish service expectations that can consistently be met.

Waiting time is the flip side of on-time delivery. Customers generally do not like to wait, but, because service capacity must be matched with demand, and because demand is often unpredictable, the time customers wait is often a function of how much extra capacity exists in the system (which is an efficiency issue). But because waits often significantly affect customers' overall perceptions of a service, waiting time is as much a measure of effectiveness as it is of efficiency.

Of course, customers may have to wait for service even if the service *is* delivered on time. For example, if a patient has an appointment for an annual physical examination scheduled for 10:00 A.M. but arrives at 9:00 A.M., he will wait for one hour. But that hour of waiting will generally feel more tolerable to the patient than if he arrived at 10:00 and waited until 11:00. Similarly, most people probably expect to wait for a minute or two before being served at a fast-food restaurant—the "promise" to the customer is fast service, not immediate service—but few customers would tolerate a wait of 30 minutes or more.

View from the Top

George W. Bush, President of the United States

"Americans demand top-quality service from the private sector. They should get the same top-quality service from their government . . . I will work with Congress to build a government that is responsive to the people's needs, and responsible with our people's money."[1]

George W. Bush, who earned an MBA from Harvard Business School, is the first U.S. president to hold a management degree. He is emphasizing performance in government, focusing on decreasing costs and also on increasing quality, flexibility, speed, and innovation.

One way President Bush hopes to improve performance is to privatize many of the processes historically managed by government agencies by encouraging federal agencies and private firms to compete to perform work currently done by federal workers. Who wins the competition is based on well-understood and measurable performance goals and holding the winners responsible for improving their processes and achieving their goals. In other words, they will be responsible for getting results.

Furthermore, President Bush wants to link program performance to agencies' budgets. In the federal 2002 budget, he supported the 1993 Government Performance and Results Act (GPRA). He planned to start testing the ability of government agencies to set goals, measure performance, and use the information to improve results. To participate in the test, agencies had to meet five criteria set by the Office of Management and the Budget (OMB).

• Clearly state a specified, desired outcome that can be measured.

• Examine different processes for achieving that outcome to identify the best possible process.

• Clearly identify the results of the program and how the agency will assess performance.

• Develop a list of required inputs, including not just budget numbers but also personnel, time, effort, and other resources required to complete the work.

• Identify the cost per output to determine if the investment in resources is worth the result.

Initially many agencies had difficulty defining the right goals and measurements, focusing instead on fixing the consequences of problems rather than addressing their causes. But as the president wrote in his 2002 Management Agenda, "Government likes to begin things—to declare grand new programs and causes. But good beginnings are not the measure of success. What matters in the end is completion. Performance. Results. Not just making promises, but making good on promises. In my administration, that will be the standard from the farthest regional office of government to the highest office in the land."[2]

Sources: Diane Frank, "OMB Turns Up Heat on Performance," *Federal Computer Week,* June 25, 2001; Adrian Moore, "Privatization: Competition Yields Quality," *Washington Times,* May 1, 2002; and Miles Benson, "Bush Embarks on Latest Effort to Reform Government, but Experts are Skeptical," *Newhouse News Service,* 2002.

Financial Measures

Financial measures such as return on assets (ROA), return on investment (ROI), contribution, and profit are all measures that can be applied to service organizations. There are no magic or ideal numbers for any of these measures; each should be compared to both the business plan for the service and industry standards.

The Impact of Technology

Technology has made collecting information about and analyzing service processes easier than ever. Tollbooths, for example, measure the number of vehicles that go through each gate as well as how much toll money is collected. Electronic cash registers note the time of each transaction so that demand at different hours of the day and on different days of the week can be tracked. Phone systems collect data on the number of calls, busy signals, waiting times, and hang-ups that occur, and websites track hits, transactions, and even which pages are visited and in what order!

[1] George W. Bush, Radio Address of the President to the Nation, August 25, 2001.
[2] "The President's Management Agenda," Executive Office of the President, Office of Management and Budget, Fiscal Year 2002, August 2001.

Technology also increases the capacity of many services: bar code scanners allow cashiers to process groceries more accurately and quickly; fast lanes collect tolls from more cars/hour than traditional tollbooths with attendants.

Technology has also enabled the creation of new processes. Just a few years ago, online banking, securities trading, shopping, and even information retrieval were just a dream. Expert systems technology has helped physicians make difficult diagnoses and loan officers determine the creditworthiness of loan applicants. Each of these new processes has different inputs and transformation steps than the process it replaced and possibly different measures of performance. For example, online banking transactions require a user-friendly interface, access to the main customer databases, and server capacity. In-person banking services require space inside the bank, a teller, access to databases, and perhaps a variety of paper forms. Other ancillary inputs may also be important for in-person banking customers: a place to park their cars, a pleasant decor, and a comfortable and fair waiting environment. Because labor costs are usually significant, the cost of online bank transactions are usually much lower than the cost of in-person bank transactions—in other words, they may be more efficient. Customer satisfaction may be high (or low!) with either process, depending on the customer's needs. Less computer-savvy customers, for example, may be very uncomfortable with even a well-designed online process and may be more comfortable with the in-person process. Similarly, computer-savvy customers may be more comfortable with the privacy and anytime-access to online banking services. Whatever the process, it is important to determine what measures are important and to monitor performance regularly.

Summary

Process flow diagrams show the relationship between tasks, decisions, and waits in any process. There are several measures of service process efficiency, which indicate how well resources are being used, and effectiveness, which indicate how well customers' needs are met. Efficiency measures include capacity utilization, productivity, and cost measures. Yield, delivery time, waiting time, and financial measures are indicators of both efficiency and effectiveness. Effectiveness measures include customer satisfaction, such as customer retention, customer loss, percent of new customers, sales volume, and market share. Customer complaint volume and internal measures of the technical quality of the service that can be evaluated only by professionals, employee satisfaction, and service volume and service content bandwidth are also effectiveness measures. Each of these measures is important for service managers because each provides insight into a different dimension of service performance and the strength and viability of the organization in the long run.

Key Terms

absenteeism: percentage of employees who call in sick or fail to report to work. *(p. 281)*
bandwidth: ability of a service to tolerate wide variation in demand for its services. *(p. 281)*
bottleneck: the task in a sequential process that has the least capacity. *(p. 274)*
capacity: how much of a resource is available per unit of time. *(p. 273)*
capacity utilization: measure of how much of the available capacity is being used. *(p. 275)*
elapsed time: time required for a customer or unit of output to pass through an operating unit, including task time and waits. *(p. 275)*
granularity: degree of detail. *(p. 273)*
effectiveness: how well process objectives are being met. *(p. 272)*
efficiency: how well resources are used. *(p. 272)*
idle time: time a worker spends not working. *(p. 274)*
process flow diagram: a tool for analyzing processes that depicts tasks, flows, waits, and decision points in the process. *(p. 272)*
productivity: work done by a worker, a work unit, or a piece of equipment per time period.
yield: the percentage of the ouput of a process that is good. *(p. 281)*

Review and Discussion Questions

1. Describe the purpose and elements of a process flow diagram.
2. Define capacity and how it is determined.
3. Define capacity utilization and how it is determined.
4. If you were the manager of a 911 phone facility, how would you evaluate performance? How would that differ from performance measures for a bookstore?
5. Define efficiency and effectiveness. List some measures of each.

Internet Assignment

Using your favorite Internet browser, search for "process flow diagram." Visit several sites and compare at least three of the process flow diagrams you find. How well have they described the process to you? What creative elements did they employ? Did the creative elements enhance your understanding of the process or reduce it?

Solved Problems

1. Suppose you are serving customers at a movie ticket counter, and a customer is served, on average, every 30 seconds (the task time).

   a. What is the capacity of your work center in customers per hour?

   $$\text{Capacity} = \text{Time available} \div \text{Task time}$$

   Time available = 60 Minutes/hour $\times$ 60 Seconds/minute = 3,600 Seconds/hour
   Task time = 30 Seconds/customer

   $$\text{Capacity} = 3{,}600 \text{ Seconds/hour} \div 30 \text{ Seconds/unit} = 120 \text{ Customers/hour}$$

   b. Suppose you are serving customers who use different modes of payment. Cash payment has a service time of 20 seconds, credit card payment has a service time of 50 seconds, and payment by check has a task time of 80 seconds. Which expression of capacity (units per unit of time or time) is most useful here? Why?

   Solution
   Because more than one type of customer can be served, it can be difficult to express capacity in units, so expressing capacity in time is more useful.
   If, however, the proportion of each type of payment was fairly consistent, you could calculate a weighted average task time for the service mix. For example, assume the mix is 50 percent cash, 30 percent credit card, and 20 percent check. The weighted average task time would be:

20 seconds $\times$ .5	=	10 seconds
50 seconds $\times$ .3	=	15 seconds
80 seconds $\times$ .2	=	<u>16 seconds</u>
Weighted average	=	41 seconds

   The capacity of your work center is now:

   $$3{,}600 \text{ Seconds/hour} \div 41 \text{ Seconds/customer} = 87.8 \text{ Customers/hour}$$

2. Suppose you are a physician and the average length of time required to meet and examine a new patient is one hour and the average time required to meet and examine a return patient is 15 minutes. On any given day, the mix of new and return patients is unpredictable. How would you express capacity? Why?

   Solution
   As above, because you are uncertain of the mix, it would be more useful to express capacity in time, rather than in units. For example, if the physician is available to see patients four days each week for six hours each day, the capacity in hours per week would be:

   $$4 \text{ Days/week} \times 6 \text{ Hours/day} = 24 \text{ Hours/week}$$

3. You are the manager of a surgical center that performs minor surgical cases. The center has five operating rooms, and, on average, each case takes 60 minutes to perform. After each case, cleanup requires 20 minutes. If the center schedules its first case for 8:00 A.M., no cases are performed between noon and 1:00 P.M., and the last case must be completed by 5:00 P.M., what is the daily capacity of the center in cases? Identify two ways you can increase the capacity of the center?

Solution

Here, the total time for each case is the task time of 60 minutes plus the cleanup time of 20 minutes, or 80 minutes. Each operating room has four hours in the morning and four hours in the afternoon that can be scheduled for cases.

4 Hours × 60 Minutes/hour = 240 Minutes/half-day operating session

240 Minutes/session ÷ 80 Minutes/case = 3 Cases/session

3 Cases/session × 2 Sessions/day/room × 5 Rooms = 30 Cases/day

The two basic ways to increase capacity are (1) to increase the time available each day by either being open for longer hours or adding more operating rooms, or (2) to shorten the length of time it takes to do the surgery and cleanup for each case. Because the day is broken into two four-hour sessions, the total time required for each case (operating time plus clean up time) cannot exceed 60 minutes to increase the capacity by one case each session. If more than 60 minutes is required, the one-hour lunch is violated.

4. An automated check-clearing process has five tasks, as shown in the table below. At each of the five tasks, some checks cannot be processed using the automated process and are removed at that task. All machines are used for each task. A shift consists of eight actual work hours. Calculate the yield for the process overall, assuming units that cannot be processed at each step are identified through inspection and removed for processing before the next task is performed. Calculate the shift capacity, in units, for each task.

Task	Yield	Task Time for Each Machine	Number of Machines	Shift Capacity (units)
1	0.95	6 minutes	3	
2	0.82	4 minutes	1	
3	0.97	2 minutes	2	
4	0.92	3 minutes	4	
5	0.89	6 minutes	3	

What task is the bottleneck of this process?

You are the office manager and you want to double output. What steps would you take? What issues would you need to consider?

Solution

The overall yield for the process, when checks that cannot be processed automatically are removed (similar to being scrapped), is calculated by multiplying the yields for each step (.95 × .82 × .97 ×.92 × .89 = 61.9%). The logic here may be easier to see if you think in terms of units. If you start out at task 1 with 1,000 checks, you will be able to process only 950 checks to go on to task 2; of those 950 checks, task 2 will yield only 779 (950 × .82) to go on to task 3, and so on.

To complete the rest of the table, you need to consider the number of machines at each task to determine the theoretical shift capacity in units for each task. It is also appropriate to consider the yield at each step and calculate the actual capacity at current yields for each task. (There are hidden dangers in either calculation. If you calculate only the theoretical capacity, which assumes that you can process all checks at each step, you are overstating what you can actually do with current yields. If, however, you calculate capacity factoring in current yields, you may be, in effect, assuming that the yields are fixed and that your capacity is necessarily constrained to those levels.)

Incorporating yields into the calculation of total capacity is a bit complicated, because yield rates before the true bottleneck task don't affect the overall capacity, but yield rates at each task after the bottleneck task do. The results are shown in the table below.

Task	Yield	Task Time for Each Machine	Number of Machines	Shift Capacity (units)	Shift Capacity (units × yield)
1	.95	6 minutes	3	240	228
2	.82	4 minutes	1	120	98
3	.97	2 minutes	2	480	465
4	.92	3 minutes	4	640	588
5	.89	6 minutes	3	240	213

Identifying the bottleneck here is a little tricky. The longest task times are at tasks 1 and 5, so they might be expected to define the bottleneck task. Because there is more than one machine at several tasks, the bottleneck is the task with the least capacity. Therefore, task 2 is the bottleneck task.

To double output, you need to look to the bottleneck, because the capacity at that task determines the capacity for the overall process. The capacity at task 2 is 120 units per shift so you could either add a machine or think about adding a shift for that task. If you identified the need to consider yield as affecting capacity here, which is correct, you would need to demonstrate what you would do to change it. Other issues to consider are equipment cost, labor cost, space, and market demand.

Problems

1. A service has five tasks, performed in sequence. When there is more than one worker assigned to a task, each worker performs the entire task.

Task	Task Time per Worker	Number of Workers	Hourly Capacity in Units
1	2 minutes	2	
2	6 minutes	2	
3	10 minutes	2	
4	4 minutes	1	
5	15 minutes	5	

   a. Complete the table above to indicate the hourly capacity in units for each task.
   b. What is the capacity of the process as a whole?
   c. What is the bottleneck of the process?
   d. Where would you expect customers to wait?

2. If you are the operations manager of any service process, how do you determine a "good" capacity utilization?

3. A professor has only five hours to grade exams for 20 students. If it takes 30 minutes to grade each of the first five exams, how fast must the professor grade each of the 15 remaining exams to finish in the five hours?

4. A barbershop offers three different types of haircuts:

Type of Cut	% of Customers	Time
Buzz cut	50	10 minutes
Razor cut	20	15 minutes
Scissor cut	30	30 minutes

   a. How many customers can be served each hour, on average?
   b. There are three barbers on duty when the shop opens and four customers are waiting to be served. You are the fourth customer. How long will you have to wait for service?

5. You are a very successful tax accountant and your firm, which has grown to 20 full-time accountants, experiences huge demand between January 1 and April 15 each year. During peak season last year, your accountants worked 80-hour weeks. This year, the accounting staff members have made it clear they are unwilling to work such outrageous hours. What are your options for managing this supply/demand imbalance?

CASE   Massbay Medical Center: Lab Central Receiving Area*

"They're *your* people!" thundered Bob DiGiacomo, supervisor of the chemistry department at MassBay Medical Center. "The reason why we have such poor laboratory specimen* turnaround is because *your* staff are unprofessional. They're more concerned about having a good time than they are about their work. And I'll tell you, it's affecting patient care. Some of those blood samples sit needlessly in your area for hours, and they're spoiled by the time they reach the lab for testing. If it were *my* department, I'd get rid of them all and start over with a new crew that was dedicated to getting the job done. This can't continue! I want a solution to this problem and I want it fast!"

DiGiacomo stormed out. As his words sank in, Jim LaForte, manager of the lab's Central Receiving Area (CRA), knew that something had to be done. Could DiGiacomo be right? LaForte had always been pleased about the high morale in CRA. Could it be that his staff was really just having a good time?

Central Receiving Area Work Flow

CRA processed specimens 24 hours a day, seven days a week, although the volume of specimens varied considerably by day of the week and time of the day (Exhibit 1). Each worker was scheduled to work 8.5 hours a day. Out of that time, workers took an unpaid half-hour lunch and two paid 15-minute breaks. The work in CRA was very important, but it was also very monotonous. The people who worked there got along well, however, and what made the monotony of the CRA job bearable was the opportunity to interact with co-workers.

Six workers staffed the two processing lines at any given time and other workers answered phone requests for test results. LaForte chose Friday as a representative day for the data collection (Exhibit 2).

Specimens were received in special containers or tubes stored within a plastic bag. Attached to the bag was a requisition that recorded the patient's medical identification number, the patient's ward or clinic, and the test to be performed. Each specimen was also labeled with its priority status: either "STAT," which meant that testing was to be performed immediately upon receipt of the specimen, or "routine," which indicated that a specimen could be batch-processed with other similar tests, often performed at scheduled times during the day. Some tests required specimens to be fresher than others, however, so workers used a priority sort system, called triage, to prioritize which routine specimens needed to be processed first.

CRA used two processing lines. One was dedicated solely to processing routine samples, and the other was used primarily for STAT tests. The volume of STAT tests was considerably lower than that of routine tests, however, so the STAT line also processed routine samples.

Each line had three stations: a shared unwrapping station and separate typing and labeling stations. At the unwrapping station (also called triage), a worker removed the specimen from the bag, checked to make sure the name on the specimen matched the name on the requisition, and placed the specimen and the requisition together on a table (Exhibit 3). The average time for the unwrapping task was four seconds per specimen.

At each typing station, a worker sitting at a computer terminal entered the patient's medical record number, the time the specimen was collected, the location of the inpatient unit or clinic where the specimen had been collected, the name of the physician ordering the test, and a four-digit test code. The computer assigned a specimen number and printed a sticky paper label on a printer at the next station. The typing task required, on average, 32 seconds per specimen. Only two computer terminals were available for the sorting process.

This case was prepared by Janelle Heineke and Joseph Restuccia on the basis of data collected by Daniel R. Buck. Modified June 2002. Copyright Heineke & Restuccia.

* A specimen is a sample taken from a patient for testing, such as blood or urine.

EXHIBIT 1
Average Specimen
Arrivals at CRA
(based on six weeks
of data)

Hour Ending	Sun.	Mon.	Tues.	Wed.	Thurs.	Fri.	Sat.
0:00	6	5	13	11	14	11	3
1:00	6	5	13	11	14	11	3
2:00	6	5	13	11	14	11	3
3:00	15	15	23	17	14	17	13
4:00	30	29	52	35	38	37	32
5:00	31	24	39	33	34	34	30
6:00	35	28	46	32	32	36	33
7:00	19	23	35	35	17	22	30
8:00	41	55	95	80	91	87	40
9:00	63	72	84	87	91	90	58
10:00	42	112	109	116	127	133	36
11:00	47	107	101	143	99	135	40
12:00	38	105	76	111	119	127	45
13:00	33	92	104	129	118	104	34
14:00	38	108	164	123	113	114	41
15:00	35	116	109	149	140	135	36
16:00	36	105	103	114	140	98	45
17:00	25	91	101	119	110	78	32
18:00	27	76	92	108	75	72	26
19:00	16	41	66	47	45	36	16
20:00	19	33	50	43	38	44	25
21:00	19	29	49	28	44	30	19
22:00	26	28	47	33	30	34	25
23:00	19	18	38	24	25	23	18
Total	672	1,322	1,622	1,639	1,582	1,519	683

EXHIBIT 2
CRA Staffing

Hour Ending	Sun.	Mon.	Tues.	Wed.	Thurs.	Fri.	Sat.
0:00	2	1	2	2	2	2	2
1:00	2	1	2	2	2	2	2
2:00	2	1	1	1	1	1	1
3:00	2	1	2	1	1	1	1
4:00	2	1	2	2	2	2	2
5:00	2	2	3	3	3	3	2
6:00	2	2	3	3	2	2	2
7:00	3	3	2	1	1	2	3
8:00	2	3	2	2	2	2	2
9:00	3	5	5	5	5	5	2
10:00	3	5	5	5	5	5	3
11:00	3	5	5	5	5	5	3
12:00	3	5	5	5	5	5	1
13:00	2	3	5	5	5	5	2
14:00	2	5	5	5	5	5	2
15:00	2	5	5	5	5	5	2
16:00	1	5	5	5	5	5	1
17:00	1	2	3	3	3	3	1
18:00	1	2	3	2	3	3	1
19:00	1	3	3	3	3	3	1
20:00	1	2	2	2	2	2	1
21:00	1	2	2	2	2	2	1
22:00	1	1	2	1	1	2	1
23:00	1	1	2	2	1	2	1

*Time away from CRA for paid and unpaid breaks is not shown.

EXHIBIT 3
Central Receiving
Area Layout

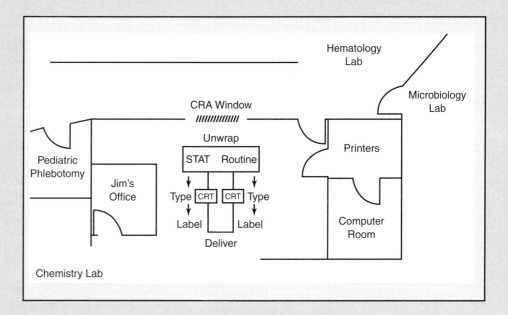

At the labeling station, a worker affixed a label onto each specimen and separated the tubes and requisitions according to which laboratory would perform the test. Labeling required, on average, 10 seconds per specimen.

When workers performed all three tasks, the total time to process a specimen was 51 seconds, somewhat more than the sum of the three individual task times. LaForte attributed the difference to the fact that a worker performing only one task became more efficient at that particular task but, when asked to perform others, might be slower at performing the new task than a worker who focused on that task only.

After specimens had been processed by CRA, they were delivered to the appropriate labs.

Questions

1. What is the key problem in CRA?

2. Describe the demand for CRA specimen processing.

3. What is the capacity of CRA to process specimens?

4. What are the capacity utilizations for the CRA workers, given typical demand patterns?

5. What should LaForte do?

6. What other variables should be considered?

CASE   University Bookstore—Textbook Department

Most of the year was "library-like" at the Textbook Department, according to Marilyn Copp, the department manager. But the two weeks after Labor Day and the second two weeks of January were quite the opposite. She explained:

> Semester start-ups put enormous pressure on us. Last semester, in the twelve 9 A.M. to 9 P.M. workdays of those two weeks, we served 21,600 customers. I must admit, we didn't serve them all as well as I'd have liked. I am hoping to do much better in January.

> A study done this past fall shows that we can expect 10% of our early semester customers to buy one book, 20% to buy two, 25% to buy three, 30% to buy four, and 15% to buy five books. Customers who come in can ask for help at the information desk, but the shelf areas for the many schools, departments and courses are clearly marked, so most customers help themselves. Then they come to the cash registers to check out. That's where we feel the most pressure. (See Figure 1.)

The checkout counter had four electronic cash registers. The cashiers' task included:

1. Keying into the register an inventory code number and a price for each book (Time required: 0.1 minutes per book); and

2. Bagging books and receiving payment either by
   a. collecting cash and making change (Time: 0.4 min per customer),
   b. waiting while the customer wrote a check, then taking down the customer's identification data (Time: 1.2 min per customer), or
   c. running a credit card through the register's automatic approval device, filling out a charge slip while waiting for an approval code, getting the customer's signature, and returning the card (Time: 1.0 min per customer).

Store records indicated that about 40 percent of textbook customers paid cash, 40 percent paid by check, and 20 percent by credit card.

Demand during the first two weeks was fairly level, except during the first two days. Ms. Copp estimated that the first two days were by far the busiest, with their total volume per day double the average daily volume of the twelve-day period. The busiest hours on those two peak days were between noon and 4:00 P.M., when students came to buy books just after attending their first classes. Ms. Copp said that customer arrivals during those peak hours ran at three times the average rate over the twelve days. "That's when the department gets its reputation for poor service," she remarked. "Those two afternoons each year can make or break my career with this company. This January I want to manage them much better than I did last fall. Can you help?"

FIGURE 1
Textbook Department
Floorplan

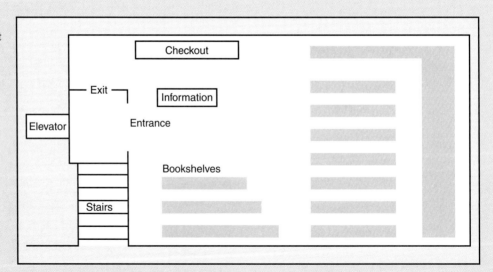

This case was prepared by Duncan C. McDougall and Thomas E. Vollmann. Copyright by Boston University and the authors.

Questions

1. What is the capacity of the bookstore checkout stations in customers per hour?

2. What is the average hourly demand during the peak periods of the first two weeks of the semester?

3. What should the manager at the bookstore do?

Selected Bibliography

Benson, Miles. "Bush Embarks on Latest Effort to Reform Government, but Experts Are Skeptical." *Newhouse News Service,* 2002.

Frank, Diane. "OMB Turns Up Heat on Performance." *Federal Computer Week,* June 25, 2001.

Keltner, Brent, David Finegold, Geoff Mason, and Karin Wagner. "Market Segmentation Strategies and Service Sector Productivity." *California Management Review* 41, no. 4 (Summer 1999), pp. 84–102.

Moore, Adrian. "Privatization: Competition Yields Quality." *Washington Times,* May 1, 2002.

Newcombe, Tod. "Documenting the Tax Byte." *Government Technology,* January 2002.

Newcombe, Tod. "How Big States Use Tax Imaging." *Government Technology,* January 1998.

"The President's Management Agenda." Executive Office of the President, Office of Management and Budget, Fiscal Year 2002, August 2001.

"Process Analysis Note—1995." This note was originally prepared by D. C. McDougall, J. G. Miller, and T. E. Vollmann. It was revised in 1992 by Peter Arnold, Janelle Heineke, and Jay Kim, and revised and expanded in 1995 by Janelle Heineke, Peter Arnold, and J. Robb Dixon.

Quinn, J. B., and M. Baily. "Information Technology: Increasing Productivity in Services." *Academy of Management Executive* 8, no. 3 (1994), p. 28.

Van Biema, M., and B. Greenwald. "Managing Our Way to Higher Service-Sector Productivity." *Harvard Business Review,* July–August 1997, p. 87.

CHAPTER TWELVE

Understanding Service Quality

Learning Objectives

- Distinguish between the quality of tangible goods and the quality of services.

- Identify the different dimensions of quality for goods and for services.

- Introduce the major components of quality theory and the theorists who contributed to it.

- Distinguish between technical quality and functional quality.

- Understand how customer expectations affect perception of quality.

- Present the role of certification and awards for recognizing outstanding quality.

Elizabeth Renee Day Spa: What the Customer Wants

EyeWire / Getty Images

The day spa at Elizabeth Renee Esthetics understands what customers want. The spa, established in 1991 by owner and licensed aesthetician Elizabeth Kosky, is located in Wellesley, Massachusetts, a quiet suburban college town 10 miles west of Boston.

Spa staff members pride themselves on being the "ingredients experts." They match specific skin care products to each customer's unique skin characteristics, combining a variety of ingredients to relax and calm the customer as well as to cleanse, soften, and smooth the skin. They incorporate aromatherapy, nutrition, cosmetic formulation, and makeup artistry, providing treatments in a "relaxed, friendly (never intimidating) environment." The French-country decor is elegant yet comfortable and the aestheticians are knowledgeable, warm, and friendly.

Elizabeth Renee's website invites customers to, "Come . . . relax . . . kick back . . . and enjoy an experience which will sooth your mind, de-stress your body, and rekindle your spirit . . . ahhhh . . . spa!"

Source: http://www.erespa.com/dayspa.htm.

The Customer's Perspective

You and a few friends decide to go out for dinner and are discussing the quality of different restaurants you've eaten at recently. One of the group members suggests Louie's—and the confusion begins!

Bill says, "I think Louie's is great! Terrific quality!"

Josh replies, "How can you say that? They seem to have a very broad menu, but the entrées are almost all meat items—with only one or two fish or vegetarian dishes."

"You're right," Martha agrees, "but everything on the menu is good and the portions are generous. They have a great dessert selection, too."

"I like Louie's because the servers are so friendly and once you're at your table they seem to know just when you need something," Bill adds.

Jen counters with, "Sure, but that's once you're seated! There's no parking, they don't take reservations, and the waiting area is cramped and uncomfortable."

Peter says, "Fair enough, but the atmosphere in the restaurant is so nice—relaxed but still nice enough for a special occasion."

"That's true," Josh says. "And it *is* in our price range."

In the end you decide that Louie's is where you'll go, but each of you enters the restaurant with a better understanding of what matters to the others in your group. You realize that "quality" doesn't necessarily mean the same thing to all of you, and you are each on the watch for the quality elements that are important to your friends as well as the ones that have always mattered to you.

Quality does mean something different to each of us, and it even can mean something different to the same person in different service environments. Customers of services are not always aware of the individual dimensions of quality. Rather, they view quality in light of the experience as a whole.

Managerial Issues

Quality will always matter to customers, so it should always be a high priority for every service manager. At the same time, service quality is often very difficult to manage, for a variety of reasons. Managing service quality requires knowing exactly what customers want, designing services to meet their needs, developing and monitoring processes that deliver the services, training workers, and measuring customer satisfaction. But unlike product quality, which is fairly objective, service quality is highly subjective, varying from customer to customer even under identical circumstances. As we saw above, good quality to one customer may be seen as poor quality by another. Even a single customer's quality requirements may change under different circumstances. For example, a business executive staying at a hotel on a weekday has different needs than the same person staying at the same hotel for a weekend on vacation with his family.

"Quality" service itself is a very broad concept that encompasses many dimensions, including the friendliness of the servers, the ease of access to service, the knowledgeability of the server, the speed of the service, and the length and comfort of the wait for service.

Good managers manage service quality very carefully, because keeping existing customers is easier—and more profitable—than finding new ones.

Another reason managers should be concerned with quality is that quality and cost are closely related. Every time a customer is dissatisfied with the way a service is provided, the organization is likely to incur three significant costs. First, dealing with customers who are unhappy takes time—time that can't be used to serve other customers. Second, customers who are unhappy with the service they receive are likely to tell others, which will hurt the reputation of the service provider. Third, and perhaps most important, every time a customer is dissatisfied with a service, there is a good chance that he or she will not return to that service organization again and the organization will lose the entire future stream of service opportunities—and its potential profits—from that customer.

Quality as a Strategic Element

Within a firm, quality can be viewed from an operational level as an element that must simply be controlled in the processes of producing goods and services, or it can be viewed from a strategic level with a long-term perspective. The mind-sets of these two views are fundamentally different. In the operational quality control view, the quality focus is only on identifying defects or addressing customer complaints. In the strategic view, quality is seen as a factor that can lower the costs of producing goods by reducing waste and rework, plus high quality can justify higher prices to customers because the products or services are differentiated from others in the marketplace. Furthermore, if the quality produced is consistent and the organization strives for continued product/service improvements, customers tend to be more loyal and the organization will be more successful in the long term.

But *quality* is a vague word. *The American Heritage Dictionary*[1] defines quality as "an inherent or distinguishing characteristic; a property," which is not a definition that is very helpful for understanding what quality means in business. To manage quality as an important strategic element, a manager needs to be able to define what quality means, to measure it, and to consistently deliver it to customers. Because *quality* can mean so many different things to different people at different times, it is important to develop a quality vocabulary that will help service managers and workers understand what their customers want and how to consistently meet their needs. If a service firm can't specifically define what quality is, it probably can't do a good job of managing it.

Virtually all organizations, in both the manufacturing and the service sectors, compete to some extent on the basis of service, so understanding and effectively managing service quality is critically important for the creation and maintenance of competitive advantage.

Product Quality versus Service Quality

Chapters 1 and 2 defined services as intangible and simultaneously produced and consumed. These characteristics make defining and managing the quality of services much more difficult than for tangible goods, which can be seen and touched and reexamined. However, much of the theory of service quality has evolved from the theory on product quality. It is therefore important to show the relationship between the two.

Dimensions of Product Quality

Viewing quality from a strategic perspective, David Garvin identified eight dimensions of product quality, each different from the other and each important to customers. This frame-

[1] *The American Heritage® Dictionary of the English Language,* 4th ed. (Boston: Houghton Mifflin, 2000).

work permits managers and workers to think about and discuss the elements of quality in more precise terms. Firms can then focus on the dimensions that are especially important to the markets they serve. These eight dimensions are (*a*) performance, (*b*) features, (*c*) reliability, (*d*) durability, (*e*) conformance, (*f*) serviceability, (*g*) aesthetics, and (*h*) perceived quality.[2]

Performance

Performance quality relates to a product's primary operating characteristics and can be objectively measured along some scale. For example, performance quality for a computer is related to the computing speed and the memory capability. For a car, performance can be defined by acceleration ("zero to 60 in 4.5 seconds") or gas mileage.

Features

Features are a product's "bells and whistles," the secondary characteristics or options that supplement or enhance a product's basic function. The Internet keys and key "action" on your computer's keyboard, the heated seats, the moon-roof and sound system in your car, and the easy-lace eyelets on your new boots are examples of features. Although they are not the primary operating characteristics of the product, they are important to customers, and individual customers determine *which* features are important to them.

Reliability

Reliability is defined as the probability of a product's malfunctioning or failing within a specified time. Some measures of reliability are mean time to first failure (MTFF), mean time between failures (MTBF), and failures per unit of time. Reliability is very important, especially for goods that are expected to last a long time, because downtime and maintenance become more expensive. For example, a car's reliability is determined by how often it needs repairs. Good examples of products with high reliability are Sears' Diehard battery and Maytag kitchen appliances.

Durability

Durability is a measure of a product's life: how long a product lasts before it must be replaced. A washing machine that lasts for 15 years is more durable than a washing machine that lasts for only 10. Durability can also be measured in units other than time. For example, the measure of durability of automobile tires is the number of miles they can be driven before they need to be replaced. The measure of durability for a lightbulb is the number of hours it can be expected to produce light before it burns out.

Conformance

Conformance quality is the degree to which a product's design and operating characteristics meet established standards or specifications. For example, if a car radio is ordered with certain physical dimensions so that it can fit into a dashboard, the radio must conform to those specifications: it can be neither too large nor too small. Process control and statistical sampling techniques are used to assure high levels of conformance quality.

Serviceability

Serviceability is related to the ease of repair of a product. For example, when you buy a new car, you will probably be concerned about how easy it will be to get to the dealership for ongoing service. From the product design perspective, serviceability relates to how easy it is to access the working elements of the product when repairs are necessary. Serviceability also relates to the speed, courtesy, and competence of service providers.

---

[2] D. Garvin, "Competing on the Eight Dimensions of Quality," *Harvard Business Review,* November–December 1987.

Aesthetics

Aesthetic quality is very individual and relates to sensory appeal: how a product looks, feels, smells, or sounds. The color, weave, and design of a sweater may be very appealing to one customer and not at all appealing to another; the scent of one cologne may be alluring to one customer and repelling to another. Customer differences in perception of aesthetic quality provide opportunities for small firms to focus on the sensory preferences of a particular segment, as illustrated by the rapidly growing microbrewing industry.

Perceived Quality

Perceived quality is brand image and is related to the reputation of the firm that produces the product (marketers often refer to perceived quality as brand equity). Some customers will purchase particular brands because they perceive them to be better than others. For example, a car purchaser may think, "If it's a Mercedes-Benz, it must be a good car," or a computer purchaser may think, "If I purchase a Compaq I'm likely to have fewer problems than if I purchase a no-name clone."

These quality dimensions are not completely discrete and discernible. For example, while one computer user may consider an extra-large monitor screen to be an optional feature, a graphics designer may consider an extra-large monitor to be a necessary standard operating characteristic: Some software programs may be virtually unusable without an extra-large screen. Managers need to recognize that the word *quality* incorporates many dimensions; when we talk about product quality we should be very specific about which dimension(s) we are really addressing.

Dimensions of Service Quality

Parasuraman, Berry, and Zeithaml conducted the most systematic and thorough work on quality in services. They categorized service quality into five major dimensions: (*a*) reliability, (*b*) tangibles, (*c*) responsiveness, (*d*) assurance, and (*e*) empathy.[3] Of these five dimensions, reliability is primarily concerned with the service *outcome,* whereas the other four dimensions are primarily concerned with the service *process.* However, all five dimensions emphasize the customer's perception of the service rather than the service provider's view of how the service should be delivered.

Reliability

Reliability in services is defined differently from reliability in products. In services, **reliability** relates to the ability to perform the promised service dependably and accurately. For example, are your shirts returned from the cleaners with the right amount of starch and by the date promised every time? Does your monthly checking account statement from your bank arrive on time and is it correct?

Tangibles

Tangibles are the physical aspects of a service and include the appearance of physical facilities, equipment, personnel, and communications materials. Because the service is intangible, customers often rate the quality of the service by its tangible components. For example, is the restaurant clean? Does it offer an ambience that is appropriate for its price range? Are the menus clear? Is the staff well groomed? Are servers wearing tuxedos or aprons? Tangibles are often used to demonstrate that service was provided: The car inspection tag on the rear view mirror in a rental car indicates that the car has been inspected,

---

[3] A. Parasuraman, L. L. Berry, and V. A. Zeithaml, *Understanding, Measuring, and Improving Service Quality: Findings from a Multiphase Research Program* (New York: The Free Press, 1990).

and the chocolates on the pillow in the hotel room show that an employee has performed the turndown service.

Responsiveness

Responsiveness is the willingness of service providers both to help customers and to provide prompt service. For example, does someone answer the customer service line for your credit card company quickly? Is the customer service representative helpful when you ask questions?

Assurance

Assurance relates to the knowledge and courtesy of employees and their ability to convey trust and confidence. For example, does your accountant ask questions and provide answers that make you confident that he is up-to-date on tax laws and deductions? Or when you ask questions, does he or she seem uncertain about the answers?

Empathy

Empathy is the ability to show caring, individualized attention to customers. For example, do you feel like just one more customer when you go to your hair salon, or does the stylist make you feel that he or she is concerned about what you want and how you feel about the haircut?

The Evolution of Quality Thinking

Every organization that wants to be successful needs to care about what its customers want. Quality has always mattered and will always matter. However, the systematic study of quality began in earnest during World War II, when it was necessary to produce reliable goods, particularly vehicles and weapons, quickly. To provide a background on how quality has evolved, we introduce some key elements of quality management and the theorists who developed them.

The Challenge of Variation

Variation, which is inherent in every process, is what makes managing every process difficult. Even if processes could be developed that always performed exactly the same way, factors change and new factors are introduced. The importance of variation in processes was first recognized by Walter A. Shewhart, a statistician at Bell Laboratories who studied randomness in industrial processes. He developed a system that permitted workers to determine whether the variability of a process was random or caused by specific factors that could be identified (called assignable causes). If a process exhibited only random variation, it was considered to be "in control"; if a process exhibited nonrandom variation, it was considered to be "out of control," and the cause for the variation had then to be identified and addressed for the process to be brought back into control.

All processes vary, and it is the variation that makes them challenging to manage. Think of it: If all customers always wanted the same things and all workers were always able to provide exactly what customers wanted, managing service delivery would be easy. But customers don't all want the same things, and workers are not equally capable. Tastes vary. Circumstances vary. Demand varies. Even service times vary for the same worker. Because of variation, even a seemingly simple system can become very complex to manage.

Understanding variation is central to being able to manage services well—perhaps even more so than in manufacturing environments because many services require the customer to participate in the service, and because each individual customer is different from every other customer. Even in the most mundane services—the ticket window at a movie theater, for example—the individuality of each customer affects the service environment. Some customers go to the window, ask for some number of tickets for a particular film, pay in cash, and quickly move away from the window. Others ask questions: How long will the movie last? How full is the theater? Is a particular actor in the film? Is it a good movie for children? Others fumble with their wallets or purses to find cash or a credit card. Still others are members of groups who talk among themselves at the window, trying to decide among the different movie alternatives.

The servers at the window also exhibit variability. Some are faster than others with the process. Some are more knowledgeable about movies. Some are outgoing and interact warmly with customers, which may take longer, while others are curt. And each server and each customer is not only inherently different, but is also affected by the circumstances of the day. Some feel well, others are under the weather. Some are having good days and will be satisfied with any service they give or receive, others got out of the wrong side of the bed and are ready to be dissatisfied no matter what happens in the service interaction. Additionally, each interaction between a customer and a service provider is unique.

Still other kinds of variability exist. Some days are busy, others are slow. Sometimes the variability in demand can be predicted—Saturday nights at the movies are likely to be busier than Tuesday nights—but sometimes it is more difficult. Are rainy days going to be busier because outside recreation options are more limited, or slower because people don't want to go out in the rain? Which movies will bring huge crowds and which will be box-office busts?

If variability can be so significant in a service that is as "easy" or "straightforward" as a movie theater ticket window, think of the amount of variability inherent in more individualized types of service environments like computer stores (where options are broader, there are likely to be many more technical questions, and prices are much higher), hair salons (where every person's hair and face shape is different and the skills and personalities of the stylists make a big difference in the perception of the service), and hospitals (where the services are very customized and highly emotional because they affect health and well-being, where anxiety is likely to be high, and where real risks exist).

Understanding the variability in customer needs, service capabilities, and customer demand is critically important in managing services well and consistently meeting customer needs. When some of the causes of variability are understood, the firm can improve the quality of the services provided to customers.

Management as a System

"The basic cause of sickness in American industry and resulting unemployment is failure of top management to manage."[4]

Perhaps the most famous of the quality gurus is W. Edwards Deming, who, influenced by Shewhart's work on variation, applied notions of statistical variation to industrial processes and later to U.S. production processes during World War II.

After the war, Deming worked with Japanese managers to build quality into their production processes. He was convinced not only that quality control techniques could change both the quality and the productivity of organizations, but also that top management commitment was needed to maintain a quality emphasis. His philosophy was directed specifically to managers, but he also emphasized the tools of statistical quality control and sampling.

The most central of Deming's messages is that every process must be managed as a system and that everyone involved in the process must understand his or her role within that

[4] W. E. Deming, *Out of the Crisis* (Cambridge, MA: Massachusetts Institute of Technology, Center for Advanced Engineering Study, 1984).

system. In services, this is particularly important because customers are very often part of the service system. Service workers must know the "big picture" so they can make the right decisions when they serve customers. Awareness of the customer's needs is an important part of management as a system: Workers need to be aware of the needs of their customers so that they can satisfy those needs. Customers can be either external customers, who purchase the goods or services of the firm, or internal customers, who are employees who use the output of the stage in the process that precedes theirs.

When Deming visited Boston University in 1993, he used a story to describe management as a system. As he sat on stage behind a large table, he said, "I may be the best table washer in the world, but I can't wash this table unless I know why I'm washing it. If I'm washing it so I can eat lunch here, it's clean enough! But if I'm washing it so that an operation can be performed on it, I need to use special cleansers and equipment. I need to scrub it on top and underneath. I need to wash the floor all around it. If I know why I am washing the table I can do a good job, and I can take joy in my work."

Deming's table washing story is a good service example. Every worker in a service system needs to know his or her place in the system; Deming also understood that workers want to feel good about their work.

Deming summarized his philosophy in his famous 14 points, shown in Exhibit 12.1.

Deming's 14 points all seem very straightforward the first time you read them, but the more you think about each point, the more significant it appears to be—and the more challenging! Each of the 14 points requires managers to be consistent, to be vigilant for opportunities to improve, to consider the input and knowledge of the workforce, and to establish an organizational culture that works continuously toward meeting customers' needs.

EXHIBIT 12.1   Deming's 14 Points

1. Create constancy of purpose toward improvement of product and service, with the aim to become competitive and to stay in business, and to provide jobs.
2. Adopt the new philosophy. We are in a new economic age. Western management must awaken to the challenge, must learn their responsibilities, and take on leadership for change.
3. Cease dependence on inspection to achieve quality. Eliminate the need for inspection on a mass basis by building quality into the product in the first place.
4. End the practice of awarding business on the basis of price tag. Instead, minimize total cost. Move toward a single supplier for any one item, on a long-term relationship of loyalty and trust.
5. Improve constantly and forever the system of production and service, to improve quality and productivity, and thus constantly decrease costs.
6. Institute training on the job.
7. Institute leadership. The aim of supervision should be to help people and machines and gadgets to do a better job. Supervision of management is in need of overhaul as well as supervision of production workers.
8. Drive out fear, so that everyone may work effectively for the company.
9. Break down barriers between departments. People in research, design, sales, and production must work as a team, to foresee problems of production and in use that may be encountered with the product or service.
10. Eliminate slogans, exhortations, and targets for the work force asking for zero defects and new levels of productivity. Such exhortations only create adversarial relationships, as the bulk of the causes of low quality and low productivity belong to the system and thus lie beyond the power of the work force.
11. a. Eliminate work standards (quotas) on the factory floor. Subtitute leadership.
    b. Eliminate management by objective. Eliminate management by numbers, numerical goals. Substitute leadership.
12. Remove barriers that rob people in management and in engineering of their right to pride of workmanship. This means, inter alia, abolishment of the annual merit rating and of management by objective.
13. Institute a vigorous program of education and self-improvement.
14. Put everybody in the company to work to accomplish the transformation. The transformation is everybody's job.

Armand Feigenbaum was another quality theorist concerned with quality being the job of everyone in an organization. He proposed "total quality control," stressing interdepartmental communications, particularly with respect to design control, incoming material control, and production control. The implications of Feigenbaum's approach to quality management for services are clear: Everyone in a service organization needs to understand that satisfying customers requires everyone to be involved. Since customers are so often present in service systems, totally leaving quality up to a quality control department is not an option, at least not one that is likely to lead to customer satisfaction.

Feigenbaum is president of the General Systems Company, a consulting firm in Pittsfield, Massachusetts. The Massachusetts Quality Control Award is named after him to recognize his significant contribution to the field of quality management.

The Costs Associated with Poor Quality

Mistakes in services are costly. Most of us recognize intuitively the highest cost of not meeting a customer's needs: losing the customer! But there are many other costs of poor quality, and service managers need to have a clear understanding of what they are and how to manage them.

Fundamentally, the cost of poor quality is the difference between the actual operating cost and what the operating cost would have been if there had been no errors or failures by either the systems or the staff.[5] Continuing with our earlier movie theater ticket window example, imagine that the customer ordered three tickets to *Shrek,* but the ticketer provided three tickets to *Pearl Harbor,* which was playing at the same time. The customer notices immediately and a new set of tickets is produced. It takes another minute or so to complete the transaction. The cost of the error is the extra time it took to correct the error, which can be calculated as the labor cost per ticket, and the aggravation felt by the customers, which could be mitigated by an apology and a positive attitude on the part of the ticketer but which could also negatively affect the customers' perception of the theater and their future theatre choices.

Joseph Juran introduced a framework that defined categories of quality costs because he understood that managers would pay attention to quality if they understood how costly poor quality can be. In 1951, Juran published the *Quality Control Handbook,* which first outlined his now famous cost of quality framework, which is a managerial guide for determining how much to spend on quality improvement at any one point. Fundamentally, this framework states that no matter how quality is achieved, there are associated costs. Juran described those costs in each of four categories, which are presented in Exhibit 12.2. The costs associated with preventing and finding quality problems (prevention and appraisal) can be balanced against the costs associated with the quality problems themselves (internal failures, which are quality problems that are discovered and addressed by the firm before customers are aware of them, and external failures, which are quality problems that are discovered by the customer), as shown in Exhibit 12.3. In our theater ticket example, the cost of the error was an external failure cost. A manager would be able to think about how much he or she is willing to spend on prevention (such as ticketer training or improved processes, for example) to prevent such errors.

Exhibit 12.3 clearly shows that there is an optimal quality level: a point at which it is more costly to solve a quality problem than it is to deal with the effects of the problem. But Juran would not have said that an organization should stop trying to solve its quality problems, only that the monetary decisions about how much to spend at any given time can be quantified and understood using the trade-off framework. Again, in our theater example, if ticket errors are rare, it might not be worthwhile to invest in additional training or process

---

[5] F. M. Bland, J. Maynard, and D. W. Herbert, "Quality Costing of an Administrative Process," *The TQM Magazine* ii (1999), pp. 221–30.

EXHIBIT 12.2
Categories of Quality Costs

Prevention Costs

The costs associated with preventing poor quality are usually expended before a product or service is produced. Prevention costs include the costs of:
Quality planning
- Developing the organization's quality plan
- Developing procedures
- Preparing manuals that communicate the plan and procedures

Design review
- Evaluating and modifying new product designs
- Testing new products and processes

Education and training
- On-the-job training for quality
- Training for quality in formal programs

Process control: Controlling the process to achieve fitness for use of the product or service (not for safety or for productivity)
Quality data acquisition and analysis, information systems costs
- Collecting quality data
- Running the quality system
- Analyzing data to identify problems

Quality reporting
- Summarizing quality data
- Reporting quality data to managers and workers in the firm

Improvement projects
- Developing programs for defect reduction or quality motivation
- Implementing programs

Working with suppliers before manufacture

Appraisal Costs

Appraisal costs are those that are incurred for inspection and testing to determine the condition of the product during and after its production but before it is released to the customer. These costs include:
Incoming materials inspection
- Inspecting materials upon receipt
- Inspecting materials at the source

Inspection and test (in-process and final)
- Checking the product or service at various points during its production
- Testing of new products before they are installed at the customer site (field testing)

Maintaining accuracy of test equipment: Keeping test equipment in calibration
Materials and services consumed: Using up or destroying products or services in the testing process
Evaluation of inventories: Testing products in storage to evaluate spoilage or degradation

Continued

changes. But if ticket errors are common, and customers are voicing complaints, the additional investment in prevention probably makes sense.

Because services are often produced in the presence of the customer, the most significant quality cost in services is usually external failure because customers are aware of errors as they happen in any service interaction. As managers begin to recognize the lifetime value of a customer, they also become aware of the true cost of external failures and are able to more readily justify increased efforts to reduce or eliminate problems in their service processes.

Phillip Crosby used a different approach to understanding quality costs. His notion of striving for "zero defects" arose out of his experience at the Martin Company building missiles. The Martin Company had achieved a reputation for quality, earned primarily through

EXHIBIT 12.2
Categories of Quality
Costs (Continued)

Internal Failure Costs

Internal failure costs are the costs of producing defective products or services before they reach the customer. These include:
  Scrap: Labor and materials costs associated with products or parts that must be thrown out (because they cannot be repaired or used)
  Rework: Correcting defectives to make them fit for use
  Retest: Reinspecting and retesting products that have been reworked
  Downtime: Idle equipment time associated with defective products
  (for example, the time the machine is off-line because defective output is being investigated for root cause)
  Yield losses: Overfilling of containers
  Disposition
  • Reviewing defective materials
  • Deciding what to do with defective materials

External Failure Costs

External failure costs are incurred when defective products or services are received by customers. These are generally quite difficult to quantify well and tend to be underestimated. External failure costs include:
  Complaint adjustment: Investigating and addressing customer complaints about defective products or services
  Returned material: Receiving and replacing returned products
  Warranty charges: Serving customers according to warranty agreements
  Allowances: Price reductions offered to customers to induce them to accept products that are substandard or defective
  Loss of future business
  Lawsuits

J. M. Juran, *Quality Control Handbook* (New York: McGraw-Hill, 1951).

EXHIBIT 12.3
The Cost of Quality
Framework

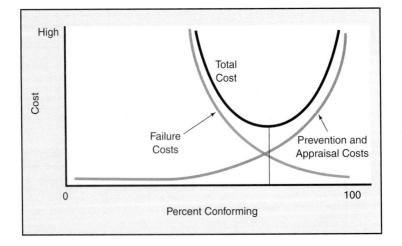

massive inspection. At one point, however, a Pershing missile was promised to Cape Canaveral (on a tight timeline) with no defects. Knowing there would be no time for the usual inspection process, management asked workers to do it right the first time—and they did! Crosby celebrated the concept in his book *Zero Defects,* which emphasizes quality awareness, motivation, and employee recognition. Crosby's definition of quality is conformance to specifications, and he says that although it is not a gift, quality is free. Like Juran, Crosby emphasizes the cost of failure and proposes eliminating those costs by producing the good or service without defects so there is no need for rework and no possibility that customers will be dissatisfied. Again, the significance of this notion for services is clear: when the customer is present in the service interaction, the customer *will* know when the service is not delivered correctly and the organization will incur unnecessary costs.

Another quality theorist, Genichi Taguchi, was concerned with the cost of quality not only to the firm, but also to society. He pointed out not only the cost to the firm that produces and delivers a defective product, but also the cost to the firm that accepts it, the customer that receives it, and on and on. This philosophical perspective offers a view of how much is really lost when products fail to meet specifications, and it "ups the stakes" for managers and workers who are concerned with the quality of their products and services.

The implications for services of the cost to society notion are clear. Many service workers, particularly those who are on the front lines interacting with customers every day, are not highly paid and their jobs may not be prestigious. But knowing what is important to customers can be highly motivating for service workers. For example, the clerks who file X-rays in the basement of Children's Hospital in Boston have very low absenteeism and turnover, and they care about making sure that each and every document is properly labeled and filed so that it can be quickly found when needed. When asked why they care so much about their jobs, they respond, "We do it for the kids. We know that physicians need the X-ray information we file to treat sick children, so our job is an important part of caring for them." These clerks are not directly involved with caring for the sick children, but they understand that their work is a critical part of the overall process, and they understand that society pays a price when their work is not done correctly.

Despite what is theorized and what is known about quality costs in services, research in this area has been mixed on whether expenditures on service quality can be linked to profits. There are a number of reasons investments in quality cannot be easily linked to profits. First, many other factors besides quality affect profits, including advertising, changes in the economy, and competition. Second, investing in the right quality improvements is important, in contrast to spending on quality in general. Finally, the relationship is not a short-term one; the effects of investment in quality are likely to add up over time. Other recent studies have demonstrated a direct relationship between quality improvement and the market value of firms[6] and overall corporate performance.[7]

Assessing Quality

Every decision about quality should be based on data. Therefore, how data are analyzed and depicted is important if the data are to be useful for decision making. Kaoru Ishikawa developed many problem-solving tools for quality management, among them the cause-and-effect, or "fishbone," diagram. Ishikawa was very specific about the role of managers and their focus within the organization. He believed that the first concern of any company should be the happiness of people who are connected with it. If the people do not feel happy and cannot be made happy, the company does not deserve to exist. He thought that employees deserve to have an adequate income and to have their humanity respected, and they also deserve the opportunity to enjoy their work and lead a happy life. Furthermore, Ishikawa believed that consumers deserve to be satisfied and pleased when they buy and use goods and services and that shareholders deserve to earn a profit on their investment. Ishikawa understood that if workers are happy and satisfied in their jobs, they are more likely to be able to satisfy their customers and if customers are more satisfied, the firm will be more profitable and better positioned for long-term success.

[6] K. B. Hendricks and V. R. Singhal, "Does Implementing an Effective TQM Program Actually Improve Operating Performance: Empirical Evidence from Firms That Have Won Quality Awards," *Management Science* 44, no. 9 (1997), pp. 1258–74.

[7] G. S. Easton and S. L. Jarrell, "The Effects of Total Quality Management on Corporate Performance," *Journal of Business* 71 (April 1998), pp. 253–308.

Implications for Service Quality

While each of the major quality theorists has made specific contributions to the way we think about and manage product quality, they are more alike than different. At heart, the quality theorists discussed here all emphasize the basic tenets of what has come to be known as total quality management, or TQM—top management commitment, worker involvement and empowerment, management by data, and customer focus—but each had a particular perspective. Ishikawa, Garvin, and Feigenbaum emphasized the importance of total organizational involvement in quality and the strategic role that quality can play. Garvin and Parasuraman, Zeithaml and Berry systematized the quality vocabulary; Taguchi focused on both quality control and quality costs; Deming focused on leadership commitment and quality control. Crosby focused on leadership commitment and cost, and Juran emphasized cost as the way to get management's attention. Exhibit 12.4 shows the key elements of quality management and where the quality theorists focused their individual efforts.

These basic tenets are the foundation upon which service quality frameworks have been built. But there are some fundamental differences between product quality and service quality.

EXHIBIT 12.4
Quality Theory: Putting It All Together

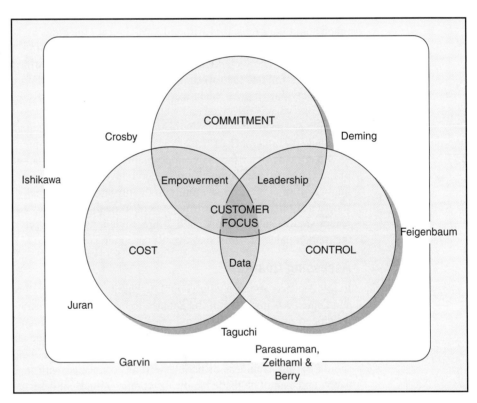

Defining Service Quality

Technical versus Functional Quality

In service operations, as in manufacturing operations, it is important to distinguish between **technical quality,** which relates to the core element of the service, and **functional quality,** which relates to the customers' perception of *how* the service is delivered. For example, the appropriateness of the medical treatment ordered by a physician for a patient's ailment is a measure of the technical quality of the care. The physician's "bedside manner"—how empathetic he or she is, how well he or she listens and explains, how much care he or she takes to make the patient comfortable both physically and psychologically—is a measure of the functional quality of the care.

Customers can readily assess functional quality because it relates primarily to their interaction with the service providers. Technical quality, however, may not be something that customers can properly assess because they do not have the technical knowledge to do so. For example, unless customers know a great deal about auto repair, they can be uncertain about whether a mechanic has appropriately identified and solved their car problems. Similarly, most of us who are not trained in dentistry are unable to tell whether our dentists know a cavity in a tooth from a hole in the wall! To compensate for not having the knowledge required to assess technical quality, customers will often adopt other measures that they hope are objective to help them make those assessments. For example, when we evaluate the quality of physicians, we may consider where they trained, how much experience they have, and whether they are certified by a specialty board. When we evaluate an MBA program, we may look at whether the school is accredited and what percentage of faculty hold doctoral degrees as measures of technical quality. The inability of most customers to assess technical quality in service operations makes functional quality all the more important. Good service managers address both aspects of quality.

Expectations and Perceptions

Another approach to defining quality in services is to measure how satisfied the customer is with the service result. Customers' satisfaction with service is related to both their prior expectations about the service and their perceptions of how well the service was provided. Customers develop a certain set of expectations based on a variety of inputs. They consider their previous experiences with services in general and with each specific kind of service they have encountered. For example, you might have expectations about service in a retail clothing store that gives you some sense of what you should expect when you speak with a service provider on the phone, as well as when you are served in another retail clothing store. Customers also develop expectations when they hear about services from others. If you hear that your friend was delighted with her stay at a particular hotel, you're more likely to expect that same level of service if you stay there. Customers also form expectations based on a service provider's advertisements and promotions. Promises of positive service bring in customers, but a promise isn't enough. Customers will be satisfied only if the service meets or exceeds their expectations. For example, if a restaurant advertises that you will be served your lunch in 15 minutes or less, you are likely to be satisfied if it is served in 12 minutes, but dissatisfied if it is served in 18 minutes.

However, the customer's satisfaction with the service performance is also affected by the customer's perceptions of the quality of service. As a result, the relationship between satisfaction, the perception of service performance, and expectations can be described in the following equation:

$$\text{Satisfaction} = (\text{Perception of performance}) - (\text{Expectation})$$

Customers will be satisfied when their perceptions of performance exceed their expectations, and they will be more likely to return in the future. This equation suggests there are two ways to increase satisfaction: improve the customers' perceptions of performance or decrease their expectations. But what happens to expectations for the next service encounter when satisfaction is high? It is likely that the customer will expect that same high level of service again, thereby raising the stakes for the service provider.

This equation is therefore a dynamic one: Each encounter affects customer expectations for the next encounter, so managing both performance and expectations is important for continuously achieving high levels of customer satisfaction. Before managers can think about managing service performance, however, they must understand what service quality is. What is it that their customers really want, and how can their needs be consistently met?

Identifying Service Quality Problems

There is usually more than one possible cause for service quality problems. We have already defined customer satisfaction as the gap between expected and perceived service. Parasuraman, Berry, and Zeithaml developed the service quality gap model, which is presented in Exhibit 12.5. This model identifies the possible gaps between elements in the design and delivery of services that can ultimately affect the relationship between expected and perceived service.[8] As Exhibit 12.5 shows, the gap between expected and perceived service is denoted as gap 5. Gap 5 is directly related to the four other gaps identified in the model.

Gap 1 is the difference between the customer's expectations and management's perceptions of those expectations. One key factor contributing to gap 1 is inadequate use of marketing research within the service firm. This could mean that (a) the firm does not do enough market research, (b) it doesn't consider the market research findings when making important decisions, or (c) there is a lack of interaction between management and customers. For example, the medical staff in an emergency room may believe that patients and their families expect not to wait for services. Because zero waiting time may not be possible, they may assume there is nothing that they can do to improve patient/family satisfaction with their waits. Most patients and families do expect to wait in emergency rooms, especially if it is evident that others have needs more urgent than theirs. They also expect clear communication about what is happening, when they can expect to be seen, and what will happen while they are there. Failure to understand these expectations can result in failure to provide what the customers really want.

Gap 2 results from managers' inabilities to translate their understanding of customer expectations into specific target levels of service quality. This might happen for many reasons. It could be that managers are not really committed to service quality, or that they believe achieving high levels of customer satisfaction is impossible. Gap 2 also occurs when

[8] Parasuraman, Berry, and Zeithaml, *Understanding, Measuring, and Improving Service Quality.*

EXHIBIT 12.5   **The Service Quality Gap Model**

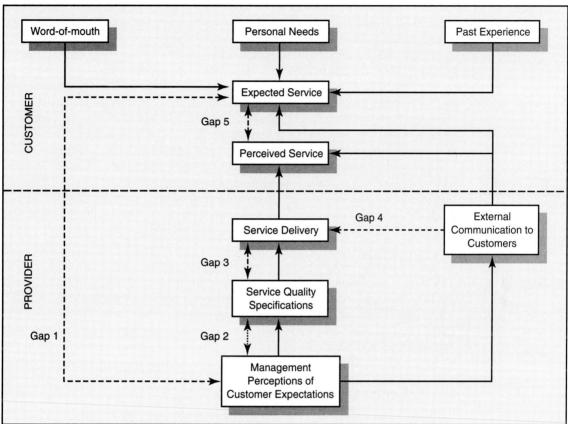

tasks are not standardized, so that the delivery of satisfactory service may vary according to who is providing the service. For example, when you go to a fine-dining restaurant, you may find that one server may be attentive and thoughtful and interacts positively, while another server, although he takes your order correctly, is curt or condescending in his attitude. The service provided is therefore inconsistent and, as a result, the customers' experiences can be dramatically different.

Gap 3 is also called the service performance gap because the actual delivery of the service does not meet the specifications set by management. This can result when employees have not been adequately trained to understand their roles, or when they experience a conflict within their roles. It can also result when employees are not rewarded for their performance, or when employees fail to work together to accomplish the service goals. An example would be the retail clerk who was trained to greet customers when they enter the store, but fails to do so, perhaps because the training was not reinforced or because some customers reacted negatively to the greeting.

Gap 4 is defined as the difference between the service actually delivered and what is communicated to customers about the service. This gap occurs when there is inadequate communication between functions in the service system, particularly between marketing and operations, or when there are different policies at different branches of an operation. This gap also occurs when the organization overpromises to customers and simply cannot deliver on those promises. For example, if a fast-food restaurant states in its ads that the menu can be customized ("have it your way") but servers react negatively to requests to make changes in the basic product, customers are likely to be less satisfied than if they were never led to believe that customization was possible. The same is true for a retail tire company that promises to install your tires in less than an hour, but very often takes longer.

Gap 5, the gap between expected and perceived service, is clearly related to the four other gaps, each of which contributes both to the customer's perception of the service's performance and to the way expectations about future service develop.

The service quality gap model provides a framework for focusing on customer needs and the elements that need to be managed to consistently meet those needs. To deliver good service, it is important to have effective and capable people in the customer contact positions. To keep costs low, however, many service firms are willing to tolerate some level of employee dissatisfaction, which leads to high absenteeism and high turnover, which ultimately produces lower levels of service and customer satisfaction. Leonard Schlesinger and James Heskett have called this self-perpetuating phenomenon the cycle of failure.[9] As the cycle progresses, the service firm experiences continuing deterioration of service quality. In the long term, these firms experience declines in sales and profits.

Recognizing Quality: Certification and Awards

This chapter has described many challenges customers have in defining quality. Customers can have more confidence in the quality of the goods and services produced by firms when a third party assesses the firm's processes and outputs. The third-party assessment can be in the form of either certifications or awards. Quality certification and award programs have also increased the recognition of the importance of quality and established some consistency regarding quality between companies and even between countries.

Quality Certification

Certification typically verifies that an organization has met some baseline set of standards in either its processes or its outcomes. One type of certification with which we are all familiar is the diploma: We rely on high school diplomas, college degrees, graduate degrees, and professional degrees to verify that the individuals that hold them have met some basic standards of knowledge and capability. For example, we expect that a medical school degree and a specialty certificate in internal medicine mean that a physician is qualified to diagnose and treat our health problems. Similarly, we expect that accreditation from the Joint Commission on the Accreditation of Healthcare Organizations (JCAHO) means that a hospital has met basic procedural standards.

ISO 9000

Most industries have their own certification processes, but there are so many of them and the standards so different, particularly across national borders, that the certifications can be confusing. One certification process, ISO 9000, has attempted to standardize the certification of processes in all types of organizations and between countries. For example, Ryder, a world leader in transportation and logistics, has been ISO certified since 1993 and now has certified operations in Brazil, Canada, England, Mexico, and the United States. Today, it has achieved 100 percent compliance for all its automotive clients.

ISO 9000 certification has been a significant factor in the European business community for years, and it is increasingly becoming a necessary qualification for firms throughout North America.

---

[9] L. A. Schlesinger and J. L. Heskett, "Breaking the Cycle of Failure in Services," *Sloan Management Review* 32, no. 3 (Spring 1991), pp. 17–29.

During the 1980s and into the 1990s, organizations around the world became more concerned about efficiently and effectively meeting the needs of their customers. Increasing international trade made universal standards for quality more important, but until 1987 there was no standardized way for supplier organizations around the world to demonstrate their quality practices or to improve the quality of their manufacturing or service processes. In that year, the International Organization for Standardization (ISO) published its first standards for quality management.

The International Organization for Standardization ISO, headquartered in Geneva, Switzerland, is made up of representatives from each of the national standards bodies from over 90 countries. ISO and the International Electrotechnical Commission (IEC), both nongovernmental organizations, work together to develop and publish voluntary standards, introducing as many as 800 new and revised standards each year. In 1986, after several years of development, ISO Technical Committee 176 completed the ISO 9000 series quality standards. It immediately became apparent that the ISO 9000 standards were different from the usual engineering standards, which often related to units of measure, standardization of terminology, and methods of testing. These new standards incorporated the belief that management practice can be standardized to the benefit of both the producers of goods and services and their customers.

The ISO 9000 Series of Standards The purpose of the ISO 9000 standards is to satisfy the customer organizations' quality assurance requirements and to increase the level of confidence of the customer organizations in their suppliers. The first major revisions to the ISO 9000 standards were completed in December 2000 with the issuance of the following three new standards that replaced the previously existing standards:[10]

- *ISO 9001:2000—Quality Management Systems—Requirements.* This standard is used to demonstrate the conformity of a quality management system to meet the requirements of customers and third parties and certifies a firm's quality management systems.

- *ISO 9004:2000—Quality Management Systems—Guidelines for Performance Improvement.* This standard provides guidelines that can be used to establish a quality management system that is focused not only on meeting customer requirements but also on improving performance.

- *ISO 9000:2000—Quality Management Systems—Fundamentals and Standards.* This standard provides the terminology and definitions used in the first two standards.

ISO 9000 standards played a particularly important role in the formation of the European Union because they promoted a single worldwide quality standard that would foster international trade and cooperation. Before long, organizations recognized that service management also could be improved through the application of the fundamentals of management practice that were set forth in the ISO 9000 standards.

Toward a Global Market Today, over 40,000 companies are ISO certified, with the vast majority of them located within the 12 nations that currently make up the European Union. When customer organizations have an objective way to evaluate the quality of a supplier's processes, the risk of doing business with that supplier is significantly reduced. When quality standards are truly standardized around the world, customer firms can be more confident that supplier firms will produce the goods and services that will satisfy their needs.

[10] John E. West, "Implementing ISO 9001:2000," *Quality Progress,* May 2001, pp. 65–70.

The ISO 9000 standards have been important enablers of the European Community and of the development of worldwide markets. When customer organizations have an objective way to evaluate the quality of a supplier's processes, the risk of doing business is reduced. When quality standards are truly standardized around the world, customer firms can be more confident that supplier firms will produce the goods and services that will satisfy their needs.

Quality Awards

Another way for customers to get a third-party evaluation of quality is to see which organizations have won awards. Like certifications, there are a plethora of awards in every industry and for every type of product or service. In the United States, the Malcolm Baldrige National Quality Award was designed to recognize quality processes and outcomes across all industries and in all sectors of the economy.

The Malcolm Baldrige National Quality Award

On August 20, 1987, President Ronald Reagan signed Public Law 100-107, commonly called the Malcolm Baldrige National Quality Improvement Act. This groundbreaking legislation established an annual award to recognize total quality management in U.S. industry. The Malcolm Baldrige National Quality Award (MBNQA), named after the secretary of commerce who served from 1981 until his death in 1987, represents the U.S. government's endorsement of quality as an essential part of successful business strategy.

By establishing the MBNQA, Congress sought to encourage greater U.S. competitiveness in global markets through the recognition and commendation of exceptional quality in American business. The MBNQA seeks to:

1. Stimulate companies to improve quality and productivity for the pride of recognition while obtaining a competitive advantage through decreased costs and increased profits.

2. Establish guidelines and criteria that can be used by business, industrial, governmental, and other organizations to evaluate their quality improvement efforts.

3. Recognize the achievements of companies that improve the quality of their goods and services and make them examples for others.

4. Provide guidance for other American organizations that wish to learn how to manage for high quality by making available detailed information on how winning organizations were able to change their cultures and achieve quality eminence.

Without question, the MBNQA and its criteria have had a considerable impact. The MBNQA is awarded in five categories: manufacturing, service, small business, health care, and education. Exhibit 12.6 lists the MBNQA winners in services.

EXHIBIT 12.6
Malcolm Baldrige National Quality Award Winners in Services

Year	Winner
2000	Operations Management International, Inc.
1999	The Ritz-Carlton Hotel Company, L.L.C.
1997	Merrill Lynch Credit Corporation
	Xerox Business Services
1996	Dana Commercial Credit Corporation
1994	AT&T Consumer Communications Services
	GTE Directories Corporation
1992	AT&T Universal Card Services
	The Ritz-Carlton Hotel Company
1990	Federal Express Corporation

The Baldrige Criteria   To evaluate and recognize effective quality systems, Baldrige administrators created a comprehensive review process and a set of quality criteria based on the comments and observations of experts throughout the country. The Baldrige criteria are designed to be flexible, evaluating quality on three broad dimensions: (1) the soundness of the approach or systems, (2) the deployment or integration of those systems throughout the organization, and (3) the results generated by those systems.

Since the award's inception, the criteria have been revised and simplified to capture the key elements of process quality. The criteria are organized into seven broad topical areas (see Exhibit 12.7) that are dynamically interrelated (see Exhibit 12.8).

The Baldrige criteria create an integrated set of indicators of excellence. In the Baldrige view, total quality is a value system. It is a way of life, an approach to doing business that affects every corporate decision and permeates the entire organization.

When a company applies for the Baldrige award or uses the Baldrige criteria internally to evaluate its quality program, it must address 16 subcategories, each weighted according to importance. A maximum of 1,000 points can be earned, about half allocated to quality processes and about half to quality outcomes. The processes should be leading indicators of the results that will be achieved. In turn, the results verify that the appropriate processes are in place and are being used effectively.

Application of the Baldrige Quality Criteria   As a practical tool for assessing an organization's operations, the Baldrige guidelines can be used:

EXHIBIT 12.7
The Malcolm Baldrige National Quality Award Criteria

2001 Categories		Point Values
1. Leadership		120
1.1 Organizational leadership	80	
1.2 Public responsibility and citizenship	40	
2. Strategic planning		85
2.1 Strategy development	40	
2.2 Strategy deployment	45	
3. Customer and market focus		85
3.1 Customer and market knowledge	40	
3.2 Customer relationships and satisfaction	45	
4. Information and analysis		90
4.1 Measurement and analysis of organizational performance	50	
4.2 Information management	40	
5. Human resource focus		85
5.1 Work systems	35	
5.2 Employee education, training, and development	25	
5.3 Employee well-being and satisfaction	25	
6. Process management		85
6.1 Product and service processes	45	
6.2 Business processes	25	
6.3 Support processes	15	
7. Business results		450
7.1 Customer-focused results	125	
7.2 Financial and market results	125	
7.3 Human resource results	80	
7.4 Organizational effectiveness results	120	
Total		1,000

EXHIBIT 12.8
Baldrige Award Criteria Framework: A Systems Perspective

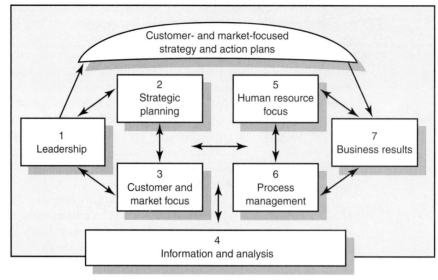

Source: 2002 Criteria for Performance Excellence, U.S. Department of Commerce, National Institute of Standards and Technology, p. 5.

1. To help define and design a total quality system.

2. To evaluate ongoing internal relationships among departments, divisions, and functional units within an organization.

3. To assess and assist outside suppliers of goods and services to the company.

4. To assess customer satisfaction.

Companies in the early stages of quality management development can use the Baldrige criteria as a checklist for getting started. Middle-stage companies can use the criteria as a road map for continued improvement. Companies that are advanced in their management of quality can use the criteria as a tool to help them fine-tune their quality programs.

The Baldrige criteria also provide a common language for discussion of quality within or across organizations. Better communication about quality can lead to a shared understanding of quality that can be built into the organization's goals and policies and that can be a foundation for the organization's value system. So deeply does Motorola care about the value of total quality control that it ordered all its 2,500 suppliers to apply for the Baldrige award as evidence of their commitment to total quality management—or lose Motorola's business.

Award Process   The Baldrige applications are scored by quality experts from business, consulting, and academia. Of the 1,000 points that can be earned, none of the applicants has received higher than a 751, awarded in 1994. A good company usually earns points in the 500 range.

Only about 10 percent of MBNQA applicants become finalists and receive site visits from a team of examiners. From this group of finalists, winners are chosen. All companies that apply for the award receive feedback from the examiners' written reports, an important element in the MBNQA's commitment to quality improvement in all organizations.

The Impact of Technology

Technology has made it possible for organizations to easily collect data about their customers' needs and how well they are being met. The Ritz-Carlton Hotel customizes ser-

Using Technology to Create Value

The Ritz-Carlton Hotel Company

You've had a long trip. When you arrive at your hotel, you're greeted with a welcoming smile and an efficient check-in procedure. As the desk clerk hands you your key, he says, "Thank you for staying at the Ritz-Carlton, Mr. Miller. You'll find two extra-firm pillows in your room and an additional blanket. Would you like me to send up a bottle of Chardonnay?" While you're delighted by the personalized service, you're not really surprised; after all, the Ritz-Carlton is renowned for "going the extra mile" to satisfy customers.

The Ritz-Carlton Hotel Company is the only two-time recipient of the Malcolm Baldrige National Quality Award in the service category. One reason why it continues to provide excellent service quality is that it has established a measurement system to chart progress toward its goal of elimination of all customer problems, no matter how minor.

To cultivate customer loyalty, the Ritz-Carlton has instituted an approach of "customer customization," which relies on extensive data gathering and capitalizes on the capabilities of advanced information technology. Information gathered during various types of customer contacts, such as responses to service requests by overnight guests or post-event reviews conducted with meeting planners, is entered into a database, which holds information about almost a million customers. Accessible to all Ritz-Carlton hotels worldwide, the database enables hotel staff to anticipate the needs of returning guests and to initiate steps that will help to ensure a high-quality experience.

The Ritz-Carlton also uses its database to continuously improve performance. The company employs a well-documented and systematic method for collecting and analyzing data and establishes standards for all processes. It also analyzes each process carefully to determine where problems are likely to occur so they can be prevented. Analysis has shown there are 970 opportunities for a problem to arise in interactions with overnight guests and 1,071 during interactions with meeting event planners!

The Ritz-Carlton's commitment to quality has paid off. Both meeting planners and overnight guests report levels of satisfaction higher than for any competitor. Financial performance is also increasing. Most financial measures of performance have nearly doubled since 1995, and revenue per available room continues to grow, exceeding the industry average by more than 300 percent.

Source: http://www.nist.gov/public_affairs/bald99/ritz.htm.

vices for its customers by maintaining a worldwide database. The 85-year-old Stop & Shop grocery chain, which has more than 275 stores in New England, New York, and New Jersey, provides scan cards that track customer purchases and produce customized coupons based on purchasing preferences. As an incentive to use the card, Stop & Shop customers receive discounts on purchases when the card is presented. In addition, customers are told on their receipts how much they have saved year-to-date from using the card. Companies now collect data on hits to various pages of their websites and Web transaction data to get a sense of what customers want.

Technologies are evolving rapidly, enabling companies to collect huge amounts of data about their customers, but many companies have not learned how to turn that data into information that can help them make decisions that produce the results they want.[11] What is still vitally important is *thinking* about the data. Thinking about what is important and what needs to be monitored enables the next step, which is analyzing the data and converting it into useful information that can be used as the basis for sound decision making.

Technology has unquestionably helped organizations to understand how their customers define quality and what dimensions of quality are important to them. Successful service organizations will learn how to connect their people with the information so that the quality of their services really can be a strategic advantage.

[11] Thomas H. Davenport, Jeanne G. Harris, David W. De Long, and Alvin L. Jacobson, "Data to Knowledge to Results: Building an Analytic Capability," *California Management Review* 43, no. 2 (Winter 2001), pp. 117–38, and Lawrence A. Crosby and Sheree L. Johnson, "Customer Relationship Management," *Marketing Management* 9, no. 3, p. 4.

Summary

Quality will always matter to customers, so it should be a high priority for every service manager. Service quality is particularly challenging to manage because so much of the evaluation of service quality is subjective, varying substantially from customer to customer. Service quality also has many dimensions and is affected by the variation inherent in service demand, in service delivery, and in customers. Theorists have approached quality management from a number of perspectives, including a focus on quality as an effect of how a system is managed and on the costs of poor quality.

Customers will be satisfied when their perceptions of performance exceed their expectations. The service quality gap model identifies five possible gaps between elements in the design and delivery of services that can affect the relationship between expected and perceived service.

Quality awards and certification processes have also provided frameworks managers can use to understand and manage quality in their organizations. Technology has enabled managers to track quality data and to focus on the dimensions of quality that are important to their customers.

Key Terms

assurance: the knowledge and courtesy of employees and their ability to convey trust and confidence. *(p. 299)*

empathy: the provision of caring, individualized attention to customers. *(p. 299)*

functional quality: the customer's perception of the service, involving, in large part, the interaction between the customer and the service provider. *(p. 306)*

reliability: the ability to perform the promised service dependably and accurately. *(p. 298)*

responsiveness: the willingness to help customers and to provide prompt service. *(p. 299)*

tangibles: the appearance of physical facilities, equipment, personnel, and communications materials. *(p. 298)*

technical quality: the quality of the service rendered from the perspective of experts in the area; difficult for customers to assess. *(p. 306)*

Review and Discussion Questions

1. What are the costs to the firm of poor quality? How are quality costs in service environments likely to be different from quality costs in manufacturing environments?

2. As a manager of a service organization, how would you use the notion of "management as a system"?

3. Define the difference between functional and technical quality. Why is this distinction important to managers?

4. How does the theory that developed from product quality relate to service quality?

5. What are the five potential gaps in service quality? What actions should a manager take to minimize each gap?

Internet Assignment

1. Go to your favorite Internet browser and enter the keywords *service quality*. You'll find many different kinds of URLs.
   - Identify at least two URLs for sites that advertise quality assessment or training services. Find out what services they offer and in what industries or sectors.
   - Identify at least two URLs for sites that update thinking about defining or measuring quality. Are they related to any of the theorists discussed in this chapter?

2. Enter the keywords *cost of quality*. What kinds of sites come up?

3. Enter the name of at least one of the quality theorists highlighted in this chapter. What can you find about his or her work?

CASE   Jose's Authentic Mexican Restaurant

"Two bean tacos, a chicken burrito grandé, and a side order of Spanish rice please," Ivan called his table's order into the kitchen as he prepared the beverage order. Business was brisk. Ivan liked it that way. Lots of customers meant lots of tips and, as a struggling graduate student, he greatly appreciated the extra income. Lately, however, Ivan's tip revenue had been decreasing.

Jose's is a small, 58-seat restaurant that offers a reasonably broad range of Mexican food prepared and presented in a traditional Mexican style. It is located in New England in a mature business district on the margin of a large metropolitan area. The site is on a central artery and offers limited free off-street parking. The restaurant's interior decoration promotes the Mexican theme: The walls appear to be made of adobe and are draped with serapes, the furniture is Spanish-Mexican style, and flamenco guitar music plays in the background.

Patrons enter the restaurant through a small vestibule that opens directly into the dining area; there is no separate waiting area. Upon arrival, they are greeted by a hostess and either seated directly or informed of the expected wait. Seating at Jose's is usually immediate except for Friday and Saturday nights when waits of up to 45 minutes can be encountered. Because there is very limited space inside for waiting, patrons must remain outside until their party is called. Jose's does not take reservations.

When patrons are seated, the hostess distributes the menus, fills the glasses with water, and, if standards are being met, the waiter assigned to the table greets the patrons within one minute of being seated. (As this is a traditional Mexican restaurant, all servers are male.) When meeting the table, the waiter introduces himself, announces the daily specials, and takes the beverage order. When the beverages are delivered, the meal order is obtained.

The menu consists of 23 main entrées that are assembled primarily from eight basic ingredients (chicken, beef, beans, rice, corn tortillas, flour tortillas, tomatoes, and lettuce). Before the dining hours begin, the cook prepares the basic items so that they can be quickly combined and finished to complete the requested meals. The typical time to complete a meal once it is ordered is 12 minutes. Since a good portion of this is final cooking time, several meals can be in the preparation process at once. As can be imagined, a good cook needs to be able to schedule the production of the various meals ordered at a table so that they are ready at approximately the same time. Once all the meals and any side dishes are completed by the cook, the waiter checks to see that all meals are correct and are pleasing to the eye, corrects any mistakes, and adds any finishing touches. When everything is in order, he assembles

them on a tray and delivers them to the table. From this point on, it is the waiter's duty to keep an eye on the table to detect when any additional service or assistance is needed.

When the diners at the table appear to be substantially finished with their main meal, the waiter approaches, asks if he can clear away any dishes, and takes any requests for dessert and/or coffee. When the entire meal is completed, the waiter presents the bill and shortly thereafter collects payment. Jose's accepts cash or major credit cards but no checks.

Ivan believes that his relationship with the cook is quite important. Since the cook largely controls the quality of the food, Ivan wants to stay on good terms with him. He treats the cook with respect, tries to place the items on his order slip in the sequence of longest preparation time, and makes sure to write clearly so that the orders are easy to read. Although it is not his job, he helps by fetching food from the refrigerator or the storage area when the cook is busy and by doing some of the food preparation himself.

The cook has been irritable lately, complaining of the poor quality of some ingredients. Last week, for example, he received lettuce that appeared wilted, and chicken that was tough and more bone than meat. During peak times, it can take more than 20 minutes to get good meals delivered to the table.

Ivan had been shown the results of a customer survey that management conducted last Friday and Saturday during the evening mealtime. The table below shows a summary of the responses received.

Customer Survey Results

Were you seated promptly?	Yes 70	No 13
Was your waiter satisfactory?	Yes 73	No 10
Were you served in a reasonable time?	Yes 58	No 25
Was your food enjoyable?	Yes 72	No 11
Was your dining experience worth the cost?	Yes 67	No 16

As Ivan carried the tray of drinks to his table, he wondered if the recent decline in tips was due to anything he was able to control.

Questions

1. How should quality be defined at this restaurant?

2. What are the restaurant's costs of poor quality?

Source: This case was prepared by Larry Meile, Boston College, as a basis for classroom discussion. Copyright Larry Meile.

Selected Bibliography

American Society for Quality Control. *Quality Costs—What and How.* 2nd ed. (Milwaukee: American Society for Quality Control), 1971.

Bland, F. M., J. Maynard, and D. W. Herbert. "Quality Costing of an Administrative Process." *The TQM Magazine* ii (1999), pp. 221–30.

Crosby, Lawrence A., and Sheree L. Johnson. "Customer Relationship Management." *Marketing Management* 9, no. 3, p. 4.

Crosby, P. B. *Quality Is Free.* New York: Mentor/New American Library, 1979.

Davenport, Thomas H., Jeanne G. Harris, David W. De Long, and Alvin L. Jacobson. "Data to Knowledge to Results: Building an Analytic Capability." *California Management Review,* Winter 2001, pp. 117–38.

Deming, W. E. *Out of the Crisis.* Cambridge, MA: Massachusetts Institute of Technology, Center for Advanced Engineering Study, 1984.

Deming, W. E. *Quality, Productivity, and Competitive Position.* Cambridge, MA: Massachusetts Institute of Technology, Center for Advanced Engineering Study, 1982.

Easton, G. S., and S. L. Jarrell. "The Effects of Total Quality Management on Corporate Performance." *Journal of Business* 71 (April 1998), pp. 253–308.

Feigenbaum, A. *Total Quality Control.* New York: McGraw-Hill, 1961.

Garvin, D. *Managing Quality.* New York: The Free Press, 1988.

Garvin, D. "Competing on the Eight Dimensions of Quality." *Harvard Business Review,* November–December 1987, pp. 101–109.

Greising, D. "Quality—How to Make It Pay." *Business Week,* August 8, 1994, pp. 54–59.

Hendricks, K. B., and V. R. Singhal. "Does Implementing an Effective TQM Program Actually Improve Operating Performance: Empirical Evidence from Firms That Have Won Quality Awards." *Management Science* 44, no. 9 (1997), pp. 1258–74.

Ishikawa, K. "How to Apply Companywide Quality Control in Foreign Countries." *Quality Progress,* September 1989.

Ishikawa, K. *What Is Total Quality Control? The Japanese Way.* Englewood Cliffs, NJ: Prentice Hall, 1985.

Juran, J. M. *Juran on Planning for Quality.* New York: The Free Press, 1988.

Juran, J. M. *Quality Control Handbook.* New York: McGraw-Hill, 1951.

Juran, J. M., and F. M. Gryna. *Quality Planning and Analysis.* New York: McGraw-Hill, 1980.

Parasuraman, A., L. L. Berry, and V. A. Zeithaml. *Understanding, Measuring, and Improving Service Quality: Findings from a Multiphase Research Program.* New York: The Free Press, 1990.

Schlesinger, L. A., and J. L. Heskett. "Breaking the Cycle of Failure in Services." *Sloan Management Review* 32, no. 3 (Spring 1991), pp. 17–29.

Schlesinger, L. A., and J. L. Heskett. "The Service Driven Service Company." *Harvard Business Review,* September–October 1991.

Taguchi, G. *Introduction to Quality Engineering: Designing Quality into Products and Processes.* Tokyo: Asian Productivity Organization, 1986.

Taguchi, G., and D. Clausing. "Robust Quality." *Harvard Business Review,* January–February 1990.

Walton, M. *The Deming Management Method.* New York: Putnam Publishing Group, 1986.

Zahorik, A. J., and R. T. Rust. "Modeling the Impact of Service Quality on Profitability: A Review." In *Advances in Service Quality and Management,* vol. 1. Ed. Terry Schwartz. Greenwich, CT: JAI, 1992.

Zeithaml, V. "Service Quality, Profitability, and the Economic Worth of Customers: What We Know and What We Need to Learn." *The Academy of Marketing Science Journal* 28, no. 1 (Winter 2000), pp. 67–85.

Quality Control Tools for Process Improvement

Learning Objectives

- Introduce the basic tools for analyzing processes and quality.

- Describe acceptance sampling and when it can be used to control quality in services.

- Introduce statistical process control and describe how and when it can be used to analyze service processes.

- Define the types of sampling errors that can occur when statistical sampling is used.

- Distinguish between the statistical analysis of attributes and of variables.

Six Sigma at GE Card Services

The General Electric Company, under the leadership of CEO Jack Welch, adopted the Six Sigma quality program in 1995 and has achieved significant improvement in all its divisions. The GE Card Services division was formed in 1932 to provide consumer financing for GE appliances. GE Card Services now provides credit services to retailers and consumers, serves more than 70 million cardholders, and has grown to over $18 billion in assets. Six Sigma has enabled GE Card Services to reduce telephone waiting times, improve operators' interactions with customers, and ensure that bills and payments are correct. Each year, the division receives 36 million phone calls; each day, it sends out 1.1 million bills and receives 850,000 payments.

According to Robert Binnie, GE Card Services senior vice president of quality, GE spent $600 million in 2001 to train employees in Six Sigma quality and achieved some amazing improvements, such as reduction in operator turnover rate from 45 percent per year to 25 percent per year. Overall, the benefits to GE in 2001 from Six Sigma initiatives were estimated to be $3.4 billion.

Source: www.ge.com, and Richard Lee, "Six Sigma Fills Gaps in GE's Customer Service," *The Advocate,* June 13, 2002.

Managerial Issues

Managers need to be concerned about quality because customers are concerned about quality, but being "concerned" is not enough. To improve quality, data must be gathered and analyzed so that opportunities for improving quality can be identified and decisions can be made about what actions to take.

Many managers fall into the trap of believing that they don't need data, that they already understand all there is to know about their business. Other managers collect large amounts of data and may even perform a variety of analyses, but then file both the data and the analyses away, never to be seen or used again. Effective managers, on the other hand, understand that it is critical to regularly collect data about the organization and its performance. But just collecting data is not enough. Careful analysis transforms raw data into information that can be used for making decisions that will make the process more effective or efficient.

The Seven Basic Quality Tools

Managers can use a number of tools to collect, depict, and analyze data about any kind of processes, including service processes. Many of the tools are simple and straightforward to use. Among these are the seven basic quality tools: (*a*) process flow diagrams, (*b*) check sheets, (*c*) histograms/bar charts, (*d*) Pareto charts, (*e*) scatter plots, (*f*) run charts, and (*g*) cause-and-effect diagrams. Other tools, such as statistical process control, require a basic understanding of statistics to use them to their greatest advantage. Whatever tools are used, the goal is always to provide managers with insight so they can make better decisions about how to design and improve process performance.

EXHIBIT 12S.1 **Process Flow Diagram: Dry-Cleaning Service**

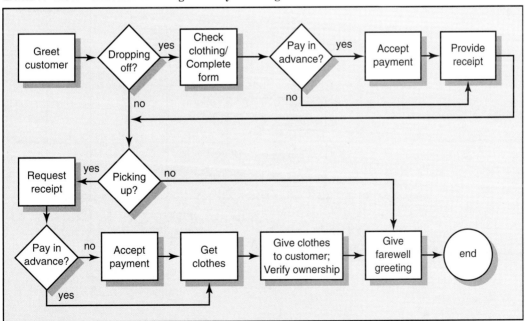

Process Flow Diagram

Process flow diagrams, or flowcharts, depict each of the steps that are required to produce either a good or a service. As presented in Chapter 11, tasks in a process flow diagram are typically depicted as rectangles, waits or inventories as inverted triangles, and decision points as diamonds. Arrows connecting these activities show the direction of flow in the process. As we saw in Chapter 7, in service operations flowcharts are often referred to as "service blueprints."

There is an element of creativity in constructing a process flow diagram, but the goal is always to clearly depict the steps in the process, their relation to each other, and where the decision points occur. Sometimes it is also useful to show other information. The process flow diagram in Exhibit 12S.2, for example, shows the many handoffs among the staff in a college graduate admissions department. Showing which staff members perform each task provides insight into how people and roles affect the applications review process.

EXHIBIT 12S.2   **Process Flow Diagram: Graduate Admissions Process**

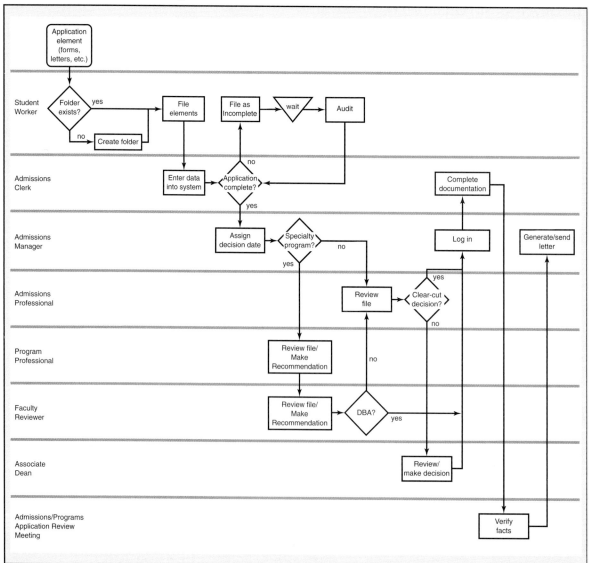

Check Sheets

Most of us have collected data on some process by noting the time an event occurs and making a tick mark for a particular category in a check sheet. For example, as a hotel manager, you may want to collect information about the types of calls taken at the front desk so that you can determine how to train new clerks more effectively. To collect the data, you might ask the clerks to identify the types of calls they take during a shift, as shown in Exhibit 12S.3.

In check sheets, categories should not overlap and all categories should be identified and listed; in other words, categories should be *mutually exclusive* and *collectively exhaustive.* An example of a confusing check sheet in a restaurant would be one that, instead of listing party size, listed "couples, families, and groups of friends." These categories don't capture all possibilities (business groups, for example, might not fit into any of those categories) and it is likely that the categories would overlap (families with friends). In addition, different people collecting the data might make different decisions about which category to place a particular party in. As a result, the data, when finally collected, might not be very useful.

Bar Charts and Histograms

Bar charts and histograms are two tools that visually display data variation. A bar chart is used to graph nominal data (also called *categorical* or *attribute* data), which are data that can be categorized and counted, rather than measured. For example, one can count the number of customers from various countries at a popular college-area lunch spot, as shown in Exhibit 12S.4.

Histograms, rather than bar charts, are used to display continuous data, that is, data that can be measured. For example, one can measure the length of time it takes a restaurant's

EXHIBIT 12S.3
Check Sheet

Call Type	Count
Location question	ⅢⅠ
Rate question	卌 卌 卌 卌 Ⅲ
Complaint	卌 卌 Ⅱ
Reservation	卌 卌 卌 卌 卌 卌 Ⅰ
Service question	卌 卌 卌
Guest call	卌 Ⅱ
Other	Ⅱ

EXHIBIT 12S.4
Example of a Bar Chart

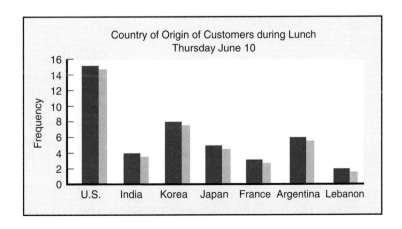

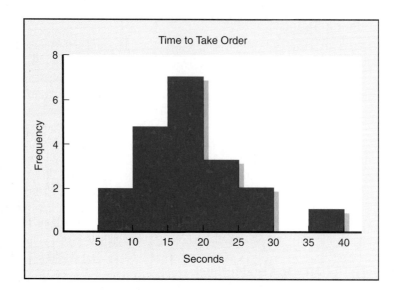

staff to take a meal order. Because the scale for time is continuous, we first need to determine how to divide the time scale into intervals to show the variation in length of time for a number of customers. For example, we could use intervals of 1 minute, 5 minutes, or 10 minutes, depending on how much detail we wanted to show and how much variation in waiting time there is in our sample. Histogram intervals (which are also referred to as *buckets* or *bins*) must all be the same size and must not overlap. Exhibit 12S.5 provides an example of a histogram that shows how long it takes to take an order. The histogram uses five-second intervals. It is easy to see that most orders are taken in 15 to 20 seconds, but some orders take more or less time.

Pareto Charts

Pareto charts are specialized bar charts in which the frequency of occurrence of items is sorted in descending order. A cumulative percent line is typically added to make it easy to determine how the categories add up. Pareto charts are useful for establishing priorities for action, focusing attention on the categories of variables that occur most frequently.

Exhibit 12S.6 illustrates a Pareto chart that shows the responses to an internal hospital survey about what factors needed to be changed in emergency room processes.

There are times, however, when the frequency of occurrence by itself does not determine how important a factor might be. For example, when making a bar chart of student complaints about a university food service, it might be known that complaints about waiting in line are twice as common as complaints about food availability, but that students consider food availability to be five times more important than waiting. In this case, the Pareto diagram weights the factors being considered to enable managers to take action on those items that most need attention. Exhibit 12S.7A shows the weights FedEx uses for delivery-related problems in a large region for the month of July 2002.[1] The weights indicate the relative importance of each error type. Problems that are likely to be most important to customers, such as lost or damaged packages, are weighted most heavily.

Exhibit 12S.7B shows the Pareto chart using unweighted problem frequencies. Exhibit 12S.7C shows the Pareto chart when the weights of the problems are considered. The rel-

---

[1] The weights are those actually used by FedEx; the frequency values are disguised.

EXHIBIT 12S.6
Example of a Pareto Chart

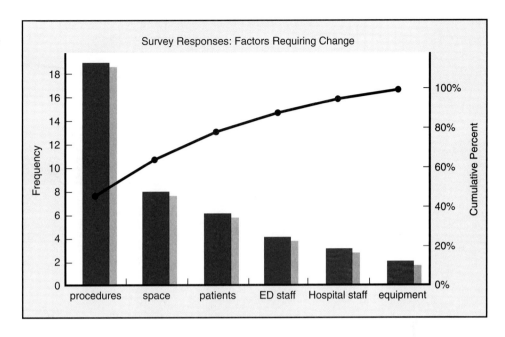

EXHIBIT 12S.7A
Fedex Weights for Delivery Problems: Region Four, July 2002

Weight	Item	Occurrence	Occurrence × Weight
50	Lost package	1	50
30	Damaged package	1	30
10	Overnight wrong day late	2	20
10	Other wrong day late	2	20
3	Traces	5	15
10	International priority inbound wrong day late	1	10
10	Complaint reopened	1	10
3	Late pickup stops	3	9
3	Package not cleared for international destination	2	6
1	Abandoned calls	4	4
1	Domestic right day late	2	2
1	Missing proof of delivery	2	2
1	International right day late	1	1
1	Invoice adjustment	1	1

ative weights for the delivery problems result in different Pareto charts. The priority for process improvement action would be very different if the data are depicted using the weighted frequencies rather than using only the frequencies.

Scatter Plots

Scatter plots show the relationship between two measured (not counted) variables. For example, as a manager in an upscale restaurant, you may want to understand the relationship between how long customers wait to have their orders taken and how satisfied they are with their service. You could measure the waiting time before ordering in minutes and you could assess customer satisfaction on a scale of 1 to 10. It is likely that you would see a relationship like the one shown in Exhibit 12S.8: Customers are less satisfied when waits are either too short or too long. If the wait is too short, customers may feel that they do not have enough time to

EXHIBIT 12S.7B
Pareto Chart of Fedex Delivery Problems, by Frequency

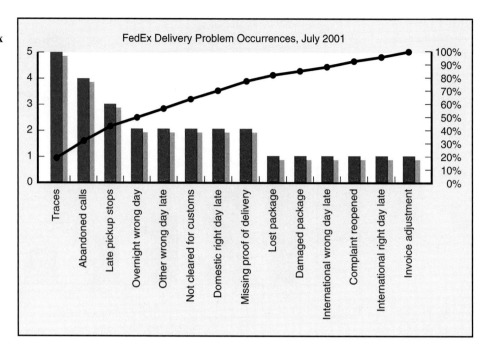

EXHIBIT 12S.7C
Pareto Chart of Fedex Delivery Problems, by Weighted Frequency

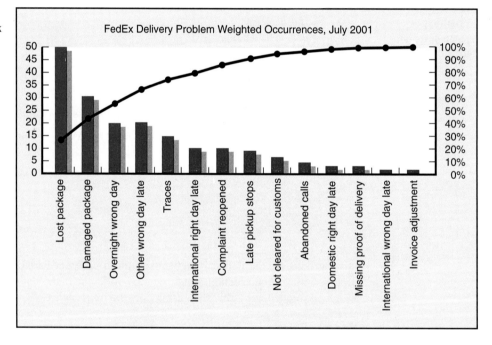

study the menu and make a decision about what they want to order; if the wait is too long, they may be frustrated with the lack of responsiveness of the service staff.

Run Charts

Run charts show the behavior of a variable over time. Continuing with the restaurant example, as a manager you also want to study how the pre-seating waiting time varies through the evening. You could record the time a party enters the restaurant and the time the party

EXHIBIT 12S.8
Example of a Scatter Plot

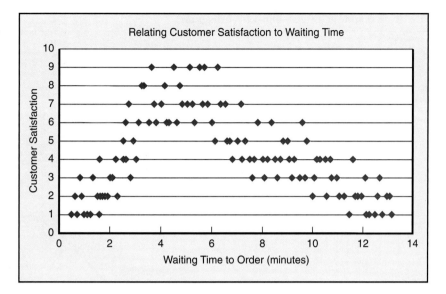

EXHIBIT 12S.9
Example of a Run Chart

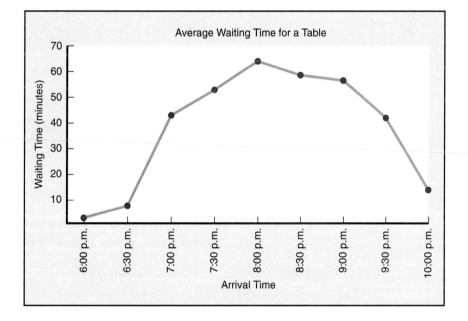

is seated and plot the average waiting time on a run chart in half-hour increments as shown in Exhibit 12S.9. The run chart shows that at 6:00 P.M. there is no wait for a table, but, as more customers arrive, the wait increases. As the dinner hour passes, the wait decreases.

Cause-and-Effect Diagrams

Cause-and-effect or fishbone diagrams (also called Ishikawa diagrams, after their inventor) are used to identify the causes that lead to a particular outcome or effect. Major categories of causes are identified, then for each cause, "why?" is asked until the root cause for that category can be identified. Consider Exhibit 12S.10, a cause-and-effect diagram for customer dissatisfaction with the experience in a restaurant. In the major cause "server attitude," there are several possible subcauses. If customers complain about server rudeness,

EXHIBIT 12S.10   **Example of a Cause-and-Effect Diagram**

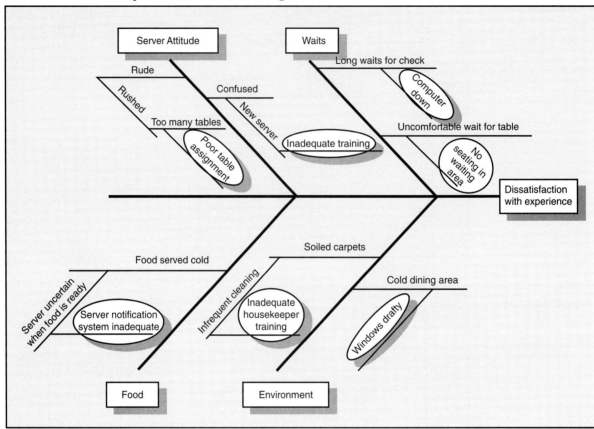

the cause of the rudeness must be discovered before any action can be taken. In this example, servers are rude because they are rushed, and they are rushed because they are assigned too many tables. The table assignment process, therefore, should be the target of managerial action, rather than admonishing servers to be more polite.

Relationships between the Basic Quality Tools

Organizations that focus on quality use the quality tools in combination to collect and depict data and to identify root causes for problems, to collect further data, and to identify new causes and so on. Exhibit 12S.11 illustrates an eight-step quality improvement process, patterned on the plan/do/check/act cycle developed by Walter Shewhart and popularized by W. Edwards Deming (see Chapter 12 for a discussion of their contributions to quality theory).

Once a problem has been identified, for example, customer dissatisfaction with a service, data on customer complaints may be collected using a check sheet. The next step would be to depict the data using a bar chart to show the frequency of different complaint types. The bar chart may be sorted using an importance weighting, becoming a Pareto chart that can help to prioritize the action to be taken. The manager may convene a staff meeting to discuss the causes for the most important complaints, producing a fishbone diagram. The staff may then work together to develop a new flowchart for the improved process. After the solution has been implemented, more data should be collected to determine whether the problem has been solved. After review of the new data, additional im-

EXHIBIT 12S.11
The Eight-Step
Quality Improvement
Process

PDCA	#	Step/Description	Tools
P l a n	1	Identify the Problem	
	2	Collect Data Analyze the Problem	Check Sheets
	3	Analyze the Problem	Scatterplots Pareto Charts Histograms/Bar Charts Flowcharts Run Charts
	4	Identify Root Causes	Cause-and-Effect Diagrams
	5	Develop a Solution and Action Plan	Flowcharts
D o	6	Implement the Solution	
C h e c k	7	Review and Evaluate	Scatter Plots Pareto Charts Histograms Flowcharts Run Charts Control Charts
A c t	8	Standardize the Process	Flowcharts Control Charts

provements may be made and the process can be standardized. After the process is improved, the whole cycle begins again, resulting in a continuous improvement cycle.

Data may, of course, be collected in different ways. Customer surveys and interviews, electronic data collection tools, and direct observation may be used to collect data about processes in a service organization. Which tools managers decide to use to depict the data depends on the nature of the data and what they want to learn. For example, if the data collected pertain to customer waits on the telephone at a call center, the data could be presented in a histogram that shows the variation in waits overall or plotted on a run chart, which would provide information about how the waits were distributed over time.

Using the data to make improvements is important. Data become information that can guide decision making only when the data are thoughtfully analyzed and used. The visual depiction of the data using the seven basic quality tools tends to lead to more questions. Why is there a spike in waiting time at 4:00 P.M. every day at the call center? Why are customers complaining about the ticket process at the aquarium? How important is a lost roll of film at the film processing center versus prints that were finished in three hours when two-hour processing was promised?

Statistical Quality Control

Chapter 12 emphasized the strategic importance of quality for service organizations. To assure that the goods and services produced are meeting customer needs, a firm must regularly assess those goods and services. One way to do this is to evaluate every single good or service produced. Total, or 100 percent, inspection can be justified in situations when the cost of having *any* bad output is greater than the cost of the inspections. This could be true for services for which there are life-and-death consequences of failure (such as major surgery), but it can also be true for more mundane services if the total cost of inspection is lower than the total cost associated with having customers receive defective services.

Philips Medical Systems Collects Information on Patients with Congestive Heart Failure

Philips Medical Systems uses technology to provide data to healthcare providers on their patients with congestive heart failure. Patients enrolled in the service receive and are taught to use the Patient Measurement set, which may include a blood pressure unit, a scale with safety handles, and a heart rhythm strip recorder. Each day, patients use the equipment as instructed, and the findings are sent immediately to their care providers.

When clinicians log on to the system, they find up-to-date information on their patients' vital signs, heart rhythm, blood pressure, and weight. Clinicians are able to review trends and produce reports that show a patient's progress over time. If the clinical data indicate that the clinician should contact the patient, telephone and address information, stored in the system, are immediately available.

The results have been impressive. As their brochure states, "One program with 29 patients reduced actual emergency room visits from 17 to 3 per year, while the average hospital readmission rate went from 1.5 to .13 per year." In addition to reduced healthcare costs, patients feel safer and more confident and care providers get the information they need to make the best decisions for their patients.

But testing every service produced to assess quality is both time consuming and expensive. In many situations, it is not even possible to evaluate every single service output or interaction. For example, if every burger at your favorite fast-food restaurant was inspected for taste, there wouldn't be any burgers to sell!

However, a well-designed methodology for collecting and statistically analyzing samples of data can make it possible for firms to manage quality costs and at the same time collect the information they need to assure high-quality output and customer satisfaction. There are two basic models for statistical quality control: **acceptance sampling,** which involves testing samples after the goods or services have been produced, and **statistical process control (SPC),** which involves testing samples of goods or services as they are being produced. Both methods are used to evaluate the quality of the output of repetitive processes that produce large volumes of goods or services that have similar characteristics.

Acceptance Sampling

Acceptance sampling involves collecting samples from goods or services that have already been produced to determine whether they meet specifications. Sampling plans can be developed to evaluate either attributes, which are characteristics that are counted, or variables, which are characteristics that are measured. An acceptance sampling example for attributes in a service environment might be a grocery store that inspects a delivery of produce from its suppliers to ensure that the quality is acceptable before it is signed for and unloaded. An acceptance sampling example for variables in a service environment might be measuring the raw weight of hamburgers that are used in Quarter Pounders at McDonald's. When the hamburgers are delivered, a sample is drawn and the average weight of the sample is calculated. If the average weight of the sample is within the acceptable range, the delivery is accepted; otherwise, it is rejected. These two examples refer to *facilitating goods* in a service environment rather than the intangible services themselves. Because of the intangibility of services and the simultaneity of production and consumption of services, acceptance sampling of the service act itself is not possible.

The Sampling Plan

The purpose of a sampling plan is to provide a decision rule to determine whether a batch (called a lot) of a product should be accepted or rejected. When sampling for attributes, the sampling plan is defined by N, the size of the lot; *n*, the number of units in the sample; and *c,* the critical value or the maximum number of defective items that can be found in the sample before the lot is rejected. Values for *n* and *c* are determined by the interaction of four factors that quantify the objectives of the product's producer and consumers, as well as the trade-offs between the two.

The objective of the producer is to minimize the producer's risk, which is having the consumer reject a good lot. The probability of producer risk is expressed as a percentage that is denoted by the Greek letter alpha (α) and is called **Type I error.** A lot is defined as good if it contains no more than a specified level of defectives, termed the *acceptable quality level (AQL).* In contrast, the objective of the consumer is to minimize the consumer's risk, which is accepting a bad lot. The probability of consumer risk is expressed as a percentage that is denoted by the Greek letter beta (β) and is called **Type II error.** A lot is defined as bad if the percentage of defectives is greater than a specified level, called the *lot tolerance percent defective (LTPD).* The selection of specific values for AQL, α, LTPD, and β is based on the cost trade-offs for both the producer and consumer. Exhibit 12S.12 shows the relationships between the actual quality of the population from which the sample is drawn and the results of the sample test.

An **operating characteristic (OC) curve** shows the probability of accepting lots given the actual percentage of defective units in the lot. Each sampling plan has a unique OC curve. The simplest way to think about OC curves is that given a particular sampling plan, the curve provides the probability that a lot will be accepted (vertical axis) as a function of the defect rate (horizontal axis). In other words, the acceptance probability is based on what the actual percentage of defects in the lot is.

Consider Exhibit 12S.13. This OC curve was constructed based on a lot size (N) of 100, a sample size (*n*) of 15, a critical value (*c*) of 1, and an AQL of 2 percent. The OC curve is drawn by calculating the probability of accepting a lot for each possible number of defects in the lot. The horizontal line marked α is the probability of accepting a lot whose true percentage defective is equal to 2 percent. For this sampling plan, that probability is equal to 85 percent; therefore the probability of making a Type I error (α) is $1 - .85 = .15$. The LTPD for this example is 10 percent. The horizontal line marked β is the probability of accepting a lot whose true percentage defective is equal to 10 percent. This corresponds to a probability of 22 percent; therefore the probability of making a Type II (β) error is 22 percent. The producer and the consumer would want to balance these probabilities against the costs of different sampling plans.

The appropriate values of α and β are a function of the risk sensitivity of the producer and consumer. The producer may be subject to great expense if a lot is rejected. There may be contractual penalties, increased inspection costs, replacement costs, and other such expenses. At the same time, the consumer may be subject to higher than anticipated rework

EXHIBIT 12S.12

Relationships between Population Quality and Sample Findings

		What the Population Quality Actually Is	
		Good	**Bad**
What the Sample Finding Is	**Good**	Good Lot Accepted: No Error	Bad Lot Accepted: Type II Error or β
	Bad	Good Lot Rejected: Type I Error or α	Bad Lot Rejected: No Error

EXHIBIT 12S.13   Operating Characteristic Curve

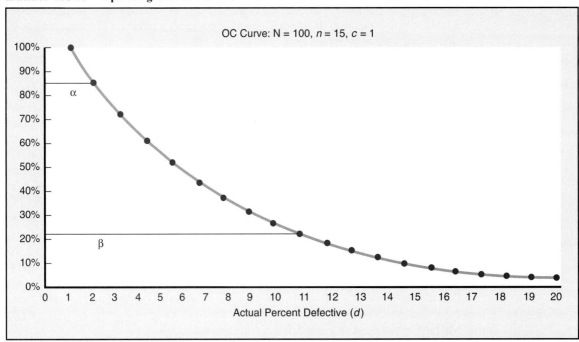

OC Curve: N = 100, n = 15, c = 1

Actual Percent Defective (d)

costs and many of the same costs experienced by the producer. Because the risks are different for each sampling plan, one way to determine the risk is to enumerate all possible sampling plans. This is a tiresome process unless the user has some idea what the relationships are between α, β, and the sampling parameters N, n, and c.

For a given sample size n, as c gets larger there is a higher probability of acceptance, which makes sense, because as the number of defectives permissible in the sample increases, more lots will be accepted. Also not surprisingly, for a given c, as the sample size n increases, the probability of making a Type I error increases and the probability of making a Type II error decreases.

Statistical Process Control

Statistical process control (SPC) is a quantitative method for monitoring an ongoing repetitive process to determine whether the process is operating as it is expected to operate, that is, it is *in control.* SPC uses process data collected and analyzed in real time and compares current measures to baseline process performance measures. It then applies simple statistical techniques to determine whether or not the process has changed. SPC allows management and workers to distinguish between random fluctuations inherent in the process and variation that might indicate that the process has changed.

At its core, SPC is about understanding process variation. Every process varies in a way that is characteristic of that process. Some processes vary a great deal, some vary only slightly, but a careful analysis of the inherent variation in a given process makes it possible to compare current performance with the way the process is *expected* to perform based on past performance.

For example, every month, a financial services manager wants to monitor customer satisfaction with the services provided. From a monthly sample of 200 customers, the manager determines that the service is rated as "very good" or "excellent" 90 percent of the time, on average. Every month, however, the sample does not show exactly a 90 percent rating of "very good/excellent." The manager has noticed that the "very good/excellent" rating varies from about 84 percent to about 96 percent, but within that range, she has not been able to discover what drives the variation.

She has noticed, however, that there are specific instances when customer satisfaction levels change. When the firm hires new financial counselors who are tentative about financial options because they are in training, the satisfaction level may be significantly lower. Also, when the firm introduces a new financial product that is difficult to explain to customers, the manager may see the same thing—customers' satisfaction with the service may be significantly lower, on average, than the 90 percent that would normally be expected.

This simple example illustrates the difference between inherent, random variation in a particular process and nonrandom, or *assignable,* causes of variation. Assignable causes can usually be categorized as relating to the worker, to the equipment being used, or to the materials being used, as identified in a fishbone diagram.

Sampling in SPC

SPC uses statistics—in particular, the power of sampling—to refine this basic understanding of variation in processes. The **central limit theorem** states that no matter what the shape of a distribution, when samples of a given size are drawn from that distribution, the sample means will be normally distributed when plotted on a graph. (If you are not convinced of this, think about a deck of cards. If each of the cards takes its face value (an ace = 1, numbered cards take their number value, a jack = 11, a queen = 12, and a king = 13), the deck represents a uniform distribution of cards: there are four of each value. The overall average value of a card in a deck would be seven. If you draw samples of size four from the deck, how many combinations of cards will have a mean value of one? It can only happen one way—four aces—and it will be a very rare sample that contains four aces. How many combinations of cards will have a mean value of 13? Again, only four kings will produce that sample mean, so that outcome will be very rare. On the other hand, think of how many ways a sample mean of seven could be produced: four sevens, three sixes and one nine, and so on in many different combinations. If you shuffle the deck, draw a sample, calculate its mean, plot the sample mean on a graph, reshuffle the deck and begin again, you will find that your sample mean distribution will quickly take on the shape of a bell curve, rather than the uniform flat shape of the underlying distribution of cards in the deck.)

What about distributions other than the uniform? Does the central limit theorem still hold true? Yes! You can do the same experiment again with cards, assigning the value of 4 to all red cards and 10 to all black cards, simulating a bimodal distribution, still with an overall or grand mean of 7. Draw samples as before, calculate the mean value of each sample, plot the means on a graph, and the graph will shortly begin to look bell-shaped, or similar to the normal distribution. Of course, the larger the sample size, the smoother the curve will be.

The Normal Distribution

If the distribution of sample means is normal, we can use the well-understood properties of the normal distribution to understand variation in processes. For example, as illustrated in Exhibit 12S.14, we know that if we have a normal distribution:

- The distribution is symmetrical about its mean (that is, bilaterally symmetrical).

- 68.26 percent of the distribution lies between plus and minus one standard deviation from the mean.

EXHIBIT 12S.14
The Normal Distribution

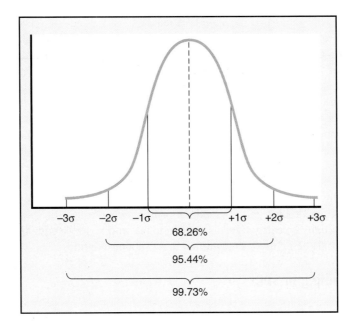

EXHIBIT 12S.15
Normal Distribution with the Same Mean but Different Standard Deviations

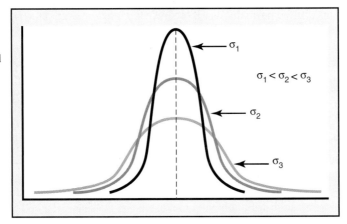

- 95.44 percent of the distribution lies between plus and minus two standard deviations from the mean.

- 99.73 percent of the distribution lies between plus and minus three standard deviations from the mean.

A normal distribution is defined by two parameters: the mean (depicted by the Greek letter mu, μ), or average of the distribution, and the standard deviation (depicted by the Greek letter sigma, σ), a measure of the distribution's spread or variation. Exhibit 12S.15 shows three normal distributions with the same mean but different standard deviations.

If we plot the means of successive samples drawn from a process whose long-run pattern of variation is known, we can look at the pattern of the sample means and decide whether the process is behaving the way we expect it to behave, or whether it has changed.

Statistical control means that a process is exhibiting only its inherent random variation and not signs of "assignable," or nonrandom, variation. Statistical control does *not* mean that a process is producing goods or services that are good or bad. Whether the output of a process is good or bad is determined by the customer, who provides the specifications for the product or service. In other words, it is very possible to have a process that is statistically in control, but nevertheless produces goods or services that are unacceptable to customers.

Process Capability

Before SPC can be properly implemented, a process capability study should be undertaken to determine whether the process can produce what the customer requires, given the inherent variation in the process. The purpose of the process capability study is to compare the inherent variation of the process to the customer's requirements (the specifications). A study involves two basic steps:

1. Collect data on the process while the process is operating without known causes of variation. For example, you would not collect data to understand how long it takes to serve customers in a restaurant during a week when three of its seven servers were just hired and are in training. Rather, you would collect data when the staffing is stable. Using these data, calculate the long-run mean and standard deviation of the process.

2. Compare the customer's requirements to the inherent variation of the process. If the customer's specifications fall within the three standard deviation points for the process, we can conclude that for some predictable percentage of the time, the process will produce output that will not meet the customer's needs.

For example, you hire a neighborhood teenager, Pat, to chop wood for your fireplace, and your specifications state that you want the pieces of wood to be 12 inches long, on average. Your fireplace can accommodate a piece of wood that is 18 inches long and you would prefer to have no pieces shorter than 6 inches because they're harder to stack. Your specifications, then, are pieces of wood that are 12 inches long, ± 6 inches.

Pat chops a stack of wood and you look at the variation in the output and compare it to your specifications. The first graph (A) in Exhibit 12S.16 shows a process that is capable: the output of the process is consistently within the customer's specifications. The second

EXHIBIT 12S.16   Capability Study

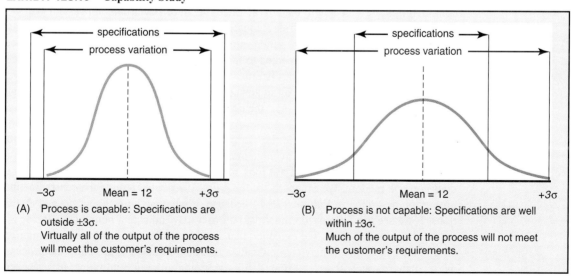

(A)   Process is capable: Specifications are outside ±3σ.
Virtually all of the output of the process will meet the customer's requirements.

(B)   Process is not capable: Specifications are well within ±3σ.
Much of the output of the process will not meet the customer's requirements.

EXHIBIT 12S.17
Six Sigma Quality

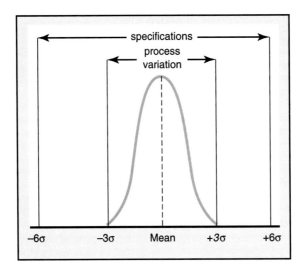

graph (B) shows a process that is not capable; some of the output of the process is outside the customer's specifications when the process varies as it inherently does.

If the process is capable of meeting the customer's needs, the process can begin to produce the goods or services for the customer and use SPC to monitor the process.

If a process is not capable, the only way to discover when the customer's requirements are not being met is to inspect all the output. Six Sigma quality programs, described in Chapter 13, are based on the notion that the variation in a process should be so much less than what a customer requires that the specifications are as far out as ± 6 standard deviations from the mean (see Exhibit 12S.17). With Six Sigma quality, a process would have to be wildly out of control to produce services that did not meet customer requirements.

SPC Charts

SPC charts are specialized run charts based on the central limit theorem. The mean value for the process is calculated (from past performance), and, for the sample size being used, control limits are calculated, usually at three standard deviations above and below the mean, because plus and minus three standard deviations from the mean value encompasses 99.73 percent of the distribution. When samples are drawn from the output of the process, the means of the samples are expected to fall between plus and minus three standard deviations. The x axis of the SPC chart is time; the y axis is the variation from the mean value for the process. The center line of an attribute chart is the long-run average for that attribute (such as percent defective), and the center line of a variables chart is the target value for the process.

For each sample, we calculate the sample mean (either the percentage of an attribute that occurs in the sample or the average measured value) and plot that point on the graph. As each sample mean is plotted, we look to see if the process is exhibiting variation that does not look random. We expect to see the points distributed around the center line in the proportion described in Exhibit 12S.14 because of what we know about normal distributions. If we see too little or too much variation, it may indicate a nonrandom factor is affecting the process. If we see evidence that the points are not distributed symmetrically around the center line, it may also indicate a nonrandom factor is affecting the process. If we see patterns such as several points in a row going up or several points in a row going

EXHIBIT 12S.18
Statistical Process
Control Chart

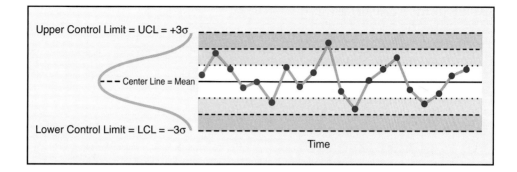

down, it may again indicate a nonrandom factor is affecting the process. When we read an SPC chart, we are looking for evidence of nonrandom behavior—that the process is behaving in a way we don't expect. Exhibit 12S.18 shows a statistical process control chart for a process that is exhibiting only random variation. Most of the points fall between ±1 standard deviation from the mean of the process (the center line), but about one-third of the points fall between +1 and +2 standard deviations or −1 and −2 standard deviations and that one point in the 20 (5 percent) falls either between +2 and +3 standard deviations or −2 and −3 standard deviations.

Because points on an SPC chart are plotted sequentially in real time as the samples are drawn, the ambiguity of "too little or too much variation" or "evidence of a nonrandom pattern" has prompted the development of some rules of thumb for interpreting control charts, which are presented in Exhibit 12S.19. These decision rules, or *heuristics,* are simply guidelines for standardizing the ways in which the variation in a control chart can be interpreted.

A process that exhibits nonrandom variation is said to be *out of control.* (*Out of control* does not mean the process is producing bad output. A process can be out of control and producing fewer defects than usual. The point here is that the process is not behaving in the way it is expected to behave given what is known about the process.) When we see evidence of nonrandom variation in a process, we look for the factors that may have caused that variation. In other words, we look for an assignable cause: changes in workers, equipment, materials, or something else.

Remember that SPC is done in real time as the services are being produced. As soon as the sample is taken, its mean is plotted and the control chart evaluated so that appropriate action can be taken. In a manufacturing environment, this means drawing samples randomly throughout the day and making sure the process has not changed. In a service environment, samples are collected in real time but may not be evaluated until the end of a service period. For example, in a restaurant, customer response cards may be collected throughout the day, but are probably not going to be reviewed and analyzed until the end of the day. In contrast, customer waiting times at a call center are tracked in real time.

As with acceptance sampling, two types of errors can be made when interpreting control charts. The first is that a process is considered to be out of control when it is really not. This type of error, as noted earlier, is a Type I error, or producer risk, because it is costly to stop a process and look for causes of variation when the variation is random. The second is that the process is considered to be in control when it is really not. As also noted earlier, this type of error is a Type II error, or consumer risk, because if an out-of-control process is not investigated, there is a chance that the process is producing output that does not meet the customer's specifications. Control limits are typically set at three standard deviations to balance the risk of Type I and Type II errors.

EXHIBIT 12S.19   **Control Chart Decision Rules**

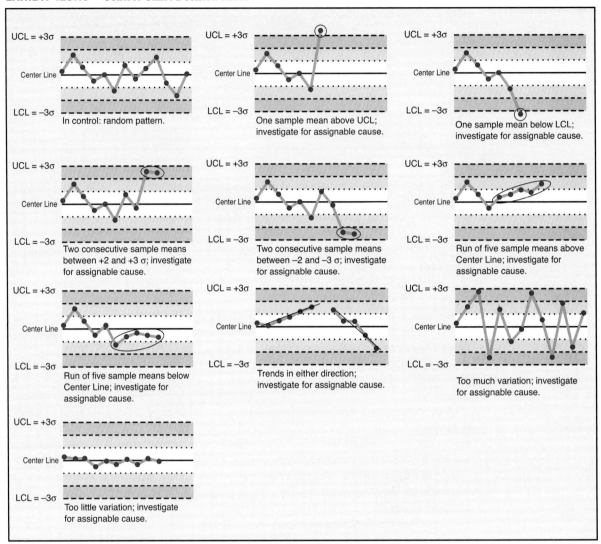

Source: Bertrand L. Hansen, *Quality Control: Theory and Applications* (Englewood Cliffs, NJ: Prentice Hall, 1963), p. 65.

As with acceptance sampling, there are two major categories of SPC: SPC using attribute measures, that is, data that are counted, and SPC using variables, that is, data that are measured. SPC using attribute data is described in the next section; SPC using variables data requires another step, which is described later in this chapter.

SPC Using Attribute Measurements

Attribute data are data that are counted, such as the number of customers in a sample who rate service as "very good" or "excellent." If we draw samples during the month, we can count, for each sample, the number of customers who rate the service as "very good" or "excellent." If the long-run percentage of customers who rate services "very good" or "excellent" is 95 percent, we can compare the percentage of those customers in each sample to that long-run percentage to see if our service process is behaving the way we expect it to behave. We expect the process to behave the way it usually behaves: 95 percent "very good" or "excellent," on average.

It is important to emphasize that a process can be in control and produce bad output. For example, if the long-run percent dissatisfaction for a particular process is 20 percent, that means 20 percent of the customers are dissatisfied! The process may continue to produce the same level of dissatisfaction—in other words, be in control—but the dissatisfaction is still dissatisfaction. On the other hand, if a process usually produces 20 percent dissatisfaction and something changes so that the process now produces only 5 percent dissatisfaction, the process is out of control, but has improved! The goal is to find the cause of any nonrandom variation and either eliminate it, if it is producing more negative output, or sustain it, if it has resulted in a process improvement.

Calculating Control Limits

The center line for an attribute chart is the long-run average for the attribute in question. Because the long-run attribute percentage is critical to the calculation of the center line and the control limits for the SPC chart, it is important to have adequate historical information about the process. For example, for a *p*-chart, or percent defective chart, the center line is *p,* the long-run average percent defective. The upper control limit and the lower control limit are set at plus and minus three standard deviations from *p*:

$$\text{Center line} \quad = \quad p \quad = \quad \frac{\text{Count of attribute}}{\text{Total count (long-run)}}$$

$$\text{Standard deviation} \quad = \quad s_p \quad = \quad \sqrt{\frac{p\,(1-p)}{n}}$$

$$\text{Upper control limit} \quad = \quad \text{UCL} \quad = \quad p + 3s_p$$

$$\text{Lower control limit} \quad = \quad \text{LCL} \quad = \quad p - 3s_p$$

If the calculated lower control limit is a negative number, zero becomes the lower control limit.

Sample Size in Attribute SPC

The size of a sample is extremely important for successful SPC implementation. If attribute data are being collected, the sample must be large enough to be able to count the attribute. For example, if we know that a service process produces, on long-run average, 5 percent dissatisfied customers, we are very unlikely to be able to answer the question "Is the process producing defects at the rate it usually does" if we have a sample of size five. The usual rule of thumb for attribute SPC is that the sample should be large enough to be able to include the attribute twice, on average. So if the dissatisfaction rate is 5 percent, the sample size would need to be at least 40 to expect to count two dissatisfied customers. Of course, since we are not looking at every unit, some samples will, by chance, have more than two dissatisfied customers, and some will have fewer than two. What we are looking for is a pattern of dissatisfaction in the samples over time to tell us whether the process is exhibiting nonrandom variation.

Variable SPC Charts Using X-bar and R Charts

Variable data are data that are measured, such as length, weight, or time. Because variable data are more specific than attribute data, smaller sample sizes can be used. However, because the data are measured, there are two ways the process can change from the expected pattern of the process: the mean can shift or the variation in the process can change, as illustrated in Exhibits 12S.20 and 12S.21. Therefore, when variable data are used for SPC, two charts must be constructed and interpreted simultaneously to be certain the question

EXHIBIT 12S.20
**Changes in Mean
and Variation
of Sample Mean
Distributions**

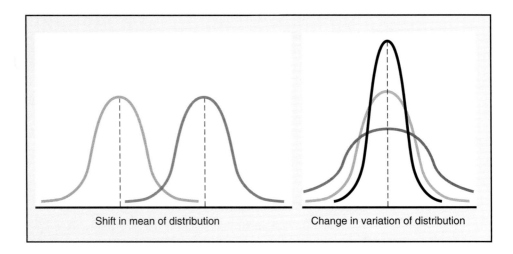

Shift in mean of distribution | Change in variation of distribution

EXHIBIT 12S.21
**X-bar and R Charts
for Variables SPC**

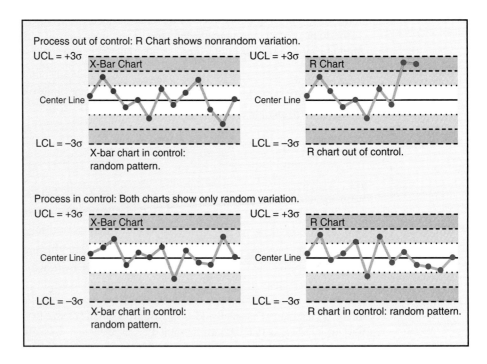

"Is the process behaving the way we expect it to behave, given what is known about the process?" can be answered.

The two charts used for variables are usually the mean chart, or $\bar{X}$ chart (pronounced "X-bar") and the range chart, or R chart. The sample mean is plotted on the $\bar{X}$ chart; the sample range (maximum value minus minimum value) is plotted on the R chart.

Summary of Acceptance Sampling and SPC

The purpose of SPC is to focus attention on process variation. If the inherent variation of a process is understood, managers and workers can watch the process to make sure that it is performing as expected. When the process exhibits nonrandom variation, the cause of the variation needs to be sought (assignable cause) and eliminated (if the process has deteriorated) or continued (if the process has improved). Because variation can easily be seen on an SPC chart, managers and workers can look for nonrandom variation and its assignable causes.

There are many opportunities to use attribute SPC in services: percentage of customer complaints, percentage of late loan application reviews, percentage of no-shows in an ambulatory medical clinic. There are fewer obvious applications for variables SPC. One possibility, you might think, would be waiting times, but it is more likely that a service system would monitor waiting times in real time and take action (adding or removing checkers in a grocery store, for example) without taking samples and plotting data.

Acceptance sampling also focuses on variation. In services, this variation is usually related to inputs such as facilitating goods. It is useful to be aware of the potential applicability of these tools in services. More detailed information on the mechanics of these tools can be found in an introductory operations management or statistics text.

The Impact of Technology

Technology has made it much easier for service managers to collect, analyze, and use data for better decision-making. Software programs can quickly construct process flow diagrams, histograms, Pareto charts, scatterplots, run charts, and even cause-and-effect diagrams. Other programs collect data in real time and automatically analyze the data. For example, telephone systems used in call centers inform service representatives and managers of how many customers are on hold, how long the average waiting time is, and how long it takes to process each call taken.

Statistical process control software is also available, eliminating the need to calculate control limits and sample means. Workers simply input sample data and the software can even apply the interpretation heuristics to assess whether the process has changed. Technology has made the collection of data so much easier that many of the sampling-based methodologies are no longer necessary because data can be collected on every service interaction. Complete information in real time provides a tremendous support for decision making.

Summary

Service managers can use a variety of tools to collect and analyze information for better decision making. The seven basic quality tools, process flow diagrams, check sheets, bar charts/histograms, Pareto charts, scatterplots, run charts, and cause-and-effect diagrams, are simple graphical depictions of data that show patterns and interactions among factors in a service process. When these tools are used in an organized framework such as the eight-step quality improvement process, the manager has a simple but effective approach for collecting data and understanding service processes and customers.

Sampling is used as the basis for acceptance sampling and statistical process control. These methods compare sample data against expected population characteristics, enabling the manager to ask whether the process has produced the expected performance characteristics. The goal of sampling methods is to reduce the cost of monitoring quality without compromising the quality itself.

Management decisions based on data should lead to better decision making and to the production of higher-quality services.

Key Terms

acceptance sampling: a statistical tool for evaluating the quality of a lot or batch of goods or services after they are produced. *(p. 330)*

central limit theorem: the means of samples will be normally distributed no matter what the shape of the underlying population distribution. *(p. 333)*

operating characteristic curve (OC) curve: shows the probability of accepting lots given the actual percentage of defective units in the lot. *(p. 331)*

statistical process control (SPC): a tool used for analyzing the output of repetitive processes in real time. *(p. 330)*

Type I error: producer risk, the risk of rejecting a good lot (in acceptance sampling) or of calling a process out of control when it is in control (in SPC). *(p. 331)*

Type II error: consumer risk, the risk of accepting a bad lot (in acceptance sampling) or of calling a process in control when it is out of control (in SPC). *(p. 331)*

Review and Discussion Questions

1. List the seven basic quality tools and describe why they are used.
2. You are the manager of a coffee shop. Lately your servers have reported lower tips than usual. What quality tools might you use to understand what might be causing this change?
3. Describe under what circumstances acceptance sampling should be used for quality management.
4. Describe under what circumstances SPC should be used for quality management.
5. Define Type I error and Type II error and explain why there is a trade-off between the two.
6. Explain what it means when a process is *in control* or *out of control.*
7. Can a process be in control and still produce output that does not meet customer requirements? Explain.

Internet Assignments

1. Go to your favorite Internet browser and do a keyword search on *statistical process control.* Find at least one site related to application of SPC in a service environment. Describe the sites. Are they service sites (consulting, training)? Resource sites (information)? Professional organization sites? What does the goal of the site appear to be? What information can you find about SPC that supports the information in this chapter? What new information can you find?
2. Go to your favorite Internet browser and do a keyword search on *statistical process control software.* Find a site that has either free downloads or online demos you can play with. Identify the product and describe some of the product features.

Solved Problem

Completed forms from a particular department of an insurance company were sampled on a daily basis as a check against the quality of performance of that department. The long-run percent of errors was 3 percent. To monitor quality on an ongoing basis, one sample of 100 units was collected each day for 15 days, with these results:

Sample	Sample Size	Number of Forms with Errors
1	100	4
2	100	3
3	100	5
4	100	0
5	100	2
6	100	8
7	100	1
8	100	3
9	100	4
10	100	2
11	100	7
12	100	2
13	100	1
14	100	3
15	100	1
Average	100	3.07

    a. Develop a *p*-chart using 3 standard deviation control limits.

    b. Plot the percent errors for the 15 samples collected.

    c. What comments can you make about the process?

Solution

a. To answer this question, first we must calculate the standard deviation for the sample mean distribution. The formula is:

$$\text{Standard deviation} = s_p = \sqrt{\frac{p\,(1-p)}{n}}$$

Here, the long-run percent defective is 3 percent and the sample size is 100:

$$\text{Standard deviation} = s_p = \sqrt{\frac{.03(.97)}{100}} = 0.0170 \text{ (or } 1.7\%)$$

The next step is to find the upper and lower control limit for the control chart:

$$\text{Upper control limit} = \text{UCL} = p + 3s_p = .0307 + 3(0.017) = 0.0817$$

$$\text{Lower control limit} = \text{LCL} = p - 3s_p = .0307 - 3(0.017) = -0.0217$$

Since the LCL is less than zero, the LCL is 0.

b. The next step is to plot the sample means:

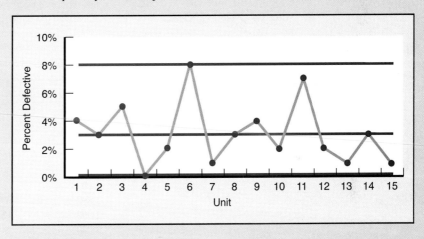

c. The process is *wildly* out of control. The variation is much greater than we would expect given the mean and standard deviation for the process.

Problems

1. You are a newly appointed assistant vice president at a local teaching hospital that is under increasing competition to maintain market share, especially from community hospitals that claim to provide better patient amenities. As one of the most important amenities is the quality of patient meals. You decide that your first project is to investigate the quality of the meals served by the food service department. Over the past year, patient surveys have indicated that 50 in 1,000 meals on average are considered to be unsatisfactory. You conducted a 10-day survey of patients, asking that they check off whether the meal was satisfactory or unsatisfactory. To facilitate calculations, assume that 1,000 questionnaires were returned each day. The results are as follows:

Date	Sample Size	Number of Unsatisfactory Meals
Dec. 1	1,000	74
Dec. 2	1,000	42
Dec. 3	1,000	64
Dec. 4	1,000	80
Dec. 5	1,000	40
Dec. 6	1,000	50
Dec. 7	1,000	65
Dec. 8	1,000	70
Dec. 9	1,000	40
Dec. 10	1,000	75

a. Construct a p-chart based on the questionnaire results, using 3 standard deviation control limits.

b. What comments can you make about the results of the survey?

2. The state and local police departments are trying to analyze crime rates in different areas so they can shift their patrols from decreasing-rate areas to areas where rates are increasing. The city and county have been geographically segmented into areas containing 20,000 residences. The police recognize that all crimes and offenses are not reported; people either do not want to become involved, consider the offenses too small to report, are too embarrassed to make a police report, or do not take the time, among other reasons. Every month, because of this, the police are contacting by phone a random sample of 1,000 of the 20,000 residents for data on crime (the respondents are guaranteed anonymity). The data collected for the past 12 months for one area are as follows:

Month	Sample Size	Crime Incidence
January	1,000	7
February	1,000	9
March	1,000	7
April	1,000	7
May	1,000	7
June	1,000	9
July	1,000	7
August	1,000	10
September	1,000	8
October	1,000	11
November	1,000	10
December	1,000	8

a. Construct a p-chart for using 3 standard deviation control limits and plot each of the months.

b. If the next three months show the number of crime incidences (out of 1,000) sampled in this area as January = 10, February = 12, March = 11, what can you say about the crime rate?

3. Pat and Doug own a small restaurant in Burlington, Vermont. Because they are also students at the University of Vermont, there are times when neither of them can be at the restaurant. Recently, they have been receiving a large number of customer complaints about the quality of their restaurant's food.

a. Draw a fishbone diagram for the restaurant's operation and identify potential causes in each of the major categories (for example, methods, materials, equipment, and labor). Be specific.

b. What other quality control tool(s) would you use to reduce the number of customer complaints as quickly as possible?

4. Allison Genivive, the manager of the toll-free reservation service for a nationwide chain of luxury hotels, is concerned about the productivity of her operation. Analysis of past data shows that

it should take an average of five minutes to properly process a reservation and that the standard deviation is 30 seconds. Every day, Allison randomly samples how long it takes to make each of 25 reservations.

a. Set up a process control chart with 3 standard deviation control limits.

b. If the sample results show that the average reservation time is significantly above the upper control limit, what might be some of the causes for the longer reservation times? How would you correct the problems?

c. Should Allison have any concern if the average reservation time was significantly below the lower control limits? Why?

5. Is the following p-chart in control or out of control? Why or why not?

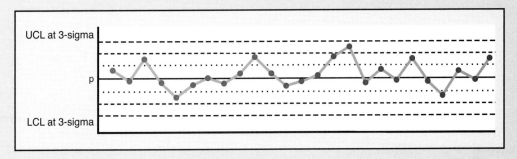

6. What is your opinion about the following process?

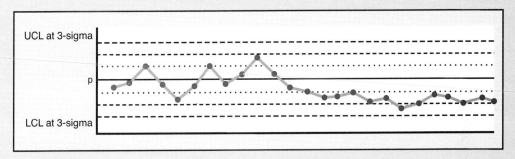

7. You are the manager of a luxury hotel in New York City and have collected the following data on customer complaints over the last month.

Cause	Frequency
Long check-in times	16
Slow room service (food)	11
Rude staff	27
Late room cleaning	42
Early room service closing	4

   a. Draw a fishbone diagram for the potential causes of one of the items in the table.
   b. Draw a Pareto diagram for the data in the table, labeling the axes appropriately. How may this information help the manager to improve service quality?

8. As a careful spender, you always use the self-serve pump at your local gas station. Draw a process flow diagram for filling your gas tank. Include decision points, waits, and task steps.

9. You are a new health researcher interested in understanding the relationship between height and weight and age and weight. You collect the following information:

Person	Height	Weight	Age	Zip Code
1	71	180	40	01945
2	71	174	36	01803
3	69	165	37	01748
4	62	108	41	01742
5	71	130	39	03062
6	63	115	44	01746
7	73	180	50	01719
8	68	165	33	02173
9	69	140	37	02172
10	65	107	35	02146
11	72	215	35	02864
12	68	145	44	04062
13	68	180	35	03031
14	72	205	44	02235
15	72	190	36	04074
16	70	180	30	02172
17	73	220	29	02129
18	62	118	35	01760
19	71	180	37	01940
20	74	210	46	01746

   a. Construct a scatterplot showing the relationship between weight and height. Remember that the dependent variable should be plotted on the x-axis. How would you interpret this plot?
   b. Construct a scatterplot showing the relationship between age and weight. Remember that the dependent variable should be plotted on the x-axis. How would you interpret this plot?
   c. What would you expect to see if you plotted the relationship between height and zip code? Why?

10. What are some of the ways you might construct a bar chart to show characteristics of students in one of your classes? What categories might you use?

11. You want to unobtrusively collect data about customers entering your record store. You have asked your sales staff to collect the data using check sheets. Develop a check sheet you will have the staff use. Why did you choose those customer characteristics? What difficulties might you encounter with collecting data using the categories you chose?

CASE   Improving Customer Satisfaction in the Personnel Office

Joe and Mary, the director and assistant director of the personnel office at a major university, were returning to work after their first "quality lunch" and neither had much to say. They had been enthusiastic when they asked Mike, Bill, and Ann, all professors in the operations management department, to meet with them to discuss starting a quality improvement program in the personnel office, but the discussion had taken an unexpected turn.

The meeting had started out well enough with a lot of general enthusiasm about quality management concepts all around the table, but during dessert, Bill turned to Ann and asked, "Did you show Joe and Mary the case you wrote?" Ann looked a little uncomfortable, but began her story about her recent visit to the personnel office.

"This is my first year here and I'd already been through the new faculty orientation, but I still needed to get an ID card to be able to use the library and to obtain a computer account," she related. "So I called your office and made an appointment for 3:00 P.M. one afternoon. When I got there I was rather rudely told that I could not have the ID made until 3:30—and the receptionist informed me that no one would have told me that 3:00 would be possible. Finally a work-study student stepped up and admitted that he had scheduled the appointment. He also hadn't told me about needing a letter from my department chair, but they told me they would make the card for me anyway. I had to either wait or come back later, so I left and came back and then had to wait for another half-hour behind two other faculty members. Making the ID couldn't have taken more than two minutes! I was really frustrated and upset when I left, so I wrote a case about it to use in my quality management course."

Ann had been matter-of-fact in her description of the incident, but Mary was embarrassed. "The first few weeks of a new semester are always really hectic and we're usually very short staffed. We don't have the resources to deal with the peaks in demand. We only have one receptionist and she's responsible for answering phones, greeting people, making IDs, scheduling, and so on."

Mike interrupted. "Mary, that's not a quality answer. You know that there are busy times and they're pretty predictable. If you really want to serve your customers better, you'll be prepared." There was awkward silence around the table for a few seconds, then Mary said, "Ann, can I have a copy of your case?"

"Sure," Ann replied. "The real point of the case is that no one is to blame, but the system needs to be fixed to serve customers better."

Talk turned to more general quality topics and the rest of the lunch was uneventful. As Mary and Joe approached their offices, though, they agreed it was time to pay some attention to the personnel reception area. They knew, from Ann's story and from other complaints, that customer satisfaction was generally not very high and they had done enough general quality training in the department to form a quality improvement team.

The Work of the QIT

One month later, the Office of Personnel's first quality improvement team (QIT) had been formed to address issues of effectiveness and customer satisfaction in the reception area. There were four team members: Paul, Amy, Adam, and Susan, the receptionist. Four managers agreed to function as a steering committee, offering assistance and resources when necessary.

During the first team meeting, the group agreed to collect data on the tasks the receptionist performed. All the group members thought a written questionnaire to get customer feedback would be a good idea and that developing the questionnaire together would be their first joint task. Each of them would also take on another task.

- Susan would keep a checklist that identified the number of phone calls received each day by the receptionist.

- Paul and Amy agreed to observe the reception area for one hour each week to see how customers moved through the physical setting and how they acted.

- Adam agreed to identify the specific steps required to schedule and produce a faculty ID card.

The group met for one hour each week for a month. By the end of that time, the data on the phones had been tabulated (Table 1) and the questionnaire (Exhibit 1) had been developed and reviewed by Ann in the operations management department.

Adam presented the steps he had identified for producing a faculty ID. First, a mail notice was sent by the Office of Personnel to all faculty, reminding them that IDs were made on Monday and Wednesday afternoons and that appointments were necessary. Then, when a faculty member called, whoever answered the phones would check the schedule, offer a time, and write the appointment on the calendar. The faculty member was also informed that a letter verifying faculty status was required to make an initial or replacement ID.

EXHIBIT 1   **Office of Personnel Customer Satisfaction Survey**

1. Is this your first visit to the university?   ❑ Yes   ❑ No

2. Is this your first visit to the university's Office of Personnel?   ❑ Yes   ❑ No

3. Did you have a scheduled appointment?   ❑ Yes   ❑ No

4. How often do you conduct business with the Office of Personnel?
   ❑ Daily   ❑ Weekly   ❑ Monthly   ❑ Once/year or less

5. Are you: ❑ Faculty   ❑ Staff   ❑ Other   ❑ Job applicant (not employed by the university)

6. What was the purpose of your visit?

   ❑ Job Application/View Job Posting   ❑ Promotion & Transfer
   ❑ Meeting with Personnel Staff member   ❑ Application Training
       with whom?_____(optional)   ❑ Identification card
   ❑ Meeting with a member of the Administrative Services Staff   ❑ Benefits Information
       with whom? _____(optional)   ❑ Orientation
   ❑ Other

                                 Poor   Excellent

7. Evaluate the **promptness** of the service in the front office.   1   2   3   4   5

8. Evaluate the **courteousness** of the service in the front office.   1   2   3   4   5

9. What was your **overall impression** of the service in the front office.   1   2   3   4   5

10. Did you receive the information you requested?   ❑ Yes   ❑ No
    (If yes, was it helpful? Please explain. If not, please explain why it did not meet your needs.)

11. Do you have suggestions to help us better serve you?

    (Please explain below.)   ❑ Yes   ❑ No

Please use the space below to explain any of your answers or to make additional comments.
(Please feel free to use the back of this survey.)

If you would like to discuss your experience further, please leave your name and phone number and a staff member will call you.

THANK YOU FOR TAKING THE TIME TO COMPLETE THIS SURVEY.
Please drop this form in the sealed box by the exit. All information will be kept confidential and will be used solely for the purpose of improving the services delivered by the Office of Personnel.

When faculty members arrived at the Office of Personnel, the receptionist (or work-study student) would greet them and ask them to fill out a form with their name, Social Security number, title, and signature. The receptionist would then ask for their letters of verification of faculty status and, if the letters could be produced, ask them to wait until all ID customers arrived so that picture taking could be done in a "batch."

Susan began to administer the questionnaires to "customers" of the reception area one week after it was completed. During the first week, seven faculty members, 20 staff members, and 34 job applicants completed surveys. As noted in Exhibit 1, the questionnaire asked customers to evaluate the promptness, courteousness, and overall impression of their service at the reception desk on a five-point scale where 1 indicated poor service and 5 indicated excellent service. The first 11 people to complete the survey responded as shown in Table 2.

Most customers indicated they were satisfied with their experiences, but 40 customers wrote comments that indicated

TABLE 1
Calls by Day of Week

Day	Calls	Day	Calls
Monday	165	Monday	156
Tuesday	122	Tuesday	124
Wednesday	124	Wednesday	118
Thursday	126	Thursday	130
Friday	106	Friday	104
Monday	158	Monday	160
Tuesday	118	Tuesday	121
Wednesday	122	Wednesday	128
Thursday	120	Thursday	118
Friday	112	Friday	98

TABLE 2
Individual Responses to Survey Questions on Satisfaction with Promptness, Courteousness, and Overall Satisfaction

Person	Satisfaction with Promptness	Satisfaction with Courteousness	Satisfaction Overall
1	3	1	1
2	3	2	2
3	2	3	2
4	2	1	3
5	3	2	3
6	4	3	3
7	5	4	3
8	3	4	4
9	4	5	4
10	5	4	5
11	4	5	5

TABLE 3
Categories of Survey Comments

Category	Comment	Number
Information	No follow-up sent	2
	No copies of job postings	6
	No information provided by phone	2
	Jobs posted slowly	3
	Information not provided	3
Attitude	Receptionist rude	11
	Receptionist preoccupied	2
Process	ID hours poor	1
	Phones too busy	3
	No customization of service	1
	Too much work for one person	1
Decor	Lobby not cheerful	3
Other	No water fountain	2

they were displeased with the service they received. The comments were categorized by the quality improvement team as relating to information, attitude, process, decor, and other, as presented in Table 3.

Questions

1. Using the data provided in Table 1, produce a run chart of calls received in the personnel reception area for the data collection period.

2. Draw a process flow diagram of the procedure for processing faculty ID cards.

3. Produce a bar chart that shows the types of respondents to the survey.

4. Using the data in Table 2, produce scatter plots that show (*a*) the relationship between survey respondents' satisfaction with promptness and overall satisfaction and (*b*) the relationship between survey respondents' satisfaction with courteousness and overall satisfaction.

5. Using the data in Table 3, produce a Pareto diagram that shows the categories of survey comments.

6. Using the data in Table 3, produce a fishbone diagram of the causes that lead to customer dissatisfaction with the reception area in the Office of Personnel. For each cause, brainstorm items that might contribute to each cause.

7. Identify possible solutions to the causes identified in your fishbone diagram.

Selected Bibliography

Brassard, Michael, and Diane Ritter. *The Memory Jogger II.* Salem, NH: Goal/QPC, 1996.

Hansen, Bertrand L. *Quality Control: Theory and Applications.* Englewood Cliffs, NJ: Prentice Hall, 1963, pp. 65, 125–33.

Welch, Jack. Presented at the General Electric Company 1997 Annual Meeting, Charlotte, North Carolina, April 23, 1997; http://www.reims-corporate.org/ehrm/alearningcompany.htm.

CHAPTER THIRTEEN

Customer-Focused Service

Learning Objectives

- Identify the factors that affect customer satisfaction with the service encounter.

- Review the service satisfaction equation and describe how to improve customer satisfaction through managing both performance and expectations.

- Introduce the zone of tolerance concept and its implications for service delivery.

- Describe types of service encounters and the challenges they present.

- Identify sources of customer satisfaction and dissatisfaction.

- Present the concept of customer relationship management and its advantages for service firms.

- Introduce the concepts of service recovery, service guarantees, and Six Sigma quality.

Jordan's Furniture: Make Shopping Fun

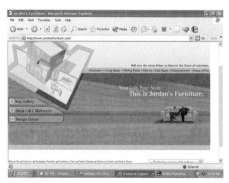

Courtesy of Jordan's Furniture

The customer is the focus at Jordan's Furniture. CEO Barry Tatelman and his brother Eliot have created a culture in their four stores that puts the experience of the customer first. Most people don't think of furniture shopping as fun, but Jordan's has tried to create an experience that makes customers want to come into the store and then makes them want to return. At the store in Natick, Massachusetts, customers walk into a re-creation of New Orleans's Bourbon Street, complete with Mardi Gras beads and animatronic performances by Louis Armstrong, Elvis, and the Beatles. Customers who shop at the Avon store can visit MOM, the Motion Odyssey Movie ride. Furniture shopping, apparently, *can* be fun!

But Jordan's is absolutely serious about selling furniture, too. The large store layouts are easy to maneuver through and display a wide variety of furniture styles. To reduce the anxiety and pressure of shopping for furniture, Jordan's never holds sales, unlike other furniture stores that hold frequent, and frequently bewildering, sales. Instead, Jordan's offers "underprices"—lower prices than most furniture stores for the same quality, all the time. Each furniture item is labeled with a detailed fact tag that provides information on the manufacturer, the item's dimensions, construction details, warranty information, and product care. Salespeople are trained to be friendly and informative, but not pushy. All purchasers receive a follow-up phone call, asking for an evaluation of their experience—from the time they enter the store to the time the furniture is delivered and set up in their homes. Each day, these results are entered into a database that permits Eliot and Barry to evaluate their sales staff, not only on volume sold, but also on the customer's perception of the overall experience.

The focus on the customer works. Jordan's sells more furniture per square foot than any furniture store in the country, and customers consistently give high marks for the service—and the fun experience—in the stores.

Source: Arthur Lubow, "Wowing Warren," *Inc Magazine,* March 1, 2000; Barry Tatelman, "You Can't Take That Away from Us," *Entreworld,* April 2002; and http://www.bbb.org/torchaward/jordans.asp.

The Customer's Perspective

You're shopping at your favorite large department store. You browse for a while and find exactly the right pair of jeans; they are just the style you are looking for, the fit is perfect, and the price is right. As you leave the dressing room, you look for a clerk to ring up your purchase, but there's no register in sight. The store is laid out to make each area seem like a smaller shop, so you make a few turns and finally see a register, but no clerk. Around another corner you encounter a young man wearing a department store name tag and you ask him if he can help you. He looks at you blankly for a moment, turns toward a register around yet another corner, nods, and says, "She'll help you over there," immediately looking down and turning away. You shrug and make your way toward the register where two young women are folding a stack of items. You walk up to the register and say, "Hi. I'd like to buy these jeans, please." The young women—their name tags identify them as Sarah and Nicole—look up but continue their conversation. Sarah, while speaking to Nicole, reaches for the jeans and hunts for the price tag. When she finds it, without making eye contact, she asks, "Cash or charge?" You respond "cash" and reach for your wallet. As Sarah bags the jeans and rings up the sale, you hear about Nicole's fight with her father last night. Sarah correctly makes your change, and, with a mumbled "thanks," hands you the bag and the receipt. Before you can respond, she turns toward Nicole and tells her own tale of aggravation with her father.

As you leave the store, you think, "I found exactly what I wanted, but I'm so frustrated now that I don't know if I'll ever come back to this store! What in the world were they thinking?!" As you drive home you calm down a bit and look forward to wearing your new jeans, but when you open the bag, you realize the security sensor is still firmly in place!

You'll have to spend another hour-and-a-half going back and forth to the mall and in and out of the store to correct *the store's* error! And they call this service?

Managerial Issues

Reliability is the most important service dimension when it comes to *meeting* customer expectations. However, the other four dimensions, which are associated mainly with the quality of the service process, are more important in *exceeding* customer expectations. In other words, service providers are expected to be reliable and to provide the service they promised with dependability and accuracy. For example, customers expect to have their reserved rooms ready when they check into a hotel. By simply providing the reserved room, the hotel just meets customers' expectations. However, the hotel has an opportunity to exceed customers' expectations along the four process dimensions of tangibles, responsiveness, assurance, and empathy (see Chapter 12). Treating customers with courtesy, responding quickly and willingly to their requirements, and generally "going the extra mile" can lead to a service that is performed at a level beyond the customers' expectations. Overall, companies must be reliable simply to compete, but if they perform well on the process dimensions they can attain and retain an advantage over competition.

The service encounter has been called "the moment of truth"[1] because it is during the encounter that the service experience is either made or broken. Most managers of service organizations believe that achieving total customer satisfaction is impossible. Regardless of whether they have achieved it or not, leading service companies identify total customer satisfaction not just as a goal but also as an imperative.

Identifying Core Customer Needs

Chapters 1 and 5 showed that services can be categorized in many ways, but with one model emphasizing the degree and nature of customer involvement in the service, or customer contact.

In low-customer-contact transactions, such as check clearing, credit card processing, or billing, customers care only about reliability: The service is satisfactory if there are no errors and the work is done on time. We are not delighted when our bank statement is accurate—we expect it. We are not wildly enthusiastic about a credit card company that bills us only for the credit card purchases we've made—we expect no less. But the psychology of high-customer-contact services is different. Our expectations encompass more than just appropriate technical quality; we expect a baseline level of human interaction as well. Benjamin Schneider and David Bowen note that customers are people first and consumers second, and they have needs that are more fundamental and compelling than their expectations as consumers. They describe three core needs as fairness, security, and esteem:[2]

- Fairness is the need for just treatment. It encompasses:

  a. The outcomes of the service. Was the service provided as promised? For example, if you hire a lawyer to make a will, you expect her to write the will and to follow any and all procedures to make sure it is binding and legal.

  b. The procedures followed. Were the practices and policies of the service organization followed in the same way for all customers? For example, if you fly first class, you expect to be treated the same as all other first-class passengers.

[1] Richard Normann, *Service Management* (New York: John Wiley and Sons, 1984), pp. 8–9.
[2] B. Schneider and D. E. Bowen, "Understanding Customer Delight and Outrage," *Sloan Management Review* 41, no. 1 (1999), pp. 35–45.

c. The interaction itself. How well did the parties involved communicate about the outcomes? For example, if you seek the services of an investment counselor, it would be important to understand what you can reasonably expect in terms of asset growth over a period of time—and what might not be a reasonable expectation.

- Security is the need to feel free from harm. For example, when customers go to a restaurant, they expect it to be clean and free from health risks, and if you take a taxi, you expect the company to screen and monitor its drivers to make sure they know and obey the rules of the road.

- Esteem is the need to protect or even enhance one's self-concept. This involves treating the customer as an important individual, not just one of many. It can also mean providing customers with enough information that they believe they have some control over the service situation. For example, if customers seek advice about loss of data on their computers, they expect that, whatever their level of expertise with computers, the service provider will provide information that will help them to understand not only what might have happened to cause the data loss, but also what might be done to prevent it in the future, without any editorial commentary about their capability with technology.

The notion of the importance of fairness dates back to Aristotle in ancient Greece. The need for security and esteem is based on early work by Maslow and Alderfer.

Ignoring the needs for fairness and security will probably result in outrage, whereas respecting those needs is likely to result in satisfaction with the service. Ignoring the need for self-esteem will also probably result in outrage, but respecting that need is likely to result in delight with the service.

Managing Customer Expectations

Chapter 12 noted that customers form expectations about service before experiencing the service, and that expectations are an important determinant of how satisfied the customer will be. Expectations are derived from many sources. Customers hear about a service from a friend and build that friend's experience into their own expectations. They may have seen the service provider's advertisements and promotions, which promise a specific level of service. Or customers may have experienced the service in the past and have expectations based on their own prior encounters. Customers will be satisfied only if the service meets their expectations, and the service performance is colored by the customer's perceptions of the quality of service. The relationship between expectations, service performance, and the perception of that performance is all captured in the following equation:

$$\text{Satisfaction} = \text{Perception of performance} - \text{Expectation}$$

The relationships in this equation imply there are two ways to increase satisfaction: (*a*) to improve the customer's perception of performance and (*b*) to decrease expectations.

Improving customer perception of performance can further be separated into improving customer *perceptions* and actually improving *performance*. In most service situations, both actual performance and perception of performance can be affected by the service organization.

If actual performance continuously improves, customer expectations rise along with performance. Speed of service is again a good example of this. Before bar-code scanning in grocery stores, customers expected to wait in line at the checkout counter, and it was fairly unusual to walk right up to a checkout counter and go straight through. Today, with much faster checkout performance, customers expect shorter waits or no waits, and they are likely to be frustrated and dissatisfied with waiting times that would once have been considered typical and tolerable.

Managing expectations is also a reasonable way to increase satisfaction. The basic notion is to set expectations low and it will be easy to satisfy the customer. This approach is widely used. For example, when you go to a crowded restaurant, the host will usually provide an estimate of how long you will have to wait for a table. Usually, the estimate is slightly higher than the actual wait will be; if you are told your wait will be 15 minutes and you are called to your table in 10 minutes, you are likely to be pleased. Of course, managing expectations has to be done with some finesse. If the same host told you the wait would be one hour and it was actually only 10 minutes, you are not likely to be pleased, you are likely to be on your way to another restaurant!

If service expectations are set too low, customers are likely to be intolerant and seek alternatives. If no alternatives exist, low expectations are helpful. For example, when most drivers renew their driver's licenses—at least if they have been through the renewal process before—they expect a long wait and bring a book. If the wait turns out to be much shorter than expected, they *are* delighted.

The Zone of Tolerance

Customer expectations are not simple "point targets," however; they are more like "expectation zones" that are defined by different expectation levels. One level of expectation is desired service, which is the level of service the customer hopes to receive and believes *should* be received. For example, when you hire a carpet cleaner, you may realistically and reasonably expect that any stains on your carpet will be removed and the overall appearance of the carpet will improve. Similarly, if you contract with an investment manager, you expect a better-than-average return on your assets.

Customers may recognize factors that limit a service's ability to deliver the desired service, and therefore they have a lower acceptable level of expectation. This level of expectation is called adequate service. To continue our carpet cleaning example, you may understand that some of the stains on the carpet cannot be completely removed, but you are satisfied if the appearance of the carpet is improved. Similarly in our investment example, if the economy has a downturn, you may not achieve the desired return on your assets, but if your portfolio performance is as good as average market performance, you are likely to find that to be acceptable.

The standards for desired service and for adequate service define the upper and lower boundaries of an expectation zone called the **zone of tolerance,** illustrated in Exhibit 13.1.

EXHIBIT 13.1
Zone of Tolerance

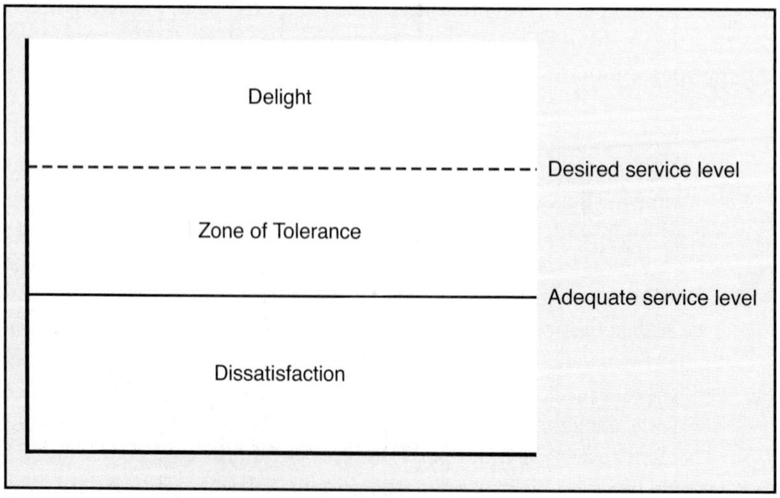

The zone of tolerance is the level at which the customer will be satisfied with the service provided. If the service performance is below the adequate level, customers will be dissatisfied, disappointed, frustrated, and even angry about the service. If the performance level is higher than the desired level of service, customers will be surprised and delighted with the service provided.

The zone of tolerance is not fixed for all customers at all times. In Chapter 12, we saw that significant variation exists in services and that understanding and managing that variation are critical to the service's success in the eyes of the customer. Some customers have very high expectations for services; others are more easygoing. Even the same customer will have different expectations at different times, affected by the many factors that make our lives different from day to day. For example, a college student customer may ordinarily be very easygoing and tolerant about service in a local Burger King restaurant, chatting with friends while waiting to order, willing to explain an order to a new counter server, and comfortable with squeezing five people into a small booth because no other tables are available. However, that same student, in a hurry to catch a train home or unsettled after a physics exam, may feel that any wait at the Burger King is interminable, service-with-a-smile is insincere, and *again* they forgot the extra ketchup!

Customer expectations and tolerance zones may be different for different service elements as well. For example, when shopping at a retail store, attentive service may be the most important factor to a customer, while waiting in line is less important. As Exhibit 13.2 shows, generally, when the factor is very important, the desired level of service tends to be higher and the customer's willingness to accept something less (the adequate level of service) is smaller, so the zone of tolerance tends to be narrower. For factors that are less important, the reverse is true: the desired service level tends to be lower and the adequate service level tends to be lower still.

The service organization can control some of the factors that affect the customer's zone of tolerance. One very important factor is price. A customer may be very satisfied with service at a particular price, but if the price is increased, expectations for both desired and adequate service levels are likely to increase as well, making it more difficult for the service organization to meet the customer's expectations.

EXHIBIT 13.2
Zone of Tolerance for Different Service Factors

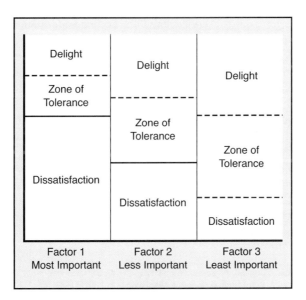

These zone of tolerance examples show that the service equation

$$\text{Satisfaction} = \text{Perception of performance} - \text{Expectation}$$

is more complicated than it first appears, and there are still further wrinkles. For example, if the first service encounter truly delights the customer, one might expect the expectations for the next encounter to be very high. But there is also the "goodwill" effect: If the second encounter does not meet expectations, the customer may think to himself, "They're so customer oriented here, this must be a fluke." Similarly, if the first encounter was very negative but the customer returns, perhaps because no alternative services are available, one might expect that service expectation may be lower and therefore the service should more easily delight, but it is just as likely that the first negative encounter has created a negative impression that will be even more difficult for the service firm to overcome—making it even harder to delight the customer. Similarly, as customers develop longer relationships with service organizations, they tend to be more tolerant of service "slips" than if they have less experience with the organization.

The Service Encounter

Types of Encounters

Customers interact with service providers in three basic ways: remotely, by phone, and/or face to face.[3] Often, service interactions involve a combination of these types of encounters.

Remote encounters occur without any direct human contact. Examples of remote encounters would include pay-at-the-pump self-service at a gas station, an automated information service such as dial-up time or weather, Web-based banking, and mail transactions such as billing and crediting payment. Within these examples, a further distinction can be made. When a firm receives a mailed check as payment for services, the transaction is remote but still requires someone to carry out at least parts of the transaction. In Web-based banking, however, the customer substitutes for the service provider, acting as a data-entry clerk. Similarly, at a pay-at-the-pump gas station, the customer conducts the entire transaction and there is no need for a service worker to be involved. As technology continues to develop, particularly Internet technology, remote service opportunities are likely to proliferate. For remote encounters, customers base their perceptions of quality primarily on the ease, accuracy, and speed of service. Providing accurate information and instructions to customers about how to use the service is imperative, whether it is to whom to write the check to pay the electric bill or exactly what steps to follow to fill your tank at the gas station.

Many service interactions occur between a customer and a worker in a service firm via the telephone. Common phone encounters include customer service support, telephone inquiries, appointment scheduling, and order taking. Phone encounters present a different set of service challenges from remote encounters because all the variation inherent in the personalities and needs of the customers and the personalities and skills of the service workers are embedded in the interaction. Customer satisfaction will depend on both the technical quality of the service interaction (how quickly and accurately the service is provided) and the functional quality of the service interaction (the worker's tone of voice, empathy, and interaction style).

The third type of service encounter is the one that takes place with the customer and the service provider face to face. Face-to-face encounters are the most complex because, like

---

[3] Lynn G. Shostack, "Planning the Service Encounter," in *The Service Encounter,* ed. John A. Czepiel, Michael R. Solomon, and Carol F. Surprenant (Lexington, MA: Lexington Books, 1985), pp. 243–54.

phone encounters, they involve both technical and functional service quality elements and because nonverbal signals play an important part in interaction. The importance of the nonverbal cues in face-to-face service interactions was made clear to a Women's Health Service manager when she walked into the reception area and observed the secretary on the phone with an anxious patient trying to schedule an appointment. The secretary, who had a very expressive face, was rolling her eyes at some of the patient's demands and generally looking very unsupportive. The manager was initially horrified by this behavior in what she had believed to be an office with a strong culture of customer service, until she closed her eyes and just listened to the interaction. With the nonverbal cues eliminated, the manager heard a perfectly supportive secretary who sounded as though she was being particularly attentive to the patient's needs. Having overheard this interaction, the manager made a point of observing several face-to-face encounters between patients and this secretary and was relieved to discover that her face-to-face encounters incorporated much more appropriate nonverbal communication!

The customer, too, affects the tone of both phone and face-to-face service encounters. In both, the customer's behavior actually plays a part in determining the level of service quality.

Sources of Customer Satisfaction

What causes customers to have either positive or negative perceptions of service encounters? Using a method called the critical incident technique, which asks customers to provide stories about service encounters that they have experienced, researchers have identified four common themes as the sources of customer satisfaction/dissatisfaction: recovery, adaptability, spontaneity, and coping.[4]

The **recovery** theme involves incidents in which there have been failures in the service delivery system and an employee must respond in some way to the customer's frustration, disappointment, or complaint. An example of a service failure is the late departure of an airplane, or the arrival of the wrong entrée in a restaurant. Service recoveries in these examples might be a coupon for a free meal in the airport restaurant or, if the flight delay is long, a coupon for a free stay at a nearby hotel. In the restaurant, service recovery might be a free dessert—or even a free meal.

The **adaptability** theme relates to the service system's ability to deal with a customer's special needs or requests. For example, adaptability might include a fairly simple request such as a substitution of one item for another on a menu, which might be very easy for the service provider to deliver, or something more complicated such as accommodations for comfort on a cross-country flight for an elderly traveler who recently suffered a stroke. Both customers and service providers may be frustrated by constraints on adaptability—real or perceived—placed on them by the service system.

The **spontaneity** theme relates to unprompted or unsolicited actions by service workers. Positive examples of spontaneity are a flight attendant bringing a special treat to a mother to offer her finicky toddler or a roofer leaving an extra bundle of shingles at no extra charge in case repairs are needed later. Negative spontaneity incident examples include the secretary who hangs up on a customer who politely requests to reschedule an appointment for a flooring installation or the gas station attendant who remarks to a bewildered middle-aged woman, "Lady, even my 10-year-old can follow those pump instructions."

The **coping** theme relates to how service employees interact with problem customers. These incidents were related by service employees themselves, rather than customers, but they illustrate how customer behavior can be the cause of customer dissatisfaction. A positive

---

[4] Mary Jo Bitner, Bernard H. Booms, and Mary Stanfield Tetreault, "The Service Encounter: Diagnosing Favorable and Unfavorable Incidents," *Journal of Marketing* 54 (January 1990), pp. 71–84.

EXHIBIT 13.3
General Service
Behavior Dos
and Don'ts

Theme	Do	Don't
Recovery	Acknowledge problem Explain causes Apologize Compensate/upgrade Lay out options Take responsibility	Ignore customer Blame customer Leave customer to fend for him/herself Downgrade Act as if nothing is wrong Pass the buck
Adaptability	Recognize the seriousness of the need Acknowledge Anticipate Attempt to accommodate Adjust the system Explain rules/policies Take responsibility	Ignore Promise, but fail to follow through Show unwillingness to try Embarrass the customer Laugh at the customer Avoid responsibility Pass the buck
Spontaneity	Take time Be attentive Anticipate needs Listen Provide information Show empathy	Exhibit impatience Ignore Yell/laugh/swear Steal from customers Discriminate
Coping	Listen Try to accommodate Explain Let go of the customer	Take customer's dissatisfaction personally Let customer's dissatisfaction affect others

Source: Valarie A. Zeithaml and Mary Jo Bitner, *Services Marketing* (New York: Irwin/McGraw-Hill, 2000).

example of coping might be the service employee who, when confronted by an angry and verbally abusive customer, acknowledges the customer's frustration and thereby "defuses" the situation. A statement like "I certainly understand why you're angry, Mr. Meile. If you take a seat, we'll get you a cup of coffee while I try to sort out the problem" could have a calming effect on some customers, but might incite others to even higher levels of rage. It should not be too surprising that the vast majority of reported incidents in this category are unsatisfactory.

Because these four themes seem to be major drivers of satisfaction or dissatisfaction with the service encounters that customers consider to be memorable, it is important that service organizations train their workers to deal with them properly. Formal training, including role-playing of challenging situations, can help workers prepare for these kinds of situations so that they are not taken by surprise and consequently unable to meet the customers' needs. Exhibit 13.3 offers some dos and don'ts for each of the four themes.

Customer Relationship Management

There is a shift in many firms away from an acquisition/transaction focus toward a retention/relationship focus.[5] The goal of customer relationship management is to "build and maintain a base of committed customers who are profitable for the organization."[6] Funda-

[5] *Journal of the Academy of Marketing Science* 23, no. 4, Special Issue on Relationship Marketing (Fall 1995).
[6] Valarie A. Zeithaml and Mary Jo Bitner, *Services Marketing* (New York: Irwin/McGraw-Hill, 2000), p. 139.

Using Technology to Create Value

Merrill Lynch Credit Corporation

Technology has made many routine office tasks faster while reducing errors, and as technology advances, it has enabled organizations to automate many more complicated tasks. At Merrill Lynch Credit Corporation (MLCC), winner of the 1997 Malcolm Baldrige National Quality Award, technology has improved both efficiency and customer satisfaction.

"Many organizations grapple with tying together disparate computer systems in an effort to create a more functional working environment," explains Mark Rizk, system architecture manager at MLCC. "The real challenge comes with re-creating the organization to take advantage of these renewed system efficiencies. Technology is the enabler. The business processes provide the real benefit to the organization."

Since 1997, Rizk and his MLCC team have redesigned the loan origination process. Their old system was fragmented, with many manual steps that led to task repetition and errors. "Our objectives were to implement a workflow management system that would improve client satisfaction through the use of a more standard and consistent loan application and approval process," Rizk says. They focused on six central goals:

1. Enhance client satisfaction by improving each loan officer's ability to respond to inquiries.

2. Reduce oversight and errors.

3. Increase productivity by queuing and prioritizing tasks.

4. Reduce fallout by minimizing loan processing time.

5. Increase productivity by reducing the learning curve.

6. Enhance management reporting capabilities.

They developed a team process that uses the workflow management system to manage the loan approval process. It produces task lists and tracks the status of each loan. "The system assigns tasks as needed and notifies each team member when the next steps are expected and where that person fits into the process," Rizk says. By coordinating their work, teams are able to process more loans.

To develop the workflow management system, MLCC first defined the ideal process. Teams were then formed to analyze how information and work flowed through the system, to review the technology then in use, and to determine how different pieces of the process were connected.

The new system was first piloted in 1998. Users have found that getting up to speed on the new system takes only a day or two and that time savings are almost immediate. One supervisor said the system's assignment of processing tasks alone saves him 30 minutes a day. The workflow management system has increased customer satisfaction by helping lending officers respond to inquiries and, because work is more consistent, by reducing errors and omissions. The system reduced loan processing time from 36 days to 22 days, which also means the same number of people can process more loans.

Rizk summarized the effect of the change in process. "The workflow management system enables each person in the organization to have a common view of the loan information. This integration has dramatically changed how MLCC does business and has enabled us to reorganize our staff. By revamping the core tenets of how we operate, we have increased our productivity and in turn our client satisfaction."

The results of MLCC's focus on process and quality had a positive effect on the bottom line, too. From 1994 to 1996, net income rose 100 percent, return on equity increased 74 percent, and return on assets improved approximately 36 percent in that same period.

But, as MLCC President and Chief Operating Officer Kevin O'Hanlon said, "Feedback is what drives how we do business." MLCC gets customer information from surveys, toll-free calling centers, the Internet, and roundtable discussions—the focus is always on the customer.

Sources: "Merrill Lynch Streamlines Loan Origination Process with Custom Workflow Management System," *Information Builders Magazine* 1, no. 1 (2000), http://www.quality.nist.gov/Merrill_Lynch_97.htm, created August 27, 2001; and Maria Carlino, "Merrill Lynch Credit Corp.," *Journal of Commerce*, October 24, 1997, p. 673.

mentally, this means targeting, through market segmentation, the customers who are likely to become long-term customers. Long-term customers are more likely to purchase additional services if they are very satisfied with current service provision. They may also help to attract new customers through word of mouth.

Benefits for Customers

Once customers are attracted into a relationship with a service provider, they are likely to remain with that provider as long as their needs are satisfied or, put another way, unless they are given a reason to want to switch. Customers who have long-term relationships with service providers receive confidence benefits, social benefits, and special treatment benefits.

Confidence benefits include feelings of trust in the service provider and a sense of what to expect in the service interaction. Most people prefer not to change service providers once a relationship is established. The established relationship is comfortable and safe. Even if the satisfaction with service is not uniformly high, many customers are of the mind that "the devil you know is better than the devil you don't know." In other words, the risk of an even less satisfactory service relationship can produce anxiety. For example, a patient may think, "My doctor doesn't have the warmest bedside manner, but I know he has a good professional reputation, I don't have trouble getting an appointment, I'm familiar with the office staff, I know how far in advance I need to call for a routine appointment, and I can generally find a parking space." When the relationship with a service provider is very strong, customers may go to great lengths to continue it. For example, one woman who moved from New England to Singapore, still kept her annual appointments with her physician in Boston.

When the service relationship is very strong, customers experience *social benefits* from the service interaction. A family with teenage children and the pediatrician who has cared for them since their birth may chat about events in their lives like old friends. A warm and friendly long-term hairdresser may be as much a part of the pleasure of the service encounter as the relaxing scalp massage. Or the owner of the Campus Trolley sandwich shop may welcome a regular customer with a warm, genuine smile and a friendly "How are you today?! Hummus sandwich with onions?" that brings a happy smile to the face of the customer and makes her feel memorable as well as well-served. Social benefits can develop in the encounter points between businesses as well.

Special treatment benefits include things such as getting a prime appointment time or a preferential price because of the long-standing relationship. While these benefits are real and appreciated by customers, research indicates they are not as important to customers as either the confidence benefits, which are most important, or the social benefits.

Benefits for the Firm

There are several benefits for the service firm in having strong relationships with customers. Most obvious is that it is less costly to keep current customers than it is to attract new ones; advertising and promotion costs are lower and the cost of "training the customer" decreases as the customer becomes more familiar with the service over time. Another clear benefit is the potential for positive word-of-mouth advertising. Customers looking for new services, especially complex or professional services such as automobile repair, accounting services, and medical services, to name a few, are likely to ask their friends for advice and referrals. Satisfied customers are likely to provide strong references for their relationship service providers when asked and to share their positive experiences with their service providers, solicited or not.

There is also some evidence that customers who have established relationships with service providers are likely to increase the amount of money they spend with that provider from one year to the next. Both business-to-business customers and consumers will tend to give more of their business to a firm when they are satisfied with the service.[7]

Another benefit of customer retention to the service firm may be employee retention, because when customers are happy, the workplace is more enjoyable for workers as well.

Customizing Services

One way of building relationships with customers is to provide services that are tailored to fit each individual's needs. Because there is so much variation in the service encounter, the

---

[7] Frederick F. Reichheld and Earl W. Sasser, *The Loyalty Effect* (Boston: Harvard Business School Press, 1996).

potential for personalization of service is high. At the same time, the variation makes predictability and quality control difficult to achieve.

There are a number of ways to approach personalization, also called mass customization.[8]

- Customizing the service around a standardized core. Weekend getaways at resort hotels or pre-theater dinner specials at theater-district restaurants are examples of slight modifications to a core product that provide enhanced service to a particular group of customers.

- Creating customizable services. Firms that use this approach offer the same service to all customers, and the customers themselves choose options that personalize the service. Buffet brunches, Web-based banking services, and pay-per-view television are examples of customizable services.

- Customizing at point of delivery. This approach permits customers to communicate with service providers and explain the service they need at the point of service delivery. Professional services such as health and dental care, personal care services, and legal services are examples of point-of-delivery customization.

- Offering standard modules that can be combined in different ways. "Day of Beauty" packages that can include services from a menu of personal care offerings, vacation tours that offer different numbers of destinations and different levels of amenities, and education programs that focus around a core curriculum and a menu of electives are all examples of this approach.

Customization may not be the best strategy for all service firms, but the core notion that customers want to feel unique and want to be able to purchase services that are well suited to their likes, their lifestyles, and their pocketbooks should be considered, if not adopted, by all service firms.

Appreciating Customers

It may be obvious, but many firms fail to let customers know that their business is appreciated. Approaches such as frequent-customer programs offer something back to regular customers—on airlines, in hair salons, or at sandwich shops. These programs provide both incentives and rewards for continued business.

Appreciating customers is all about relationships, and, as in all relationships, insincere behavior rarely produces the desired effect. While it is nice to be remembered at holidays with a card or a thank you, a more personal approach may be more successful. During recent renovations at one of its stores, for example, the Stop & Shop supermarket chain in New England provided coupons for $5 off the next purchase of $60 or more to thank customers for their patience with a disrupted store—and also printed coupons for their cardholder customers for triple manufacturer coupons during the renovation period. It is likely that the continued customer loyalty purchased with those signs of appreciation far outweighed the cost of the thank you.

Managing Difficult Customers

Is the customer always right? Anyone who has ever worked in a service environment will immediately answer, "No!" Some customers are demanding, rude, abusive, and seem generally impossible to satisfy. Because human behavior is complicated, these customers may be behaving the way they are because of factors unrelated to the service encounter. Some are under pressure or stress and are not able to control their anxiety. In health care environments, for example, it is not uncommon for patients who are concerned about their

---

[8] Joseph B. Pine, *Mass Customization* (Boston: Harvard Business School Press, 1993).

health, or for families who are concerned about the health of a loved one, to behave rudely toward service providers. While this customer behavior is not enjoyed, most providers understand the stress levels of their customers and try to put the encounters in perspective. For example, the parents who have brought their child to the emergency room for a high fever may be so anxious that they snap at the receptionist who greets them and the clerk who processes their insurance information. Those same parents may be the most delightful "customers" of health care under normal circumstances. Although health care is the ultimate example of a stressful service, legal services, financial services, dentistry, auto repair, and retail shopping may all elicit anxiety in some customers, and that anxiety can lead to less than positive service encounters.

However, customers experiencing stress are salvageable. The same parents who raised their voices at the receptionist in the emergency room when they brought in their ill toddler may return with a fruit basket the next day to thank anyone and everyone who was kind to them when they were panicked. Kind words, acknowledgment of fear and anxiety, and support and empathy from service providers can turn these negative encounters into positive ones.

But some customers just cannot be pleased. Even the most customer-focused of systems will encounter these customers periodically. Sometimes nothing can be done to change the nature of the interaction. There are times when it is best for both the customer and the server to encourage the customer to seek service elsewhere.

Recovering from Service Failures

Because of the variation inherent in services, it is virtually impossible for services to perform perfectly all the time. Research has demonstrated, however, that resolving service failures promptly and completely can lead to higher overall satisfaction than if the service had been perfect from the start.[9]

For the service provider to recover from a service failure, however, the provider needs to know about it. Some customers do not complain to either the service provider or to third parties; they "vote with their feet" and seek an alternative service elsewhere. Some customers complain to their friends and acquaintances but not to the service firm, which can have a negative effect on the service firm's reputation without any possibility of recovery with the dissatisfied customer. Some customers complain to formal third parties such as lawyers or advocacy groups.

Some customers complain later, by phone or by letter. These customers provide an opportunity for the service provider to make things right, albeit after the fact. Some customers complain immediately when they are dissatisfied with service. These customers provide an opportunity for the service provider not only to satisfy them, but also to learn about the problems in the system that will enable them to serve other customers more effectively.

When customers complain, they generally seek three specific types of justice:[10]

- Outcome fairness. Customers expect compensation that matches the level of service failure. For example, if the wrong entrée is served in a restaurant, the customer may reasonably expect that the correct entrée will be brought and that a token compensation, perhaps a free dessert, will be offered. If the rest of the service was adequate, most customers would probably be uncomfortable with overcompensation—the entire meal free, for example.

[9] Stephen S. Tax and Stephen W. Brown, "Recovering and Learning from Service Failure," *Sloan Management Review,* Fall 1998, pp. 75–88.
[10] Ibid.

- Procedural fairness. Clear, understandable, and hassle-free procedures for addressing complaints are important to all customers.

- Interaction fairness. Even beyond outcome and procedural fairness, customers expect to be treated with respect and courtesy. This relates back to the notion of esteem discussed at the beginning of this chapter.

Despite the fact that companies may not be able to prevent all service failures, they can learn to recover from them. A recent study by the U.S. Department of Consumer Affairs reveals a very strong relationship between a customer's intention to repurchase and a provider's ability to resolve a customer's problem on the spot. Specifically, 95 percent of the customers said they intend to repurchase if their problem is resolved quickly on the spot. However, if the service recovery takes even a little time, the percentage drops to 70 percent. A decrease in customer retention from 95 percent to 70 percent can have a dramatic impact on a company's bottom line.[11]

Obtaining Customer Satisfaction Information: Service Guarantees

Because some customers will not complain about service even when they are not satisfied with the service they received, many firms offer an incentive for customers to provide information about service satisfaction problems. They do this in the form of a service guarantee: offering a guarantee of 100 percent customer satisfaction or a full refund, credit, or replacement in the event of dissatisfaction. Overall, a service guarantee is a powerful tool for achieving service quality for the following five reasons:

1. Guarantees force firms to focus on what their customers want and expect from each element of the service. If all the service workers in a system know that a service guarantee has been offered, they are likely to be more attuned to serving those customers.

2. Guarantees set clear standards for both the customers and the employees of the organization. The danger of having to compensate customers for poor service will encourage managers to take guarantees seriously, because they are directly linked to the financial costs of service failures.

3. Guarantees require the development of systems for generating meaningful customer feedback and acting on it. Again, because customers do not always provide information to the service firm, it is important for the firm to seek ways to actively collect that information, to analyze it, and to act on it.

4. Guarantees force service organizations to understand why they fail, encouraging them to identify and overcome potential failure points.

5. Guarantees reduce the consumer's risk of the purchase decision and build long-term loyalty.

It is important to note that poorly designed service guarantees are unlikely to work well. If the guarantee has too many exceptions and conditions or requires customers to maneuver through a complicated procedure to collect on the guarantee, customers won't bother—and the service firm loses valuable information. For a service guarantee to work effectively, it must be: (1) unconditional, (2) easy to understand, (3) meaningful, (4) easy to invoke, and (5) easy and quick to collect on.[12]

---

[11] C. W. L. Hart, J. L. Heskett, and W. E. Sasser, Jr., "The Profitable Art of Service Recovery," *Harvard Business Review,* July–August 1990.
[12] Hart, "The Power of Unconditional Service Guaranties," *Harvard Business Review,* July–August 1988.

Six Sigma Quality

When customers complained that they weren't reaching the right person when they called GE Capital Mortgage Insurance, GE collected data to measure the impact of variables ranging from lunch breaks to the use of voice mail. It found that 24 percent of callers were hanging up, an "abandon rate" that was slashed to 0.5 percent.[13] This is just one example of how GE has used its Six Sigma quality improvement program to better satisfy its customers.

To make sure customers' needs are consistently met, organizations need to be sure they have developed systems that will produce consistent output in relation to customer needs. The managerial thrust of Six Sigma quality is to effectively use data to analyze business processes to reduce defects to no more than 3.4 defects per million. The Six Sigma process generally involves first identifying the goal of the process, then:

1. Defining the project goals and customer needs.

2. Measuring the output of the current process.

3. Analyzing the process and using quality tools and simple statistics like those presented in Chapter 12S to identify areas for improvement.

4. Improving the system to reduce defect levels.

5. Controlling the new system by monitoring the process, perhaps by using statistical process control or other real-time monitoring tools.[14]

Six Sigma, or any quality initiative, requires the commitment of top management and the alignment of incentives to succeed. At organizations such as General Electric, up to 40 percent of executive incentives are tied to Six Sigma performance, and at Motorola, quality "Black Belts" are awarded bonuses when projects succeed. Six Sigma programs also involve selecting and training the workforce throughout the organization so that the philosophy of reducing variation and improving output is a part of everyone's consciousness. Key employees (called "Black Belts" at GE, Motorola, and Allied Signal or "Variability Reduction Leaders" at Polaroid) are chosen to lead improvement projects. These Six Sigma project leaders receive intensive training in quantitative improvement tools using statistical software and are also trained on teamwork and communication.

Organizations such as Allied Signal, GE, Lockheed-Martin, Motorola, Polaroid, and Texas Instruments have all reported significant successes with their Six Sigma programs. In GE's 1998 annual report, Chairman Jack Welch stated, "We plunged into Six Sigma with a company consuming vengeance just over three years ago. We have invested more than a billion dollars in this effort, and the financial returns have now entered the exponential phase—more than three quarters of a billion dollars in savings beyond our investment in 1998, with a billion and a half in sight for 1999."[15] The *2000 Annual Report* "Letter to Stockholders" stated, "Six Sigma has turned the Company's focus from inside to outside, changed the way we think and train our future leaders and moved us toward becoming a truly customer-focused organization."

Keeping Customers: Zero Defections

One way to think about customer-focused service refers back to the notion of loyalty. In manufacturing environments, a focus on "zero defects" keeps management and workers at-

---

[13] Del Jones, "Firms Aim for Six Sigma Efficiency," *USA Today,* July 21, 1998, p. 1B.

[14] Stephen Halliday, "So What Is Exactly . . . Six Sigma?" *Works Management* 54, no. 1 (2001), pp. 15–17.

[15] Gerald J. Hahn, William J. Hill, Roger W. Hoerl, and Stephen A. Zinkgraf, "The Impact of Six Sigma Improvement—A Glimpse into the Future of Statistics," *The American Statistician* 53, no. 3 (1999), pp. 208–15.

There is no stronger advocate for outstanding service to customers than Tom Raffio, president and CEO of Northeast Delta Dental (NEDD), a nonprofit dental insurance provider covering Maine, New Hampshire, and Vermont. NEDD's Guarantee of Service Excellence (GOSE) is the cornerstone of Tom's corporate strategy. The seven-point GOSE Program, which incorporates NEDD's three major customers (dentists, subscribers, and the organizations where the subscribers work), provides ongoing feedback from customers, identifying opportunities for continuously improving NEDD's business processes.

A guarantee of service is explicitly stated for each of the seven points in the program, and, if that service is not provided, the refund level is specified. Even if the customer is not aware that service has not been properly provided, Tom encourages NEDD employees to report mistakes so they can be addressed and eliminated in the future. The refunds paid to customers for service guarantee failures are viewed as continuous improvement, and these "investments" have helped reduce administrative costs as a percentage of revenues from 18 percent in 1996 to 13 percent in 2001.

The results show that Tom is on the right track. Eighty-four percent of the dental professionals in the areas that it serves are participants. Between 1996 and 2001 the total number of NEDD subscribers increased from 147,590 to 240,992, an average annual increase of more than 10.3 percent, in an industry with little or no growth! More impressive is that NEDD covers 600,000 people in a tri-state area with a population of 3.1 million and has a customer retention rate of 95.7 percent.

1. Smooth Implementation to Northeast Delta Dental—Successful implementation will be determined by the group through the results of a survey conducted by Northeast Delta Dental.

2. Exceptional Customer Service—Northeast Delta Dental will resolve a telephone inquiry immediately or guarantee an initial update within one business day and notification upon resolution.

3. Quick Processing of Claims—During the course of a contract year, 90 percent of a group's accurately completed claim forms will be processed correctly within 15 calendar days.

4. No Inappropriate Billing by Participating Dentists—Patients will not be charged for more than the appropriate co-payments at the time of service or for any difference between a participating dentist's submitted and Northeast Delta Dental's approved amount, as indicated on the Notification of Benefits form.

5. Accurate and Quick Turnaround of Identification Cards—A pair of accurate identification cards will be mailed within 15 calendar days upon receipt of a completed enrollment form or request.

6. Timely Employee Booklets—Standard Northeast Delta Dental Summary Plan Description Booklets and/or Outline of Benefits will be mailed within 15 calendar days of request, finalized benefits change, or receipt of signed contract.

7. Marketing Service Contacts—Each group will receive at least two Marketing service contacts during a contract term.

Source: From Stephen Halliday, "So What Exactly Is . . . Six Sigma?" *Works Management,* 54, no. 1, 2001, p. 15. Reprinted by permission of the author.

---

tuned to the need to prevent quality problems rather than solve them. In the 1980s, manufacturing firms discovered that the only way to improve quality was to start measuring it. Measurement of quality enabled them to realize that poor quality has a high cost (for example, the costs associated with scrap, rework, machine downtime, etc.) and also a direct linkage to the company's bottom line. Manufacturers realized they could increase their firms' profitability by striving for zero defects.

Although problem-free service is an admirable goal, it is probably also an unrealistic one because of the tremendous variation in service systems. In services, increased profitability can be achieved through customer loyalty and retention: the notion of "zero defections."[16] Striving for zero defections means trying to retain every customer that the company can profitably serve. In recent years, service companies have recognized that existing customers cost less to serve and are generally more profitable than new ones. Because loyalty to a service results from meeting or exceeding customers' expectations, superior service quality leads to an increased rate of customer retention and improved

[16] F. F. Reichheld and W. E. Sasser, Jr., "Zero Defections: Quality Comes to Services," *Harvard Business Review,* September–October 1990.

profitability. Studies about customer loyalty have shown that even a 5 percent increase in customer retention can increase profitability from 25 percent to 85 percent. However, eliminating defections, or even reducing them, is a very challenging task. It requires the use of specific mechanisms that will enable the organization to find the customers who have ended their relationship with the company (or are about to do so) and also to analyze and act on the information they provide.

The Impact of Technology

Over the past two decades, technology has dramatically changed the nature of the service encounter. Services used to be provided exclusively face to face, with all the benefits and challenges associated with every interaction that occurs between two or more people. With the invention of the telephone, many services were offered over the phone, but the interaction was still between two people, with only the nonverbal cues absent from the interaction.

While remote service has always been available by mail, those encounters were temporally disconnected. New technologies have made it possible for customers to interact in real-time with service providers and even to become a part of the service itself. You can become a data entry clerk for your bank or your brokerage firm by conducting transactions over the Internet. You can be an order entry clerk by purchasing items from retailers over the Web or by using a Touch-Tone phone.

Never before have services been so convenient for both the service provider and the customer. Each transaction costs the firm less because fewer workers are involved. The customers enjoy greater access to service and convenience because they can conduct transactions from many locations at any time of the day or night.

But these new service encounters require a great deal of thought about what is important to customers and how the technology can provide it. Service organizations that offer new technological alternatives will pull ahead of their slower competitors, but they may not be able to keep that marketplace advantage unless they take the new encounter forms as seriously as if they had the customer in their offices face to face!

Summary

Technology has also facilitated the collection of customer satisfaction data and has provided alternate channels of communication for customers. Companies such as Seibel and CRM offer software packages that enable service firms to integrate sales, customer service and support, and marketing.

In order to be successful in the long run, service organizations need to reliably meet their customers' expectations. Customer expectations are complex, involving core needs for fairness, security, and esteem. Customer expectations are also dynamic, affected by their perception of service by one firm in particular and by all firms in general. Customer expectations can be described by "zones." When the service provides service beyond what customers desire, they are delighted. When service is adequate, but does not meet the desired service level, customers are tolerant of the service. When service does not reach the adequate level, customers are dissatisfied. These zones vary as the importance of the service to the customer varies: when the service is very important to the customer, the desired level of service is higher and the customer's willingness to accept less is smaller, so the zone of tolerance is narrower than it might be for a service that is less important to the customer.

Customer perception of service is affected by the service encounter. Service recovery, adaptability, spontaneity, and coping are themes that are important to customers and that, therefore, should be an important part of the training for service workers.

Service firms that recognize the importance of customer satisfaction are moving away from a transaction orientation toward customer relationship management. Both the service firm and the customer benefit when the relationship between service provider and customer are strong. Strong customer relationships are built on reliable service interactions.

Because variation in service systems is so significant, service firms have adopted many other strategies, among them service guarantees, Six Sigma quality programs and zero defection programs aimed at collecting information and satisfying customers.

Key Terms

adaptability: the service system's ability to deal with a customer's special needs or requests. *(p. 359)*

coping: how service workers relate to problem customers. *(p. 359)*

recovery: response to initial service failures to regain customer satisfaction. *(p. 359)*

spontaneity: unprompted or unsolicited actions by service workers. *(p. 359)*

zone of tolerance: the level at which the customer will be satisfied with the service provided. *(p. 356)*

Review and Discussion Questions

1. What are core customer needs and why are they important in service environments?

2. What are the two ways a service firm can improve customer satisfaction? How does the satisfaction equation behave dynamically?

3. Describe the zone of tolerance and its boundaries. What are some factors that cause variation in the zone of tolerance?

4. What are the three basic types of service encounters? What are the particular challenges offered by each?

5. Describe how the recovery, adaptability, spontaneity, and coping themes relate to service satisfaction. What are some service provider actions that can be taken to make these themes positive rather than negative?

6. Describe customer relationship management and its benefits to both the customer and the firm.

7. Describe some options for building customer loyalty through customization. Give examples of each option.

8. Describe the key elements of a good service guarantee and why they are important.

9. Define Six Sigma quality and its benefits.

Internet Assignments

1. Go to your favorite Internet browser and do a keyword search on *customer relationship management.* Identify at least one article published within the last year on this topic, and describe at least one firm that provides this service.

2. Go to your favorite Internet browser and do a keyword search on Six Sigma quality. Identify at least one firm that provides services related to Six Sigma quality and describe the services it offers. Find at least one implementation story. Was the implementation successful or unsuccessful?

CASE Laura Milton's Printer

On August 21, Laura Milton, a professor at Eastern Business School in Massachusetts, had just printed her fall syllabus on her PrintCo 400 printer when she saw the one-page error message. She checked the printer manual, rebooted the computer, turned the printer off and on again, checked for jams, and even checked for a blown fuse. Then she decided to call the customer service line at PrintCo. After 15 minutes on hold, she reached a very pleasant technician who suggested she insert a new printer cartridge. Laura was frustrated about having to spend $100 for a new cartridge, but she did find that the error message printed with better contrast!

When Laura called again, the technician instructed her to call a different service number to locate the nearest certified repair office. Eight minutes on hold later, Laura was given three locations: one in Pennsylvania, one in a town in Massachusetts she had never heard of, and one in Needham, Massachusetts, about a 30-minute drive from the retail store, Electronic World, at which she had purchased the printer. Laura called the Needham service center and arranged to take her printer there the next morning at 8:00.

Andrea, the technician in Needham, was very pleasant and reassured Laura that the printer would likely be ready within two working days. Laura responded that this was a rather good week for a failure, but that classes would begin the next week and she would *really* need it. Andrea promised to call with any news.

A week later, Laura had heard nothing about her printer, so she called Andrea. Andrea replied that she had been in contact with PrintCo and that a part she had replaced had made the printing error much more interesting: both sides of the printed page had wide, black, strongly contrasting lines now. She planned to continue to work closely with PrintCo to solve the problem and would call as soon as anything changed.

Another week later, Laura called Andrea again. This time, Andrea offered to ask to have PrintCo replace the six-month-old printer for Laura. Two hours later, Andrea called Laura to inform her that the printer would need to be taken back to Electronic World before any replacement could be considered. Laura drove to Needham to pick up the printer and drove the hour in the opposite direction to Electronic World to drop off the printer. The young clerk, Chris, was very pleasant and reassuring. He told Laura that these problems were handled all the time at Electronic World and that she would hear from them in no more than two business days about the printer.

A third week later, Laura had called Electronic World several times only to be put on hold, then switched to an answering machine. Finally, Chris called back to inform her that the printer was still not working, that they had replaced more parts, and that he thought sending the printer to PrintCo's New Jersey office was the right move.

Laura was getting cranky. She agreed (since she had no choice) and the printer was sent.

A fourth week later, Laura was informed that her printer had returned to Electronic World and she could come get it. She drove the half-hour to retrieve the printer, carried it up to her home office, and plugged it in. She received a new error message: No Cartridge. Her new $100 cartridge had not been returned with the machine! Laura called Electronic World, was put on hold, and routed to an answering machine. Two hours later, she was called back and informed that the cartridge must have been left in New Jersey. She asked for the New Jersey PrintCo number and called there herself to inquire about the cartridge. She was put on hold and transferred automatically to an answering machine.

The next morning, Laura bought a new printer cartridge for $100 just so she could see if the problem had been repaired. After work that day, Electronic World called to say that they had the printer cartridge after all.

Two hours later, PrintCo in New Jersey called to apologize for Laura's experience and to encourage her to call the complaint line at PrintCo that dealt specifically with retailer problems. After all, it was Electronic World's fault, not PrintCo's. Laura replied that she had no intention of taking the initiative to contact PrintCo. Twenty minutes later, the PrintCo complaint department called to interview Laura. The agent commiserated with Laura. The New Jersey PrintCo staff had been through empowerment training, she told her. Too bad Electronic World's employees hadn't been empowered to replace Laura's cartridge!

Laura held the phone away from her ear and stared, speechless!

Questions

1. Identify the customer service problems encountered by Professor Milton.

2. What kind of service guarantee might have been offered by PrintCo? By Electronic World?

3. What kind of service recovery might have been offered by PrintCo? By Electronic World?

Selected Bibliography

Alderfer, Clayton. "An Empirical Test of a New Theory of Human Needs." *Organizational Behavior and Human Performance* 4 (1969), pp. 142–75.

Bitner, Mary Jo, Bernard H. Booms, and Mary Stanfield Tetreault. "The Service Encounter: Diagnosing Favorable and Unfavorable Incidents." *Journal of Marketing* 54 (January 1990), pp. 71–84.

Cook, Lori S., David E. Bowen, Richard B. Chase, Sriram Dasu, Doug M. Stewart, and David A. Tansik. "Human Issues in Service Design." *Journal of Operations Management* 20 (2002), pp. 159–74.

Halliday, Stephen. "So What Is Exactly . . . Six Sigma?" *Works Management* 54, no. 1 (2001), pp. 15–17.

Hahn, Gerald J., William J. Hill, Roger W. Hoerl, and Stephen A. Zinkgraf. "The Impact of Six Sigma Improvement—A Glimpse into the Future of Statistics." *The American Statistician* 53, no. 3 (1999), pp. 208–15.

Hart, C. W. L. "The Power of Unconditional Service Guarantees." *Harvard Business Review,* July–August 1988, pp. 54–62.

Hart, C. W. L., J. L. Heskett, and W. E. Sasser, Jr. "The Profitable Art of Service Recovery." *Harvard Business Review,* July–August 1990, pp. 148–56.

Journal of the Academy of Marketing Science 23, no. 4, Special Issue on Relationship Marketing (Fall 1995).

Maslow, Abraham. "A Theory of Human Motivation." *Psychological Review* 50 (1943), p. 381.

Pine, Joseph B. *Mass Customization.* Boston: Harvard Business School Press, 1993.

Reichheld, Frederick F., and Earl W. Sasser. *The Loyalty Effect.* Boston: Harvard Business School Press, 1996.

Reichheld, F. F., and W. E. Sasser, Jr. "Zero Defections: Quality Comes to Services." *Harvard Business Review,* September–October 1990, pp. 105–11.

Richard, Normann. *Service Management.* New York: John Wiley and Sons, 1984, pp. 8–9.

Schneider, B., and D. E. Bowen. "Understanding Customer Delight and Outrage." *Sloan Management Review* 41, no. 1, pp. 35–45.

Shostack, Lynn G. "Planning the Service Encounter." In *The Service Encounter,* ed. John A. Czepiel, Michael R. Solomon, and Carol F. Surprenant. Lexington, MA: Lexington Books, 1985, pp. 243–54.

Tax, Stephen S., and Stephen W. Brown. "Recovering and Learning from Service Failure." *Sloan Management Review,* vol. 40, no. 1 (Fall 1998), pp. 75–88.

Zeithaml, Valarie A., and Mary Jo Bitner. *Services Marketing.* New York: Irwin/McGraw-Hill, 2000, p. 139.

CHAPTER FOURTEEN

Managing Capacity and Demand

Learning Objectives

- Introduce different strategies for managing service capacity.

- Present approaches for matching capacity and demand.

- Introduce the concept of yield management as a tool for increasing revenues and profits for service operations.

- Identify the characteristics of services that can take maximum advantage of yield management.

- Illustrate how services control capacity and manage customer demand to maximize capacity utilization.

- Identify additional approaches for maximizing capacity utilization that improve the overall long-term performance of the firm.

Yield Management Improves Revenues and Profits at National Car Rental

John Riley / Stone / Getty Images

Faced with possible liquidation in 1993 by parent company General Motors, National Car Rental was under significant pressure to produce both a substantial and a sustainable profit. To accomplish this, its senior management team decided to adopt a comprehensive revenue management (or yield management) system. Instead of a constant car rental price for all time periods, regardless of demand, the revenue management system demonstrated that a variable pricing policy, which would fluctuate with demand, would result in significantly higher profits.

The new revenue management system was implemented in two phases. The first was introduced in July 1993, with the goal of showing immediate profits—and it did. The second phase focused on developing a state-of-the-art revenue management system for the car rental industry. This phase was successfully implemented in July 1994.

With the revenue management system in place, profits increased significantly, and General Motors was able to sell National Car Rental in 1995 for more than $1 billion.

Source: Ernest Johnson, "1994 Trophy Award: National Car Rental Systems, Inc.," *Scorecard: The Revenue Management Quarterly,* First Quarter 1995, and M. G. Geraghty and Ernest Johnson, "Revenue Management System Saves National Car Rental," *Interfaces* 27, no. 1 (January–February 1997), pp. 107–27.

The Customer's Perspective

"Hyatt Hotel, O'Hare Airport. How can I help you?"

"Yes, I'd like to make a room reservation for two nights. I'll be attending the SAP Conference and would like the special conference room rate of $145 per night."

"That room rate of $145 per night is correct, Mr. Davis, but unfortunately, we are all sold out of rooms reserved at that rate. However, I can give you a room at our regular room rate."

"How much is that?"

"$245 per night."

"I'm sorry, but that's too expensive for me. I guess I'll have to stay somewhere else."

"Do you belong to AAA?"

"Yes, I do."

"I can give you a room at the AAA rate of $99 per night."

"Sounds good to me."

How often have you sat next to someone on an airline and, in the course of conversation, discovered that you paid a different price for your ticket (and usually that your ticket cost more!)? Similarly, how often have you stayed at a hotel, only to find out that the room rate you were charged differed from that of your friends or colleagues (and again, you usually paid more for your room), or that you were charged different rates for different nights that you stayed at the hotel? If you travel a lot, you will have had similar experiences with car rentals (weekend rates are typically lower than weekday rates) and cruises (last-minute reservations can cost significantly less than those made a couple of months ahead of time).

The above telephone conversation actually occurred, and although at first glance it sounds terribly confusing, there is actually some logic to it, at least from the company's perspective. There is also logic to the wide range of airfares that airlines charge and to the various rates that car rental firms charge. The rationale behind these different fares and rates is based on the principles of yield management, which is also referred to as *revenue management.* The hotel, the airline, and the car rental agency are attempting to match available capacity (as measured in rooms, seats, or cars, respectively) with the customer demand for that capacity to maximize revenues and ultimately profits.

Management Issues

Because services are both intangible and simultaneously produced and consumed, they cannot be inventoried. Consequently, managing or matching capacity and demand is a key element in the success of every service operation. Too much capacity, while providing high levels of customer service, results in unnecessarily high costs that reduce profits. Too little capacity, on the other hand, results in poor service or the inability to provide service when customers want it, resulting in the loss of both current and future customers and revenues, and again reduced profits.

The difficulty of matching capacity and demand is further complicated by the variability in demand for services, which may be dramatic from month to month, week to week, day to day, or even hour to hour. This variability often results in the underutilization of service capacity during significant periods.

To determine the proper level of capacity to provide, service managers must seek a balance between the cost of additional capacity and the cost of lost customers resulting from poor service or the inability to provide any service. At the same time, service managers need to constantly identify new ways to increase customer demand during slow periods when capacity is underutilized.

For managers of service firms that can take maximum advantage of yield management, the challenge is to determine what prices to charge and what percentage of available capacity to allocate to the different prices. Substantial amounts of capacity, be it in the form of airline seats or hotel rooms, can usually be sold in advance at rates that are significantly discounted. For example, airlines usually require that tickets be purchased at least 21 days in advance for their super-saver fares, which offer the lowest prices; similarly, organizations holding conferences usually reserve hotel rooms years in advance of their meetings, again at substantially reduced rates.

Service firms with perishable capacity offer such significant discounts because it is more profitable to sell the airplane seats, or hotel rooms, at a discount rather than to let them remain vacant. At the same time, service managers do not want to pay the opportunity cost of turning away last-minute customers who usually pay the full fare for the airline seat or the "rack rate" for the hotel room because the capacity had been previously sold at a discounted rate.

The methodology for determining the percentage of capacity to allocate to each market segment or price is called yield management. With yield management, the service manager is simultaneously managing both the availability of and the demand for the firm's capacity. Capacity is controlled by the amount that management makes available at each of the different price levels. Demand can also be controlled by different price levels: lower prices increase demand; higher prices decrease demand.

Types of Capacity

Capacity in service operations can be divided into two broad categories: fixed, or long-term, capacity and variable, or short-term, capacity.

Fixed, or Long-Term, Capacity

Fixed, or long-term, capacity consists of the physical facilities of the service, so any changes in fixed capacity usually require a major commitment of resources, both in terms of labor and finances. As a result, long-term capacity often requires a significant amount of time to change, and therefore remains relatively "fixed" over the short term. Examples of fixed capacity for various services are shown in Exhibit 14.1.

Variable, or Short-Term, Capacity

Variable, or short-term, capacity consists primarily of the labor that is required to satisfy customer demand. In many service environments, variable capacity can quickly change over relatively small increments of time, such as an hour. Managing labor capacity falls under the topic of scheduling and is addressed in detail in Chapter 10.

EXHIBIT 14.1
Examples of Fixed Capacity

Service	Examples of Fixed Capacity
Airline	Airplanes, ticket counters, gates
Hotel	Guest rooms, meeting rooms, parking
Restaurant	Tables, seats, kitchen equipment, parking
Hospital	Beds, operating rooms
College	Classrooms, dormitory rooms
Call Center	Telephone lines, workstations

To address short-term capacity issues, the service manager must acknowledge the fact that the physical capacity of the facility has already been established and acts as a constraint in the labor scheduling decision process. For example, it would not make sense for a supermarket manager to schedule nine cashiers to be on duty at the same time when there are only six checkout stations.

Capacity Strategies

Matching capacity with demand is always challenging in service environments. Managers must be able to address two general situations: the normal variation in demand for services over time and sustained growth in demand.

Managing Capacity to Address Variation

Managing capacity to address the typical variation in demand for services is primarily concerned with short-term capacity, or labor scheduling, and can be done in two basic ways: maintain level capacity and chase demand.[1]

The level capacity strategy is most often used when workers are more skilled and more highly paid. For example, although there are high demand periods in many professional services—consider flu season in pediatric services or tax season in accounting practices—professional services generally maintain a consistent workforce. Busy periods are managed by working longer hours, by scheduling less time-sensitive demand for slower periods (scheduling fewer routine annual appointments in flu season, for example), and by scheduling worker vacations during slower periods. Some service environments, such as hospital emergency rooms, expect significant variation in capacity utilizations as demand varies. For example, an emergency room may be consistently busy on Friday nights and schedule staff for the average demand, but although Fridays may be busy *on average,* any given Friday may be slow, or a block of hours within a Friday night shift may be slow. Busy periods are likely to be hectic for workers and may mean customers wait longer than they prefer to.

The chase demand strategy is used more often in services in which labor is less skilled and less highly paid. For example, additional department store sales staff are hired for the holiday season, additional hotel staff are hired during the summer on Cape Cod and during the winter at Palm Springs, California.

Managing Capacity for Growth

Again, there are two basic ways to manage capacity (both short term and long term) when demand for a service is growing: to add capacity in anticipation of demand and to add capacity when demand levels have exceeded current capacity.

[1] W. Earl Sasser, "Match Supply and Demand in Service Industries," *Harvard Business Review,* November–December 1976, p. 134.

Anticipating Growth

The first approach is to anticipate the growth in demand by adding additional capacity before it is actually needed. With this approach, short-term costs are high because capacity utilization is low and, consequently, the cost of the additional capacity is not offset right away by the increase in demand. However, this approach results in shorter customer waiting times and therefore has a positive effect on the long-term success of the firm.

Reacting to Growth

With this approach, capacity is not added until the demand for it has been clearly established. Delaying the addition of the needed capacity makes the capacity utilization of the service significantly higher than with the anticipated strategy, and, as a consequence, the revenue stream is much larger, thereby more easily justifying the cost of the additional capacity. However, with this approach, customers are likely to experience longer waiting lines. If the waits become unacceptable, they can have a negative effect on the long-term success of the firm, as customers will take their business elsewhere.

The Trade-off Between Capacity Utilization and Service

Determining the size or capacity of a service facility is a critical factor in its design. Once the service facility has been constructed, its physical capacity becomes fixed and can be changed only at great expense (if at all!).

Two primary measures relate to the physical or fixed capacity for a service facility. First, as illustrated in Exhibit 14.2, there is *maximum capacity,* which defines the maximum number of customers the physical facility can process in a given period. Examples include the number of rooms available per night in a hotel, the number of seats available in a restaurant, the number of checkout stations in a supermarket, and the number of telephone lines coming into a call center.

When customers must wait before being served there is also *optimal capacity utilization,* which is directly related to the maximum number of customers the facility can serve while still providing a desired level of service. (Typically, service levels are expressed as a percentage of customers who are served within a given time frame. For example at BostonCoach, which

EXHIBIT 14.2
Comparing Capacity and Demand for a Food Service Facility

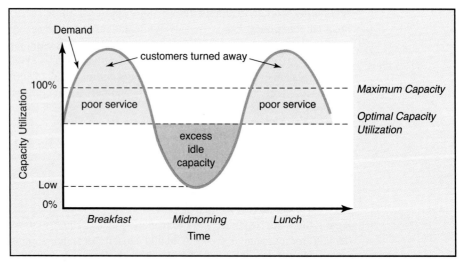

Source: Adapted from Christopher Lovelock, "Strategies for Managing Capacity-Constrained Services," *Managing Services: Marketing, Operations Management and Human Resources,* 2nd ed. (Englewood Cliffs, NJ: Prentice Hall, 1992), p. 155.

provides ground transportation services primarily for corporate clients, the service level goal for its call center is that 80 percent of all calls be answered in 20 seconds or less.)[2] Examples here include the check-in counter at an airline, an ATM, and a hotel reservations call center. To better understand how customer demand, capacity, and service level are related, Christopher Lovelock has identified four situations that service managers may encounter, as shown in Exhibit 14.2.

These four situations are:

Situation	Example
Customer demand exceeds maximum capacity causing customers to be turned away.	You receive a busy signal when you call to make a hotel reservation.
Demand causes an increase in capacity utilization beyond its optimum level, resulting in customers receiving very poor (or slow) service.	You have to wait more than an hour to be seated in a very busy restaurant.
Demand results in optimal capacity utilization.	Your wait at the supermarket checkout is short even though all of the checkout stations are being used.
Demand causes capacity utilization to be less than its optimum level, resulting in excess idle capacity.	Your telephone call is answered immediately or you are seated immediately in a restaurant.

For example, if an airline check-in counter has six stations and it takes an average of four minutes to process each passenger, then the maximum capacity of the counter is calculated as follows:

$$\text{Capacity of each station} = \frac{60 \text{ Minutes/hour/station}}{4 \text{ Minutes/passenger}} = 15 \text{ Passengers/hour/station}$$

Capacity of the counter = 15 Passengers/hour/station × 6 Stations = 90 Passengers/hour

The optimum capacity utilization for the check-in counter is determined with queuing theory, which is presented in detail in the supplement to Chapter 15. Using demand, as expressed in customers per time period, and the maximum capacity of the facility, which is also expressed in customers per time period, queuing theory can determine the level of service being provided to the customer, as measured by the average amount of time customers wait before being served.

Continuing with our check-in counter example, if, through queuing theory, we find that the optimal capacity utilization for this facility is 67.7 percent, then the customer demand that results in a 67.7 percent capacity utilization is 90 × 67.7 percent, or 60 customers per hour (which is the maximum number of customers the facility can serve while still providing the required service level).

Managing Demand

Managing customer demand in services consists primarily of trying to shift demand from peak periods, when demand exceeds the capacity of the service facility, or service is being poorly provided, to slow periods, when the capacity is underutilized. As part of this approach, managers also try to create new demand during these slow periods.

---

[2] Per conversation with Grant Mitchell, director of account development, BostonCoach, January 16, 2001.

Demand can be shifted either by time or by location. Shifting demand from one time period to another, such as in a hotel from a Thursday to a Saturday or in a restaurant from 8:00 P.M. to 5:00 P.M., can increase the utilization of the physical capacity and permit more efficient and effective service. Shifting demand to different locations is possible when several service outlets are available, such as with hotel chains. Again, the goal of shifting demand is to better utilize available physical capacity and to provide more efficient and effective service.

Specific ways in which demand can be shifted from peak periods to slow periods are discussed in detail later in this chapter, as part of the discussion on yield management. However, we present here an overview of some common approaches to managing demand in services.

Pricing

Offering price discounts for services that are provided during nonpeak periods is one obvious way to shift demand. Movie theaters offer special prices for matinees; telephone companies offer lower rates for long-distance calls on nights and weekends; toll roads in France have non-rush-hour rates; subways offer nonpeak fares.

Managers may choose to shift demand even if it means short-term decreases in revenues. For example, if peak periods are so busy that service suffers and customers are dissatisfied, it may be appropriate to shift demand by using price discounts simply to even out the demand, thereby ensuring better service. Once demand during peak periods is at its desired level, managers must look for ways to segment the market for the service to create additional demand during the slow periods.

Advertising and Promotion

Another approach to shifting demand focuses on advertising and promotion. In addition to advertising price discounts, services also inform their customers that better service can be provided during specific times when demand is significantly lower. Twenty-four-hour supermarkets promote the benefits of shopping very early in the morning or late at night, and Jordan's Furniture advertises the benefits of visiting its stores on Saturday night, suggesting that it's a good place to relax or for a date because of the entertainment they provide.

Reservations

Reservations allow service firms to manage demand along both the time and location dimensions. A restaurant, by taking reservations, can schedule diners more evenly throughout the evening, thereby better matching demand with the capacity of the dining area and kitchen. For example, a well-known, upscale restaurant in New Orleans that is always busy will take reservations only for 6:30 P.M. and 9:00 P.M. In so doing, it doubles the nightly capacity by having two turnovers per seat (in comparison to having only one turnover if it took reservations for 8:00 P.M.). As mentioned earlier, hotel chains can use reservations to shift demand from one location that is fully booked to another nearby location that still has rooms available.

Creating New Demand

Many services look to new ways to create additional demand during nonpeak periods. For example, McDonald's and Burger King introduced breakfast menus to their original hamburger operations. Likewise, some ski resorts offer alpine rides or tennis tournaments during the summer.

Yield Management

Yield management actually is not a new concept. In the 1890s, Coney Island amusement park impresario George Tillyou introduced a crude version of yield management when he cut the price of admission on slow days.[3] However, the modern version was introduced by Bob Crandall at American Airlines during the 1980s, following the deregulation of the airline industry.

Services with high fixed costs and low variable costs, such as airlines, hotels, cruise lines, and car rental companies can effectively apply yield management. Profits for these services tend to be directly related to sales because variable costs, as a percentage of sales, are very low. Consequently, the goal for these firms is to maximize sales or revenues by maximizing capacity utilization, even if it means selling some of the available capacity at reduced prices—as long as these prices are greater than the variable costs.

Yield management allows the service manager to maximize revenue and capacity utilization by simultaneously controlling both the capacity (by limiting the available capacity at certain price levels) and demand (through price changes).

To illustrate how a service firm applies yield management to manage both demand and capacity, the "Using Technology to Create Value" on airfares at American Airlines provides a sampling of the different airfares that it offers between Boston and London and the restrictions associated with each airfare. While the level of service is significantly different for first-class and business-class passengers, all passengers who travel in coach receive the same level of service regardless of the fare they paid.

The airline controls supply by allocating a specific number of seats on the plane in each price category. When those seats are sold, a customer cannot purchase a seat at that fare, even though there are still seats available on the flight. However, as we shall see later in this chapter, if the plane does not fill up as fast as initially predicted, the airline might elect to open up additional seats at the lower fare, or even at special fares that are available for a limited time.

To better understand the approaches service managers can take to apply yield management to their own operations, Sherri Kimes and Dick Chase propose a framework, as shown in Exhibit 14.3, that identifies different pricing policies—and the duration for which these policies are applicable.

[3] Joe Sharkey, "Hotels Take a Lesson from Airline Pricing," *New York Times,* December 17, 2000, p. 3.

EXHIBIT 14.3
Framework for Applying Yield Management for Different Service Industries

Duration		Pricing	
		Fixed	**Variable**
	Predictable	Movies Stadiums/Arenas Convention centers	Hotels Airlines Rental cars Cruises
	Unpredictable	Restaurants Golf course Internet service providers	Continuing care Hospitals

Source: Sheryl E. Kimes and Richard B. Chase, "The Strategic Levers of Yield Management," *Journal of Service Research* 1, no. 2 (1998), pp. 298–308.

Using Technology to Create Value

The Application of Yield Management at American Airlines

Advances in information technology have facilitated the use of yield management in the airline industry to maximize revenues and profits. American Airlines was one of the first companies to use yield management to (*a*) establish prices, (*b*) determine for a given flight what percentage of capacity it should allocate to each price, and (*c*) determine the restrictions necessary to segment the markets. Listed below is a sampling of the different prices for a round-trip flight between Boston and London.

Fare	Season	Day of Week	Advanced Purchase (days)	Other Restrictions
$ 298	Low	Tue, Wed	0	Sat. night stay
$ 338	Low	Other Days	0	Sat. night stay
$ 548	Shoulder	Midweek	7	Sat. night stay
$ 597	Shoulder	Weekend	7	Sat. night stay
$ 824	High	Midweek	7	Sat. night stay
$ 884	High	Weekend	7	Sat. night stay
$ 2,920				Unrestricted coach
$ 7,538				Business class
$11,884				First class

Definitions:

Low season:	November 1–December 17
	January 6–March 15
Shoulder season:	September 30–October 31
	March 16–June 15
High season:	December 18–January 5
	June 16–September 29
Midweek:	Monday–Thursday
Weekend:	Friday–Sunday

Source: Based on a telephone conversation on February 18, 2002, with a reservation agent with American Airlines.

Those service industries that were the first to introduce yield management are in the upper-right-hand corner, while the most recent users are those in the lower half (that is, with unpredictable duration).

An Example of Yield Management at Charlie's Barbershop

The following story of Charlie's Barbershop provides a brief introduction to the basic concepts of yield management.[4]

Charlie operated a one-chair barbershop in a small suburb outside Atlanta, where he lived for many years. He was somewhat of an institution in the local community, being both a talented hairstylist and a great person with whom to discuss current events. Businesspeople, in particular, liked to have Charlie cut their hair but dreaded visiting his shop.

[4] Charles W. Chase, Jr., "Revenue Management: A Review," *The Journal of Business Forecasting,* Spring 1999, pp. 2, 28–30.

Because many of his customers frequently traveled during the week, they would go to Charlie's only on Saturdays. Unfortunately, Saturdays were especially busy, as retirees convened there to review Friday night's high school football game and whole families waited patiently for their turn in the single barber chair. For businesspeople on a tight schedule, Saturday mornings at Charlie's were frustrating. There was often a two-hour wait to get a haircut. Many customers tried to talk Charlie into accepting appointments, so they could schedule specific times without waiting, but he did not want to change his fundamental approach and risk alienating his other customers.

One day when business was slow, Charlie read a book on the basic principles of yield management. Afterward, he summarized his situation as follows:

- The shop was overcrowded on Saturdays, but Tuesdays were very slow.

- Some of the Saturday customers could come only on Saturdays, while others were retirees and schoolchildren, who could get their hair cut any day of the week.

- His rent and utilities costs were increasing, but many of his customers would balk at an across-the-board price increase.

- He was turning away a significant number of customers on Saturday. This was lost business.

- He had considered adding another chair and a part-time barber to the shop, but he couldn't justify the cost.

Over the course of a few months, Charlie began to wonder whether he could actually increase revenues while holding his costs constant if he raised his prices on Saturdays and discounted them on Tuesday. To put this in yield management terms, these price/convenience trade-offs existed in Charlie's micro-market. But he didn't know how willing his customers would be to pay a premium on Saturdays, and how many others would gladly move to a weekday to save a few dollars. If Charlie had a large database with all the appropriate customer data, he could build a model, simulate the opportunity, optimize his alternatives, and predict the outcome. Unfortunately, Charlie's business was too small for all that technical stuff.

Here's what Charlie did: He raised the Saturday price by 20 percent and lowered the Tuesday price by 20 percent. The retirees and mothers with school-age children were delighted to move to Tuesdays because of the lower price. This filled the slack in Charlie's schedule and enabled him to serve Saturday customers who were willing to pay extra for the convenient Saturday service. He was thus able to retain many of the people who used to leave frustrated on Saturdays without getting their hair cut. Furthermore, customers who continued to get their hair cut on Saturday benefited from a waiting time that was reduced to less than 30 minutes. Most important, at the end of the first year of this arrangement, Charlie was happy to find that he had increased the overall revenue of the shop by almost 20 percent as a result of increased volume.

Benefits of Yield Management

When yield management is properly implemented, it has a major impact on revenues and profits. According to an airline industry study conducted by Don Garvett of Simat, Helliesen and Eichner, a consulting firm specializing in the transportation industry, yield management was the factor, out of 13 studied, that was most highly correlated with profits (see Exhibit 14.4). On average, yield management increased revenues as much as 4 to 8 percent. Although this appears to be a small percentage, 80 percent of that increase translates directly to the bottom line.[5]

[5] "Yield Management Systems Are the Biggest Driver of Airline Profits," *World Airline News,* May 1, 1998, p. 1.

EXHIBIT 14.4
The Impact of Various
Factors on Airline
Profits

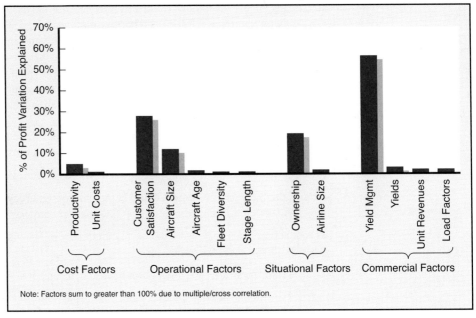

Note: Factors sum to greater than 100% due to multiple/cross correlation.

Source: Courtesy of Simat, Helliesen, and Eichner, New York.

Tim Baker and Dave Collier provide further examples of how yield management has benefitted various firms.[6] At American Airlines, for example, revenues increased between 1989 and 1991 by an estimated $1.4 billion, with net profits after taxes increasing by $892 million during that same period. Similarly, Hertz increased its annual revenue by 1 to 5 percent, Marriott improved its 1991 revenues by $25 million to $35 million, and Royal Caribbean Cruise Lines increased revenues by more than $20 million in one year.

Disadvantages of Yield Management

The primary disadvantage of yield management is that some customers perceive the associated pricing structure as being unfair, which ultimately translates into dissatisfied customers. This has become even more evident with ability to make reservations and purchase tickets on the Internet. For example, during the week of July 8–11, 2002, one of the authors, using Orbitz.com, an online travel reservations company, obtained a price of $286 for a round-trip flight between Boston and Denver on Monday. On Tuesday, the price had increased to $368. On Thursday morning of that week, the price dropped to $299, which is when the ticket was purchased. But by Thursday afternoon, the price had dropped even further, to $219, causing significant aggravation and frustration.

Services That Are Appropriate for Yield Management

To take maximum advantage of yield management, a service should have the following characteristics: (*a*) the ability to segment its markets, (*b*) high fixed and low variable costs, (*c*) product perishability, and (*d*) the ability to presell capacity.[7]

[6] Timothy K. Baker and David Collier, "A Comparative Revenue Analysis of Hotel Yield Management Heuristics," *Decision Sciences* 30, no. 1 (Winter 1999), pp. 239–63.
[7] Sheryl E. Kimes, "Yield-Management: A Tool for Capacity-Constrained Service Firms," *Journal of Operations Management* 8, no. 4 (October 1989).

Bob Crandall has long been recognized as one of the pioneers and innovators in the airline industry in the post-deregulation era. His many creative ideas include yield management; SABRE, the world's first global reservation and travel distribution system; AAdvantage, the first airline frequent flier program; and Super Saver Fares, the first implementation of differential fare pricing. He is often referred to as "The Father of Yield Management," the term having been introduced first at American Airlines. In a 1992 article that appeared in *Interfaces,* Crandall made the following comments:

> I believe that yield management is the single most important technical development in transportation management since we entered the era of airline deregulation in 1979. The development of yield management was a key to American Airlines' survival in the post-deregulation environment. Without yield management we were often faced with two unsatisfactory responses in a price competitive marketplace: We could match deeply discounted fares and risk diluting our entire inventory, or we could not match and certainly lose marketshare. Yield management gave us a third alternative— match deeply discounted fares on a portion of our inventory

and close deeply discounted inventory when it is profitable to save space for later booking higher value customers. By adjusting the number of reservations which are available to these discounts, we can adjust our minimum available fare to account for differences in demand. This creates a pricing structure which responds to demand on a flight-by-flight basis. As a result, we can more effectively match our demand to supply.

The development of the American Airlines' yield management system has been long and sometimes difficult, but this investment has paid off. We estimate that yield management has generated $1.4 billion in incremental revenue in the last three years alone. This is not a onetime benefit. We expect yield management to generate at least $500 million annually for the foreseeable future. As we continue to invest in the enhancement of DINAMO [AA's yield management system], we expect to capture an even larger revenue premium.

Source: Barry C. Smith et al., "Yield Management at American Airlines," *Interfaces,* January–February 1992.

Market Segmentation

A major issue in the successful implementation of yield management is the ability of the firm to segment its markets. Proper segmentation will prevent all the firm's customers from taking advantage of price reductions.

Market segmentation can be done in several ways. The first is to impose significant restrictions on customers who use the lower prices. For example, airlines require customers to stay over a Saturday night and/or to purchase their tickets from 7 to 30 days in advance to qualify for lower airfares. These conditions, however, prevent the business traveler, who usually travels midweek on short notice, from taking advantage of the lower fares.

Another method of segmentation is to limit lower prices to specific days of the week or times of the day. Movie theaters offer reduced ticket prices for matinees, which senior citizens can take advantage of during weekdays. Similarly, downtown hotels typically offer discounts on weekends when business travelers are home, as an incentive for tourists. Conversely, hotels in resort areas offer lower room rates during the week than they do on weekends. Exhibit 14.5 provides examples of various types of services and the strategies by which they segment markets for yield management purposes.

Markets are often segmented by price in another way on the Internet. Priceline.com is an independent e-business that auctions off excess capacities of airlines, hotels, and rental cars. The trade-off for customers is that while the prices tend to be very low, they usually have to accept some uncertainty at the time the reservation is made. For example, in the case of an airline ticket, the customer will not know the airline or the exact time of the flight until after the ticket has been purchased. Similarly, when booking a deeply discounted hotel stay

EXHIBIT 14.5
Examples of Services
and Market
Segmentation
Strategies

Service	Examples of Market Segmentation
Airlines	Weekdays vs. weekends; advanced purchase; Saturday night stay
Hotels	Weekdays vs. weekends; high season vs. low season
Toll roads	Peak vs. nonpeak hours; weekdays vs. weekends
Telephone companies	Nights vs. business hours; weekdays vs. weekends
Parking garages	Hourly vs. daily vs. monthly
Slips at a marina	Daily vs. monthly vs. seasonally
Restaurants	Early-bird menu vs. regular menu
Casinos	High minimum tables vs. low minimum tables

through Hotwire.com, a customer may not know the name or the exact location of the hotel until after the room is paid for.

The companies that are actually providing the service are also using the Internet in this manner. For example, American Airlines in December 2000 offered a round-trip fare on the Internet between Boston and Los Angeles for $331, but the lowest fare available through the American Airlines' reservation center was $384. Again there are trade-offs. The Internet fare was available for only one specific flight in each direction, while a choice of flights was available through the reservations center.

High Fixed and Low Variable Costs

A service firm with high fixed and low variable costs can offer significant discounts while still being able to cover variable costs. When a service firm has this cost structure, profits are directly related to sales. In other words, the more sales generated, the greater the resulting profits.

For example, let's assume the variable costs associated with having a hotel room cleaned are estimated to be $30 (which would include the labor to clean the room and the replacement of any material that was consumed, such as soap and shampoo, as well as fresh sheets and towels). Any price that the hotel could receive for the room above the $30 variable cost would be better financially than leaving the room empty for the night. Thus, it would be better to let a hotel guest have a room for $60 a night than to let the room remain empty, even though the regular or "rack" rate is $150 per night.

Product Perishability

The underlying reason that yield management can be applied to many types of services is the perishability of existing capacity. In other words, the capacity cannot be saved for future use. (Wouldn't it be great if the airlines could accumulate all their empty seats during the year for use during the Thanksgiving and Christmas periods?) Given that the capacity in a service operation is perishable, the service manager should try to maximize capacity utilization whenever possible, even if it means offering large discounts to attract customers—provided that the discounted prices exceed the variable cost.

Presold Capacity

A final requirement for the successful implementation of yield management is that the capacity for the lower-priced market can be sold in advance. This limits the availability of capacity to the higher-priced market segments. For example, hotels usually work with conference planners several years in advance of a conference, offering a given number of rooms at the lowest room rates. Travel groups usually plan tours within a year of when they need them and therefore also receive a discount. Finally, the last-minute customer, or "walk-in," will pay the highest or "rack rate" for a hotel room.

EXHIBIT 14.6
Example of a Booking Curve

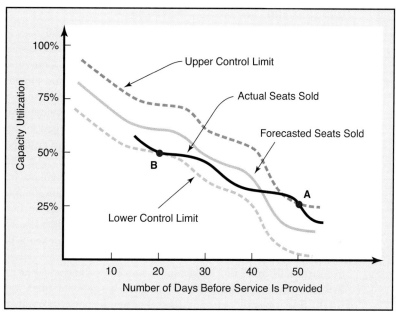

The Booking Curve

The concurrent management of both capacity and demand is a very dynamic process, with changes occurring daily or even more frequently. To facilitate this process, a tool known as the **booking curve** has been developed to assist managers both to control the availability of capacity and to manage the customer demand for that capacity. An example of a booking curve is presented in Exhibit 14.6

The horizontal axis represents the number of days before the service is to be used. For an airline, this would be the number of days before a particular flight is scheduled to take off. If a specific flight between New York City and Los Angeles is scheduled to take off on December 28, and today is December 8, then we would look at the status of the flight at the 20-day point on the horizontal axis.

The vertical axis represents the percentage of capacity that has been sold. A forecast is made using historical data to predict how much capacity will be sold as we approach the date of the flight. Because this is a forecast and not a known number, we predict within a range of values within a given confidence interval. Finally, the actual percentage of capacity that has been sold is plotted on the graph and compared with the forecast.

To illustrate how a manager would use this chart to make decisions, let's examine two points on the graph using simple examples. To begin, the airline offers two fares, a full fare with no restrictions and a discounted fare with restrictions. At point A, when there are 50 days to go before the flight, there is very strong demand and the number of seats sold exceeds the upper control limit. Management therefore decides to no longer offer any discounted fares, as there appears to be strong enough demand at that time to charge full fares and still reach 100 percent capacity utilization.

However, sales between 50 days and 20 days are relatively flat, and as a result, the lower control limit is reached at point B. This sends a signal to management that there is a need to reintroduce discounted fares to reach 100 percent capacity utilization.

This simple example has only two fares. Imagine the complexity of the problem if we have to balance capacity and fare pricing for a dozen or more different fares, and this process occurs with every flight every day.

Overbooking

Often customers will make an airline, hotel, or car rental reservation and then either not show up or cancel it at the last minute. When this occurs, the service firm finds itself with unused capacity that it cannot sell on such short notice. Consequently, many services have begun instituting new procedures with penalties that are aimed at reducing the number of no-shows. For example, airlines typically charge a $100 fee for reissuing a ticket that wasn't used as originally purchased; many hotel chains now require a cancellation notice 24 or more hours before arrival or the customer is charged for one night's stay.

Another approach to minimizing the negative impact of customer no-shows is for firms to overbook their capacity. In other words, they continue to take reservations even though the maximum capacity of their facility for a given flight or night has been reached. For example, as shown in Exhibit 14.7, a hotel may take reservations for 365 rooms on a given night even though the total number of rooms in the hotel is 350. This **overbooking** is done in anticipation of a certain number of customers either canceling their reservations at the last moment or not showing up. The amount of capacity that is overbooked is based on historical data.

However, because the amount of capacity overbooked is only an estimate based on past experience, there are times when more customers show up for an airline flight or a hotel than there are seats or rooms available. To address such situations, which can be embarrassing for the firm, several options or courses of action can be taken by the service manager.

In the case of an airline, the manager may offer, free of charge, an upgrade to business or first class for preferred customers, making additional capacity available in coach. If business or first-class seats are not available, then the manager may ask for volunteers to take a later flight. As an incentive to take the later flight, the passenger will be given either a free airline ticket for a future flight or a voucher for a specific amount of money that can be applied to the cost of a future flight. Depending on the number of seats overbooked and the length of delay until the next available flight, these monetary incentives can range from a few hundred dollars to a thousand dollars or more. The cost to the airline to issue these credits in the form of a free airline ticket or voucher is minimal. With such a service recovery system in place,

EXHIBIT 14.7
Example of Overbooking

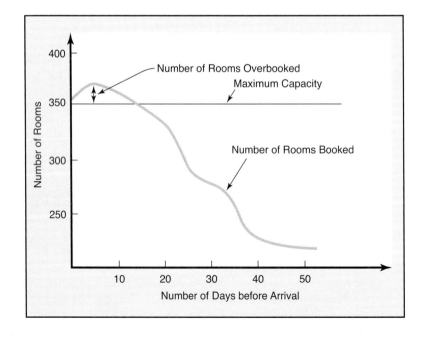

the airline will usually be willing to make a reservation for a full-fare customer at the last minute, even though all the seats for a given flight have previously been sold.

When overbooking occurs at a hotel, the manager can offer a free upgrade to a better room or suite with no additional cost to the customer. If the hotel is completely sold out on that night, the manager can offer to make a reservation for the customer at another nearby hotel at no cost to the customer. If the other hotel is some distance away, the manager can also include free transportation to and from that hotel. Under these circumstances, many customers would be more than happy to stay free of charge at another hotel, trading off the inconvenience for the free lodging. A key element in successfully turning such an awkward and unpleasant situation into a positive experience for the customer is the proper training of personnel.

Simultaneously Managing Capacity and Demand

Capacity and demand decisions described earlier in this chapter were treated as independent decisions, which is the case with many services. However, one contributing factor to yield management's success as a tool for increasing profits is that it requires that capacity and demand be managed simultaneously, thereby providing solutions that previously were not possible.

Allocating Capacity

An integral part of yield management is determining how much capacity should be allocated to each of the different prices that the firm offers. For example, how many seats on an airplane should be reserved for last-minute, full-fare coach customers; how many seats should be sold at super-saver fares; and how many should be sold at a deep discount to *consolidators.* (Consolidators are firms that purchase large amounts of capacity from services such as airlines and hotels at deeply discounted prices and then resell them to tour groups, conference planners, and other organizations.) The prices paid by consolidators are typically not available to the public, thereby providing these services with another market segment. The amount of capacity that is allocated to each of the market segments depends on both the customer demand and the price being charged in each segment.

There are several methods for determining the allocation of capacity. The one we present here uses a discrete probability distribution of forecasted customer demand with the goal of maximizing the firm's expected value.

Example

Jacob and Evan Raser own a small hotel with 65 rooms in western Massachusetts. During the summer, there are many cultural activities going on in this region, including the Boston Symphony Orchestra at Tanglewood. The maximum room rate they charge during this time is $150 per night. However, while the hotel is usually sold out on weekends, it is never sold out during the week. From historical data, the two brothers have developed the following probability table with respect to the number of rooms occupied during a weeknight (Sunday through Thursday nights):

Number of Rooms Occupied	Probability
45	0.15
50	0.30
55	0.20
60	0.35

The variable cost to clean an occupied room is estimated to be $25. The two brothers have recently been approached by a group representing retired people who are on limited incomes. The group is doing a special promotion for its spring newsletter and wants to include a hotel that would offer reduced room rates during the week if the retirees make reservations at least one month in advance. The group assures Jacob and Evan they could sell all the rooms available on a weekday night at $95 per night. How many rooms should Jacob and Evan allocate to this lower rate for weeknights?

Solution

We construct the following payoff table:

Probability	0.15	0.30	0.20	0.35	
Customer Demand	45	50	55	60	
Number of Rooms Available at $150					**Expected Profit**
45	7,025	6,750	6,475	6,200	$6,543.75
50	6,325	7,300	7,025	6,750	6,906.25
55	5,625	6,600	7,575	7,300	6,893.75
60	4,925	5,900	6,875	7,850	6,640.00

The values in the payoff table can be divided into three groups. In the first group, the number of rooms that are reserved for full rate ($150/night) exactly equals demand. The profit generated when this happens is:

$$\text{Profit} = D(SP - C) + (N - D)(DP - C)$$

where

D = Demand

SP = Standard room rate per night

DP = Discounted room rate per night

C = Variable cost to clean a room per night

N = Total number of rooms in the hotel

Thus, if we have a demand for 50 rooms and we allocate 50 rooms for the standard rate then the profit generated is:

$$\text{Profit} = 50(150 - 25) + (65 - 50)(95 - 25)$$
$$= 6,250 + 1,050 = \$7,300$$

The second group consists of those combinations where demand for the standard room rate exceeds the number of rooms allocated for this rate. Here we have to consider the opportunity cost associated with the lost revenues resulting from unsatisfied demand at the standard rate, because the rooms were sold to the retirees at the discounted rate. The opportunity cost is the difference between the standard rate and the discounted rate. The profit generated in these cases is as follows:

$$\text{Profit} = Q(SP - C) + (N - Q)(DP - C) - (D - Q)(SP - DP)$$

where

Q = Number of rooms allocated for the standard rate

If we have a demand for 60 rooms per night at the standard rate and we have only allocated 50 rooms then the resulting profit is:

$$\text{Profit} = 50(150 - 25) + (65 - 50)(95 - 25) - (60 - 50)(150 - 95)$$
$$= 6{,}250 + 1{,}050 - 550 = \$6{,}750$$

The third case is when the number of rooms we have allocated for the standard rate exceeds the demand. Here we have to take into account the opportunity cost of not selling the rooms to the retirees earlier. The net profit calculated is therefore as follows:

$$\text{Profit} = D(SP - C) + (N - Q)(DP - C) - (Q - D)(DP - C)$$

If we have reserved 60 rooms per night for the standard room rate and demand is only for 50 rooms, then the profit generated is:

$$\text{Profit} = 50(150 - 25) + (65 - 60)(95 - 25) - (60 - 50)(95 - 25)$$
$$= 6{,}250 + 350 - 700 = \$5{,}900$$

After we have determined all the values in the payoff table, we next have to calculate the expected profit associated with the number of rooms reserved for the standard rate. This is calculated by multiplying the probability associated with each level of demand by the profit generated by that demand. For example, if we decide to allocate 55 rooms for the standard rate, then the expected profit from this decision is:

$$\text{Expected profit } (55) = (0.15)(5{,}625) + (0.30)(6{,}600) + (0.20)(7{,}575)$$
$$+ (0.35)(7{,}300)$$

$$\text{EP}(55) = 843.75 + 1{,}980 + 1{,}515 + 2{,}555$$
$$= \$6{,}893.75$$

Finally, we select that number of rooms to allocate for the standard rate that yields the maximum expected profit. In this case, Jacob and Evan should allocate 50 rooms a night during the week for the standard rate and provide the retiree group with 15 rooms a night because this decision provides the maximum expected profit of $6,906.25, as shown in the table above. Below is the Excel spreadsheet solution.

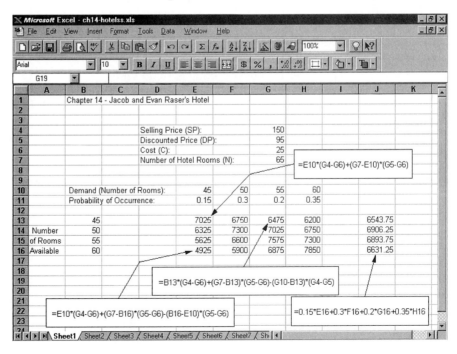

Controlling Demand

Several factors need to be considered in trying to manage demand so that it matches the allocated capacity. First, when there is significant competition, the service manager must be aware of what the competition is charging. If there is little or no difference in the service being offered by competitors, then the customer will make a choice based strictly on price. Airlines, for example, tend to charge the same price when serving the same markets. However, when those markets are different, fares can vary dramatically, depending on what the competition is charging in each of the markets. The round-trip airfare between Boston and Chicago might be $1,200 if you don't stay over a Saturday night. But a flight out of Providence, Rhode Island, which is only 50 miles from Boston, can be as much as 75 percent less, because that market is also served by Southwest Airlines, which offers discounted fares without restrictions. (Southwest Airlines does not serve the Boston market.)

Another factor that needs to be considered is the elasticity of demand for the service. Exhibit 14.8 shows, as an example, the number of seats that are forecasted to be sold at various fares, with their price points shown on the graph in Exhibit 14.9.

In deciding between points A and B, point A yields the greater total revenue, so the airline should charge $1,300 for the full coach fare. This is because the demand curve is relatively inelastic in this range. In other words, business travelers, who are usually the ones paying full fare, are most often unaffected by the fare, so it doesn't matter what the airline

EXHIBIT 14.8
Relating Demand and Price for an Airfare

Point	Fare Price	Demand	Total Revenue
A	$1,300	10	$13,000
B	$1,000	12	$12,000
C	$600	30	$18,000
D	$480	50	$24,000
E	$360	75	$27,000

EXHIBIT 14.9
Demand Curves for Various Airfares

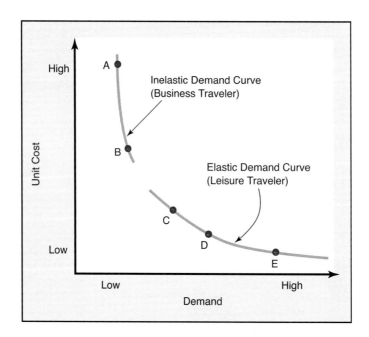

EXHIBIT 14.10
**Airfares Continue
to Increase
for Business
Travelers**

	Airfare		
Route	**1998**	**1999**	**2000**
Chicago to Denver	$341	$620	$704
Chicago to New York	$509	$514	$679
New York to Los Angeles	$918	$998	$1,123

*Based on three-day advance purchase, economy-class fare on November 18, 2000.
Source: *Business Week,* December 11, 2000, p. 42.

charges (as long as it doesn't exceed the fares charged by competing airlines). The airlines recognize the price inelasticity for business travelers and have continued to raise prices, as shown in Exhibit 14.10.

With discounted fares, on the other hand, the demand curve tends to be very elastic, as the decision to travel is usually optional for customers looking for discounts, such as leisure travelers and vacationers. In this range of the demand curve, as the price decreases, demand tends to increase significantly. The decision for the service manager here is how much capacity to sell at the discounted price. If the manager wants to sell 30 seats at a discount, then the price should be $600 per seat; if 50 seats is the goal, then the price per seat should be $480; and if the goal is 75 seats, the seat price should be $360 each.

Alternative Approaches to Increase Capacity Utilization

Initially the primary goal of yield management was to maximize revenues. However, service managers have since realized that even with yield management, there are still certain times when it is not possible to sell all their capacity, even with deeply discounted prices. Consequently, services now look for other ways to utilize unsold capacity that would benefit the firm both in the short term and long term. Three alternatives for utilizing unused capacity are (*a*) bundling, (*b*) customer loyalty programs, and (*c*) employee loyalty programs. All these approaches need to be integrated into the firm's yield management system to maximize the total benefits to the firm.

Bundling

Combining several service components and offering them as a single package at a reduced price is referred to as **bundling.** For example, firms that offer complete tour packages might include airfare, hotel accommodations, transfers between the airport and hotel, and tour guides for a single price that is less expensive than if the individual components of the tour were purchased separately. Services such as hotels and airlines participate in these package deals because they know there are times when they will not be able to sell their full capacity through normal marketing channels. Bundling provides an additional approach for selling capacity without negatively affecting sales within already existing channels. As discussed earlier, consolidators often perform the bundling in the hospitality industry.

Customer Loyalty Programs

Even with bundling, some capacity may still be unused. At these times, services can reward loyal customers with free use of the capacity. The frequent flier programs that are popular with most airlines are a good example of how services utilize unused capacity to reward loyal customers. Many of the larger hotel chains such as Marriott and Hilton have similar loyalty programs that award customers with points each time they stay at that chain.

As part of their customer loyalty programs, services often offer opportunities for upgrades. For example, Delta Air Lines will allow customers to upgrade their seats with 10,000 frequent flier miles each way. In addition, American Airlines' Gold Card members (customers who have flown a minimum of 25,000 miles in a calendar year) are awarded points that can be used to upgrade a seat to either business or first class.

Customer loyalty programs also manage demand by varying the number of miles required, depending on when the trip is taken. A customer on American Airlines can fly round trip between Chicago and Rome for as little as 40,000 frequent flier miles between October 15 and April 15. However, that same trip costs 60,000 frequent flier miles between April 15 and October 15, which is the peak travel time between the United States and Europe. Some airlines also have blackout dates during which frequent flier miles cannot be used.

Employee Loyalty Programs

Unused capacity can also be used to reward service workers. Many hotel chains offer their employees free rooms at any of their locations during times of the year when occupancy rates are low. Airlines also permit their workers (and sometimes their family members) to fly free with certain restrictions, and very often they will also allow workers from competing airlines to fly on their planes through reciprocal agreements. Providing these opportunities to employees is a major benefit that costs the firm very little.

The Impact of Technology

Technology has played a significant role in managing capacity and demand in services, enabling service managers to increase their capacity without significant changes to their physical facilities. For example, automated fare collection lanes on toll roads that require cars to have a bar-code insignia on the windshield can process many more cars per hour than can lanes with toll collectors. Similarly, bar-coded products in supermarkets and department stores speed up the checking out process, thereby increasing capacity without altering the physical facilities.

The Internet also allows customers to quickly check availability of hotel rooms and airline flights. Customers can readily compare prices and even book their own reservations. Reservation confirmations are sent via e-mail, so the entire process can be undertaken by the customer at any hour of the day or night.

The significant contribution of yield management concepts to improving the financial performance of service firms could not have been accomplished without the continued advances in information technology. Greater computing power coupled with increased speed of calculations enables services to apply highly sophisticated yield management models on a continuous basis. Thus, a firm such as American Airlines can recalculate its capacity/pricing strategy for every one of its more than 4,000 daily flights several times a day. This constant application of yield management results in increased revenues with a comparable increase in profits.

In addition, information technology has increased the ability of service facilities within an organization to communicate in real time, which greatly expands the use of **dynamic pricing.** Previously, for example, a central reservations system for a hotel chain did not have the ability to know the current status of rooms at each of its locations. To compensate for this lack of knowledge, the central reservations system might have had a block of rooms set aside at each location for reservations that were made through the corporate call center. As a result, customers might be quoted two different rates, depending on whether they called the hotel directly or the central reservations system. Today, all facilities within a major hotel chain are networked together in real time, so up-to-date information is provided throughout the chain on the status of rooms at each location, and prices can be revised on a continuous basis to meet the changing needs of the market. The real-time networking eliminates the need to maintain an inventory of rooms at the central call center, thereby improving the overall performance of the chain. The Internet has provided an additional marketing channel to service firms that segments markets by technology, with services purchased over the Internet often less expensive but also more restrictive.

Advances in information technology have expanded the use of yield management concepts into service industries where it had never been used previously. For example, several e-businesses now provide restaurants with a yield management-based service that offers potential customers discounts or bonus points that are part of a customer loyalty program during off-peak hours. These websites, working in real time with the restaurants, have instituted a form of dynamic pricing by continuously adjusting the amount of the discount or number of bonus points awarded, depending on the demand. For those times when it is difficult to make a reservation, such as Saturday nights and holiday periods, these e-businesses charge a premium to reserve a table, which is shared with the restaurant. An additional benefit to restaurants using this service is that customers who pay such premiums usually spend more per customer, further increasing revenues during peak periods of demand.

As another example of how technology enables the use of yield management in nontraditional services, Sabre, Inc., of Burlington, Massachusetts, has developed a yield management software package for the trucking industry. The objective of this software is to maximize a freight company's revenues by maximizing the capacity utilization of its trucks with that freight which earns the maximum revenue during specified time periods. This is also accomplished by balancing the network of trucks and trailers within the firm's overall network.

Summary

The successful managing of capacity and demand is a critical element in the success of every service organization. This typically requires a coordinated effort between the marketing and operations functions. In addition, the level of service that a firm can provide its customers is directly related to the capacity utilization of its operation.

For service firms that have the required characteristics, yield management is an important tool for improving their overall financial performance. Yield management simultaneously manages both the demand for the service and the amount of capacity of the service that is made available at different pricing levels.

While the primary goal of yield management is to maximize revenues, the service manager should be aware of other uses for unsold capacity that will also contribute to the long-term success of the firm. These additional uses include customer loyalty and employee loyalty programs.

Information technology has been a catalyst in the widespread use of yield management concepts to services that had not previously used yield management, such as restaurants and golf clubs. IT has also enabled the development of highly sophisticated models for firms that have been applying yield management for a long time, such as airlines and hotels.

Key Terms

booking curve: a tool that tracks the amount of capacity for a service that has been sold over time and compares it with historical data. *(p. 385)*

bundling: the grouping of several services that are then offered at a single price. *(p. 391)*

dynamic pricing: a concept in yield management that refers to the constantly changing prices of a service in an attempt to match capacity and demand. *(p. 392)*

overbooking: When a service such as a hotel or airline sells more capacity than it has available. *(p. 386)*

yield management: a quantitative analysis tool that allows management to simultaneously manage capacity and demand with the goal of maximizing profits. *(p. 379)*

Review and Discussion Questions

1. From a customer's point of view, what are some problems that might be associated with the wide variety of prices that a service charges as a result of using yield management?

2. Call a hotel in a major city that is a tourist destination and ask for the room rates for both week-days and weekends. Similarly, call a hotel located near a group of office buildings that caters to the business traveler and ask its rates for weekdays and weekends. Explain the differences in rates for weekdays and weekends between the two hotels.

3. A hotel chain advertises a fixed nightly room rate, regardless of the time of year or location of the hotel. How might such a firm utilize yield management concepts when a special event occurs near one of its locations and demand is expected to exceed the capacity?

4. When a hotel chain maintains an "inventory" of rooms at its central reservations call center, why might there be two different prices, depending on whether or not the customer called the hotel directly or went through the corporate call center?

Internet Assignment

Go to an airline website or a travel website. Pick two cities between which you would like to travel (other than Boston and London). Identify the different prices for traveling coach class between these two cities and the restrictions associated with each price.

Problems

1. Mike Coggins, owner of Bagel Maker bakery, is trying to decide how many bagels he should make each morning. He currently sells fresh bagels for $5.25 per dozen. Any bagels that are left at the end of the day are sold the next day as "yesterday's bagels" for $3.00 per dozen. Mike estimates that the material and labor to make a dozen bagels is $3.75. To help him decide how many bagels to make each morning he has collected the following information based on historical data:

	Dozens of Bagels Sold						
	12	14	16	18	20	22	24
	Probability						
Weekdays (Monday–Friday)	.15	.25	.25	.20	.15	.00	.00
Weekends (Saturday–Sunday)	.05	.15	.15	.25	.20	.15	.05

   a. How many dozens of bagels should Mike make weekday mornings?
   b. How many dozens of bagels should Mike make on weekend mornings?

2. Sonia Groves owns a parking lot in downtown Los Angeles with 100 spaces. She can offer an "early bird" special for $12.00 a day and she knows she can attract as many customers who work in downtown Boston as she is willing to allocate parking spaces at this low daily rate. The hourly rate that she charges is $6.00 and the average customer stays for about 3.5 hours. Sonia has collected the following data on how many parking spaces a day she has had occupied at the hourly rate:

Parking spaces	65	70	75	80	85
Probability	.15	.20	.25	.30	.10

   If we assume that only one hourly customer per day occupies a given parking space, how many spaces should Sonia allocate for the early-bird special to maximize her profits?

CASE BostonCoach

"I hear what you're saying, Grant, but there has to be some way we can increase the utilization of our vehicles and ultimately our bottom line. Right now the average capacity utilization rate for our cars is less than 60 percent. That means more than 40 percent of the time they are sitting idle in the garage generating no revenues. At a cost of more than $30,000 a car, that's a lot of capacity sitting idle.

"And what really gets to me is that even at the current utilization rate, there are still times when we have to turn down clients or pass them on to one of our affiliates because we can't accommodate them."

"But, Todd, that's the nature of this crazy business. Our customers are mainly corporate clients who only need us at specific times during the week. The consultants need us on Sunday nights and Monday mornings to take them to the airport and then again on Thursday and Friday nights to bring them home. Our other corporate clients need us primarily at the beginning and the end of the workday either to go to and from the airport or to go first thing in the morning from their hotels to their meetings and then back again in the afternoon or evening."

Todd Stephens had recently been appointed senior vice president for BostonCoach's Boston office and was expressing his thoughts about the current utilization rates of the sedans at the Boston location to Grant Mitchell, who was director of account development. He knew that if he could increase his capacity utilization he would significantly increase profits, but at this time he didn't have any ideas about how to accomplish that, and was looking to Grant for some suggestions.

"Let me collect some data on what we are actually doing, so we will be able to discuss this more intelligently," said Grant, as he left Todd's office.

Company Background

In 1985, Fidelity Investments, decided there had to be a better ground transportation alternative for business travelers that would be more comfortable than a taxi, and therefore also more productive for them while they were traveling. As a result, a decision was made to purchase eight Ford Crown Victorias, and Fidelity security personnel were assigned to drive them. The mission at that time was, and continues to be, to provide safe, clean, courteous, and dependable transportation.

Since that time, BostonCoach has grown to a fleet of over 5,000 company-owned and affiliate vehicles that provide an array of ground transportation services to more than 25,000 corporate accounts around the world. Today, BostonCoach is a global transportation company providing sedan service in more than 450 cities.

In 2000, BostonCoach's revenues exceeded $115 million, up significantly from $90 million in 1999, which again was a 19 percent increase over 1998's revenues.

BostonCoach Connection®

Although BostonCoach provides executive ground transportation in more than 450 cities around the world, it actually has operations in only seven cities in the United States. The remaining locations are served by affiliates, which are known as the BostonCoach Connection. These affiliate members are an extension of BostonCoach, thereby providing seamless service to BostonCoach clients. Consequently, these affiliates are required to meet the same exacting standards of quality and service that have been established by BostonCoach. Affiliates even operate in those cities where BostonCoach has established a presence, like Boston and San Francisco. In these cases, the affiliates are given those customers that BostonCoach cannot handle during its peak periods of operations. A major advantage to being an affiliate is that BostonCoach always pays within 10 days. As most of the affiliates are small individually owned operators with fleets of six cars or less, the quick payments significantly improve their cash flows, providing the necessary incentive to remain an affiliate.

The BostonCoach Connection with its worldwide affiliates provides BostonCoach with a competitive advantage with respect to its major competitors. With this network in place, a client only needs to place a single call to BostonCoach to arrange ground transportation in any of the cities around the world that are supported by its network.

The Boston Operation

The headquarters and garage for the Boston operations is located in Everett, Massachusetts, a Boston suburb. The current fleet consists of 300 cars, which are all late model Lincoln Towncars. BostonCoach caters primarily to the business executive, equating the service it provides to business class on an airplane.

The majority of business for the Boston operation is to take clients to and from Logan Airport, which is located in downtown Boston, just across the harbor from the center of the city. Grant, in collecting the data, determined that the average ride takes about an hour plus 15 minutes to pick up and drop off. In addition, the driver typically spends an additional hour driving to the pickup point (be it the airport or the client's home or hotel).

However, in taking a closer look at the data, he discovered that the actual driving time is 15 percent higher on Mondays and Fridays because of heavy traffic conditions. At the same time, the average time for Wednesdays, Saturdays, and Sundays is 25 percent less due to light traffic. Exhibit 1 shows the average number of customers that are served at various times throughout the day for each day of the week.

In addition, Grant collected the data shown in Exhibit 2 on the average number of clients that BostonCoach could not accommodate each day. As indicated in the exhibit, most of these clients were served by affiliates in the Boston area. Nevertheless, some clients still had to be denied service because the affiliates also experienced peak demand during those times.

Financial Data

The average customer is charged $60.00 per ride, although it can vary anywhere from $45.00 to $90.00, depending on the distance. Unlike a taxi's, the fare is fixed regardless of how long the actual trip may take. Drivers are paid a minimum of $12.00 per hour, although some drivers make as much as $16.00 an hour. (The average rate is about $13.00 per hour.)

The Follow-up Meeting

Grant, having collected all the above data, met again with Todd Stephens to discuss the issue of capacity utilization of the vehicles. Since their previous meeting, Todd had spoken to his counterpart at BostonCoach in Chicago about the low capacity utilization of his vehicles. The Chicago manager informed Todd that he had just instituted a service with several eye surgeons in the Chicago area who perform laser surgery to correct vision or to remove cataracts. As their patients are not physically capable of driving themselves home after the surgery, BostonCoach now provides this service, which is included in the total price of the eye operation. The charge to the physician for this service is $75.00 per patient, which includes picking up the patient before the operation and then taking the patient home afterward. These eye operations usually take place on Tuesday and Thursday mornings between 9:00 A.M. and noon. Todd thought a similar service could be provided in the Boston area. The total time required to provide this service was estimated to be 2.5 hours.

After reviewing the data with Grant, Todd posed the following questions:

1. Are there any other types of services, besides the eye surgery, that could use our services during our slow periods? If yes, what do you think we should charge for them?

2. Can you develop a method for determining exactly what our capacity utilization is for our vehicles for each of these periods between 6:00 A.M. and midnight for each day of the week? Also, what is the overall average weekly capacity utilization using this method?

3. How can we minimize the percentage of clients that are denied service without purchasing more vehicles?

4. How can we reduce the number of clients we have to refer to affiliates without purchasing more vehicles?

5. What additional ideas do you have to increase capacity utilization and revenues?

EXHIBIT 1
Distribution of the Average Number of Rides Provided during the Week

			Days of the Week					
	Sun	Mon	Tue	Wed	Thu	Fri	Sat	Totals
Average number of rides:	756	1,132	1,321	1,455	1,317	1,585	644	8,210

Time of Day	Distribution Throughout the Day (Percentages)						
6:00–8:00 A.M.	4%	21%	18%	14%	9%	4%	2%
8:00–10:00 A.M.	7	24	23	19	13	11	9
10:00 A.M.–noon	9	3	4	2	5	7	15
Noon–2:00 P.M.	13	2	3	5	8	7	20
2:00–4:00 P.M.	15	5	6	3	4	14	18
4:00–6:00 P.M.	22	13	15	12	18	23	22
6:00–8:00 P.M.	24	16	17	22	24	22	10
8:00–10:00 P.M.	4	12	13	20	17	9	3
10:00 P.M.–midnight	2	4	1	3	2	3	1
Totals	100	100	100	100	100	100	100

EXHIBIT 2
Number of Clients
Served by Affiliates
and Denied Service
in an Average Week

	Sun	Mon	Tue	Wed	Thu	Fri	Sat	Total
Total number of clients	756	1,132	1,321	1,455	1,317	1,585	644	8,210
Number of clients								
Served by affiliates	0	51	54	5	68	223	0	401
Denied service	0	0	0	0	6	34	0	40
Total	0	51	54	5	74	257	0	441
Percentage of total clients								
Served by affiliates	0.0%	4.5%	4.1%	0.3%	5.2%	14.1%	0.0%	4.9%
Denied service	0.0%	0.0%	0.0%	0.0%	0.5%	2.1%	0.0%	0.5%
Total Percentage								5.4%

Selected Bibliography

"Award for Leadership: American Airlines, Inc." *Scorecard,* First Quarter 1995, pp. 4–5.

Baker, Timothy K., and David Collier. "A Comparative Revenue Analysis of Hotel Yield Management Heuristics." *Decision Sciences* 30, no. 1 (Winter 1999), pp. 239–63.

"Bob Crandall's Brainchild." *Scorecard,* First Quarter 1993, pp. 6–8.

Chase, Charles W., Jr. "Revenue Management: A Review." *The Journal of Business Forecasting,* Spring 1999, pp. 2, 28–30.

Garvett, Donald S. "What Drives Airline Profits? A First Look." Presented to the Sixth International Airline CEO Conference, April 28, 1998.

Kimes, Sheryl E. "Yield-Management: A Tool for Capacity-Constrained Service Firms." *Journal of Operations Management* 8, no. 4 (October 1989).

Kimes, Sheryl E., and Richard B. Chase. "The Strategic Levers of Yield Management." *Journal of Service Research* 1, no. 2 (1998), pp. 298–308.

Lovelock, Christopher. "Strategies for Managing Capacity-Constrained Services." *Managing Services: Marketing, Operations Management and Human Resources.* 2nd ed. Englewood Cliffs, NJ: Prentice Hall, 1992.

Ng, Irene C. L., Jochen Wirtz, and Khai Sheang Lee. "The Strategic Role of Unused Service Capacity." *International Journal of Service Industry Management* 10, no. 2 (1999), pp. 211–38.

Palmeri, Christopher. "Revolt of the Business Class." *Business Week,* December 11, 2000, p. 42.

Sasser, W. Earl. "Matching Supply and Demand in Service Industries." *Harvard Business Review,* November–December 1976, pp. 132–38.

Schwartz, Mathew. "Software Fills Trucks, Maximizes Revenues." *Computerworld,* November 15, 1999.

Sharkey, Joe. "Hotels Take a Lesson from Airline Pricing." *New York Times,* December 17, 2000, p. 3.

Smith, Barry C., et al. "Yield Management at American Airlines." *Interfaces,* January–February 1992.

Waters, C. Dickinson. "Web Sites Vie to Bring 'Dynamic-Pricing' to Restaurants." *Nation's Restaurant News,* August 21, 2000, pp. 67–68.

"Yield Management Systems are the Biggest Driver of Airline Profits." *World Airline News,* May 1, 1998, p. 1.

CHAPTER FIFTEEN

Waiting Time Management

Learning Objectives

- Emphasize the competitive advantage associated with providing fast service.

- Show the relationship between customer expectations, customer perceptions, and customer satisfaction as they pertain to waiting time.

- Introduce the different factors that can affect customer satisfaction with waiting time, and

provide a framework for showing managers which of these factors are under their control.

- Demonstrate how service managers can design their operations to provide faster service without incurring additional costs.

- Illustrate how technology can assist companies in providing faster service to their customers.

Time Is Money at Disney's Theme Parks

Jeff Goldberg / PhotoEdit

Waiting in line at a Disney theme park is an accepted fact of life, and most people hate it.

Although Disney's philosophy is that everyone is a VIP (very important person), some people are more "VI" than others. These Disney guests can avoid waiting in most lines.

For an additional $50 to $60 per ticket (and with the necessary contacts), guests can buy a theme park VIP tour. These guests receive special services including preferred seating at shows and a personal escort at certain attractions. The VIP service isn't very widely known, however, and it is usually very difficult to obtain.

Celebrities and top business executives can also avoid long waits at Disney parks. Disney managers understand that celebrity business is good promotion, so they try to ensure that these VIPs enjoy the park without the loss of anonymity that waiting in line would bring.

Employees of companies who sponsor attractions at Disney are also considered VIPs, although they need to bring a business card and request their VIP treatment from the right Disney contacts. These VIPs may be able to enjoy similar VIP treatment at other attractions through networking.

Disney guests staying on special concierge floors in Disney hotels are VIPs, too—for an extra $300 or so a night! The concierges will do everything they can to accommodate guest wishes and provide special no-wait passes.

So what's the best way to deal with lines at a Disney park? Unless you're exceptionally rich or a true VIP, grin and bear it!

The Customer's Perspective

Virtually every day we spend much of our time waiting in lines. On our way to work in the morning, we wait in line to pay the toll on the turnpike and wait to park our car in the garage. If we use public transportation, we usually wait for the bus or the train to take us to work. We wait to be served coffee at our favorite morning eatery; we wait for our elevator to take us to our office, and all this happens before we even start work!

And we continue to wait in lines throughout the workday. We wait in line to use the copier machine, to send a fax. We wait in line on the telephone to make a hotel or airplane reservation. ("Your call is very important to us. All our customer service agents are busy with other customers. Your call will be answered in the order in which it was received. Please wait for the next available agent.") We wait for a response to an inquiry on a lost package or to a question about why our software program or computer isn't working. We even have to wait sometimes to access the Internet. (While some individuals can delegate these waits to others, the waits nevertheless still exist.)

After work, we face the reverse of the morning waits: getting out of the garage, the bus or train, the tollbooth. In addition, we may have to stop and wait at the gas station (even if it's self-service!); if we stop at the supermarket we wait in line at the checkout counter. If we are too tired to prepare dinner, we can expect to wait in line at our favorite restaurant before we are seated.

No one enjoys waiting in line. Waiting in a line is totally nonproductive, and can cause frustration and aggravation and, ultimately, a negative attitude toward the firm.

Managerial Issues

As illustrated in Exhibit 15.1, service managers face a trade-off between the cost of providing fast service and the cost of having customers wait. This trade-off between providing fast service and high levels of worker productivity results from the direct interaction of the customer with the service-producing process. Variable levels of demand contribute to the formation of waiting lines in service environments. To eliminate all waiting lines, service managers would need an infinite amount of capacity to be able to satisfactorily meet all contingencies. If this approach were taken, a portion of this capacity would remain idle and nonproductive most of the time, adding significant costs to the firm with little or no added benefit.

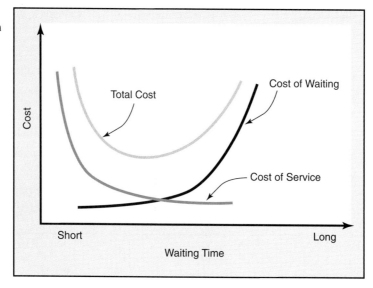

Consequently, service managers need to find a balance between short waiting times and efficient operations. To successfully accomplish this, service managers need to recognize that the management of customer waiting times involves two major elements: the **actual waiting time,** as measured in minutes and/or seconds, and the customer's **perceived waiting time.**

The Importance of Fast Service

A customer's first contact with a service organization typically involves some type of line or queue before being served. Many factors contribute to good service, including the friendliness and knowledge of workers. Nevertheless, customers' experiences with waiting lines are often their initial encounter with a firm, and therefore can significantly affect their overall level of satisfaction with the organization.

Providing ever-faster service, with the ultimate goal of having zero customer waiting time, has recently received managerial attention for several reasons. First, in the more highly developed countries, where standards of living are rising, time is becoming more valuable and, consequently, customers become less tolerant of waiting for service. As a result, customers may be willing to pay a premium price to those firms that minimize their waiting time as demonstrated in the opening vignette.

Another reason for increased emphasis on providing fast and efficient service is that organizations now recognize that how they treat their customers today significantly affects whether or not those customers will remain loyal tomorrow. In the past, the treatment of present customers was viewed as independent of any potential future revenues. This attitude persisted primarily because future customer behavior does not appear anywhere on the firm's financial statements.

Finally, advances in technology, especially in information technology, have provided firms with the ability to provide faster service than was previously possible. Fax machines, e-mail, and satellite communications provide firms with electronic networks that allow them to respond faster to the customer.

In providing fast service, however, the real goal of service managers should not be to ensure that customers are served within a specified time (that is, a stated number of minutes), but rather to ensure that customers are satisfied enough with the level of service provided so that they will want to return in the future.

Steve Rubin / The Image Works

MBNA, the Wilmington, Delaware, credit card company, has developed a very loyal customer base due, in large part, to its ability to provide outstanding service. To accomplish this, MBNA has developed 15 different measures of performance, many of which pertain directly to speed. For example, customer address changes must be processed within one day; telephones must be answered within two rings; switchboard calls must be transferred to the appropriate individual within 21 seconds.

State-of-the-art technology allows MBNA to monitor performance on a continuous basis. At any given moment it is possible to obtain a performance measurement that shows, for example, that employees are achieving "two-ring pick-up" 99.7 percent of the time. The current standard for the minimum level of service that is acceptable for each of the 15 performance measures is 98.5 percent, which was increased recently from 98.0 percent and is significantly up from 10 years ago when it was 90 percent.

Source: J. Martin and J. E. Davis, "Are You As Good As You Think?" *Fortune,* September 30, 1996.

Companies can provide faster and more convenient service to customers using the Internet. The ability to shop, make reservations, and get information at any time and without a service representative has changed how we do business.

Courtesy of Travelocity.com

Defining Customer Satisfaction

The customer's direct involvement in the service delivery system suggests a need to integrate both marketing and operations perspectives into the service system's design and evaluation. A marketing-related measure of customer reaction to waiting in line would indicate the true customer waiting costs more completely than just the actual waiting time itself. **Customer satisfaction** appears to be the marketing measure that links both perspectives.

Definition of Customer Satisfaction

Drawing on research efforts in marketing, we define customer satisfaction as being related to the comparison between a **customer's expectations** of a service's performance and that customer's perception of that performance. If the perceived performance meets expectations, then the customer is satisfied; if it exceeds expectations by a large amount, then the customer is very satisfied or delighted; if the performance falls significantly short of expectations, then the customer is dissatisfied. In marketing terminology, satisfaction is said to be directly related to the **disconfirmation** or the difference between the customer's expected and perceived performance of the service.

Customer satisfaction is a good measure of how effective the service delivery system is, because it links the level of service that the company is currently providing to its customers, the customers' perception of that service, and the customers' future behavior toward the firm. Richard Oliver suggests that customer satisfaction is part of an overall model of customer behavior that develops over time, as shown in Exhibit 15.2.

Customer Expectations

Customer expectations are defined as the customers' preconceived notions of what level of service they should receive from a particular service. Expectations can be derived from several sources.

One source of expectations is advertising. Many quick-service restaurants, for example, promise in their advertising that your lunch will be served in 15 minutes or less. Thus, if you have to wait longer than 15 minutes, you will be dissatisfied; if your wait is significantly less than 15 minutes, you will be very satisfied. Expectations can also be predicated on the cus-

EXHIBIT 15.2
**The Role
of Satisfaction
in a Customer
Behavior Model**

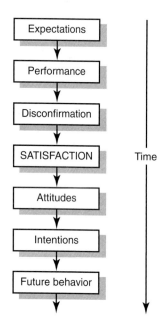

Source: Richard L. Oliver, "A Cognitive Model of
the Antecedents and Consequences of Satisfaction
Decisions," *Journal of Marketing Research* 17
(November 1980).

tomer's prior experience with the company. Additional sources of expectations include word-of-mouth and previous experiences with similar types of operations, like those of competitors.

The overall service delivery package also influences a customer's expectations regarding waiting time. People tend to associate little or no waiting with upscale or higher-priced services. These types of operations, therefore, often require appointments or reservations to ensure minimal, if any, waiting. The degree of customization provided to each customer is another factor that can influence expectations. The more a service is customized, the longer a customer might expect to wait.

Perceived Waiting Time

Perceived waiting time is the amount of time customers believe they have waited before receiving service. While this is usually directly related to the actual time a customer waits, there are often significant differences between the two. Studies have shown that perceived waiting time has a greater impact on customer satisfaction than does actual waiting time.[1] As we will present later in this chapter, management can affect a customer's perceived waiting time if it understands the factors that affect it.

To illustrate the difference between perceived waiting time and actual waiting time, we look at the example of a newly designed luxury hotel that was built with insufficient elevator capacity, especially in the morning hours when most guests were in a hurry to check out. Customer complaints about the long waits for elevators to take them to the ground floor prompted management to hire a consultant to reduce these waits. The consultant developed a scheduling algorithm for the elevators that significantly reduced the waiting times, but guest complaints continued. Another consultant suggested placing full-length mirrors on both sides of the elevator doors on every floor. This was done and the complaints stopped, even though there was no further decrease in the actual waiting time. Why? Because the guests now had something to occupy their time after pushing the elevator button, and consequently weren't as aware of their wait for the elevator.[2]

The Economics of Waiting Lines

As depicted in Exhibit 15.1, the economic trade-off between having an efficient operation and providing fast service to customers results in an "optimal waiting time" that minimizes the combined costs of waiting and providing service. Although easily understood in theory, this model is not always adaptable to real-world applications, due primarily to the difficulty associated with measuring the cost of having a customer wait.

As a first step in understanding the economic issues associated with waiting lines, we divide customers into *internal customers* and *external customers.* Internal customers are employees of the firm, while external customers are those who are not employed by the firm and who generate revenues for the firm. An example of an internal customer is a secretary waiting to use a copy machine or a server in a restaurant waiting for dinners to be completed in the kitchen. Examples of external customers include the patient waiting to see a doctor or a customer waiting on the telephone to make an airline reservation.

Cost of Waiting for Internal Customers

The cost of internal customers waiting in line is relatively easy to measure; it is the average employee waiting time multiplied by their hourly wage, which should include fringe

[1] Mark M. Davis and Janelle Heineke, "How Disconfirmation, Perception and Actual Waiting Times Impact Customer Satisfaction," *International Journal of Service Industry Management* 9, no. 1 (1998), pp. 64–73.
[2] W. E. Sasser, R. P. Olsen, and D. D. Wyckoff, *Management of Service Operations: Text, Cases and Readings* (Boston: Allyn and Bacon, 1978).

benefits. For example, we might observe in a law firm that, on average, 10 employees arrive per hour at the copier and the average waiting time per employee is four minutes. If the average hourly rate of those waiting in line is $15 per hour, then the cost to the firm of having these internal customers wait is calculated as follows:

$$10 \text{ employees} \times (4 \text{ minutes wait/employee})/(60 \text{ minutes/hour}) \times \$15/\text{hour}$$
$$= \$10/\text{hour}$$

Whether to provide faster service by adding capacity in the form of another copier is relatively easy to determine. If the cost of purchasing and installing another copier is less than the labor savings resulting from shorter waiting times, the purchase is justified. The calculations of the economics involved in these types of problems are straightforward and are presented in detail in the supplement to this chapter.

Cost of Waiting for External Customers

The determination of the cost of waiting for external customers is more complicated for several reasons. First, the value of time to each customer varies significantly and is usually unknown to the firm. More important, it is irrelevant from the firm's perspective. What is important to the firm is how the customers' perception of the value of their time translates into satisfaction or dissatisfaction with waiting in line, which, in turn, will ultimately affect their future behavior or loyalty toward the firm.

Second, the value of each customer to the firm varies significantly, from those who frequent the firm often and make large purchases to those who use the service only when a bargain is being advertised. Obviously the firm would like to provide faster service to its regular customers to ensure their loyalty, even if it is at the expense of the bargain hunters.

In addition, a customer's level of satisfaction with waiting can vary significantly from one visit to the next, depending on circumstances. For example, a customer eating in a restaurant during a workday lunch hour will be more impatient than during a leisure-time dinner. As another illustration, customers are usually more tolerant of waiting if a store is full of customers than if the store is empty and there does not appear to be any justification for the wait.

Service managers must understand a significant cost is associated with having external customers wait. Therefore, the managerial decisions that are made with respect to capacity, scheduling workers, and managing customer waiting times need to consider this cost.

The following example provides a framework for determining the cost of having external customers wait.

Example

A fast-food restaurant has an average check of $4.50 per customer with a variable cost of 70 percent, or $3.15. Thus, the contribution of each customer to overhead and profit is $1.35. A survey of customers reveals that customers visit this restaurant about once a week on average. The survey also revealed the following information about their satisfaction with respect to waiting in line:

	Percentage of Customers at Each Level of Satisfaction			
Length of Wait	Very Satisfied	Satisfied	Very Dissatisfied	Total
Less than 1 minute	100%	0%	0%	100%
1–3 minutes	10%	60%	30%	100%
More than 3 minutes	0%	30%	70%	100%

Next, let us assume that very satisfied customers will result in a 10 percent increase in business, that satisfied customers will maintain their once-a-week visit, and that dissatisfied customers will decrease their business by 10 percent. (This impact on business can occur in several ways, including more/less frequent visits, larger/smaller purchases, and positive/negative word-of-mouth advertising to friends and relatives.)

Solution

If the restaurant averages 300 customers per hour during its busy peak mealtime periods, the cost of having customers wait can be determined as follows:

Length of Wait	Number of Customers at Each Level of Satisfaction during Peak Hours of Operation		
	Very Satisfied	Satisfied	Very Dissatisfied
Less than 1 minute	300	0	0
1–3 minutes	30	180	90
More than 3 minutes	0	90	210

The cost or benefit to the firm of having customers wait various amounts of time is then calculated as follows:

Length of Wait	Cost/Benefit per Hour of Waiting during Peak Hours of Operation			
	Very Satisfied	Satisfied	Very Dissatisfied	Total
Less than 1 minute	$300 \times 1.35 \times 10\%$ = $40.50	0 0	0 0	+$40.50
1–3 minutes	$30 \times 1.35 \times 10\%$ = $4.05	0 0	$90 \times 1.35 \times (-10\%)$ = −$12.15	−$8.10
More than 3 minutes	0	0	$210 \times 1.35 \times (-10\%)$ = −$28.35	−$28.35

These totals, which are plotted in Exhibit 15.3, provide an estimate of the cost of having customers wait in line. The manager then needs to determine how many more workers are needed to reduce the waiting time to less than one minute, and what this will cost in comparison to the cost of having customers wait. Usually, scheduling additional workers to provide faster service is justified. (The number of additional workers that need to be scheduled can be determined using queuing theory, which is presented in the supplement to this chapter.)

The above example is highly simplified, but it provides a framework for estimating the cost of having an external customer wait. If anything, this framework underestimates the cost. First, it considers only a onetime impact on future business. Thus, the 10 percent increase/decrease can be interpreted to mean that the customer will show up one time more/less over the next 10 weeks, based on a once-a-week frequency. In addition, studies have shown that a negative experience with service, which includes a long wait, tends to have much more impact on a firm than does a positive one.

Factors Affecting Customer Satisfaction with Waiting[3]

As stated previously, service managers should focus on improving both the customer's level of satisfaction with waiting and the actual waiting time itself. David

[3] Adapted from Mark M. Davis and Janelle Heineke, "Understanding the Roles of the Customer and the Operation for Better Queue Management," *International Journal of Operations and Production Management* 14, no. 5 (1994), pp. 21–34.

EXHIBIT 15.3
Cost of Waiting
for External
Customers

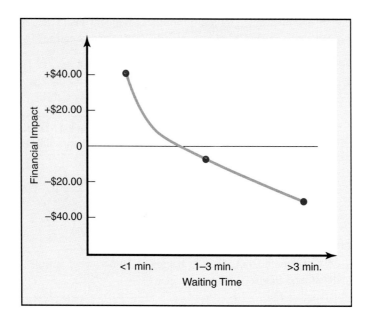

Maister[4] presented an initial framework for focusing on customer satisfaction with waiting, identifying many of the factors that can affect satisfaction. To further assist the service manager, these factors can be classified into three categories: (*a*) firm-related factors, (*b*) customer-related factors, and (*c*) a combination of firm- and customer-related factors. Such a framework permits service managers to effectively manage the customer's waiting time by allowing them to distinguish between those factors over which they have total or at least partial control from those over which they have no control.

Firm-Related Factors

Factors that fall primarily within the firm's control can be grouped into four types of waits: (*a*) unfair versus fair waits, (*b*) uncomfortable versus comfortable waits, (*c*) unexplained versus explained waits, and (*d*) initial versus subsequent waits.

Unfair versus Fair Waits

The successful management of the customer's perception of fairness with respect to waiting is dependent on queue design, service system design, and contact hours.

A popular approach, to ensure fairness, is to group all customers into a single queue or line. When more than one server is on duty, the first person in line moves to the next available server. This method has been adopted by many bank and airline check-in counters. Not only is the combined queue perceived as fairer, but the average wait has also been shown to be considerably shorter, even though the line itself is longer. However, managers also need to consider the physical elements of the operating system. For example, the physical space required by customers and their shopping carts has prevented most supermarkets from adopting the combined queue approach.

Service system design elements other than physical waiting can also affect customer perceptions of fairness. Interruptions by telephone calls during busy periods, for example, give the impression (which is correct!) that the answered call is receiving priority treatment.

So that customers do not perceive unfair treatment due to their watches being off by a few minutes, the actual hours of operation that a service is open for business should ex-

[4] David Maister, "The Psychology of Waiting Lines," in *The Service Encounter,* ed. J. A. Czepiel, M. R. Solomon, and C. F. Surprenant (Lexington, MA: Lexington Books, D. C. Heath & Co., 1985).

ceed the posted hours. For example, if a retail operation has posted hours of 10:00 A.M. to 10:00 P.M., then the store should be ready to receive customers and the doors unlocked at 9:50 A.M., and the doors should not be closed until 10:10 P.M.

Uncomfortable versus Comfortable Waits

It is common sense to recognize that when one is uncomfortable, time passes more slowly. There are many ways in which service organizations can affect customer comfort: temperature, lighting, seating, and sound levels should all be considered. Comfort and fairness can often be combined when a "take a number" system is employed. Full-service restaurants recognize the importance of comfort by providing lounges in which customers can wait before being seated. This is a good example of a win–win situation. The restaurant can gain additional sales from drinks sold to waiting customers, and the customers enjoy a pleasant and comfortable environment while they wait for their tables.

Unexplained versus Explained Waits

Customer dissatisfaction with waiting increases when the waits cannot be justified or explained. For example, when airline passengers are informed that they must wait for equipment arrival, for the weather to clear, or for the wings of their plane to be de-iced, they are less likely to be dissatisfied than if no explanation is given for the delay. However, the repeated use of the same reason, no matter how valid it is, will eventually negate any benefits gained from the explanation.

Idle workers or idle stations that are visible while customers wait increase customer dissatisfaction. Although there are many justifiable reasons for apparently idle capacity (e.g., worker rest breaks, the need to complete important off-line tasks, etc.), the customer should not be expected to recognize these. Thus, idle service workers and service stations should be "camouflaged" when not in use.[5]

Waits of unknown duration always seem longer than waits of known duration. This relates, in part, to a customer's anxiety with waiting. Thus, it is important to provide customers with an estimate of the wait. When the actual waits cannot be determined, updates or status reports can be acceptable substitutes. For example, Federal Express will report back to a customer before the close of each business day with an update on the status of the search for a lost package.

Initial versus Subsequent Waits

As David Maister points out, customers tend to become more dissatisfied with waits before entering a service delivery system than they do with waits after they are in the system. For example, waiting to place an order at a quick-service restaurant usually seems longer than waiting the same amount of time for your order to be prepared and delivered. Similarly, the wait while a telephone is ringing at a reservations call center seems longer than the same amount of time waiting after your call has been answered and you are waiting for the next available operator. Before the initial wait, customers see themselves as being outside the system, whereas after the initial service has been received they consider themselves to be within the system and know that they will, therefore, be served. Thus, firms should emphasize minimizing a customer's initial wait when designing the service delivery system.

Customer-Related Factors

A firm cannot control some factors that affect a customer's satisfaction with waiting time. For example, how customers arrive, and the various moods they are in when they do, cannot be controlled by the firm, but an awareness of these factors and how they can contribute

[5] Richard B. Chase, "The Ten Commandments of Service System Management," *Interfaces* 15, no. 3 (May–June 1985).

to dissatisfaction with waiting can help the service manager to better control those aspects of the wait that are manageable.

Solo versus Group Waits

People waiting in line by themselves tend to grow more impatient with the wait than people who are waiting in groups. Although this is not something that can be changed by the service organization, recognition of this fact may suggest service-appropriate distractions or alternatives. Ski areas, for example, often have a separate line for single skiers, and this line is typically much shorter than those for couples or larger groups.

This is another case of designing the service delivery system in such a way as to create a win–win situation. The single skier has a much shorter waiting time, and the ski area can take maximum advantage of its lift capacity during peak periods of demand by using single skiers to fill otherwise empty seats as they appear.

Waits for More Valuable versus Less Valuable Services

Customers are willing to wait longer for a service perceived to be of high value than for a service perceived to be of low value. In other words, the perceived value of the product is large enough that customers are willing to absorb some of the cost in the form of waiting time. However, in today's highly competitive environment, making customers wait extraordinarily long times can quickly result in a loss of market share to competitors that provide the same or similar products in a shorter amount of time.

Customer Value Systems

Businesses need to recognize the importance of segmenting the market by customer value systems. Customers who place a premium on obtaining fast service may not mind paying for it (as illustrated in the opening vignette), and may not want to waste their time on self-service, menu-driven service systems that many companies now use. To ensure consistency from a customer's perspective, the market focus of the firm must therefore also be incorporated into its operational strategy for waiting line management. The importance of doing this is recognized by Ritz-Carlton Hotels, which targets customers who are willing to pay prices that are in the top 5 percent of the hotel industry. A real person answers the telephone when you call to make a reservation, and you experience little or no waiting.

Customer's Current Attitude

The attitudes of customers just before they enter the service operation can have a significant effect on their level of satisfaction with the service they receive. If customers enter upset, they are more likely to be dissatisfied with their wait, regardless of its length. This type of *halo effect* will also affect the customers' perception of all facets of the services they receive.

Both Firm- and Customer-Related Factors

Some factors that relate to a customer's satisfaction with waiting are under the influence of both the firm and the customer.

Unoccupied versus Occupied Waits

As illustrated with the example of the mirrors beside the hotel elevator doors (discussed earlier in this chapter) customers who are occupied tend to tolerate longer waiting times than do customers who are unoccupied during their waits. Many options are available to occupy a customer's time in line: reading material, interesting displays, mirrors, and music have all been demonstrated to be useful. Gambling casinos do an excellent job of keeping customers occupied while they are waiting to enter their nightclubs. The waiting lines to get into these clubs wend their way through the slot machine areas of the casino, creating another win–win situation: customers are kept occupied and slot machine revenues are increased.

Under certain circumstances, customers can also be kept busy while waiting in line doing meaningful activities that can improve the efficiency of the service. For example, customers waiting in a checkout line in a retail store can be informed, through the proper signage, of what they have to do to process a payment other than cash. Another approach to keeping customers occupied while waiting is to provide a waiting environment in which they can productively work on their own tasks. Airport lounges with tables or private areas equipped with fax machines, PCs, and Internet connections, are good examples of this.

Anxious versus Calm Waits

Customer anxiety regarding the nature of the service or the uncertainty of the wait can affect customer satisfaction. Any wait in a hospital emergency room or to hear the results from an important medical test may seem interminable, regardless of the actual length of the wait. Service organizations cannot eliminate the customer's anxiety associated with these types of waits, but they can look critically at the nature of the service that they provide and take the necessary steps to try to reduce customer anxiety. Providing reading material that both occupies the wait and simultaneously explains the procedure to be followed can be very effective in reducing the customer's anxiety and the associated level of impatience with a wait.

A Focus on Providing Fast Service

Ultimately, providing ever-better and ever-faster service to customers is the responsibility of the service operations manager. From an operations perspective, this can be accomplished in several ways, beginning with good system design and proper cross-training of workers.

Previous service system design theory advocated splitting the delivery system into two cores, with the goal of reducing customer contact time, thereby increasing the speed of delivery and the efficiency of the operation. With this approach, the first core, or *front-of-the-house,* interacts directly with the customer and consequently its capacity must be available to meet peak demand when it occurs. The second core, or *back-of-the-house,* includes all those functions that can be accomplished without the presence of the customer, and therefore can be staffed to manage average demand. McDonald's provides an excellent example of this split core strategy, with packaged hamburgers in the bins acting as a buffer inventory between the two stages.

New Approach to Service System Design

To significantly reduce the worker idle time that is traditionally associated with providing fast service, the service manager and/or the service system designer need to incorporate several interrelated elements into the service delivery system design process. These elements are:

- Accurate forecasting of demand.
- Work station design.
- Reduced setup times.
- Cross-training of employees.

Accurate Forecasting of Demand

Accurately forecasting customer demand is difficult, especially in the small time increments necessary for efficiently scheduling workers. This difficulty can also be attributed to the many factors that can affect customer demand, some of which are unknown when the forecasts are made. For example, sunny weather can significantly affect demand in a restaurant (either positively or negatively, depending on the type and location of the restaurant). However, the weather for a particular day is usually unknown when workers are scheduled.

Another factor that contributes to forecasting inaccuracy is the highly variable demand for many services with dramatic changes occurring within short time periods. To capture these changes, the forecast needs to be divided into relatively small time increments. Unfortunately, the smaller the time increments, the less accurate the forecast.

Work Station Design

Although early service system design models suggested the separation of the process into two cores to increase overall efficiency, that approach usually prevents workers in the two cores from easily flowing back and forth as the workload might require. As a consequence, a very high level of staffing is required in the customer service core to accommodate both peak periods of demand and customer uncertainty.

By properly integrating back-of-the-house operations with front-of-the-house operations, front-of-the-house workers can be kept busy when there are no customers to wait on. For example, workers in a supermarket can restock shelves with groceries when there are no customers at the checkout registers. Similarly, bank tellers can process checks and conduct other financial matters when no customers are requiring service.

Managers must remember that jobs should be designed so there are non-time-dependent responsibilities in the workers' job descriptions. This will ensure that workers have sufficient work to do during slow periods throughout the workday.

Reduced Setup Times

By reducing the setup times required to begin new tasks, workers can more easily switch from one job function to another without the firm having to incur extra setup costs. These reductions in setup times allow the service manager to reassign workers from time-dependent functions, such as waiting on customers, to non-time-dependent functions such as cleaning counters in a fast-food restaurant or restocking shelves in a supermarket, and back again, as the situation dictates. The smaller the setup times, the more frequently the switching between tasks can occur. For example, if a cashier at a supermarket can log on and off a cash register quickly, then the cashier can easily close the register and perform other tasks when there are no customers to serve, and just as quickly open the register when there are customers who want to check out.

Cross-training of Employees

Providing fast and efficient service requires service worker flexibility. With broader job skills, workers can perform additional, non-customer-related tasks during idle periods. Service managers, therefore, should invest resources to cross-train workers so they can perform several tasks. Cross-training enables the firm to inventory worker skills rather than inventorying customers in waiting lines. Workers are busy more of the time and customers wait less. In the long run, both generate higher profits.

As the standard of living in any economy improves, time becomes more important to people and the cost of having customers wait for service increases significantly. Exhibit 15.4 shows that costs increase as the cost of waiting line shifts from W_1 to W_2. But service managers who properly design their delivery systems can dramatically reduce the cost of providing service without making customers wait longer. Exhibit 15.4 shows that costs decrease as

EXHIBIT 15.4
Why Faster Service Is Still "Optimal"

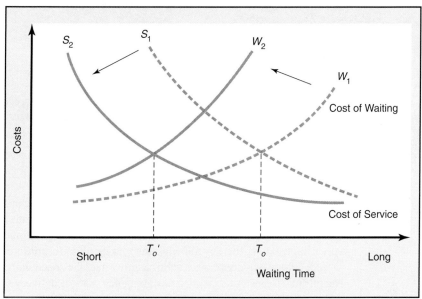

the cost of service line shifts from S_1 to S_2. The result of these two trends is the new "optimal" waiting time, T_o', that minimizes total cost and, at the same time, is lower than the initial T_o. As these trends continue, the optimal waiting time will become shorter and shorter.

The Impact of Technology

Technology can be used in many ways to reduce and, in many cases, eliminate customer waiting time. Automated teller machines (ATMs) now provide bank customers with 24-hour service, eliminating the need for customers to use banking services only during the bank's operating hours. Customers with personal computers can access their accounts any time, day or night, and perform many types of transactions. (See Using Technology to Create Value.)

Bar-code scanners at checkout counters in department stores and supermarkets reduce service processing times, thereby increasing capacity and reducing customer waiting times. Similar scanners are used on toll roads to scan each time a car passes a tollbooth. (Currently under development for use in supermarkets are scanners that will be able to scan an entire shopping cart without having to unload it!)

Technology has significantly affected how managers deal with waiting times in other ways as well. For example, to make a wait more enjoyable, many restaurants now give their customers an electronic buzzer or similar device when they put their names in for a table. With these devices, customers no longer have to listen for their names to be called. In addition, the wait can even be enjoyable, as customers are no longer restricted to the immediate area of the restaurant, but instead can visit other stores if the restaurant is located in a mall.

Information technology has also permitted companies to segment their customers and to design services to minimize waits for target customers. For example, preferred customers at Fidelity Brokerage Services and American Airlines' AAdvantage Club members can call special telephone numbers that provide faster service. However, these preferred customers often receive faster service at the expense of the company's other customers, who are complaining loudly about it.[6]

[6] Diane Brady, "Why Service Stinks!" *Business Week,* October 23, 2000, pp. 118–28.

Using Technology to Create Value

ATMs Save Time by Sprouting Wings

Cathay Pacific Airways now has ATMs onboard two of its 747 airplanes. These machines, supplied by Aero-Design Technology of Irvine, California, dispense currency for bank cards as well as for all major credit cards. In addition, these ATMs convert U.S. dollars into any one of 19 foreign currencies based on daily exchange rates that are provided by a satellite.

The airborne ATMs eliminate the need for customers to wait in ATM lines at their own banks or at the airport. They are also attractive to security-minded passengers who are uncomfortable about using ATMs in strange airports.

Source: Dennis Blank, "ATMs at 12 o'Clock High," *Business Week,* October 13, 1997, p. 8.

Bar-code scanners are also used at many airports to scan tickets as passengers board airplanes. This permits passengers to board more quickly and with less waiting time.

Menu-driven computer databases provide telephone operators with quick access to customer information, thereby allowing them to be more responsive to customer inquiries.

Technology will continue to significantly affect the speed with which service operations can respond to customers. When designing new service delivery systems, managers should always keep in mind that no wait is better than any wait!

Summary

As time becomes more critical in today's fast-paced environment, firms that can provide fast service will have a competitive advantage over firms that respond more slowly to customer requirements. Today, more than ever before, service managers need to constantly seek innovative ways to provide faster and better service to customers. Advances in technology, especially information technology, can assist the service manager in accomplishing this.

In providing faster service, however, managers should remember that it is the customer's perception of the wait that is critical, rather than the actual wait itself. Many factors can affect customer perceptions of waits, and the service manager needs to know what these factors are and which of them can be effectively managed by the firm. Such an approach will enable the manager to allocate the firm's scarce resources to ensure faster service.

Key Terms

actual waiting time: time, as measured by a stopwatch, of how long a customer has waited prior to receiving service.*(p. 400)*

customer's expectations: preconceived notions of what will occur at a service operation, often influenced by prior experience, advertising, and word-of-mouth. *(p. 402)*

customer satisfaction: measure of the customer's reaction to a specific service encounter. *(p. 402)*

disconfirmation: marketing measure of the difference between a customer's expectations from an operation and a customer's perception of its performance. *(p. 402)*

perceived waiting time: amount of time customers believe they have waited prior to receiving service. *(p. 400)*

Review and Discussion Questions

1. Compare having inventory in a manufacturing company and having customers waiting in line in a service operation.

2. What are some factors that you think might affect your degree of satisfaction with waiting in line in a supermarket checkout line late at night? In a bank during your lunch hour? At a fast-food restaurant with young children (not necessarily your own!)?

3. Calculate the opportunity cost associated with a dissatisfied customer who stops frequenting a fast-food restaurant for a year. What are your assumptions?

4. Why is it important for a service manager to be able to distinguish between the different types of factors that can affect a customer's level of satisfaction with his or her wait?

5. From your own personal experiences, cite some actual examples of both good and bad waiting line management practices.

6. For each of the different types of service operations listed below, provide specific recommendations for improving both the efficiency of the operation and the customer's level of satisfaction with the waiting time.
   - Airline check-in counter
   - Hospital emergency room
   - Department of Motor Vehicles
   - Mail-order 800 number
   - Emergency hot line
   - Upscale restaurant

Selected Bibliography

Anderson, R. E. "Consumer Dissatisfaction: The Effect of Disconfirmed Expectancy on Perceived Product Performance." *Journal of Marketing Research* 10 (February 1973).

Bearden, W. O., and J. E. Teele. "Selected Determinants of Consumer Satisfaction and Complaint Reports." *Journal of Marketing Research* 20 (February 1983).

Brady, Diane. "Why Service Stinks!" *Business Week,* October 23, 2000, pp. 118–28.

Chase, Richard B. "The Customer Contact Approach to Services: Theoretical Bases and Practical Extensions." *Operations Research* 29, no. 4 (July–August 1981).

_____. "The Ten Commandments of Service System Management." *Interfaces* 15, no. 3 (May–June 1985).

Churchill, G. A., Jr., and C. Surprenant. "Investigation into the Determinants of Customer Satisfaction." *Journal of Marketing Research* 19 (November 1982).

Davis, Mark M., and Janelle Heineke. "How Disconfirmation, Perception and Actual Waiting Times Impact Customer Satisfaction." *International Journal of Service Industry Management* 9, no. 1 (1998), pp. 64–73.

_____. "Understanding the Roles of the Customer and the Operation for Better Queue Management." *International Journal of Operations and Production Management* 14, no. 5 (1994).

Davis, Mark M., and Michael J. Maggard. "Zero Waiting Time: A Model for Designing Fast and Efficient Service." In *Advances in Services Marketing and Management Research and Practice* 3. Ed. Teresa A. Swartz, David E. Bowen, and Stephen W. Brown. Greenwich, CT: JAI Press, 1994.

Day, R. L., and E. L. Landon. "Toward a Theory of Consumer Complaining Behavior." In *Consumer and Industrial Buying Behavior.* Ed. A. G. Woodside, J. N. Sheth, and P. D. Bennett. New York: North-Holland, 1977.

Katz, K. L., B. M. Larson, and R. C. Larson. "Prescription for the Waiting Time Blues: Entertain, Enlighten, and Engage." *Sloan Management Review* 32, no. 2 (Winter 1991), pp. 44–53.

Maister, David. "The Psychology of Waiting Lines." In *The Service Encounter.* Ed. J. A. Czepiel, M. R. Solomon, and C. F. Surprenant. Lexington, MA: Lexington Books, D. C. Heath & Co., 1985.

Oliver, Richard L. "A Cognitive Model of the Antecedents and Consequences of Satisfaction Decisions." *Journal of Marketing Research* 17 (November 1980).

Sasser, W. E., R. P. Olsen, and D. D. Wyckoff. *Management of Service Operations: Text, Cases and Readings.* Boston: Allyn and Bacon, 1978.

Waiting Line Theory

Learning Objectives

- Introduce the characteristics of waiting lines and describe how they can affect a customer's waiting time.

- Identify the constraints and/or conditions that are required by waiting line theory in order to obtain valid results.

- Present waiting line theory in the form of a set of equations that represent different types of waiting line configurations.

Managerial Issues

Waiting lines occur when the capacity of a service operation is fully occupied at the exact moment when a customer wants that service. In other words, waiting lines form whenever customers arrive at a service facility that is already fully engaged serving other customers. Waiting lines take a wide variety of forms, from waiting in line at the checkout in a supermarket, to waiting in line at a tollbooth on a turnpike, to waiting on the telephone to make a hotel or airline reservation.

There are several challenges for managers with respect to the actual customer waiting times. The first is determining which type of service delivery system best meets the needs of the firm and its customers. In addition, managers must decide on how many workers to have on duty at any given time, which determines the service level that is provided. Too few workers translates into long waiting lines and dissatisfied customers that could ultimately have a negative effect on future revenues; too many workers means incurring unnecessary labor costs that negatively affect current profits. Queuing theory is the tool that provides management with the insight to achieve the proper balance between the two.

The previous chapter addressed the management of the customer's satisfaction with waiting in line. Here we focus on the management of the actual length of the waiting time. In this supplement we introduce the basic elements of waiting line problems and provide standard steady-state formulas for solving them. These queuing theory formulas enable facility designers, managers, and planners to analyze service requirements and establish service facilities appropriate to stated conditions. Queuing theory is broad enough to cover delays as dissimilar as those encountered by customers in a shopping mall or by aircraft awaiting landing slots.

Waiting Line Characteristics

The waiting line (or queuing) phenomenon consists essentially of six major components: (*a*) the source population, (*b*) the way customers arrive at the service facility, (*c*) the physical line, (*d*) the way customers are selected from the line, (*e*) the characteristics of the service facility (such as how the customers flow through the system and how much time it takes to serve each customer), and (*f*) the condition of the customers when they exit the system). These six elements, shown in Exhibit 15S.1, are discussed separately in the following sections.

Population Source

Arrivals at a service system may be drawn from either a finite or an infinite population. These two population sources are analyzed using different assumptions and equations, so the distinction between them is important for managers.

Finite Population

Some populations can be defined exactly as comprising a certain number of people. These populations are called finite populations. When a customer leaves a finite population service system, the size of the population is reduced by one—and the probability that a customer will require service is also reduced. Conversely, when a new customer enters the service system, the probability that a customer will require service increases. The total number of students that a professor teaches in a semester is a good example of a finite population.

Infinite Population

An infinite population can occur only in theory, but when the customer population of a service system is sufficiently large, any changes in the population caused by customers entering or leaving the system do not affect the probability that a customer will require service. For example, if a physician has 1,000 patients or a department store has 10,000 customers, the population source of patients or customers requiring service can be considered to be infinite.

Arrival Characteristics

Another factor in waiting line problems is the *arrival characteristics* of the queue members. As shown in Exhibit 15S.2, there are four main characteristics of arrivals: the *pattern of arrivals* (whether arrivals are controllable or uncontrollable); the *size of arrival units*

EXHIBIT 15S.1
Framework for Viewing Waiting Line Situations

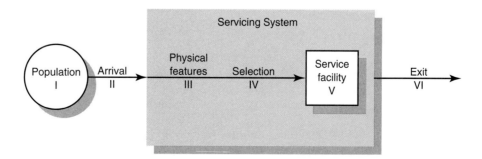

EXHIBIT 15S.2
Arrival
Characteristics
in Queues

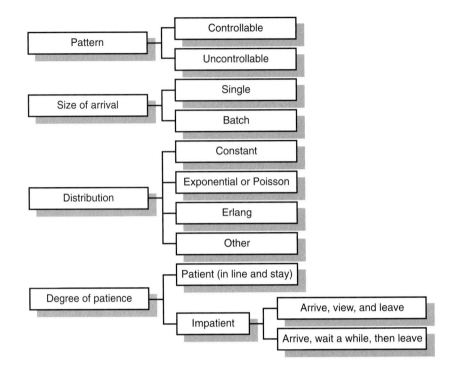

(whether they arrive one at a time or in batches); the *distribution pattern* (whether the time between arrivals is constant or follows a statistical distribution such as a Poisson, exponential, or Erlang); and the *degree of patience* (whether the arrival stays in line or leaves). We describe each of these in more detail.

Arrival Patterns

The arrivals at a system are far more *controllable* than is generally recognized. Hair salons, for example, may decrease their Saturday arrival rate (and it is hoped shift it to other days of the week) by charging more for adult haircuts or charging adult prices for children's haircuts, department stores can run sales during the off season or one-day-only sales to control demand levels, and airlines can offer excursion and off-season rates. The simplest of all arrival-control devices is the posting of business hours.

Some service demands are clearly *uncontrollable,* such as emergency medical demands on a city's hospital facilities. However, even in these situations, the arrivals at emergency rooms in specific hospitals are controllable to some extent by, say, keeping ambulance drivers in the service region informed how busy the emergency rooms of all regional hospitals are.

Size of Arrival Units

A *single arrival* may be thought of as one unit (a unit is the smallest number handled). A single arrival on the floor of the New York Stock Exchange (NYSE), for example, is 100 shares of stock. A *batch arrival* is some multiple of the unit, as a block of 1,000 shares on the NYSE or a party of five at a restaurant.

Distribution of Arrivals

Waiting line formulas require an **arrival rate,** or the average number of customers or units per time period (for example, 10 per hour). The time between arrivals is referred to as the interarrival time (such as an average of one every six minutes). A *constant* arrival distribution is periodic, with exactly the same time period between successive arrivals. In service processes, probably the only arrivals that truly approach a constant interarrival period are those that are subject to appointments. Much more common are variable random arrival distributions. The variable or random distribution patterns that occur most frequently in system models are described by the *negative exponential, Poisson,* or *Erlang* distributions.

Degree of Patience

Patient arrivals are those customers who wait as long as necessary until the service facility is ready to serve them. (Even if arrivals grumble and behave impatiently, the fact that they wait is sufficient to label them as patient arrivals for purposes of waiting line theory.)

There are two classes of *impatient* arrivals. Members of the first class arrive, survey both the service facility and the length of the line, and then decide to leave. Those in the second class arrive, view the situation, and join the waiting line, and then, after some period, depart. The behavior of the first type is termed **balking,** and the second is termed **reneging.**

Physical Features of Lines

Length

In a practical sense, an infinite line is very long in terms of the capacity of the service system. Examples of *infinite potential length* are a line of vehicles backed up for miles at a tollbooth on a turnpike and customers who must form a line around the block as they wait to purchase tickets for a rock concert.

Gas stations, loading docks, and parking lots have *limited line capacity,* which is often defined by legal restrictions or physical space. This complicates the waiting line problem not only in service system utilization and waiting line computations, but also in the shape of the actual arrival distribution. The arrival who is denied entry into the line because of lack of space may rejoin the population later or may seek service elsewhere. Either action makes an obvious difference in the finite population case.

Number of Lines

A *single line* or single file means there is only one line. The term *multiple lines* refers either to the single lines that form in front of two or more servers or to single lines that converge at some central point.

Customer Selection

Queuing Discipline

A queuing discipline is a priority rule, or set of rules (some of which are listed in Exhibit 15S.3), for determining the order of service to customers who are waiting in line. These rules can have a dramatic effect on the system's overall performance. The number of customers in line, the average waiting time, the range of variability in waiting time, and the efficiency of the service facility are just a few factors affected by the choice of priority rules.

Probably the most common priority rule, especially in service operations, is *first come, first served* (FCFS), also known as first in, first out (FIFO). This rule states that the customers in line are served in the order of their arrival; no other characteristics have any bearing on the selection process. This is popularly accepted as the fairest rule.

Reservations first, emergencies first, highest-profit customer first, largest orders first, best customers first, longest waiting time in line, and *soonest promised date* are other examples of priority rules. Each has its advantages as well as its shortcomings.

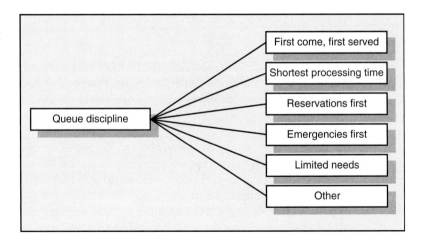

Directives such as "single transactions only" (as in a bank) or "12 items or less" express lanes (as in a supermarket) seem similar to priority rules, but in reality they are methodologies for structuring the line itself. Such lines are formed to serve a specific class of customers with similar characteristics. Within each line, however, priority rules still apply (as before) to the method of selecting the next customer to be served.

Service Facility Structure

Several types of service facility structures are presented in Exhibit 15S.4, four of which are discussed in detail in the following sections. The physical flow of items to be serviced or customers to be served may go through a single line, multiple lines, or some combination of the two. The choice of format depends partly on the volume of customers, partly on physical constraints, and partly on the restrictions imposed by requirements governing the order in which the service must be performed.

Single Channel, Single Phase

This is the simplest form of waiting line structure, and straightforward formulas are available to solve the problem for standard distribution patterns of arrival and service. When the distributions are nonstandard, the problem is easily solved by computer simulation. A typical example of a single-channel, single-phase situation is the one-person barbershop.

Single Channel, Multiphase

A car wash provides a good illustration of a series of services—vacuuming, wetting, washing, rinsing, drying, window cleaning, and parking—performed in a uniform sequence. Another example is a cafeteria line with different stations for salads, entrées, and desserts. A critical factor in the single-channel case with service in series is how much the items or customers build up in front of each service.

Because of the inherent variability in service arrival times, the most efficient use of a service station is to allow an infinite waiting line to build in front of each station. In other words, server efficiency is highest when the server never has to be idle between customers. The least efficient is when no line is permitted and only one customer at a time is allowed. When no sublines are allowed to build up in front of each station, as in a car wash, the use of the overall service facility is governed by the probability that a long service time will be required by any one of the servers in the system. This problem is common in most product-oriented systems, such as assembly lines. For example, if the person taking pay-

EXHIBIT 15S.4 **A Service Facility's Structure**

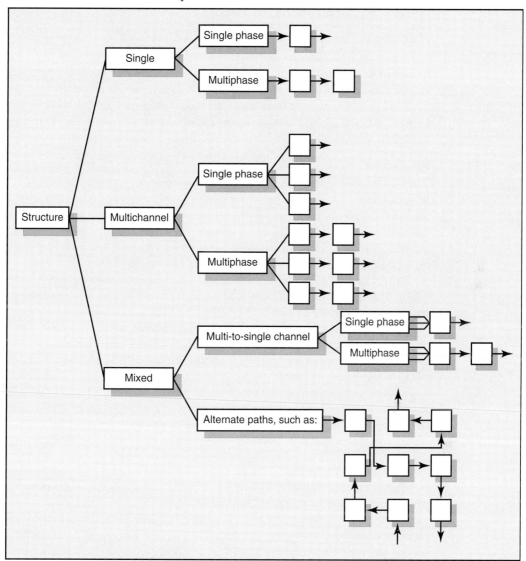

ment at the entrance to a car wash serves a customer who asks several questions, can't find the cash in his wallet, and/or fumbles for the exact change, the rest of the car wash remains idle while all this occurs. What is most efficient for the service operation, however, may not always be perceived as being very effective by the customers.

Multichannel, Single Phase

Checkout counters in supermarkets and high-volume department stores exemplify this type of structure. The difficulty with this format is that the uneven service time given each customer results in unequal speed or flow among the lines. This can result in some customers being served before others who arrived earlier as well as in some shifting between lines, called **jockeying.** Varying this structure to assure serving of arrivals in chronological order would require forming a single line, from which, as a server becomes available, the next customer in the queue is assigned. This type of line structure is now commonly used at airport ticket counters and banks.

Multichannel, Multiphase

This situation is similar to the preceding one except that two or more services are performed in sequence. The admission of patients in a hospital follows this pattern because a specific sequence of steps is usually required: initial contact at the admissions desk, filling out forms, making identification tags, obtaining a room assignment, escorting the patient to the room, and so forth. Since several servers are usually available for this procedure, more than one patient at a time may be processed.

Service Rate

Waiting line formulas generally define **service rate** as the capacity of the server in terms of the number of units served per time period (such as 12 customers per hour) and *not* as service time, which might average five minutes each. A *constant* service time rule states that each service takes exactly the same time. As in constant arrivals, this characteristic is generally limited to machine-controlled operations. (As with arrival rates, Erlang and hyperexponential distributions represent variable service times.)

The *exponential* distribution is frequently used to approximate the actual service distribution. This practice, however, may lead to incorrect results; few service situations are represented exactly by the exponential function since the service facility must be able to perform services in much less time than the average time of service.

Most other services also have some practical minimum time. A clerk in a checkout line may have a three-minute average service time but a one-minute minimum time. This is particularly true when another checkout aisle provides a quick service. Likewise in a hair salon, while the average service time may be 30 minutes, a customer is rarely finished in less than 20 minutes or more than an hour. Hence, these and similar types of services that have strong time dependency are poorly characterized by the exponential curve.

Capacity Utilization

The percentage of time that a service station is busy attending to the needs of a customer is referred to as the **capacity utilization** of that station. The remainder of the time there are no customers to be waited on and the station is, therefore, idle. In single-channel service systems, the capacity utilization is simply the ratio of the arrival rate to the service rate. For example, if customers arrive into a system at the rate of eight per hour and the service rate is 12 customers per hour, then the capacity utilization of this service station is 8/12 or 66.7 percent. To determine the capacity utilization for a station, both the arrival rate and the service rate must be expressed in the same units.

Exit

After customers are served, they exit in one of two ways: (*a*) the customer may return to the source population and immediately become a competing candidate for service again or (*b*) there may be a low probability of reservice. The first case can be illustrated by a patient with a chronic illness who has to visit a doctor routinely but can become seriously ill at any time; the second can be illustrated by a customer who buys a personal computer or a major kitchen appliance but has a low probability of a similar type of purchase in the near future. We might refer to the first as the "recurring-common-cold case" and to the second as the "appendectomy-only-once case."

When the population source is finite, any change in the service performed for customers who return to the population modifies the arrival rate at the service facility. This, of course, alters the characteristics of the waiting line under study and necessitates further analysis of the problem.

Waiting Line Equations

To underscore the importance and wide range of applications of waiting line analysis, we describe in this section six different waiting line systems and their characteristics (Exhibit 15S.5), and present their respective steady-state equations (Exhibit 15S.6). The definitions of the terms used in these equations are presented in Exhibit 15S.7.

In addition to these equations, two more formulas are important for understanding the relationships among the steady-state performance measures. First, the average total time in the system is equal to the average waiting time in the system plus the average service time or:

$$\bar{t}_s = \bar{t}_l + 1/\mu$$

The average total number of customers in the system is directly related to the total time in the system, or:

$$\bar{n}_s = \lambda \, \bar{t}_s$$

This well-known relationship is known as Little's Law. To illustrate how these models can be applied, we solve two sample problems and their solutions for the first two of the six models presented. (There are more types of models than these six, but the formulas and solutions become quite complicated and those problems are generally solved using computer simulation.) Keep in mind that these formulas are steady-state formulas which assume that the process under study is ongoing. Thus, they may provide inaccurate results when applied to initial operations such as the start of a new business day by a service firm.

EXHIBIT 15S.5 **Properties of Some Specific Waiting Line Models**

Model	Layout	Service Phase	Source Population	Arrival Pattern	Queue Discipline	Service Pattern	Permissible Queue Length	Typical Example
1	Single channel	Single	Infinite	Poisson	FCFS	Exponential	Unlimited	Drive-in teller at bank, one-lane toll bridge
2	Single channel	Single	Infinite	Poisson	FCFS	Constant	Unlimited	Roller coaster rides in amusement park
3	Single channel	Single	Infinite	Poisson	FCFS	Exponential	Limited	Ice cream stand, cashier in a restaurant
4	Single channel	Single	Infinite	Poisson	FCFS	Discrete distribution	Unlimited	Empirically derived distribution of flight time for a transcontinental flight
5	Single channel	Single	Infinite	Poisson	FCFS	Erlang	Unlimited	One-person barbershop
6	Multi-channel	Single	infinite	Poisson	FCFS	Exponential	Unlimited	Multiple-lane toll bridge or turnpike

EXHIBIT 15S.6
Equations for Solving Six Model Problems

Model 1

$$\bar{n}_l = \frac{\lambda^2}{\mu(\mu-\lambda)} \qquad \bar{t}_l = \frac{\lambda}{\mu(\mu-\lambda)} \qquad P_n = \left(1-\frac{\lambda}{\mu}\right)\left(\frac{\lambda}{\mu}\right)^n$$

$$\bar{n}_s = \frac{\lambda^2}{\mu-\lambda} \qquad \bar{t}_s = \frac{1}{\mu-\lambda} \qquad p = \frac{\lambda}{\mu}$$

Model 2

$$\bar{n}_l = \frac{\lambda^2}{2\mu(\mu-\lambda)} \qquad \bar{t}_l = \frac{\lambda}{2\,\mu(\mu-\lambda)}$$

$$\bar{n}_s = \bar{n}_l + \frac{\lambda}{\mu} \qquad \bar{t}_s = \bar{t}_l + \frac{1}{\mu}$$

Model 3

$$\bar{n}_l = \left(\frac{\lambda}{\mu}\right)^2 \left[\frac{1 - Q\left(\frac{\lambda}{\mu}\right)^1 + (Q-1)\left(\frac{\lambda}{\mu}\right)^Q}{\left(1-\frac{\lambda}{\mu}\right)\left(1-\left(\frac{\lambda}{\mu}\right)^{Q+1}\right)}\right]$$

$$\bar{n}_s = \left(\frac{\lambda}{\mu}\right)\left[\frac{1 - (Q+1)\left(\frac{\lambda}{\mu}\right)^Q + \left(Q\left(\frac{\lambda}{\mu}\right)^{Q+1}\right)}{\left(1-\frac{\lambda}{\mu}\right)\left(1-\left(\frac{\lambda}{\mu}\right)^{Q+1}\right)}\right] \qquad P_n = \left[\frac{1-\frac{\lambda}{\mu}}{1-\left(\frac{\lambda}{\mu}\right)^{Q+1}}\right]\left(\frac{\lambda}{\mu}\right)^n$$

Model 4

$$\bar{n}_l = \frac{\left(\frac{\lambda}{\mu}\right)^2 + \lambda^2\sigma^2}{2\left(1-\frac{\lambda}{\mu}\right)} \qquad \bar{t}_l = \frac{\frac{\lambda}{\mu^2}+\lambda\sigma^2}{2\left(1-\frac{\lambda}{\mu}\right)}$$

$$\bar{n}_s = \bar{n}_l + \frac{\lambda}{\mu} \qquad \bar{t}_s = \bar{t}_l + \frac{1}{\mu}$$

Model 5

$$\bar{n}_l = \frac{K+1}{2K}\cdot\frac{\lambda^2}{\mu(\mu-\lambda)} \qquad \bar{t}_l = \frac{K+1}{2K}\cdot\frac{\lambda}{\mu(\mu-\lambda)}$$

$$\bar{n}_s = \bar{n}_l + \frac{\lambda}{\mu} \qquad \bar{t}_s = \bar{t}_l + \frac{1}{\mu}$$

Model 6

$$\bar{n}_l = \frac{\lambda\mu\left(\frac{\lambda}{\mu}\right)^M}{(M-1)!\,(M\mu-\lambda)^2}P_0 \qquad \bar{t}_l = \frac{P_0}{\mu\,M\,M!\left(1-\frac{\lambda}{\mu M}\right)^2}\left(\frac{\lambda}{\mu}\right)^M$$

$$\bar{n}_s = \bar{n}_l + \frac{\lambda}{\mu} \qquad \bar{t}_s = \bar{t}_l + \frac{1}{\mu}$$

$$P_0 = \frac{1}{\displaystyle\sum_{n=0}^{M-1}\frac{\left(\frac{\lambda}{\mu}\right)^n}{n!} + \frac{\left(\frac{\lambda}{\mu}\right)^M}{M!\left(1-\frac{\lambda}{\mu M}\right)}} \qquad P_w = \left(\frac{\lambda}{\mu}\right)^M \frac{P_0}{M!\left(1-\frac{\lambda}{\mu M}\right)}$$

EXHIBIT 15S.7
Notations for
Equations (Exhibit
15S.5)

Infinite Queuing Notation

σ = Standard deviation

λ = Arrival rate

μ = Service rate

$\dfrac{1}{\mu}$ = Average service time

$\dfrac{1}{\lambda}$ = Average time between arrivals

ρ = Potential capacity utilization of the service facility (defined as λ/μ)

$\bar{n}_l$ = Average number waiting in line

$\bar{n}_s$ = Average number in system (including any being served)

$\bar{t}_l$ = Average time waiting in line

$\bar{t}_s$ = Average total time in system (including time to be served)

Q = Maximum queue length

M = Number of channels

Two Typical Waiting Line Situations

Here is a quick preview of the two problems we will use to illustrate the first two waiting line models in Exhibits 15S.5 and 15S.6.

Problem 1: Customers in line. A bank wants to know how many customers (or cars) are waiting for a drive-in teller, how long they have to wait, the utilization of the teller, and what the service rate would have to be so that 95 percent of the time there would not be more than three cars in the system at any one time.

Problem 2: Equipment selection. A franchisee for Robot Car Wash must decide which equipment to purchase out of a choice of three. Larger units cost more, but wash cars faster. To make the decision, costs are related to revenue.

The two problems are solved using the equations in Exhibit 15S.6 with the notations defined in Exhibit 15S.7.

Problem 1: Customers in Line

Example

Western National Bank wants to provide a drive-through service for customers. Management estimates that customers will arrive in their cars at the rate of 15 per hour. The teller who will staff the window can serve customers at the rate of 20 per hour.

Assuming Poisson arrivals and exponential service, find the:

a. Capacity utilization of the teller.

b. Average number of cars in the waiting line.

c. Average number in the system.

d. Average waiting time in line.

e. Average time in the system, including service.

Solution

a. The average capacity utilization of the teller is

$$\mu = 20 \text{ customers/hour}$$
$$\lambda = 15 \text{ customers/hour}$$

$$\rho = \frac{\lambda}{\mu} = \frac{15}{20} = 75 \text{ percent}$$

b. The average number of cars in the waiting line is

$$\bar{n}_l = \frac{\lambda^2}{\mu(\mu - \lambda)} = \frac{(15)^2}{20(20 - 15)} = 2.25 \text{ cars}$$

c. The average number in the system is

$$\bar{n}_s = \frac{\lambda}{\mu - \lambda} = \frac{15}{20 - 15} = 3 \text{ cars}$$

d. Average waiting time in line is

$$\bar{t}_l = \frac{\lambda}{\mu(\mu - \lambda)} = \frac{15}{20(20 - 15)} = 0.15 \text{ hour, or 9 minutes}$$

e. Average time in the system is

$$\bar{t}_s = \frac{1}{\mu - \lambda} = \frac{1}{20 - 15} = 0.2 \text{ hour, or 12 minutes}$$

Example

Because of limited space and a desire to provide an acceptable level of service, the bank manager would like to ensure, with 95 percent confidence, that not more than three cars will be in the system at any one time. What is the present level of service for the three-car limit? What level of teller use must be attained and what must be the service rate of the teller to assure the 95 percent level of service?

Solution

The present level of service for three cars or less is the probability that there are 0, 1, 2, or 3 cars in the system.

From Model 1, Exhibit 15S.6:

$$P_n = \left(1 - \frac{\lambda}{\mu}\right)\left(\frac{\lambda}{\mu}\right)^n$$

at $n = 0$	$P_0 = (1 - 15/20)$	$(15/20)^0 = 0.250$	
at $n = 1$	$P_1 = (1/4)$	$(15/20)^1 = 0.188$	
at $n = 2$	$P_2 = (1/4)$	$(15/20)^2 = 0.141$	
at $n = 3$	$P_3 = (1/4)$	$(15/20)^3 = \underline{0.105}$	
		0.684 or 68.4 percent	

The probability of having more than three cars in the system is 1.0 minus the probability of three cars or less ($1.0 - 0.684 = 0.316$ or 31.6 percent).

For a 95 percent service level to three cars or less, this states that $P_0 + P_1 + P_2 + P_3 =$ 95 percent.

$$0.95 = \left(1 - \frac{\lambda}{\mu}\right)\left(\frac{\lambda}{\mu}\right)^0 + \left(1 - \frac{\lambda}{\mu}\right)\left(\frac{\lambda}{\mu}\right)^1 + \left(1 - \frac{\lambda}{\mu}\right)\left(\frac{\lambda}{\mu}\right)^2 + \left(1 - \frac{\lambda}{\mu}\right)\left(\frac{\lambda}{\mu}\right)^3$$

$$0.95 = \left(1 - \frac{\lambda}{\mu}\right)\left[1 + \frac{\lambda}{\mu} + \left(\frac{\lambda}{\mu}\right)^2 + \left(\frac{\lambda}{\mu}\right)^3\right]$$

We can solve this by trial and error for values of λ/μ. If $\lambda/\mu = 0.50$:

$$0.95 \stackrel{?}{=} 0.5(1 + 0.50 + 0.25 + 0.125)$$

$$0.95 \neq 0.9375$$

With $\lambda/\mu = 0.45$,

$$0.95 \stackrel{?}{=} (1 - 0.45)(1 + 0.45 + 0.203 + 0.091)$$

$$0.95 \neq 0.9592$$

With $\lambda/\mu = 0.47$,

$$0.95 \stackrel{?}{=} (1 - 0.47)(1 + 0.47 + 0.221 + 0.104) = 0.95135$$

$$0.95 \approx 0.9514$$

Therefore, with the utilization $\rho = \lambda/\mu$ of 47 percent, the probability of three cars or fewer in the system is 95 percent.

To find the rate of service required to attain this 95 percent service level, we simply solve the equation $\lambda/\mu = 0.47$, where λ = number of arrivals per hour. This gives $\mu = 31.92$ or about 32 per hour.

That is, the teller must serve approximately 32 people per hour—a 60 percent increase over the original 20-per-hour capability—in order to be 95 percent confident that not more than three cars will be in the system. Perhaps service can be accelerated by modifying the method of service, adding another teller, or limiting the types of transactions available at the drive-through. (Many banks limit each customer to a maximum of three transactions at the drive-up window.) Note that with the condition of 95 percent confidence, three or fewer cars will be in the system and the teller will be idle 53 percent of the time.

Problem 2: Equipment Selection

Example

The Robot Car Wash Company franchises combination gas and car wash stations throughout the United States. Robot gives a free car wash with a gasoline fill-up or, for a wash alone, charges $5.00. Past experience shows that the number of customers that have car washes following fill-ups is about the same as for a wash alone. The average gross profit on a gasoline fill-up is about $7.00, and the cost of the car wash to Robot is $1.00. Robot Car Wash stations are open 14 hours a day.

Robot has three power units with drive assemblies, and a franchise must select the unit preferred. Unit I can wash cars at the rate of one every five minutes and is leased for $120 per day. Unit II, a larger unit, can wash cars at the rate of one every four minutes but costs $160 per day. Unit III, the largest, costs $220 per day and can wash a car in three minutes.

The franchisee estimates that customers will not wait in line more than five minutes for a car wash. A longer time will cause Robot to lose both gasoline sales and car wash sales.

If the estimate of customer arrivals resulting in washes is 10 per hour, which wash unit should be selected?

Solution

Using Unit I, calculate the average waiting time of customers in the wash line (μ for Unit I = 12 per hour). From the Model 2 equations (Exhibit 15S.6),

$$\bar{t}_l = \frac{\lambda}{2\mu(\mu - \lambda)} = \frac{10}{2(12)(20 - 10)} = 0.208 \text{ hour, or } 12\tfrac{1}{2} \text{ minutes}$$

For Unit II at 15 per hour,

$$\bar{t}_l = \frac{10}{2(15)(15 - 10)} = 0.067 \text{ hour, or 4 minutes}$$

If waiting time is the only criterion, Unit II should be purchased. However, before we make the final decision, we must look at the profit differential between the units.

With Unit I, some customers would balk or renege because of the 12½-minute wait. And although this greatly complicates the mathematical analysis, we can gain some estimate of lost sales with Unit I by inserting $\bar{t}_l$ = 5 minutes or $\frac{1}{12}$ hour (the average length of time customers will wait) and solving for λ. This would be the effective arrival rate of customers:

$$\bar{t}_l = \frac{\lambda}{2\mu(\mu - \lambda)}$$

$$\lambda = \frac{2\bar{t}_l \mu^2}{1 + 2\bar{t}_l \mu}$$

$$\lambda = \frac{2(1/12)(12)^2}{1 + 2(1/12)(12)} = 8 \text{ per hour}$$

Therefore, since the original estimate of λ was 10 per hour, an estimated two customers per hour will be lost. Lost profit of two customers per hour × 14 hours × ½ ($7.00 fill-up profit + $4.00 wash profit) = $154.00 per day.

Because the additional cost of Unit II over Unit I is only $40 per day, the loss of $154.00 profit obviously warrants the installation of Unit II.

The original constraint of a five-minute maximum wait is satisfied by Unit II. Therefore, Unit III is not considered unless the arrival rate is expected to increase.

Capacity Utilization and Waiting Time

As the capacity utilization of a service facility increases, the average waiting time for that facility increases. To illustrate this relationship, we use the formula for Model 1 (in Exhibit 15S.6) to calculate the capacity utilization and average waiting time for a single server facility. The results are shown in the table in Exhibit 15S.8 and plotted in the graph in Exhibit 15S.9. As a rule, when the capacity utilization of the service facility with random customer arrivals is greater than 75 to 85 percent, the lines become unacceptably long for the vast majority of customers. (Scheduled services can have higher capacity utilizations.)

EXHIBIT 15S.8
Calculating the Relationship between Capacity Utilization and Waiting Time

Arrival Rate	Service Rate	Capacity Utilization	Waiting Time (hr)	Waiting Time (min)
10	60	16.7%	0.003	0.20
20	60	33.3%	0.008	0.50
30	60	50.0%	0.017	1.00
40	60	66.7%	0.033	2.00
45	60	75.0%	0.050	3.00
50	60	83.3%	0.083	5.00
55	60	91.7%	0.183	11.00
56	60	93.3%	0.233	14.00
57	60	95.0%	0.317	19.00
58	60	96.7%	0.483	29.00

EXHIBIT 15S.9
The Relationship between Capacity Utilization and Waiting Time

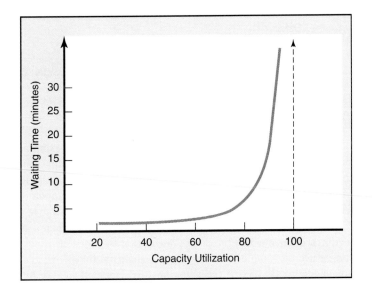

The Trade-off between Balking and Reneging

Service managers, in designing their facilities, need to recognize the trade-off between having a large waiting facility for customers and the customer dissatisfaction associated with waiting too long before being served. The larger the waiting area, the less likely a customer will balk or not enter the facility. At the same time, for a given arrival rate (λ) and service rate (μ), the larger the waiting area, the longer the average waiting time for the customer. This trade-off is shown in Exhibit 15S.10.

If the wait is so long that the customer eventually reneges or leaves the line, then the customer is likely to be more dissatisfied than if he had balked. For example, you are likely to be very dissatisfied if you call to make an airline reservation and have to wait on the phone for such a long time that you eventually hang up; you would probably be less dissatisfied if you get a busy signal, and then call back later. Similarly, you will likely be more dissatisfied if you have to wait such a long time for a table in a restaurant that you finally leave before you are seated than if you found the parking lot full and decided to come back another time.

EXHIBIT 15S.10
The Trade-off between Balking and Reneging for a Given λ and μ

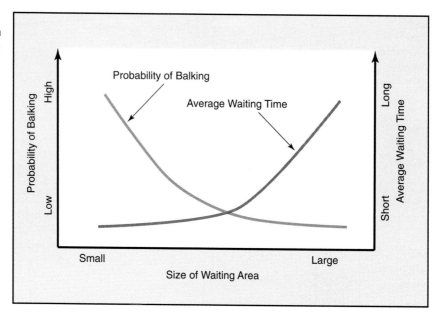

Computer Simulation of Waiting Lines

Some waiting line problems that seem very simple on first examination turn out to be extremely difficult or impossible to solve. We have been treating waiting line situations that are independent; that is, either the entire system consists of a single phase, or each service that is performed in a series is independent. (This could happen if the output of one service location is allowed to build up in front of the next one so that, in essence, the first service becomes a calling population for the next service.) When a series of services is performed in sequence where the output rate of one becomes the input rate of the next, we can no longer use the simple formulas. This is also true for any problem where conditions do not meet the conditions of the equations, as specified in Exhibit 15S.7. The analytical technique best suited for solving this type of problem is computer simulation.

The Impact of Technology

The major effect technology has had on waiting line theory is in the continued development and application of queuing theory software. For example, queuing theory software plays an integral role in the management of call centers. These software packages range from very simple models to highly sophisticated applications. Some software packages include a forecasting component, which helps managers estimate future customer demand.

Summary

Waiting line problems present both a challenge and a frustration to those who try to solve them. The main concern in dealing with waiting line problems is what procedure or priority rule to use in selecting the next customer to be served.

Many queuing problems appear simple until an attempt is made to solve them. This supplement has dealt with the simpler problems. When the situation becomes more complex, such as when there are multiple phases and/or where services are performed only in a particular sequence, computer simulation is usually necessary to obtain a good solution.

Key Terms

arrival rate: rate at which customers arrive into a service delivery system, usually expressed in terms of customers per hour. *(p. 416)*

balking: when a customer sees a long line and leaves without entering it. *(p. 417)*

capacity utilization: percentage of time a service station is busy serving a customer. *(p. 420)*

jockeying: when a customer shifts from one line to another because it is shorter. *(p. 419)*

reneging: when a customer enters a long line and then leaves some time later. *(p. 417)*

service rate: capacity of a service station, usually expressed in terms of customers per hour. The reciprocal of the service rate is the average time to serve a customer. *(p. 420)*

Review and Discussion Questions

1. How many waiting lines did you encounter during your last airline flight?
2. Distinguish between a *channel* and a *phase*.
3. Which assumptions are necessary to employ the formulas given for Model 1?
4. In what way might the first-come, first-served rule be unfair to the customers waiting for service in a bank or hospital?
5. Identify the different types of waiting lines you encounter in a "normal" day.

Solved Problems

1. Quick Lube, Inc., operates a fast lube and oil change garage. On a typical day, customers arrive at the rate of three per hour, and lube jobs are performed at an average rate of one every 15 minutes. The mechanics operate as a team on one car at a time.

   Assuming Poisson arrivals and exponential service, determine the:
   a. Utilization of the lube team.
   b. Average number of cars in line.
   c. Average time a car waits before it is lubed.
   d. Total time it takes a car to go through the system (i.e., waiting in line plus lube time).

Solution

$\lambda = 3, \mu = 4$

a. Utilization $(\rho) = \dfrac{\lambda}{\mu} = \dfrac{3}{4} = 75\%$.

b. $\bar{n}_l = \dfrac{\lambda^2}{\mu(\mu - \lambda)} = \dfrac{3^2}{4(4 - 3)} = \dfrac{9}{4} = 2.25$ cars in line.

c. $\bar{t}_l = \dfrac{\lambda}{\mu(\mu - \lambda)} = \dfrac{3}{4(4 - 3)} = \dfrac{3}{4} = .75$ hour = 45 minutes in line.

d. $\bar{t}_s = \dfrac{1}{\mu - \lambda} = \dfrac{1}{1} = 1$ hour total time in the system (waiting + lube).

Problems

1. Burrito King is a new fast-food franchise that has automated burrito production for its drive-up fast-food establishments. The Burro-Master 9000 requires a constant 45 seconds to produce a burrito (with any of the standard fillings). It has been estimated that customers will arrive at the drive-up window according to a Poisson distribution at an average of 1 every 50 seconds.
   a. What is the expected average time in the system?
   b. To help determine the amount of space needed for cars in line at the drive-up window, Burrito King would like to know the average line length (in cars) and the average number of cars in the system (both in line and at the window).

2. Big Jack's drive-through hamburger service is planning to build another store at a new location and must decide how much land to lease. Leased space for cars will cost $1,000 per year per space. Big Jack is aware of the highly competitive nature of the quick-service food industry and knows that if his drive-through is full, customers will go elsewhere. The location under consideration has

a potential customer arrival rate of 30 per hour (Poisson). Customers' orders are filled at the rate of 40 per hour (exponential) since Big Jack prepares food ahead of time. The average profit on each arrival is $0.60, and the store is open from noon to midnight every day. How many spaces for cars should be leased?

3. To support National Heart Week, the Heart Association plans to install a free blood pressure testing booth in El Con Mall for the week. Previous experience indicates that, on the average, 10 persons per hour request a test. Assume arrivals are Poisson from an infinite population. Blood pressure measurements can be made at a constant time of five minutes each. Assume that the queue length can be infinite with FCFS discipline.

   a. How many people will be in line, on average?
   b. How many people will be in the system, on average?
   c. On average, how long can a person expect to spend in line?
   d. On average, how much time will it take to measure a person's blood pressure, including waiting time?
   e. On weekends, the arrival rate can be expected to increase to nearly 12 per hour. What effect will this have on the number in the waiting line?

4. A company has a self-service coffee station for the convenience of its workers. Arrivals at the station follow a Poisson distribution at the rate of three per minute. To serve themselves, workers take about 15 seconds, which is exponentially distributed.

   a. How many customers would you expect to see on the average at the coffee station?
   b. How long would you expect it to take to get a cup of coffee?
   c. What percentage of time is the coffee station being used?
   d. What is the probability that there would be three or more people at the station?
   If an automatic machine is installed that dispenses coffee at a constant time of 15 seconds, how does this change your answers to a and b?

5. Dr. L. Winston Martin is an allergist who has an excellent process in place for handling his regular patients who come in for allergy injections. Patients arrive for an injection and fill out a name slip, which is then placed in an open slot that passes into another room staffed by one or two nurses. They prepare the specific injections and call the patient through a speaker system into the room to receive the injection. At certain times during the day, the patient load drops and only one nurse is needed to administer the injections.

   When there is one nurse, assume that patients arrive in a Poisson fashion and the service rate of the nurse is exponentially distributed. During this slower period, patients arrive with an interarrival time of approximately three minutes. It takes the nurse an average of two minutes to prepare and administer the injection.

   a. What is the average number of patients you would expect to see in Dr. Martin's facilities?
   b. How long would it take for a patient to arrive, get an injection, and leave?
   c. What is the probability that there will be three or more patients on the premises?
   d. What is the utilization of the nurse?

6. The NOL Income Tax Service is analyzing its customer service operations during the month before the April 15 filing deadline. On the basis of past data, it has been estimated that customers arrive according to a Poisson process with an average interarrival time of 12 minutes. The time to complete a return for a customer is exponentially distributed with a mean of 10 minutes. On the basis of this information, answer the following questions.

   a. If you went to NOL, how much time would you allow for getting your return done?
   b. On average, how much room should be allowed for the waiting area?
   c. If the NOL service were operating 12 hours per day, how many hours on average, per day, would the office be busy?
   d. What is the probability that the system is idle?
   e. If the arrival rate remains unchanged but the average time in the system must be 45 minutes or less, what would need to be changed?
   f. Software has been developed for preparing the new "simplified" tax forms. If the service time became a constant nine minutes, what would total time in the system become?

7. The law firm of Larry, Darryl and Darryl (L, D & D) specializes in the practice of waste disposal law, and is interested in analyzing the caseload. Data were collected on the number of cases received in a year and the times to complete each case. The partners consider themselves a dedicated firm and will take on only one case at a time. Calls for their services apparently follow a Poisson process with a mean of one case every 30 days. Given the fact that L, D & D are outstanding in their field, clients will wait for their turn and are served on a first-come, first-served basis. The data on the number of days to complete each case for the last 10 cases are 27, 26, 26, 25, 27, 24, 27, 23, 22, and 23.

   Determine the average time for L, D & D to complete a case, the average number of clients waiting, and the average wait for each client.

8. There is currently only one tollbooth at one of the smaller exits of a state turnpike. On average it takes about 40 seconds for the toll collector to take the money from the driver and, if necessary, return change. Cars arrive at the tollbooth at an average rate of 70 cars per hour.
   a. What is the average waiting time for a car before it pays the toll?
   b. What is the capacity utilization of the toll collector?
   c. The turnpike authority has decided to install another toll collection station that is equipped with an electronic scanner that can scan stickers on the windshields of cars. The scanning time is estimated to be 5 seconds, which is constant. It is estimated that 40 percent of the people will use the stickers. What will be the average waiting time for cars with stickers and for cars without stickers?

9. Inndependents.com is a start-up company that provides a network for small independently owned inns and hotels. This network makes guest reservations and provides technical support for the managers of these properties. To begin operations, one customer service representative has been hired to answer telephone calls. (In other words, this is a one-person call center.) It is estimated that the average call will take about three minutes to answer, and that initially the demand is forecasted to be 50 calls per day over an eight-hour day.
   a. What will be the average waiting time before a call is answered?
   b. What is the capacity utilization of the customer service representative?
   c. After one week of operation, demand is exceeding the forecast and is now averaging 80 calls per day. To provide better service, another customer service representative is hired. In addition, the calls are segmented by guest reservations and technical support, with each representative assigned to answer only one type of call. Based upon the first week's data, 75 percent of the calls are for reservations while only 25 percent are for technical support. Additional data show that the average time to make a reservation is two minutes while the time to answer a technical support question averages six minutes. With this additional information, determine the average waiting time for each type of call and the capacity utilization for each customer service representative.

10. An agricultural cooperative consists of a group of farmers that invest in a common business venture, which is often a processing facility for their farm products. Ocean Spray in Massachusetts (cranberries), Tillamook in Oregon (cheese), and Cabot in Vermont (cheese) are all good examples of agricultural cooperatives. The farmers who own the cooperative share in the costs and/or profits that it generates.

   A grape cooperative in California, which processes grapes for wine making, has one unloading dock at its facility. During the fall harvest, trucks arrive from the vineyards at an average rate of three per hour throughout the 12 hours that the facility is open every day. The growers rent these trucks with drivers at a cost of $75 per hour.

   Joe Newpol, the manager of the processing plant, is trying to decide how big a crew he should hire to unload the trucks. As a first step, he has estimated the following average times that it will take to unload a truck for different crew sizes:

Crew Size	Average Unload Time (minutes)
4	18
5	15
6	12
7	10

He pays workers $16 per hour, which includes benefits. Based on this information, how big a crew should he hire to minimize total costs?

Selected Bibliography

Bartfai, P., and J. Tomko. *Point Processes Queuing Problems.* New York: Elsevier-North Holland Publishing, 1981.

Bruell, Steven C. *Computational Algorithms for Closed Queuing Networks.* New York: Elsevier-North Holland Publishing, 1980.

Gorney, Leonard. *Queuing Theory: A Solving Approach.* Princeton, NJ: Petrocelli, 1981.

Hillier, Frederick S., et al. *Queuing Tables and Graphs.* New York: Elsevier-North Holland Publishing, 1981.

Newell, Gordon F. *Applications of Queuing Theory.* New York: Chapman and Hall, 1982.

Solomon, Susan L. *Simulation of Waiting Lines.* Englewood Cliffs, NJ: Prentice Hall, 1983.

Srivastava, H. M., and B. R. Kashyap. *Special Functions in Queuing Theory: And Related Stochastic Processes.* New York: Academic Press, 1982.

Vinrod, B., and T. Altiok. "Approximating Unreliable Queuing Networks under the Assumption of Exponentiality." *Journal of the Operational Research Society,* March 1986, pp. 309–16.

INDEX